Lecture Notes in Computer Science 7977

Commenced Publication in 1973
Founding and Former Series Editors:
Gerhard Goos, Juris Hartmanis, and Jan van Leeuwen

T0223915

Florian Daniel   Peter Dolog   Qing Li (Eds.)

Web Engineering

13th International Conference, ICWE 2013
Aalborg, Denmark, July 8-12, 2013
Proceedings

 Springer

Volume Editors

Florian Daniel
University of Trento
Department of Information Engineering and Computer Science
Via Sommarive 5, 38123 Povo, Italy
E-mail: daniel@disi.unitn.it

Peter Dolog
Aalborg University
Department of Computer Science
Selma Lagerloefs Vej 300, 9220 Aalborg, Denmark
E-mail: dolog@cs.aau.dk

Qing Li
City University of Hong Kong
Department of Computer Science
83 Tat Chee Ave., Kowloon, Hong Kong, China
E-mail: itqli@cityu.edu.hk

ISSN 0302-9743   e-ISSN 1611-3349
ISBN 978-3-642-39199-6   e-ISBN 978-3-642-39200-9
DOI 10.1007/978-3-642-39200-9
Springer Heidelberg Dordrecht London New York

Library of Congress Control Number: 2013941133

CR Subject Classification (1998): H.3.5, H.3.3, H.3, H.4, D.2.1, D.2, J.1, H.5.3, H.5, H.2.8, I.2.6

LNCS Sublibrary: SL 3 – Information Systems and Application, incl. Internet/Web and HCI

Typesetting: Camera-ready by author, data conversion by Scientific Publishing Services, Chennai, India

Printed on acid-free paper

Springer is part of Springer Science+Business Media (www.springer.com)

Preface

This volume collects the research articles, tool demonstrations, posters, tutorials, and keynote speeches presented at the 13th International Conference on Web Engineering (ICWE 2013). The discipline of Web engineering is a special branch of the broader area of software engineering that specifically focuses on the World Wide Web and the Internet. The year 2013, in this respect, is an important year: it's the 30th birthday of the Internet! In fact, its official launch dates back to the year 1983, in which the Advanced Research Projects Agency Network (ARPANET) officially adopted the so-called TCP/IP stack of protocols with the Transmission Control Protocol (TCP) and Internet Protocol (IP) at its core, turning into what became the Internet. The second enabler of Web engineering, the World Wide Web, is only slightly younger: it dates back to the year 1989, in which the physicist Tim Berners-Lee at CERN, Switzerland, founded the World Wide Web with its HyperText Transfer Protocol (HTTP) able to transmit interlinked hypertext documents over a network. Since then, both the Web and the Internet have experienced tremendous adoption and evolution, with Web 3.0, the Semantic Web, IPv6, Internet of Things, and Cloud Computing being only some of the latest buzzwords produced by the unstoppable fermentation that characterizes the biggest network of our planet.

In this context, the International Conference on Web Engineering (ICWE) aims to be a premier fair and discussion forum of the latest developments, concerns, and challenges that occupy industry and academia alike. ICWE specifically aims to promote scientific and practical excellence in Web Engineering and to bring together researchers and practitioners working on all aspects regarding the engineering of Web-based software systems. The conference contributes to the advancement of the state of the art of technologies, methodologies, programming languages, algorithms, models, protocols, tools, and metrics and specifically looks for excellent research contributions, cutting-edge engineering practices, and empirical insights.

ICWE 2013 was held during July 8–12 in Aalborg, Denmark. It was the 13th edition of the conference series, following prior editions held in Berlin, Germany (2012); Pahpos, Cyprus (2011); Vienna, Austria (2010); San Sebastian, Spain (2009); Yorktown Heights, NY, USA (2008); Como, Italy (2007); Palo Alto, CA, USA (2006); Sydney, Australia (2005); Munich, Germany (2004); Oviedo, Spain (2003); Santa Fe, Argentina (2002); and Caceres, Spain (2001).

This year's calls for research and industry papers jointly attracted 92 submissions from 31 countries, covering a wide spectrum of topics, such as, among others: Web mining and knowledge extraction, semantic and linked data management, crawling and Web search, model-driven Web engineering, component-based Web engineering, Rich Internet Applications (RIAs) and client-side programming, Web services, and end-user development. All submissions were carefully reviewed by the Program Committee, consisting of renowned experts and practitioners in the field of Web engineering coming from 20 different countries. As a result, 21 submissions were accepted as full research papers and four as industry papers, resulting in a 24.7% acceptance rate for full research papers and a 27.2% overall acceptance rate of full papers. In addition to full papers, 11 submissions were accepted as short papers with an extra 12.9% rate for short papers. The scientific program was completed with seven workshops, six demonstrations and posters, as well as with four tutorials and three keynote talks by Wil van der Aalst (Technische Universiteit Eindhoven, The Netherlands), Sean Wang (Fudan University, Shanghai, China), and Jan Borchers (RWTH Aachen, Germany).

Of course, such a rich program would not have been possible without the collaboration of a large number of people. First of all, we would like to thank the 250 authors who submitted their work to ICWE 2013 for evaluation. They are the very reason for this conference to exist. Then, we would like to thank all the Program Committee members and external reviewers, who provided valuable and constructive feedback to the authors and important assessments to the Program Chairs for the selection of papers. We would like to thank the Workshop Chairs, Industry Track Chairs, Demo/Poster Chairs, Tutorial Chairs, PhD Symposium Chairs, and local organizers for their professional work. We would like to express our gratitude to the keynote speakers for their availability and insights, as well as to Geert-Jan Houben, who acted as liaison to ISWE and the ICWE Steering Committee. The final thanks go to Aalborg University and all the ICWE 2013 sponsors that contributed to making this event happen.

July 2013

Florian Daniel
Peter Dolog
Qing Li

Organization

The ICWE 2013 edition was organized by the Intelligent Web and Information Systems Group at the Computer Science Department of Aalborg University in cooperation with Visit Aalborg.

General Chair

Peter Dolog   Aalborg University, Denmark

Program Chairs

Florian Daniel   University of Trento, Italy
Qing Li   City University of Hong Kong SAR, China

Industry Track Chairs

Erik Wilde   EMC Corporation, USA
Cesare Pautasso   University of Lugano, Switzerland

Workshop Chairs

Michael Sheng   The University of Adelaide, Australia
Jesper Kjeldskov   Aalborg University, Denmark

Tutorial Chairs

Maristella Matera   Politecnico di Milano, Italy
Benjamin Satzger   Microsoft, USA

Demo and Poster Chairs

Marcos Baez   University of Trento, Italy
Alessandro Bozzon   TU Delft, The Netherlands

PhD Symposium Chairs

Oscar Diaz   University of the Basque Country, Spain
Marco Winckler   ICS-IRIT, Paul Sabatier University, France

ICWE Steering Committee Liaison

Geert-Jan Houben   TU Delft, The Netherlands

Local Arangements Chair

Hanne Christiansen   Visit Aalborg, Denmark

Program Committee

Silvia Abrahão   Polytechnic University of Valencia, Spain
Marcos Báez   University of Trento, Italy
Ladjel Bellatreche   LIAS/ISAE-ENSMA, France
Boualem Benatallah   University of New South Wales, Australia
Davide Bolchini   University of Indiana, USA
Niels Olof Bouvin   Aarhus University, Denmark
Alessandro Bozzon   Politecnico di Milano, Italy
Marco Brambilla   Politecnico di Milano, Italy
Jordi Cabot   INRIA, Nantes, France
Yi Cai   South China University of Technology, China
Coral Calero   University of Castilla-La Mancha, Spain
Cinzia Cappiello   Politecnico di Milano, Italy
Fabio Casati   University of Trento, Italy
Sven Casteleyn   Polytechnic University of Valencia, Spain
Wei Chen   Beijing Institute of Technology, China
Dickson Chiu   Dickson Computer Systems, Hong Kong SAR,
                            China
Antonella De Angeli   University of Trento, Italy
Olga De Troyer Vrije   Universiteit Brussel, Belgium
Óscar Díaz   University of the Basque Country, Spain
Damiano Distante   Università Telematica TELMA, Italy
Schahram Dustdar   Vienna University of Technology, Austria
Federico M. Facca   CREATE-NET, Italy
Flavius Frasincar   Erasmus University Rotterdam,
                            The Netherlands
Piero Fraternali   Politecnico di Milano, Italy
Martin Gaedke   Chemnitz University of Technology, Germany
Yunjun Gao   Zhejiang University, China
Irene Garrigos   University of Alicante, Spain
Dragan Gasevic   Athabasca University, Canada
Athula Ginige   University of Western Sydney, Australia
Kaj Groenbaek   Aarhus University, Denmark
Michael Grossniklaus   Portland State University, USA
Volker Gruhn   Universität Duisburg-Essen, Germany
Han Hao   National Institute of Informatics, Japan

Simon Harper   University of Manchester, UK
Olaf Hartig   Humboldt-Universität zu Berlin, Germany
Bernhard Haslhofer   Cornell University, NY, USA
Martin Hepp   Universität der Bundeswehr München,
                                Germany
Geert-Jan Houben   Delft University of Technology,
                                The Netherlands
Patrick Hung   University of Ontario Institute of Technology,
                                Canada
Jesper Kjeldskov   Aalborg Universtity, Denmark
In-Young Ko   Advanced Institute of Science and Technology,
                                Korea
Nora Koch   LMU Munich, Germany
Frank Leymann   University of Stuttgart, Germany
An Liu   University of Science and Technology of China
Steffen Lohmann   University of Stuttgart, Germany
Xiangfeng Luo   Shanghai University, China
Maristella Matera   Politecnico di Milano, Italy
Nikolay Mehandjiev   University of Manchester, UK
Santiago Meliá   University of Alicante, Spain
Anders Møller   Aarhus University, Denmark
Hamid Motahari   HP Labs Palo Alto, USA
Wolfgang Nejdl   University of Hannover, Germany
Tobias Nestler   SAP Research Dresden, Germany
Axel-Cyrille Ngonga   University of Leipzig, Germany
Moira Norrie   ETH Zurich, Switzerland
Luis Olsina   National University of La Pampa, Argentina
Satoshi Oyama   Hokkaido University, Japan
George Pallis   University of Cyprus, Cyprus
Oscar Pastor   Polytechnic University of Valencia, Spain
Fabio Paternò   ISTI-C.N.R., Italy
Cesare Pautasso   University of Lugano, Switzerland
Vicente Pelechano   Polytechnic University of Valencia, Spain
Alfonso Pierantonio   University of L'Aquila, Italy
Xiaojun Quan   City University of Hong Kong SAR,
                                China
I.V. Ramakrishnan   Stony Brook University, USA
Florian Rosenberg   IBM T.J. Watson Research Center, NY, USA
Gustavo Rossi   UNLP, Argentina
Fernando Sánchez-Figueroa   Universidad de Extremadura, Spain
Daniel Schwabe   PUC-RIO, Brazil
Quan Z. Sheng   University of Adelaide, Australia
Sören Auer   Universität Leipzig, Germany
Giovanni Toffetti-Carughi   IBM Haifa Research, Israel
Takehiro Tokuda   Tokyo Institute of Technology, Japan
Riccardo Torlone   Roma Tre University, Italy

Jean Vanderdonckt	Université Catholique de Louvain, Belgium
Xiao Wei	Shanghai University, China
Shiting Wen	Ningbo Technological Institute of Zhejiang University, China
Marco Winckler	Paul Sabatier University, France
Bin Xu	Tsinghua University, China
Yi Zhuang	Zhejiang Gongshang University, China
Qingguo Zhou	Lanzhou University, China

Poster/Demo Track Program Committee

Fabio Casati	University of Trento, Italy
Sven Casteleyn	Universidad Politécnica de Valencia, Spain
Alessio Gambi	Università Della Svizzera Italiana, Switzerland
Andrea Mauri	Politecnico di Milano, Italy
Santiago Meliá	Universidad de Alicante, Spain
Maristella Matera	Politecnico di Milano, Italy
Marcello Leida	Khalifa University of Science, Technology and Research, United Arab Emirates
Nora Koch	Ludwig Maximilians University of Munich, Germany
Marco Brambilla	Politecnico di Milano, Italy
Stefan Pietschmann	TU Dresden, Germany
Devis Bianchini	University of Brescia, Italy
William Van Woensel	Vrije Universiteit Brussel, Belgium
Javier Luis Cnovas Izquierdo	INRIA, Ecole des Mines de Nantes, France
Gustavo Rossi	University of La Plata, Argentina
Richard Chbeir	University of Bourgogne, France
Fernando Sánchez Figueroa	Universidad de Extremadura, Spain
Flavius Frasincar	Erasmus University of Rotterdam, The Netherlands

External Reviewers

Saeed Aghaee	University of Lugano, Switzerland
Jose Alfonso Aguilar Calderón	University of Alicante, Spain
Liaqat Ali	Athabasca University, Canada
Cristobal Arellano	The University of the Basque Country, Spain
Mohsen Asadi	Athabasca University, Canada
Vikas Ganjigunte Ashok	Stony Brook University, USA
Moshe Chai Barukh	University of New South Wales, Australia
Seyed-Mehdi-Reza Beheshti	University of New South Wales, Australia
Sebastian Bress	LIAS/ISAE-ENSMA, France
Hugo Brunelière	INRIA, Nantes, France

Javier Luis Canovas Izquierdo	INRIA, Nantes, France
Olexiy Chudnovskyy	Chemnitz University of Technology, Germany
Jose Maria Conejero	Universidad de Extremadura, Spain
Adrin Fernández	Polytechnic University of Valencia, Spain
Marco Fisichella	University of Hannover, Germany
Miriam Gil	Polytechnic University of Valencia, Spain
Allel Hadjali	LIAS/ISAE-ENSMA, France
Matthias Heinrich	Chemnitz University of Technology, Germany
Michael Krug	Chemnitz University of Technology, Germany
Angel Lagares	University of New South Wales, Australia
Marino Linaje	Universidad de Extremadura, Spain
Jose-Norberto Mazón	University of Alicante, Spain
Salvador Martnez	INRIA, Nantes, France
Sujith Mathew	University of Adelaide, Australia
Bardia Mohabbati	Athabasca University, Canada
Hernan Molina	GIDIS Web, Universidad Nacional de La Pampa, Argentina
Rober Morales-Chaparro	Universidad de Extremadura, Spain
Abdallah Namoun	University of Manchester, UK
Arun Nampally	Stony Brook University, USA
Stefan Negru	University of Stuttgart, Germany
Talal H. Noor	University of Adelaide, Australia
Andreas Papadopoulos	University of Cyprus, Cyprus
Yury Puzis	Stony Brook University, USA
Yongrui Qin	University of Adelaide, Australia
Bene Rodriguez-Castro	Universität der Bundeswehr München, Germany
Roberto Rodríguez-Echeverría	Universidad de Extremadura, Spain
Seung Ryu	University of New South Wales, Australia
Melody Siadaty	Athabasca University, Canada
Stalo Sofokleous	University of Cyprus, Cyprus
Jean Stéphane	LIAS/ISAE-ENSMA, France
Alex Stolz	Universität der Bundeswehr München, Germany
László Török	Universität der Bundeswehr München, Germany
Stefano Tranquillini	University of Trento, Italy
Demetris Trihinas	University of Cyprus, Cyprus
William Van Woensel	Vrije Universiteit Brussel, Belgium
Stefan Wild	Chemnitz University of Technology, Germany
Yang Yang	Ningbo Technological Institute of Zhejiang University, China
Lina Yao	University of Adelaide, Australia
Yong Xu	University of Adelaide, Australia

Sponsoring Institutions

Otto Monsted Fond, Denmark,
Det Obelske Famieliefond, Denmark

Table of Contents

Component-Based User Interfaces

Mashups and End-User Development

Navigation Analysis and Collaboration

Web Information Retrieval

Crawling and Revisitation

Semantic Data Search and Interlinking

Web Services and Cloud Computing

Industry Papers

Demonstrations and Posters

Tutorials

Challenges in Service Mining:
Record, Check, Discover

Wil M.P. van der Aalst[1,2]

[1] Architecture of Information Systems, Eindhoven University of Technology,
P.O. Box 513, NL-5600 MB, Eindhoven, The Netherlands
w.m.p.v.d.aalst@tue.nl
[2] International Laboratory of Process-Aware Information Systems, National
Research University Higher School of Economics (HSE),
33 Kirpichnaya Str., Moscow, Russia

Abstract. Process mining aims to discover, monitor and improve real processes by extracting knowledge from event logs abundantly available in today's information systems. Although process mining has been applied in hundreds of organizations and process mining techniques have been embedded in a variety of commercial tools, to date these techniques have rarely been used for analyzing web services. One of the obvious reasons is that cross-organizational event data cannot be shared easily. However, (1) messages exchanged between services tend to be structured, (2) service-orientation continues to be the predominant implementation paradigm, and (3) the most substantial efficiency gains can often only be achieved across different organizations. Hence, there are many possible applications for *service mining*, i.e., applying process mining techniques to services. If messages are recorded, then one can discover a process describing interactions between services. If, in addition, descriptive or normative models are available, one can use process mining to check conformance and highlight performance problems. This extended abstract aims to provide pointers to ongoing work on service mining and lists some of the main challenges in this emerging field.

1 From Process Mining to Service Mining

Process mining is an enabling technology for service mining. Process mining can be used to *discover* processes from raw event data, *check* the conformance of observed and modeled behavior, *enhance* models by improving or extending them with knowledge extracted from event logs [2]. The uptake of process mining is not only illustrated by the growing number of papers, but also by commercial analysis tools providing process mining capabilities, cf. Disco (Fluxicon), Perceptive Process Mining (Perceptive Software, before Futura Reflect and BPMone by Pallas Athena), ARIS Process Performance Manager (Software AG), ProcessAnalyzer (QPR), Interstage Process Discovery (Fujitsu), Discovery Analyst (StereoLOGIC), and XMAnalyzer (XMPro).

Web services have become one of the main paradigms for architecting and implementing business collaborations within and across organizational boundaries

F. Daniel, P. Dolog, and Q. Li (Eds.): ICWE 2013, LNCS 7977, pp. 1–4, 2013.

[10,20]. The functionality provided by many of today's business applications is encapsulated within web services, i.e., software components described at a semantic level, which can be invoked by application programs or by other services through a stack of Internet standards including HTTP, XML, SOAP, WSDL and UDDI [10,20]. Once deployed, web services provided by various organizations can be inter-connected in order to implement business collaborations, leading to composite web services.

In the context of web services, typically all kinds of *events* are being recorded. It is possible to record events related to *activities inside services* or *interactions between services* (e.g., messages) [6,8,9]. The autonomous nature of services and the fact that they are loosely coupled makes it important to monitor and analyze their behavior. In this paper, we will refer to this as *service mining*.

Starting point for process mining is an *event log*. Each event in such a log refers to an *activity* (i.e., a well-defined step in some process) and is related to a particular *case* (i.e., a process instance). The events belonging to a case are ordered and describe one "run" of the process. Event logs may store additional information about events. In fact, whenever possible, process mining techniques use supplementary information such as the *resource* (i.e., person, device, or software component) executing or initiating the activity, the *timestamp* of the event, and other *data attributes* (e.g., the size of an order). As mentioned before, three types of process mining can be distinguished: (1) *process discovery*, (2) *conformance checking*, and (3) *model enhancement*. See [2] for an introduction to the corresponding techniques.

The *correlation of messages* is a particular challenge for service mining [3]. Process models always describe the behavior of cases, also referred to as process instances. Without correlating messages, it is impossible to discover causalities. Another challenge is to *use additional information provided by such messages*. In case of asynchronous messages with sender and receiver information we can exploit knowledge about distributed processes, e.g., choices need to be communicated. For example, service x cannot expect the service y to take action because x did *not* send a message to y. Thus far, these insights are not used in process discovery [16].

2   Related Work on Service Mining

In this section, we provide some pointers to papers on services mining and related topics. Given space restrictions, we do not aim to be complete. For additional references we refer the interested reader to [3].

In [9] a concrete application of process mining to web services is described. IBM's WebSphere product is used as a reference system and its CEI (Common Event Infrastructure) logs are analyzed using ProM.

An approach to check the conformance of web services was described in [6]. The paper includes a description of various experiments using Oracle BPEL. The token-based replay techniques presented in [18] were used to measure conformance.

In [8] an LTL-based approach to check conformance was proposed. This approach uses a graphical declarative language to describe the normative behavior of services. Rather than modeling a detailed process, this approach allows for checking graphically specified constraints such as "a payment should always be confirmed".

The topic of event correlation has been investigated in the context of system specification, system development, and services analysis. In [7] and [11] various interaction and correlation patterns are described. In [17] a technique is presented for correlating messages with the goal to visualize the execution of web services. In [16] so-called operating guidelines are exploited for conformance checking.

Dustdar et al. [12,14] proposed techniques for services interaction mining, i.e., applying process mining techniques to the analysis of service interactions.

Nezhad et al. [15] developed techniques for event correlation and process discovery from web service interaction logs. The authors introduce the notion of a "process view" which is the result of a particular event correlation. However, they argue that correlation is subjective and that multiple views are possible. A collection of process views is called the "process space".

In [19], Simmonds et al. propose a technique for the run-time monitoring of web service conversations. The authors monitor conversations between partners at runtime as a means of checking behavioral correctness of the entire web service system. This is related to the earlier work on conformance checking [4,6,18] mentioned before.

Within the ACSI project the focus is on many-to-many relationships between instances. So-called "proclets" [5] are used to model artifact centric models. A conformance checking approach for such models is presented in [13] and implemented in ProM.

In [1] the topic of "cross-organizational mining" was introduced. Here the goal is not to analyze interacting services but to compare services that are variants of one another. Cross-organizational mining can be used for benchmarking and reference modeling.

Acknowledgements. This work was supported by the Basic Research Program of the National Research University Higher School of Economics (HSE).

References

1. van der Aalst, W.M.P.: Configurable Services in the Cloud: Supporting Variability While Enabling Cross-Organizational Process Mining. In: Meersman, R., Dillon, T.S., Herrero, P. (eds.) OTM 2010. LNCS, vol. 6426, pp. 8–25. Springer, Heidelberg (2010)
2. van der Aalst, W.M.P.: Process Mining: Discovery, Conformance and Enhancement of Business Processes. Springer, Berlin (2011)
3. van der Aalst, W.M.P.: Service Mining: Using Process Mining to Discover, Check, and Improve Service Behavior. IEEE Transactions on Services Computing (in print, 2013), http://doi.ieeecomputersociety.org/10.1109/TSC.2012.25

4. van der Aalst, W.M.P., Adriansyah, A., van Dongen, B.: Replaying History on Process Models for Conformance Checking and Performance Analysis. WIREs Data Mining and Knowledge Discovery 2(2), 182–192 (2012)
5. van der Aalst, W.M.P., Barthelmess, P., Ellis, C.A., Wainer, J.: Proclets: A Framework for Lightweight Interacting Workflow Processes. International Journal of Cooperative Information Systems 10(4), 443–482 (2001)
6. van der Aalst, W.M.P., Dumas, M., Ouyang, C., Rozinat, A., Verbeek, H.M.W.: Conformance Checking of Service Behavior. ACM Transactions on Internet Technology 8(3), 29–59 (2008)
7. van der Aalst, W.M.P., Mooij, A.J., Stahl, C., Wolf, K.: Service Interaction: Patterns, Formalization, and Analysis. In: Bernardo, M., Padovani, L., Zavattaro, G. (eds.) SFM 2009. LNCS, vol. 5569, pp. 42–88. Springer, Heidelberg (2009)
8. van der Aalst, W.M.P., Pesic, M.: Test and Analysis of Web Services. In: Specifying and Monitoring Service Flows: Making Web Services Process-Aware, ch. 2, pp. 11–56. Springer, Berlin (2007)
9. van der Aalst, W.M.P., Verbeek, H.M.W.: Process Mining in Web Services: The WebSphere Case. IEEE Bulletin of the Technical Committee on Data Engineering 31(3), 45–48 (2008)
10. Alonso, G., Casati, F., Kuno, H., Machiraju, V.: Web Services Concepts, Architectures and Applications. Springer, Berlin (2004)
11. Barros, A., Decker, G., Dumas, M., Weber, F.: Correlation Patterns in Service-Oriented Architectures. In: Dwyer, M.B., Lopes, A. (eds.) FASE 2007. LNCS, vol. 4422, pp. 245–259. Springer, Heidelberg (2007)
12. Dustdar, S., Gombotz, R.: Discovering Web Service Workflows Using Web Services Interaction Mining. International Journal of Business Process Integration and Management 1(4), 256–266 (2006)
13. Fahland, D., de Leoni, M., van Dongen, B.F., van der Aalst, W.M.P.: Conformance Checking of Interacting Processes with Overlapping Instances. In: Rinderle-Ma, S., Toumani, F., Wolf, K. (eds.) BPM 2011. LNCS, vol. 6896, pp. 345–361. Springer, Heidelberg (2011)
14. Gombotz, R., Dustdar, S.: On Web Services Workflow Mining. In: Bussler, C.J., Haller, A. (eds.) BPM 2005. LNCS, vol. 3812, pp. 216–228. Springer, Heidelberg (2006)
15. Montahari-Nezhad, H.R., Saint-Paul, R., Casati, F., Benatallah, B.: Event Correlation for Process Discovery from Web Service Interaction Logs. VLBD Journal 20(3), 417–444 (2011)
16. Müller, R., van der Aalst, W.M.P., Stahl, C.: Conformance Checking of Services Using the Best Matching Private View. In: Lohmann, N. (ed.) WS-FM 2012. LNCS, vol. 7843, pp. 49–68. Springer, Heidelberg (2013)
17. De Pauw, W., Lei, M., Pring, E., Villard, L., Arnold, M., Morar, J.F.: Web Services Navigator: Visualizing the Execution of Web Services. IBM Systems Journal 44(4), 821–845 (2005)
18. Rozinat, A., van der Aalst, W.M.P.: Conformance Checking of Processes Based on Monitoring Real Behavior. Information Systems 33(1), 64–95 (2008)
19. Simmonds, J., Gan, Y., Chechik, M., Nejati, S., Farrell, B., Litani, E., Waterhouse, J.: Runtime Monitoring of Web Service Conversations. IEEE Transactions on Services Computing 2(3), 223–244 (2009)
20. Zhang, L.J., Zhang, J., Cai, H.: Services Computing, Core Enabling Technology of the Modern Services Industry. Springer, Berlin (2007)

How to Share Data Securely

X. Sean Wang

School of Computer Science, Fudan University, Shanghai, China
xywangCS@fudan.edu.cn

Data is increasingly available in a digital form, and data about us is being
continuously collected. Such data has made possible many interesting and useful
applications, and in essense made it possible for the Web to exist in the current
form. Sharing this data makes a lot of sense for many reasons. However, personal
privacy has become a concern. In this talk, I will touch upon a recent study of
the privacy data leakage problem of mobile apps in China, and discuss various
ways to protect user data.

However, completely locking up data is neither desirable nor necessary. How
to share our data in a secure way becomes an interesting question. Privacy
protection of data has been a research problem for decades, with many interesting
results emerging in the last 15 or so years. In this talk, I will discuss a framework
for secure data sharing, linking many of the existing solutions under a unified
principle. The hope is to develop new insights and better data sharing methods.

F. Daniel, P. Dolog, and Q. Li (Eds.): ICWE 2013, LNCS 7977, p. 5, 2013.
© Springer-Verlag Berlin Heidelberg 2013

An Internet of Custom-Made Things: From 3D Printing and Personal Fabrication to Personal Design of Interactive Devices

Jan Borchers

Media Computing Group, RWTH Aachen University, Aachen, Germany
borchers@cs.rwth-aachen.de

In the homes of bleeding-edge tinkerers around the world, a revolution is happening that, as many predict, will overshadow the PC and internet revolutions that began with home computers in the 70's: Personal Fabrication. Sub-$1000 3D printers are a reality, and other computer-controlled digital fabrication tools such as lasercutters are close behind. Research labs are printing anything from molecules to entire houses, and Fab Labs around the world are introducing the public to the possibilities and dangers of this new era in production.

On the one hand, these tools are bringing exciting changes to the way we teach and do ubicomp and HCI research: Instead of merely creating on-screen prototypes, students are now able to rapidly create actual working, networked hardware prototypes with little effort, driving home the message that successful interactive products today require software and hardware design to go hand in hand. As personal fabrication technologies evolve to include multiple materials and even electronics in custom-made objects, their interface will likely be mediated via online services, leading to new challenges for how to create the appropriate web-based architectures for an Internet of Custom-Made Things. On the other hand, it is still largely unclear how users at home should create those 3D models to print or otherwise fabricate on their desktop factory of the near future: For example, will they download and customize online designs, specifying their search queries for object models via hand shape gestures in mid-air? This is a major challenge for HCI that calls for radically new user interface approaches, paradigms and interaction techniques for what I call "Personal Design", before we'll arrive at something like the MacPaint of Digital Fabricationp

F. Daniel, P. Dolog, and Q. Li (Eds.): ICWE 2013, LNCS 7977, p. 6, 2013.
© Springer-Verlag Berlin Heidelberg 2013

MockAPI: An Agile Approach Supporting API-first Web Application Development

José Matías Rivero[1], Sebastian Heil[2], Julián Grigera[1],
Martin Gaedke[2], and Gustavo Rossi[1]

[1] LIFIA, Facultad de Informática, UNLP, La Plata, Argentina
{mrivero,julian.grigera,gustavo}@lifia.info.unlp.edu.ar
[2] Department of Computer Science, Chemnitz University of Technology, Germany
{sebastian.heil,martin.gaedke}@informatik.tu-chemnitz.de

Abstract. In the last years, agile development methodologies have been widely adopted. However, they still lack support for API requirements while, at the same time, public RESTful APIs are fueling a rapid growth of web applications providing services built on other services. On the other hand, whereas Model-Driven Development techniques successfully increase the productivity in the development of data-intensive web applications, they lack the agility required when developing heterogeneous web applications with frequent requirement changes. In this paper we introduce MockAPI, an approach based on annotating user interface mockups that combines the advantages of agile approaches and Model-Driven Development. We introduce a metamodel for annotations and demonstrate how to derive running API prototypes as starting point for agile development. RESTful API best practices and API-first development are introduced into the agile process. The MockAPI approach defines a set of constraints to accelerate the development of web applications. We also show the results of a brief validation applying MockAPI to popular web sites.

Keywords: API, Model-Driven Development, Agile Development, Prototyping.

1 Introduction

Agile development methodologies have shown a massive adoption [1] because they allow to adapt quickly to changing requirements, effectively shorten the development cycle and include end-users more intensively in the development process, in order to reduce risks during projects. However, these development approaches are lacking support for API-related requirements (i.e. stating what the applications should provide as a service and how), since their advantages are not efficiently applied when gathering and implementing requirements that are not strictly related to user interaction (like user interface or business logic), i.e. not related to *what the user can see* [2].

Infrastructure-as-a-Service (IaaS) and Software-as-a-Service (SaaS) are transforming the way of providing services in the Cloud, and at the same time dropping the costs. On the one hand, IaaS provides a fast, easy and cost effective way of requesting infrastructure (processing, storage, data transfer, etc.) as needed to implement and

F. Daniel, P. Dolog, and Q. Li (Eds.): ICWE 2013, LNCS 7977, pp. 7–21, 2013.

scale applications. On the other hand, SaaS provides working software over the Cloud at a low cost, avoiding higher cost of deployment and maintenance associated with custom on-site installations. In this way, IaaS is providing an important cost reduction for software developers while SaaS is providing a similar reduction for software end-users. As a consequence, since both trends are intended to avoid an on-site installation of infrastructure and software, they provide APIs to facilitate critical operations like servers instantiations, storage increment requests (IaaS), data exportation/importation or special data operations (SaaS) [3].

On the application level, APIs are commonly used for different purposes. A common API layer is usually built to fulfill the business requirements of applications that run on different platforms and front-ends (web, desktop, mobile, etc.). Besides, making APIs publicly available is a well-known way of extending the impact and use of popular applications. Main examples of this approach are Facebook through its Facebook Graph API[1], and Twitter[2].

The development of APIs is getting more attention because they speed up the development process allowing reusing already existing software and infrastructural power to deliver software faster through integration of existing components. As the API becomes more important from the strategy and technology point of view and is part of the requirements, the challenge is to either help the end-users understand the concept and hidden complexity of distributed systems, or to provide a way for retrieving the necessary information for the API design with common requirement gathering techniques. Current agile methodologies do not provide a way of gathering and structuring this kind of requirements. Agile methodologies leave all the APIs definition work for developers without any guidance. Since in API-First[3] development the implementation of a core API is a blocking task delaying other tasks like frontend development, the entire development process is slowed down.

In this paper we provide a structured way of dealing with the definition of APIs, from requirements gathering to implementation. In addition to textual user stories, we use annotated user interface sketches (mockups) of the different front-ends of the application. We do so in order to gather a general overview of the underlying API of the application being built. The annotations placed over mockups can be easily applied to textual user stories as well, working as a story *stereotyping* strategy.

The rest of the paper is organized as follows: in Section 2 we analyze related work and background of the fundamental concepts used in our proposal, Section 3 details the core features of our approach including procedural and technical features. In Section 4 we explain implementation details and Section 5 summarizes the results of a validation experiment featuring popular real-world web sites. Finally, in Section 6 we conclude the paper and envision future work.

---

[1] Facebook Graph API - https://developers.facebook.com/docs/reference/api/, last accessed on 06-March-2013.

[2] Twitter Developers - https://dev.twitter.com, last accessed on 23-Feb-2013.

[3] API-First development - http://www.api-first.com

2   Background and Related Work

2.1   State of the Art in Web Applications Development

When developing software through direct coding, extensive tool support and well-known practices are often available to make the development process faster and less error prone for developers. Dependency management tools, Integrated Development Environments (IDEs), build and deployment environments among many other remarkable tools are available to assist the development team daily. In the same sense, a plethora of technologies, patterns, practices and processes have been defined to cope with complexities in software development like Design Patterns, Aspect-Oriented Programming, Test-Driven Development, etc. However, while they substantially help developers in the process, there are still many challenges related to coding software by hand: writing it syntactically and semantically correct according to the elicited requirements, writing tests to check whether the application meets them, use the same patterns, practices, programming style and frameworks in the correct way, etc. To make things worse, integration between newly developed software and SaaS applications (from social networking like Facebook or Twitter to infrastructural services as provided by Amazon[4], Microsoft[5] or Google[6]) are becoming increasingly required in industry. This introduces the problem of interacting with other software using particular communication channels and data formats.

Not specifically focused on APIs, Model-Driven Development (MDD) [4] solutions have been defined to cope with such challenges. In MDD, software is defined as a set of high-level models and derived automatically using code generators, respecting a previously agreed architecture, patterns and platform defined by the software architects or developers. The main problem in MDD is that it only allows specifying software features by concepts included in the high-level language. When a special feature has to be included in the application, either the language has to be extended in order to express and further derive this features or the generated code has to be modified manually. MDD can be suitable for specific types of development such as data-intensive web applications [5]. However, MDD is less applicable for developing heterogeneous applications. This is due to the cost of personalizing the MDD infrastructure to cope with detailed and rapidly changing requirements and implementations. In a previous work we explore the possibility of bringing an agile approach to MDD [6], starting from mockups to gather requirements and generating prototypes.

On the other hand, software scaffolding solutions like Ruby on Rails[7] propose an intermediate solution: they allow generating the structural parts of the applications expressed in some simplistic specification language (sometimes using standards like XML or YAML). Once generated, they have to be manually refined by developers,

---

[4] Amazon Web Services - http://aws.amazon.com/, last accessed 23-Feb-2013.

[5] Windows Azure - http://www.windowsazure.com/en-us/, last accessed 23-Feb-2013.

[6] Google App Engine - https://developers.google.com/appengine/, last accessed 23-Feb-2013.

[7] Ruby on Rails - http://rubyonrails.org/, accessed on 28-Feb-2013.

discarding the initial specifications. Such approaches force a specific platform and architecture with the advantages of automatic code generation to speed-up the initial stages of the development. Similar to scaffolding approaches, user interface prototype annotations like Canonical Abstract Prototypes [7] intend to model common UI patterns and propose a semi-automatic code generation. However, since they focus on user interface implementation – that is inherently complex – they only allow generating a limited subset of features, leaving the task of dealing with the generated UI code to the programmer.

An additional issue in all three approaches is the need to manually translate requirements (expressed usually as user stories, use cases, natural language narratives, etc.) to code or models only observing the requirements artifacts; that is, no assistance is provided to guide this process. In this work, we present a Model-Driven process that allows defining and quickly generating an initial API for a Web Application to speed-up the initial iterations in the development. This allows developing the application frontend that uses the API through direct coding speedily in order to obtain a fully functional running version of the application that can be tested with end-users as soon as possible. Finally, the generated API can be further partially or totally implemented as necessary in the following iterations. Thus, our approach intends to combine classic code-based development with Model-Driven and Scaffolding processes.

2.2   Agile Development Style Meets Service-Oriented Architecture

In agile development, the focus on a rapid implementation of functionality that yields a visible business value can be unfavorable in the context of service-oriented architecture [8]. While user stories are customer-oriented, architectural aspects like identification and modeling of services, data resources or API design are not covered in agile development [9–11]. Though there are proposals to tackle service related features in the early requirements gathering stage, e.g., using use cases [12], they do not use requirement artifacts fully understandable for end-users, which are at the same time, unambiguous and technically sound for developers [13]. Approaches like [11] advocate using architectural knowledge bases for decision making and evaluation, however, they do not focus on accelerating the process to create early running versions.

Advantages of the API-first paradigm cannot be fully leveraged. Ideally, common functionality and resources for different application platforms are consolidated at the service layer. This enables independent parallel development of applications for different devices and facilitates serendipity through the development of third-party applications benefiting from the exposed service layer [14].

As API development requires a lot of experience and knowledge about best practices [15], API quality in agile development is highly dependent on the developer team's skill level. There is no process-intrinsic guidance or widely accepted concept available that supports agile developers in using best practices.

Agile development teams encounter difficulties when applying a service-oriented architecture style. Particularly, there is a gap between requirements represented by customer-oriented stories and application architecture, which can produce poorly designed APIs. Application of best practices for a clean, usable API is highly dependent on the experience of the development team as there is no further guidance provided. For better support of applying service-oriented architecture style in agile development, a refined approach is required bridging the gap between requirements and architecture by combining the most promising elements of various development approaches employed today and providing enhanced guidance regarding API best practices to the agile developer.

3   The MockAPI Approach

In this section we describe motivation, procedural and technical aspects of our approach that allows quickly specifying and generating APIs using requirement artifacts that are easily understood by both developers and customers: user interface mockups.

3.1   The Approach in a Nutshell

To overcome the issues mentioned in Section 2, we proposed an approach called *MockAPI*. MockAPI aims at helping developers in an agile environment to design service-oriented applications. The proposed process starts by eliciting requirements through user stories and their related user interface mockups. Such mockups represent an intermediate language between developers and customers, being technically sound to developers and fully understandable by customers [13]. Mockups are then annotated with simple but formal specifications that we use to automatically generate a first API implementation. This API is intended to help building the first iterations of the different application front-ends, reducing the requirements-to-software time and effort, though it might be later replaced by the definitive one. In this paper we focus on generating APIs for service-backed web applications, however, the same annotation approach can be used to generate other artifacts like interaction descriptions related to mockups (that can be checked by end-users) or data layer schemas and configurations.

3.2   MockAPI Process

To exemplify the approach within an agile methodology we chose Scrum, since it is one of the most widely adopted in industry [1]. The Scrum process starts with the construction of a Product Backlog, listing Stories, ordered by value delivered to the customer. Then, the product is built iteratively in Sprints. Every Sprint starts with a Planning Meeting in which Stories are selected from the Product Backlog according to their priority and broken down into Tasks, forming the Sprint Backlog. A short Daily Meeting is held every work day to gain awareness of work progress/problems. At the end of each Sprint, a potentially shippable application is demonstrated to the Product Owner and customer [16].

The MockAPI Scrum process in Fig. 1 proposes using mockups in all steps. Since a mockup represents the user interface/interaction required to satisfy a story, mockups form an intermediate tool between abstract stories and concrete tasks. Therefore, we propose to add mockups to the Sprint Backlog. Mockups must be built and annotated with stakeholder participation; developers can explain semantics if needed.

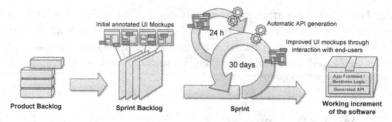

Fig. 1. An overview of the MockAPI Scrum process

The developer team starts with coding the application front-end. An initial API implementation can be derived from annotated mockups to speed-up the process. Thus, in early iterations, the development team can focus on interaction and presentation allowing for early feedback. Front-ends for different devices (e.g. cellphones, tablets, PCs) can be built in parallel with API support from the outset.

Although changes in mockups are frequent, they do not require strong re-implementation effort: the API can be re-generated from updated annotations.

3.3   Mockup Building and Annotation

MockAPI relies on annotating mockups to discover and specify features related to the required API. Annotations can serve both as requirements and implementation specification. In the following subsections we describe the structure of the annotations MockAPI defines to specify API-related features.

3.3.1   Dealing with Content

One of the basic specifications required to define an API is its content (in terms of types and relationships) and the way it is accessed. To deal with these concerns, MockAPI proposes the following annotation types, depicted in Fig. 2 over sample mockups for a conference management system:

List(ItemName): describes a list of items in a mockup, of the type *ItemName*. For instance, the List(conference) tag in the leftmost mockup from Fig. 2 denotes a list of conference objects. From these tags, we can infer the existence of resources called *ItemName* (objects of type ItemName) aggregated in a list.

Item(ElementName): expresses that the annotated mockup shows a user interface containing representation of a single item called *ElementName*. A mockup showing the details of a conference is annotated with Item(conference).

Viewing/Editing: describe access type to resources; we identified two basic resource access patterns: viewing and editing. Both are included as tags in MockAPI. viewing represents read-only access, editing represents Create, Read, Update, Delete functionality.

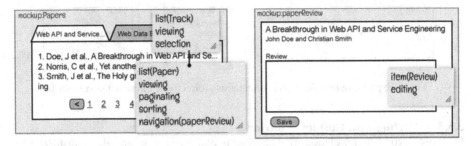

Fig. 2. Sample annotated mockups for a conference management system

Although there are other combinations of CRUD actions, in order to keep our approach simple, the two combinations described by our resource access patterns cover most actions used in web applications. If other particular combinations are required, a user story is added and the respective API has to be manually configured. Used with Item, viewing implies the content cannot be changed, while editing allows creating new instances, updating their content and deleting them. Used with List, editing additionally allows removing/reordering elements.

Associations. Since the structure of mockups can be arbitrarily complex, several content annotations can be present in a single mockup. Thus, MockAPI allows defining and relating different *Item* or *List* annotations. For this purpose, we introduce the concept of *Associations*. Each Association represents a directed relationship between two content annotations in the mockup and is graphically expressed by an arrow connecting them.

Sorting, Ordering, Filtering, Selection and Pagination. These 5 tags can only be applied to List to indicate it supports element sorting (e.g. by price), ordering (e.g. list prioritization using drag & drop), filtering elements (e.g. filtering by name), selecting elements (e.g. to apply some operation like deleting them) or pagination.

3.3.2   Dealing with Navigation

Navigation is another important aspect to define in web applications. It defines how interaction and data from the UI is fractioned and simplified in presentation units like pages, windows or menus, which can have an indirect impact in the API. For instance, a complex UI that displays a lot of data will be presented faster to the end-user if the API supports to get all the required information in a single request instead of many. This kind of relationship may be directly specified from one annotation to the other within the same mockup, as illustrated in Fig. 3a, where selecting a specific conference produces the tracks list to update. To relate data across two different mockups instead, an indirect navigation relationship can be defined between them, as shown in figure 3.b. To specify these navigations MockAPI includes the following annotation:

Navigation(DestinationMockupName). Indicates an element in the present mockup navigates to another mockup identified by *DestinationMockupName*, as seen in Fig.3b from *mockup1* to *mockup2*. Depending on the tooling used, the destination mockup can be identified by its name using different strategies like its filename.

Fig. 3. Expressing relationships in annotations (directly or through a navigation)

3.3.3 Dealing with Custom Behavior

Features beyond manipulation of data objects and navigation are also considered in the approach. The underlying functionality cannot be generated automatically, but they can be modeled and added to the mockup to be implemented as separated user stories to be coded later, without breaking the annotation abstraction and requiring to make extensive language and code generation improvements. This kind of features can be introduced with the `SpecialFeature()` tag:

SpecialFeature(Description). Represents a complex feature that must be implemented in the API through direct coding, described in plain text (Description).

3.3.4 The MockAPI Metamodel

In order to abstract the structure of MockAPI annotations from their representations, we defined a detailed metamodel which structure can be observed in Fig. 4.

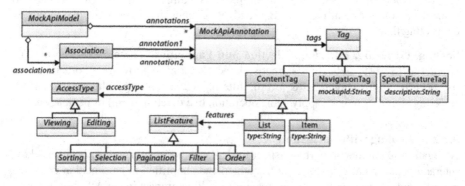

Fig. 4. Structure of the MockAPI metamodel

A MockAPI model (`MockAPIModel`) is composed by a list of annotations (`MockAPIAnnotations`) and associations (`Association`). An annotation is composed by a list of tags (`Tag`), which can be of type content (`ContentTag`), navigation (`NavigationTag`) or a special feature (`SpecialFeatureTag`) according to the types previously introduced. A `ContentTag` can be a `List` or `Item` and can have a specific `AccessType` (`Viewing` or `Writing`). In addition, a list can feature sorting (`Sorting`), selection (`Selection`), etc. A `NavigationTag` stores the id of the destination mockup and `SpecialFeatureTag` includes the description of the special behaviour to be implemented. Though not directly expressed in the metamodel, `MockAPIAnnotation` can only contain one instance of each `Tag` type but `SpecialFeatureTag`.

In 3.4 we describe how to generate API prototypes for set-based resources by analyzing content annotations, i.e. instances of the metamodel. The tags detailed in this section can be combined to form annotations placed over mockups. Fig. 5. shows a sample mockup of a conference manager with editable data of a conference, its editable and selectable tracks and read-only papers per tracks. Papers can be sorted and paginated. Clicking a paper navigates to another mockup called trackDetails.

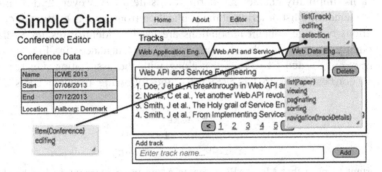

Fig. 5. Annotated conference manager mockup

3.4   Generating APIs from MockAPI

The MockAPI approach focuses on CRUD features of applications based on RESTful Web services; therefore, it constrains the supported design space. Providing guidance for these basic aspects supports agile developers in a frequent and time-consuming yet important part of work. Martin Fowler argues that "[d]isappointing as it is, many of the use cases in an enterprise application are fairly boring 'CRUD' (create, read, update, delete) use cases on domain objects" [17]. Any functionality beyond CRUD access to API resources, e.g., calculations, complex queries and statistical report generation, is handled in the usual agile way by creating a corresponding story. MockAPI simply sets the stage for developers to start implementing the missing functionality.

From an instance of our metamodel, the basic outline of the RESTful API can be inferred. Best practices for RESTful Web services [15] and the set-based navigation pattern [18] are applied to the modeling. The two central tags regarding content are List and Item. List tags are used to identify API resources and corresponding URIs. In the example shown in Fig. 5 List(track) implies the existence of:

/tracks

following the "Plural nouns and concrete names" principle described in [15]. Furthermore, tags defining user interaction aspects such as Selection and Ordering also influence the API. For instance adding a Selection tag in addition to the previous List(track) tag defines the items of the list, i.e. single tracks, to be individually selectable elements. Inferring resource URIs would additionally yield:

/track/<id>

This allows for access to the entire list as well as to a single item of the list identified by its id [15]. Although the same API can be achieved with List(track) and Item(track) – because to display a single list item it has to be identifiable in the API – the Selection tag additionally documents the user interaction requirement of selecting items from the list. The same applies to Ordering, which, only considering the API, is implied by List(conference) with access pattern editing as allowing update of a list implicitly enables reordering of its items. However, Ordering also specifies implementing list ordering at the application frontend e.g. by drag & drop.

Associations between content annotations are used to identify resource relationships explicitly visible in the UI mockups. For instance in Fig. 5, from Item(conference) and List(track) along with the association, i.e. the arrow from Item(conference) to List(track), the following resource URIs can be inferred:

```
/tracks
/tracks/<id>
/conferences/<id>/track
```

It is important to note that MockAPI assumes a one-to-many relationship by default when Item and List are related. However, if an inverse one-to-many relationship is found in another mockup, the entire relationship is interpreted as many-to-many. Relationships between Lists are always assumed as many-to-many.

Further associations can be inferred even between annotations in separate mockups, using the Navigation tags. For instance, if an Item(conference) defines a navigation to a List(track) in a different mockup, a relationship between conferences and tracks will be inferred. In general, when annotations specify navigation to other mockups, the root content annotation is identified and an association is created between both content elements. The root content annotation of a mockup is an annotation with no incoming associations. If only one root annotation is present, the association is inferred automatically; otherwise it has to be refined manually.

4   Implementation

To assist the process, we devised tools that help through the main steps, as depicted in Fig. 6, starting from bare mockups to the generated API prototype.

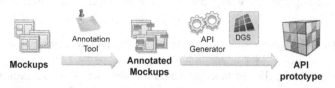

Fig. 6. MockAPI process with tooling support

In the following we explain process and tools for annotation automatic generation.

4.1   The Interactive Annotation Tool

While the structured annotations previously introduced can be applied manually over physical mockups to add semantics to the plain UI structure that they represent, semi-automatic API generation is not possible directly from them. To assist the annotation process and also to have a digital representation of the proposed annotations that can be used to generate the API, we developed a web annotation tool[8]. This tool allows importing any mockup image – e.g. hand-drawn or from image export capabilities present in mockup tools like Balsamiq[9] – and allows adding annotations over it. Fig. 7 shows a screenshot of the tool. During annotation, the tool parses the annotations to validate their structure and generates the underlying MockAPI model concepts.

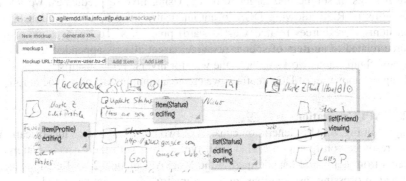

Fig. 7. Annotating a hand-drawn mockup with the MockAPI annotating tool

Once mockups have been correctly annotated, the tool provides a way of exporting an XML representation of the MockAPI model represented by the annotations. This model is used to further derive and configure the API automatically. Thus, the annotation tool works as the initial stage in the semi-automatic annotation-to-API process.

4.2   Generating APIs from MockAPI

In the following section we describe the implementation of a supporting tool that automatically generates a running API prototype from a set of annotated mockups by processing the XML representation of a MockAPI model. This tool applies the rules described in 3.4 to infer involved resources, access patterns and relationships.

4.2.1   WebComposition/DataGridService

In order to transform annotated mockups into a running API prototype, we employ the WebComposition/DataGridService (DGS) [19], which allows defining, creating and configuring resources at runtime and access via a RESTful interface. Our API Generator sets up the API prototype by configuring DGS XML resources.

---

[8] Available at: http://agilemdd.lifia.info.unlp.edu.ar/mockapi/
[9] Balsamiq Mockups - http://www.balsamiq.com/, last accessed 23-Feb-2013.

HTTP methods GET, POST, PUT and DELETE are supported on both resource and item level. Child elements of the XML root of the resource are treated as items of this resource, facilitating full read/write access to each of them separately. Additionally, DGS provides service and resource metadata maintained as RDF[10]. Configuration of the DGS and its resources is available through adding RDF statements to the metadata of the service or resource. Configuration on resource level includes the possibility to blacklist HTTP methods defining resource access policy. XML schema can be declared per resource to provide validation when HTTP-Requests attempt to modify the resource. On service level, relationships between resources can be declared consisting of source and target resource, a predicate, optionally an inverse predicate, source and target alias. Predicate is the RDF predicate to represent the relationship between items of source and target resource. Using inverse predicates, we leverage the benefits of RDF allowing DGS to automatically infer inverse relationships between items of resources related via (forward) predicates. To query items of target resource related to an item of source resource, target alias is appended to the source item path. Source alias works in the same way for inverse relationships.

Using the above set of DGS features we create a running API prototype at runtime.

4.2.2   API Generation

As shown in Fig. 8, API Generation consists of two phases: resource identification (1-5) and resource configuration (7-14). All types along with their access patterns are collected from items and lists defined in the MockAPI model (2-3). Relationships are identified processing associations and cardinality is determined as described in 3.4 (5).

Processing the derived set of types with access pattern information, the corresponding resources are created in the DGS, one per type (08). We pursue a set-based approach declaring the resources assuming containers of elements of the identified type. The container resource name follows the scheme <TypeName>s. While any occurrence of access pattern editing causes a type to be defined editable, only those types with all occurrences of viewing across all mockups are considered read-only. For each type identified read-only we configure DGS to restrict access to the corresponding resource accordingly denying HTTP methods POST, PUT and DELETE (10).

A default XML Schema is created per list (11) defining the root element matching the above name scheme and its content as sequence of elements named after the type, zero to unbounded occurrences. Currently, the content of the list elements is specified as *xs:any*, zero to unbounded, in order to allow for arbitrary data structures. However, the XML Schema can be easily adapted to incorporate specification of concrete data structures in future. For instance, a semi-natural language approach with statements like "A conference consists of name, location, startDate and endDate" is desirable.

Following the rules described in 3.4 relationships between resources are configured (14). Predicate names are created from a combination of resource names, e.g. mkapi:ConferenceHasTracks or mkapi:TrackBelongsToConference.

---

[10] RDF Primer - http://www.w3.org/TR/rdf-primer/, last accessed 29-Apr-2013.

```
01 foreach type Type with access Access in mockups
02    Types.Add Type
03    Accesses.Add (Type, Access)
04 foreach association (Source, Target) in mockups
05    Relationships.AddOrUpdate (Source, Target)
06
07 foreach type Type in Types
08    resource = DGS.CreateResource Type
09    if not Accesses.Contains (Type, "Editing")
10       resource.Deny [POST,PUT,DELETE]
11    resource.SetSchema DefaultXMLSchema(Type)
12 foreach relationship (Source, Target, Card)
13 in Relationships
14    DGS.DefineRelationship (Source, Target, Card)
```

Fig. 8. API Generation

Source and target alias are set to the resource name of the forward/inverse related resources. For instance `/conferences/<cid>/tracks` yields all tracks related to the conference with id `<cid>` via the `mkapi:ConferenceHasTracks` predicate. For the inverse relationship using `mkapi:TrackBelongsToConference` the generated URI path is `/tracks/<tid>/conference`.

5   Validation

In order to evaluate our proposed approach and identify potential shortcomings we conducted a brief validation. We tested the applicability of MockAPI in state-of-the-art websites by creating mockups for the most relevant user interfaces of 10 of the most popular websites based on the Alexa ranking [20]. To demonstrate the versatility of MockAPI, we used pen and paper mockups as well as digital mockup tools. The resulting mockups have been annotated using our interactive annotation tool and API prototypes have been generated using the MockAPI DGS API Generator.

MockAPI does not claim to create complete and mature APIs ready for productive use. Instead, we aim at providing a starting point for agile development by creating functional API prototypes. Therefore, an indirect metric is employed to evaluate our approach. We call this metric *coverage metric* and define it as follows:

Let M be a mockup and $P(M) = P_S \cup P_D$ the set of panels of M which provide user interface functionality. $P(M)$ can be subdivided into P_S, the set of panels which are static, and P_D, the set of dynamic panels. For instance, P_S includes navigation menus and buttons triggering predefined actions and P_D includes panels that dynamically depend on content or calculations such as lists of breaking news or displays of current time. Let A be the set of annotations added to M. Then $C(M) = \frac{|A|}{|P_D|}$ is the coverage metric of M. In other words, the coverage metric C is the ratio of coverage of dynamic panels with MockAPI annotations. The main motivation behind this metric is to validate how much of the dynamic content can be modeled and further API generated automatically using the MockAPI infrastructure. Static content (P_S) is excluded from the evaluation as it is rendered directly, without making use of any API. Since some sites adjust static content to user preferences, we checked that panels remain the same for at least 3 different users to consider them as truly static.

We calculated C for each mockup of the popular websites used for validation. For the top 10 sites according to Alexa, we created 38 mockups and identified 150 dynamic data panels[11]. 134 of these panels could be covered by our annotations, which results in an average coverage metric of 89%. This indicates that the majority of dynamic panels in the most popular websites can be described using MockAPI annotations. Among those that could not be cover we identified 4 recurring groups: (1) results of calculations such as counting views, converting units etc., (2) results of foreign Web Service invocations such as weather information etc., (3) trending entities that are results of activity monitoring and access statistics such as trending news, tweets, hashtags etc. and (4) related entities that are results of similarity heuristics such as related articles, searches, news etc.

The high coverage for the rest of the panels shows that most features in the evaluated web applications can be specified as API operations. We found generated APIs to be surprisingly simple in comparison to the API and infrastructure of real web sites. However, since MockAPI is meant to speed up the development process, we argue that the functionality automatically generated from mockups is enough for the development team to start creating the application's front-end without wasting time coding the operations that the API must implement.

6   Conclusions and Future Work

We presented MockAPI, an approach based on mockup annotations which combines the advantages of agile and Model-Driven Development and demonstrated how to derive running API prototypes as starting point for agile development using our annotation metamodel. The brief validation indicated that MockAPI can cover most of the functionality found in the user interfaces of popular web sites.

In future work, we will focus on improving the ease of use and expressivity of our annotations. For instance, while currently annotations are simple lists of keywords, the proposed approach is a first step towards documentation and agile development support for technically less experienced stakeholders. Therefore, we want to evolve the annotation syntax to facilitate a semi-natural language description of UI elements and content in general and the structure of data in particular.

Moreover, we plan to extend the approach to cover additional aspects such as navigation, security or user interaction and consolidate the idea of constraint-based development with recent advances in mashup research to provide an environment for rapid development of web applications based on re-usable components.

---

[11] Analyzed data is available at http://agilemdd.lifia.info.unlp.edu.ar/mockapi/validation

Acknowledgments. This project is partially supported by the DAAD – MINCYT project 54367460 / DA/11/11.

References

1. VersionOne Inc.: State of Agile Survey (2011)
2. Rodríguez, P., Yagüe, A.: Some findings concerning requirements in Agile methodologies. Product-Focused Software Process Improvement 32, 171–184 (2009)
3. Leymann, F., Fritsch, D.: Cloud computing: The next revolution in IT. In: Proceedings of the 52th Photogrammetric Week (2009)
4. Kelly, S., Tolvanen, J.-P.: Domain-Specific Modeling: Enabling Full Code Generation. Wiley-IEEE Computer Society (2008)
5. Ceri, S., Fraternali, P., Bongio, A.: Web Modeling Language (WebML): a modeling language for designing Web sites. Computer Networks 33, 137–157 (2000)
6. Rivero, J., Grigera, J., Rossi, G., Luna, E., Koch, N.: Improving agility in model-driven web engineering. In: CAiSE Forum (2011)
7. Constantine, L.L.: Canonical Abstract Prototypes for Abstract Visual and Interaction Design. In: Jorge, J.A., Jardim Nunes, N., Falcão e Cunha, J. (eds.) DSV-IS 2003. LNCS, vol. 2844, pp. 1–15. Springer, Heidelberg (2003)
8. Papazoglou, M.P., Traverso, P., Dustdar, S., Leymann, F.: Service-Oriented Computing: State of the Art and Research Challenges. Computer 40, 38–45 (2007)
9. Kruchten, P.: Software architecture and agile software development. In: Proceedings of the 32nd ACM/IEEE International Conference on Software Engineering, ICSE 2010, pp. 497–498. ACM Press, New York (2010)
10. Abrahamsson, P., Babar, M.A., Kruchten, P.: Agility and Architecture: Can They Coexist? IEEE Software 27, 16–22 (2010)
11. Eloranta, V.-P., Koskimies, K.: Aligning architecture knowledge management with Scrum. In: Proceedings of the WICSA/ECSA 2012 Companion Volume on - WICSA/ECSA 2012, p. 112. ACM Press, New York (2012)
12. Millard, D.E., Davis, H.C., Howard, Y., Gilbert, L., Walters, R.J., Abbas, N., Wills, G.B.: The Service Responsibility and Interaction Design Method: Using an Agile Approach for Web Service Design. In: Fifth European Conference on Web Services (ECOWS 2007), pp. 235–244. IEEE, Halle (2007)
13. Mukasa, K.S., Kaindl, H.: An Integration of Requirements and User Interface Specifications. In: 6th IEEE International Requirements Engineering Conference, pp. 327–328. IEEE Computer Society, Barcelona (2008)
14. Medrano, R.: Welcome To The API Economy. Forbes Online: CIO Network (2012)
15. Mulloy, B.: Web API Design: Crafting Interfaces that Developers Love. Apigee (2012)
16. Schwaber, K.: Scrum development process. In: Proceedings of the Workshop on Business Object Design and Implementation at the 10th Annual Conference on Object-Oriented Programming Systems, Languages, and Applications (OOPSLA 1995) (1995)
17. Fowler, M.: Patterns of Enterprise Application Architecture. Addison-Wesley (2012)
18. Rossi, G., Schwabe, D., Lyardet, F.: Improving Web information systems with navigational patterns. Computer Networks 31, 1667–1678 (1999)
19. Chudnovskyy, O., Gaedke, M.: Development of Web 2.0 Applications using WebComposition/Data Grid Service. In: The Second International Conferences on Advanced Service Computing (Service Computation 2010), pp. 55–61. Xpert Publishing Services (2010)
20. Alexa: Alexa Top Sites, http://www.alexa.com/topsites

Semantic Data Driven Interfaces for Web Applications

Vagner Nascimento and Daniel Schwabe

Department of Informatics, PUC-Rio,
Rua Marques de Sao Vicente, 225. Rio de Janeiro, RJ 22453-900, Brazil
{vnascimento,dschwabe}@inf.puc-rio.br

Abstract. Modern day interfaces must deal with a large number of heterogeneity factors, such as varying user profiles and runtime hardware and software platforms. These conditions require interfaces that can adapt to the changes in the <user, platform, environment> triad. The Model-Based User Interface approach has been proposed as a way to deal with these requirements. In this paper we present a data-driven, rule-based interface definition model capable of taking into account the semantics of the data it is manipulating, especially in the case of Linked Data. An implementation architecture based on the Synth environment supporting this model is presented.

Keywords: SHDM, HCI, Interface, Adaptation, Semantic Web, Data-driven design.

1 Introduction

The design and implementation of the interface component of applications, and in particular Web applications, consumes over 50% of the development effort, as first reported by, Myers and Rosson in the nineties [11]. Since then, their figures have surely increased, due to the evolution of the computing platforms, the advent of the Internet and the Web, and the now popular gestural and vocal interface modalities. Sources of heterogeneity affecting application development include:

- Different computing platforms – desktops, laptops, tablets, smartphones, embedded devices - affording a variety of interaction modalities – typing, voice, motion sensing, (multi)touch - and diverse input/output capabilities - keyboard, mouse, (multi)touch sensitive surfaces, motion sensors, cameras, even head-mounted displays/cameras;
- Multiple, often dynamically varying contexts of use, be it at a desktop with a wired network or a smartphone or Google Glass-like device on the go, wirelessly connected in a variety of underlying network infrastructures. These contexts also includ diverse working environments, that may have high degree of noise, and sometimes restricted bandwidth;
- Multiple, ever evolving set of tasks that must be supported, derived from an increasing number of different workflows that users adopt and must be supported by the application;

F. Daniel, P. Dolog, and Q. Li (Eds.): ICWE 2013, LNCS 7977, pp. 22–36, 2013.

- Highly diverse types and profiles of end users, ranging from very novice to experts, being from many different cultures and speaking a multitude of languages,

Not only these sources of heterogeneity exist, but often the context of use, i.e., each component of the triad <user, platform, environment> (the context) changes dynamically while the application is being used, which calls for so-called Plastic UIs [3], capable of adapting while preserving the "user experience" while the user is engaged with the application.

The Model-Based User Interface (MBUI) development approach has been used to address these challenges and maintain or decrease the level of effort necessary to develop applications, and more specifically, user interfaces, under these conditions.

The Cameleon Reference Model is a current reference framework for User Interfaces gaining adoption [2], the result of several years of research of a major European research project, which proposes four abstraction levels for modeling UIs: Task and Domain, Abstract Interface, Concrete Interface, Final User Interface.

The Domain model describes the domains of the application, and the Task model describes the sequence of steps needed to perform the tasks (with respect to interactions with the User Interface).

The Abstract Interface model describes the composition of interface units in an implementation and modality independent way.

The Concrete Interface model describes the interface in terms of platform-dependent widgets, but still modality- and implementation language independent.

The Final User Interface is the actual running code that the end user accesses when interacting with the application.

A more recent trend has been the dissemination of the Semantic Web, and the availability of data sources expressed in its formalisms – RDF, RDFS, OWL, in particular the Linked Data Initiative (LOD)[1], and the emergence of Linked Data Applications (LDAs for short), that access, enrich and manipulate linked data. There are some proposals of development environments or frameworks for supporting the development of LDAs, such as CubicWeb[2], the LOD2 Stack[3], and the Open Semantic Framework[4]. In addition, semantic wiki-based environment such as Ontowiki[5], Kiwi[6], and Semantic Media Wiki[7] have also been used as platforms for application development over Linked Data.

While useful, they do not present a set of integrated models that allow the specification of an LDA, and the synthesis of its running code from these models. Therefore, much of the application semantics, in its various aspects, remains represented only in the running implementation code.

---

[1] http://linkeddata.org

[2] http://www.cubicweb.org

[3] http://lod2.eu/WikiArticle/TechnologyStack.html

[4] http://openstructs.org/open-semantic-framework

[5] http://ontowiki.net/Projects/OntoWiki

[6] http://www.kiwi-project.eu

[7] http://www.semantic-mediawiki.org/wiki/Semantic_MediaWiki

We have been working in the past years in the Semantic Hypermedia Design Method (SHDM) [6] and its implementation environment Synth [1], which aims to allow Model-Based development of Linked Data Applications. While SHDM includes a proposed Abstract Interface Model, it lacks more refined models capable of dealing with the complexities of UIs as outlined above.

In this paper we present a new set of User Interface models and its implementation architecture similar to the Cameleon Framework proposal, addressing some of the challenges outlined earlier.

We present our approach in this paper as follows. After describing the example we are going to use through the paper in Section 2, we present our approach for interface modeling in Section 3. We discuss the implementation in Section 4. Section 5 presents the related work and with Section 6 we draw some conclusions and discuss future work.

2   Running Example

To help illustrate the concepts discussed in the paper, we use a running example of a fictitious online hotel-booking site. Suppose the user navigated to a given hotel's page, but has not yet entered the date, then the page should include fields to allow her/him to enter the desired dates, as shown in **Fig. 1** and **Fig. 2**.

When the dates have been informed, the application must show the rates for each type of room, their availability, and a warning is there is low availability for a certain type of room.

Notice that these conditions depend both on Domain Model information, and on the interaction state. The actual screen layout and interaction options depend also on the device; **Fig. 1** and **Fig. 2** show here the interface meant for desktop computers.

Fig. 3 shows the same application when accessed from a mobile device, with a different layout and different interaction capabilities (e.g., scrolling through swiping across the screen).

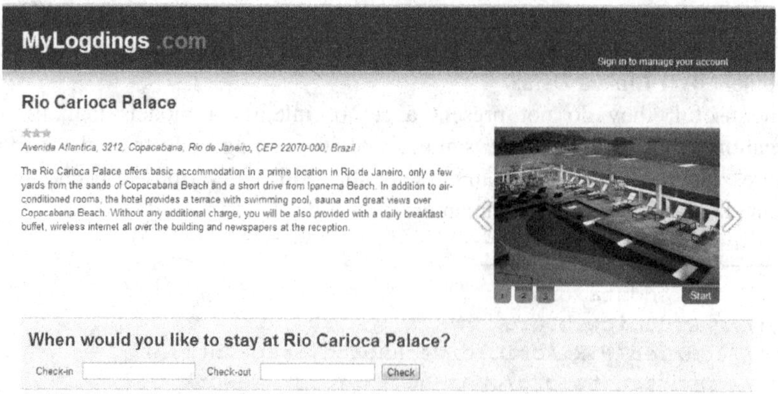

Fig. 1. Example hotel details page, with fields to inform check-in and checkout dates

Fig. 2. – Details of available hotel rooms if the dates have been provided

Fig. 3. – Mobile device version of the hotel-booking example interfaces

3   A Semantic Interface Model

In this section we present the new set of models for specifying interface in SHDM[8]. As mentioned earlier, SHDM follows the basic abstraction levels of the Cameleon Reference Model. The Domain Model, in SHDM is simply a set of RDF triples, which form a graph, and may include RDFS or OWL definitions. It is often the case

---

[8] A video illustrating the use of these models in Synth is available in
`http://www.tecweb.inf.puc-rio.br/synth`

that there does not exist any schema definitions in the Domain Model, only instances of resources representing information items.

The Abstract Interface Model [14] focuses on the roles played by each interface widget in the information exchange between the application and the outside world, including the user. It is abstract in the sense that it does not capture the look and feel, or any information dependent on the runtime environment. The Concrete Interface model is responsible for the latter.

Summarizing the Abstract Interface meta-model, an abstract interface is a composition of abstract interface elements (widgets). These in turn can be an `ElementExhibitor`, which is able to show values; an `IndefiniteVariable`, which is able to capture an arbitrary input string; a `DefinedVariable`, which is able to capture input values (one or several) from a known set of alternatives; and a `SimpleActivator`, which is able to react to an external event and signal it to the application.

Consider the interfaces shown in **Fig. 1**-**Fig. 3**. From them we can see that a hotel page has

- A header with a title and an anchor to the login operation;
- Hotel data, including name, address, category, description;
- A set of hotel images;
- A table of room types and respective rates, their availability, and an anchor to book it;
- A form to input check-in and checkout dates.

The corresponding abstract interface describing this is (as a nested list of attribute-value pairs)

```
{name: "main_page", widget_type: "AbstractInterface", children:[
  {name: "header", widget_type: "CompositeInterfaceElement",
children: [
    {name: "title", widget_type: "ElementExhibitor"},
    {name: "account_anchor", widget_type: "SimpleActivator"},
  ] },
  {name: "content", widget_type: "CompositeInterfaceElement",
children:[
    {name: "hotel_name", widget_type: "ElementExhibitor"},
    {name: "hotel_images", widget_type:
"CompositeInterfaceElement", repeatable: true, children: [
      {name: "hotel_image", widget_type: "ElementExhibitor"}
      ]},
    {name: "hotel_category", widget_type: "ElementExhibitor"},
    {name: "hotel_address", widget_type: "ElementExhibitor"},
    {name: "hotel_description", widget_type:
"ElementExhibitor"},
    {name: "rates", widget_type: "CompositeInterfaceElement",
children: [
      {name: "rates_title", widget_type: "ElementExhibitor"},
      {name: "rates_by_room", widget_type:
"CompositeInterfaceElement", repeatable: true,
```

```
     children: [
        {name: "room", widget_type:
"CompositeInterfaceElement", children: [
           {name: "room_type", widget_type:
"ElementExhibitor"},
           {name: "price", widget_type: "ElementExhibitor"},
           {name: "availability", widget_type:
"ElementExhibitor"},
           {name: "book", widget_type: "SimpleActivator"}
        ]},
        ]},
     ]},
   {name: "search_rates", widget_type:
"CompositeInterfaceElement", children: [
     {name: "search_rates_title", widget_type:
"ElementExhibitor"},
     {name: "label_checkin", widget_type: "ElementExhibitor"},
     {name: "checkin", widget_type: "IndefiniteVariable"},
     {name: "label_checkout", widget_type: "ElementExhibitor"},
     {name: "checkout", widget_type: "IndefiniteVariable"},
     {name: "search", widget_type: "SimpleActivator"}

   ]}
  ]}
 ]}
```

Fig. 4. - Abstract Interface specification of the Interfaces in **Fig. 1**-**Fig. 3**

Notice that this Abstract Interface represents both interfaces; each specific one can be seen as a special case of this one, where some elements have been omitted. The Abstract Interface also adds the widget types, indicating their role in the information flow.

A mapping specification made by the designer determines how each abstract widget will be mapped onto one or more Concrete Interface elements, and onto which Operations. The latter are the primitives in SHDM used to specify the business logic i.e., the application behavior to achieve the desired tasks.

Here we start introducing the new features in the existing model. Previously, the designer would determine, for each operation, which abstract interface would be used to exhibit its results. Furthermore, the composition of widgets in each abstract interface was specified statically at design time, the same being true for its mapping to concrete interfaces.

The new model instead uses rules to determine each of these aspects. Thus, instead of statically defining which abstract interface should be used, how that interface is composed, and how it is mapped onto the concrete interface, the designer now establishes *rules*, which, in a model- (and data-) driven fashion will assemble the final user interface that will be used. **Fig. 5** shows how the Interface Models are related to each other, and how the actual interface is defined.

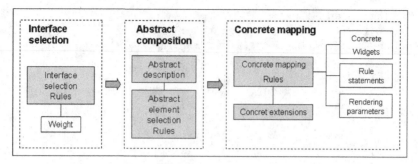

Fig. 5. – Relation between Interface Models in SHDM

The first step is the selection of the abstract interface, determined by its own set of rules. The result of executing these rules is a ranked list of candidate Abstract Interfaces, based on a weighting function defined by the UI designer.

The highest-ranking Abstract Interface is then chosen. Its own composition is again determined by executing another set of rules, which may include or exclude widgets from the initial base Abstract Interface composition defined by the designer.

Next, a third set of rules is executed to determine how each Abstract Interface widget will be mapped onto concrete interface widgets, and in some cases also extend the concrete widget compositions to allow interaction between them.

This rule-driven approach has several advantages:

1. It allows taking into account actual runtime data and context information in determining which interface should be used. Since the rules can refer to actual input data to be exhibited through it, as well as to the Domain Model, it is fair to say that the interface definition is now Semantic, in the sense of being aware of the data types and values of the data it is exposing;
2. It allows adapting the interface to both the user and to the execution environment, allowing a user experience that is in tune with the user's device and environment capabilities. Once again, such rules may take into account the semantics of the user or context model to alter the concrete interface.
3. It becomes a design choice whether the adaptation process will be run only at design time, or also during runtime. Running them during the application execution provides maximum flexibility, as the interface can change dynamically in reaction to several context changes, such as change of device, reduced bandwidth, loss of modality due to either circumstantial reasons (e.g., no visual access during driving) or due to hardware failure (e.g., display failure).

3.1   Rules and Interface Definition Parameters

Before going into more detail on how each part of the Interface Model is specified, it is useful to summarize the different types of information that are the input parameters for the definition.

- Rules follow the Condition-Action format. The conditions can reference
  - Any of the other models in SHDM, namely, Domain, Hypertextual Navigation, and Operations. For instance, it can test the type and value of a data item, or whether the element being exhibited is a hypertextual link;

o   Hypertextual parameters received in an http request;
o   Browser header information, including browser, platform, operating system, etc.
o   Environment variables, e.g., date and time of day, location
- Mapping specifications are a different type of rule, which use data both to establish the concrete interface to be activated, and to pass rendering parameters as needed. These include hypertextual navigation information, including sets of values to be iterated over.

All this information is converted into <object, property, value> triples which are input to the rules facts database. The pre-condition of each rule simply tests the presence or absence of a triple pattern in the facts database.

When an Operation (a behavior specification in SHDM) activates the Interface Engine to render its results, it also passes parameters needed for the rendition. Such parameters typically include the Domain Model data values and any input parameters it has received itself.

We next discuss each type of rule, illustrating it with the running example.

3.2   Abstract Interface Selection Rules

The first step in defining the Interface is establishing the selection rules for the Abstract Interface. The pre-condition in these rules define when each Abstract Interface is applicable, allowing, for instance, to

- Select the interface only if the user is logged in;
- Select the interface only if the application is being accessed from a mobile device;
- Select the interface only for certain types of data passed as input during runtime. Notice that this is often necessary if one wants to deal with "raw" data in RDF, which may not have any schema or vocabulary information associated with it.

In our example, the Abstract Interface selection rules are

```
set{
  has "params", "action", "hotel"
  has "params", "id", :_
}
```

The first line in the set tests whether we are exhibiting a `hotel` page; the second tests whether a specific hotel (i.e., `id` has some value) was passed as a parameter.

3.3   Abstract Interface Element Selection Rules

The Abstract Interface is a composition of elements. Each element may have rules associated to it, which determine if that element will be included in the final Abstract Interface composition or not.

Consider the rates element in the Abstract Interface shown in **Fig. 4**. It should be shown only if the check-in and checkout dates have been defined; conversely, the input fields for those dates (the search_rates element) should be shown if they have not been defined. The following rules capture this. The neg condition is the same as not has.

```
set "rates" do                    set "search_rates" do
  has "params", "checkin", :_       neg "params", "checkin", :_
  has "params", "checkout", :_      neg "params", "checkout", :_
end                               end
```

3.4   Concrete Interface Mapping Rules

For each Abstract Interface widget, there is a mapping rule that determines how it is mapped onto concrete widgets. Below we show some of the rules that map the Abstract Interface in **Fig. 4** onto the concrete interfaces of **Fig. 1**-**Fig. 3**.

Each rule starts with `maps-to`, includes the name of the abstract widget it applies to; the concrete widget to which it maps; parameters needed by the concrete widget; and a rule block delimited by `do-end` used to determine under which conditions the mapping is applicable. Rules are applied in order; once a rule has been applied to an element, other subsequent rules applying to that same element are ignored.

```
1. maps_to abstract: "main_page", concrete_widget: "HTMLPage" ,
   params: { title: "myLogdings.com - #{hotel[:name]}",
   include_css: "/stylesheets/hotel_mob.css" }do
2. has "user_agent", "mobile", true end
3. maps_to abstract: "main_page", concrete_widget: "HTMLPage" ,
   params: { title: "myLogdings.com - #{hotel[:name]}",
   include_css: "/stylesheets/hotel.css" }
```

```
# Header block
```

```
4. maps_to  abstract: "header", concrete_widget:
   "HTMLComposition"
```

```
5. maps_to  abstract: "title", concrete_widget: "HTMLHeading",
   params: { content: "MyLogdings" }
```

```
6. maps_to  abstract: "account_anchor", concrete_widget:
   "HTMLAnchor", params: { content: "Sign in to manage your
   account", url: "/signin" }
```

```
7. maps_to  abstract: "content", concrete_widget:
   "HTMLComposition"
```

```
# Hotel Data
```

```
8. maps_to  abstract: "hotel_name", concrete_widget:
   "HTMLHeading", params: { size: 2, content: hotel[:name] }
```

```
   # Images slider
9. maps_to  abstract: "hotel_images", concrete_widget:
   "JQueryAnythingSlider", params: { collection:
   hotel[:images], as: :hotel_image }
```

```
10. maps_to  abstract: "hotel_image", concrete_widget:
    "HTMLImage", params: { content: hotel_image }
```

```
...
# Rates
```

```
11. maps_to  abstract: "rates", concrete_widget:
    "HTMLComposition"
```

```
...
#== Availability
12. maps_to  abstract: "availability", concrete_widget:
    "HTMLSpan", params: {content: "Sold out", css_class:
    "highlight"}do
13. equal room[:status], 'sold-out' end
14. maps_to  abstract: "availability", concrete_widget:
    "HTMLSpan", params: { content:
    "Only #{room[:rooms_available]} left!", css_class:
    "highlight"}do
15. equal room[:status], "few-rooms" end
16. maps_to  abstract: "availability", concrete_widget:
    "HTMLSpan", params: {content: "Available", css_class: "col3"
    }
17. maps_to  abstract: "book", concrete_widget:
    "HTMLFormButton", params: {content: "Book", css_class:
    "col4"} do
18. diff room[:status], "sold-out"
19. has "user_agent", "mobile", true end
20. maps_to  abstract: "book", concrete_widget:
    "HTMLFormButton", params: {content: "Book Now", css_class:
    "col4"} do
21.   neg "user_agent", "mobile"
22.   diff room[:status], "sold-out" end
# Search rates
23. maps_to abstract: "search_rates", concrete_widget:
    "HTMLForm", params: {method: "get" }
24. maps_to  abstract: "search_rates_title", concrete_widget:
    "HTMLHeading", params: {size: 2, content: "When would you
    like to stay at #{hotel[:name]}?"}
25. maps_to  abstract: "label_checkin", concrete_widget:
    "HTMLLabel", params: {content: 'Check-in' }
26. maps_to  abstract: "checkin", concrete_widget:
    "JQueryDatePickerInput" , params: {date_format: "d M, y",
    min_date: 0 }
27. maps_to  abstract: "label_checkout", concrete_widget:
    "HTMLLabel", params: {content: 'Check-out' }
28. maps_to  abstract: "checkout", concrete_widget:
    "JQueryDatePickerInput" , params: {date_format: "d M, y",
    min_date: 0 }
29. maps_to  abstract: "search", concrete_widget:
    "HTMLFormButton", params: {content: "Check" }
```

Some concrete widgets, such as HTMLHeading, HTMLSpan, HTMLForm, etc... correspond directly to their counterparts in HTML. We make additional comments highlighting the interesting uses of the rules.

- Lines 1 and 3 show two possible mappings for the main page. The first is selected when the user agent is a mobile device, tested in line 2. Otherwise, the mapping in line 3 applies. This is how the proper choice for generating of the interfaces in **Fig. 1**- **Fig. 3** is made.
- The expression `#{hotel[:name]}` in line 1 retrieves the value of the "name" property of the hotel instance being shown;
- The expression `url: "/signin"` in line 6 generates a (REST) call to the `signing` Operation, defined in the Behavior Model (not shown);
- Line 9 shows the use of a Javascript component, `JQueryAnythingSlider`, capable of exhibiting a set of elements, including images. The actual set of elements is passed as a parameter, the result of the expression `collection: hotel[:images]` that retrieves from the Domain Model the set of image values associated with the hotel being exhibited. Lines 26 and 28 map the input form fields for the check-in and checkout dates to a library component, `JQueryDatePickerInput`.
- Line 12 shows a conditional element. If the value of the `room[:status]` property is `"sold out"`, this element (a warning text "Sold out") will be shown, with a CSS style `"highlight"`.
- Lines 14-15 show another conditional element. If the value of the `status` property of `room` is `"few-rooms"`, a highlighted warning showing the number of rooms left (`"Only #{room[:rooms_available]} left!"`) is shown; otherwise it is omitted.
- The `book` element defined in Line 17 is only included if there are rooms available, as specified in the condition in line 18. There are two different CSS styles used, one when the user agent is a mobile device (tested in line 19), the other when it is not (tested in line 21).

An interesting point is raised by the flexibility of the mapping rule language. Since any valid DSL expression (see [12] for a discussion on the embedded DSL offered by Synth) can be used in the test clause of the condition, we could have inserted the test for low availability in the rule itself, e.g., `{room[:rooms_available]} < 3}`. This, however, would imply including parts of the Business Logic in the interface, which is undesirable. Rather, this condition is actually implemented as an inference rule in the Domain Model, which concludes the fact `<"room", "status", "few-rooms">` from the number of rooms available, according to the application's Business Rules.

In addition to these mapping rules, it is sometimes necessary to define Extensions to the Concrete Interface Model to allow interactions between concrete widgets. A common example is when the value set to one widget must be used as an input to another widget.

Consider the check-in and checkout date widgets specified in lines 26 and 28. It would be user-friendlier (and semantically correct) that once the check-in date has been filled, the checkout date should be a date at least one day later. The extension shown below encapsulates this behavior:

```
extend nodes: ['checkin'], extension: 'JQueryCopyDateTo',
params: { target: "checkout", string_format: "d MMM, yy",
add_days: 1 }
```

Extensions are wrappers around Concrete Interface elements. Typically, they will call Domain model operations to determine Domain-dependent integrity constraints normally enforced by these communications between widgets.

3.5   Concrete Widgets Definitions

As seen from the examples in the mapping rules, concrete widgets are treated as software components outside the model itself; different concrete widgets should be defined for different runtime platforms. In this sense, we diverge from the Cameleon model, as Concrete Widgets are rendered directly to the Final User Interface.

A Concrete Widget should be self-contained, and capable of self-rendering based only on their input parameters. Any potential dependencies they may have with other widgets should be parameterized as well. For example, the `JQueryDatePickerInput` is capable of receiving an initial date, as used by the extension discussed above in the case of check-in and checkout dates.

Concrete Widgets are described in Manifest declarations, containing their name; version; description; list of compatible abstract widgets (i.e., abstract widgets that can be mapped to it); list of other widgets it depends on; list of parameter; and a text with examples of use.

4   Implementation Architecture

The conceptual architecture that integrates the models defined in Section 3 is show in **Fig. 6**.

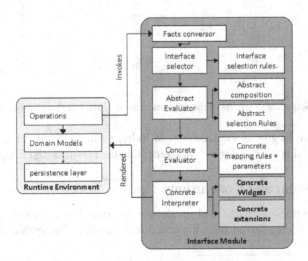

Fig. 6. – The conceptual implementation architecture for Interfaces

The Facts Convertor component is responsible for extracting the model definitions from the knowledge base, and converts them into facts - <object, property, value> triples - that will be used by the rules engine. The Interface Selector runs the Selection rules, returning a ranked list of interfaces. The Abstract Evaluator runs the composition rules, resulting in the actual Abstract Interface to be used; abstract widgets without associated rules are included by default. The Concrete Evaluator runs the mapping rules to generate the concrete interfaces, adding applicable extensions, and the results are interpreted using the concrete widget definitions to generate the final running interface.

The Concrete Interface Interpreter receives a composition tree of concrete widget specifications, including their parameters and extensions. It does a depth-first traversal of the tree, and for each node instantiates (i.e., generates the code) for the corresponding concrete widget.

Fig. 7 shows the actual sequence of events within the Interface Engine in Synth.

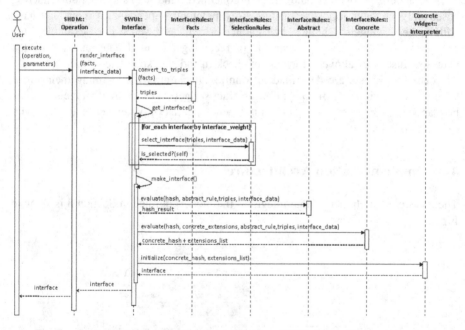

Fig. 7. – Sequence of events in the implementation of the Interface Engine in Synth

The Interface Engine is implemented in Ruby, as is the Synth environment. The rules engine used is *Wongi-Engine*[9], implementing the classical RETE algorithm.

5   Discussion and Conclusions

We have described a data- and model-driven rule based model and runtime architecture. It is data-driven since the actual interface is self-assembled as a result of

---

[9] https://github.com/ulfurinn/wongi-engine

the execution of the various rule-sets that use the instance data in the various models in SHDM (Domain, Hypertextual Navigation, Behavior) to determine the final interface. It is model-driven because all Synth models are available as data as well (as discussed in [1]). For example, a rule can determine the inclusion of an abstract widget if the data item being exhibited is of a certain type, and/or if it has a certain property, e.g., "it is of any Class that has a Discount property".

The work presented here is related to a very large number of models and approaches that have been proposed in the literature (see, for example, [10]); it would be beyond the scope of this paper to make a comparison with every one of them. Several of the Interface Models in SHDM, e.g., the Abstract Interface and the Concrete, have counterparts in the many proposed models, e.g., Maria [13], UsiXML [9], UIML [7], among many, as well as those in Hera [5], UWE [8] and WebML [4], differing mostly in the level of abstraction and on the underlying formalism (e.g., XML vs RDF). Each has advantages and disadvantages, a discussion of which would require another paper altogether. A similar observation can be made regarding the use of rules (e.g. [15], the difference still remaining in the underlying models.

The major distinguishing original contribution is the use of data- and model-driven rules integrated seamlessly with the various other models within the SHDM approach, directly supported by an implementation environment. Our approach leads to explicating design decisions associated to the various levels of abstraction, as they become explicit in the rules, as opposed to embedded in the interface code.

As an example, consider the problem of adapting the hotel-booking interface to a mobile environment. The designer has some choices to make: The first is to define a *different* Abstract Interface altogether for each device family; the second is to define a *generic* interface, and specialize it for each device family; and the third is a combination of both – define intermediary abstract interfaces for groups of families of devices based on common properties, and specialize one of them for each specific family. Our approach allows all three alternatives, allowing a better comparison among them, e.g., based on the complexity of the models used for each approach.

One frequent concern with rule-based architectures is performance. We are now in the process of systematically evaluating the performance overhead introduced by our approach. Nevertheless, within the Synth architecture[10], we have already observed that the overall application performance is not significantly affected by this interface architecture, because of the much larger performance hit caused by database access and inferencing while executing the business logic operations.

We are continuing this work in several directions. The first is to continue the evaluation of the approach, both in terms of performance, but also in terms of its expressivity and usability for developers. Second, we want to explore the design trade-offs for multi-platform applications, along the lines discussed in this section. Finally, we plan to extend the rule-based adaptation engine to encompass all models in SHDM besides the Interface Model, to achieve fully adaptive applications.

Acknowledgments. Daniel Schwabe was partially supported by CNPq (WebScience INCT).

---

[10] Synth currently uses the BigOWLIM RDF store.

References

1. de Souza Bomfim, M.H., Schwabe, D.: Design and Implementation of Linked Data Applications Using SHDM and Synth. In: Auer, S., Díaz, O., Papadopoulos, G.A. (eds.) ICWE 2011. LNCS, vol. 6757, pp. 121–136. Springer, Heidelberg (2011)
2. Calvary, G., et al.: The CAMELEON Reference Framework, CAMELEON Project (September 2002),
   `http://giove.isti.cnr.it/projects/cameleon/pdf/`
   `CAMELEON%20D1.1RefFramework.pdf`
3. Coutaz, J., Calvary, G.: HCI and Software Engineering for User Interface Plasticity. In: Jacko, J. (ed.) Human Computer Handbook: Fundamentals, Evolving Technologies, and Emerging Applications, 3rd edn. Taylor and Francis Group Ltd. (May 2012)
4. Ceri, S., Fraternali, P., Bongio, A.: Web Modeling Language (WebML): a modeling language for designing Web sites. In: Proc. of the WWW9 Conf., Amsterdam (May 2000)
5. Frasincar, F., Houben, G.J., Barna, P.: Hypermedia Presentation Generation in Hera, Information Systems, vol. 35(1), pp. 23–55. Elsevier Science Ltd., Oxford (2010)
6. Lima, F., Schwabe, D.: Application Modeling for the Semantic Web. In: Proceedings of LA-Web 2003, Santiago, Chile, pp. 93–102. IEEE Press (November 2003)
7. Helms, J., Schaefer, R., Luyten, K., Vermeulen, J., Abrams, M., Coyette, A., Vanderonckt, J.: Human-Centered Engineering with the User Interface Markup Language, Human-Centered Software Engineering, ch. 7, pp. 141–173. Springer, London (2009)
8. Koch, N., Knapp, A., Zhang, G., Baumeister, H.: UML-based Web Engineering: An Approach based on Standards (book chapter). In: Rossi, G., Pastor, O., Schwabe, D., Olsina, L. (eds.) Web Engineering: Modelling and Implementing Web Applications, ch. 7, pp. 157–191. Springer, HCI (2008)
9. Limbourg, Q., Vanderonckt, J., Michotte, B., Bouillon, L., López-Jaquero, V.: USIXML: A Language Supporting Multi-path Development of User Interfaces. In: Feige, U., Roth, J. (eds.) EHCI-DSV-IS 2004. LNCS, vol. 3425, pp. 200–220. Springer, Heidelberg (2005)
10. Meixner, G., Paternó, F., Vanderonckt, J.: Past, Present, and Future of Model-Based User Interface Development. i-com 10(3), 2–11 (2011)
11. Myers, B., Rosson, M.B.: Survey on User Interface Programming. In: Proc. 10th Annual ACM CHI Conference on Human Factors in Computing Systems, pp. 195–202 (2000)
12. Nunes, D.A., Schwabe, D.: Rapid prototyping of web applications combining domain specific languages and model driven design. In: Proc. 6th International Conference on Web Engineering (ICWE 2006), pp. 153–160. ACM (2006) ISBN 1-59593-352-2
13. Paterno, F., Santoro, C., Spano, L.D.: Maria:A Universal, Declarative, Multiple Abstraction Level Language for Service-Oriented Applications in Ubiquitous Environment. ACM Transactions on Computer-Human Interaction (TOCHI) 16(4) (November 2009)
14. Silva de Moura, S., Schwabe, D.: Interface development for hypermedia applications in the semantic web. In: Proc. WebMedia and LA-Web, Ribeirão Preto, Brazil, pp. 106–113. IEEE Press (October 2004)
15. Virgilio, R., Torlone, R., Houben, G.J.: Rule-based Adaptation of Web Information Systems. In: Proc. 7th International Conference on Mobile Data Management (MDM 2006), Nara, Japan, May 10-12. Springer Science (2006)

Integrating Component-Based Web Engineering into Content Management Systems

Stefania Leone[1,*], Alexandre de Spindler[2], Moira C. Norrie[2], and
Dennis McLeod[1]

[1] Semantic Information Research Laboratory, Computer Science Department, USC
Los Angeles, CA, 90089-0781, USA
{stefania.leone,mcleod}@usc.edu
[2] Institute for Information Systems, ETH Zurich
CH-8092 Zurich, Switzerland
{despindler,norrie}@inf.ethz.ch

Abstract. Popular content management systems such as WordPress and Drupal offer a plug-in mechanism that allows users to extend the platform with additional functionality. However, plug-ins are typically isolated extensions defining their own data structures, application logic and user interface, and are difficult to combine. We address the fact that users may want to configure their applications more freely through the composition of such extensions. We present an approach and model for component-based web engineering based on the concept of components and connectors between them, supporting composition at the level of the schema and data, the application logic and the user interface. We show how our approach can be used to integrate component-based web engineering into platforms such as WordPress. We demonstrate the benefits of the approach by presenting a composition plug-in that showcases component composition through configurable connectors based on an eCommerce application scenario.

Keywords: Component-based Web Engineering, Content Management System, WordPress.

1   Introduction

Popular content management systems (CMS) such as WordPress[1] and Drupal[2] greatly facilitate the task of designing and developing web applications for small companies and individuals. These systems offer a graphical administrator interface, where users can author content, upload media, customise the layout and integrate a wide variety of plug-ins to extend the platform core with additional functionality. The WordPress Plug-in Directory[3] hosts thousands of plug-ins

---

* Stefania Leone's work is supported by the Swiss National Science Foundation (SNF) grant PBEZP2_140049. The research has also been funded in part by the Integrated Media Systems Center (IMSC) of the University of Southern California (USC).
[1] http://wordpress.org
[2] http://drupal.org/
[3] http://wordpress.org/extend/plugins/

F. Daniel, P. Dolog, and Q. Li (Eds.): ICWE 2013, LNCS 7977, pp. 37–51, 2013.
© Springer-Verlag Berlin Heidelberg 2013

developed by the community, providing functionality ranging from site access statistic, over sophisticated photo galleries to eCommerce solutions. Plug-ins may define their own data structure, application logic and user interface. Although extremely powerful, plug-ins are simply extensions of the platform core. They are typically isolated and it is difficult to compose them with other plug-ins. For example, a company that runs their online shop based on a WordPress eCommerce plug-in, such as WooCommerce[4], might want to perform a customer satisfaction survey by using a survey plug-in, e.g. WordPress Simple Survey[5]. Ideally, for the participant profile data, the survey plug-in could directly make use of the customer data managed as part of the eCommerce plug-in. However, the current WordPress application model would require the user to familiarise themself with the code of the eCommerce plug-in and to programatically extract and map the customer data from the eCommerce plug-in to the participant format defined by the survey plug-in. This is a task that generally goes beyond the skills of a typical, non-technical WordPress user.

In this paper, we present an approach and a well-defined component model that supports end-users, both non-technical as well as more advanced ones, in performing such composition scenarios. The presented work is in line with recent research on end-user development, where they not only consider how to make web information systems easy to use, but also easy to develop [1]. Our approach enhances and generalises the application model of CMS such as WordPress to support component-based web engineering. Our model is based on the concept of components and explicit connectors between them. A component adheres to a well-defined component structure exposing interfaces for component composition at various levels. To build an application, components are composed through configurable connectors between them. We introduce different connector types to support composition at various levels, i.e. composition at the schema and data level, at the level of the application logic, and at the level of the user interface. We have realised our approach based on WordPress and present a composition plug-in that supports component composition based on configurable connector types. Finally, as proof of concept, we show how an eCommerce solution could be extended and combined with other plug-ins using our composition plug-in.

This paper is structured as follows. We give an overview of the background in Sect. 2, followed by our approach in Sect. 3. We introduce the component and composition model in Sect. 4. Section 5 presents the application of our approach using WordPress, followed by the presentation of the composition plug-in in Sect. 6 and the validation of our approach in Section 7. Concluding remarks are given in Sect. 8.

2   Background

Over the years, numerous frameworks and approaches for designing and developing web information systems have been introduced. Model-driven web

---

[4] http://wordpress.org/extend/plugins/woocommerce/

[5] http://wordpress.org/extend/plugins/wordpress-simple-survey/

engineering approaches, e.g. [2, 3] offer systematic methodologies based on models describing the structural, navigational and presentation aspects of a Web information system. Models are typically defined graphically and most methodologies offer a platform for application generation and deployment according to the defined models. These solutions, however, were targeted at collaborating groups of database architects, web developers and graphic designers, and explicitly supported the separation of concerns in terms of their roles by providing separate models for the different levels of a web information system.

In parallel, CMS became a popular way for non-technical users, including individuals and small companies, to create websites and publish their content. Platforms such as WordPress and Drupal provide graphical administrator interfaces, which support the website design of content and structure in terms of general publishing units and presentation styles. The extensibility mechanism inherent to these platforms allows for the integration of arbitrary data and services to support the creation of complex web information systems. The configuration and use of plug-ins is typically also performed through the administrator interface. However, as already stated, these extensions, while extremely powerful, cannot easily be combined or mashed-up. Plug-ins are typically isolated units developed by community members, and there is little control or conventions with respect to the plug-in internals. In the case of WordPress, developing and composing plug-ins requires knowledge of PHP as well as a detailed understanding of the WordPress platform and its inner workings.

A number of approaches support web application development from reusable components. With WebComposition [4], web applications are built through hierarchical compositions of reusable application components. Similarly, web mashups are composed through the orchestration of reusable, self-contained services, which interact at the message level and may span multiple applications and organisations. Various mashup editors offer graphical tools as an alternative to programmatic interfaces to do the composition process, both for general, e.g. [5–7] and domain-specific mashup creation, e.g. [8, 9]. While some mashup editors help users to integrate information from distributed sources, others provide infrastructure for building new applications from reusable components. For example MashArt [7] enables advanced users to create their own applications through the composition of user interface, application and data components. The focus is on supporting the integration of existing components based on event-based composition, where components can react to events of other components.

We build on and extend these ideas for the CMS domain targeting non-technical users. In contrast to previous work, our approach offers component-based web engineering based on the definition and configuration of explicit connectors that encapsulate the collaboration logic between components. As stated in [10], one of the main challenges of modular system development lies in the fact that modular units may not be compatible for composition. As a consequence, our component model is inspired by the Architecture Description Language (ADL) [11, 12], an approach to component-based software engineering, where the component model consists of components and explicit connectors between them. Through the definition of explicit connectors between components, we circumvent the problem of component incompatibility. Connectors encapsulate the composition logic, exhibiting functionality ranging from simple message passing, to complex collaboration logic, such as data transformation operations, and, consequently, would allow for the composition of arbitrary components. We introduce different types of connectors, which can be configured to define the composition for a particular composition scenario. For example, a schema connector type could be configured to support the structural composition of the eCommerce and survey plug-ins.

Our approach and model is not dissimilar to the application model introduced by the Google Android platform[6] for developing and running mobile applications. Their application model propagates the reuse of different types of application components across applications, where applications are configured through so-called intents that define the glue code between the various components. While intents allow base values to be passed in the form of key-value pairs between components, our connectors generalise this approach and may define arbitrary complex collaboration logic between components.

3   Approach

We introduce a component-based approach to web engineering based on ideas of ADL where applications are modelled based on reusable components and explicit connectors between them. Components may provide arbitrary functionality and define their own data structure, application logic and user interface.

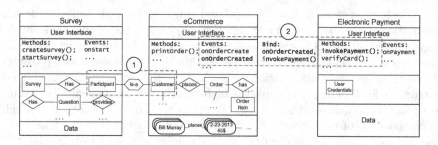

Fig. 1. Composition Scenario

We will introduce our approach based on the example of a company that makes use of a CMS extended with an eCommerce component for their online business. Figure 1 gives an overview of the scenario. The eCommerce component, in the centre, allows users to create and manage an online store, including product, customer and order management. The component defines a schema that represents the eCommerce application domain by means of entity types and relationships,

---

[6] http://developer.android.com/guide/

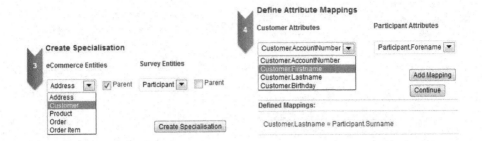

Fig. 2. Specialisation Screenshot   **Fig. 3.** Attribute Mapping Screenshot

and manages data structured accordingly. Furthermore, the component defines application logic by means of methods and events, which implement the online store functionality, and this functionality is made available to the user through a graphical user interface.

To evaluate customer satisfaction, the company decides to perform a customer satisfaction survey and they would like to make use of their customer data when performing the survey. For this purpose, they have selected a survey component, shown on the right, that offers the required functionality to define and run surveys. The survey component, in turn, consists of a user interface, application logic and a schema, and the component may manage data structured accordingly. However, they want to avoid having two separate user entities and therefore want to create a connection between the eCommerce customer and the survey participants.

Connector ①, on the left in Fig. 1, defines the composition between the two components. It is a specialisation connector that defines an `is-a` relationship between the `Customer` entity of the eCommerce component and the `Participant` entity of the survey component. Through this specialisation connector, the customer data can automatically be used as participant data for the survey.

Figures 2 and 3 illustrate, based on screenshots, how a user configures a specialisation connector through a graphical composition wizard. We assume that the user has already selected the components to be composed as well as the connector type. Figure 2 shows how the user creates the actual `is-a` relationship by selecting the `customer` entity of the eCommerce component and the `participant` entity of the survey component. The user also defines that the `customer` entity should become the parent entity by checking the *parent* checkbox. Next, the user has the possibility to define attribute mappings between the matching/overlapping attributes of the two entity types. In our example, both entities participant and customer define `name` attributes. Figure 3 shows how such mappings are created. Here, the user is about to create a mapping between the `User.firstname` and the `Participant.forename` attributes. At the bottom of the figure, the list of defined mappings is shown, where the attribute `User.lastname` was mapped to `Participant.surname`. With these mappings, the specialisation connector ensures that each time the name of a survey

Fig. 4. Binding Creation Screenshot   **Fig. 5.** Parameter Mapping Screenshot

participant is accessed, the corresponding customer name from the eCommerce component is retrieved and displayed. Note that, in this example, the specialisation does not require any data mappings, since the survey component does not yet manage data. However, when composing two components with data, the specialisation definition also requires the definition of a data mapping and a conflict resolution strategy, also supported through our composition wizard.

While this is the basic functionality provided by the specialisation connector, advanced users are free to extend the configured connector programatically. For example, the connector could be extended to perform data mining by defining queries that combine survey data with customer data to answer questions such as "Do customers who selected answer (a) in question 4 buy similar products?".

In a second step, the company decides to offer support for electronic payment, a functionality that is not provided by the eCommerce component. For this composition, the eCommerce component is composed with an electronic payment component, shown on the right of Fig. 1. The event handler registration connector ② operates at the application logic level, based on events and callback methods. Figure 4 and 5 show the steps involved in configuring this connector. Again, we assume that the user has already selected the components to be composed and the connector type. Furthermore, the user has decided that the electronic payment component should be invoked as a result of an event that occurs in the eCommerce component. The screenshot in Fig. 4 shows how a user defines that binding by selecting events and methods. In the current example, the user has selected the `onOrderCreated` event from the survey component. According to the description shown below the drop-down menu, the event gives access to the created order and its attributes. On the left, the user has selected the `invokePayment` method of the electronic payment component and the description of the method and its parameters is displayed, saying that the method takes two parameters `amount` and `currency`.

After creating the basic binding, the user may define mappings between the event object attributes and the method parameters, as shown in Fig. 5. In the current example, the user intends to map the `price` attribute of the order to the `amount` parameter of the `invokePayment` method. Also, at the bottom, a list of created mappings is illustrated. The user has already created a static mapping for the currency parameter by assigning it the default value "USD". Note that users are free to define such default values for parameters in cases where the attributes and parameters do not match or are incompatible and we support basic type transformation.

As these two composition examples illustrate, connectors provide the glue between components and are configured by the user to adhere to a particular composition scenario. We offer different types of connectors that support composition at various levels of a component. Figure 6 gives an overview of the composition levels and shows, from left to right, that connectors may be used at the data level, the schema level, the application logic level and the user interface level. We provide connector types for all these levels and will present our component model including the various connector types in the next section.

Data Level		Schema Level		Application Logic Level		User Interface Level	
User Interface	User Interface	User Interface	User Interface	User Interface	User Interface	User Interface	User Interface
Application Logic	Application Logic	Application Logic	Application Logic	Application Logic	Application Logic	Application Logic	Application Logic
Schema	Schema	Schema	Schema	Schema	Schema	Schema	Schema
Data	Data	Data	Data	Data	Data	Data	Data

Fig. 6. Composition Levels

4   Component Model

A component is an application providing arbitrary functionality to its users. Components may be composed with other components using explicit connectors between them to form more complex applications. The general component model along with the composition interface is shown on the left in Fig. 7, while the eCommerce component introduced in Sect. 3 is shown on the right as an example following this model.

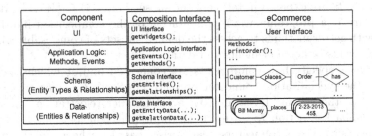

Fig. 7. Component Example

Formally, a component is defined as a tuple of the four elements

$$Component = \langle Schema, Data, Application\ Logic, User\ Interface \rangle$$

The *Schema* is a data model instance describing the component *Data* in terms of a set of entity types $\{E_1, \ldots, E_M\}$ and relationships $\{R_1, \ldots, R_N\}$. The *Application Logic* includes a set of methods $\{m_1(), \ldots, m_U()\}$ implementing the application logic and events $\{e_1, \ldots, e_V\}$ related to these methods. Components typically contain basic CRUD methods supporting the management of their entity types and relationships, as well as higher-level methods providing domain-specific functionality. Component developers are free to define an arbitrary number of events triggered by the execution of such methods. For example, a component may define events marking the start and end of CRUD method executions.

Finally, the *User Interface* defines the graphical user interface. In CMS, the user interface is typically specified by layout themes defining the general presentation of the provided publishing units for the complete web site. As part of the user interface, components may define a set of widgets $\{W_1, \ldots, W_N\}$ displaying specific component data or providing component services to the users. Widgets represent complete user interfaces including user interface controls, layout and style templates. Note that components do not necessarily specify multiple or all of these four elements. For example, while the eCommerce component specifies *Schema*, *Application Logic* and *Widgets* elements, other components may for example only specify *Application Logic* and *Schema* elements.

Components expose a composition interface which defines in which way they may be composed with other components. In order to implement such an interface, component developers need to specify which of the component elements they wish to make available for composition. Component interfaces do not need to expose component elements at all levels. At the schema-level, the interface specifies the subset $\{E_i, \ldots\} \subseteq \{E_1, \ldots, E_M\}$ of composable entity types and the subset $\{R_j, \ldots\} \subseteq \{R_1, \ldots, R_N\}$ of composable relationships. The specification of the data available for composition consists of a query Q over the composable schema elements. Similar to the schema interface definition, application logic made available for composition is defined in terms of subsets $\{m_k(), \ldots\} \subseteq \{m_1(), \ldots, m_U()\}$ and $\{e_l(), \ldots\} \subseteq \{e_1, \ldots, e_V\}$. Finally, user interface widgets are exposed in terms of the subset $\{W_i, \ldots\} \subseteq \{W_1, \ldots, W_N\}$.

In Figure 7, a programmatic representation of the composition interface is shown, with getter methods to access the defined subsets of composable widgets, methods, events, schema elements and data.

Connectors specify how components are connected and at which level. For example, the specialisation connector presented in Sect. 3 defines an is-a relationship at the schema level, and the event handler registration component binds a callback function to an event at the application logic level. Figure 8 shows the basic types of connectors—categorised based on the composition level. The widget connector, shown at the top, supports composition at the UI level through the integration of widgets between components. The connector forms the union of widgets defined as *User Interface* := $\{W_1, \ldots\} \subseteq UserInterface_A \cup UserInterface_B$. In the example in Fig. 8, the connector integrates a widget of component A into the user interface of component B.

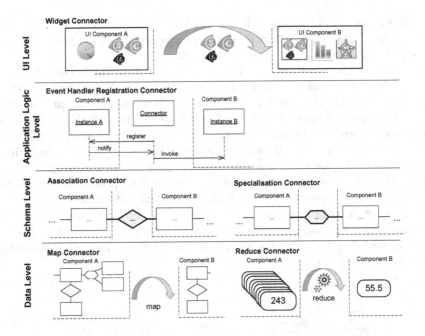

Fig. 8. Basic Connector Types and Composition Scenarios

At the application logic level, Fig. 8 illustrates the Event Registration Connector based on a UML sequence diagram that reflects the collaboration between components and connectors in an event-based setting. The connector is specified as *Application Logic* $:= \{m_1()\{e_i \rightarrow m_j()\}, \ldots\}$ defining functions binding events from one component to methods of another component.

Schema-level connectors compose components based on schema elements, such as specialisation and associations [13]. As shown in Fig. 8, a specialisation connector defines an `is-a` relationship establishing a specialisation relationship among entity types from different component schemata and an association connector defines a relationship between two entity types from different components. More generally, a schema connector may define arbitrary schema elements among component entities *Schema* $:= \{\{E_1, \ldots\}, \{R_1, \ldots\}\}$.

Finally, data connectors allow data from one component to be reused by another component. As shown in Fig. 8, data reuse may be defined by a mapping connector that maps the schema of one component to the schema of another component, or by a reduce connector that transforms data from one component to a format specified by another component. Generally, data connectors may be defined as combinations of map and reduce functions of the form *Application Logic* $:= \{map()\{E_i.a_j \leftarrow reduce(E_k.a_n, E_l.a_m)\}, \ldots\}$. Such map and reduce functions may in turn be bound to data mapping connector events to define whether the mappings should occur once, multiple times or periodically.

Note that we have given a minimal specification of the various connector types, but they may define richer functionality. For example, the association connector may also define application logic in the form of CRUD methods to create associations, as well as a widget that allows new associations to be graphically created and viewed. Similarly, a reduce connector may define a user interface, where the reduce function could be configured.

As seen with these examples, connectors consist of the same building block as general components and, therefore, can be seen as a special type of components, where the functionality is not targeted at the application domain, but rather at the composition of domain-specific application units. Figure 9 shows the meta-model of our component model. A component defines a user interface, application logic, schema and data, and, depending on the implementation technology, these elements may be realised in different ways. A connector is a sub-type of component, and therefore, they can in turn be composed. Connectors are classified according to their supported composition level, which defines the access points of a connector. A concrete connector is an instance of such a connector type and is instantiated with values that are particular to a composition scenario. For example, a specialisation connector will be instantiated with an **is-a** relationship between two entity types.

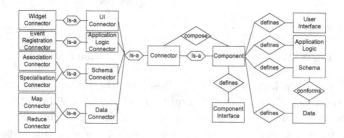

Fig. 9. Component Metamodel

5   WordPress Extension

We have extended WordPress with our approach and component model to support component-based web engineering. We will first give a short introduction to the WordPress plug-in mechanism before presenting our extension.

The WordPress plug-in mechanism allows the original blogging model to be extended in terms of data structure, application logic and user interface widgets by hooking into the WordPress core. A number of such hooks are provided, which allow plug-ins to inject additional functionality, data structures and presentation into the WordPress core execution environment. Hooks may represent plug-in lifecycle events such as their installation or uninstallation, as well as administrative or end-user activities including the creation, manipulation, retrieval, selection, display and deletion of posts, pages or plug-in-specific data. Typically, the plug-in code includes functions for creating and deleting database tables, for inserting and selecting table data and the assignment of these functions to particular hooks. Users are free to define their own hooks, which allows plug-ins to react to events of other plug-ins. For the user interface, plug-ins rely on the WordPress publishing process and themes that define the structure and layout of the complete web site. A plug-in may, however, define widgets that can be placed in various places of the user interface. To install a plug-in, the files containing the plug-in code, typically one or more PHP files and JavaScript, are uploaded into the target WordPress platform through the WordPress administrator dashboard and can be activated and deactivated. Upon activation, the additional functionality, data structures and presentation facilities become part of WordPress and are available for immediate use.

We have extended the WordPress plug-in model to adhere to our approach. On the level of the application logic and user interface, the WordPress plug-in model matches our component model. At the level of the user interface, plug-ins may define widgets and the WordPress core handles the generation of the user interface from themes including the placement of such widgets. Application logic is represented by PHP functions and events. At the data and schema level, however, WordPress only supports a basic notion of types and data may be stored in any possible way and format. Also, plug-ins do not define a composition API, as defined by our approach. We therefore build on our previous work [14] where we introduced DataPress, a WordPress plug-in which supports the generation of tailored WordPress plug-ins from user-defined ER models. With DataPress, a user graphically defines an application domain by means of ER models through the dashboard and DataPress automatically generates a plug-in that allows data to be managed accordingly. For each defined entity type and relationship, Data-Press generates data structures, CRUD methods and user interface components to create and manage the data.

By building on this approach, we not only gain support for ER modelling, but we could also extend the automatic generation of plug-ins to conform to our component model. We additionally generate two hooks for each of the generated CRUD operations—a before and after hook. For example, for the creation of an order entity, the two hooks `onOrderCreate` and `onOrderCreated` are generated. Also, we generate a configuration file that represents the composition API that gives access to the composable plug-in elements. The file lists the names of the entities, relationships, methods, events and widgets defined by a plug-in and the user can simply remove elements that should not be offered for composition. The configuration of a connector for a particular composition scenario is based on these names defined in the respective plug-in configuration files.

6   Composition Plug-in

To support composition by non-technical users, we provide a composition plug-in that supports the composition process graphically, as illustrated in the screenshots in Sect. 3. Figure 10 gives an overview of the composition plug-in architecture. The composition plug-in, shown in the centre, is a regular WordPress plug-in that is integrated into the dashboard. It provides access to locally installed plug-ins, shown on the left, and the connector type plug-ins, shown on the

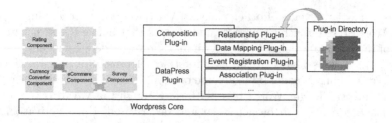

Fig. 10. Composition Plug-in Architecture

right. It builds on an extended version of DataPress and supports the generation of plug-ins from user-defined ER models structured according to our component model. Using the composition plug-in, new plug-ins can be composed with the installed ones by configuring one of the provided connector types. Assuming that all plug-ins would be structured according to our approach, a user could also download, install and compose plug-ins from the Wordpress Plug-in directory, shown on the left.

Each connector type has been realised as parameterised plug-in, which gets "instantiated" upon composition. The composition plug-in automatically generates and installs the configured connector plug-ins. Below, we show a configured version of the event handler registration connector that corresponds to the configuration shown in Figs. 4 and 5. Through the configuration process, the connector has been named *Payment Connector* and the event and method names to be bound, have been injected into the plug-in template. In WordPress, the `add_action` method registers a specific hook with a specific method. The `add_action` method further defines the priority of the method invocation, as well as the numbers of arguments that are passed from the event to the method. While WordPress assumes that the number and types of attributes provided by the hook match the parameters of the callback method, we have generalised this approach by giving the user the possibility to define attribute-parameter mappings, as shown in Fig. 5. In this example, the event `onOrderCreated` defines four attributes while the method `invokePayment` only takes two parameters.

```
/* Plug-in Name: PaymentConnector*/
...
add_action('onOrderCreated', 'invokePaymentTemp', 1, 4);
add_action('onPayedElectronically', 'redirectToShop');

function invokePaymentTemp($orderID, $date, $price, $noItems){
    $currency=''USD'';
    invokePayment($price, $currency);
}
function redirectToShop(){...}
```

The mappings are reflected in the connector code. Upon `onOrderCreated`, a helper method `invokePaymentTemp` method is invoked, accepting the four attributes defined by the `onOrderCreated` event as parameters. The method realises the defined attribute mappings and invokes the actual payment method using these mappings. Here, the attribute `$price` from `onOrderCreated`, and the attribute `currency` set to the default value "USD" are used as parameters.

Note that more advanced users are free to extend a configured connector plug-in with additional code. In the current example, the user has also defined a second binding, which, upon completion of the electronic payment, invokes the locally defined method `redirectToShop` to automatically redirect the customer back to the eCommerce component.

While the configured event registration connector plug-in only defines application logic between two components, other connectors also define schema, data and widgets. For example, the association connector creates a database table as part of its installation process where associated pairs of entities are stored. Furthermore, it also defines a widget allowing users to graphically create associations and, as part of the connector configuration, the user decides whether the widget may be visible along with one or both composed components as part of a dynamic sidebar injected into the layout theme, or as part of the dashboard. The widget connector is realised in a similar way: A configured widget connector injects a widget from one component into the user interface of another component, based on a user's configuration, by placing them in a dynamic sidebar.

7 Scenario

We have used the composition plug-in to compose an extended eCommerce application from various components. Figure 11 illustrates the various composition scenarios. As a first step (1), the eCommerce component has been composed with the survey component through a specialisation connector as described in Sect. 3. On the left, the specialisation is defined by means of an `is-a` relationship and the two attribute mappings.

In a second step, the eCommerce component has been composed with a review component to allow products to be reviewed by customers. The composition is based on an association connector, shown in (2). The connector defines the association between the product and the review entity including the cardinality constraints. A product may have *0* or *n* reviews and a review is for exactly one product. The connector also defines a widget, illustrated by the editor icon on the left. The connector is configured in such a way that the widget is displayed alongside the product view, allowing customers to write and view reviews while browsing products. Next, the eCommerce component is extended with electronic payment support, by composing it with an electronic payment component at the level of the application logic, shown in (3). The connector configuration defines the binding of the `onOrderCreate` event with the `invokePayment` method.

As the customer base of the company becomes more international, the company decides to make use of a currency converter component. In (4) the composition of the eCommerce component with a currency converter component is shown. The composition takes place at the user interface level: the connector defines that the currency converter widget is to be displayed along with products and orders, so that customers can make use of it when browsing products or to convert the price of an order.

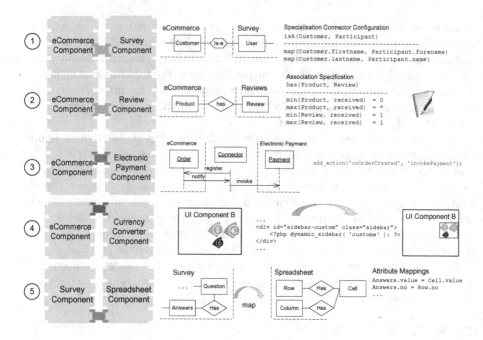

Fig. 11. Scenario Application

Finally, the company would like to evaluate the outcome of the survey using a spreadsheet component. To do so, the data of the survey component is mapped to the data format of the spreadsheet component, as shown in (5). The mapping is specified by a number of attribute mappings between the entities of the survey component and the entities of the spreadsheet component, where the survey questions and answers are mapped to the spreadsheet format.

8   Conclusion

Our approach, model and implementation is a practical solution to enhance today's content-management systems with support for component-based web engineering. By defining components and explicit connectors between them, we not only circumvent possible incompatibilities between components, but we also make sure that composed systems are resilient to plug-in updates, since the composition logic is completely encapsulated within the connector code.

We see our work as a further step towards providing systems that are easy to develop. While we target non-technical end-users and support the composition process through graphical user interfaces, this approach is clearly more limited than the programmatic definition and extensions of connectors, as can be done by more experienced users. However, the presented scenario has shown that a small set of relatively simple connector types covers a wide range of composition scenarios allowing for the design of relatively complex applications through graphical user interfaces. As a next step, we plan to conduct a user study to further validate and refine our approach. We also note that our approach is extensible, and new connector types could be added at any level.

References

1. Lieberman, H., Paterno, F. (eds.): End User Development. Human-Computer Interaction Series. Springer (2006)
2. Ceri, S., Fraternali, P., Bongio, A.: Web Modeling Language (WebML): A Modeling Language For Designing Web Sites. Computer Networks 33(1-6) (2000)
3. Vdovják, R., Fräsincar, F., Houben, G.J., Barna, P.: Engineering Semantic Web Information Systems in Hera. Journal of Web Engineering 1(1-2) (2003)
4. Gellersen, H.W., Wicke, R., Gaedke, M.: Webcomposition: An object-oriented support system for the web engineering lifecycle. Computer Networks 29(8-13), 1429–1437 (1997)
5. Ennals, R., Brewer, E., Garofalakis, M., Shadle, M., Gandhi, P.: Intel Mash Maker: Join the Web. ACM SIGMOD Record 36(4), 27–33 (2007)
6. Murthy, S., Maier, D., Delcambre, L.: Mash-o-Matic. In: Proc. ACM Symposium on Document Engineering (DocEng 2006) (2006)
7. Daniel, F., Casati, F., Benatallah, B., Shan, M.-C.: Hosted Universal Composition: Models, Languages and Infrastructure in mashArt. In: Laender, A.H.F., Castano, S., Dayal, U., Casati, F., de Oliveira, J.P.M. (eds.) ER 2009. LNCS, vol. 5829, pp. 428–443. Springer, Heidelberg (2009)
8. Imran, M., Soi, S., Kling, F., Daniel, F., Casati, F., Marchese, M.: On the Systematic Development of Domain-Specific Mashup Tools for End Users. In: Brambilla, M., Tokuda, T., Tolksdorf, R. (eds.) ICWE 2012. LNCS, vol. 7387, pp. 291–298. Springer, Heidelberg (2012)
9. Chudnovskyy, O., Nestler, T., Gaedke, M., Daniel, F., Fernández-Villamor, J.I., Chepegin, V.I., Fornas, J.A., Wilson, S., Kögler, C., Chang, H.: End-user-oriented Telco Mashups: The OMELETTE Approach. In Proc. World Wide Web Conf. (WWW 2012) (Companion Volume) (2012)
10. Shaw, M.: Modularity for the Modern World: Summary of Invited Keynote. In: Proc. Intl. Conf. on Aspect-Oriented Software Development (AOSD 2011) (2011)
11. Medvidovic, N., Taylor, R.N.: A Classification and Comparison Framework for Software Architecture Description Languages. IEEE Trans. Softw. Eng. 26(1), 70–93 (2000)
12. Clements, P.C.: A Survey of Architecture Description Languages. In: Proc. Intl. Workshop on Software Specification and Design (IWSSD 1996) (1996)
13. Leone, S., Norrie, M.C.: Building eCommerce Systems from Shared Micro-Schemas. In: Meersman, R., Dillon, T., Herrero, P., Kumar, A., Reichert, M., Qing, L., Ooi, B.-C., Damiani, E., Schmidt, D.C., White, J., Hauswirth, M., Hitzler, P., Mohania, M. (eds.) OTM 2011, Part I. LNCS, vol. 7044, pp. 284–301. Springer, Heidelberg (2011)
14. Leone, S., de Spindler, A., Norrie, M.C.: A Meta-Plugin for Bespoke Data Management in WordPress. In: Wang, X.S., Cruz, I., Delis, A., Huang, G. (eds.) WISE 2012. LNCS, vol. 7651, pp. 580–593. Springer, Heidelberg (2012)

Hidden-Web Induced by Client-Side Scripting: An Empirical Study

Zahra Behfarshad and Ali Mesbah

University of British Columbia,
Vancouver, BC, Canada
{janab,amesbah}@ece.ubc.ca

Abstract. Client-side JavaScript is increasingly used for enhancing web application functionality, interactivity, and responsiveness. Through the execution of JavaScript code in browsers, the DOM tree representing a webpage at runtime, can be incrementally updated without requiring a URL change. This dynamically updated content is hidden from general search engines. In this paper, we present the first empirical study on measuring and characterizing the hidden-web induced as a result of client-side JavaScript execution. Our study reveals that this type of hidden-web content is prevalent in online web applications today: from the 500 websites we analyzed, 95% contain client-side hidden-web content; On those websites that contain client-side hidden-web content, (1) on average, 62% of the web states are hidden, (2) per hidden state, there is an average of 19 kilobytes of data that is hidden from which 0.6 kilobytes contain textual content, (3) the DIV element is the most common clickable element used (61%) to initiate this type of hidden-web state transition, and (4) on average 25 minutes is required to dynamically crawl 50 DOM states. Further, our study indicates that there is a correlation between DOM tree size and hidden-web content, but no correlation exists between the amount of JavaScript code and client-side hidden-web.

1   Introduction

General web search engines cover only a portion of the web, called the visible or indexable web, which consists of the set of web pages reachable purely by following URL-based links. There is, however, a large body of valuable web content that is not accessible by simply following hypertext links. Well-known examples include dynamic server-side content behind web forms [3,19] reachable through application-specific queries. This portion of the web, not reachable through search engines, is generally referred to as the invisible or hidden web, which, in 2001, was estimated to be 500 times larger than the visible web [4]. More recently, form-based hidden web content has been estimated at several millions of pages [3,12].

With the wide adoption of client-side programming languages such as JavaScript and AJAX techniques to create responsive web applications, there is a new type of hidden-web that is growing rapidly. Although there has been

F. Daniel, P. Dolog, and Q. Li (Eds.): ICWE 2013, LNCS 7977, pp. 52–67, 2013.
© Springer-Verlag Berlin Heidelberg 2013

extensive research on detecting [3,14,19] and measuring [4,11] hidden-web content behind web forms, hidden-web induced as a result of client-side scripting has gained limited attention so far.

JavaScript is the dominant language for implementing dynamic web applications. Today, as many as 97 of the top 100 most visited websites [1], have client-side JavaScript [20], often consisting of thousands of lines of code per application. JavaScript is increasingly used for offloading core functionality to the client-side and achieving rich web interfaces. JavaScript code interacts with and incrementally updates the Document Object Model (DOM) in an event-based style. Changes made dynamically to the structure, contents or styles of the DOM elements are directly manifested in the browser's display. This event-based style of interaction is substantially different from the traditional URL-based page transitions through hyperlinks, where the entire DOM is repopulated with a new HTML page from the server for every user-initiated state change.

The goal of our paper is to measure the pervasiveness and characterize the nature of *hidden-web content induced by client-side JavaScript* in today's web applications. For simplicity, we will refer to this type of hidden-web content as **client-side hidden-web** throughout this paper. To the best of our knowledge, we are the first to conduct an empirical study on this topic. Our empirical data shows that as high as 95% of the 500 websites we analyzed contain hidden-web content, and on average 62% of the 50 states we crawled for each website are hidden due to client-side scripting.

2   Background and Motivation

Client-Side Hidden-Web Content. Client-side scripting empowers achieving dynamic and responsive web interfaces in today's web applications. Through JavaScript, the client-side runtime DOM tree of asear web application can be dynamically updated with new structure and content. These updates are commonly initiated through event-listeners, AJAX callbacks, and timeouts. The new content, either originated from the server-side or created on the client-side, is then injected into the DOM through JavaScript to represent the new state of the application.

Although DOM manipulation through JavaScript increases responsiveness of web applications, these dynamically mutated states end up in the hidden-web portion of the web. The main reason is that crawling such dynamic content is fundamentally more challenging and costly than crawling classical multi-page web applications, where states are explicit and correspond to pages that have a unique URL assigned to them.

Client-side state is determined dynamically through changes in the DOM that are only visible after executing the corresponding JavaScript code. The major search giants have currently little or no support for dynamic analysis of JavaScript code due to scalability and security issues. They merely extract hypertext links and index the resulting HTML code recursively.

```
1   $(document).ready(function() {
2     $('div.update').click(function() {
3       var updateID = $(this).attr('rel');
4       $.get('/news/', { ref:updateID },
5       function(data) {
6         $(updateID+'Container').append(data); }); }) });
```

Fig. 1. JavaScript code for updating the DOM after a click event

```
<body><h1>Sports News</h1>
 <p><span id="sportsContainer"></span></p>
 <div class="update" rel="sports">Update!</div>
</body>
```

Fig. 2. The initial DOM state

Hidden-Content Example. We present a simple example of how JavaScript code can induce hidden-web content by dynamically changing the DOM tree. Figure 1 depicts a JavaScript code snippet using the popular jQuery library.[1] Figure 2 illustrates the initial state of the DOM before any modification has occurred. Once the page is loaded (line 1 in Figure 1), the JavaScript code attaches an `onclick` event-listener to the `DIV` DOM element with class attribute 'update' (line 2). When a user clicks on this `DIV` element, the anonymous function associated with the event-listener is executed (lines 2–8). The function then sends an asynchronous call to the server (line 4), passing a parameter read from the `DIV` element (i.e., 'sports') (line 3). On the callback, the response content from the server is injected into the DOM element with ID 'sportsContainer' (line 6). The resulting updated DOM state is shown in Figure 3. All the data retrieved and injected into the DOM this way will be hidden content as it is not indexed by search engines. Although the effect of client-side scripting on the hidden-web is clear, there is currently a lack of comprehensive investigation and empirical data in this area.

3   Related Work

Crawling the Hidden-Web. Crawling techniques have been studied since the advent of the Web itself. Web crawlers find and index millions of HTML pages daily by searching for hyperlinks. Yet a large amount of data is hidden behind web queries and therefore, extensive research has been conducted towards finding and analyzing the hidden-web – also called deep-web – behind web forms [3,7,8,14,15,19]. The main focus in this line of research is on exploring ways of detecting query interfaces and accessing the content in online databases, which is usually behind HTML forms. This line of research is merely concerned with server-side hidden-web content (i.e., in databases).

On the contrary, exploring the hidden-web induced as a result of client-side scripting has gained very little attention so far. Alvarez et al. [2] discussed the

---

[1] http://jquery.com

```
<body>
  <h1>Sports News</h1>
  <p><span id="sportsContainer">
    <h3>US GP: Vettel fastest in Austin second practice</h3>
    <p>Vettel produced an ominous performance</p></span></p>
  <div class="update" rel="sports">Update!</div>
</body>
```

Fig. 3. The updated DOM tree after clicking on 'Update!'

importance and challenges of crawling client-side hidden-web. Mesbah et al. [17] proposed an automated crawler, called CRAWLJAX, for AJAX-based web applications. Duda et al. [9] presented how DOM states can be indexed. The authors proposed a crawling and indexing algorithm for client-side state changes.

Measuring the Hidden-Web. Researchers have reported their results of measuring the hidden-web behind forms. In 2001, Bergman [4] reported a study indicating that the hidden-web was about 500 times larger than the visible web. In 2004, Chang et al. [5] measured hidden-web content in online databases using a random IP-sampling approach, and found that the majority of the data in such databases is structured. In 2007, He et al. [11] conducted a study using an overlap analysis technique between some of the most common search engines such as Yahoo!, Google, and MSN and discovered that 43,000-96,000 deep websites existed. They presented an informal estimate of 7,500 terabytes of hidden data, which was 500 times larger than the visible web, which supported the earlier results by Bergman.

All this related work focuses on measuring server-side hidden-web behind forms. To the best of our knowledge, we are the first to study and measure client-side hidden-web.

4   Methodology

Our main objective is to gain an understanding of how much dynamic client-side content is unsearchable for end-users on the Web. To that end, we conduct a quantitative empirical study to measure the pervasiveness and characterize the nature of hidden-web content induced by client-side scripting. Our research questions are formulated as follows:

RQ1 How pervasive is client-side hidden-web in today's web applications?
RQ2 How much content is typically hidden due to client-side scripting?
RQ3 Which clickable elements contribute most to client-side hidden-web content?
RQ4 Are there any correlations between the degree of client-side hidden-web and a web application's characteristics?

4.1   Experimental Objects

In this study, we analyze 500 unique websites in total. To obtain a representative pool of websites, similar to other researchers [13,20], we select 400 unique websites from Alexa's Top Sites [1] (henceforth referred to as ALEXA). For multiple instances of the same domain on Alexa's top list (e.g., *www.google.com*, *www.google.fr*), we only include and count one instance in our 400 objects list. In addition, we gather another 100 random websites using Yahoo! random link generator (henceforth referred to as RANDOM), which is also used in other studies [6,16]. All the 500 websites (henceforth referred to as TOTAL) were crawled and analyzed throughout February-March 2013.

4.2 Experimental Design

To investigate the pervasiveness of hidden content due to client-side scripting (**RQ1**), we examine all the 500 websites and count the percentage of websites that exhibit client-side hidden-web content. In addition, for each of the websites that contains hidden-web content, we measure what portion of the crawled (50) states is client-side hidden-web. To measure the amount of content that is hidden (**RQ2**), we compute the total and average in terms of textual *differences* between each hidden state and its previous state. To address **RQ3**, we classify the type of clickable elements, which clicking them results in a hidden state in our analysis. We assess what type of DOM elements are commonly used in practice by web developers that induce this type of dynamic JavaScript-driven state change. In order to answer **RQ4**, we analyze possible correlations between the client-side hidden-web content and the average DOM size and custom JavaScript code of each website examined, for 100 websites randomly chose from our pool of 500 websites. In the next section, technical details of our analysis approach are presented.

5   Client-Side Hidden-Web Analysis

We have implemented our client-side hidden-web analysis approach in a tool called JAVIS, which is available for download, along with all our empirical data.[2]

Figure 4 depicts our client-side hidden-web content analysis technique which is composed of three main steps: (1) dynamically crawling each given website, (2) classifying the detected state changes into visible and hidden categories, and (3) conducting characterization analyses of the hidden states. Each step is described in the subsequent subsections.

5.1   Event-Driven Dynamic Crawling

State Exploration. Our approach for automatically exploring a web application's state space is based on our CRAWLJAX [17] work. CRAWLJAX is a crawler capable of automatically exploring JavaScript-induced DOM state changes through an event-driven dynamic crawling technique. It exercises client-side code, detects and executes clickables that lead to various dynamic states of Web

---

[2] http://salt.ece.ubc.ca/content/javis/

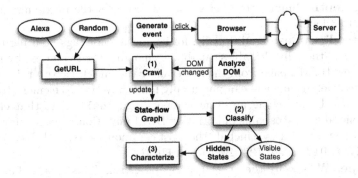

Fig. 4. Overview of our client-side hidden-web analysis

2.0 AJAX-based web applications. By firing events on the web elements and analyzing the effects on the dynamic DOM tree in a real browser before and after the event, the crawler incrementally builds a *state-flow graph* (SFG) capturing the client-side states and possible event-based transitions between them. This state-flow graph is defined as follows:

Definition 1. *A **state-flow graph** SFG for an AJAX-based website* **A** *is a labeled, directed graph, denoted by a 4 tuple* $< r, V, E, \mathcal{L} >$ *where:*

1. r *is the root node (called Index) representing the initial state when* **A** *has been fully loaded into the browser.*
2. V *is a set of vertices representing the states. Each* $v \in V$ *represents a runtime DOM state in* **A**.
3. E *is a set of (directed) edges between vertices. Each* $(v_1, v_2) \in E$ *represents a clickable* c *connecting two states if and only if state* v_2 *is reached by executing* c *in state* v_1.
4. $\mathcal{L}$ *is a labelling function that assigns a label, from a set of event types and DOM element properties, to each edge.*
5. *SFG can have multi-edges and be cyclic.*

CRAWLJAX is also capable of crawling traditional URL-based websites. It is fully configurable in terms of the type of elements that should be examined or ignored during the crawling process. For more details about the architecture, algorithms or capabilities of CRAWLJAX the interested reader is referred to [17,18].[3]

Crawling Configuration. We have extended, modified, and configured CRAWLJAX for this study as follows:

Maximum states. Dynamic crawling is quite expensive and time consuming. To constrain the state space and still acquire a representative sample for our analysis in a timely manner, we define an upper limit on the number of states to dynamically crawl for each website, namely, 50 unique DOM states.

---

[3] http://crawljax.com

Crawling depth. Similar to other studies [11], we set the maximum crawling depth to 3 levels.

Candidate clickables. Traditionally, forms and anchor tags pointing to valid URLs were the only clickables capable of changing the state (i.e., by retrieving a new HTML page from the server after the click). However, in modern websites, web developers can potentially make any HTML element to act as a *clickable* by attaching an event-listener (e.g., onclick) to that element. Such clickables are capable of initiating DOM mutations through JavaScript code. In our analysis, we include the most commonly used clickable elements, namely: A, DIV, SPAN, IMG, INPUT and BUTTON.

Event type. We specify the event type to be click. This means the crawler will generate click events on DOM elements that are spotted as candidate clickables, i.e., elements potentially capable of changing the DOM state. Note that there are other types of events (e.g., onmouseover) that can generate hidden-web content. Our study is currently targeted towards the click event, which is the mostly commonly used event-type in web applications.

Randomized crawling. In order to get a simple random sample, we randomize the crawling behaviour in terms of selecting the next candidate clickable for exploration. Hence, the crawler clicks on any of the defined candidate clickable types (e.g., DIV, A, etc) randomly while crawling.

Once the tool is configured, we automatically select and crawl each website, and save the resulting state-flow graph containing the detected states (DOM trees) and transitional edges (clickables).

5.2   Classification

As shown in Figure 4, for each website crawled, we classify the detected states into two categories: visible and hidden. Our client-side hidden-web analysis is largely based on the following two assumptions:

1. A valid URL-based state transition can be crawled and indexed by general search engines and, therefore, it is visible;
2. A non-URL-based state transition is not crawled nor indexed by general search engines and thus, it ends up in the hidden-web; For instance, the DOM update presented in Figure 3, as a result of clicking on the DIV element of Figure 2, is hidden.

To classify the crawled states into the visible or hidden group, we traverse the inferred state-flow graph of each website. For each state, we analyze all the incoming edges (i.e., clickables). If the incoming edges is a valid URL-based transition, we consider that state to be visible, otherwise it is hidden.

Each edge contains information about the type of clickable element that caused a state change. Our classification uses that information to decide which resulting states are hidden as follows:

Anchor tag (A). The anchor tag can produce both visible and hidden states, depending on the presence and URL validity of the value of its `HREF` attribute. For instance, clicking on `<A HREF='www.eg.com/news/'>` results in a visible state, whereas `<A HREF='#' onclick= 'updateNews();'>` can produce a hidden state.

IMG. The image tag is also interesting since it can result in a visible state when embodied in an anchor tag with a valid URL; For every edge of `IMG` type, we retrieve the parent element from the corresponding DOM state. If the parent element is an anchor tag with a valid URL, then we categorize the resulting state as visible, otherwise the state is hidden.

Other element types. Per definition, `DIV`, `SPAN`, `INPUT`, and `BUTTON` do not have attributes that can point to URLs, and thus, the resulting state changes are all categorized as hidden.

5.3   Characterization Analysis

Hidden-Web Quantity. Once the explored states are categorized, we annotate the hidden states on the state-flow graph to measure the amount of hidden-web data in those states. We traverse the annotated state-flow graph, starting from Index, and for each annotated hidden state, we compute the differences between the previous state (which could be a visible or hidden state) and the annotated hidden state using a differencing engine. To measure the amount of data that can be hidden, the differencing method computes merely the *additions* in the target (hidden) state. For each website, JAVIS saves all the differences in a file and measures the total size in bytes. We also compute the pure textual content in the total differences.

Clickable Types. To investigate which clickable type (i.e., `A`, `DIV`, `SPAN`, `IMG`, `INPUT` and `BUTTON`) contributes most to inducing hidden-web content in practice, JAVIS examines the annotated state-flow graph and gathers the edges that result in hidden states. It then calculates, for each element type, the mean of its contribution portion to the hidden-web percentage.

Correlations. Further, we measure the average DOM string size as well as the custom JavaScript code (excluding common libraries such as jQuery, Dojo, Ext, etc) of each website. To examine the relationship between these measurements and the client-side hidden-web content, we use R [10] to calculate the non-parametric Spearman correlation coefficients (r) as well as the p-values (p), and plot the graphs.

6   Results

Table 1 provides a representative small sample (20 websites) of the kind of websites we have crawled and the type of data we have gathered, measured, and analyzed in this study. These websites are randomly selected from our total pool of 500 websites. The first 10 are taken from ALEXA and the second 10 from

Table 1. Hidden-web Analysis Results. The first 10 are from ALEXA, and the remaining 10 from RANDOM.

ID	Site Name	States (#)	Clickables			Clickable Types								Size		Hidden				Time Elapsed (S)
			Total	Visible	Hidden	A (Visible)	A (Hidden)	Div	Span	Img (Visible)	Img (Hidden)	Input	Button	JavaScript (KB)	DOM (KB)	States (%)	Total (KB)	Total Content (KB)	Average (KB)	
1	Google	50	49	3	46	3	0	29	16	0	1	0	0	329	210	94	906	13	18	228
2	ESPN	50	49	12	37	6	0	26	2	6	9	0	0	161	196	75	4358	120	89	7565
3	AOL	50	49	8	41	5	1	18	22	3	0	0	0	203	170	82	4626	140	64	4727
4	Youtube	50	49	7	42	7	0	7	17	0	7	0	17	286	153	84	4230	153	86	530
5	Aweber	50	49	24	25	16	1	20	0	8	4	0	0	41	31	65	38	0	0.78	740
6	Samsung	50	49	3	46	2	0	42	3	1	0	0	1	96	267	92	1381	21	28	1274
7	USPS	50	49	8	41	5	1	33	7	3	0	0	0	200	258	82	563	6	11.5	317
8	BBC	50	49	41	8	25	0	3	3	16	2	0	0	142	112	16	293	6	6	794
9	Alipay	50	49	2	47	2	7	33	7	0	0	0	0	200	72	94	77	0	1.5	828
10	Renren	50	49	0	49	0	0	49	0	0	0	0	0	100	47	100	1613	3	33	152
11	EdwardRobertson	50	49	1	48	1	2	45	1	0	0	0	0	120	64	98	154	7	3.14	161
12	Rayzist	50	49	31	18	31	1	16	0	0	1	0	0	329	54	37	257	38	5.2	976
13	Metmuseum	50	49	3	46	3	0	2	0	0	44	0	0	54	87	94	935	68	19	364
14	JiveDesign	50	49	0	49	0	0	49	0	0	0	0	0	241	202	100	369	0	7.5	322
15	MTV	50	49	0	49	0	0	19	0	0	30	0	0	242	200	100	530	14	10.8	417
16	Challengeair	50	49	0	49	0	0	49	0	0	0	0	0	176	28	100	22	0	0.45	145
17	Mouchel	50	52	52	0	51	0	0	0	1	0	0	0	20	60	0	0	0	0	535
18	Sacklunch	50	49	45	4	3	0	3	0	42	1	0	0	121	83	8	166	6	3.39	236
19	Pongo	50	49	3	46	3	0	46	0	0	0	0	0	61	463	94	4229	58	83.3	713
20	MuppetCentral	50	49	17	32	8	0	32	0	9	0	0	0	254	224	65	4807	272	98.1	966

RANDOM. The complete set of our empirical data is available for download.[4] It should be noted that Total column in the table refers to both the hidden DOM structure and the textual content while the Total Content only refers to the hidden textual content. The Average is the average hidden content and DOM structure per state.

6.1   Pervasiveness (RQ1)

95% (476/500) of the websites we analyzed exhibit some degree of client-side hidden-web content, i.e., they have at least one or more client-side hidden states.

To gain deeper knowledge of what percentage of the 50 states crawled from each of these websites actually contain hidden-web content, each web application is analyzed individually. Figure 5 presents three box plots illustrating the hidden-web state percentages for ALEXA, RANDOM, and TOTAL.

Alexa. For the 400 websites from ALEXA, on average 65.63% of the 50 states we analyzed were client-side hidden-web. This high number can be explained by the nature of such websites perhaps. They are among the top most visited sites in the world. As such, developers of many of these websites use the latest Web

---

[4] http://salt.ece.ubc.ca/content/javis/

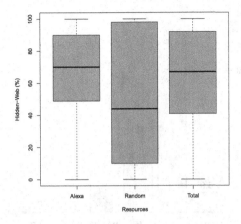

Fig. 5. Box plots of the percentage of client-side hidden-web states in ALEXA, RANDOM, and TOTAL. 50 states (pages) are crawled from each website.

Table 2. Descriptive statistics of the average hidden-web content for all states and per state

	Textual hidden content (KB)			All hidden content (KB)		
Hidden-Web	**Min**	**Mean**	**Max**	**Min**	**Mean**	**Max**
Per State	0	0.60	11.65	0	18.91	286.4
All States	0	27.6	536	0	869.7	13170

2.0 technologies, such as JavaScript, DOM, Ajax, and HTML5, to provide high quality features that come with rich interaction and responsiveness. As we have discussed in Section 2, these Web 2.0 techniques contribute enormously to the creation of client-side hidden-web.

Random. An average of 50.6% of the states from the RANDOM websites constitute hidden states. These websites were purely randomly chosen on the web. In other words, we do not know about their rankings nor their popularity among end users. The lower percentage is perhaps due to the fact that many websites on the web might still are quite classical in nature, meaning they use more URL-based links for state transitions, rather than using JavaScript. However, although the percentage is not as high as the websites on ALEXA, the rather high 50.6% in the wild still points to the pervasiveness of client-side hidden-web on the web.

Total. When the results of ALEXA and RANDOM are combined in TOTAL, the total hidden-web state percentage is 62.52%. It should be noted that both ALEXA and RANDOM contain websites that have as low as 0% and as high as 100% hidden-web states, regardless of any rankings.

On average, per website 25 minutes was required to dynamically crawl 50 states. It took JAVIS 211 hours ($\approx$ 8.8 days) to crawl and classify all the 500 websites (each with 50 states).

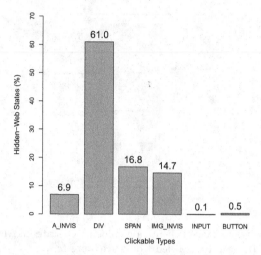

Fig. 6. Barplot of hidden-web percentage behind different types of clickables. 'A_INVIS' represents anchor tags without a (valid) URL. 'MG_INVIS' represents IMG elements not embedded in an anchor tag with a (valid) URL.

6.2 Quantity (RQ2)

In order to gain an understanding of the quantity of content in the client-side hidden-web states, we measured the amount of hidden data as described in Section 5.3. Table 2 shows the amount of client-side hidden-web content for all of the crawled hidden-web states, and per hidden-web state. It shows descriptive statistics for all the hidden content including DOM structures and textual content as well as only textual, natural language content, extracted from the DOM elements.

Per Hidden-Web State. Per hidden-web state, on average 19 kilobytes of DOM and textual content exist while 0.6 kilobytes was only textual content. Some states have as high as 286 kilobytes of hidden content.

All Hidden-Web States. For all the states crawled together, we measured an average of 870 kilobytes of client-side hidden-web content including both DOM and textual content while the textual content was around 27.6 KB. The minimum and maximum are 0, 13170 kilobytes, and 0 and 536 kilobytes respectively.

We manually examined some of the hidden textual content to understand why type of information would be hidden to end-users. The nature of the hidden textual content is a combination of singular words, numbers, short messages or whole sentences. The short messages are mostly informative descriptions of the websites or advertisements. The larger sentences range from descriptions of a particular subject, questions/answers, news items, and discussions in various domains such as health, science, animals, videos and images, actors and stars, sports and so on.

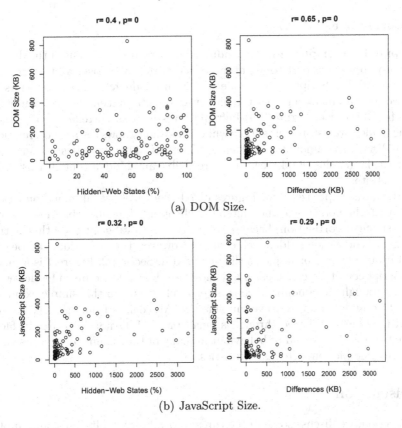

(a) DOM Size.

(b) JavaScript Size.

Fig. 7. Scatter plots of the average DOM and JavaScript size versus the hidden-web state percentage and content. r represents the Spearman correlation coefficient and p is the p-value.

6.3 Induction (RQ3)

To better understand what type of clickable elements web developers use in today's websites that induce state changes in the browser, we analyzed how much each clickable type contributes to the measured hidden-web state percentage.

As discussed in Section 5.3, the anchor tag (A) and the image element (IMG) can induce both visible and hidden states; For this part, we only consider the ones that cause hidden-states in our analysis. Figure 6 depicts a barplot of the different clickable types versus the associated hidden-web state percentage. We can see that the DIV has the highest contribution to the hidden-web state percentage (61%), followed by SPAN (16.8%). Interestingly, the IMG and A element types are also used quite often to induce client-side hidden content, with 14.7% and 6.9% each, respectively. Finally, BUTTON and INPUT contribute to less than one percent of the hidden-web states. This shows that while crawling, it is not sufficient to simply focus on the anchor tags of a website, any longer.

6.4   Correlations (RQ4)

DOM and JavaScript Size. We conducted a correlation analysis of the degree of hidden-web with respect to (1) average DOM size, taken over all the crawled states, and (2) JavaScript custom code size. Figure 7 depicts the scatter plots of these two measurements against the hidden-web state percentage and content.

For the DOM size, Figure 7(a)-Left indicates a weak correlation ($r = 0.4$) with the hidden-web state percentage while 7(a)-Right shows a strong correlation ($r = 0.65$) with the amount of hidden-web content. This comes as no surprise, because the larger the DOM tree, the more visible and hidden content there will be in a website.

For the JavaScript size, both Figures of 7(b) indicate a weak monotonic correlation with the percentage and amount of client-side hidden-web. We expected to see a stronger correlation, because after all, it is JavaScript code that is the root cause of client-side hidden-web content. However, this behaviour can be explained using a simple example as the one used in Section 2: Figure 1 is a piece of JavaScript code that can cause many hidden-web states and much hidden-web content, although the amount of code is relatively small; In this simple example all the state updates are retrieved in small HTML deltas from the server, and injected into the DOM tree through a small piece of JavaScript code. In fact, we have witnessed this kind of behaviour in many of the examined websites that have client-side hidden-web characteristics.

7   Discussion

In this section, we discuss some of the threats to validity, limitations, and implications of our findings.

Client-Side Scripting. Plugin-based Rich Internet Applications (RIA) such as Adobe Flash and Silverlight have their own client-side scripting languages that induce hidden-web content. The main focus of our work, however, was standard-based technologies and therefore we limited our study to only JavaScript initiated client-side hidden-web content.

Clickable Types. Through JavaScript event-driven programming any HTML element can potentially become a clickable item. In this study, we included six of the most common HTML elements used as clickables. We made our selection based on a small pilot study we conducted on ten Alexa websites. Other clickable types (e.g., P, TD) could also potentially induce client-side hidden-web content, which we have not analyzed. The inclusion of other clickable types can probably marginally increase the hidden-web percentage.

Crawler. We extended and used CRAWLJAX [17] to crawl client-side hidden-web content. Using a different crawler could result in different outcomes. However, to the best of our knowledge, CRAWLJAX is currently the only available open source tool capable of crawling JavaScript-based applications.

Event Types. Our study is constrained to the click event type. We believe this is the most commonly used event type in practice for making event-driven transitions in Web 2.0 apps. However, the DOM event model has many other event types, e.g., *mouseover*, *drag and drop*, which can potentially lead to hidden-web states. This is part of our future work.

Number of States Examined. To be able to have a fair analysis in a timely manner, we constrained the maximum number of states to crawl for each website to 50. There were a few websites that did not have that many states to crawl. In those cases, we analyzed the websites according to the number of states available. Choosing a different maximum number could theoretically impact our evaluation results, although we do not have any evidence that that would be the case (because of the randomization).

Representativeness. We have collected data for 500 websites. To obtain a representative sample and minimize selection bias, we collected 400 URLs from ALEXA and 100 randomly from the wild. For the same reason, we randomized the candidate clickable selection while crawling, to make the state exploration of each website unbiased.

Reproducibility. Our tool implementation, JAVIS, the list of all websites used in our study, as well as all the empirical data are available for download, making the study fully replicable.

Implications. Our study shows that there is a considerable amount of data that is *hidden* due to client-side scripting. The hidden content is increasing rapidly as more developers adopt modern Web 2.0 techniques to implement their web applications. We believe more research is needed to support better understanding, analysis, crawling, indexing, and searching this new type of hidden-web content. In addition, web developers need to realize that by using modern techniques (e.g., JavaScript, AJAX, HTML5), a large portion of their content becomes hidden, and thus unsearchable for their potential users on the web.

8   Conclusion

With the advent of Web 2.0 technologies, an increasing amount of the web application state is being offloaded to the client-side browser to improve responsiveness and user interaction. Through the execution of JavaScript code in the browser, the DOM tree representing a webpage at runtime, is incrementally mutated without requiring a URL change. This dynamically updated content is inaccessible through general search engines, and as a results it becomes part of the hidden-web portion of the Web.

In this paper, we presented the first empirical study on measuring and characterizing the hidden-web induced as a result of client-side scripting. Our study shows that client-side hidden-web is omnipresent on the web. From the 500 websites we analyzed, 476 (95%) contained some degree of hidden-web content. In those websites, on average 63% of the states were hidden, and per hidden state, we measured an average of 19 kilobytes of hidden content from which 0.60 kilobytes is pure textual content. The DIV element is the most commonly used clickable to induce client-side hidden-web content, followed by the SPAN element.

This points to the importance of including the examination of such elements in modern crawling engines and going beyond link analysis in anchor tags.

In future work, we will expand the list of websites in our analysis. We also intend to study the effects of other event-types (e.g., mouseover) and HTML5 (e.g., canvas) on the amount of client-side hidden-web content.

References

1. Alexa top sites, http://www.alexa.com/topsites/
2. Alvarez, M., Pan, A., Raposo, J., Vina, A.: Client-side deep web data extraction. In: Proc. of the Int. Conf. on E-Commerce Technology for Dynamic E-Business, pp. 158–161. IEEE Computer Society (2004)
3. Barbosa, L., Freire, J.: An adaptive crawler for locating hidden-web entry points. In: Proc. of the 16th Int. Conf. on World Wide Web (WWW), pp. 441–450. ACM (2007)
4. Bergman, M.: White paper: the deep web: surfacing hidden value. Journal of Electronic Publishing 7(1) (2001)
5. Chang, K.C.-C., He, B., Li, C., Patel, M., Zhang, Z.: Structured databases on the web: observations and implications. SIGMOD Rec. 33(3), 61–70 (2004)
6. Choudhary, S.R., Versee, H., Orso, A.: WebDiff: Automated identification of cross-browser issues in web applications. In: Proc. of the 26th IEEE Int. Conf. on Softw. Maintenance (ICSM 2010), pp. 1–10 (2010)
7. Dasgupta, A., Ghosh, A., Kumar, R., Olston, C., Pandey, S., Tomkins, A.: The discoverability of the web. In: Proc. of the Int. Conf. on World Wide Web (WWW), pp. 421–430. ACM (2007)
8. de Carvalho, A.F., Silva, F.S.: Smartcrawl: a new strategy for the exploration of the hidden web. In: Procs. of the ACM Int. Workshop on Web information and Data Management, pp. 9–15. ACM (2004)
9. Duda, C., Frey, G., Kossmann, D., Matter, R., Zhou, C.: Ajax crawl: making Ajax applications searchable. In: Proc. Int. Conf. on Data Engineering (ICDE 2009), pp. 78–89 (2009)
10. Gentleman, R., Ihaka, R.: The R project for statistical computing, http://www.r-project.org
11. He, B., Patel, M., Zhang, Z., Chang, K.: Accessing the deep web. Communications of the ACM 50(5), 94–101 (2007)
12. Hsieh, W., Madhavan, J., Pike, R.: Data management projects at Google. In: Proc. of the Int. Conf. on Management of Data (SIGMOD), pp. 725–726 (2006)
13. Krishnamurthy, B., Wills, C.: Cat and mouse: content delivery tradeoffs in web access. In: Proc. of WWW, pp. 337–346. ACM (2006)
14. Lage, J.P., da Silva, A.S., Golgher, P.B., Laender, A.H.F.: Automatic generation of agents for collecting hidden web pages for data extraction. Data Knowl. Eng. 49(2), 177–196 (2004)
15. Madhavan, J., Ko, D., Kot, L., Ganapathy, V., Rasmussen, A., Halevy, A.: Google's deep web crawl. Proc. VLDB Endow. 1(2), 1241–1252 (2008)
16. Mesbah, A., Mirshokraie, S.: Automated analysis of CSS rules to support style maintenance. In: Proc. of the 34th ACM/IEEE Int. Conf. on Softw. Eng. (ICSE), pp. 408–418. IEEE Computer Society (2012)

17. Mesbah, A., van Deursen, A., Lenselink, S.: Crawling Ajax-based web applications through dynamic analysis of user interface state changes. ACM Transactions on the Web (TWEB) 6(1), 3:1–3:30 (2012)
18. Mesbah, A., van Deursen, A., Roest, D.: Invariant-based automatic testing of modern web applications. IEEE Trans. on Softw. Eng. (TSE) 38(1), 35–53 (2012)
19. Raghavan, S., Garcia-Molina, H.: Crawling the hidden web. In: Proc. of the Int. Conf. on Very Large Data Bases (VLDB), pp. 129–138 (2001)
20. Yue, C., Wang, H.: Characterizing insecure JavaScript practices on the web. In: Proc. of the Int. World Wide Web Conf (WWW), pp. 961–970. ACM (2009)

Discovering Implicit Schemas in JSON Data*

Javier Luis Cánovas Izquierdo and Jordi Cabot

AtlanMod, École des Mines de Nantes – INRIA – LINA, Nantes, France
{javier.canovas,jordi.cabot}@inria.fr

Abstract. JSON has become a very popular lightweigth format for data exchange. JSON is human readable and easy for computers to parse and use. However, JSON is schemaless. Though this brings some benefits (e.g., flexibility in the representation of the data) it can become a problem when consuming and integrating data from different JSON services since developers need to be aware of the structure of the schemaless data. We believe that a mechanism to discover (and visualize) the implicit schema of the JSON data would largely facilitate the creation and usage of JSON services. For instance, this would help developers to understand the links between a set of services belonging to the same domain or API. In this sense, we propose a model-based approach to generate the underlying schema of a set of JSON documents.

1 Introduction

With the emergence of the Web 2.0, asynchronous-based web technologies are becoming mainstream mainly thanks to their ability to provide richer, faster and more interactive web experiences [1]. AJAX-based web applications (e.g., Google Maps, Gmail or Facebook to cite some popular ones) are good examples of such technology. For a long time, these applications have been using XML as interchange format, however, in the last years the JavaScript Object Notation (JSON[1]) has been gaining in popularity since it provides a lightweigth data exchange format with a significant performance improvement [2].

JSON is a human readable format consisting in sets of objects (i.e., types or concepts) described by name/value pairs (i.e., fields or attributes). JSON is schemaless, i.e., there is no a schema specifying the internal structure of JSON objects, instead the schema is implicit. Schemaless data is particularly interesting in cases dealing with non-uniform data (e.g., non-uniform types or custom fields) or in schema migration [3], however, it can become a burden in data integration scenarios (e.g., consuming JSON-based APIs) where it becomes necessary to discover at least partially the underlying structure in order to properly process the data.

Therefore, web developers must often interact with APIs publishing a set of JSON-based services and face the problems of undertanding and managing the JSON documents returned by those services. The problem gets worse when developers need to

---

* This work has been supported by the European Commission under the ICT Policy Support Programme, grant no. 317859.

[1] www.json.org

F. Daniel, P. Dolog, and Q. Li (Eds.): ICWE 2013, LNCS 7977, pp. 68–83, 2013.

compose several JSON-based services since their implicit structure can differ. For instance, digesting the data returned by a query service to call another service later on.

A first attempt to formalize JSON data is being performed by the *JSON schema* initiative [4], but it is still far from a wide adoption. So far, most APIs are only documented by means of natural language explanations and a few use case examples. Thus, developers must invest a lot of time to grasp the kind of information an API provides and how to use the API services to get that information. We believe that a mechanism able to provide a (visual) higher-level view of the data provided by the API services would be a significant improvement.

In this sense, this paper proposes a discovery process for JSON-based services. Given a set of JSON documents, our approach returns a model describing their implicit schema. We follow an iterative process where new JSON documents (from the same or different services within the API) contribute to enrich the generated model. The model helps to both understand single services and to infer possible relationships between them, thus suggesting possible compositions and providing an overall view of the application domain. The use of a model-based approach enables to reuse the plethora of existing model-driven engineering techniques for further processing of the JSON model. An implementation of the approach is also provided.

The paper is organized as follows. Section 2 motivates the problem and presents a running example. Sections 3 and 4 describes the approach and its application to discover service dependencies, respectively. Section 5 describes the implemented tool. Finally, Section 6 presents the related work and Section 7 ends the paper.

2 What is Behind JSON Data

Nowadays, a considerable number of web applications provide an external API consisting in a set of JSON-based services (more than 40% of the APIs included in ProgrammableWeb[2] return JSON data) where all services are interrelated. Indeed, each service gives access to a subset of the application domain and developers must combine them to build any kind of non-trivial functionality on top of that API. Since JSON data is a schemaless format, deducing the right way of combining those services is not a trivial task. Next we will illustrate this problem with the TAN running example that we will use along this paper.

TAN is the public transportation entity of the city of Nantes, France, and provides a REST API composed of a set of JSON-based services to query the bus/tram transportation system (e.g., the nearest bus stop to a given geolocation, which buses stop in a bus stop, etc.). Figure 1 shows the JSON output obtained when querying two of services of the TAN API (meaningful strings have been translated into English for the sake of comprehension). Figure 1a shows the JSON document coming from the first service, which returns the bus/tram stops close to a position (i.e., latitude/longitude) given as input. On the other hand, Figure 1b shows the JSON document coming from the second service, which returns the waiting times for a particular bus/tram stop given as input. To simplify, we will refer to the first service as *closeStop* and the second one as *waitingTime*.

---

[2] http://www.programmableweb.com/

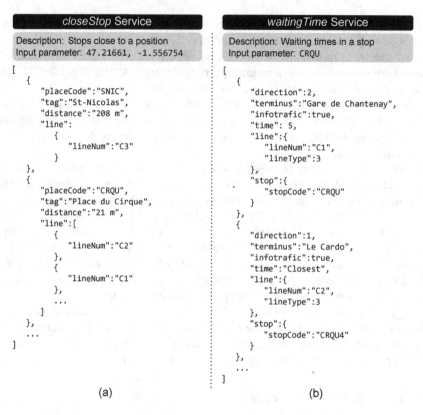

Fig. 1. JSON documents from two TAN API services: (a) the *closeStop* service, which returns the closest bus/tram stops to a geolocation, and (b) the *waitingTime* service, which returns waiting times for a particular bus/tram stop

By looking at the JSON data we can quickly identify some concepts and relationships of the domain, that is, the implicit structure of the data returned by each service. Regarding the *closeStop* service, the returned data includes an array composed of several objects (list of elements inside the square brackets surrounded by curly braces) with a set of name/value pairs. Each object represents a bus/tram stop and includes a code (see `placeCode`), a tag (see `tag`), the distance to the stop (see `distance`) from the position given as input to the service and a set of bus/tram lines (see `line`) passing by such a stop, which is a complex value composed by a set of objects, each one representing a line number (see `lineNum`). The *waitingTime* service returns an array of objects describing the waiting time, expressed by means of a sequence of buses/trams passing by the stop. Thus, each object describes a transport line (see `line`) and the time remaining (see `time`). For the sake of simplicity, we do not comment all the name/value pairs. On the other hand, since the two service calls are part of the same application, it is also possible to identify some relationships between the returned JSON objects. For instance, both services include information about bus/tram lines (see `line`).

However, the concepts and relationships previously identified are only a partial view of the underlying structure. Each call to a service provides some useful insight on that structure and only by combining them we can get an approximation to the complete picture of the application domain exposed through the API. For instance, one may think that for each stop there is a single bus line passing by (if this happens to be the case for the specific stop passed as input for the service call) while later calls may prove this assumption wrong (see line in *closeStop* service). A similar thing happens with the data type of the time value in the *waitingTime* service, which may look like as an integer value until one call returns closest as a (string) value. Moreover, dealing with several JSON documents is crucial to discover relationships between matching concepts across different services. Different names in name/value pairs from two calls may suggest unrelated concepts but a closer look may reveal that in fact those names hold always an overlapping set of values. For instance, this happens with the stop code, which is represented either as placeCode in the *closeStop* service or stopCode in the *waitingTime* service.

Clearly, an automated discovery process is needed to reveal the whole domain model behind the application. In the following sections we will describe such automatic process and the benefits the generated model can bring to the developers interested in working with the API.

3   Schema Discovery in JSON

To discover the schema information from JSON documents we propose a model-based process composed of three phases: (1) pre-discovery phase extracting low-level JSON models out of JSON documents, (2) single-service discovery phase aimed at obtaining the schema information for a concrete service (inferred from a set of low-level JSON models output of different consecutive calls to the service), and (3) multi-service discovery phase in charge of composing the schema information obtained in the previous phase in order to get an overall view of the application domain.

This schema information will be represented as a class diagram representing the concepts (i.e., classes) and relationships (i.e., attributes and associations) of the domain. In particular, we will use the EMF framework[3], which allows representing such elements by means of Ecore models. Ecore models conform to the Ecore metamodel, where concepts are represented as EClass elements while features are represented as StructuralFeature elements, which can be either attributes (EAttribute elements) or references (EReference elements).

Figure 2 illustrates the proposed process. Given an application with one or more JSON-based services, the pre-discovery and single-service processes are applied to each set of JSON documents returned by the services. The pre-discovery phase works at the sintactical level, changing the representation format so that JSON documents can be dealt as models, which are then analyzed by the single-service discoverer to obtain new models describing the domain. Next, the multi-service discoverer takes those domain models as input and combines them to obtain the application domain model. During the process, the discovery phases (i.e., single-service and multi-service) are performed by

---

[3] http://www.eclipse.org/emf

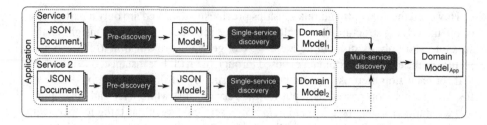

Fig. 2. Process of discovering schema information from JSON documents

means of model transformations. In the following sections, we describe in detail each phase of the process.

3.1 Pre-discovery Phase

The pre-discovery phase can be seen as a bridge between the two involved technologies. On the one hand, JSON documents conform to the JSON grammar (i.e., grammarware technical space). On the other hand, models conform to metamodels, which represent the modelware technical space. Thus, to obtain models out of JSON documents it is required to build a bridge between the grammarware and the modelware spaces.

To build this bridge, we used Xtext[4], which allows defining textual DSLs. From a Xtext grammar-based language definition the tool automatically generates its metamodel (i.e., the abstract syntax of the language) and the tooling required to obtain models conforming to such metamodel (i.e., the injector) from a language instance. Therefore, Xtext can take textual documents (conforming to a grammar G) as input and generate models (conforming to a metamodel M which is derived from the grammar G) representing those documents as output.

We have defined the JSON grammar in Xtext, which is shown in Figure 3a. As can be seen, a JSON document (see `Document` rule) can be composed of either an object or an array of objects. An object (see `Object` rule) is composed of name/value pairs (see `Pair` rule). A name/value pair has a name (see `Name` rule) and the a value (see `Value` rule) that can be either of primitive type (i.e., string, number, boolean or null) or complex (i.e., array or object). The grammar rules also include annotations to guide the generation of the language metamodel. Thus, from this grammar definition, the corresponding metamodel of the language (see Figure 3b) and the JSON model injector have been generated. Figure 3c illustrates the pre-discovery phase, where JSON models conforming to the JSON metamodel are injected from JSON documents conforming to the JSON grammar. From now on, any JSON document can be dealt as a model whose elements conform to the JSON metamodel elements, which actually resemble the JSON grammar elements. We will use the term "JSON document" to refer to both the grammar-based view and the model-based view of the document indistinctely.

---

[4] http://www.eclipse.org/xtext

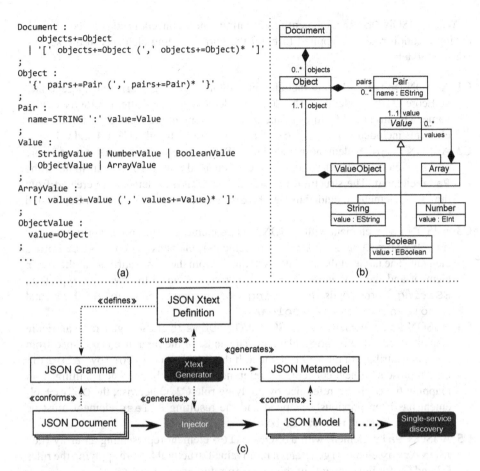

```
Document :
    objects+=Object
  | '[' objects+=Object (',' objects+=Object)* ']'
;
Object :
  '{' pairs+=Pair (',' pairs+=Pair)* '}'
;
Pair :
  name=STRING ':' value=Value
;
Value :
    StringValue | NumberValue | BooleanValue
  | ObjectValue | ArrayValue
;
ArrayValue :
  '[' values+=Value (',' values+=Value)* ']'
;
ObjectValue :
  value=Object
;
...
```

(a)

(b)

(c)

Fig. 3. (a) Excerpt of the JSON grammar defined in Xtext. (b) Metamodel generated by Xtext. (c) Pre-discovery process.

3.2 Single-Service Discoverer

JSON documents include both metadata (i.e., the name of the object name/value pair elements) and data (i.e., their value). Note that, however, two objects in the same or different JSON documents generated by a call to the same service do not necessarily have the same exact structure, e.g., it is possible that some of them include only a subset of the metadata/data, thus removing some name/value pairs (e.g., to reduce network traffic). Therefore, the accuracy of the single-service discovery increases when a number of JSON Object elements to infer their common structure are analyzed.

The single-service discovery process is therefore launched for each JSON Object element and has two execution modes: creation and refinement. The former creates a root concept from an Object representing a concept not yet existing in the service schema created so far whereas the latter enriches/refines an already existing concept with information coming from new Object elements representing such concept.

When a JSON `Object` element representing a new concept is considered, the following creation rules are applied to build the corresponding elements in the service domain model:

C1 A JSON `Object` element included in a JSON `Definition` element generates an Ecore `EClass` element. The `EClass` element is named after the JSON service name. The structural features of the `EClass` element are created from the `Pair` elements included in the `Object` element according to rules C3, C4 and C5.

C2 A JSON `Object` element included in a JSON `Pair` element generates an Ecore `EClass` element. The `EClass` element is named after the `name` attribute of the `Pair` element. The structural features of the `EClass` element are created from the `Pair` elements included in the `Object` element according to rules C3, C4 and C5.

C3 A JSON `Pair` element with a JSON `Value` element representing a primitive type (i.e., `String`, `Number` or `Boolean` elements) generates an Ecore `EAttribute` element. The name of the attribute is obtained from the `name` attribute of the `Pair` element and the type is the Ecore one corresponding to the primitive type (i.e., `EString` corresponds to `String`, `EInt` corresponds to `Number` and `EBoolean` corresponds to `Boolean`).

C4 A JSON `Pair` element with a JSON `ValueObject` element generates an Ecore single-valued `EReference` element. The name of the reference is obtained from the `name` attribute of the `Pair` element. If the JSON object referred by `ValueObj ect` represents a new concept, the reference type will be the one resulting from mapping the `object` reference by applying rule C2. Otherwise, the `Object` element has been previously mapped and the resulting `EClass` element must be refined (see refining rules R1-R3 below).

C5 A JSON `Pair` element with a JSON `Value` element representing an array (i.e., JSON `Array` element) generates a multivalued structural feature applying the rules C3 and C4 for the elements of the `values` reference.

Figure 4 shows the service domain models resulting from applying the previous mappings to the injected models from the JSON documents provided by the two services of the running example. For the sake of clarity and conciseness, we show the JSON document textually (instead of showing the injected JSON model) for the *closeStop* service. In the *closeStop* service, the single-service discoverer receives the first JSON `Object` of the resulting array as input (see Figure 1). As it is a new concept which is included in a `Document` element (i.e., included in the root of the JSON document), the rule C1 is applied, thus generating the `Stop` element. Next, each `Pair` element of the `Object` is considered. The first three `Pair` elements generate the attributes `placeCode`, `tag`, `distance`, all of them typed as String, according to rule C3. The last `Pair` element includes a JSON `ValueObject` element so the rule C4 is applied, thus generating a new reference called `line`. Since the JSON object referred by the `ValueObject` element represents a new concept and is included in a pair, rule C2 is applied, thus generating the element `Line`. Finally, each pair element of the object included in the `line` pair is considered. In this case, there is only one pair, for which the rule C3 is applied, thus generating the string-based attribute `lineNum` in the element

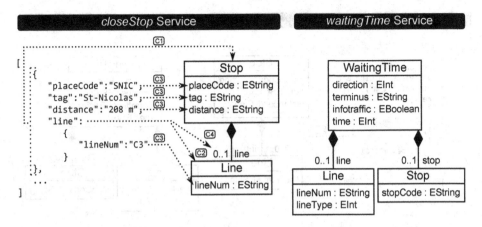

Fig. 4. Ecore models created by the single-service discovery process from the JSON documents shown in Figure 1

Line. Figure 4 also includes the model created from the JSON document coming from the *waitingTime* service, which will be used later in Section 3.3.

When a JSON Object element represens a concept already created, the corresponding concept (i.e., the EClass element) is recovered and enriched according to the following refining rules:

R1 A JSON Pair element with a JSON Value element representing a primitive type (i.e., String, Number or Boolean elements) refines the EAttribute named after the name value of the Pair element. If the EAttribute does not exists in the EClass element, it is included according to rule C3. If the EClass element already includes an attribute with the same name, the specified attribute type is compared with the one for the current object, if they do not match, the type of the attribute will be refined to EString (the most generic type), otherwise nothing is changed.

R2 A JSON Pair element contained in a JSON Object element with a JSON Value Object element refines the EReference named after the name value of the Pair element in the EClass obtained from such Object. If the EReference already exists, do nothing. Otherwise the EReference is included into the EClass definition according to rule C4.

R3 A JSON Pair element contained in a JSON Object element with a JSON Array element refines a multivaluated feature, following the rules R1 and R2. If the feature is already included in the EClass, the cardinality is updated to be multivaluated. Otherwise, a new feature is created according to rules C3 and C4.

Figure 5 shows the refined models for the running example. As done before, we show the JSON text for the first service. In the *closeStop* service, the single-service discoverer receives the second JSON Object of the resulting array as input (see Figure 1). As the object represents a concept already considered in the process, it is used to refine the existing concept. The element Stop is retrieved and the Pair elements of the

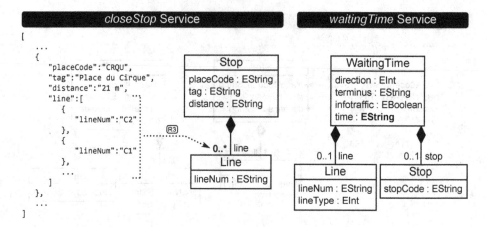

Fig. 5. Ecore models refined by the single-service discovery process from the JSON documents shown in Figure 1. Changes are highlighted in bold.

`Object` are traversed to refine the concept. The first three `Pair` elements trigger the rule R1, but no change is done because the attribute types match with the type of the existing `EAttributes`. The last `Pair` element triggers the rule R3, which refines the reference `line` to be multivalued and retrieves the `Line` element to be refined. Rule R1 is triggered for each `lineNum` pair element, but no change is done because the attribute type matches with the type of the existing `EAttribute`. Figure 5 also includes the refined metamodel for the *waitingTime* service, in which the type of the attribute `time` of the class `WaitingTime` is refined to `EString` according to rule R1. Thus, the refined version of these models complies with the data and metadata described in the JSON documents. With these models, developers can see and understand easily the domain accessible from each service.

3.3   Multi-service Discoverer

As commented before, many applications provide a complete JSON-based API, including several complementary services, each one offering a distinct viewpoint on the application data. In the previous section we described the process to discover the structural information (represented as Ecore models) regarding a single service. In this section we will show how to obtain a composite model including each single service viewpoint. The resulting model will therefore provide a general overview of the application domain.

To be able to compose a set of models coming from different services, it is necessary that such models share some elements, thus allowing establishing semantic relationships among them.

The discovery of differences and similaritires (i.e., correspondences) between models is not an easy task since it relies on model matching, which can be reduced to the problem of finding correspondences between two graphs (i.e., graph isomorphism). This problem has been proved as NP-hard [5] and the available approaches can only approximate the exact solution (several model matching approaches have been proposed in [6]). However, in the context of this work, since we are dealing with services defined in the same application domain, it is expected that the number of similarities (i.e., concept, attributes and reference names matching) to be high, thus decreasing the complexity of the process.

The multi-service discovery process starts by first creating a new model being the union of all the service-specific models. From there, the following rules try to link/merge the different submodels:

M1 Two classes $c1$ and $c2$ contained in different submodels represent the same concept if $c1.name = c2.name$. The classes will be merged into a new one called c where $c.name = c1.name$. The structural features of c will initially be the union of the structural features of $c1$ and $c2$ (further matching rules on them may apply).

M2 Two attributes $a1$ and $a2$ are defined to be the same if they are contained in an EClass representing the same concept (see rule M1) and $a1.name = a2.name$. The two attributes will be merged into a new one called a where $a.name = a1.name$. The type of a will be $a1.type$ if $a1.type = a2.type$, or the more general otherwise. Regarding the cardinality of a, the lower bound will be set to the lowest of $a1.lowerCardinality$ and $a2.lowerCardinality$ while the upper bound will be set to the highest of $a1.upperCardinality$ and $a2.upperCardinality$.

M3 Two attributes $a1$ and $a2$, where $a.name <> a1.name$, are considered the same if they are contained in an EClass representing the same concept (see rule M1) and there are matching values in the JSON value/pair elements. The two attributes will merged into a single one a where $a.name = a1.name$ and both the type and cardinality will be inferred as done in rule M2.

M4 Two references $r1$ and $r2$ are considered the same if they are contained in an EClass representing the same concept (see rule M1) and $r1.name = r2.name$. The type of r will be $r1.type$ if $r1.type = r2.type$, otherwise an error will be raised. Regarding the cardinality of r, the lower bound will be set to the lowest of $r1.lowerCardinality$ and $r2.lowerCardinality$ while the upper bound will be set to the highest of $r1.upperCardinality$ and $r2.upperCardinality$.

Note that these rules apply merging heuristics and therefore may be manually adapted to each specific scenario.

Figure 6 shows in the center the resulting model after applying the rules to the models obtained in the previous phase (shown on the sides of the figure). The multi-service discovery process begins with a model containing all the elements of the models obtained from the single-service phase, thus repetitions may occur (e.g., Stop and Line elements). The mapping rules are applied then, forcing some elements to merge. For instance, Line elements are merged according to rule M1, the lineNum attribute is merged according to rule M2 whereas the lineType attribute is simply added. Stop elements are merged according to rule M1 while placeCode and stopCode are merged according to rule M3 (some values of these attributes match in the JSON document, as can be seen in Figure 1), and tag and distance attributes, and line reference are added.

We refer to the resulting model as application domain model since it offers a clear view of the domain accessible by the two JSON services of the running example.

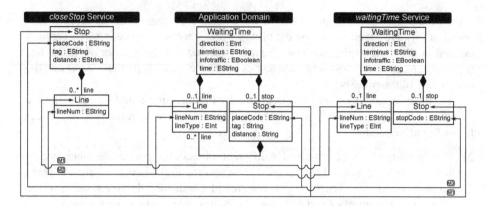

Fig. 6. The multi-service discovery process where the *Application Domain* model is obtained from the *closeStop* and *waitingTime* service domain models

As can be expected, these matching rules do not cover all the possible cases and may be improved by other model matching approaches, as commented in Section 6. Note that individual JSON documents can now be represented as instances of the application domain model, thus promoting the integration of JSON with model-based applications.

4   Discovering Service Dependencies

We believe the generated application domain model offers a valuable and helpful view to understand the information managed through and reachable from a set of JSON services, thus facilitating the creation of applications and other services on top of them.

Nevertheless, this data-centric view is only part of the solution. Once developers know what data is available the next question is how to query the services to get it. To help in this task, we add *coverage information* to the application domain model. This coverage information highlights the elements in the application domain model returned by each services. Therefore, a developer could quickly identify the set of services that could be potentially used to get the data he/she is interested in.

Furthermore, coverage models can be manually annotated to visualize not only the output of the service but also the input parameters required to call them, when those parameters are also part of the application domain model. This helps to automatically discover dependencies between the services, for instance, possible execution chains (if the input of a service X is covered by the output of a service Y, then they can be executed in sequence). For instance, Figures 7a and 7b show in grey the coverage for the two services of the running example. Figure 7b also highlights the input element of the *waitingTime* service, which is the attribute `placeCode` of the class `Stop`. As can be seen, there is an overlapping in the inputs/outputs of the services: the output of the *closeStop* service includes the `placeCode` attribute, which is the input of the *waitingTime* service. Thus, it could be possible to chain both services by using the *closeStop* service to find the closest stop to our position and then use the returned *placeCode* as input of the *waitingTime* service to get the waiting time for that stop.

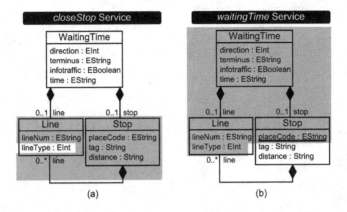

Fig. 7. Coverage model for the (a) *closeStop* and (b) *WaitingTime* services

Service dependencies could even be used to create a dependency graph to identify, given a set of available input data and a target output information, which is the shortest path (i.e., the least number of chained service calls) to reach that output. The initial candidate services would be those that can be executed using the starting input data and from there the overlappings (the edges in the graph) would be taken into account to calculate which services can be executed next.

5 Implementation

Our approach has been implemented in Java and distributed as an open source Eclipse plug-in[5]. The tool includes both the pre-discoverer developed in Xtext and the two discoverers (single and multi-service) mentioned in Section 3. Furthermore, the tool can also instantiate the discovered models by using the set of initial JSON documents.

This plugin has been contributed to MoDisco[6], an official Eclipse project aimed at providing a common framework for Model-Driven Reverse Engineering (MDRE) processes and tools. MoDisco includes a set of discoverers to obtain models from different software artefacts such as Java or XML files. Our tool has therefore been incorporated as a new type of discoverer dealing with JSON files. Figure 8 shows a snapshot of the enviroment including the metamodels of the *closeStop* and *waitingTime* service, and the application domain model.

Our implementation also supports the notion of coverage models (Section 4). Coverage models have been defined as a new type of models consisting in a set of links that relate the service domain model with the whole application domain model as a way to know how the service contributed to the composed model. This is also useful to then analyze the relationships among the different services, e.g., allowing inferring possible services chain uses, as comented in Section 4.

Coverage models conform to the coverage metamodel, shown in Figure 9a. The coverage of a service (Coverage metaclass and its service attribute) is defined by

---

[5] https://code.google.com/a/eclipselabs.org/p/json-discoverer
[6] http://www.eclipse.org/MoDisco

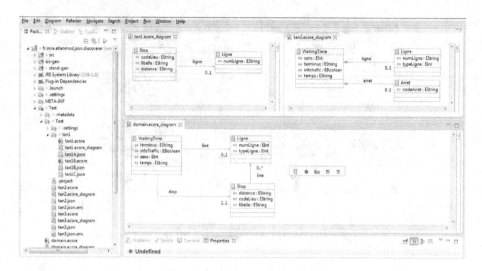

Fig. 8. Snapshot of the developed tool

a set of coverage mappings (`CoverageMapping` metaclass), which link attributes (`AttMapping` metaclass), references (`RefMapping` metaclass) and concepts (i.e., classes) (`ConceptMapping` metaclass) between the application domain model and the service model. Optionally, the input of the service can also be represented (`input` reference) regardless this input is part or not of the output JSON data itself.

Figure 9 shows the model representing the coverage of the *closeStop* service (i.e., illustrated in Figure 7a). For the sake of simplicity, Ecore models are represented as class diagrams and not as instances of Ecore metamodel.

6 Related Work

JSON schema discovery is related to works aimed at the general problem of obtaining structured information from unstructured data, such as [7]. Some of their ideas have been integrated in our approach.

In the field of web engineering, there are a number of approaches to extract the structure (e.g., navigational model, MVC pattern elements, etc.) from web sites [8–11] but none of them focuses on the discovering/representing the structure of the data those applications exchange with external services. Our tool could be integrated in these approaches to improve their support for JSON-based data. Trang[7] follows a similar approach to ours but is restricted to XML documents.

On the pure modeling side, there are some tools such as Texo[8], and the *emfjson*[9] and *xmi-to-json*[10] GitHub projects, that provide a bridge between the two technical spaces,

---

[7] https://code.google.com/p/jing-trang/
[8] wiki.eclipse.org/Texo
[9] www.github.com/dsevilla/xmi-to-json
[10] www.github.com/ghillairet/emfjson

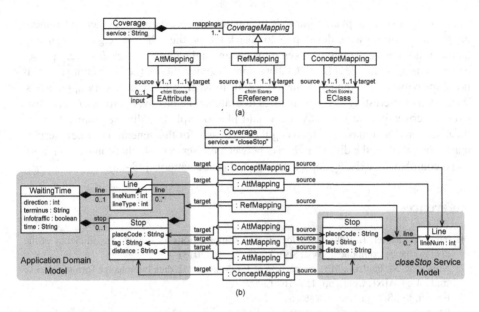

Fig. 9. (a) Metamodel to represent coverage information. (b) Coverage links between the application domain model and the *closeStop* service model.

thus allowing exporting models as JSON documents and viceversa. The functionality provided by these tools correspond to our pre-discovery phase, i.e., the mapping is always a one-to-one mapping applied on single elements, there is no attempt to infer more complex data structures.

Finally, several works [12–17] cover the automatic matching of modeling elements. These works could help us to improve our multi-service process discovery phase, enriching our set of heuristics to deal with very complex scenarios.

7 Conclusion and Future Work

Many web applications consume/publish JSON data coming from different sources. Integrating such JSON services is a challenging task mainly due to the schemaless nature of JSON which forces developers to peruse the (generally poor and little) available documentation to guess the best way to extract from those documents the data they need.

To improve this situation, we have presented an approach to automatically discover an implicit schema from a set of JSON documents coming from the same or different providers. We use model-driven techniques to devise a process where initial schema excerpts are discovered from each individual service and then are combined to obtain a composite model describing the underlying domain model of the application, which facilitates the understanding of the JSON-based services to interact with. The approach has been implemented in Java and contributed to the MoDisco open source Eclipse reverse engineering framework.

As future work, we plan to improve the quality and precision of the generated models by means of allowing developers to enrich the partial schemas (e.g., by manually adding links among them to be taken into account in the multi-service discovery phase) and by reusing some ideas from database normalization theory (i.e., to evalute the relationships between the model elements) and from XML schema discovery approaches. We find also interesting to define metrics to evaluate the discovery process (e.g., effectiveness, coverage, etc.). Finally, we would like to explore additional applications of the discovered schemas, e.g., by using them as basis for the generation of new service mash-ups based on the discovered links between the services. In this context, our work could complement existing approaches on API usage patterns [18–20].

References

1. Ying, M., Miller, J.: Refactoring legacy AJAX applications to improve the efficiency of the data exchange component. Syst. Soft. 86(1), 72–88 (2013)
2. Nurseitov, N., Paulson, M.: Comparison of JSON and XML data interchange formats: A case study. In: CAINE Conf., pp. 157–162 (2009)
3. Fowler, M.: Schemaless data structures,
   http://martinfowler.com/articles/schemaless
4. IETF: A json media type for describing the structure and meaning of json documents. Standard Draft v3
5. Lin, Y., Gray, J., Jouault, F.: DSMDiff: a differentiation tool for domain-specific models. Europ. Inf. Syst. 16(4), 349–361 (2007)
6. Kolovos, D.S., Di Ruscio, D., Pierantonio, A., Paige, R.F.: Different models for model matching: An analysis of approaches to support model differencing. In: CVSM Conf., pp. 1–6 (2009)
7. Nestorov, S., Abiteboul, S., Motwani, R.: Inferring structure in semistructured data. ACM SIGMOD Record 26(4), 39–43 (1997)
8. Chang, C., Kayed, M.: A survey of web information extraction systems. IEEE Trans. Knowl. Data Eng. 18(10), 1411–1428 (2006)
9. Arasu, A., Garcia-Molina, H., University, S.: Extracting structured data from Web pages. In: SIGNMOD Conf., p. 337. ACM Press (2003)
10. Crescenzi, V., Mecca, G.: Automatic information extraction from large websites. Journal of the ACM 51(5), 731–779 (2004)
11. Hernández, I., Rivero, C.R., Ruiz, D., Corchuelo, R.: Towards Discovering Conceptual Models behind Web Sites. In: Atzeni, P., Cheung, D., Ram, S. (eds.) ER 2012. LNCS, vol. 7532, pp. 166–175. Springer, Heidelberg (2012)
12. Ohst, D., Welle, M., Kelter, U.: Differences between versions of UML diagrams. In: ACM SIGSOFT Conf., pp. 227–236 (2003)
13. Alanen, M., Porres, I.: Difference and union of models. In: Stevens, P., Whittle, J., Booch, G. (eds.) UML 2003. LNCS, vol. 2863, pp. 2–17. Springer, Heidelberg (2003)
14. Melnik, S., Garcia-molina, H., Rahm, E.: Similarity Flooding: A Versatile Graph Matching Algorithm. In: DE Conf., pp. 117–128 (2002)
15. Selonen, P., Kettunen, M.: Metamodel-Based Inference of Inter-Model Correspondence. In: CSMR Conf., pp. 71–80 (2007)
16. Treude, C., Berlik, S., Wenzel, S., Kelter, U.: Difference computation of large models. In: ESEC/FSE Conf., p. 295 (2007)

17. Whang, S.E., Garcia-Molina, H.: Joint entity resolution. In: ICDE Conf., pp. 294–305 (2012)
18. Xie, T., Pei, J.: MAPO: Mining API usages from open source repositories. In: MSR Workshop, pp. 54–57 (2006)
19. Robillard, M.P., Bodden, E., Kawrykow, D., Mezini, M., Ratchford, T.: Automated API Property Inference Techniques. IEEE Trans. Soft. Eng., 1–1 (2012)
20. Bruch, M., Monperrus, M., Mezini, M.: Learning from examples to improve code completion systems. In: ESEC/FSE Conf., pp. 213–222 (2009)

The SWAC Approach for Sharing a Web Application's Codebase Between Server and Client

Markus Ast, Stefan Wild, and Martin Gaedke

Chemnitz University of Technology, Germany
`{firstname.lastname}@informatik.tu-chemnitz.de`

Abstract. A Web application's codebase is typically split into a server-side and a client-side with essential functionalities being implemented twice, such as validation or rendering. For implementing the codebase on the client, JavaScript, HTML and CSS are languages that all modern Web browsers can interpret. As the counterpart, the server-side codebase can be realized by plenty of programming languages, which provide facilities to implement standardized communication interfaces. While recent developments such as Node.js allow using JavaScript as a client-side programming languages outside the browser in a simple and efficient way also on the server-side, they lack offering a common codebase for the entire Web application. We present a flexible approach to enable sharing of presentation and business logic between server and client using the same codebase. Our approach aims at reducing development efforts and minimizing coding errors, while taking characteristic differences between server and client into account. We show the impact of our solution during an evaluation and in comparison to related work.

Keywords: Development Tools, HTML5 and Beyond, Web Standards and Protocols.

1 Introduction

More and more of today's dynamic Web applications imitate behavior, look and feel of desktop applications by moving large parts of their business and presentation logic from the server-side to the client-side[1]. This trend was accelerated by the Internet's increasing speed and coverage for mobile devices as well as advances in standards, which made the Web more dynamic in the last couple of years [1,5,13]. Development methodologies like progressive enhancement have additionally blurred the line between desktop and Web applications. Progressive enhancement focuses on Web applications that are universally accessible, intuitive and usable by realizing all Web content and functionality only using semantic Hypertext Markup Language (HTML). Enhancements such as advanced

---

[1] While in our scenarios clients are mostly represented by browsers, other applications e.g., Firefox OS or WebView Components in Android and iOS are also valid clients.

F. Daniel, P. Dolog, and Q. Li (Eds.): ICWE 2013, LNCS 7977, pp. 84–98, 2013.

Cascading Style Sheet (CSS) or JavaScript are layered unobtrusively on top of HTML [12]. Web-enabled devices like search engines or gaming systems do only provide limited or no support for further enhancements. By following this development methodology, they are also enabled to access corresponding Web applications. New devices like latest browsers benefit from this additional technological layer by improvements to style and interaction.

Progressive enhancement can be accomplished by duplication, i.e., realizing parts of the application for both server and client. Duplicating the business and presentation logic entirely, however, is inadequate as it decreases not only development efficiency, but also makes the application more error-prone and harder to maintain. Besides the problem of technically establishing a server/client compatible codebase[2], we identified four key differences between both sides that have to be treated separately: view, routing, data access and state transfer.

Unlike the view on the server-side that is commonly string-based and generated on-demand, the client-side view is based on the Document Object Model (DOM). This difference also affects the routing because the view on server-side is built from scratch on every request, i.e., on every route. In addition to this, the business logic of routes cannot be reused for the client-side without further regard. As the client-side is generally more vulnerable to malicious manipulations, unveiling data exchange logic to the client-side has potential security issues. The state established during the initial request consisting of data, view bindings and precompiled fragments acts as origin and as basis for all further user interaction. As a consequence, the state needs to be transferred from the server to the client in order to continue on the client where left off on the server.

In this paper we present a framework providing both dynamic functionalities and progressive enhancement without having to implement an application twice on server and client. We focus on coping with characteristic client/server differences using a technically compatible codebase, supporting client- and server-side generated views, implementing a server/client compatible routing as well as establishing mechanisms for data access and state transfer.

This paper is organized as follows: We begin in Section 2 with an example demonstrating the features of our framework. Section 3 provides an overview of our approach and describes the resulting framework. We detail the routing, the view, the data access and the state transfer. In Section 4 we evaluate our framework. We position our approach to related work in Section 5 and conclude our work in Section 6.

2   Example

In this section we present an example for developing a simple task & document management application. We apply our proposed framework and best practices to implement a single codebase for the entire Web application and realize progressive enhancement.

---

[2] The term "codebase" refers to the whole source code of an application.

Consider a simple application for managing tasks and documents as shown in Figure 1. There are tasks, documents and projects. Tasks and documents are both assigned to projects and each project can contain several tasks and documents. There are five routes associated to these elements, i.e., one to the project list, a second to a specific project, a third to the tasks associated to a project, a fourth to the documents within a project, and another route acting as an entry point for the application. Four separate views are rendered on the basis of these routes, i.e., the layout, the project, the tasks and the documents.

Fig. 1. Screenshot of Sample Web application

Our framework enables developers of such a task & document management application to combine these five distinct routes into one, which itself is split into five hierarchical pieces, as shown in Figure 2. Therefore, we have consolidated the business logic of these routes: (1) the root route rendering the layout, (2) the projects route loading and rendering the list of projects, (3) the project route loading a specific project and (4) tasks and documents routes to render all tasks and documents of the selected project. That is, the tasks and documents routes reuse logic introduced with the project route (1-3).

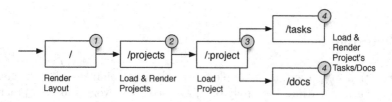

Fig. 2. Route Hierarchy of Sample Application

On the client-side, this separation relieves us from the need to execute the whole route once a project is selected. Furthermore, the separation enables moving through a route step by step to execute only the necessary parts of a route, e.g., projects, tasks or documents. The presentation logic is responsible for reflecting changes based on the business logic addressed by these routes. To achieve this without re-rendering, our framework allows splitting the view into pieces called fragments. These fragments are used to construct the view step by step or to update parts of the view once underlying data changes. As shown in Figure 3, the sample application consists of a fragment for the project list, the task collection, the document collection and one for each project, task and document.

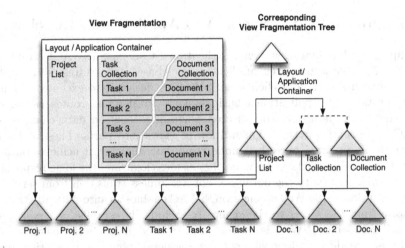

Fig. 3. View Fragmentation of Sample Application

Having implemented the routes and the view as described, requesting the list of projects from the server would be as follows: each route up to the projects route is executed automatically by our framework, and the layout and the project list are rendered accordingly. The result of this request not only contains the rendered view composed of the layout and the project list. It also contains the state consisting of the underlying data, the bindings, the fragment's precompiled templates[3] and their positions inside the view. The bindings are established to re-render fragments on data changes like creating, renaming or removing projects.

At this point in time, most of the application's functionalities can be executed decoupled from the server-side, i.e., only data access and manipulation operations have to involve server communication. It is important to note that in our framework, the logic responsible for the data exchange with the database is not shared with the client because of potential security concerns. As the data logic remains on the server all the time, our framework automatically provides an

---

[3] A precompiled template is a JavaScript function responsible for creating HTML for the data provided in the fragment.

appropriated API allowing client-side data access to be proxied through. In the example, selecting a project on the client-side would work as follows: The client makes an AJAX request to the server to get the tasks of the selected project. Additionally, the client requests the precompiled fragments of the tasks template, which are used for the appropriate rendering. The resulting fragments ensure that the task items can be re-rendered once their underlying data changes, e.g., selecting another project results in the execution of the associated route part. This would cause re-rendering view fragments of the task items.

Demonstration: This sample application created with the SWAC framework is available at: `http://vsr.informatik.tu-chemnitz.de/demo/swac/`

3   Approach for Sharing a Web Application's Codebase

Our approach for Sharing a Web Application's Codebase (SWAC) establishes server/client compatible Web application codebases and addresses the differences between server- and client-side. SWAC is designed to execute only necessary parts of an application's business logic by defining routes as a route hierarchy. To update only the affected parts of a view on data changes, the SWAC approach supports fragmentation of views into parts. These parts are automatically updated once their underlying data changes. It achieves data security by an additional layer between the business logic and the logic responsible for communicating with the database. For a seamless transition from server- to client-execution of the Web application, SWAC enables to automatically transfer the state from the server to the client. To technically establish a server/client compatible codebase, SWAC is entirely implemented in JavaScript using Node.js on the server-side. The following subsections detail both the theoretical background and the actual implementation of the SWAC approach.

3.1   Routing

A route hierarchy is an essential part of the business layer as it defines the relationship of routes in an application to each other. SWAC utilizes such a route hierarchy to determine the necessary parts to be executed for reflecting changes between two user interactions. That is, it expects the URL to be hierarchical, which is also considered a best practice [4]. There is no standalone business logic for each complete route. Instead, the business logic is separated into parts, where each part reflects the changes necessary to move from one route to an immediately following one. This allows executing only the necessary parts to reflect the changes required to navigate from one route to another on the client-side. To handle scenarios of routes requiring logic that is incompatible to both sides, e.g., logic provided by third-party frameworks like jQuery and Dojo, every route can consist of an additional client-only part. While the client-only part is optional, the server/client compatible part is always required.

The SWAC framework covers three different routing schemes, where each schema is distinct in terms of handling the route hierarchy tree: 1) the route is executed on the server-side, 2) the client is initialized to take off the application and 3) the client-side navigates through the route hierarchy tree. The following terminology is applied to describe the routing algorithm: We define $G(V, E)$ as a directed graph representing the route hierarchy, $u \in V$ as a route and $(x, y) \in E$ as a directed edge connecting dependent routes. Additionally, we define $A(u)$ as a subset of G, with each node $x \in A$ being an ancestor of u. A node $a \in A$ is called a common ancestor of u and v if a is an ancestor of both of them, $w(u, v)$ is called the lowest common ancestor of u and v. In analogy to $A(u)$, we define $D(u)$ as a subset of G, with each node $x \in D$ being a descendent of u. We define $T(u)$ as a tree inside G with $u \in T$. Other trees like $T(k)$ can also exist within $G(V, E)$. These definitions are illustrated in Figure 4.

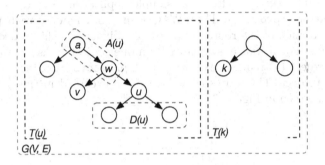

Fig. 4. Routing Terminology

Server-Side Execution. The server-side of our framework is stateless, i.e., a request to the server always requires executing the whole logic responsible for providing the desired result. Calling a route v on the server-side results in the execution of v and all ancestors of v, i.e., all nodes being an element of $A(v)$. These routes are executed in the order they are specified in.

Client-Side Initialization. The initial request is always completely processed on the server-side. Afterwards, our framework can execute most of the application's functionality decoupled from the server on the client-side. Therefore, the client-only parts of the current route are executed. This is done by applying the same method as used for the server-side execution with the difference of executing the client-only and not the server/client compatible part of the route.

Client-Side Execution. On the client-side, only the routes that are responsible for the changes between two user interactions are executed. There are four sub-scenarios for the client-side execution. They take different positions of the target route into account. If the target route v is not an element of the tree $T(u)$ of the starting position u, the execution works the same way as on the server-side. That is, v and all ancestors $A(v)$ are executed in their appropriate order. Otherwise, the target route v is an element of $T(u)$. If $v \in T(u)$, v could be an ancestor of u, i.e., $v \in A(u)$, v could be a descendant of u, i.e., $v \in D(u)$ or otherwise, v is inside another branch of $T(u)$. In case v is an ancestor of u, only v is executed. If v being a descendant of u, every route from u down to v is executed. Otherwise, every route from the lowest common ancestor $w(u,v)$ down to v is executed. $R(u,v)$, as the set of routes to be executed, is built using the following method:

$$R(u,v) = \begin{cases} A(v) \cup \{v\} & \text{if } v \notin T(u), \\ v & \text{if } v \in T(u) \wedge v \in A(u), \\ [A(v) \cap D(u)] \cup \{v\} & \text{if } v \in T(u) \wedge v \in D(u), \\ [A(v) \cap D(w(u,v))] \cup \{v\} & \text{if } v \in T(u) \wedge v \notin A(u) \wedge v \notin D(u). \end{cases}$$

Example. Consider the route from our sample application (Figure 2). There we use a parameter (`:project`). The SWAC framework handles each parameter as a distinct branch of the route hierarchy (cf. Figure 5). This is necessary for correct routing. For instance, switching from one project tasks (u) to the tasks of another project (v) requires executing the `/projects/:project` route again for the new project. The routes that have to be executed in this scenario are highlighted in green in Figure 5.

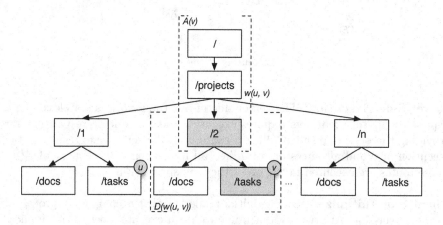

Fig. 5. Routing example $T(u)$ (1)

Figure 6 covers two additional scenarios for this route hierarchy. On the left hand side, target route v is an ancestor of the current route u. On the right hand side, target route v is a descendant. As in the previous example, the highlighted routes are executed.

3.2   View

The view on the client-side facilitates executing only the necessary presentation logic instead of re-rendering the entire view on every data change. While every

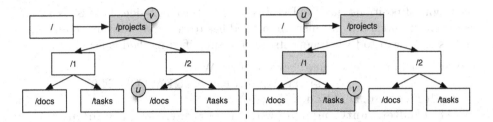

Fig. 6. Routing example $T(u)$ (2)

single part of a view can be directly updated on the client-side via DOM, this is impossible using a string-based template as normally done on the server-side. Due to the fact that parsing the whole template is expensive, having a full-fledged DOM on the server-side would negatively affect the performance [10].

As we are interested in creating an efficient and compact partition similar to DOM for string-based templates on the server-side, we utilize embedded JavaScript. We achieve the fragmentation by wrapping parts of the template into an appropriated block expression, as exemplary shown below:

```
<div>
    @fragment(function() {
        Self-updating fragment
    })
</div>
```

The re-rendering of a fragment consists of three steps: 1) delete the fragment's content, 2) re-render the fragment and 3) reinsert it into the DOM. Step 1 and 3 require knowledge about the position of the fragment. For this reason, the position of a fragment needs to be tracked. This could be easily accomplished by wrapping fragments into HTML elements, which are identified and accessed via IDs. However, this approach has several issues, e.g., HTML elements like <title> do not support child nodes [2]. HTML table rows are another example for elements, which do not allow container tags. Considering a collection, where each item is represented through two HTML rows, there is no valid way to wrap each of these two <tr> rows into their own container [2]. Only the comment node, which is allowed to reside inside every HTML element, fits our purpose. Since a comment cannot wrap content that should be rendered, they have to act as start and end markers for a fragment, as exemplary shown below:

```
<div>
    <!-- -{1 -->
        Self-updating fragment
    <!-- -1} -->
</div>
```

On the server-side, these comments are just parts of the rendered string and they only share their syntax with a DOM comment. This requires initializing the fragment positions once the DOM is built on the client-side. That is, as soon as the client builds the document, a method has to detect all relevant comments and assigns them to their fragments. Such a simplified method is listed below:

```
var walker = document.createTreeWalker(
                start , NodeFilter.SHOW_COMMENT)
while(walker.nextNode()) {
  if (!isRelevantComment(walker.currentNode)) continue
  // assign comments to their fragments
  fragment[isStartNode(walker.currentNode.nodeValue)
   ? 'startNode' : 'endNode'] = walker.currentNode
}
```

The bindings ensure that fragments update themselves on appropriate data changes. They have to be created once the data got accessed. To achieve this without making the API inconvenient, properties used inside a fragment have to be enabled to interact with the fragment they are accessed from. The SWAC framework uses the JavaScript function's caller property for this purpose. This property points to the object which called the function the property was accessed from [8]. We achieved this by making each data property a getter that binds itself to the fragment it is called from:

```
Object.defineProperty(model, prop, {
  get: function get() {
    if (typeof get.caller.fragment !== 'undefined')
      this.on('change.' + prop, get.caller.fragment.refresh)
    return value
  }, set: [...] , enumerable: true
})
```

Although this Function.caller property is not part of the ECMA standard [3], it is currently supported by all major browsers (Firefox, Safari, Chrome, Opera and Internet Explorer) [16].

3.3 Security

Since the goal of this framework is to reuse an application's codebase between server and client every part of the application's logic is shared between server and client unless it is explicitly declared as server-only logic. Nevertheless, the communication between the business logic and the database is always executed on the server-side. We achieved this by splitting the business tier into two layers: the service layer and the business layer. The service layer provides the API for the communication with the database and is never shared with the client, i.e., the client-side cannot directly access the database. However, both sides share the same API. Data API calls executed on the client-side are proxied through an automatically provided RESTful API on the server, as illustrated in Figure 7. That is, authentication and authorization logic for data access is always executed in a privileged environment on the server-side.

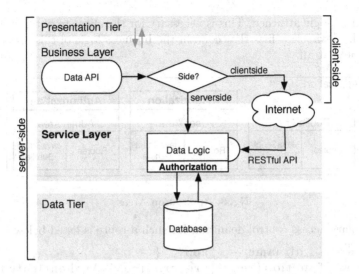

Fig. 7. Service Layer

Due to the fact that the actual authentication/authorization logic is not pre-defined, the SWAC framework provides hooks for injecting custom logic. This facilitates implementing such logic using already existing Node.js packages, e.g., for OAuth or OpenID. An exemplary API usage, which only allows update, delete and read access to the user model by the owner, is shown below:

```
swac.Model.define('User', function() {
  this.allow({
    all: function(request, user) {
      return request.user.id == user.id
    },
    post: function(request) {
      return true
    }
  })
})
```

There are two options for establishing route security. First, avoiding route sharing is the most secure way for routes referring to proprietary algorithms. We suggest only using this option if absolutely necessary because the benefit of the SWAC framework results from the ability of sharing code. Second, for shared routes, the SWAC framework provides hooks for both authentication and authorization logic. Executing this logic on the client-side is useless because of vulnerability to malicious manipulations. SWAC enables developers to divide applications into several areas, as shown in Figure 8. Since these areas are isolated from each other, navigating between them triggers requests to the server. A client requesting a route of such an area must pass the authentication/

authorization logic attached. This is necessary for the client to obtain the area's bundle (the JavaScript files that contain the business logic of this area) and to call the route at all.

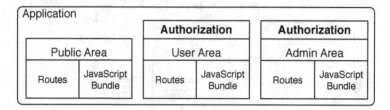

Fig. 8. Application Areas

An exemplary access control definition for such a route is listed below:

```
swac.area(__dirname + '/app', {
    allow: function(req) { return req.isAuthenticated() }
})
```

These areas provide a way to support the separation of an application into different security levels and enable responding to users who try to access application parts they are not authorized to.

3.4   State Transfer

The initial request is processed and rendered completely on the server. Enabling the client to take off the application's execution requires making this state available to the client. The state includes the following information:

- data contained in models and collections
- fragment positions
- events and their listeners
- precompiled templates

Such state information is necessary to update the view on the client-side on data changes caused by user interactions. Although the client can always retrieve data from the server, it would be unnecessary to retrieve data twice - once on the server-side and once the client takes off the application. Fragments can update themselves on certain events, e.g., data changes. Bindings between fragments and events are established once a fragment is rendered for the first time, i.e., on the server-side. To automatically reflect data changes, bindings must be transferred to the client. Since a fragment's position and template are required for fragment re-rendering, associated data is also transferred to the client. To avoid compiling templates again on the client-side, they are transferred in a precompiled form.

Transferring the state requires serialization. Possible formats for this purpose are textual ones, like the JavaScript Object Notation (JSON) and the Extensible Markup Language (XML), or binary ones, like the MessagePack[4] and

---

[4] http://msgpack.org/

the Protocol Buffers[5]. There is no direct support for buffers in browser-based JavaScript [9]. Deserializing a buffer format on the client-side would be slow and error-prone. Therefore only textual formats are qualified for a server/client compatible serialization and deserialization. As JSON is supported by JavaScript directly [3], it is the textual format we use.

Regardless of this format choice, serialization of complex objects asks for additional logic to cope with circular references, functions as well as closures. There is no built-in mechanism available that allows serialization of all kinds of JavaScript objects [3]. The SWAC framework achieves sufficient object serialization by resolving circular references, avoiding closures and utilizing the service locator pattern to restore object instances. SWAC resolves circular references by tagging an object as visited on its first occurrence. This allows identifying references to objects that are already part of the state. The framework replaces further occurrences of objects with a JSONPath[6] to their first occurrence. To serialize functions we avoid closures and use string representations of functions via their toString() method. For restoring objects created built using a constructor, we implement the service locator pattern. Constructors are registered to the service locator and all objects created with such a registered constructor are tagged appropriately. This enables restoring such objects on deserialization. These approaches in combination are a powerful toolkit to deserialize/serialize complex JavaScript objects.

4   Evaluation

In order to demonstrate the benefits of our solution, we made a small coding contest: the development of a simple single-page task application capable of adding, removing, editing and changing the state of tasks. For this purpose, we compared a combination of a common back-end and a common front-end framework with the SWAC framework. As a challenge for our approach, we chose Rails[7] as the back-end framework, which facilitates the development of back-ends due to its scaffolding functionalities. For front-end implementation, we used Backbone.js[8]. Both Rails and Backbone.js are necessary to provide the features the implementation with SWAC provides. Although a Rails-only implementation using its JavaScript Adapter would allow fast development, only a few functionalities are supported. This might be sufficient for a simple application like this, but is inappropriate for the use cases our framework is aiming at, e.g., execution of business logic on the client-side or automatic view binding.

While developing the application with Rails/Backbone.js required an average time of 52 minutes, the task was done on average in 22 minutes with SWAC. As shown in Figure 9, the development of this simple task application is about 60%

---

[5] http://code.google.com/p/protobuf/
[6] http://goessner.net/articles/JsonPath/
[7] http://rubyonrails.org/
[8] http://backbonejs.org/

faster when SWAC is used in comparison to the use of different frameworks for back- and front-end. As a result of Rails maturity and scaffolding functionalities, the back-end only development is indeed faster than using SWAC.

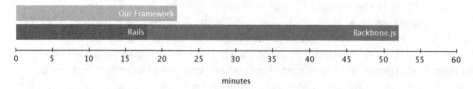

Fig. 9. Time comparison for Rails/Backbone.js vs. SWAC framework

The comparison of the amount of source lines of code (SLOC) necessary to implement the application shows a significant difference, as illustrated in Figure 10. While the implementation with SWAC only required about 60 SLOC, Rails and Backbone.js required at least 190 SLOC (Rails: 75, Backbone.js: 115).

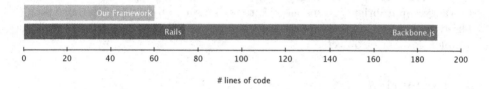

Fig. 10. SLOC comparison for Rails/Backbone.js vs. SWAC framework

The SWAC framework and Rails require nearly the same SLOC. However, Backbone.js' DOM based view updates needed some extra lines of code for their implementation. Although the evaluation shows that the SWAC framework improves the development efficiency of dynamic and "progressively enhanced" Web applications, both comparisons should only be considered as an orientation. This is because time consumed as well as lines of code required for the development depend on the knowledge and experience with a framework.

5   Related Work

In this section, we analyze the work related to our solution. This analysis focuses on frameworks that aim for creating dynamic Web applications through establishing a technically compatible client/server codebase. The key differences between server and client, we identified in Section 1, are used as main analysis criteria. The analysis is based upon the following criteria:

- Technically compatible codebase
- Progressive enhancements
- State transfer from server- to client-side

- Data logic separation and access control
- Business logic routing
- Intelligent presentation logic, e.g., automatically updating view fragments

Derby [14], as a WebSocket-based framework, focuses on real-time and collaborative applications. Despite its facility to completely render the result of the first request, it is not progressively enhanced. Since Derby uses WebSockets for all data manipulations, submitting data without WebSockets is impossible. A Web application's client-side implemented with Derby cannot be executed left-off from the server because the state remains on the server. However, WebSockets can be used to propagate state changes. Derby solves separation of data logic and access control similar to our solution [11]. While business logic is only executed on the server-side, Derby dynamically initiates routing from the client-side.

As another framework in this context, Meteor [6] can create technically compatible Web application codebases using JavaScript. However, Meteor does not achieve complete compatibility between server- and client-side because the framework lacks built-in routing functionalities, i.e., business logic is triggered through DOM events. Meteor utilizes Fibers, i.e., one thread per request, to create synchronous APIs. Even though this is good for simplicity, it breaks with Node.js event-based characteristic. For protecting the data logic, sensitive functions can be executed in a privileged environment on the server-side. Meteor supports rendering via DOM simulation on the server-side [7] taking Google's AJAX crawling specification into account. While this is beneficial for search engines, for common visitors Meteor renders the Web application only on the client-side. That is, Meteor is not suitable for developing progressively enhanced Web applications. As Meteor Web applications are executed on client-side only, there is no state to be transferred from the server-side.

Compared to the frameworks analyzed so far, the API of Yahoo! Mojito [15] is quite different from familiar back-end frameworks in the sense that it does not provide a homogenous data API for both the server- and client-side. Although Mojito can be used to build technically compatible Web application codebases, it lacks native support for client-side routing, i.e., HTML5 History [2] is not used. Mojito presentation logic allows updating view fragments on data changes.

Although the analyzed frameworks allow sharing parts of the codebase between server and client, they do not offer facilities to automatically create progressively enhanced Web applications.

6 Conclusion

With the SWAC approach we provided a solution for sharing a Web application's codebase between server and client. Although we accomplished the technical compatibility of the codebase on both server- and client-side using JavaScript, the characteristic differences between server and client made it necessary to create a business and presentation logic compatible to string- and DOM-based views. This was realized by splitting routes into hierarchical parts. As a consequence of this action, we had to adjust the presentation logic to be compatible, too. Therefore, we added a mechanism to split the view into fragments, which are updated automatically once underlying data changes. In addition to these contributions, we integrated a facility into our framework allowing the client to seamlessly take over the application after the state was transferred automatically from the server to the client. While the data exchange logic is not shared by the SWAC framework because of security concerns, we enabled the client to unobtrusively proxy its database calls through the server.

In future work, we intend to perform an evaluation with a larger set of frameworks. We assume that the evaluation results will help to identify advantages as well as shortcomings of our current solution that need to be addressed in further contributions. We plan implementing modularity improvements, e.g., making fragments compatible to third party template engines or enabling authorization per data property. In addition to these enhancements, we will investigate collaborative editing scenarios asking for facilities such as data push.

Acknowledgment. This work was funded by the European Commission (project OMELETTE, contract 257635).

References

1. Belson, D., Leighton, T., Rinklin, B.: The State of the Internet, vol. 5(3) (2012)
2. Berjon, R., Leithead, T., Doyle Navara, E., O'Connor, E., Pfeiffer, S.: HTML5 Specification, Editor's Draft 6 (October 2012)
3. Ecma International: ECMA-262 ECMAScript Language Specification 5.1 Edition (2011)
4. Masinter, L., Berners-Lee, T., Fielding, R.T.: Uniform Resource Identifier (URI): Generic Syntax (2005), http://tools.ietf.org/html/rfc3986
5. Meeker, M., Wu, L.: 2012 Internet Trends (2012)
6. Meteor Development Group: Meteor, http://docs.meteor.com/
7. Meteor Development Group: Meteor - Search engine optimization, http://meteor.com/blog/2012/08/09/search-engine-optimization
8. Mozilla Developer Network: Function.caller https://developer.mozilla.org/de/docs/ JavaScript/Reference/Global_Objects/Function/caller
9. Mozilla Developer Network: JavaScript typed arrays, https://developer.mozilla.org/en-US/docs/JavaScript_typed_arrays
10. Nicola, M., John, J.: XML Parsing: A Threat to Database Performance. In: Proceedings of the 12th International Conference on Information and Knowledge Management, pp. 175–178. ACM Press (2003)
11. Noguchi, B., Smith, N.: Racer Access Control, https://github.com/codeparty/racer/tree/master/lib/accessControl
12. Parker, T., Jehl, S., Wachs, M.C., Toland, P.: Designing with Progressive Enhancement: Building the Web that Works for Everyone. New Riders Publishing (2010)
13. Smith, A.: Cell Internet Use 2012 (2012)
14. Smith, N., Noguchi, B.: Derby, http://derbyjs.com/
15. Yahoo! Inc.: Yahoo! Mojito, http://developer.yahoo.com/cocktails/mojito/
16. Zaytsev, J.: ECMAScript extensions compatibility table, http://kangax.github.com/es5-compat-table/

DireWolf - Distributing and Migrating User Interfaces for Widget-Based Web Applications

Dejan Kovachev, Dominik Renzel, Petru Nicolaescu, and Ralf Klamma

Advanced Community Information Systems (ACIS) Group,
RWTH Aachen University,
Ahornstr. 55, 52056 Aachen, Germany
{kovachev,renzel,nicolaescu,klamma}@dbis.rwth-aachen.de,
http://dbis.rwth-aachen.de

Abstract. Web applications have overcome traditional desktop applications especially in collaborative settings. However, the bulk of Web applications still follow the "single user on a single device" computing model. Therefore, we created the DireWolf framework for rich Web applications with distributed user interfaces (DUIs) over a federation of heterogeneous commodity devices supporting modern Web browsers such as laptops, smart phones and tablet computers. The DUIs are based on widget technology coupled with cross-platform inter-widget communication and seamless session mobility. Inter-widget communication technologies connect the widgets and enable real-time collaborative applications as well as runtime migration in our framework. We show that the DireWolf framework facilitates the use case of collaborative semantic video annotation. For a single user it provides more flexible control over different parts of an application by enabling the simultaneous use of smart phones, tablets and computers. The work presented opens the way for creating distributed Web applications which can access device specific functionalities such as multi-touch, text input, etc. in a federated and usable manner.

1 Introduction

People increasingly interact with a collection of heterogeneous computing devices attached to their daily lives. However, most Web applications fail to combine devices' features into a cohesive symbiotic way to convey a single user task in a collaborative fashion. One of the reasons behind this failure is the lack of tools and methodologies required to develop applications spreading user interfaces across multiple devices available to a particular user or group of users. Personal computing is no longer confined to a single device. PCs together with commodity smartphones, tablets, eBook readers, gaming consoles and interactive TVs can be federated over the Internet to create collaborative multi-device interactive systems which can benefit from the diverse device capabilities. An individual can interact in different ways with such symbiotic computing environments, consisting of personal devices.

F. Daniel, P. Dolog, and Q. Li (Eds.): ICWE 2013, LNCS 7977, pp. 99–113, 2013.

As a consequence, monolithic single-device *user interfaces* (UI) devolve to *Distributed User Interfaces (DUI)*. DUIs separate, migrate and merge seamlessly between devices. Additionally, they can adapt to different platforms [1] and account for changes in device availability to achieve a continuous application experience [2].

Developing distributed user interfaces is challenging [3]. From the user perspective, two challenges are salient. First, users should be supported to adapt the distribution to their needs. Second, users should experience seamless UI migration. Migrated UI components preserve state and remain consistent with the whole application context. Concerning the use of multiple devices, current Web applications can be well rendered on different platforms. However, most of them ignore the possibility of using multiple personal computing devices. Cooperation between such devices related to distributed interfaces is scarce and mostly limited to device-specific static interface separation.

Fig. 1. An example of distribution of user interface components (widgets) to diverse (mobile) computing devices

To address these challenges, we present DireWolf, a framework for distributed Web applications based on widgets. We have chosen to work with Web widgets because they represent interface components with limited, but clear-cut functionality, dedicated to smaller tasks. Widgets can be shared, reused, mashed up and personalized between applications. By splitting the interface into separate widgets and enabling them to exchange information, customizable Web applications can be developed. Whereas previous work [4,5] on widget applications and mashups considers single-end devices only, we examine the concept of widget-based Web applications combined with device awareness, session mobility and cross-device cooperation.

To illustrate the concept, we shortly describe a semantic video annotation application (cf. Figure 1). This application was transformed from a typical Web application into a widget-based one, thus validating the feasibility of our approach. A semantic video annotation application is an ideal candidate for extended UI interactions: users watch videos, annotate them at certain time points or for specific time intervals and navigate through a video using the annotations. Various types of available semantic annotations (agent, time, concept, object type) can be added using text input and interacting with a video player. Place annotations can be pinpointed on a map. However, e.g. full screen mode of the video player hides all other UI controls on one device. In an annotation scenario, distributing the UI enhances user experience. Users can play the video in full screen on one device and can use additional devices to annotate it or to browse through the video. Moreover, they can use device-specific features for each of the UI elements, e.g. multi-touch on a smartphone for interacting with a digital map. Preserving UI state across devices is also required for such a scenario, e.g. resume at current position instead of restart after migration of a video player, continue annotating, etc. Our paper brings forward the following contributions:

- a framework for easy browser-based distribution of Web widgets between multiple devices
- facilitation of extended multi-modal real-time interactions on a federation of personal computing devices
- provision of continuous state-preserving widget migration

DireWolf helps managing a set of devices and handles communication and control of distributed parts of the Web application. The conceptual and implementation details of the DireWolf framework, together with the possibility of integration into existing widget platforms is detailed in the next sections.

The rest of the paper is structured as follows. In Section 2, relevant literature related to our approach is presented. In Section 3 we introduce current widget-based Web applications as a starting point for our DUI framework. Sections 4 presents the DireWolf framework in detail with a focus on the framework concept and continuous widget migration. Section 5 provides implementation details. Evaluation results are discussed in Section 6. Section 7 concludes this work and provides an outlook to future research.

2   Related Work

Our DUI approach is related to work in two research domains, namely mechanisms for distributing and migrating Web UI, and frameworks for using multiple personal computing devices to perform a single user task.

Distributing Web UIs means ungrouping Web document elements and presenting them separately without compromising application functionality. The granularity of UI splitting can range from arbitrary partitions to pre-defined UI blocks. Ghiani et al. [6] provide a mechanism to select a part of a Web page which can be migrated and shown on a mobile device. However, this approach is only feasible for the adaptation of Web pages and does not support presentation of different UI components on multiple devices at the same time. Model-based approaches [2,7,8] define different abstract UI configurations at design time and generate concrete UI presentations at runtime. These works demonstrate dynamic distribution of Web interfaces among heterogeneous platforms. But reusability and extensibility of sub-services/components are major shortcomings in these approaches. A new UI schema needs to be fixed for a complete application. Sub-service definitions cannot be separated. Consequently, the services of an application cannot be ported with ease. Learning to use the schema for an application induces additional development effort. Moreover, if a new application joins the system, new UI schema files must be written, and the root UI schema must be modified. In contrast, we consider Web applications composed of widgets using open Web standards.

Dynamic DUIs should support runtime component migration. Necessary steps for a successful migration are presented in the Roam project [9]. Roam preserves the application execution state information such as heap, stack, network sockets, etc. at the start of the migration and restores them after migration. For continuous Web browsing, Alapetite et al. [10] migrate Web sessions across mobile devices using 2D-barcodes captured by cameras. A dedicated State Mapper is also developed in [11] for state recovery during UI migration between mobile phones and digital TVs. Inspired by these approaches, our framework realizes complete continuous migration tailored to Web widgets.

Multi-device collaboration means that multiple devices can join the same application scope and that these devices can complete tasks together. Early approaches have focused on supporting desktop applications with devices such as PDAs and handheld computers over wired or wireless connections. Pebbles [12] extends computing and I/O functionalities by involving heterogeneous devices. The extended UIs are native applications specially tailored for each computing platform and each functionality. Thus, multi-device UI are tightly coupled with the computing hardware. Melchior et al. [13] present a P2P framework that helps deploy distributed graphical user interfaces. All devices must install the framework before they can create components or import remote components directly from other devices. Many projects consider one-to-one mappings between users and devices, which is more applicable for collaborative scenarios. MarcoFlow [14,5] uses modular UI to represent the relevant controls and information to the user, but it focuses on the orchestration of business processes involving multiple users with different data views. Pierce and Nichols [15] use the idea of ownership to address personal computing devices and to enable seamless user experience over multiple devices. Their prototype simplifies the development of applications that are aware of a user's devices but it does not support UI migration. The DireWolf framework supports any device with an available modern Web browser. There is no need for pre-installed components or configurations. In the following, we first introduce Widget-based Web applications to clarify the context in which DireWolf was developed.

3   Widget-Based Web Applications

Important prerequisites for distributing individual elements of complete Web applications are a clear separation into conceptual and functional units, a context for managing separation, and cross-device communication between these units. In this section we briefly introduce *widget-based Web applications* and discuss why they fulfill the above prerequisites and thus served as foundation for the DireWolf framework.

The basic building block is a *widget*. Conceptually, a widget is a self-contained mini-application with limited, however clean-cut functionality. Widgets are usually designed to accomplish small stand-alone tasks, which may recur in multiple different applications. Furthermore, widgets are usually designed with limited display size, such that multiple widgets fit on one desktop browser screen or single widgets fit on limited-size mobile device screens. By design, widgets are reusable for multiple purposes in different applications. As such, widgets strongly resemble mobile applications. Technically speaking, existing widget standard specifications define widgets as packaged Web applications including means of configuration and access to dedicated widget application programming interfaces. Principally, any existing Web application can be "widgetized". However, the form factor of limited display size often requires an adapted design. In practice, widgets usually serve as minimal frontends to more complex Web services. For our work, widgets perfectly serve as the functional units to be migrated across devices.

Complex applications can be achieved by orchestrating multiple widgets in a dashboard fashion in *widget containers*. Research towards the effective integration of widgets to complete collaborative Web applications resulted in additional layers on top of widget containers that make use of the DireWolf framework, i.e. *widget spaces* and *inter-widget communication*.

First, combinations of multiple widgets require a working context and technical support to manage such contexts. In our work, we employ the concept of a *widget space* [4] as working context. A widget space is a collaboration context, in which multiple users collaboratively manage and operate sets of widgets and additional resources to create custom applications for different purposes. For this work, we extended widget spaces by the additional notion of multiple devices per user.

Second, the integration of multiple widgets to complete applications requires an interoperable communication mechanism between widgets, referred to as *Inter-widget Communication (IWC)*. With such a usually publish-subscribe-based mechanism, messages can be broadcasted from any widget and possibly dispatched by other widgets, thus allowing the orchestration [16] and tighter integration of multiple widgets to complete applications. Most existing approaches only support local IWC, i.e. communication between widgets within one single browser instance. An additional feature of our complete IWC approach includes remote communication between widgets across different browser instances and users [17]. For this work, we use both forms of IWC as carrier for message exchange between different parts of our DUI framework within and across devices.

Figure 2a depicts the initial setting from which this work departed. In the following section we elaborate on the extensions contributed by our DUI framework in detail, thus leading to the situation in Figure 2b.

4   DireWolf Framework

Based on the state-of-the-art in widget-based Web applications discussed in the previous section, we now introduce the DireWolf framework. First, we discuss the particular requirements for such a framework, which are not yet covered by existing widget-based Web application frameworks.

The DUI framework is involved in every layer of the widget-based Web application. As shown in Figure 2b, components should be created for widgets, client browsers, backend services as well as the data storage. Framework client components are included in the widget application document rendered in the Web browser. They manage communication and synchronization between widgets on one device but also between widgets on other devices. The framework server components extend the functionality of common widget spaces with services for data persistence, user device profiles and shared application state.

The DUI framework provides management services for device profiles and widgets when the user owns multiple devices. The inner workings of a widget are out of concern of the DUI framework. A requirement is that a mobile device needs to host some modern Web browser such as those found on most commodity

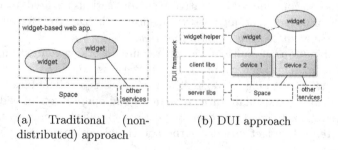

(a)   Traditional   (non-distributed) approach

(b) DUI approach

Fig. 2. Widget-based Web applications

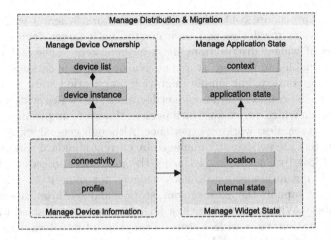

Fig. 3. Requirements to a dynamic widget-based DUI framework

smartphones and tablets. The use cases focus on creating, getter/setter and operating on resources (widgets).

4.1 Requirements Analysis

As a first step, we performed a requirements analysis with the goal of improving deficiencies found in existing work on DUIs (cf. Section 2), thereby taking into account the current state-of-the-art in widget-based Web applications (cf. Section 3). Figure 3 provides a high-level overview of the main identified requirements for a DUI framework, grouped into four interrelated categories: *device information, device ownership, distribution & migration, application state* and *widget handling*.

A DUI framework must enable the management of general and context-specific device information. General information includes information on device *connectivity* and *profile*. A device profile captures information on device type (e.g. smartphone, tablet, laptop) and capabilities (e.g. operating system, display size, in/output modalities, browser type) required for device recognition and adaptation purposes. Device connectivity describes the current availability of the device for collaboration and should be updated in real time. Context-specific information includes *device location*, i.e. in which context the device is currently active and *displayed widgets*, i.e. which widgets are displayed on the device in the current context.

Furthermore, a DUI framework must dynamically capture and manage *device ownership*. With the ever dropping prices of mobile devices, a person's device portfolio is likely to change often. Each user should thus be enabled to dynamically manage a personal *device list*. Thereby, each device instance describes a virtual device which can be bound to a real device. The introduction of virtual devices provides additional flexibility, i.e. multiple configurations for a single device and switching between real devices.

Obviously, a DUI framework must support distribution and migration of widgets across devices within a given context. In its simplest form, migration is a synchronized procedure controlled by the framework, where a widget is first removed from a source device and then created on a target device. However, constellations of widget distributions must be persistent. Thus, a DUI framework must be enabled to manage, store and synchronize application state within a given working context. For simple migration, application state must include information on the context and on widget locations, i.e. which widgets are currently residing on which device for which person. However, simple migration does not guarantee a seamless working experience. Although general widget configuration parameters are persistently managed by current standard widget engines, a widget will lose its internal state during the migration procedure. For some widgets this is not an issue (e.g. a clock widget), for some it is. Thus, a DUI framework must support the management, storage and synchronization of internal widget state. With such measures, a DUI framework is enabled to support continuous migration, i.e. a widget stores a snapshot of its internal state before removal from a source device and restores internal state after its creation on the target device.

4.2   Framework Design

Figure 4 depicts the key architecture features of the DireWolf framework. As mentioned in Sec. 3, the DUI framework requires a real-time communication mechanism to "glue" all distributed UI components into one cohesive application. The *Message Router* server component provides bi-directional asynchronous message exchange between the client components and the server.

DUI Client is a widget helper component to be included as a JavaScript library in the widget namespace. DUI Client usage in widgets is optional (e.g. legacy widgets). These widgets can still be distributed and migrated. However, the DUI Client enhances DUI-related features for the widget and provides an API to interpret and create framework messages and events. DUI Client has additional methods to store widget state as part of application state at the server-side service component. It sends requests, and server components send back responses as well as broadcast notifications to all other Web clients if necessary.

DUI Manager is the central DUI component on the client browser. All features/functionalities are directly or indirectly related to it. DUI Manager connects to other components of the framework in three ways: request-response communication, local and remote IWC. For example, DUI Manager uses requests-response communication to retrieve user profile and space information from server-side services. Local IWC is used for communicating with widgets running in the same browser context. Remote IWC provides the message-exchange mechanism for widgets and DUI Managers located at different devices.

At start, the DUI manager fetches the user profile which contains the device list and the device profiles. The connectivity of a user's devices is monitored constantly after the DUI manager is activated. The user can choose one virtual device per real device. If a device is not listed, the framework attempts to recognize it by using cookies, HTTP User-Agent headers and user input.

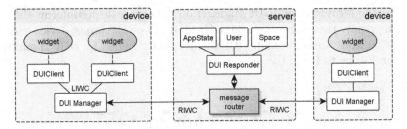

RIWC - Remote inter-widget communication
LIWC - Local inter-widget communication

Fig. 4. Abstract architecture of the DUI framework

DUI Responder is the server-side central DUI component. All DUI relevant requests are redirected to this component. The main tasks of DUI Responder are to maintain DUI-relevant data and keep all DUI managers on client browsers synchronized.

4.3 Widget Migration

By using a widget approach, the dynamic transition of UI components from desktop to mobile devices is simpler. Widgets resemble mobile device screen sizes by design. Rendering a widget on smartphone or a tablet only requires adaptation of the widget containing element.

Considering the failover, since mobile devices can go offline unexpectedly, widgets can become inactive. The DUI Responder considers a widget to be inactive if it cannot find an active device displaying the widget. Different procedures are provided to inactive widgets and active widgets. Figure 5 illustrates the case of continuous migration. When a DUI Manager initiates a widget migration on any device, the DUI Responder looks for the widgets on all devices of the requesting user. If the widget is found to be inactive, the DUI Responder switches the widget location from no device or an inactive device to the migration target device. Then, it sends out a message to perform the migration procedure on all DUI Managers.

During continuous migrations, widget state is saved right before migration. The widget can retrieve state as a snapshot for continuing the task. DUI-supported widgets can be either inactive or active. DUI Manager tries to restore the state for inactive widgets and guarantees the continuity for active widgets. For inactive widgets, the steps are the same as the non-continuous migration of inactive widgets, except that DUI Manager sends the last saved state of the widget.

For continuous migration of active widgets, DUI Manager asks the widget's DUI Client to collect the widget state for the incoming migration. On receiving the command for migration, DUI Manager on the source device informs the DUI Client to prepare the widget removal. DUI Manager on the target device extracts information from the command. DUI Client is then guided by DUI Manager to run several steps to finish the migration.

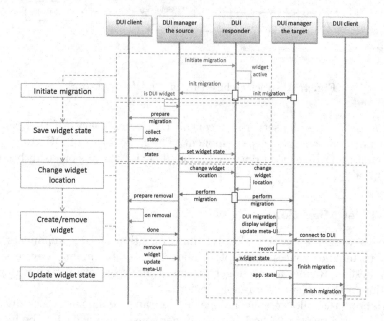

Fig. 5. Sequence diagram for continuous migration of active widgets

5   Implementation

The implementation of the DireWolf framework builds upon the Open Source Java-based ROLE SDK[1] including a platform for hosting and managing Widget-based Web applications as described in Section 3. As basic widget engine, the ROLE platform employs the standard OpenSocial [18] container Apache Shindig[2]. On top of Shindig, the platform implements a set of RESTful services for *user management* and *personal and collaborative widget space management*. It should be noted that the space concept is currently standardized in the OpenSocial 3.0 specification. Consequently, it will be implemented in Shindig and will possibly become part of other Shindig-based widget platforms such as Apache Rave[3]. Furthermore, the platform supports secure authentication and

---

[1] http://sourceforge.net/projects/role-project/
[2] http://shindig.apache.org/
[3] http://rave.apache.org

authorization by employing OpenID and OAuth. A real-time service realizes the integration with a standard XMPP [19] server providing support for multi-user chat conversations in widget spaces and publish-subscribe support for remote IWC. Associations between modules are realized by injection. For our work we strongly employ IWC, using HTML5 Web Messaging [20] for local IWC. An additional feature of our complete IWC approach includes remote communication between widgets across different browser instances and users [17] using the XMPP protocol [19] and its publish-subscribe extension [21]. We use both forms of IWC as a carrier for message exchange between different parts of our DUI framework within and across devices.

On client side, the platform provides an AJAX browser frontend based on HTML/JavaScript/CSS and jQuery[4]. For client-side real-time support the ROLE platform employs strophe.js[5], a robust XMPP library for JavaScript including support for XMPP over WebSocket [22] in modern browsers. Widget spaces are used as context for IWC. In collaboration with user and space management services, the platform real-time service manages one dedicated publish-subscribe channel per space for IWC including whitelist-based access control. On client side, every widget space is instrumented with a DUI Manager including an *IWC proxy*, which routes outgoing IWC messages to the affiliated XMPP server via the strophe-based XMPP connection and incoming messages to all widgets in the space via HTML5 Web Messaging [20]. Widgets can be equipped with IWC support by simply importing a small *IWC client* library and implementing functions for publishing and processing IWC messages. The DUI Client library extends the plain IWC library by a set of functions related to storage and retrieval of internal widget state.

Given that many technical prerequisites for DireWolf were already fulfilled by the ROLE platform, we chose an integration approach. In its current version, DireWolf is an extension of the existing ROLE platform and its components. The DUI Responder is realized as an additional RESTful service for managing device migration-specific data such as personal device lists, device profiles, and user and space-related application states. Client side components such as DUI Manager and DUI Client communicate application state and initiate widget migration by simple HTTP requests to the DUI Responder, which in turn controls the synchronization process and initiates real-time synchronization necessary for migration. All migration-related communication between individual components (Message Router, DUI Manager, DUI Clients) is handled via ROLE IWC over a separate publish-subscribe channel to avoid interference with regular developer-defined IWC messages.

For convenient control of widget distribution and device registration DireWolf provides a set of user interface components as frontend to the DUI Manager. Figure 6 shows the main component integrated into the side panel of a widget space's view in the overall ROLE platform user interface . The upper *Device Manager* button bar provides shortcuts to a device manager console for personal

---

[4] http://jquery.com/
[5] http://strophe.im/strophejs

Fig. 6. DUI manager user interface in a widget space sidebar panel

device management including detailed configuration and debugging options. The *Current Device* resp. *Remote Devices* sections list all widgets displayed on the current device resp. remote devices along with device connectivity. In the example in Figure 6, the current widget space contains six widgets, distributed to four devices with different profiles (PC, iPad, iPhone and Mac). Only two devices are currently active, indicated by the green circle next to the device name. Thus, only five widgets are currently visible. One widget was previously migrated to the user's iPhone, which is currently disconnected, indicated by a grey marker. By using drag and drop, widgets can be (re-)distributed between active devices.

6 Evaluation

The focus of our experiments was to research how distributing widget-based user interfaces in Web applications across different personal user devices can be achieved. In this section, we briefly present performance evaluation results regarding widget migration.

The migration component of the DireWolf framework was tested on a wireless local area network, simulating the home or office conditions. The ping latency of the network (of 6ms) was considered negligible. Two setups were considered. The first setup measured migration between two desktop machines (Mac OS, Windows 7), using the Google Chrome browser (version 23). The second setup measured migration between desktop machines and an iPad 1 with iOS 5.0, using the Safari Web browser.

Tests were conducted with widgets with simple functionality, measuring the time between two consecutive migrations across two devices. In order to avoid noise induced by local time inconsistencies between devices, a reverse operation was automatically executed after initial migration, and total round-trip time was recorded. For consistency reasons, two kinds of migrations - simple migration (non-state-preserving) and continuous migration (state-preserving) - were evaluated. Round trip times for 100 migrations (i.e. 50 rounds) were measured.

Overall, our prototype achieved good performance results. Average migration time for simple migration was around 362.6 ms for a "hello world" widget with a standard deviation of 48.9 ms. Continuous migration requires two more steps than simple migration, i.e. storing widget state and rendering the widget with the Apache Shindig rendering engine. Average time for continuous migration between the MacBook and the desktop computer was 1305 ms, with a standard deviation of 147.2 ms. The results show higher average migration time between the MacBook and the iPad, i.e. an average time of 2069 ms and the standard deviation of 222.6 ms. This is due to the hardware differences and the time needed to load all the dependencies. By decomposing the time necessary for the migration and observing the interval needed by each component of our framework, the results show that the initiation and the widget rendering process take more time than the migration itself. The Shindig server's Javascript library loading and the widget rendering steps require approximatively 69% of the time. In contrast, the loading time needed by the DUI components is less than 25% of the overall time.

The presented evaluation is limited to technical properties of the widget migration feature. However, we conducted an extensive user study for assessing the usability of the DireWolf framework, which due to space limitations could not be discussed in this paper. In addition, DireWolf is currently being tested on a bigger range of devices. Even though DireWolf has been derived from the existing ROLE Widget SDK, as described in Section 5, it is not yet included into an existing official SDK release. Encouraged by the small overhead and latency that the framework introduces, the next step is to integrate DireWolf into the future versions of the SDK.

7   Conclusions and Future Work

In this paper, we try to leverage the lack of dynamic interactive environments based on Web technologies which can take advantage of the various personal devices used by an individual. We provide a framework that can facilitate user interactions on a federation of personal computing devices, by making use of distributed user interfaces. Furthermore, we believe that a widget-based approach to encapsulate UIs and application functionalities benefits Web developer communities already familiar with this programming model. Apache Rave and Shindig are examples of such open-source communities. Since widgets can be grouped, shared, reused and personalized, our approach ensures unique user experiences with DUI applications. Our framework also provides features for distributing and migrating widgets, at the same time hiding the complexity of device awareness, communication and session mobility. As initial evaluation indicates, the framework adds only small overhead to the overall widget rendering process.

The framework we present here paves the way for many interesting experiments. We are already testing complex interaction modalities within the semantic video annotation application illustrated in Figure 1. Furthermore, we envision our framework in the domains of technology-enhanced learning and interactive smart television. We also consider using the emerging WebRTC project[6] for real-time browser-to-browser communication without a server intermediate. As a next step beyond the personal multi-device distributed computing environment, we will extend DireWolf to support multi-device multi-user collaboration. Further research must address security and privacy issues in message exchange across devices and users. We are committed to open source development and we aim to integrate the IWC and DireWolf within an open source project, such as Apache Rave. We plan to provide tutorials, Web casts and code snippets with intention to form a sustainable developer community around our solution.

Acknowledgements. The research leading to these results has received funding from the European Commission's Seventh Framework Programme (FP7/2007-2013) under grant agreements no 231396 - Responsive Open Learning Environments (ROLE) project and no 318209 - Learning Layers: Scaling up Technologies for Informal Learning in SME Clusters and the Excellence Initiative of German National Science Foundation (DFG) within the research cluster Ultra High-Speed Mobile Information and Communication (UMIC). We thank Ke Li for his framework implementation.

References

1. Lòpez-Espin, J.J., Gallud, J.A., Lazcorreta, E., Peñalver, A., Botella, F.: A Formal View of Distributed User Interfaces. In: Distributed User Interfaces CHI 2011 Workshop, University of Castilla-La Mancha, Spain, pp. 97–100 (2011)
2. Vandervelpen, C., Vanderhulst, G., Luyten, K., Coninx, K.: Light-Weight Distributed Web Interfaces: Preparing the Web for Heterogeneous Environments. In: Lowe, D.G., Gaedke, M. (eds.) ICWE 2005. LNCS, vol. 3579, pp. 197–202. Springer, Heidelberg (2005)
3. Blumendorf, M., Roscher, D., Albayrak, S.: Distributed User Interfaces for Smart Environments: Characteristics and Challenges. In: Distributed User Interfaces CHI 2011 Workshop, University of Castilla-La Mancha, Spain, pp. 25–28 (2011)
4. Bogdanov, E., Salzmann, C., Gillet, D.: Contextual Spaces with Functional Skins as OpenSocial Extension. In: The Fourth International Conference on Advances in Computer-Human Interactions, ACHI 2011, pp. 158–163 (2011)
5. Daniel, F., Soi, S., Tranquillini, S., Casati, F., Heng, C., Yan, L.: Distributed Orchestration of User Interfaces. Information Systems 37(6), 539–556 (2012)
6. Ghiani, G., Paternò, F., Santoro, C.: On-demand Cross-Device Interface Components Migration. In: Proceedings of the 12th International Conference on Human Computer Interaction with Mobile Devices and Services (MobileHCI 2010), pp. 299–308. ACM Press (2010)
7. Baillie, L., Schatz, R., Simon, R., Anegg, H., Wegscheider, F., Niklfeld, G., Gassner, A.: Designing Mona: User Interactions with Multimodal Mobile Applications. In: Proceedings of 11th International Conference on Human-Computer Interaction (HCI International), pp. 22–27. Lawrence Erlbaum Associates (2005)

---

[6] http://www.webrtc.org/

8. Luyten, K., Coninx, K.: Distributed User Interface Elements to support Smart Interaction Spaces. In: Proceedings of the Seventh IEEE International Symposium on Multimedia, ISM 2005, pp. 277–286. IEEE Computer Society (2005)
9. Chu, H.H., Song, H., Wong, C., Kurakake, S., Katagiri, M.: Roam, a Seamless Application Framework. Journal of Systems and Software 69(3), 209–226 (2004)
10. Alapetite, A.: Dynamic 2D-barcodes for Multi-Device Web Session Migration Including Mobile Phones. Personal Ubiquitous Computing 14(1), 45–52 (2010)
11. Paternò, F., Santoro, C., Scorcia, A.: User Interface Migration Between Mobile Devices and Digital TV. In: Forbrig, P., Paternò, F. (eds.) HCSE/TAMODIA 2008. LNCS, vol. 5247, pp. 287–292. Springer, Heidelberg (2008)
12. Myers, B.A.: Using Handhelds and PCs Together. Communications of the ACM 44(11), 34–41 (2001)
13. Melchior, J., Grolaux, D., Vanderdonckt, J., van Roy, P.: A Toolkit for Peer-to-peer Distributed User Interfaces: Concepts, Implementation, and Applications. In: Proceedings of the 1st ACM SIGCHI Symposium on Engineering Interactive Computing Systems, pp. 69–78. ACM Press (2009)
14. Daniel, F., Soi, S., Tranquillini, S., Casati, F., Chang, H., Li, Y.: MarcoFlow: Modeling, Deploying, and Running Distributed User Interface Orchestrations. In: Proceedings of the 8th International Conference on Business Process Management Demo Track, pp. 23–27. Springer (2010)
15. Pierce, J.S., Nichols, J.: An Infrastructure for Extending Applications' User Experiences Across Multiple Personal Devices. In: Proceedings of the 21st Annual ACM Symposium on User Interface Software and Technology (UIST 2008), pp. 101–110. ACM Press (2008)
16. Zuzak, I., Ivankovic, M., Budiselic, I.: A Classification Framework for Web Browser Cross-Context Communication. CoRR abs/1108.4770 (2011)
17. Govaerts, S., Verbert, K., Dahrendorf, D., Ullrich, C., Schmidt, M., Werkle, M., Chatterjee, A., Nussbaumer, A., Renzel, D., Scheffel, M., Friedrich, M., Santos, J.L., Duval, E., Law, E.L.-C.: Towards responsive open learning environments: the ROLE interoperability framework. In: Kloos, C.D., Gillet, D., Crespo García, R.M., Wild, F., Wolpers, M. (eds.) EC-TEL 2011. LNCS, vol. 6964, pp. 125–138. Springer, Heidelberg (2011)
18. OpenSocial and Gadgets Specification Group: OpenSocial Specification 2.5.0, http://opensocial-resources.googlecode.com/svn/spec/2.5/ (Online: last accessed March 2013)
19. Saint-Andre, P.: RFC 6121: Extensible Messaging and Presence Protocol (XMPP): Instant Messaging and Presence. Technical report, XMPP Standards Foundation (2011)
20. Hickson, I.: HTML5 Web Messaging. Working draft, W3C (2011)
21. Millard, P., Saint-Andre, P., Meijer, R.: XEP-0060: Publish-Subscribe Version 1.13, Draft. Technical report, XMPP Standards Foundation (2010)
22. Hickson, I.: The WebSocket API. Editor's draft, W3C (2013)

Awareness and Control for Inter-Widget Communication: Challenges and Solutions

Olexiy Chudnovskyy[1], Stefan Pietschmann[2], Matthias Niederhausen[3],
Vadim Chepegin[5], David Griffiths[4], and Martin Gaedke[1]

[1] Chemnitz University of Technology, Germany
{olexiy.chudnovskyy,gaedke}@informatik.tu-chemnitz.de
[2] Technische Universität Dresden, Germany
stefan.pietschmann@tu-dresden.de
[3] T-Systems Multimedia Solutions GmbH, Germany
matthias.niederhausen@t-systems-mms.com
[4] University of Bolton, UK
d.e.griffiths@bolton.ac.uk
[5] TIE Nederland B.V., the Netherlands
vadim.chepegin@tiekinetix.com

Abstract. Recently, widget-based Web applications, i. e., mashups have
gained momentum, as they make it possible to address the "long tail" of
software needs. By enabling data and control flow among widgets – inter-
widget communication (IWC) – integration of data and functionality can
be defined by the end users themselves. However, IWC entails several
problems that may reduce the overall user confidence in a system. Based
on the results of user studies on the OMELETTE mashup platform,
this paper analyzes the problem space and evaluates possible solutions
to improve user perception of IWC. Further, a discussion of promising
techniques is offered and pending challenges are identified.

Keywords: mashup, widget, inter-widget communication.

1 Introduction

The vision of users who drag-and-drop and combine applications from any location on the Web, local drive, or cloud storage, in their own workspaces has never
been so close to becoming a reality. The modern Web offers powerful mashup
platforms which enable end users to create their own situational applications on
the fly without the intervention of developers. Research on such *User Interface
Mashups* (UI Mashups) has made significant progress towards this vision. One of
the most important concepts in this field is that of *widgets* – interactive components which provide the end user with access to data, services, and application
logic. A number of initiatives have been proposed, addressing the emerging need
for simple, flexible, and powerful composition environments, e.g. [8,12].

Their main goal is to enable end users to aggregate data and functionality
from various sources on one screen or *workspace*. One of the key features of

F. Daniel, P. Dolog, and Q. Li (Eds.): ICWE 2013, LNCS 7977, pp. 114–122, 2013.

these platforms, *inter-widget communication* (IWC), allows widgets to exchange events and data. Depending on the communication paradigm, solutions differ in their degree of *automation* (manual effort may be required to establish connections), *end user suitability* (usability and complexity of IWC configuration vary) and *generality* of the approach (e. g., compatibility between widgets of different vendors is not guaranteed).

The success of IWC-aware platforms is highly dependent on the degree to which they support the above characteristics. Although all of them are significant and desirable from the end users' point of view, in practice it is hard to optimize all three simultaneously. Moreover, recent research on domain specific mashups shows that, to some extent, *generality* contradicts *end user suitability* [4].

The OMELETTE project [2] has been working on finding an appropriate trade-off between the first two aspects, namely automation and end user suitability. The results of this work were incorporated into a mashup environment with IWC implemented by means of a publish-subscribe messaging pattern (pub/sub). A recent user study [13] conducted with 44 participants in Germany and China revealed a number of issues, some of which are the result of the underlying mashup approach. The goal of this paper is to elaborate on these findings by presenting a survey of approaches in which similar problems have been tackled and discussing the most promising techniques in the context of mashup platforms.

2   Towards End-User Friendly IWC: Existing Challenges

In contrast to other approaches, in which mashup developers have to deal with abstract control flow and data flow models, in OMELETTE there is no difference from a user perspective between design and execution. Mashup composition takes place at run-time and its results are immediately evident to users. A distinct feature of OMELETTE is that users are not required to establish explicit connections between widgets. Communication, i. e., data flow emerges as soon as widgets are placed together within a workspace. This is achieved by means of the messaging bus: widgets subscribe and publish messages on different communication channels, known as *topics*. The decision to apply pub/sub was motivated by recent findings, which highlighted the importance of working "out-of-the-box" [5] and the usability issues of wiring approaches for end users [10].

Thus the OMELETTE solution implies that the complex issues of composition and wiring widgets are best left to skilled developers of widgets. This, however, implies a lack of *awareness* and *control* by end users – an implication which was confirmed in the interviews and observations during the user studies. Thus, the focus of this paper is on challenges and problems from an *end user perspective*.

2.1   Problem Space: Awareness

The first problem space comprises the challenges that users face when interacting with a pre-defined workspace. It may be split into the following sub-categories:

Cold Start Problem. Upon opening a workspace, end users do not know which of the widgets are actually inter-connected. Users have to learn the data and control flows as they use a mashup and explore it. While in general this may merely frustrate users, such "exploratory" interaction can also affect live data, causing undesired side effects.

IWC Transitivity. Similarly, it is very hard for users to distinguish direct and transitive connections between widgets. The latter occur when one widget triggers action in another, which in turn triggers a third widget. While this behavior may be intended, it can negatively affect users in their understanding of the resulting functionality: First, users may see relationships when there are none, and misinterpret their findings. Second, widget reuse and workspace refactoring will result in unpredictable behavior, e. g., the loss of functionality whenever the "linking" widget is missing.

Data Ignorance. Users typically do not see the data being transferred between widgets. Instead, they only perceive the effects of their transfer, i. e., that a receiving widget is updated with new data. While one can argue that providing this information may overburden users, data ignorance still leads to three problems: users can only guess which widgets are compatible and work together; mistaken expectations of the data transferred lead to misinterpretations of the application behavior; possibly untrusted widgets might receive sensitive data without the user's consent.

2.2   Problem Space: Control

The second set of problems stems from the need of users to modify how a mashup works. IWC connections established implicitly, i. e., based on the pub/sub paradigm, greatly simplify the start of work with a mashup but also lead to a loss of control.

Lack of Extensibility. Users cannot explicitly establish new connections between widgets. Due to the potentially large number of widgets developed by independent parties, it is both impossible to foresee all valid widget combinations and impractical to try and guarantee their interoperability. Thus, users will often want previously unconnected widgets to work together and to establish a link between them manually.

Rigidity. In pre-configured workspaces, it may be necessary to change the control or data flow, i. e., the way widgets are connected by default. This can be supported in its full complexity, as with wiring tools, or by offering more subtle actions, such as allowing users to isolate widgets as senders or receivers of data. There are many possible reasons for this, e. g., because a widget is untrusted, does not work as expected, or simply because it should hold an intermediary result to be saved for later.

Clunkiness. Establishing a temporary data flow can be desirable and more convenient than setting up a permanent connection. The studies revealed that many end users intuitively work with the data in the widgets by trying to drag-and-drop from source to receiver. This user-triggered temporary data flow is usually not foreseen by IWC mechanisms – be they wiring or pub/sub approaches – and platforms.

Addressing these challenges is crucial in order to boost end user acceptance and to promote the use of widget mashups in business environments. The next section will evaluate possible solutions.

3   Analysis of Existing Approaches

The following survey presents state-of-the-art techniques from the End User Development domain (EUD) in the context of the above problem spaces. The approaches are compared based on the degree of technical skill required by end users to employ them in mashups.

3.1   Solutions for Problem Space: Awareness

Self-Descriptive Design (SDD). Systems employing SDD mechanisms try to make users aware of functional dependencies between widgets at the application layer by the means of annotations or visual markup. Whenever users are confronted with new (e.g., shared) mashups, looking at individual widgets very often does not provide the "big picture", i.e., the overall functionality. SDD-based approaches address this problem by making mashups as self-explanatory as possible. Therefore, they provide annotation tools to be used in the phase of mashup creation. In [3], the authors suggest to make internal knowledge explicit by usage of *implicit, explicit* and *literate* annotations.

Additive Views (AV). One of the common practices for increasing user awareness in software systems is to provide various views on the application. Using suitable metaphors, these views enable users to explore the internal characteristics of the application, i.e., structure, components, data and control flows. Additive views are usually implemented either in an *integrated* or in a *separated* fashion. Integrated views try to avoid the "break" between usage and programming modes. In the EDYRA mashup environment [12], a running mashup can be augmented by dedicated overlays. Users are also able to highlight direct and transitive connections between components, raising the overall awareness of IWC in the mashup.

Surprise-Explain-Reward Strategy (SER). A surprise-explain-reward strategy aims at communicating non-obvious behavior of a system to end users and letting them engage in further exploration activities [14]. Information about inscrutable activities appears in ways that grab users' attention (*surprise*) and entice them to learn more about the causes. An appropriate help system supports the learning process and opens new perspectives on the possibilitites of the system (*explain*). Having applied the newly learned technique, users benefit from advanced platform capabilities (*reward*). In the Forms/3 project [1], this idea has been applied to ensure data integrity in end-user-created spreadsheets.

Question Asking Strategy (QA). This strategy is applied to find the causes of unexpected or non-obvious application behavior. Based on explicit knowledge about the structure of an application, the system is able to provide answers to specific types of user inquires. A dialog often takes place in natural language and does not require the user to learn any programming formalisms or debugging techniques. The WhyLine tool [6] applies this technique to enable unskilled developers to test their algorithms. Using menus and pictograms of objects involved, users can construct "why did" and "why did not" questions in order to explore the system's behavior. A user study showed that developers were more efficient with this system than with traditional debugging tools. The HANDS project [9] conducted several user studies in order to understand how people without programming skills think of and express software design. After implementing their findings using natural language in question building and answering, the authors claimed that even ten-year-olds were able to create meaningful programs.

3.2   Solutions for Problem Space: Control

Parametrization (PAR). Along with interface customization, *parametrization* is one of the simplest and most common forms of EUD. It assumes that software is designed in a way that enables modification of its behavior by changing the values of a pre-defined set of parameters, e.g. the location of a news feed. Netvibes and iGoogle successfully employ the mechanism in widget-based dashboards. The way in which the parametrization view is exposed differs: it can be offered by widget developers or by the composition platform. The latter is done by portals based on explicit parameter declarations in widget descriptors. Netvibes and iGoogle support both parametrization modes.

Programming by Demonstration (PBD). This is a well-proven technique that enables end users to specify desired functionality by providing examples of its behavior [7]. Based on demonstrated activities and data samples, a PBD system tries to generalize user actions and to derive an algorithm. One of the open challenges facing PBD systems is how to represent the captured algorithm and to facilitate its future adaptation by end users. The CRUISe project [11] proposes an extension to the interface between widgets and mashup platform. Widget authors can notify the platform of user interactions, e. g., when users drag data beyond a widget's perimeters. The platform monitors further user interactions, e. g., the data being dropped onto other widgets. This way, users can implement ad hoc data exchange and also establish permanent connections.

Programming by Specification (PBS). This comprises EUD approaches that enable users to create mashups by defining the data/control flow themselves. This process of EUD is predominantly based on *visual programming* languages involving metaphors such as "Lego" constructors or electrical circuits. Similar techniques are used in the majority of mashup platforms, such as Yahoo Pipes[1] or JackBe Presto[2]. In [4], the authors propose sacrificing the generality of mashup tools in favor of simplicity and comprehensiveness of the system by applying

---

[1] http://pipes.yahoo.com
[2] http://mdc.jackbe.com/products/mashboard.php

domain-specific composition tools. A user study of the ResEval platform has confirmed this assumption, showing that end users understand the composition paradigm and can master the development of mashups if they are focused on single domains and unburdened from data transformation issues.

4 Comparison of Approaches and Drawn Guidelines

Table 1 presents a comparison of the previously discussed techniques based on the expert evaluation.

Table 1. Applicability of EUD techniques to the widget mashup domain

Criteria/Approach	SDD	AV	SER	QA	PAR	PBD	PBS
Cold Start Problem	oo	●	–	●●	–	–	–
IWC Transitivity	oo	●	●●	●●	–	–	–
Data Ignorance	oo	oo	●●	●●	–	–	–
Rigidity	–	–	–	–	●●	o	●
Clunkiness	–	–	–	–	–	●●	●
Lack of Extensibility	–	–	–	–	–	●●	●

●● – applicable without deep understanding of data types and control flows,
● – applicable with basic knowledge on data types and control flows,
oo – limited applicability without deep understanding of data types and control flows,
o – limited applicability with basic knowledge on data types and control flows,
— – not applicable

The *Surprise-Explain-Reward* strategy differs from the Question-Asking approach in that users are notified about internal mashup activities right before or right after they happened. This implies that the *cold start problem* is not addressed appropriately, i.e., users are unable to explore connections or exchanged data before the real communication takes place. This disadvantage can be crucial for cost- or load-causing widgets. The approach requires the platform to include appropriate notification mechanisms and an explicit declaration of the mashup structure including widget capabilities and IWC configuration.

Additive Views can address all of the awareness-related problems by enabling end users to explore the internals of a mashup at any time. The main challenge here is to find a compromise between complexity and usability, i.e., to identify suitable abstractions and to adjust the view according to user skills. Recent research proposes to implement overlay views to lower the cognitive load while working with alternative mashup representations [12]. Some familiarity with the "wiring" concept is required to understand connections. To facilitate AV, the platform needs to access mashup configuration and widget interface descriptions.

The applicability of *Self-descriptive Design* is constrained as it is hard to design descriptive graphics for a mashup if the screen size is not fixed. Accordingly, the layout of mashups is not completely consistent between platforms, and it is not possible to predict the degree to which users can change the position of widgets. The adoption of this approach implies (a) that the container makes design tools available to the author, (b) that the design of the container needs to be considered at the same time as the design of mashup functionality, and (c) that this work will need to be repeated whenever the mashup is deployed in a new container.

Within the *Control* problem space, *Parametrization* is the most promising approach with a focus on end users. Although it does not cover the *lack of extensibility* and *clunkiness* of a mashup, the *rigidity* of composition can be influenced if the IWC capabilities of a component are configurable. This, however, goes at the expense of simplicity for the user. To lower the learning curve, all configuration options should be exposed in a uniform manner, e.g., by avoiding all widget-internal configuration dialogs.

Programming by Demonstration addresses the *lack of extensibility* and *clunkiness* problems and enables the definition of new communication paths in an end-user-friendly way. Drag-and-drop has been successfully applied in many instances and is well understood by end users. Also, observation of user interaction with a mashup can be utilized to derive new connections between widgets. In the context of the *rigidity* problem, PBD poses new challenges, such as end-user-friendly representations of generalized algorithms and appropriate modification facilities. Additionally, user interactions with widgets have to be made explicit, e. g., by notifying the observation engine about starting drag'n'drop operations.

Programming by Specification strives to enable end users to design and modify existing software artifacts. However, in targeting all three problems from the *Control* problem space, it assumes that users are able to write behavior specifications and are familiar with basic programming concepts. Projects which utilized this technique have achieved varying degrees of usability. Environments based on natural languages and domain specific vocabularies were more efficient and comprehensive for end users than general purpose composition tools. To apply PBS efficiently, supportive EUD techniques such as instant feedback, decision support and integrity checks should be incorporated into the system.

Based on the above analysis, the following suggestions are made regarding the combination of techniques to address the identified problems:

Cold Start Problem. Provide overlay views on the widget composition, visualizing possible communication paths (AV). These views can be layered (one layer per widget) to use the screen estate efficiently. A help system can also be provided, enabling the user to explore the composition through questions in natural language (QA).

IWC Transitivity. In the overlay view, enable users to discern the direction of communication paths. During data transfer between widgets, visualize active communication paths and enable their exploration and configuration (SER). Empower the help system to answer questions in natural language regarding directions of IWC paths (QA).

Data Ignorance. Enable users to explore possible data flows within the IWC overlay view (AV). During active communication, notify users about ongoing data exchange and enable exploration or modification of this communication path (SER). Extend the help system to answer questions regarding data being transferred between widgets (QA).

Lack of Extensibility. Use observation of user-widget interactions to derive new possible connections between widgets (PBD).

Rigidity. Provide enable/disable parametrization of communication paths and the possibility of isolating widgets from IWC (PAR).

Clunkiness. Provide a drag-and-drop infrastructure to enable one-time communication between widgets (PBD).

5   Conclusions

This paper demonstrates that end-user friendly IWC is needed, but is also difficult to achieve. To tackle this problem, the typical challenges for IWC solutions were derived from user studies conducted within the OMELETTE project and literature review. Based on the findings, the next steps will be to implement the chosen IWC mechanisms using as a basis the open source OMELETTE platform and to evaluate the new features with end users.

Acknowledgment. This work was supported by the European Commission (project OMELETTE, contract 257635).

References

1. Burnett, M., Atwood, J., Walpole Djang, R., Reichwein, J., Gottfried, H., Yang, S.: Forms/3: A first-order visual language to explore the boundaries of the spreadsheet paradigm. Journal of Functional Programming 11(2), 155–206 (2001)
2. Chudnovskyy, O., Nestler, T., Gaedke, M., Daniel, F., Ignacio, J.: End-User- Oriented Telco Mashups: The OMELETTE Approach. In: WWW 2012 Companion, pp. 235–238 (2012)
3. Dinmore, M.: Documenting problem-solving knowledge: Proposed annotation design guidelines and their application to spreadsheet tools. In: Proceedings of EuSpRIG 2009, pp. 57–68 (2009)
4. Imran, M., Soi, S., Kling, F., Daniel, F., Casati, F., Marchese, M.: On the systematic development of domain-specific mashup tools for end users. In: Brambilla, M., Tokuda, T., Tolksdorf, R. (eds.) ICWE 2012. LNCS, vol. 7387, pp. 291–298. Springer, Heidelberg (2012)
5. Isaksson, E., Palmer, M.: Usability and inter-widget communication in PLEs. In: Proceedings of MUPPLE 2010 (2010)
6. Ko, A., Myers, B.: Designing the whyline: a debugging interface for asking questions about program behavior. In: Proceedings of CHI 2004, vol. 6, pp. 151–158 (2004)
7. Lieberman, H.: Your Wish is My Command: Programming By Example (Interactive Technologies). Morgan Kaufmann (2001)
8. Lizcano, D., Soriano, J., Reyes, M., Hierro, J.J.: A user-centric approach for developing and deploying service front-ends in the future internet of services. International Journal of Web and Grid Services 5, 155–191 (2009)
9. Myers, B., Pane, J., Ko, A.: Natural Programming Languages and Environments. Communications of the ACM 47(9), 47–52 (2004)

10. Namoun, A., Nestler, T., De Angeli, A.: Service Composition for Nonprogrammers: Prospects, Problems, and Design Recommendations. In: Proceedings of ECOWS 2010, pp. 123–130. IEEE (December 2010)
11. Pietschmann, S., Voigt, M., Meißner, K.: Rich communication patterns for mashups. In: Brambilla, M., Tokuda, T., Tolksdorf, R. (eds.) ICWE 2012. LNCS, vol. 7387, pp. 315–322. Springer, Heidelberg (2012)
12. Rümpel, A., Radeck, C., Blichmann, G., Lorz, A., Meißner, K.: Towards do-ityourself development of composite web applications. In: Proceedings of ITS 2011, pp. 330–332 (2011)
13. The OMELETTE Project (FP7/2010-2013 GA n 257635). D7.4 - evaluations of demonstrators report. Public deliverable (2013), http://goo.gl/oOJFG
14. Wilson, A., Burnett, M., Beckwith, L., Granatir, O., Casburn, L., Cook, C., Durham, M., Rothermel, G.: Harnessing curiosity to increase correctness in end-user programming. In: Proceedings of CHI 2003, pp. 305–312 (2003)

Heuristic Role Detection
of Visual Elements of Web Pages

M. Elgin Akpınar[1] and Yeliz Yeşilada[2]

[1] Middle East Technical University, Ankara, Turkey
[2] Middle East Technical University Northern Cyprus Campus,
Kalkanlı, Güzelyurt, Mersin 10, Turkey
{elgin.akpinar,yyeliz}@metu.edu.tr

Abstract. Web pages are typically designed for visual interaction – they include many visual elements to guide the reader. However, when they are accessed in alternative forms such as in audio, these elements are not available and therefore they become inaccessible. This paper presents our ontology-based heuristic approach that automatically identifies visual elements of web pages and their roles. Our architecture has three major components: 1. automatic identification of visual elements of web pages, 2. automatic generation of heuristics as Jess rules from an ontology and 3. application of these heuristic rules to web pages for automatic annotation of visual elements and their roles. This paper first explains our architecture in detail and then presents our both technical and user evaluations of the proposed approach and architecture. Our technical evaluation shows that complexity is an important performance factor in role detection and our user evaluation shows that our proposed system has around 80% receptive accuracy, but the proposed knowledge base could be further improved for better accuracy.

Keywords: Web Accessibility, Knowledge Engineering, Ontology, Heuristics, Rule Engine, User Study.

1 Introduction

Web pages are typically designed for visual interaction, including many visual elements to guide the reader. As web technologies develop, they enable developers to create more unique and technically sophisticated web pages. However, far too little attention has been paid to accessibility issues. When pages are accessed in alternative forms such as in audio with assistive technologies, these visual elements are not available and therefore web pages become inaccessible.

In order to provide better accessibility, having deep understanding of the structure of web pages along with the role of visual elements is important. Once we identify the role of visual elements, these roles can be used to transcode the page by removing unnecessary elements or reorganise the page structure to improve the accessibility not only for disabled people but also for small screen device users. Furthermore, such understanding could also be used in improving the accuracy of information retrieval and data mining [1], better presenting pages for small screen devices [2, 3], or designing better intelligent user interfaces [4]. However, due to the flexible syntax of HTML and CSS,

F. Daniel, P. Dolog, and Q. Li (Eds.): ICWE 2013, LNCS 7977, pp. 123–131, 2013.

developers can create the same visual layout with different underlying coding, which means automating the role identification can be a challenging task [5]. There exist studies that propose a range of roles for visual elements, but the approaches tend to be simplistic and there is no work that provides a deep understanding of visual elements (Section 2). Some standards such as ARIA from W3C [6], and HTML5 do provide much stronger and better list of roles, but they still do not cover deep understanding of the visual elements of web pages.

This paper presents our ontology-based heuristic approach that automatically identifies visual elements of web pages and their roles (Section 3). It proposes an ontology that captures detailed knowledge about visual elements and presents an architecture with three main components. First of all, visual elements are automatically identified by using both the visual rendering and the underlying source code and a visual elements tree is generated. Then, heuristics are generated as rules from our ontology. Due to the flexible nature of HTML and CSS, we cannot fully and absolutely describe objects and their definite properties and do direct reasoning with the ontology over the visual elements. To address this problem, a probabilistic approach was constructed, in which, a visual element may accomplish all of the requirements of a heuristic role, or it may satisfy a set of properties of the role. The more attributes of a role a visual element satisfies, the more likely that the visual element has the corresponding role. Therefore, the proposed ontology describes the roles and their properties, which is then converted to rules. Finally, these heuristic-based rules are applied to visual elements for automatic annotation of their roles, generating a visual element tree with role assignments. Technical and user evaluations are also produced to validate the proposed approach and architecture (Section 4).

2   Related Work

There are different approaches for automatically identifying visual elements (some refers to them as segments or blocks) and discovering their roles [5] in different fields to serve different purpose.

Role identification has been proposed to better adapt web pages for small screen devices [2, 3, 7, 8]. Proposed roles tend to be simple lists which include roles such as lists content, related links, navigation and support, advertisement, etc. As opposed to these simple lists, Chen et al. [9] introduce a very comprehensive model called Function-Based Object model which hierarchically categorises objects as basic and composite objects. Even though the proposed model is very comprehensive, it does not take into account how an end-user would understand and use a web page.

Creating intelligent user interfaces also require good understanding of web page structures, meaning that it can more intelligently displayed on different devices and systems. Xiang and Shi [4] only proposes two kinds of visual elements: nontext blocks (buttons, images, inputs, etc) and text blocks. This simplistic approach does not provide a deep understanding of web page elements.

Role detection has also been explored for information retrieval and web data mining [1, 10–13]. Proposed roles include informative and redundant content blocks, heading, subtitle, paragraph, data, etc. Web accessibility is another field where role identification has been explored. Takagi et al. [14] proposes the following roles for

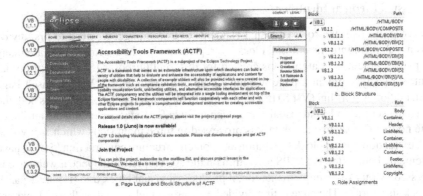

Fig. 1. The Home Page of ACTF

fragments: proper content, updated index, general index, norole, header, footer, advertisement, delete, layout table. Even though this looks like a comprehensive list, there still some roles that are missing. These roles also give the impression they were created to only guide the transcoding rather than semantically describing a web page.

In brief, discovering roles of visual elements of web pages is an important task in many fields. Even though, different research refers to different roles of visual elements, unfortunately, existing research typically focus on a small set of roles and there is no work that provides a deep understanding of visual elements.

3   Ontology Based Heuristic Role Detection

Our work aims to address the shortcomings and limitations of the existing work and provide a knowledge base that includes detailed information about visual elements of web pages and their properties. In our previous work, an ontology was created called "WAfA (Web Authoring for Accessibility)" [15] to capture knowledge about visual elements which has been mainly used to annotate web pages manually [16] such that it can be used to re-engineer web pages for better accessibility for visually disabled people [17, 18]. However, there has been no work on automatically processing a web page to identify the roles specified in WAfA Ontology. The overall architecture of our proposed system to automate the process has the following components:

1. *Visual element identifier* takes a web page and uses its visual presentation and source code to automatically divide it into visual elements in a tree structure.
2. *Rule generator* component takes our knowledge base, implemented in an OWL ontology and generates heuristic rules for visual elements.
3. *Role detector* component takes rules and tree of visual elements, generated by our first component and returns a labeled tree of visual elements.

Our system has been implemented on the Accessibility Tools Framework (ACTF) of Eclipse Foundation[1].

---

[1] http://www.eclipse.org/actf/

3.1 Visual Element Identifier

In order to discover the roles of visual elements in a web page, we need to first divide a given web page into meaningful blocks to represent visual elements. There are many web page segmentation algorithms created for different purposes [5, 19–21]. In order to automatically segment a page, we have used and extended the Vision Based Page Segmentation Algorithm (VIPS) [5]. Compared to other approaches, VIPS uses both the underlying source code and visual cues which include font, size, color and tag attributes of the nodes. The segmentation task is processed in three main steps which are: visual block extraction, visual block separation and content structure construction [5]. We have implemented our extended VIPS algorithm on the ACTF platform. Once a web page is processed by our VIPS implementation, it produces a visual block tree (Figure 1 part b - "block structure"). The page is first divided into large blocks and then these blocks are further divided into a smaller blocks. In our implementation, the visual element identifier generates a tree visual elements and for each visual element an XPATH is also created.

3.2 Rule Generator

WAfA Ontology was created to capture shared understanding of visual elements of web pages [15]. Even though, WAfA is a very rich knowledge resource, our initial experiments with WAfA showed that, the characteristics of the concepts described in WAfA are too specific; therefore, automating the process based on such definitions may have resulted in false positive role assignments. Therefore, WAfA Ontology was selected as the base ontology and a new ontology, named as eMine Ontology [2], has been developed to be used for automated role detection.

Knowledge Representation. In order to systematically characterise the roles of visual elements and their properties, popular web pages, long-tail pages and also popular web pages from different genres listed in Alexa have been investigated and analysed. In these investigations, it was observed that the following properties are affecting how visual elements are used and presented: 1. underlying tag (HTML/HTML5 or ARIA [6]), 2. children and parent elements in the underlying DOM tree, size of the element, 3. border and background color of the element, 4. position of the element, 5. some attributes including onclick, for, onmouseover, etc., 6. CSS Styles (font-size, color, etc.) of the elements, 7. some specific keywords which appear in the textual content and in the id, class, src, background-image attributes of the element. In Figure 1, VB.1.1.1 represents a *Header* block. *Header* blocks are generally placed at the top of the page and contains a *Logo*, *Search Engine* or *Menu* block. In general use, HTML tag of a *Header* block is either header or div. Also some specific keywords such as 'header' or 'hdr' occur in their id or class attributes. It is possible to extend these characteristics.

The eMine ontology consists of two main classes: atom and chunk. All roles are defined as subclasses of either atom or chunk classes. In order to extend the coverage of the roles given originally in WAfA, eMine Ontology was also compared to ARIA Ontology [6], and similarities and differences between them were identified. After this analysis, some concepts were also introduced to eMine Ontology from ARIA.

---

[2] http://emine.ncc.metu.edu.tr/ontology/emine.owl

We mainly followed an iterative approach to develop this ontology. With the initial experiments, we have noticed that object properties are required to be classified. This classification takes in two parts. The first classification is between the object properties, so that, object properties which affect the decision more than other properties have higher factor values. The second classification is in the values of object properties. In this classification, three levels of object properties for each attribute are defined. For example, must_have_tag, has_tag and may_have_tag were required where must_have_tag has the highest factor value and may_have_tag has the lowest factor. In manual evaluation, it was observed that this kind of enhancement gave more accurate results.

The ontology was parsed and processed to construct heuristic rules to apply on visual elements. After retrieving all roles and their properties from the ontology, they were converted to Jess rules in appropriate syntax and saved in a local CLP file for later use in role detection [22].

3.3 Role Detector

For detecting the roles of visual elements, Jess which is a Java based rule engine and scripting environment, is used [22]. The reason of using Jess is that it provides a rule engine to assert the visual elements and fire a set of rules on asserted elements. After a web page is segmented to its visual elements, each element in the tree was accepted as an individual. Each individual visual element was converted to facts in Jess rule engine. The collection of the facts, is called working memory. Every fact has a template, which defines its name and the set of its slots. These slots keep the attributes of a fact, in this case, the visual element attributes corresponding to the object properties in the ontology.

In order to detect the heuristic role of a visual element, following process is applied: First of all, a rule engine object is created. By loading the CLP file into the working memory of the engine, block template for facts and likelihood scores for each role were constructed in the memory. Likelihood scores are defined as global variables, and initially set to 0. Then, a set of heuristic rules, which are called defrules, are defined. These rules are based on the object properties of roles in ontology. Following statement illustrates a rule definition for the role given for a Header block:

```
(defrule Header00 (block (has_child $? /.*logo.*/ $?))
            => (bind ?*Header* (+ "2" ?*Header*)))
```

The first part after rule name denotes which object type the rule applies and in which condition it is fired. In this example, rule is applied on block objects and it is fired if visual element contains a *Logo*. Second part, which comes after '=>' operator, denotes the action if the visual element satisfies the required condition in the first part. In this example, the likelihood score for *Header* is incremented by 2, which is the value of factor annotation for this rule.

Template definition, global variables and defrules are stored in the CLP file and they are all generated by using the eMine ontology. Facts which will be asserted to the rule engine, are based on the visual elements of segmented web pages and they are constructed in each program execution. This assertion and firing process is repeated for each block in the web page. After each iteration, visual element tree is updated to represent assigned role to visual elements. Figure 1 (part c - "role assignments") shows how the tree of visual element is annotated with the roles. For example, VB.1.1.1 is labelled as *Header*.

4 Evaluation

In order to validate our proposed approach, we have conducted both technical and user evaluations. Technical evaluation mainly investigates the performance and the user evaluation investigates how people perceive the role of visual elements, and how good is our system in identifying the perceived roles automatically.

User Evaluation. Our user evaluation[3] was conducted online to reach more with diverse backgrounds. The procedure followed in the survey included four main parts: 1. included an overview page with some information about the anonymity and the tasks to be completed. 2. collected some demographics information about participants, e.g., gender, experience in web design, education, age range, etc. 3. included a web page in different levels of segmentation, and participants were asked to rate and rank these levels. 4. Based on the best level they have chosen, they were asked to assign roles to the visual segments in that level. The participants were provided a list of roles in our knowledge base; however, if the participants could not find the proper role in the list, they also had the chance of entering the role in free form text. In overall, the survey application was designed to repeat the last two steps for randomly selected nine pages.

Table 1. Accuracy and Performance Results

Complexity Group	System-Expert Evaluation (%)	Receptive Evaluation (%)	Total Memory (KB)	Total Time (ms)	Avr. Memory per Block (KB)	Avr. Time per Block (ms)	Block Count
Low Comp.	79.82	73.68	8,369	6,576	244.29	102.29	65
Medium Comp.	88.28	79.77	7,013	23,799	36.44	102.12	237
High Comp.	88.47	85.53	9,165	54,837	34.28	101.95	569
Overall	86.83	80.82	8,176	29,157	100.20	102.11	298

The complete survey was designed to include nine randomly chosen web pages from a group of 30. In order to choose these 30 pages, we have investigated the complexity of top 100 web from Alexa by using the Visual Complexity Rankings and Accessibility Metrics (VICRAM) framework [23], which assigns a Visual Complexity Score (VCS) for a given page. For 100 pages, we calculated their VCS and grouped these pages into three: low complexity ($VCS < 3$); medium complexity ($3 \leq VCS \leq 7$); and high complexity ($VCS > 7$). We randomly selected 10 pages from each complexity level by grouping these pages based on their VCS. Moreover, ramdom page selection algorithm was designed to select at least one page from all complexity levels in three pages.

Technical Evaluation. With a technical evaluation, we have mainly investigated the technical feasibility of the proposed approach and implementation in the ACTF platform. We checked the performance characterised in terms of total memory usage, time elapsed for role detection of complete pages and total number of blocks calculated. The technical evaluation has been performed on a machine which has following features: Intel®Core™2 Duo CPU T9600 @ 2.80 GHz processor, 2.071.34 MB memory, NVIDIA GeForce GT 220M videocard and Windows 7 32 Bit operating system.

---

[3] http://emine.ncc.metu.edu.tr/eval/survey/

4.1 Results

In this section, we present the preliminary analysis of our results based on the data collected in two weeks after the survey was announced. In overall, of 220 participants, only 25 of them have completed at least three pages, provided that, they evaluated at least one page from each complexity level. Of our 25 participants, 10 were female and 15 were male. 7 participants were aged between 18-24, 8 of them were 25-34, 8 of them were 25-54 and 2 of them were aged over 55. 5 participants completed high/secondary school, 2 completed associate's degree, 6 completed bachelor's degree, 7 completed master's degree and 5 completed doctorate. 18 participants have worked in web design and development, 4 of them studied this subject and 3 of them are interested in web design as a hobby. 7 participants describe their level of expertise in web design and development as professional, 13 as intermediate and 5 as novice/beginner. All of the participants use internet daily.

In overall, 1,946 role assignments have been made and 1,458 were considered in our evaluation as valid assignments since their assigners satisfied the minimum requirement of labelling at least three pages. 232 roles assigned to low complexity pages, 580 to medium complexity pages and 646 to high complexity pages. Analyzing the assignments, we have noticed that there were disagreements between our participants. In order to eliminate this, we have applied majority rule to decide about the role assigned. When majority rule applied, %32.58 of the assignments had more than %50 of agreement.

Table 1 presents both performance results and accuracy results obtained from the preliminary analysis of the data collected from the participants. The success rate of each complexity group and overall result was calculated proportional to the number of visual segments evaluated in each page. System - Expert evaluation consists of the comparison of the system results and expert responses with respect to the concept described in the ontology. As can be seen from this table, in overall the system has an accuracy of 86.83% accuracy. Strict string comparison between the roles assigned by the system and participants gave us an average of 28.86% (low complexity pages - 26.32%, medium complexity - 28.99% and high complexity - 29.92%) accuracy. This is mainly because participants use slightly different versions of the role text to label visual elements. Therefore, we have manually analyzed the role assignments given by our participants and compared them with our system assignments. These results shown as "receptive evaluation" in Table 1. In overall, the accuracy rate is 80.82%.

Although, performance results presented in Table 1 is specific to our configuration of test machine, they still provide significant information about the overall performance. Total memory usage and time elapsed in role detection process of a whole page and a single block are given with the average block count for each complexity level.

4.2 Discussion

Our receptive evaluation shows that our proposed system has more than 80% accuracy rate; however, when we do strict string comparison this accuracy becomes around 30%. Moreover, majority rule application to the data collected from participants shows that, only %32.58 of the role assignments have the majority of participants' agreements.This could be explained by different reasons. First of all, people were not asked to complete tasks and they were just shown screenshots. Task specification could affect the role assignments. Furthermore, in our survey, we have explicitly asked participants to check the underlying source code of web pages and associated CSS files by providing links to the pages. Nevertheless, participants may not have analysed the DOM structure or interacted with segments; their overall assessment may have been formed only on the visual representation of the segments. One unanticipated finding from this evaluation was that, although we asked participants to choose only one role in our survey, some blocks have more than one role in page layout or they are combinations of different sub-blocks which have different roles. While some participants tend to assign multiple roles, many of them selected only one of them, omitting the remaining meaningful roles.

Average time elapsed for role detection of a single block has close values in each complexity level and total time is proportional to the number of blocks in the page. Total memory consumed for a page has close values for each complexity group, showing that, larger amount of the memory consumed for shared resources. Therefore, average memory consumed decreases while the number of blocks increases.

In summary, the results of this study suggest that, the roles of visual segments in web pages may differ with respect to the aim of usage and user point of view, since, the majority rule applies only on a small portion of the role assignments. Moreover, this study can be used to improve our knowledge base, by extending the role set according to responses of the participants.

5   Conclusion

This paper presented an ontology-based heuristic approach to automatically identify visual elements in a web page and their roles. This approach relies on a probabilistic model, in which, the role of the visual element is detected based on the number of its attributes which satisfy the requirements of a role. The proposed system consists of a visual element identifier, a knowledge base and a role detector module.

The proposed approach was evaluated with technical performance and user evaluations. According to results in performance evaluation, response time is related to the complexity of the page, while memory consumption is independent of the complexity if shared resources are used. In order to measure the accuracy of the system, an online survey based user evaluation was performed which shows that our proposed system has around 80% receptive accuracy; however, the proposed knowledge base could be further improved for better accuracy.

In conclusion, the research presented in this paper contributes an effective method for detecting roles of visual elements in web pages automatically by using heuristics. The findings of this research can be used in different fields including information retrieval, web accessibility, intelligent web user interfaces, web page transcoding or data mining. Proposed approach also provides a modifiable knowledge base to adapt changing web design trends and task specific applications.

References

1. Kovacevic, M., Diligenti, M., Gori, M., Milutinovic, V.: Recognition of common areas in a web page using visual information: a possible application in a page classification. In: ICDM 2002, pp. 250–257. IEEE Computer Society, Washington, DC (2002)

2. Yin, X., Lee, W.S.: Understanding the function of web elements for mobile content delivery using random walk models. In: WWW 2005, pp. 1150–1151. ACM (2005)
3. Chen, Y., Xie, X., Ma, W.Y., Zhang, H.J.: Adapting web pages for small-screen devices. IEEE Internet Computing 9(1), 50–56 (2005)
4. Xiang, P., Shi, Y.: Recovering semantic relations from web pages based on visual cues. In: IUI 2006, pp. 342–344. ACM (2006)
5. Cai, D., Yu, S., Wen, J.R., Ma, W.Y.: Vips: a vision based page segmentation algorithm, MSR-TR-2003-79, Microsoft Research (2003)
6. Craig, J., Cooper, M.: Accessible rich internet applications (WAI-ARIA) 1.0 (2010), http://www.w3.org/TR/2010/WD-wai-aria-20100916/complete (retrieved on January 15, 2013)
7. Ahmadi, H., Kong, J.: Efficient web browsing on small screens. In: AVI 2008, pp. 23–30. ACM (2008)
8. Xiao, Y., Tao, Y., Li, W.: A dynamic web page adaptation for mobile device based on web2.0. In: ASEA 2008, pp. 119–122. IEEE Computer Society, USA (2008)
9. Chen, J., Zhou, B., Shi, J., Zhang, H., Fengwu, Q.: Function-based object model towards website adaptation. In: WWW 2001, pp. 587–596. ACM (2001)
10. Lin, S.H., Ho, J.M.: Discovering informative content blocks from web documents. In: SIGKDD 2002, pp. 588–593. ACM (2002)
11. Burget, R., Rudolfova, I.: Web page element classification based on visual features. In: ACI-IDS 2009, pp. 67–72 (April 2009)
12. Liu, B., Chin, C.W., Ng, H.T.: Mining topic-specific concepts and definitions on the web. In: WWW 2003, pp. 251–260. ACM (2003)
13. Yi, L., Liu, B., Li, X.: Eliminating noisy information in web pages for data mining. In: SIGKDD 2003, pp. 296–305. ACM (2003)
14. Takagi, H., Asakawa, C., Fukuda, K., Maeda, J.: Site-wide annotation: reconstructing existing pages to be accessible. In: SIGACCESS 2002, pp. 81–88. ACM (2002)
15. Harper, S., Yesilada, Y.: Web authoring for accessibility (WAfA). JWS 5(3), 175–179 (2007)
16. Yesilada, Y., Harper, S., Goble, C., Stevens, R.: Screen readers cannot see. In: Koch, N., Fraternali, P., Wirsing, M. (eds.) ICWE 2004. LNCS, vol. 3140, pp. 445–458. Springer, Heidelberg (2004)
17. Plessers, P., Casteleyn, S., Yesilada, Y., Troyer, O.D., Stevens, R., Harper, S., Goble, C.: Accessibility: A web engineering approach. In: WWW 2005, Chiba, Japan, pp. 353–362 (2005)
18. Yesilada, Y., Stevens, R., Harper, S., Goble, C.: Evaluating DANTE: Semantic transcoding for visually disabled users. ACM TOCHI 14(3) (2007)
19. Alcic, S., Conrad, S.: Page segmentation by web content clustering. In: WIMS 2011, pp. 24:1–24:9. ACM (2011)
20. Kohlschütter, C., Nejdl, W.: A densitometric approach to web page segmentation. In: CIKM 2008, pp. 1173–1182. ACM (2008)
21. Yu, S., Cai, D., Wen, J.R., Ma, W.Y.: Improving pseudo-relevance feedback in web information retrieval using web page segmentation. In: WWW 2003, pp. 11–18. ACM (2003)
22. Friedman-Hill, E.: Jess the rule engine for the java platform (2008), http://herzberg.ca.sandia.gov/ (retrieved on November 27, 2012)
23. Michailidou, E.: ViCRAM: Visual Complexity Rankings and Accessibility Metrics. PhD thesis (2010)

Performance-Aware Design
of Web Application Front-Ends

Dennis Westermann[1], Jens Happe[1],
Petr Zdrahal[2], Martin Moser[2], and Ralf Reussner[3]

[1] SAP Research, Karlsruhe, Germany
{dennis.westermann,jens.happe}@sap.com
[2] SAP AG, Walldorf, Germany
{petr.zdrahal,martin.moser}@sap.com
[3] Karlsruhe Institute of Technology (KIT), Karlsruhe, Germany
reussner@kit.edu

Abstract. The responsiveness of web applications directly affects customer satisfaction and, as a consequence, business-critical metrics like revenue and conversion rates. However, building web applications with low response times is a challenging task. The heterogeneity of browsers and client devices as well as the complexity of today's web applications lead to high development and test efforts. Measuring front-end performance requires a deep understanding of measurement tools and techniques as well as a lot of manual effort. With our approach, developers and designers can assess front-end performance for different scenarios without measuring. We use prediction models derived by a series of automated, systematic experiments to give early feedback about the expected performance. Our approach predicts the front-end performance of real-world web applications with an average error of 11% across all major browsers.

1 Introduction

Recent industrial studies [4] show that the responsiveness of web applications directly affects customer satisfaction and, as a consequence, business-critical metrics like revenue and conversion rates. Guidelines on how to optimize front-end performance, such as those published in the books of Steve Souders [7,8], are very popular among web developers. Also, tools like WebPageTest [2] or YSlow [3] are more and more adopted to support the implementation of performance best practices and to help identifying performance problems. For the development of web-based enterprise applications, companies often rely on JavaScript libraries that provide a uniform appearance, as well as a set of UI elements and utility functions commonly used in this kind of applications. Besides the classical challenges addressed by the guidelines and tools mentioned before, UI developers and designers need to evaluate the impact of the design of a screen on front-end performance. This involves questions like „How many columns and rows can I add to a table of type X in my web application without violating performance requirements?"or „What is the impact of backend call Y on front-end

F. Daniel, P. Dolog, and Q. Li (Eds.): ICWE 2013, LNCS 7977, pp. 132–139, 2013.

performance?". Theoretically, these questions could also be answered with the existing performance measurement and analysis tools. However, practically the effort for applying measurement-based approaches to these kind of questions is too high, which hinders the flexible, performance-aware construction and evaluation of screen designs. Moreover, the development of a screen's design is usually conducted before the screen is actually implemented (e.g., using wireframe or mockup tools). As a consequence, early performance feedback (prior to implementation) is essential to drive the deployment of fast web applications [5].

In this paper, we present an approach that enables performance-aware design of web application front-ends. Our main contribution is a methodology that allows performance experts to efficiently derive prediction models for UI libraries. These models can, for example, be integrated in design tools in order to give early performance feedback to the large amount of designers and developers that use the library. To get the early feedback about the expected front-end performance of their design, developers neither need to implement the web application, nor do they need to conduct performance measurements.

The main challenge in deriving the performance prediction models is to deal with the huge design space that is spanned by a UI library. To overcome this challenge, we build on the results of our previous research on automated performance evaluation experiments [9,10] and propose an experiment-based prediction model construction process. In our case study, we evaluated the impact of different screen design alternatives on front-end performance for applications developed with the JavaScript library SAP UI5 [1]. Based on the experiment results, we derived a set of assumptions and heuristics and developed a prediction model that allows estimating the impact of screen designs on performance for three major browsers (Internet Explorer, Chrome, and Firefox). While the experiment results and the prediction model are specific for the SAP UI5 library, we also describe our systematic process that can be applied for the efficient construction of such prediction models in other scenarios.

We validate our approach by comparing predictions to measurements using screens of two real-world enterprise web applications. Both have been developed with the SAP UI5 library. The results show that we can predict the front-end performance for the screens of these applications with an average prediction error of 11% across all studied browsers.

2   Prediction Model

The performance prediction model introduced in this section quantifies the relationship between the construction of SAP UI5 based web application screens and the browser CPU time consumed by the screens in different browsers. Moreover, we outline a process that allows to derive such a model efficiently.

Based on the results of a set of upstream experiments, we define the following assumptions and heuristics:

- The browser CPU time is a stable metric to describe front-end performance costs of a web application. Moreover it abstracts from influences that are hard to control such as network latency.
- The browser CPU time consumed to process different UI element types is additive (i.e., there is no interdependency between control types).
- The browser CPU time differs significantly between different UI element types.
- The properties of complex control types can significantly contribute to the browser CPU time consumed to process a UI element.
- The placement of UI elements on a screen does not have a significant effect on CPU time (at least if the nesting level stays in a reasonable range).

Utilizing these assumptions and heuristics, we define a performance prediction model as well as a process to derive a concrete instance of this prediction model for SAP UI5.

If a screen S of a web application consists of the UI elements $e_1, ..., e_n$, we write: $S = e_1 \cdot ... \cdot e_n$ where $\cdot$ denotes the composition of UI elements (e.g. a screen that consists of tables, buttons, and text fields). Hence, when a UI developer creates a screen S, he evaluates $e_1 \cdot ... \cdot e_n$. We assume this composition as associative and commutative (i.e., the UI elements can be arbitrarily placed on the screen).

Furthermore, we define $\phi(S)$ as the front-end performance of screen S which is in our case expressed as the browser CPU time consumed to load the full screen. Following the additivity and placement assumptions, we state that the performance of the UI element composition is the sum of the performance values of the individual UI elements $(\phi(e_1), ..., \phi(e_n))$ and a constant offset (ϵ_S).

$$\phi(S) = \phi(e_1 \cdot ... \cdot e_n) + \epsilon_S = \phi(e_1) + ... + \phi(e_n) + \epsilon_S \qquad (1)$$

The offset ϵ_S describes the browser CPU time consumed to load an empty screen. This includes for example the CPU time required to load the UI libraries and the CSS files (i.e. all components of a screen that are independent of a certain UI element).

Depending on its properties $p_1, ..., p_k$ (e.g., number of columns and rows of a table), a UI element e yields different front-end performance characteristics. We estimate the performance value of UI element e as

$$\phi_{type}(p_1, ..., p_k) \qquad (2)$$

In order to derive an instance of such a prediction model for the SAP UI5 library and the three major browsers, we developed a systematic process. The process is implemented in a set of automatically executable experiments. Having this set of automatically executable experiments has the benefits that (i) the manual effort to create a model instance is limited to a minimum (i) the model instance can be easily updated for new browser or UI library versions and (iii) the procedure can be reused to derive model instances in similar setups.

In the following, we give a detailed description of the process and demonstrate how we implemented this process.

Deriving the Screen Offset (ϵ_S):   As a first step, we determine the CPU time consumed by the browser to process the basic screen layout in which we place the different UI element types for our experiments. Therefore, we define and run an experiment that measures an empty screen. As a result we get the ϵ_S for the three browsers: $\epsilon_{S_{CH}} = 300ms$ | $\epsilon_{S_{FF}} = 420ms$ | $\epsilon_{S_{IE}} = 290ms$

Analyzing UI Element Types: To deal with the vast amount of UI element types, we group them in simple types and complex types. As simple types we define those UI elements with a performance cost per instance of less than 5 ms. For these elements, we do not conduct a detailed evaluation of the properties. Instead, we just determine a general fixed performance value for each instance of a UI element type that is considered as simple. Examples for such simple UI element types in our study are buttons, text views, or labels and the performance value per instance that we assigned to this group is 2 ms. Hence, we estimate the performance value of a simple UI element with the function: $\phi_{simple}() = 2 \times \#simpleUIelements$. That value is approximated based on a small set of experiments. We use the same value for all three browsers as we did not observe a significant difference between the browsers for processing these kind of UI elements.

The complex UI element types are those that significantly contribute to the browser CPU time when added to a screen. Examples for such UI element types are tables, service calls and row repeaters. For these UI element types, we run two experiment series. In the first series of experiments, we determine which property of the UI element significantly influences the browser CPU time. And in the second series, we derive $\phi_{type}(p_1, \ldots, p_k)$ for those properties that are considered as performance-relevant. To determine the performance-relevant properties in the first series of experiments, we apply standard statistical designs such as *One-at-a-Time* or *Plackett-Burman* designs in combination with statistical correlation analysis methods. The selection of the actual design is based on the size of the parameter space spanned by the number of UI element properties and their potential values. As an example, for the table UI element type, the number of columns (#cols) and rows (#rows) have been identified as the only performance-relevant properties. With the second series of experiments we aim at quantifying the relationship between the different manifestations of a table (combinations of #cols and #rows), and the browser CPU time (*CPUtime*). If we set the possible value ranges for the two variables in this example to #rows : 1..20 and #cols : 1..20, we run into the curse of dimensionality and even for this small example it would take $20 * 20 = 400$ experiments to measure the complete space. In our setup, this would mean that we would have to measure one week to determine only this relationship for the three browsers. To reduce the number of required experiments we apply advanced statistical inference approaches [10] that automatically determine which experiments to execute in order to get an accurate prediction function. As a result we get a multi-dimensional regression function such as the one outlined below (derived for Firefox).

$$CPUtime_{FF} = 584 + 30 * max(0; \#cols - 5) - 33 * max(0; 5 - \#cols)$$
$$+ 25 * max(0; \#rows - 5) - 29 * max(0; 5 - \#rows) \quad (3)$$

Deriving this function for a single browser takes approx. 2-8 hours depending on the complexity of the underlying function. Limiting the number of experiments by manually restricting the potential space is also a possible approach that can be sufficient for simple functions but implies a higher risk that important combinations have not been measured [10].

In order to predict any combination of table manifestations on a screen, we proceed as follows: We subtract the offset of a blank screen ($\epsilon_{S_{FF}} = 420$) from the function outlined in Equation 4 in order to remove this offset from the estimation. We use the resulting function as the implementation of $\phi_{type}(p_1, \ldots, p_k)$. Thus, we estimate the Firefox browser CPU time for the UI element type *table* with the following function:

$$\phi_{table}(\#cols, \#rows)_{FF} = 164 + 30 * max(0; \#cols_i - 5) - 33 * max(0; 5 - \#cols_i)$$
$$+ 25 * max(0; \#rows_i - 5) - 29 * max(0; 5 - \#rows_i) \quad (4)$$

Construct Prediction Model Instance. Once all components of the prediction model instance are determined they can be composed according to Equation 1 in order to predict the browser CPU time for a screen S. For example:

$$\phi(S)_{FF} = \epsilon_S + \phi_{simple}()_{FF}$$
$$+ \phi_{table}(\#cols, \#rows)_{FF} + \phi_{jsoncall}(datasize)_{FF} + \ldots \quad (5)$$

For our study, we derived a prediction model that contains most of the simple and complex UI element types used in enterprise applications built with SAP UI5.

Validate Prediction Model. The constructed prediction model instance is an abstraction of the real behaviour that is based on assumptions, heuristics and statistical inference. Hence, it has to be validated that the estimated performance values sufficiently reflect the behaviour of the real screens. In the following section, we validate our prediction model as well as the prediction model instances that we derived for the SAP UI5 library and the three browsers.

3   Validation and Discussion

The goal of our validation is to judge prediction accuracy and thus the utility of our heuristics and the practicability of our approach. Therefore, we compare our predictions with actual performance measurements. We selected twelve real-world pages built with the SAP UI5 library. Six pages are taken from demo applications. These pages cover a broad spectrum of different manifestations of the two most important control types in business applications. The other six pages are taken from a real application called Networking Lunch which is a social enterprise application where people can search for other people interested in the same topic and setup a joint lunch meeting.

3.1 Results

In Figure 1(a) we show the results for the twelve validation screens. The average prediction error across all screens and browsers is 11%. For 72% of the predictions, the relative prediction error is less than 15% and there is only one real outlier with an error higher than 30%. The predictions for Chrome (8% average error) and Firefox (7% average error) have been better than those for Internet Explorer (18% average error). Between the two applications, we could not observe a general difference with respect to prediction accuracy (average error for both applications is 11%).

	Chrome				Firefox				InternetExplorer			
Page	Measured	Predicted	Abs. Error	Rel. Error	Measured	Predicted	Abs. Error	Rel. Error	Measured	Predicted	Abs. Error	Rel. Error
nwlunch1	944 ms	1024 ms	80 ms	8%	905 ms	983 ms	78 ms	9%	663 ms	733 ms	70 ms	10%
nwlunch2	1107 ms	1147 ms	40 ms	4%	1060 ms	1135 ms	75 ms	7%	811 ms	805 ms	-6 ms	1%
nwlunch3	1233 ms	1119 ms	-114 ms	9%	1178 ms	1129 ms	-49 ms	4%	1357 ms	794 ms	-563 ms	41%
nwlunch4	960 ms	1034 ms	74 ms	8%	874 ms	984 ms	110 ms	13%	788 ms	764 ms	-24 ms	3%
nwlunch5	763 ms	938 ms	175 ms	23%	764 ms	888 ms	124 ms	16%	608 ms	603 ms	-5 ms	1%
nwlunch6	951 ms	1069 ms	118 ms	12%	960 ms	1079 ms	119 ms	12%	913 ms	729 ms	-184 ms	20%
demo1	485 ms	463 ms	-22 ms	5%	780 ms	740 ms	-40 ms	5%	453 ms	487 ms	34 ms	8%
demo2	874 ms	875 ms	1 ms	0%	1295 ms	1315 ms	20 ms	2%	780 ms	1013 ms	233 ms	30%
demo3	888 ms	880 ms	-8 ms	1%	1356 ms	1282 ms	-74 ms	5%	803 ms	1039 ms	236 ms	29%
demo4	491 ms	502 ms	11 ms	2%	811 ms	810 ms	-1 ms	0%	468 ms	584 ms	116 ms	25%
demo5	1591 ms	1858 ms	267 ms	17%	2348 ms	2641 ms	293 ms	13%	2340 ms	2900 ms	560 ms	24%
demo6	1373 ms	1460 ms	87 ms	6%	1973 ms	2009 ms	36 ms	2%	1638 ms	2079 ms	441 ms	27%

(a) Validation results.

The highest error is 41% for screen 3 of the Networking Lunch application in Internet Explorer. Although this screen has nearly the same characteristics as screen 4 (for which the error is only 3%), we underestimate the browser CPU time by 563ms. We could not yet figure out the root cause of this difference. It is interesting that we did not observe such a large deviation for this screen in the other browsers. The weaknesses in the predictions for the Internet Explorer is also visible for the demo application screens. However, for these screens we overestimate the browser CPU time. This overestimation is most likely caused by the estimation function for the odata service calls as these contribute largely to the estimated overall CPU time for the screens. Hence, we have to run further experiments to improve the regression function for odata calls in Internet Explorer.

In general, the results demonstrate that our assumptions are valid and that the introduced abstractions and heuristics do not significantly compromise the prediction accuracy.

3.2 Threats to Validity

The results presented in Section 3.1 demonstrate that our approach can accurately predict the front-end performance of enterprise web applications. However, it is important to note the threats to validity of our approach in order to understand its applicability in practice. The main restrictions we currently see are:

Small Validation Set. The screens evaluated in Section 3.1 are only part of two web applications. However, both are very different in type and front-end performance. One represents a typical enterprise web application for processing data, the other a social enterprise application. Even though the predictions complied to measurement for the case studies presented in Section 3.1, a broader set of validation scenarios is required, to ensure its general applicability.

Single Library. In our industrial case study at SAP, developers of web applications usually use only the SAP UI5 library to build a web application front-end. The library encapsulates other common JavaScript libraries. In other development environments, especially non-enterprise web application development, it is often the case that multiple libraries are combined to develop the front-end code. Moreover, additional style definitions can affect front-end performance in standard web sites [7] which could have been neglected for the enterprise web applications developed with the SAP UI5 library and the corresponding pre-defined styles. However, the experiment-based evaluation process presented in this paper, as well as the experiment automation tooling [6] can be used to efficiently derive prediction models for other libraries.

Custom JavaScript Code. Our prediction focuses on the influence of UI elements and service calls on front-end performance. This is a reasonable assumption for typical enterprise applications. However, developers often add custom JavaScript code to process data, to create new controls or to change configuration. This custom code will add to the browser CPU time and thus to front-end performance. While such custom code played only a minor role in the case studies presented in Section 3.1, it may have huge effects on front-end performance in other cases. However, our goal is to give early feedback on front-end performance, thus, we cannot consider such effects in our prediction.

Effort. The efforts necessary to implement the approach, i.e., to create and maintain the prediction models are a crucial factor for the practical applicability of the approach. These tasks should be performed by a small team of UI library and performance experts. Our experiment automation tooling [6] supports and guides the team in the course of the prediction model construction process which limits the efforts to a minimum. The decision if a software vendor wants to invest the efforts in constructing a prediction model for his libraries depends on the number of designers and developers that can benefit from the feedback provided by the models.

4   Conclusions

In this paper, we presented an approach that shifts performance evaluation efforts to a small team of UI library and performance experts. We introduced a methodology that enables the expert team to efficiently derive prediction models for UI libraries used by the development groups. The bulk of developers and designers in an organisation benefit from the model by getting early performance feedback that is, for example, integrated in design tools. The feedback allows designers and developers to evaluate the front-end performance of web applications prior to implementation. They can assess different design alternatives and chose the one with the best trade off between performance and user experience (which does not necessarily have to be a trade off).

We applied the approach at SAP by creating a prediction model for the SAP UI5 library and validated the accuracy of the model by comparing the predictions to measurements of real web application screens. We integrated the derived prediction model in an easy-to-use tool that is used by SAP UI5 developers to easily evaluate the performance of their screen designs and by performance trainers to raise the performance-awareness in developer training sessions.

In our future work, we are going to derive prediction models for web application screens that run on mobile devices. Moreover, we plan to investigate other popular JavaScript libraries.

References

1. Sap ui5: Ui development toolkit for html5,
   http://scn.sap.com/community/developer-center/front-end
   (last visited March 2013)
2. Webpagetest, http://www.webpagetest.org/ (last visited March 2013)
3. Yslow, http://developer.yahoo.com/yslow/ (last visited March 2013)
4. Bixby, J.: Web performance today,
   http://www.webperformancetoday.com/2010/07/01/
   the-best-graphs-of-velocity/
   (last visited March 2013)
5. Brad Frost. Performance as design (2013),
   http://bradfrostweb.com/blog/post/performance-as-design/
   (last visited March 2013)
6. sopeco.org. Software performance cockpit, sopeco (2013), http://sopeco.org (last visited March 2013)
7. Souders, S.: High Performance Web Sites: 14 Steps to Faster-Loading Web Sites. O'Reilly (2007)
8. Souders, S.: Even Faster Web Sites: Performance Best Practices for Web Developers. O'Reilly (2009)
9. Westermann, D., Happe, J., Hauck, M., Heupel, C.: The Performance Cockpit Approach: A Framework for Systematic Performance Evaluations. In: 36th EUROMICRO SEAA Conf., pp. 31–38. IEEE CS (2010)
10. Westermann, D., Happe, J., Krebs, R., Farahbod, R.: Automated inference of goal-oriented performance prediction functions. In: 27th IEEE/ACM Int. Conf. on Automated Software Engineering, ASE 2012, pp. 190–199. ACM, New York (2012)

CapView – Functionality-Aware Visual Mashup Development for Non-programmers

Carsten Radeck, Gregor Blichmann, and Klaus Meißner

Technische Universität Dresden, Germany
{carsten.radeck,gregor.blichmann,klaus.meissner}@tu-dresden.de

Abstract. Building mashup applications from existing web resources becomes increasingly popular, and, in theory, accessible even for end users without programming skills. Current proposals for end user development of mashups mainly focus on visual wiring of component interfaces supplemented by recommendations on composition steps and a certain degree of automation. However, it is still a major challenge to provide an appropriate level of functional abstraction in order to visualize the functionality of a mashup and its components, and for composing on a functional level instead of merely assembling structural units. This becomes crucial, especially when non-programmers are the intended target group. In this paper, we propose CapView, a novel functionality-aware development view on running composite applications. CapView is part of the EDYRA platform and provides a functional overview of the mashup by abstracting from interface and wiring details. It enables users to understand mashup development as an assembly process that is centered on the capabilities of components and mashup fragments. We evaluate the concepts in a user study and present lessons learned.

Keywords: mashup, end user development, non-programmers.

1 Introduction

Powered by the growth of available web resources and application programming interfaces, the emerging mashup paradigm enables loosely coupled components to be reused in a broad variety of application scenarios to fulfil the long tail of user needs. Thus, mashups and end user development (EUD) complement each other quite well. However, when supporting non-programmers, their limited understanding of technical concepts and experience on development practices have to be considered. In addition, it is hard for non-programmers to map their problem, for which they probably know a solution in terms of necessary tasks or activities, to a composition of components.

In order to empower non-programmers to build applications on their own, EUD tools have to fulfil several essential requirements as pointed out in the literature, e. g., [9,4]. Technical details, concepts and terminology have to be hidden from the user. Furthermore, there is a need for user guidance and automation throughout the composition procedure, for instance, recommendations

F. Daniel, P. Dolog, and Q. Li (Eds.): ICWE 2013, LNCS 7977, pp. 140–155, 2013.
© Springer-Verlag Berlin Heidelberg 2013

on composition steps and support for correctly connecting components when solving heterogeneity issues. In addition, there should be immediate feedback on a user's composition actions and, as proposed by [9], task-oriented user interfaces should be applied instead of technology-led ad hoc visualizations.

However, prevalent mashup solutions mostly build up on purely wiring component interfaces. With respect to the requirements above, we argue, that this technical view is still too complicated for end users without programming knowledge. Although wirings allow to retrace data flow, understanding what actually happens in a mashup, or what functionality recommendations offer, requires manual investigation by the user or depends on community-provided documentation. Therefore, a more abstract way of building mashup applications is required, which focuses on the functionality to achieve rather than the technical solution in terms of component interfaces and composition glue.

Thus, we propose **CapView**, a novel functionality-aware development view on (running) composite applications. It is part of the EDYRA platform, which extends CRUISe [12] concepts and allows for live sophistication of mashups. Thereby, the mashup runtime environment becomes the authoring tool, seamlessly interweaving mashup design and usage, to provide for instant feedback for end user's development actions [15]. CapView provides a functional overview of the mashup abstracting from interface and wiring details.

The CapView essentially helps non-programmers to (1) realize "components" as task-solving entities, (2) investigate functionalities provided by a mashup, by its components and by recommendations, and (3) to manipulate a mashup through visually composing component functionalities.

The **contribution** of this work are manifold:

- We present capabilities, a semantic description of component functionality, and define generic rules for deriving natural language labels from capabilities.
- We introduce the CapView supporting non-programmers with a functional abstraction of composition details when developing a mashup independently.
- We evaluate the efficiency of the CapView via a user study.

The remaining paper is structured as follows. First, we discuss related approaches in Sect. 2. Then, Sect. 3 describes the conceptual foundation of our work. We introduce CapView in Sect. 4 and show the results of our evaluation in Sect. 5. Finally, Sect. 6 summarizes the paper and outlines future work.

2   Related Work

Similar to our approach, Yahoo Pipes[1] uses a mainly data flow oriented visual wiring paradigm via drag&drop in conjunction with highlighting possible connections while creating a pipe. However, there is a hard break between development and usage, and the user has to understand data structures and technical

---

[1] http://pipes.yahoo.com/pipes/

concepts. IBM mashup center[2] allows to combine building blocks, including widgets, and to use the mashup while developing it. Connections are created through dialogues and are shown in a dedicated view, but functionality provided by components or compositions cannot be explored. Similarly, in Jackbe Presto wiring takes place via drag&drop, but the user is not supported in establishing correct or even useful connections, and in identifying transitive connections. A drawback is the required knowledge about technical interfaces of blocks and data types.

In academia, several projects have addressed some of the identified challenges of EUD for non-programmers. Similar to our approach, mashart [7] utilizes universal composition and a component model, but neglects semantic annotations. At development time, the components, their event-based composition and layout can be defined using drag&drop metaphors. Despite a preview, there is a separation between development time and run time, and the user is not supported by recommendations. ResEval Mash [8] is a mashup platform dedicated to the research evaluation domain. In a data flow oriented way, components of different type like sources or visualizations are coupled. A domain-specific appearance of those types on the modelling canvas may indicate implicit functionality, but there is no activity-based abstraction. The ServFace Builder [10] enables users to visually compose web services. Thereby, form-based front ends are generated from service descriptions. The data flow can be defined using drag&drop at development time, and is visible to the user. Again, only a technical view on the resulting application is provided. In MyCocktail[3] forms serve for configuration of components at design time, but there is no support regarding correctness while establishing connections. Understanding the functional interplay of the components is impeded by missing visualization of connections. Similar to our conceptual foundation, the FAST platform [2] utilizes semantically described components which are assembled to gadgets, so called screens. The latter can again be combined to screenflows using input/outputs. The functionality of gadgets is expressed by pre- and postconditions, rather concerning input and output than the activities provided. Yet, it lacks a smooth transition between run time and design time and the user has to be familiar with interface concepts. The Omlette Live Environment [17] provides interwoven runtime and development time. The user is supported with advice on patterns mined from existing mashups, and by automated integration of selected patterns. However, there is nothing comparable to our abstracting view and the recommended pattern are mainly visualized by the incorporated components. In line with our approach, DashMash [5] allows for manipulating a mashup during usage, and addresses similar users. However, to understand the data flow of a mashup, users have to inspect a dialog listing connections for a certain component, and establishing connections takes place on interface level. EnglishMash [1] shares a similar basic idea: abstracting from technical details through natural language. However, it provides restricted means for exploration of components' functionalities and no formal component model. DEMISA [16] proposes a task-oriented methodology to

---

[2] http://www.jackbe.com

[3] http://www.ict-romulus.eu/web/mycocktail/home

develop mashups. A task model has to be defined first which is semi-automatically transformed to an executable mashup composition. However, due to the top-down approach, there is a hard break between development and usage. Recently several proposals focus on semantic annotations, e. g. [3], and mediation, e. g. [11], for mashups. Therein, recommendations can be achieved based on semantic matching of annotations. Further, community-driven recommender systems, e. g. [6], have been proposed. We build up on similar techniques, but focus explicitly on functionality-centered visualization of recommendations.

To sum up, in current proposals, understanding the provided functionality of recommendations, components or even the mashup highly depends on mean-ingful naming and descriptions of interfaces, and is further impeded by missing highlighting of connections. Current tooling lacks task-oriented visualization and composition metaphors for running mashups. It is too interface-oriented, and, thus, features no sufficient level of abstraction for non-programmers.

3 Preliminaries

Within the EDYRA project we adhere to universal composition, which allows for platform and technology independent composition of arbitrary web resources and services [12]. This section outlines the underlying concepts of the CapView.

A declarative **composition model** defines all aspects of a mashup: compo-nents or templates for context-sensitive selection of matching components, their configuration, event-based communication, and layout [12]. For inter-component data exchange, several types of communication patterns are applicable: fire-and-forget according to the publish-subscribe paradigm via *Links*, request-response via *BackLinks*, and synchronization of properties using *PropertyLinks* [13].

In our **semantic component model**, web resources are encapsulated by black-box components. Furthermore, components with or without a UI (service components) are characterized by three abstractions, namely parametrized op-erations and events as well as properties. As a declarative descriptor implement-ing the component model, we use the Semantic Mashup Component Description Language (SMCDL) [11]. SMCDL covers non-functional properties, like qual-ity aspects and authors, and the public component interface consisting of the abstractions mentioned above, see Fig. 1. In order to specify data semantics of those interface parts, references to ontology concepts, like classes and object-properties, are annotated. Thereby, we can leverage semantic matching and me-diation techniques. To describe functional semantics in a formal, yet simple way, we have extended SMCDL with **Capabilities**. Basically, a capability is a tuple

$$<activity,\ entity,\ requiresInteraction>$$

and can be defined at component and operation/event level. In the latter case, capabilities complement the input and output parameters. *Activity* and *entity* refer to ontology concepts, for example act:Contact foaf:Person and, com-bined, express which action is performed on a domain object. If the user is involved in the activity, this is stated by *requiresInteraction*. This way we get

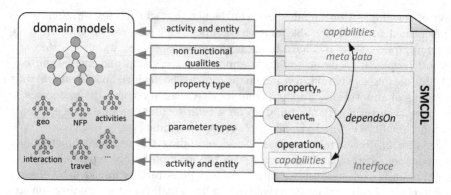

Fig. 1. Overview of the SMCDL

a tag-like descriptor of component functionality, backed by clear semantics to overcome ambiguity of tagging approaches. While the concepts referenced by entity and activity are typically domain-specific, we build up on an upper ontology for activities including generic concepts like *Calculate*, *Create*, and *Display*.

To express intra-component functional dependencies, events reference the capabilities that cause their occurrence using *dependsOn*. For sake of simplicity, or-semantics applies in case of several referenced capabilities. For instance, an event publishing results of an operation call refers to the operation's capability.

Two capabilities are **connectible** if the parameters of the underlying interface parts are semantically compatible. This either means that annotated concepts match perfectly (e. g. location → location) or can be mediated (e. g. latitude + longitude → location). Suitable mediation techniques are not in the scope of this paper, but we extend our work proposed earlier [11]. Connectibility of properties is more restrictive and requires equal or identical semantic types.

4   A Capability-Centered View for Non-programmers

The overall architecture of our platform is illustrated by Fig. 2. There are several repositories, depicted on the right. Components are managed by their SMCDL, whole mashups are represented by composition models. Certain composition fragments are mined from existing mashups or determined on the fly based on semantic annotations. Such composition fragments, like a coupling of two components or a more complex part of a composition model, are reactively or proactively queried and filtered by the recommendation manager, as part of the runtime environment [14]. Then, the fragments are presented to the end user, and, after selection, woven into the running mashup by the adaptation system.

There are different views on the mashup. The *LiveView* presents the running UI components integrated in the mashup while channels are hidden. For users with the necessary skills, the *ProfessionalView* provides a state-of-the-art wiring view which overlaps the first. The novel CapView is focused on capabilities in order to abstract from technical details. As with all views, CapView incorporates recommendations. Providing proper functionality-centered presentation for recommendations and for composition logic, CapView utilizes a *label generator*, which derives descriptions from semantic annotations of components and, thus, composition fragments. Every necessary mapping to the technical implementation in terms of the composition model is automatically performed by the runtime environment and completely hidden from the user.

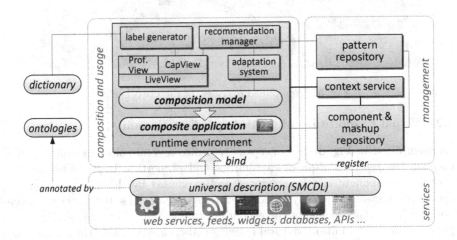

Fig. 2. Architectural overview of the EDYRA platform

4.1   Overview

In contrast to the ProfessionalView, the CapView does not explicitly display the operations and events of components. Instead, based on annotated capabilities, tasks that can be fulfilled using the component are clustered and visualized. To ease the correlation between LiveView and CapView, those tasks overlay the corresponding components. Our basic assumption is, that a mashup and its components are offering a set of functionalities. For execution, these functionalities may require inputs or produce outputs, which can be provided or consumed by other functionalities in a data flow based manner. This reflects the underlying component model (c. f. Sect. 3) and leads to tuples $<<A, E, iR>,P_{in},P_{out}>$ where $<A, E, iR>$ denotes a capability as defined in Sect. 3. $P_{in|out}$ are optional sets of the parameters of the operation or event, which correspond to the capability. Besides capabilities, components' properties are part of CapView, since we argue, that it is intuitive that objects are characterized by attributes.

An overview is shown in Fig. 3. The main part shows the overlaying CapView that lists capabilities and properties of components in the mashup, as well as connections. On the right is the **recommendation menu**, giving advice on composition fragments represented by the capabilities they offer.

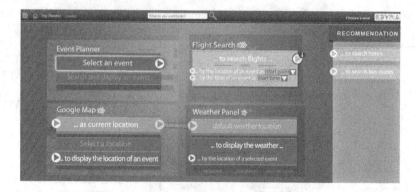

Fig. 3. Exemplified overview of the CapView

4.2   Visual Exploration of a Mashup's Functionality

As exemplified in Fig. 3, we conceptually utilize several colors in order to distinguish the *representation* of capabilities and properties. Representations for a certain component can be collapsed and expanded by the user. Further, to couple components implicitly by connecting representations, the latter can have ports as interaction elements corresponding to the inputs required and/or outputs provided. In addition, natural language labels are provided throughout the CapView, derived from semantic annotations. Thereby, several generic rules apply in order to label capabilities and properties. We go in more detail on the rules in Sect. 4.3 including examples.

Capabilities at component level are grayed out and carry no connection ports if no event refers to them via *dependsOn*. This way, the user is aware of the component's capability and the fact that it cannot be coupled. Otherwise the capability is colored according to the *requiresInteraction* (blue in Fig. 3 if *true*, else orange) and has an output port. *Capabilities at operation level* adhere to the same coloring scheme. Input ports are always visible, and their counterparts appear if at least one event refers to the capability. *Properties* are always colored uniformly (green in Fig. 3) and can have input and output ports.

A user can select a capability or property, denoted representation r_0. The **1-layer** L is defined as the set of all connectible capabilities or properties in the CapView that can directly provide input ($S \subseteq L$) for or handle output ($T \subseteq L$) of a representation. In order to avoid cycles, we assume that a certain representation cannot be in S and T of r_0. Self-connections of a component are prohibited, i.e., there is no r belonging to its own 1-layer. Established connections between representations are visualized, too. The appearance differs depending on r_0.

When selecting r_0, all $r_i \in L_0$ are highlighted and renamed, see Fig. 3 where r_0 is Select an event. The renamed labels are visually highlighted as well for several seconds to allow for awareness. Channels not connected to r_0 are grayed out in order to improve clarity. In addition to direct channels, indirect connections are highlighted as well in a less bright appearance. This way, a user can follow transitive data flow easier. For instance, if a compatible $r_j \in T_0$ is not yet connected with r_0 but with an $r_q \in T_j$, transitive highlighting $r_j \rightarrow r_q$ also applies. However, label adaptation exclusively changes the 1-layer.

Highlighting possible ports can be understood as a seamless visualization of recommendations. Besides this inline presentation, the recommendation menu lists capabilities of components not part of the mashup yet. In any case, we utilize stars to emphasize the three best rated recommendations.

4.3   Context-Sensitive Label Generation

How labels for representations are derived is subject of this section. The notion used thereby incorporates functions and indices, which we briefly explain now.

- $dLabel()$ and $aLabel()$ return a human readable description of an annotated property type or capability entity respectively activity. Thereby, either the name of the concept, extracted from its URI, or its `rdfs:label` is used.
- $art()$ inserts a correct article
- index pp denotes the past participle, queried from the dictionary
- index $norm$ indicates the "normalized" concept, i. e. `rdfs:range` of an object property, else the concept itself
- As part of recommended composition fragments, there is always a **mapping definition** $map_{P_1 \rightarrow P_2}$ that defines how interfaces have to be coupled possibly incorporating mediation techniques. For more complex fragments, there can of course be multiple definitions, one per channel in the fragment.

The generation process distinguishes essentially two cases. First, the basic case where nothing is selected by the user. The basic configuration for *properties* leverages the label or the name of the ontology concept annotated as type. To ease understanding for the user, the current value of the property is shown as well if it is set. A capability $<A, E, iR>$ is displayed utilizing the human-readable labels given for A and E, e. g. search a route, following the scheme:

$$aLabel(A) \; art() \; dLabel(E)$$

Secondly, labels are adapted to the user selection which serves for clarifying cause and effect. The algorithm built upon a generic rule set takes the 1-layer of r_0 and determines the label for representations on the 1-layer rather than r_0 itself. Thereby, $r_j \in S$ and $r_i \in T$ are treated differently. Further, dots are appended or prefixed to clarify the reading direction.

A Property Is Focused. When selecting r_0, re-labelling the 1-layer of a property distinguishes properties and capabilities.

$r_j \in S$ or $r_i \in T$ *is a property.* When connecting two properties is possible, it depends on whether r_0 is the target or source of the connection. In the first case a $r_j \in S$ is renamed according to the scheme

$$\text{Use } dLabel(Val_{prop}^j | Type_{prop}^j) \text{ as } \cdots$$

where $Type_{prop}$ denotes the type concept and Val_{prop} the currently set value of a property. In the other case, the rule slightly differs, and a $r_i \in T$ is labeled:

$$\text{Use } dLabel(Val_{prop}^0 | Type_{prop}^0) \text{ as } dLabel(Type_{prop}^i)$$

For illustration, consider the examples listed in the following table.

$r_j \in S$	r_0	$r_i \in T$
$Type_{prop} = Location$	$Type_{prop} = hasCenter$	$Type_{prop} = Location$
Use location (Dresden) as ...	Center	Use center as location

$r_i \in T$ *is a capability.* The selected property r_0 can serve as input for a representation $r_i = << A^i, E^i, iR^i >, P_{in}^i, P_{out}^i >$, where $map_{Type_{prop} \rightarrow P_{in}^i}$ is a injection and $Type_{param}$ denotes the single matched parameter's type. Hereby, we distinguish whether the normalized entity and the normalized type of the single parameter are mediable. If not and if the $Type_{param,norm}$ is equal to or super-concept of $Type_{prop,norm}$, we utilize the following scheme:

$$aLabel(A^i) \ art() \ dLabel(E^i) \text{ using } art() \ dLabel(Type_{prop})$$

Another option is, that $Type_{param}$ is part of the concept $Type_{prop,norm}$ and can be queried from instance data at runtime (**SplitRule**).

$$aLabel(A^i) \ art() \ dLabel(E^i) \text{ using } art() \ dLabel(Type_{param}) \text{ of } art()$$
$$dLabel(Type_{prop})$$

r_0	$r_i \in T$
$Type_{prop} = hasCurrentLocation$	$<<$Search, Hotel, $\perp >$, {Location, Time} $>$
Current location	Search a hotel using the current location
$Type_{prop} = Event$	$<<$Display, Hotel, $\top >$, {Location, Time} $>$
Event	Search a hotel using the location of the event

Contrary, if entity and parameter are mediable, a shorter rule applies to provide more compact labels (**CompRule**). Analogously, the SplitRule is used.

$$aLabel(A^i) \ art() \ dLabel(Type_{prop})$$

r_0	$r_i \in T$
$Type_{prop} = hasCenter$	$<<$Display, Location, $\top >$, Location $>$
Center location	Display the center location
$Type_{prop} = Event$	$<<$Display, Location, $\top >$, Location $>$
Event	Display the location of the event

If the capability represented by r_i offers multiple parameters ($|P_{in}^i| > 1$), there may of course be several possible mappings between the property and those parameters. Then, the options are declared via the suffix (**SuffixRule**):

$$\text{as } dLabel(Type_{param})$$

r_0	$r_i \in T$
$Type_{prop} = hasCenter$	$<<$Search, Route, $\perp >$, {hasStart, hasDest} $>$
Center	Search a route using the center as start
	Search a route using the center as destination

$r_j \in S$ is a capability. The selected property r_0 can consume the output of a representation $r_j = \; << A^j, E^j, iR^j>, P^j_{in}, P^j_{out} >$, where $map_{P^j_{out} \to Type_{prop}}$ is a injection and $Type_{param}$ denotes the single matched parameter's type.

Use $art()$ $aLabel(A^j)_{pp}$ $dLabel(E^j)$ as $art()$ $\ldots$

Use $art()$ $dLabel(Type_{prop})$ of $art()$ $aLabel(A^j)_{pp}$ $dLabel(E^j)$ as $art()$ $\ldots$

$r_j \in S$	r_0
<<Select, Location, ⊤ >, Location >	$Type_{prop} = hasCenter$
Use the selected location as the $\ldots$	center location
<<Select, Event, ⊤ >, Event >	$Type_{prop} = hasCenter$
Use the location of the selected event as the $\ldots$	center location

It is possible that not all $p \in P_{\{in|out\}}$ of a representation are covered. However, this is not subject to the label generation, but visualized via an exclamation-mark at the connection after the latter has been established.

A Capability Is Focused. If a $r_j \in S$ or a $r_i \in T$ is a property, the rules presented previously apply. Thus, only the case of coupling two capabilities is discussed in detail now. As with properties, we check whether the condition for CompRule holds. To this end, both entities have to be equal, identical or in inheritance relation. The same condition is checked for the mapped parameters' types. The resulting pattern is:

$\ldots$ to $aLabel(A^i)$ $art()$ $aLabel(A^0)_{pp}$ $dLabel(E^0)$

r_0	$r_i \in T$
<<Select, Location, ⊤ >, Location >	<<Display, Location, ⊤ >, Location >
Select a location	$\ldots$ to display the selected location

In the case CompRule is not applicable, the scheme shown below is used, and SplitRule and SuffixRule are utilized as required. In principle, depending on the mapping definition, there may be n by- and k as-parts (the latter are omitted if $k = 1$) in the resulting label, where n and k are the number of matched parameters in P^0_{out} respectively in P^i_{in}.

$$\ldots \text{to } aLabel(A^i)\, art()\, dLabel(E^i) \left(\text{ by } art() \left[dLabel(Type^{0,n}_{param}) \text{ of } art() \right] \right.$$
$$\left. aLabel(A^0)_{pp}\, dLabel(E^0) \left[\text{ as } dLabel(Type^{i,k}_{param}) \right]_k \right)_n$$

For some examples, consider the following table.

r_0	$r_i \in T$
<<Select, Location, ⊤ >, Location >	<<Search, Hotel, ⊥ >, Location >
Select a location	. . . to search a hotel by the selected location
<<Select, Event, ⊤ >, Event >	<<Search, Hotel, ⊥ >, Location >
Select an event	. . . to search a hotel by the location of the selected event
<<Select, Location, ⊤ >, Location >	<<Search, Route, ⊥ >, {hasStart, hasDest} >
Select a location	. . . to search a route by the selected location as start

Similarly, capability representations providing input for r_0 are handled, where n and k are the number of matched parameters in $P_{out,j}$ respectively in $P_{in,0}$.

$$\left(\ldots \text{by } art() \left[dLabel(Type^{j,n}_{param}) \text{ of } art() \right] aLabel(A^j)_{pp} \ dLabel(E^j) \right.$$
$$\left. \left[\text{ as } dLabel(Type^{0,k}_{param}) \right]_k \right)_n$$

$r_j \in S$	r_0
<<Select, Location, ⊤ >, Location >	<<Display, Location, ⊤ >, Location >
. . . by a selected location	Display location
<<Select, Event, ⊤ >, Location >	<<Search, Hotel, ⊥ >, Location >
. . . by the location of a selected event	Search a hotel

Analogously to property rules, if there are parameters of the underlying interface part that are not covered yet, a hint is shown to the user.

4.4 Interaction Mechanisms to Establish Connections

Creating connections between two representations requires an active selection r_0. The procedure can be started by selecting the input or the output port to activate it. For convenience, if there is exactly one port, it is directly activated. Then, recommended connections are further restricted according to S or T of r_0.

Since there may exist several similar capabilities whose only difference is the parameter signature of the underlying operation or event, **clustering** takes place. Thereby, all representations for a particular component with the same activity and entity are grouped. The weather panel, see Fig. 3, offers two operations annotated with capability $<Display, Weather, ⊤>$. One requires a location parameter and the second an additional date. Different outputs, i.e., events of a clustered capability are transparently handled for the user and are not shown explicitly. When determining recommendations the events are investigated separately, and the correct one is chosen before implementing the channel in the mashup. A major advantage of our approach is this possibility to abstract from interface details, like heterogeneous signatures and overloaded operations.

When clustering is required, the user has to choose the alternative he desires. Furthermore, in case there is no unambiguous parameter mapping possible, the user has to confirm or adapt it. To this end, as introduced in Sect 4.3, different by- and as-parts are determined by the label generator. Those options are displayed and set to a probable configuration as delivered by a recommendation. However, due to space limitations and in order to preserve spatial correlation, instead of revealing the complete label, representations hide details in a collapsed state at first. Therein, only the essential part of the label is shown, and on mouse-over, the representation expands. Consider the represented capability with label . . . to search flights. . . in Fig. 3, where the expanded state is illustrated. It shows several ports for each matching parameter of r_0, and options for the corresponding parameters of the target capability. In the collapsed state, the label would be a concise . . . to search flights and no options would be visible. Similarly, capability representations $r_j \in S$ are handled.

After clicking the desired port or via drag&drop, the data flow oriented connection is created. Subsequently, the platform checks whether the new connection is "sufficient". If, for example, a parameter of the underlying operation is not assigned, an exclamation mark appears (c. f. Fig. 3) and provides general hints and the possibility to request recommendations. When cancelling the current selection, all labels are reset to their base configuration.

5   Evaluation

5.1   Methodology

We conducted a user study utilizing the think aloud protocol. 10 users in the age of 22 – 37 participated and were asked to fill a questionnaire to gather demographic and skill-related data. They are students from different fields like mechanical or electrical engineering, media and computer science, and logic. The participants had no or very basic knowledge about mashups, but frequently use web applications. 5 users described their programming skills as average, so that we could evaluate the suitability of CapView not only for non-programmers.

After a short introduction to mashups and the CapView, two scenarios of increasing complexity in the travel planning domain, each comprising five tasks, were presented by the interviewer. Based on a click prototype similar to Fig. 3 covering core UI and interaction concepts, each scenario includes a mashup application with UI and service components. In the first scenario, comprising four UI and one service component, the basic understanding of the exploration and interaction mechanisms was checked. Thereby, task like identifying which components can help to search flights, and connecting capabilities so that it is possible to search and book hotels had to be solved. The second scenario focused on the concepts for creating and manipulating connections using parameter mappings and extends the first scenario to confront the participants with a non-trivial mashup. Participants were asked to extend the mashup to be able to find events in the target location, search public transportation from the hotel to the event location and display the weather. Thereby, users had to reconfigure connections and handle multiple parameters. According to the think aloud protocol, while task solving, they were encouraged to express what they are doing and why, and what system behavior they expect. The interviewer observed and supported them if necessary. We were interested in whether participants are able to solve the tasks. Additionally, after completing their tasks, users were asked to fill out a questionnaire about their perceived task load and their assessment of the CapView's suitability using the System Usability Scale (SUS). Further, users were encouraged to comment on things they liked or disliked.

5.2 Results

As an important result, all participants were able to solve the tasks. Speed and efficiency differs depending on the user's background. In general, key concepts of CapView were perceived very positive. The basic idea of CapView to provide a functional abstraction for non-programmers was approved by all participants. Since CapView overlays the LiveView, the spatial correlation to live components is facilitated and eased the understanding of component functionality.

Further, natural language labels of capabilities were considered sufficiently intuitive (70%) to understand the functionality of components and to realize a mashup as a task-solving entity. 80% of the participants found highlighting connectible ports very helpful and even stated that they would not have been able to succeed without it. In line with this, the proposed context-sensitive adaptation of labels supported the understanding of connectibility. The combination of all exploration means (focusing, highlighting, label generation, appending or pre-fixing dots to build sentences, component name) eased the hurdles significantly. Due to reduced complexity and to improved clarity, 80% of the participants liked the overview and detail metaphor of expanding and collapsing representations.

We observed, that users used both approaches the concept offers to establish connections, i. e., starting with input respectively output ports. This underlines the necessity to provide both approaches to not constraint the user.

However, we discovered that users repeatedly faced the following difficulties. First, it is hard for non-programmers to understand the concept of service components. This lead to misinterpretations of capabilities, for example, a user assumed that search flights (see Fig. 3) directly displays the results as well. Thus, those details should be appropriately abstracted as well in future work.

In addition, it became evident that the expectations on components' functionalities are highly influenced by the users' experience with web applications like Google Maps. As a consequence, meaningful capabilities have to be provided. In this regard, we found that users interpreted input and output ports differently: In a more human-centered perspective, they expected that, for example, select an event only has an input. This partly contradicted with the system-oriented perspective we used when annotating components, where select an event provides output. However, after a short time they grew familiar with our perspective. Few users had problems to realize that CapView abstracts from instance data. Thus, LiveView and CapView should be stronger interwoven.

To get a widely-accepted evaluation scale, we additionally surveyed the SUS score as well as the Task Load Index. The average SUS score equals 78.5, with a maximum of 92.5 and a minimum of 70. We consider this as a good result with regard to the preliminary status of our prototype. In more detail, 80% of the participants would like to use the system frequently in their daily life. The system's complexity was stated as low by 90%. 90% found it easy to use, too, and 70% attested a quick learnability. The positive user feedback was confirmed by the Task Load Index. For instance, mental demand and effort was assessed between low and medium and the frustration level as very low. With regard to their overall performance, users were very content. Due to the nature of our study, physical and temporal demand have limited significance.

6 Conclusion and Future Work

Today, the mashup paradigm is widely-accepted as promising approach for end user development of web applications. However, prevalent solutions only partly meet the strict requirements of non-programmers. Mostly, interface-oriented wiring is used, requiring technical understanding of the application. In this paper, we propose CapView, a novel functionality-aware development view on running mashups. It provides an overview of the capabilities and properties of components and recommended composition fragments. CapView abstracts from composition and implementation details.

Natural language labels for capabilities are derived and adapted with respect to the current selection of the user. Thereby, short sentences are formed in order to emphasize the functional interplay of components. This approach causes stronger dependency on useful annotations, and may be less precise than a extensive textual description. However, in our opinion the main advantage is genericity. Even unforeseen constellations of components can comprehensively be covered, which is important to meet the long tail of user needs. Further, the dependency on human-provided documentation of every component or recommendation lessens since ontological knowledge can be reused.

Consequently, non-programmers are empowered to explore the functionality of a mashup and its building blocks, and to manipulate the mashup through visually composing capabilities. We evaluate the CapView via a user study, and outline the results as well as identified future challenges.

Based on the concepts introduced in this paper and the lessons learned from the user study, we are working on stronger interweaving CapView and LiveView. Using the CapView's level of abstraction, we strive for an intuitive way for the user to express his/her goal. Further, we want to derive capabilities and their relationships from more complex composition fragments, and elaborate functionality-based visualization of recommendations in LiveView and CapView.

Finally, after finishing the integration of the CapView in our demo prototype, we plan to conduct an extensive user study to evaluate the overall platform in comparison to existing mashup platforms.

Acknowledgments. Funding for the EDYRA project is provided by the Free State of Saxony and the European Union within the European Social Funds program (ESF-080951805).

References

1. Aghaee, S., Pautasso, C.: Englishmash: Usability design for a natural mashup composition environment. In: Grossniklaus, M., Wimmer, M. (eds.) ICWE Workshops 2012. LNCS, vol. 7703, pp. 109–120. Springer, Heidelberg (2012)
2. Alonso, F., Lizcano, D., Lopez, G., Soriano, J.: End-user development success factors and their application to composite web development environments. In: Sixth Intl. Conf. on Systems (ICONS 2011) (2011)
3. Bianchini, D., Antonellis, V.D., Melchiori, M.: A recommendation system for semantic mashup design. In: DEXA Workshops, pp. 159–163. IEEE (2010)
4. Cappiello, C., Daniel, F., Matera, M., Picozzi, M., Weiss, M.: Enabling end user development through mashups: Requirements, abstractions and innovation toolkits. In: Piccinno, A. (ed.) IS-EUD 2011. LNCS, vol. 6654, pp. 9–24. Springer, Heidelberg (2011)
5. Cappiello, C., Matera, M., Picozzi, M., Sprega, G., Barbagallo, D., Francalanci, C.: Dashmash: A mashup environment for end user development. In: Auer, S., Díaz, O., Papadopoulos, G.A. (eds.) ICWE 2011. LNCS, vol. 6757, pp. 152–166. Springer, Heidelberg (2011)
6. Roy Chowdhury, S., Daniel, F., Casati, F.: Efficient, interactive recommendation of mashup composition knowledge. In: Kappel, G., Maamar, Z., Motahari-Nezhad, H.R. (eds.) Service Oriented Computing. LNCS, vol. 7084, pp. 374–388. Springer, Heidelberg (2011)
7. Daniel, F., Casati, F., Benatallah, B., Shan, M.-C.: Hosted universal composition: Models, languages and infrastructure in mashart. In: Laender, A.H.F., Castano, S., Dayal, U., Casati, F., de Oliveira, J.P.M. (eds.) ER 2009. LNCS, vol. 5829, pp. 428–443. Springer, Heidelberg (2009)
8. Imran, M., Kling, F., Soi, S., Daniel, F., Casati, F., Marchese, M.: Reseval mash: a mashup tool for advanced research evaluation. In: 21st Intl. Conf. companion on World Wide Web (WWW 2012), pp. 361–364. ACM (2012)
9. Namoun, A., Wajid, U., Mehandjiev, N.: Service composition for everyone: A study of risks and benefits. In: Dan, A., Gittler, F., Toumani, F. (eds.) IC-SOC/ServiceWave 2009. LNCS, vol. 6275, pp. 550–559. Springer, Heidelberg (2010)
10. Nestler, T., Feldmann, M., Hübsch, G., Preußner, A., Jugel, U.: The servface builder - a wysiwyg approach for building service-based applications. In: Benatallah, B., Casati, F., Kappel, G., Rossi, G. (eds.) ICWE 2010. LNCS, vol. 6189, pp. 498–501. Springer, Heidelberg (2010)
11. Pietschmann, S., Radeck, C., Meißner, K.: Semantics-based discovery, selection and mediation for presentation-oriented mashups. In: 5th Intl. Workshop on Web APIs and Service Mashups (Mashups), pp. 1–8. ACM (2011)
12. Pietschmann, S., Tietz, V., Reimann, J., Liebing, C., Pohle, M., Meißner, K.: A metamodel for context-aware component-based mashup applications. In: iiWAS 2010, pp. 413–420. ACM (2010)
13. Pietschmann, S., Voigt, M., Meißner, K.: Rich communication patterns and end-user coordination for mashups. In: Brambilla, M., Tokuda, T., Tolksdorf, R. (eds.) ICWE 2012. LNCS, vol. 7387, pp. 315–322. Springer, Heidelberg (2012)

14. Radeck, C., Lorz, A., Blichmann, G., Meißner, K.: Hybrid recommendation of composition knowledge for end user development of mashups. In: ICIW 2012, pp. 30–33. XPS (2012)
15. Rümpel, A., Radeck, C., Blichmann, G., Lorz, A., Meißner, K.: Towards do-it-yourself development of composite web applications. In: Proceedings of the Intl. Conf. on Internet Technologies & Society 2011 (ITS 2011), pp. 231–235 (2011)
16. Tietz, V., Pietschmann, S., Blichmann, G., Meißner, K., Casall, A., Grams, B.: Towards task-based development of enterprise mashups. In: iiWAS 2011, pp. 325–328. ACM (2011)
17. Wilson, S.: D3.3 prototype implementation of the omelette live environment: Phase 1. Tech. rep., ICT Omelette (2012)

Social Spreadsheet

Juan José Jara Laconich, Fabio Casati, and Maurizio Marchese

University of Trento, Dept. of Information Engineering and Computer Science Via
Sommarive 5, 38123 Povo (TN), Italy
{juan.jara,casati}@disi.unitn.it, maurizio.marchese@unitn.it

Abstract. Social media data is growing exponentially, to the point
where it is already hard to analyze. Consequently, there is a need to
increase the number of people analyzing this data, to make sense out of
it and, if possible, react to it. However, accessing this data is not simple
because it is behind a knowledge barrier, which can only be overcome
either with learning or with money. To considerably lower this barrier,
we implemented the Social Spreadsheet, which is a spreadsheet template
that we extended with functions that make simple the retrieval of social media data. Moreover, the collected data is ready to be analyzed
by end-users, who can use formulas, custom functions, charts, and other
commonly known spreadsheet features to create visualizations similar to
the ones offered by commercial applications. To validate our work, we
demonstrate how end-users can easily implement the same dashboards
as the ones offered by popular social media analysis tools.

Keywords: Spreadsheet-based Applications, Social Media Analysis,
End-user Programming.

1 Introduction

The adoption of smartphones exploded and, with it, the use of social networks,
which in turn caused an exponential growth of the already available social media
data. Social media data is the data that is obtained from the different social networks like Facebook, Twitter, YouTube and others. The types of social media
data that are most used are the ones that indicate demographic information,
location, interactions and user preferences.[1] People from different fields (marketing, health, sociology, etc.) are looking forward to access this data, to analyze
it and use it for different purposes like performing prediction analysis, improving advertising campaigns, getting feedback for a service or product, obtaining
communities insights and so on.

Currently, the people interested in accessing to social media data have to
choose between two options to get it. The first option is to get the data through
one of the multiple available web applications like Simply Measured [1], Social
Bakers [2], Sprout Social [3] or other social media analytics web applications.

---

[1] http://www.emarketer.com/Article/
Marketers-Use-Social-Media-Data-Drive-Campaigns/1009682

F. Daniel, P. Dolog, and Q. Li (Eds.): ICWE 2013, LNCS 7977, pp. 156–170, 2013.
© Springer-Verlag Berlin Heidelberg 2013

The problem is that these applications usually charge a fee for the data or put some constraints to the request or to the provided data. The second option is to develop an application that will get directly the data from the social network. The problem with this option is that is available only to the people with programming knowledge and, moreover, most social networks (like Facebook) do not allow data extraction for personal use.

There are a few applications for social network analysis that get data for free from social networks, like NodeXL [4]; unfortunately, this data is specifically for social network analysis and thus, is of little use for doing other types of analysis.

In this context, we implemented the Social Spreadsheet, which is our approach to provide a user-friendly environment for working with social media data.

In order to meet our objectives, we need to overcome some challenges:

- *The representation of social network entities in the spreadsheet tabular layout:* A **social networks entity** is a complex data, it can have single-valued attributes (like name, gender or birthday), multi-valued attributes (like spoken languages or interests) and it can be related to other entities (e.g., a user has friends, photos, etc.). The challenge here is defining a mapping for these complex entities into the simple typed cells (string, number, date) of the spreadsheet and its tabular layout.
- *Abstract the social network API (Application Programming Interface) model into the spreadsheet function model:* we need to use spreadsheet functions to connect to social networks APIs and get data from them. Some of the characteristics of spreadsheet functions (like cell referencing or automatic refresh) can affect negatively the user experience (like unnecessary or unwanted calls to the social networks APIs). The challenge here is in deciding which characteristics we want to keep, change or avoid to provide a user-friendly experience without deviating too much from the spreadsheet paradigm.

In our proposal, we define custom functions that abstract from the users the calls to the social networks APIs. These functions, which are common to the spreadsheet paradigm, provide to users a familiar method to access social media data. The combination of these functions and the spreadsheet features creates an environment where users can create visualizations similar to the ones found in the market. More specifically, with the Social Spreadsheet we provide:

- A **conceptual model** for representing the entities for which we can get data from the social networks,
- A **set of functions** that abstract the social network API model and that offer to spreadsheet users a more familiar method for getting social media data, and
- A **process** for providing extra-features that support the reuse of user-designed visualizations and creation of time series reports and charts.

We provide all the above in the well-known spreadsheet environment. Spreadsheets are intuitive, easy to use and are specifically designed for the manipulation and visualization of data.

The remainder of this paper is organized as follows. In the next section we explain our motivation for doing this work. In Section 3, we explain the state of the art on obtaining data from social networks and presenting it on spreadsheets. In Section 4, we present our proposal for a Social Spreadsheet. In Section 5, we describe how we implemented our proposal. In Section 6, we introduce some related work and compare them to our proposal. In Section 7, we validate our approach by implementing data visualizations similar to the ones offered by commercial applications for social media analysis. In Section 8 we discuss future works.

2   Background and Design Principles

People working in health, sociology, marketing and other fields need to constantly analyze data related to their respective target groups and communities [5,6,7]. The source of this data is usually the result of census, surveys, questionnaires or other similar sources which gather the data manually. Lately, with the boom of social networks, the people who analyze social data noticed that the data gathered by social networks in months was far richer than the data gathered by their usual sources in years.

At this point, it was evident that the interesting data was in the hand of businesses, and therefore, the people interested in working with it had to use the tools provided by these businesses. Sometimes, this situation resulted in people using a tool for doing one type of work when the tool was designed for doing another type, e.g., using a social network analysis tool for doing social media analysis.

Among the most popular tools for the manipulation and analysis of data are the spreadsheet applications. In fact, the characteristics of the spreadsheet paradigm make the spreadsheet an environment where is easy and intuitive for users to view and interact with data [8,9,10,11]. Among the spreadsheet characteristics defined in [8], the most important are:

- The **tabular layout** that makes easy to visualize and manipulate collections of entities,
- The **operators** for creating or modifying cell contents, which can be applied to a single cell or to a range of cells (such as an entire row), and
- The **dependencies between cells** that manage the propagation of changes between referenced cells, i.e., when a cell is modified, the content of its dependent cells will be updated automatically.

The work in [12] estimates that by 2012 there will be approximately 55 million spreadsheet users, and this is only in the United States. This does not mean that all these people will benefit from our proposal, but for the ones that will work doing social media analysis, our proposal will be of great help and will lower the entrance barrier to the field of social media analysis.

Spreadsheets are one of the most successful end-user programming applications. For example, a user creates a spreadsheet and uses formulas to solve some calculations. Later, the user can reuse the spreadsheet for new calculations just by changing the values of the input cells, that is, the user is able to abstract the algorithm from the data.

On the basis of the above considerations, in our work we focused our attention on the spreadsheet paradigm. Our goal is to give users the ability to create spreadsheet reports, charts and visualizations similar to the ones available in the commercial tools by facilitating to these users the access to the data that they need (social media data) in a spreadsheet environment (considered the most suitable environment for doing data manipulation and analysis).

3   State of the Art

In this section we explain the works and proposals that we found related to the retrieval of social media data from social networks and the presentation of this data on spreadsheets. We start explaining the methods for representing social media data in the tabular layout of the spreadsheets and then, the different approaches for using custom functions to call social networks APIs.

3.1   Represent Social Media Data in Spreadsheets

To copy data from social networks to spreadsheets, we need to define a mapping that indicates to the application how to put the obtained data into the spreadsheet cells. We found two approaches for defining these mappings in the applications and proposals that we studied:

- The first approach defines a straightforward mapping of the entities to the spreadsheet cells, i.e., each entity attribute is mapped to one cell. If the entity has an attribute that represents a collection, the attribute is mapped as a new entity and printed separately (usually in a different sheet). Most of the tools and proposals that we found use this approach, e.g., [4,1].
- The second approach defines a mapping where a single cell contains the representation of a whole entity (with its instances). The data of the entity can be accessed using a formula language that allows a cell to reference a specific attribute of a specific instance of the entity. A detailed explanation of this approach can be found in [11,13].

3.2   Call APIs with Spreadsheet Custom Functions

In the spreadsheet paradigm, a formula or function can take as input the reference to a cell or to a range of cells (this is besides the normal parameters that are usually passed to the function). The result or output of the function has a similar behavior; the result can be a single value that will be printed in the same cell where the function is defined or, the result can be a set of values that will be printed in the cell where the function is defined plus the cells to its bottom and its right (depending on the range of the result). In some of the analyzed works, we found interesting proposals for custom functions that combine the previous input/output options with the interconnection to other applications APIs.

In [10], the authors define (single cell input and single cell output) custom functions that use the cell value to call applications APIs. The authors then propose to define data flows between services by making custom functions reference cells that contains other custom functions and thus, allowing users to easily construct service mashups. If the input of the first function in the data flow is modified, the rest of the values in the data flow will be updated automatically due to the dependency between cells, a well-known characteristic of the spreadsheet paradigm.

The work in [11] allows users to associate a function with a web data service (the data service represents a single entity). Each time the function is used it will get from its related source a collection of entities (a function with no cell input but a multi cell output). The entity attributes, the number of items in the collection and how the data will be visualized are configured by the user. What is interesting from this approach is the implementation of a framework that supports the update of the data on the spreadsheet whenever the data in the source changes. The framework also supports the update in the other direction, i.e., when the data in the spreadsheet is modified by the user, the corresponding data in the source is also updated, when possible.

The functions in both cases take into account the active cell when they print their results and thus, they follow the standard behavior of functions of the spreadsheet paradigm. The work in [4] implements functions that do not follow this standard behavior. These functions get data from applications APIs and print their results in cells predefined by the functions algorithms without taking into account the active cell position.

4   Social Spreadsheet

Our proposal consists of extending spreadsheet-based applications with custom functions for accessing social media data. We think that the combination of these functions with the characteristics of the spreadsheet paradigm creates a user-friendly environment for the design and creation of social media data visualizations.

We start with the presentation of a conceptual model for representing the social media data that we get from social networks. Then, we present the functions that connect the entities from our model with the social network APIs. Finally, we introduce two special templates; one for recording the execution of functions in a script that can be executed later to produce the same layout using different data sources; the other for computing periodically metrics that will allow users to easily create time series charts and reports.

4.1   Social Media Conceptual Model

In this section we focus on the creation of visualizations for social media analysis, and thus, we limit the data that we get from social networks to the data that is most useful for this type of analysis. We designed our conceptual model based on the Facebook API model[2] because at the moment Facebook is the most used social network.

We show our social media conceptual model in Fig. 1. The entities that we abstracted are the following:

- **User:** this entity represents the current user (the user that is using the tool). Some of the attributes that we get for the current user (if available) are its name, gender, current location, birthday, relationship status, etc. The user can have friends, albums, photos and posts.
- **Friends:** this entity represents a social network user that has a friend connection with the current user. The attributes that we get for friends are the same attributes that we get for the current user. The friends can have albums, photos and posts.
- **Pages:** this entity represents a business or brand profile in a social network. Some of the attributes that we get for pages (if available) are their name, page link, page category, and business website. Moreover, we get two attributes that are very popular in the social media analysis field, the likes count and the people talking about this count.[3] The page can have albums, photos and posts.
- **Albums:** this entity represents a photo album defined by a user or page. Some of the attributes that we get for albums (if available) are their name, photo count, description, link, cover photo, etc. An album can contain photos.
- **Photos:** this entity represents a photo uploaded to the social network by a user or page. Some of the attributes that we get for photos (if available) are their name, link, time of upload, etc.
- **Posts:** this entity represents a message post created by a user or page. Some of the attributes that we get for posts (if available) are their name, type, message, link, etc.

Figure 1 shows the entities that we model from social networks and how they relate to each other. We consider these relations when we define the spreadsheet functions that we present in the next section. We do not do a complex mapping of the entity with the spreadsheet cells like in [11], we just map each entity attribute to one cell.

The conceptual model was designed based on the Facebook entities but it could be used to some extent to get the entities of other social networks. For example, social networks like twitter and Google+ have the user entities which are similar to our user entity and the attributes of these entities can be mapped to the attributes of our model. Also, our post entity is similar to the activities entity of Google+ or the Tweets entity of Twitter. For the friends entity we need to extend the model because in Twitter and Google+ this relationship is

---

[2] http://developers.facebook.com/docs/reference/api/

[3] For more details about these attributes check
http://developers.facebook.com/docs/reference/api/page/

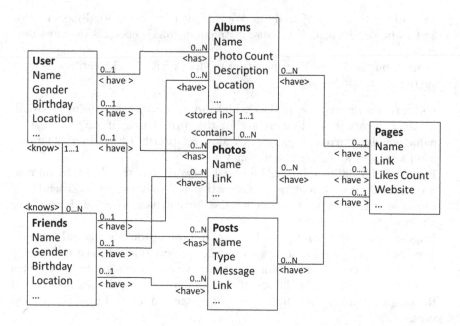

Fig. 1. The social media conceptual model

asymmetrical (if user A is a friend of user B it does not mean that user B is a friend of user A).

4.2 Spreadsheet Social Functions

We defined two types of custom functions for getting data from social networks into spreadsheets. The data functions, which are functions used to get the instances of an entity from the social network, and the metric functions, which are functions that computes a metric for an instance of an entity.

Figure 2(a) shows a generic form of a data function. The characteristics of this type of functions are the following:

- **Name:** the name of the function indicates the type of the retrieved instances, e.g., friends, photos, albums, etc. The entities available for retrieval are the ones that are present in the conceptual model.
- **Input:** this type of functions takes one input parameter that represents the *id* of the owner of the retrieved instances, e.g., in Fig. 2(b) the function will get all the photos for the user which *id* is 112233. If the *id* is null or empty the function will get the instances that belong to the current user.
- **Output:** this type of functions produces a multi-valued result. The range of the result depends on the number of attributes (one column per attribute) and the number of instances (one row per instance) that is retrieved.

– **Cell dependency:** cell dependency is not activated for this type of functions, i.e., the API to get the instances will be called only one time, if the input parameter changes the API will not be called again and the results will still correspond to the old input.

Figure 2(c) shows a generic form of a metric function. The characteristics of this type of functions are the following:

– **Name:** the name of the function indicates the metric that will be computed, e.g., number of likes, number of comments, number of female friends, etc. The available metrics were implemented according to the most popular metrics found in several social analysis tools.
– **Input:** this type of functions takes one input parameter that represents the *id* of the instance for which the metric will be computed, e.g., in Fig. 2(d) the function will get number of likes for the photo which *id* is 446677.
– **Output:** this type of functions produces a single-valued result.
– **Cell dependency:** cell dependency is activated for this type of functions, i.e., the metric will be computed each time the input value changes.

(a) = getEntity (instanceID)   **(b)** = getPhotos (112233)

(c) = getMetric (instanceID)   **(d)** = getNumberOfLikes (446677)

Fig. 2. (a) Generic data function. (b) Data function that gets the list of photos for the friend with id=112233. (c) Generic metric function. (d) Metric function that counts the number of likes for the photo with id=446677.

4.3   Special Purpose Templates

As examples on how to support the users in the manipulation and visualization of social media data we designed two sheet templates; one to support the automatic creation and reuse of user visualizations and, the other to support the creation of time series reports and charts.

The *template that supports the creation and reuse of user visualizations* uses the first and second column of sheet. The first column is used to record all the user actions (which include data manipulation and execution of functions) and the second column is used to store the position where the action occurred. Figure 3 shows an example of this template. The purpose of this template is to create a script that describes the process of creation of a visualization layout. The script can be used later to generate the same layout but using a different data source, this is done by changing either the executed function or the function parameter. This feature can be used to compensate the lack of cell dependency of the data functions.

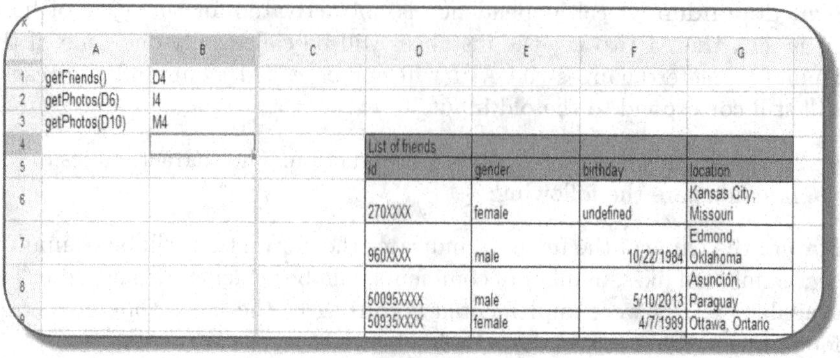

Fig. 3. Template for recording and executing action scripts

The *template that supports the creation of time series reports and charts* uses the first row and, the first to third columns. The first column is used to store the ids of the entity instances for which a metric will be computed. The second column is used to store the description of the entity instances whose ids are in the first column, this will save time to the user that will not need to search all over the spreadsheet to which instances correspond the ids in the first column. The third column is used to store the metrics that will be computed for the entity instances of their corresponding rows. This template has an associated function that is executed periodically (the interval is defined by the user). The periodic function, on each execution, gets the first not used column and prints the current timestamp on the first row of that column. Then, for each row, executes the metric function specified in the third column using as input parameter the id specified in the first column. Finally, the result of the metric computation is printed on the column where the last timestamp was stamped. Figure 4 shows an example of this template. After some executions of the periodic function the template will have the necessary data for the creation of time series reports and charts.

5   Implementation

We implemented the Social Spreadsheet by extending a Google spreadsheet with the functions described in Sec. 4.2 using the Google App Script scripting language. The spreadsheet is public and can be used by anyone with a Google account.

We published the Social Spreadsheet in the Google template gallery[4]. The template can be found by typing Facebook Analytics Template in the search template box. To use the template, users need to get an access token from our application website[5]. In the next section we explain how to get the access token and why it is needed.

---

[4] https://drive.google.com/templates

[5] https://comealong.me/fb/sp/socialspreadsheet/

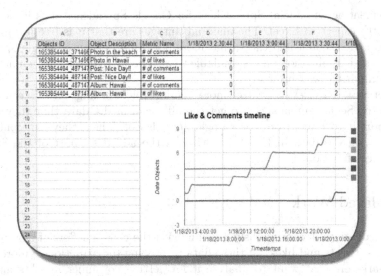

Fig. 4. Template for computing metrics periodically

5.1 Authentication with Social Networks

In order to interact with social networks, applications need to authenticate themselves with the social networks. If the authentication process is successful, the social network gives an access token to the authenticated application. The application can now interact with the social network passing with each request the given access token.

In our implementation, the authentication process is implemented outside of the spreadsheet. We did not include the authentication process in the spreadsheet due to a limitation of the scripting language at the moment of the implementation of the Social Spreadsheet. We continuously monitor the language updates to check if this limitation has been removed.

To get the access token to make the spreadsheet functional, users need to go to the application website and do the authentication process there, at the end of the process they will get the access token for the spreadsheet. The token expires after two months, after that it can be refreshed just by visiting the application website.

5.2 Google Spreadsheet vs. Excel

Why we choose Google Spreadsheet instead of Excel for the implementation of the Social Spreadsheet? We actually started to implement the Social Spreadsheet for Excel because we consider Excel as a more mature and more complete spreadsheet tool than Google Spreadsheet. However, we found that some critical functions that were available for the Windows version of Excel were missing for the Mac version of Excel. For this reason we changed the implementation tool to Google Spreadsheet.

Implementing the Social Spreadsheet for Google Spreadsheet has its advantages with respect to Excel. The main advantages are that it is free for anyone with a Google account and that it has more portability because Google Spreadsheet is a web application and is available to anyone with an internet connection and a compatible web browser.

Either way, for users that feel more comfortable working with Excel, they can use the Social Spreadsheet to get the all social media data that they need and export it to Excel from the Google Spreadsheet. Then, they can continue working with the data in Excel but without the added support of the Social Spreadsheet functions.

6   Related Work

Social media data is continuously growing with the constant flow of new posts, comments, tweets and likes; all these data is drawing the attention of more and more marketers that want to analyze it for getting consumer insights among other information. This growing interest in social media data did not go unnoticed by the software market, which increased its offer on applications for content analysis, dashboards and reports based on the analysis of social media data.

There is an extensive list of web applications for social media analysis. We selected and investigated some of the applications that are considered the most interesting according to a few blogs and articles that we found on the web.[6][7][8] From the applications that we investigated, the following are the ones that we consider most relevant: Simply Measured [1], Social Bakers [2], Inside Network [14], Sprout Social [3] and Page Lever [15]. All of them offer several reports, charts and dashboards. Table 1 shows the classification of these tools according to the following features:

- **Data provision capability:** indicates to what extent they provide social media data on spreadsheets. The possible values are:
  - *None*, which means that they do not provide data at all;
  - *Limited*, which means that they provide data but limited with constraints to the request or to the provided data and;
  - *Full*, which means that they provide all the requested data.
- **Pricing:** indicates under what payment model the data is being provided. The possible values are:
  - *Free*, which means that no money is paid for getting the data and;
  - *Subscription*, which means that a periodic fee is paid for getting the data.

---

[6] http://www.convinceandconvert.com/social-media-tools/
the-39-social-media-tools-ill-use-today/

[7] http://thenextweb.com/socialmedia/2011/09/02/
the-best-new-social-media-analytics-tools-of-the-year-so-far/

[8] http://thenextweb.com/socialmedia/2012/03/18/
50-mostly-free-social-media-tools-you-cant-live-without-in-2012/

Table 1. Classification of social media analysis tools according to their data provision capability and payment model

Pricing\ Data provision capability	None	Limited	Full
Free	Social Bakers Inside Network Sprout Social Page Lever	Simply Measured	
Subscription	Social Bakers		Simply Measured Inside Network Sprout Social Page Lever

Currently, the Social Spreadsheet does not provide all the complex charts and reports as the previous classified tools. Instead, the Social Spreadsheet provides the needed data in a suitable and user-friendly environment for the creation of similar visualizations and for free.

We found other related works that get data from the web to spreadsheets using spreadsheet functions but the scope of these works are different than ours:

- NodeXL [4], which is an Excel template that gets data from social networks but with the only scope of doing social network analysis. Moreover, the entities that can be obtained are fixed; users can only choose the entity attributes they want to get.
- In [10], the authors propose the creation of service mashups by concatenating spreadsheet functions using the cell dependency characteristic of spreadsheets. The defined functions get data from public APIs that do not require authentication and, take a single-valued input and produce a single-valued output.
- Finally, in [11], the authors also propose the creation of mashups using spreadsheet functions. The authors propose spreadsheet functions that get data from public APIs that do not require authentication, take none or a single-valued input and produce a multi-valued output and, propagates data changes between the data source and the spreadsheet (the propagation can be bidirectional if it is allowed by the source).

7   Validation

In this section we validate our proposal by implementing one data visualization that is similar to the ones offered by commercial applications (like the ones mentioned in the previous section).

In this example, we show the process for building a bar chart visualization for comparing two popular soda brands using two metrics, the *likes count* and the *people talking about this count*. Figure 5 shows all the data necessary to build the visualization and the resulting chart. Each step of the explanation will use as reference the data shown in Fig. 5:

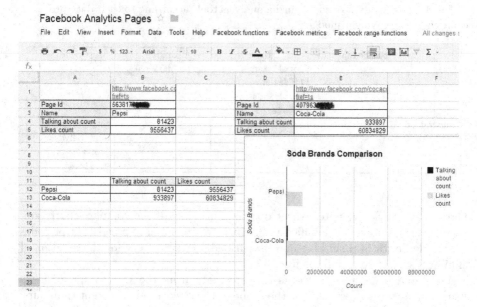

Fig. 5. Bar chart for comparing two soda brands using the *likes count* and the *people talking about this count* metrics

1. We copy the links of the Facebook pages of the desired brands in the first row.
2. We get the data for each page by positioning the active cell on the cell where the page link is and then we select the menu item Get Page under the Facebook functions menu. The page data will be copied under the cells where the page link is (as shown by Fig. 5).
3. We put the data in a format that is accepted by the bar chart. We need to put all the brand names as row headers and the metric names as column headers (columns A, B, C and rows 11- 13 of Fig. 5).
4. We select the range of the table created in step 3 and select the option to add a bar chart. The result should be similar to the observed in Fig. 5.

The above 4 steps illustrate how simple is to create one of the most popular visualizations. More examples can be found in our application website[9].

8   Conclusion and Future Work

With our proposal we demonstrated how end-users can create visualizations similar to the ones offered by commercial tools. This also served to demonstrate the great potential of spreadsheet applications as end-user programming tools.

---

[9] https://comealong.me/fb/sp/socialspreadsheet/

Spreadsheet applications can be easily extended by the addition of custom functions. However, if the targets of the extended application are end-users, the functionality added should be minimal and, if possible, comply with the characteristics of the spreadsheet paradigm. This is to maintain the simplicity and familiarity that end-users are accustomed to find when working with spreadsheets.

The proposed conceptual model is based on the Facebook data model. As a part of our future research we need to study how to abstract or extend more the conceptual model to comply with the data models of other popular social networks like Twitter or Google+. Furthermore, we want to conduct a usability study to evaluate how actual end-users perceive our proposal and to receive feedback of features or functionality that we could have omitted.

Acknowledgments. This work was supported by funds from the BPM4People project (http://www.bpm4people.org) of the EU FP7 Capacities program.

References

1. Social Media Analytics, From Data to Deliverables, http://simplymeasured.com/
2. Socialbakers: Social Media Marketing, Statistics & Monitoring Tools, http://www.socialbakers.com/
3. Sprout Social: Social Media Management, Social CRM for Business, http://sproutsocial.com/
4. NodeXL: Network Overview, Discovery and Exploration for Excel, http://nodexl.codeplex.com/
5. Mackay, H.: Information and the Transformation of Sociology: Interactivity and Social Media Monitoring. tripleC-Cognition, Communication, Co-operation 11(1), 117–126 (2012)
6. Hansen, D.L., Rotman, D., Bonsignore, E., Milić-frayling, N., Rodrigues, E.M., Smith, M., Shneiderman, B., Capone, T.: Do You Know the Way to SNA?: A Process Model for Analyzing and Visualizing Social Media Data. Group 56(3), 1–10 (2009)
7. Thackeray, R., Neiger, B.L., Hanson, C.L., McKenzie, J.F.: Enhancing promotional strategies within social marketing programs: use of Web 2.0 social media. Health Promotion Practice 9(4), 338–343 (2008)
8. Chi, E.H., Riedl, J., Barry, P., Konstan, J.A.: Principles for information visualization spreadsheets (1998)
9. Ballinger, D., Biddle, R., Noble, J.: Spreadsheet visualisation to improve end-user understanding. In: Proceedings of the Asia Pacific Symposium on Information Visualisatio, vol. 24, pp. 99–109. Australian Computer Society, Inc. (2003)
10. Hoang, D.D., Paik, H.Y., Benatallah, B.: An analysis of spreadsheet-based services mashup. In: Proceedings of the Twenty-First Australasian Conference on Database Technologies, ADC 2010, vol. 104, pp. 141–150. Australian Computer Society, Inc., Darlinghurst (2010)
11. Kongdenfha, W., Benatallah, B., Vayssière, J., Saint-Paul, R., Casati, F.: Rapid development of spreadsheet-based web mashups. In: Proceedings of the 18th International Conference on World Wide Web, WWW 2009, pp. 851–860 (2009)

12. Scaffidi, C., Shaw, M., Myers, B.: The 55M End-User Programmers Estimate Revisited. Technical Report February, Carnegie Mellon University (2005)
13. Saint-Paul, R., Benatallah, B., Vayssière, J.: Data services in your spreadsheet? In: Proceedings of the 11th International Conference on Extending Database Technology: Advances in Database Technology, pp. 690–694. ACM (2008)
14. Research and Analysis of the Facebook & Mobile App Ecosystems, http://research.insidenetwork.com
15. PageLever: Analytics & Social Marketing Tools for Facebook Pages, http://pagelever.com/

User-Driven Automation of Web Form Filling

Oscar Diaz, Itziar Otaduy, and Gorka Puente

Onekin Research Group, University of the Basque Country (UPV/EHU),
San Sebastián, Spain
{oscar.diaz,itziar.otaduy,gorka.puente}@ehu.es

Abstract. Form-intensive Web applications are common among institutions that collect bulks of data in a piecemeal fashion. European funding programs or income tax return illustrate these scenarios. Very often, most of this data is already digitalized in terms of documents, spreadsheets or databases. The task of manually filling Web forms out of these resources is not only cumbersome but also prone to typos. It does not benefit from the fact that the data is already in electronic format. Alternatively, externally-fed autofilling scripts can be programmed (e.g. using *iMacros* and *Visual Basic*) to code once, and enact many times. Unfortunately, this approach is programming intensive and fragile upon upgrades in either the website or the structure of the external source. This moves these tools away from users with scarce programming skills. We strive to empower these users by abstracting the way feeding solutions are realised. Since external sources tend to be structured, they offer the chance to be abstracted in terms of models. Autofilling scripts can then be generated as weavings between the external data model and the website model. We describe *WebFeeder*, a plugin for *iMacros* that introduces *autofilling-script models* as first-class artifacts in *iMacros*. The synthesis, enactment and maintenance of these script models are handled without leaving *iMacros*, minimizing users' cognitive load and involvement.

Keywords: autofilling, MDE, web forms, iMacros.

1 Introduction

Websites can be classified based on the quantity of data they request. If the requested data is mainly personal and limited, autofilling mechanisms are available to alleviate the tiresome task of periodically providing this information (card holder, visa number, etc.) [1,2]. On the other side of the spectrum, some institutional websites request a large quantity of data. We qualified websites as *"form-intensive"* when they account for numerous web forms spread along several pages. In these scenarios, the manual approach is not only cumbersome but also prone to typos. Neither does it help the use of traditional autofilling mechanisms (e.g. *Firefox autofill*) where the filling data comes from previously filled forms but they do not benefit from external data sources. Indeed, it is very common in these scenarios for the required data to be already available within the organization. As an example, consider the application for R&D projects.

F. Daniel, P. Dolog, and Q. Li (Eds.): ICWE 2013, LNCS 7977, pp. 171–185, 2013.
© Springer-Verlag Berlin Heidelberg 2013

The schedule, personnel, budget, etc, are all data that might well be prepared in advance and stored as spreadsheets, documents or databases (e.g. if a wiki or a document management system is used). In addition, the same institution (e.g. a university) might present different projects to the same funding agency, which results in navigating the same website many times.

So far, only script-based approaches offer a solution. Scripts can be programmed using *ad hoc* languages (e.g. *iMacros* [3], *Selenium* [6]). These tools act like a record-replay device recording the interactions of the user during a session in terms of a script. This script can next be replayed at user's will. For external sources, the strategy rests on creating a program that consults the external source (e.g. a spreadsheet), assigning the returned values to variables, and next, enacting the script which was previously parametrized with these variables. This permits to tap into existing data sources while automatizing repetitive data entries.

For form-intensive websites, this approach offers a great potential. However, its benefits are hindered by:

- requiring an important upfront investment. Form-intensive websites necessarily lead to large scripts. This increases the chances of being affected by upgrades. Script development is programming intensive. The user has to code both the access to the external sources and the script using general-programming languages. In addition, this code shows external dependencies with the structure of both the external sources and the HTML pages. If upgrades are made on the structure on either the data source or the website, this code risks to fall apart,
- affordability. Form filling is a clerical work. Clerks manage the documents, spreadsheets and database applications that contain the data that will eventually feed the website. They know the site map, the possible flows for introducing the information as well as any directive concerning the feeding process. They are the domain experts as far as the feeding process is concerned. Unfortunately, clerks do not usually have programming skills, so current scripting tools are not affordable enough for this type of users.

This paper addresses **the empowering of end users to create externally-fed autofilling scripts** (hereafter just "scripts"). The approach rests on abstracting scripts from code to models. This stands for a decrease in human error and misunderstanding while improving efficiency and affordability. As a proof of concept, the paper describes how *iMacros* has been leveraged from managing script code to script models. Moving to the model realm improves *iMacros* affordability so that end users can now synthesise, run and maintain script models without requiring programming skills.

The paper starts by revising the related work and giving a brief about *iMacros*. Section 4 outlines the approach to abstract from script code to script models, which is later detailed throughout Sections 5, 6 and 7. Section 8 focuses on upgrades. Conclusions end the paper.

2   Related Work

Autofilling is defined as a feature of a computer program that allows filling in forms without requiring user intervention. Aside from providing personal information, the autofilling feature can be useful in a large number of scenarios [14]. Table 1 compares different solutions along four dimensions: mapping approach, data origin, user involvement and process concerns.

Mapping Approach. Autofilling implies a mapping between the data and the form fields. Three main solutions stand out to automatically infer this mapping. First, *string matching* based on HTML field attributes (e.g. name, label or id). This approach is illustrated by Google Toolbar [2] or Firefox Autofill Forms [1]. Second, *semantic annotation* e.g. using Microformats [4]. Microformats can make a website machine-readable by adding special markup to mark recognizable data items (such as events, contact details or geographical locations). Firmenich et al. propose the use of Microformats to set up the mapping between HTML rendered elements and the data source [12]. A similar approach but using HTML5 features rather than Microformats is introduced in [13]. Third, *conceptual mapping*. Unlike the previous techniques, now the mapping is achieved at the conceptual level. Form clues (e.g. id, label) are mapped to lexical words which are next compared with ontologies that contain synonyms and abbreviations, such as *WordNet* or *DBpedia*. *Carbon* [7] is a case in point. This application is "able to extract relevant metadata from the previously filled forms, semantically enrich it, and use it for aligning fields between web forms". Four, *script-based mapping*. Previous approaches trade accuracy for user involvement. That is, they reduce the engagement of the user at the expense of less precise results. If user collaboration is possible, the mapping can be recorded as a client-side script using tools such as *iMacros* [3] or *Selenium* [6]. These tools act like a record-replay device. Once recorded, the script can replay the interactions at user's will. This is useful if the user wants to fill out one form with different values (i.e. distinct replays) but it does not serve to automatically fill out new forms.

Data Origin. Feeding data can be obtained from previous feeding processes or existing documentation. The former is illustrated by Google Toolbar or Firefox

Table 1. Autofilling approaches

	Mapping Approach	Data Origin	User Involv.	Process Concerns
Firefox Autofill	string matching	previous fillings	none	filling
Carbon	conceptual mapping	previous fillings	none	filling
iMacros	script-based	external sources	high	filling & navigation
WebFeeder	script-based	external sources	high	filling & navigation

Autofill Forms. Alternatively, forms can be filled out from external sources. For example, *Safari* permits to tap into the *Address Book* [5] while *CoScripter Tables* [9] uses spreadsheets. In the commercial side, both *iMacros* and *Selenium* permit populating web forms from databases and text files.

User Involvement. This dimension admits three values based on the contribution of the user: (1) *no-involvement*: no additional effort is required from the user as data is automatically collected from the filling of other forms (e.g. *Google Toolbar*), (2) *low involvement*: the user provides an example that is later used to fill out similar forms, and (3), *high involvement*: the user facilitates a script that can be parametrized and replay with different values.

Process Concerns. The filling process can tackle different concerns. It can only focus on the *filling*, include *data validation*, or allow to be extended along different pages then, addressing page *navigation* as well. Most autofilling applications concentrate on form filling, though *iMacros* and *Selenium* also support navigation.

Table 1 frames our approach to related work. We focus on form-intensive websites. In this setting, feeding scripts from external sources offers an attractive solution to tap into existing resources within the organization. In addition, user involvement should be reduced on the search for making clerks self-sufficient. This rules out the manual programming of the scripts. Moreover, automatically obtaining the mapping using semantic closeness also turned out to be difficult when addressing a whole website. The main insight of this work is *to tap into the information structure of the external sources to abstract and guide the mapping process so as to make it affordable to clerks*. Therefore, the challenge is not so much about feasibility but affordability. Before delving into the details, we provide a brief on *iMacros*, the framework that underpins our approach.

3   A Brief on iMacros

Figure 1 depicts a web form for project application at the CDTI website, a Spanish funding body. Let us consider a scenario where: (1) the data has already been digitalized in terms of databases or spreadsheets, and (2) the organization (e.g. a university) applies for different projects, and hence, the very same forms need to be filled out over and over again. As in other software settings, repetitive tasks are worth being automatized through macros.

iMacros is an extension for the main web browsers which adds record and replay functionality for a web session. The autofilling life cycle is conducted along two steps: (1) *record* the autofilling script as the user navigates throughout the site; and (2), *replay* the script at wish. Broadly, *iMacros* scripts are a sequence of navigation commands (e.g. the *URL* command opens a new webpage) and automated interactions on the current page (e.g. the *TAG* command performs some action on a web element). Autofilling wise, *iMacros* admits three strategies: (1) the data is provided at *recording* time as a script constant; (2) the data is provided at *replaying* time by prompting the user; and (3), the data is obtained

Fig. 1. CDTI form example. Parametrized *iMacros* script (top) and its *VBS* script configuration counterpart (bottom).

at *replaying* time by querying external sources. If data is provided at recording time, the autofilling follows the life cycle: *"record > play"*. If data is to be obtained from external sources, the life cycle is enlarged with two additional steps: *"record > parametrize > configure > play"*. Parametrize basically means to turn values for data input into variables. Configuration implies to code a program that instantiates these variables.

Figure 1 shows an example for the CDTI form sample. At the top, the *iMacros* script once parametrized as denoted by the expressions *{{variable}}*. At the bottom, the configuration step which is realized through *Visual Basic Script* (VBS) code. Configuration mainly involves four concerns: querying the database (line 1), validating the data format (line 11), establishing database-to-script variable mappings (lines 7-10, 12) and enacting the *iMacros* script (line 13). By far,

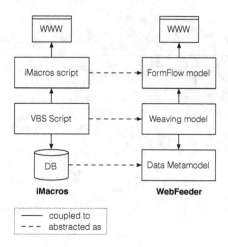

Fig. 2. From script coding to script modeling

establishing the mapping is the most complex task. Notice that parametrization and configuration are not supported by *iMacros* but handled externally (e.g. using a *VBS* editor).

From a corporate perspective, the use of this solution for feeding form-intensive websites rises two issues. First, this solution might require an important upfront investment (e.g. the script for the CDTI case study took more than 20 hours to develop). This investment can be put in jeopardy if the structure of either the web pages or the external sources are upgraded. Second, affordability. Clerks are the domain experts as far as the feeding process is concerned. They know about the documents, spreadsheets and database applications that contain the data that will eventually feed the website. They also know about the site map, the possible flows for introducing the information as well as any directive concerning the feeding process. However, they cannot set the solution by themselves: *VBS* is strange to them. Even a tiny change in the website (potentially breaking the script) makes them dependent on the availability of the always-busy computing department.

Configuration (i.e. the manual coding of the *VBS* script) is the Achilles' heel of this solution. The question is whether this code can be abstracted in terms of a model. This would bring modelware benefits to the realm of Web autofilling: simpler development, lower required skills, faster delivery, etc [8]. This grounds the development of *WebFeeder*.

4   From iMacros to WebFeeder: From Coding to Modeling

WebFeeder is a plugin for *iMacros*. *iMacros* is realized as a sidebar where artifacts (i.e. *iMacros* scripts) can be *recorded*, *edited* and *played*. We extended *iMacros* with a second type of artifact: **feeders** (see Figure 3). *Feeders* are abstractions of form filling scripts (i.e. script models). *Feeders* can be **synthesised** from *iMacros* scripts, and **run**, i.e. transformed from models into macros,

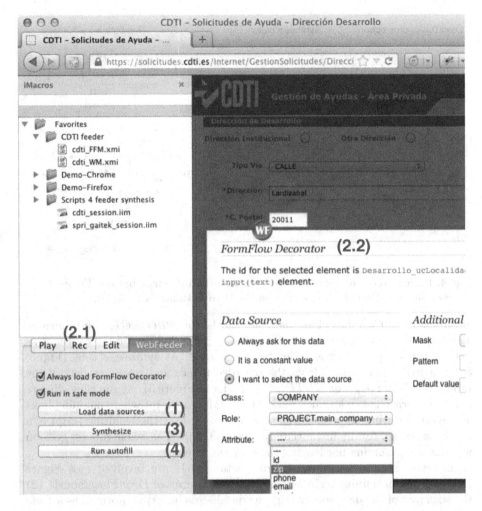

Fig. 3. *WebFeeder* extends *iMacros* to support the life cycle of *feeders*: **record** (2.1), **weave** (2.2), **synthesise** (3) and **run** (4)

and next, enacted. This round-trip from scripts to *feeders* yields the very same script if all data is constant and provided by the user at recording time. However, we extended *iMacros* with a configuration parameter: the external data sources (Figure 3(1)). This permits *WebFeeder* to obtain a rudimentary conceptual model from this external source before recording. At recording time (Figure 3(2.1)), when an input field is detected, the user is prompted to set the mapping between the entry field and the conceptual model. Figure 3(2.2) shows this layered menu for the sample case. The *C.Postal* input field is mapped to the *zip*

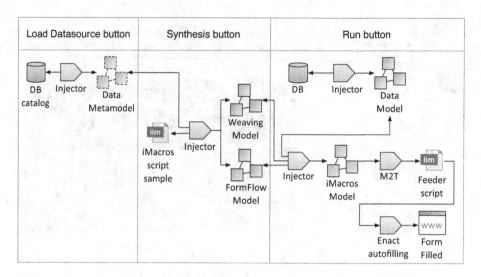

Fig. 4. Pushing the buttons in iMacros: the **LoadDataSource** button (Figure 3(1)), the **Synthesis** button (Figure 3(3)), and the **Run** button (Figure 3(4)).

attribute of the *Company* class when playing the role *PROJECT.mainCompany*. The important point to notice is that this mapping information is captured as part of the sample iMacros script being recorded. At synthesise time (Figure 3(3)), a *feeder* is obtained from the recorded macro and stored as part of the *iMacros* artifacts (e.g. the *CDTI_feeder* folder in Figure 3). At run time (Figure 3(4)), the *feeder* is transformed back into an iMacros script where mapping links are resolved during the transformation process so that the resulting script is a totally valid (i.e. totally instantiated) *iMacros* script. The whole process goes on without programming nor leaving the *iMacros* sidebar.

Implementation wise, three Ecore (meta)models are involved (see Figure 2(right)): (1) form filling scripts are abstracted in terms of *FormFlow* models, (2) the structure of the data source (e.g. the database schema) is captured as a *Data* metamodel, and (3), the VBS script is mainly expressed as a weaving model between a *FormFlow* model and a *Data* metamodel. The aforementioned **feeders** are realized as pairs *(FormFlow* model, *Weaving* model*)* (see the *CDTI_feeder* folder in Figure 3).

Feeders can be **synthesised** and **run**. Figure 4 depicts the processes triggered when pushing the namesake button in iMacros. During **synthesis**, injectors are used to obtain the *FormFlow* model (i.e. the platform-independent model (PIM)) and the *Weaving* model out of the sample iMacros script. At **run** time, the *feeder* is enacted, i.e, *(i)* references to external sources are resolved, *(ii)* an *iMacros* model (i.e. the platform-specific model (PSM)) is generated merging the information contained into the *FormFlow*, the *Weaving* and the *Data* models, *(iii)* this *iMacros* model is transformed into an *iMacros* script, and *(iv)* this script is run. Next sections introduce the main models that comprise the *WebFeeder* system and their extraction processes.

5 Abstracting the External Sources

The Data Metamodel. It stands for the elements and structure of the external source. If a database then, the *Data* metamodel captures the database schema as represented in the database catalogue. If a spreadsheet then, the *Data* metamodel denotes the tabular structure where data is ordered along different sheets and columns.

Injection. No matter the data source, the challenge is twofold. First, we need "a metamodel injector" that automatically obtains the *Data* metamodel out of the structure of the data source (e.g. the database schema, the spreadsheet file structure). Second, we require a "model injector" which harvests models out of a data source according to a given metamodel.

In a previous work [11], we studied model injection for databases, providing a language, *Schemol*, for defining database-to-model injectors. *Schemol* also permits to perform an automatic extraction of a metamodel based on a database schema. This feature, called *bootstrap*, transforms tables into metaclasses, columns into attributes, and foreign keys into references between metaclasses. This work has been extended to permit data sources other than databases. The approach is based on defining appropriate "drivers" that permit to conceptualize spreadsheets as databases, where sheets are the tables counterparts. The *Schemol* engine is the same but the driver changes. So far, drivers are available for *Excel* spreadsheets. Figure 5(right) shows the *Data* metamodel automatically obtained by *Schemol* for our sample database (Figure 5(left)). Each project has a main company, a set of participating companies, a manager and a set of users. Meanwhile, each employee is associated with the company he works for. Both companies and employees can be associated with several projects.

6 Abstracting the Form Filling Process

The FormFlow Metamodel. A *FormFlow* model abstracts the process of filling in a specific web form. This process abstracts a valid sequence of user interactions with the aim of form filling. The model includes: (*i*) the elements that compose the web form (e.g., type of inputs, ids), (*ii*) the order of the interactions (e.g., which input comes after another, when do we have to click a button, etc.) and (*iii*) the existence of loops (i.e. a set of pages that can be filled more than once during the same process, e.g. adding many users to a project).

A *FormFlow* model abstracts a filling process through a **Session** class (see Figure 6). A *session* is a sequence of **PageVisits** which in turn, are conceived as sequences of **Interactions**. Interactions can be **AtomicInteractions** or **CompoundInteractions**. Atomic interactions are classified as mouse **Click** or data **Input**. Clicks act upon *Hyperlinks* or *Buttons*, and they are usually used for page navigation. *Input* elements require the user to introduce data. On the other hand, a compound interaction stands for a meaningful unit of interactions (e.g. an HTML form element). **Loops** can be defined when many similar elements need to be introduced through the same section of the web form (e.g. adding

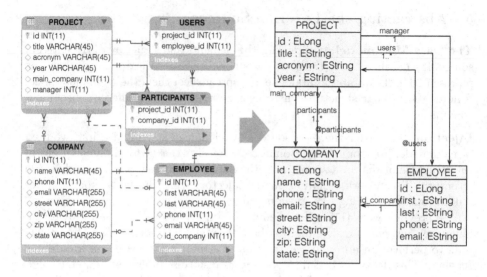

Fig. 5. Harvesting the *Data* metamodel out of database catalogues

users to a project). Each *loop* contains a reference to its trigger interaction (i.e. the button to access the first form in the loop) and the set of involved *pageVisits*.

Injection. *FormFlow* models can be *automatically* obtained from *iMacros* scripts. This process goes through the recorded macro and for each action, creates the corresponding *FormFlow* model element. For each *URL* or *TAG* command performed on a button or hyperlink, a *Click* element is created. On the other hand, when a TAG command is performed on an HTML input field, an *Input* element is generated. If the system detects that one command has been enacted in a different page than the previous one, a new *PageVisit* is generated. Within each visited page, for each different HTML form element whose fields have been enacted a *CompoundInteraction* is created. Besides, if the transformation detects that a concrete set of pages have been filled out more than once, it automatically creates the corresponding *Loop* element. Figure 7 depicts the *FormFlow* model obtained from the *iMacros* script in Figure 1.

7   Abstracting the Mapping

The Weaving Metamodel. A mapping sets a *feed* relationship from attributes in the *Data* metamodel to input fields in the *FormFlow* model. This mapping is captured as *"link"* elements along an AMW model [10]. A link states a nexus (in this case, a *feed* relationship) that indicates which data is to feed what input field.

Injection. Weaving data is collected as part of the recording process. That is, we prompt the user for the weaving information when iMacros encounters an input field. This is achieved through the *FormFlowDecorator* (see Figure 3(2.2)). When

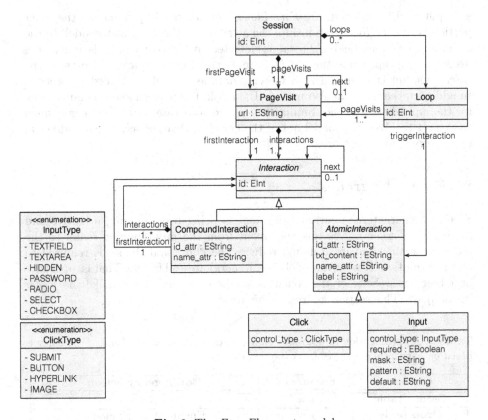

Fig. 6. The *FormFlow* metamodel

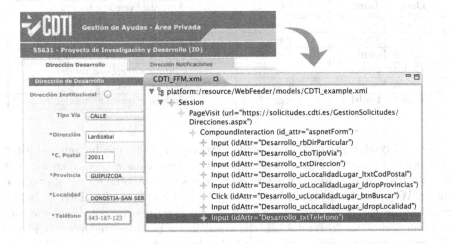

Fig. 7. Harvesting the *FormFlow* model out of iMacros scripts

an input field is detected, the *FormFlowDecorator* pops up to collect the other participant in the *link* relationship: the attribute of the *Data* metamodel. In the example, the input field *C.Postal* is detected in a web form. This makes the decorator pop up, requesting its *Data* metamodel counterpart. In this way, the *iMacros* script is leveraged with weaving data as part of the recording process. In addition, the user can also provide the mask, the pattern and a default value for the input field at hand. Similar to the previous cases, an injector is defined to extract the *Weaving* model out of the enriched iMacros script. No additional user intervention is required.

8   Facing Upgrades

Section 3 characterises current solutions as being programming intensive and fragile. *WebFeeder* moves this endeavour from the programming realm to the modeling realm, and in so doing, reduces the effort and the skills required to obtain a solution. However, models (i.e. *feeders*) are still fragile. That is, upgrades on either the website or the structure of the data source can make the *feeder* break apart. This section addresses this issue.

Table 2. A classification of upgrades for websites and database schema. Frequency is based on anecdotal evidences from the test case.

Change	Frequency	Contingency action
Create table	low	None
Drop table	low	Update Weaving model
Add column	high	None
Drop column	high	Update Weaving model
New Page	low	Regenerate the *feeder* from start
Delete Page	low	Regenerate the *feeder* from start
New Form	low	Update *FormFlow* model
Delete Form	low	Update *FormFlow* model
New Field	high	Update *FormFlow* model
Delete Field	high	Update *FormFlow* model

Table 2 typifies some of the possible changes. Upgrades can be handled using corrective or preventive actions. A corrective action deals with an upgrade that has occurred, and a preventive action addresses the potential for an upgrade to occur. We opted for a preventive strategy for tackling upgrades. That is, before running the *feeder*, we first check whether an upgrade occurred. If so, the user is prompted so as to reestablish the consistency between the *feeder* and the external dependencies (i.e. the website or the database schema). To this end, we introduce the **"safe mode"** for running *feeders*. Microsoft Windows' safe mode is a boot method that facilitates to diagnose problems. Likewise, when upgrades are expected, *feeders* can be run in "safe mode". Compared with the normal execution, this mode introduces two main differences as for the *feeder-to-iMacros* transformation, namely:

– the transformation is not enacted as a single shot but it processes one *PageVisit* at a time. This introduces a kind of "lazy evaluation" where the transformation of *pageVisit* elements and the enactment of the resulting iMacros scripts are intermingled: *transform(pageVisit_ 1, scriptOutput_ 1), enact(scriptOutput_ 1), transform(pageVisit_ 2, scriptOutput_ 2), enact(scriptOutput_ 2)*, etc. The rationales are twofold. First, this permits to phrase *upgrade detection* in terms of model differences between the existing *pageVisit* model and the current *pageVisit* model as extracted from the current page . Second, *upgrade resolution* is also handled at the page level, hence facilitating the intervention of the user at the time and at the place where the mismatch is detected (see next point).
– the transformation is leveraged with "caution clauses". Two types of caution clauses are introduced to handle each type of upgrades. For upgrades on web pages, a caution clause is introduced before the generation of the corresponding iMacros script. On loading, the clause obtains the *FormFlow* model only for the page at hand: the current *"pageVisit"* model. This model is compared for the namesake page in the existing *FormFlow* model: the stored *"pageVisit"* model. If mismatches, the *FormFlowDecorator* pops up for the user to restore the consistency. Second, for upgrades on external sources, a caution clause is introduced after the update of each *pageVisit*. This clause checks the mapping established on the Weaving model with the existing *Data* metamodel elements. If a reference does not match any *Data* metamodel element, the user is prompted to restore the consistency by providing a new mapping. Once these models are updated, the autofilling for the current page is enacted.

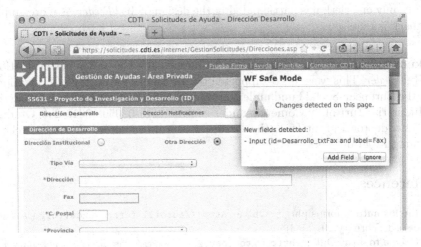

Fig. 8. Upgrading the sample form with a new field

Figure 8 illustrates the case of upgrading the sample form with a new field. *WebFeeder* detects a mismatch between the current *FormFlow* model and the *pageVisit* model as extracted from the current page. The execution stops and the user is prompted to provide a data weaving for the new field (if appropriate). Next, the execution resumes.

The bottom line is that *feeder* co-evolution is handled using the very same mechanisms that those of *feeder* construction, hence minimizing the cognitive burdens. Clerks can cope with (small) upgrades by themselves without turning to technical staff. Disruptive upgrades like introducing new tables or adding or deleting pages, require re-generating the *feeder* from scratch.

9 Conclusions

We address the feeding of form-intensive websites from external sources. Current solutions such as *iMacros* are characterized as programming intensive and fragile, hence, moving these tools away from their more likely audience: clerks. We strive to empower back clerks by abstracting the way at which feeding solutions are realized. The approach abstracts the development effort from the coding of *iMacros* scripts to the conception of models (i.e. *feeders*) from which these scripts are generated. In addition, *feeder* co-evolution (i.e. propagating website/data structure upgrades to the *feeder*) is handled using the very same mechanisms that those of *feeder* construction, hence minimizing the cognitive burdens. Clerks can cope with (small) upgrades by themselves without resorting to technical staff. The approach is realized through *WebFeeder*, a plugin for *iMacros*. *WebFeeder* introduces script models (i.e. *feeders*) as first-class artifacts in *iMacros*. *Feeder* synthesis, enactment and maintenance is handled without leaving *iMacros*. Next follow-on includes to conduct studies on the robustness and affordability of *WebFeeder*. A detailed account of the typology of website upgrades and their likelihood, will serve to better assess *WebFeeder* robustness. So far, only one clerk has participated in the design of *WebFeeder*. A more ample feedback is required.

Acknowledgments. Thanks are due to Inmaculada Cacho for her evaluation of *WebFeeder*. This work is co-supported by the Spanish Ministry of Education, and the European Social Fund under contract TIN2011-23839, and the Ministerio de Industria, Turismo y Comercio under contract TSI-020500-2010-206. Otaduy enjoys a doctoral grant from the Basque Government under the "Researchers Training Program".

References

1. Firefox autofill forms plugin. Online, http://autofillforms.mozdev.org (last accessed February 19, 2013)
2. Google toolbar. Online, http://toolbar.google.com/ (last accessed February 19, 2013)

3. iMacros. Online, http://www.iopus.com/iMacros/ (last accessed February 19, 2013)
4. Microformats. Online, http://microformats.org// (last accessed February 19, 2013)
5. Safari - autofill. Online http://www.apple.com/safari/ (last accessed February 19, 2013)
6. Selenium plugin. Online, http://docs.seleniumhq.org (last accessed February 19, 2013)
7. Araujo, S., Gao, Q., Leonardi, E., Houben, G.-J.: Carbon: Domain-Independent Automatic Web Form Filling. In: Benatallah, B., Casati, F., Kappel, G., Rossi, G. (eds.) ICWE 2010. LNCS, vol. 6189, pp. 292–306. Springer, Heidelberg (2010)
8. Brambilla, M., Cabot, J., Wimmer, M.: Model-Driven Software Engineering in Practice. Synthesis Lectures on Software Engineering. Morgan & Claypool Publishers (2012)
9. Cypher, A.: Automating Data Entry for End Users. In: 2012 IEEE Symposium on Visual Languages and Human-Centric Computing (VL/HCC), pp. 23–30 (2012)
10. Fabro, M.D.D., Bézivin, J., Valduriez, P.: Weaving Models with the Eclipse AMW Plugin. In: Eclipse Modeling Symposium, Eclipse Summit Europe, Citeseer, vol. 2006 (2006)
11. Díaz, O., Puente, G., Izquierdo, J.L.C., Molina, J.G.: Harvesting Models from Web 2.0 Databases. Software & Systems Modeling 12(1), 15–34 (2013)
12. Firmenich, S., Gaits, V., Gordillo, S., Rossi, G., Winckler, M.: Supporting Users Tasks with Personal Information Management and Web Forms Augmentation. In: Brambilla, M., Tokuda, T., Tolksdorf, R. (eds.) ICWE 2012. LNCS, vol. 7387, pp. 268–282. Springer, Heidelberg (2012)
13. Heinrich, M., Gaedke, M.: WebSoDa: A Tailored Data Binding Framework for Web Programmers Leveraging the WebSocket Protocol and HTML5 Microdata. In: Auer, S., Díaz, O., Papadopoulos, G.A. (eds.) ICWE 2011. LNCS, vol. 6757, pp. 387–390. Springer, Heidelberg (2011)
14. Scaffidi, C., Cypher, A., Elbaum, S., Koesnandar, A., Myers, B.: Using Scenario-based Requirements to Direct Research on Web Macro Tools. Journal of Visual Languages & Computing 19(4), 485–498 (2008)

Generating Feature Usage Scenarios
in Client-Side Web Applications

Josip Maras[1], Maja Štula[1], and Jan Carlson[2]

[1] University of Split, Croatia
{josip.maras,maja.stula}@fesb.hr
[2] Mälardalen University, Sweden
jan.carlson@mdh.se

Abstract. Client-side web applications are highly-dynamic event-driven GUI applications where the majority of code is executed as a response to user-generated events. Many software engineering activities (e.g. testing) require sequences of actions (i.e. usage scenarios) that execute the application code with high coverage. Specifying these usage scenarios is a difficult and time-consuming activity. This is especially true when generating usage scenarios for a particular feature because it requires in-depth knowledge of application behavior and understanding of the underlying implementation. In this paper we present a method for automatic generation of feature usage scenarios. The method is based on dynamic analysis and systematic exploration of the application's event and value space. We have evaluated the approach in a case study, and the evaluation shows that the method is capable of identifying usage scenarios for a particular feature. We have also performed the evaluation on a suite of web applications, and the results show that an increase in coverage can be achieved, when compared to the initial coverage obtained by loading the page and executing registered events.

Keywords: Web Applications, Symbolic Execution, GUI Testing.

1 Introduction

The client-side of a web application is a highly dynamic, event-driven environment where features manifest at runtime, triggered by sequences of user events – usage scenarios. Specifying these usage scenarios is a difficult and time-consuming activity and in the client-side web application domain, it is made even more complicated due to the fact that the application is a result of interplay of three conceptually different languages (HTML, CSS, and JavaScript), where the most complex one – JavaScript is a highly dynamic scripting language. This makes it difficult to understand feature behaviors and to specify usage scenarios that capture the complete behavior of particular features.

Usage scenarios are most often used in web application testing. Current state of practice is that developers create tests either manually, or with tools such as Selenium[1], which enable recording and replaying usage scenarios designed to

---

[1] http://docs.seleniumhq.org/

F. Daniel, P. Dolog, and Q. Li (Eds.): ICWE 2013, LNCS 7977, pp. 186–200, 2013.

test certain features. This is a time-consuming activity and automating it would offer considerable benefits. Usage scenarios can also be used for reuse – in our recent work [7] we have developed methods for identifying and extracting code and resources of client-side features based on the dynamic analysis of execution traces recorded while executing user-specified usage scenarios. This means that the quality of the extracted feature is highly dependent on the quality of usage scenarios. For this reason, automatic generation of high-coverage usage-scenarios for particular features would be beneficial.

In this work we define a method for generating usage scenarios for a particular feature in a client-side web application. The user selects parts of the page where the target feature manifests, and the process generates usage scenarios that achieve high coverage with respect to the selected parts of the page. The method is based on dynamic analysis and systematic exploration of the application's event and value space. Initial scenarios are created based on events registered during the initialization of the page, and new scenarios are added by executing and dynamically analyzing the execution of already generated scenarios. During scenario execution, all input parameters are symbolically tracked, and all event registrations, as well as all data dependencies between code expressions are logged. New scenarios are generated by modifying event input parameters, and by extending existing scenarios with registered events. Finally, the executed usage scenarios are filtered to reduce their number, with the criteria of still achieving high coverage.

We have evaluated the method on a case-study application, and the evaluation shows that the method is able to generate usage scenarios that target particular application features. We have also run the evaluation on a suite of web applications, and the evaluation shows that an increase in coverage, when compared to the straight-forward approach of loading the page and executing all registered events, is achieved by using systematic exploration of the application's event and value space.

This paper is organized as follows: Section 2 describes related work, while Section 3 presents a conceptual model of client-side web applications that helps us reason about the relationships between features and usage scenarios. Section 4 gives an overview of the feature usage scenario generation process, while Sections 5 and 6 go into more detail about generating and filtering usage scenarios. Section 7 describes the evaluation, while Section 8 presents the conclusion and possible future work.

2   Related Work

Our approach is based on client-side web application testing, where the goal is to create sequences of events that achieve high code coverage.

In [9], Mesbah et. al. describe their approach for automatic testing. The method is based on a crawler [8] that infers a state-flow graph for all client-side user interface states. New states and transitions are created by executing existing event handlers, analyzing the structure of the application and determining if it is changed enough to warrant a new state. The crawling phase is directed either with randomly generated input values or with user-specified values. Various errors are detected (DOM validity, error messages, etc.) by analyzing possible client-side user interface states.

Saxena et al. [10] present a method and a tool – Kudzu. The approach explores the application's event space with GUI exploration (searches the space of all event sequences with a random exploration strategy), and the application's value space by using dynamic symbolic execution. In the process, they have developed a string constraint solver capable of taking into account the specifics of string constraints present in JavaScript programs.

Artemis [2] is an approach for feedback directed testing of JavaScript applications from which we have derived most insights when developing our approach. The approach is based on dynamic analysis of web application execution – the application execution is monitored and all event registrations logged. New test cases are created by extending already existing tests with event registrations and by generating variants of the event input parameters. For generating new event input parameters they use randomly chosen values, and constants collected during the dynamic execution. They also introduce prioritization functions which influence the order in which generated test cases are analyzed.

None of the introduced client-side web application testing approaches enable developers to target specific client-side features, nor do they enable the filtering of generated scenarios in order to minimize the number of necessary usage scenarios. Also, in order to improve coverage, we use the systematic exploration of the application's event-space (similar to [2]) and combine it with symbolic execution (similar to [10]). On top of this, we track application dependencies by the means of a dependency graph [7], which enables us to accurately capture dependencies between different events, and to create event chains.

In the domain of testing server-side web applications, there exists the SWAT tool [1], which uses search-based testing. In their approach, random inputs to the web application are generated with additionally incorporated constant seeding (gathered by statically analyzing the source code), and by dynamically mining values from the execution. Although some parts of the approach could be adopted to fit the domain of client-side applications, their method is specially developed to deal with constraints inherent in server-side applications.

3　A Conceptual Model of the Client-Side Application

In this section we present a conceptual model of client-side web applications (Figure 1) that will be used to reason about generating usage scenarios for a particular feature. A feature is an abstract notion representing a distinguishable part of the system behavior that is manifested at runtime, when a user preforms a certain sequence of actions, i.e. a usage scenario [3].

A client-side application can be viewed as a collection of visually and behaviorally distinct UI elements (or UI controls). A UI control is primarily defined in terms of its structure, but it also includes the behavior on that structure. For

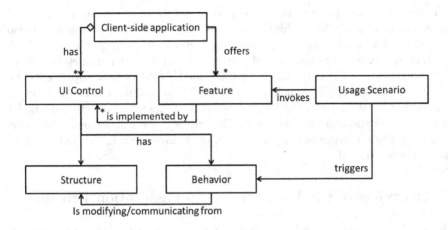

Fig. 1. Client-side web application conceptual model

example, in the case study shown in Figure 3, Section 7, each marked section of the page can be considered as a UI control.

A client-side application offers a number of features. Since client-side web applications are UI applications to server-side applications, a feature is manifested through a number of structural changes on the client-side and/or communications with the server-side. Because a UI control encapsulates structure and the behavior on that structure, and since features can cross-cut between different parts of the application, we define that a single feature is implemented by at least one UI control (Figure 1). A UI control implements a feature by reacting to user-generated events by modifying its structure, and/or communicating with the server from that structure. We utilize this relationship between features and UI controls – since features are abstract, and UI controls concrete, when generating usage scenarios for a particular feature, we are generating usage scenarios for the implementing UI controls.

3.1 Terminology

An event e is defined as a tuple $e = \langle h, t \rangle$, where h is an object on which the event occurs (e.g. an HTML node, or the global window or document objects), and where t an event type. At run-time, when an event is raised it is parametrized with properties of three different types [2]: *i)* event properties – a map from strings (property names) to numbers, booleans, strings and DOM nodes, *ii)* form properties, which provide string values for HTML form fields, and *iii)* the execution environment properties, which represent values for the browser's state that can be influenced by the user (e.g. window size). A parametrized event e^p consists of an event e and parameters p associated with that event.

The goal of the process is to compute a set U of usage scenarios: $U = \{u_0, u_1, ..., u_n\}$ that achieves high coverage of a given feature. A usage scenario u_i is defined as a sequence of parametrized events $u_i = \langle e^p{}_0, e^p{}_1, ..., e^p{}_m \rangle$. A scenario u_i exercises the behavior of a given feature if every parametrized event $e^p{}_i \in \langle e^p{}_0, e^p{}_1, ..., e^p{}_m \rangle$ is related to at least one UI control that implements the feature. A parametrized event is related to a UI control if: *i)* it is called on an html node that is a part of the UI control; *ii)* it modifies the structure of the UI control; *iii)* in the case of ajax events, if there is a data dependency from the request to the structure of the UI control, *iv)* it influences the execution of an event related to a UI control.

4   Overview of the Usage Scenario Generation Process

Client-side applications are highly dynamic and event-driven, and the appropriate way of reasoning about their control-flow is through dynamic analysis. As input the process receives the source code of the application, and a set of UI control selectors (e.g. css selectors, xPath expressions) that specify the UI controls that implement the feature of interest. The process consists of two phases: *i)* generating usage scenarios, and *ii)* filtering usage scenarios (Figure 2).

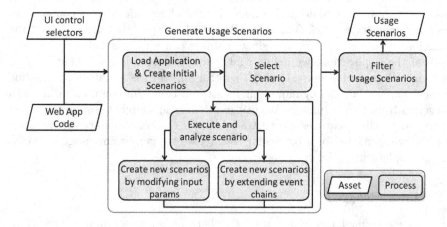

Fig. 2. The process of generating feature usage scenarios

The phase of usage scenario generation starts by initializing the web page – a stage of the execution not dependent on user input. During page initialization, a number of events can be registered, and these events are the basis for the creation of initial usage scenarios. For each event registered in the initialization phase, a new usage scenario, with default event parameter values is created.

Our approach then proceeds by selecting a usage scenarios, executing it, and dynamically analyzing the execution. New usage scenarios are created in two different ways: *i)* by modifying the usage scenario event input parameters – we track how the event input parameters influence the control-flow, and new usage scenarios are generated by modifying those inputs; *ii)* by extending event chains, either with new instances of previously executed events whose execution depends on the variables and objects modified during the execution of the scenario, or with newly registered events with default parameter values. New usage scenarios are created and analyzed until a certain coverage is achieved, a given time-budget expended, or a target number of scenarios have been generated.

In the second phase – usage scenario filtering – execution traces of all executed usage scenarios are analyzed, and the computed set of usage scenarios is filtered by removing scenarios that do not contribute to the feature behavior, and scenarios whose removal does not lower the overall coverage.

5   Generating Usage Scenarios

In this section we give a detailed description of how new usage scenarios are created, and for this we will use the example shown in Listing 1.1.

The example application has two features: Feature 1, implemented with the UI control defined by the first square (node with id *fc*, line 7), which consists of two behaviors: *i)* when the user clicks on the square with the left mouse button, the application subscribes to the mouse move events which change the color of the first square background depending on the position of the mouse, *ii)* counts the number of middle mouse button clicks on the first square, and outputs whether this number is even or odd; and Feature 2, implemented with the UI control defined by the second square (node with id *sc*, line 7), with a behavior: *i)* when the user clicks on the second square it outputs the current mouse position. This is an example of an event-driven application where code coverage depends both on the events raised by the user, and the properties of the raised events (e.g. which mouse button was clicked). Throughout this section we will show how the process generates usage scenarios that target the first feature.

5.1   Generating Initial Usage Scenarios

The start of the whole process is the execution of the page loading phase with the goal of obtaining registered events which will be used as a basis for defining initial usage scenarios (Algorithm 1).

For each event registered at the end of the loading phase, the process assigns default parameters to the event (e.g. for mouse clicks this means setting the pressed button to the left mouse button, the position of the mouse to the middle of the clicked on element; setting empty strings for HTML input elements, etc.), and creates a usage scenario (*u*) with that parametrized event.

```
1   <html><head>
2    <style>
3     .c{ width: 100px; height: 100px;}
4     #fc{background:rgb(255,0,0);} #sc{background:rgb(0,0,255);}
5    </style></head>
6   <body>
7    <div id="fc" class="c"></div><div id="sc" class="c"></div>
8    <script>
9     var fc = document.getElementById("fc");
10    var sc = document.getElementById("sc");
11    var fs = document.getElementById("fs");
12    var clicks = 0;
13    fc.onmousedown = function(e) {
14     if(e.which == 1)
15      fc.onmousemove = function(e) {
16       var val = e.pageX % 256;
17       this.style.background="rgb("+val+","+val+","+val+")";
18      }
19     else if(e.which == 2)
20      if(++clicks % 2 == 0)
21       this.textContent = "Even";
22      else
23       this.textContent = "Odd";
24    }
25    sc.onclick = function(e) {
26     this.textContent = e.pageX + ";" + e.pageY;
27    }
28   </script></body></html>
```

Listing 1.1. Example application

Algorithm 1. generateInitialScenarios($webAppCode$)

1: $executionInfo \leftarrow$ loadPage($webAppCode$)
2: $U \leftarrow$ empty
3: **for all** e : getEventRegs($executionInfo$) **do**
4:     $e^p \leftarrow$ parametrizeWithDefaults(e)
5:     $u \leftarrow$ createEmptyScenario()
6:     $u \leftarrow$ appendEventToScenario(u, e^p)
7:     $U \leftarrow$ appendScenario(U, u)
8: **end for**

Example. In the example from Listing 1.1 this means the creation of two usage scenarios with one event, based on the *onmousedown* event registration from line 13, Listing 1.1 – $u_0 = \langle \langle \#fc, onmousedown \rangle, \{which : 1\} \rangle$ (left mouse button is the default button in mouse events, represented by the value 1 of the *which* property), and based on the *onclick* mouse registration from line 25, Listing 1.1 – $u_1 = \langle \langle \#sc, onclick \rangle, \{pageX : 50, pageY : 150\} \rangle$ (the click is initially executed in the middle of the element).

5.2 Generating Scenarios by Exploring the Value Space

In order to generate scenarios by exploring the value space, we modify event parameters by using concolic testing [4,11]. The main idea is to execute the usage scenario both with concrete (e.g. default values for the initially created usage scenarios) and symbolic values for event input parameters. During the execution all encountered control-flow branches (e.g. if statements, conditional expressions, etc.) whose branching conditions are expressions that contain symbolic variables are added to the so called path-constraint, which carries information about how the control-flow of the execution depends on the input parameters. In order to build a scenario that exercises another path through the application we have to modify the input parameters based on the path constraint. This is usually done by systematically negating the constraints that compose the path-constraint, and in our approach we use generational search [5]. Constraints obtained in this way are solved with a constraint solver, which gives new event input parameter values that exercise different execution paths. Currently we are using Choco [6] – an of the shelf constraint solver.

Algorithm 2. createByModifyingPathConstraint(u, U, *executionInfo*)

1: **for all** *invertedFormula* : getInvertedFormulas(getPathConstraint(*executionInfo*)) **do**

2:    *result* $\leftarrow$ solveFormula(*invertedFormula*)

3:    **if** *result* $\neq$ *null* **then**

4:       $\langle e_0, e_1, ..., e_n \rangle \leftarrow$ getAffectedEvents(u, *result*)

5:       $\langle e^p_0, e^p_1, ..., e^p_n \rangle \leftarrow$ parametrizeEvents($\langle e_0, e_1, ..., e_n \rangle$, *result*)

6:       $U \leftarrow$ appendScenario(U, createScenario($\langle e^p_0, e^p_1, ..., e^p_n \rangle$))

7:    **end if**

8: **end for**

Determining default parameter domains – In addition to the constraints gathered during concolic execution, some of the event parameters always fall into a certain domain (e.g. the *which* property of the mouse event handler can have only three values: 1, 2, or 3; or the mouse position parameters, such as pageX and pageY, are constrained by the position of the element the event occurs upon). For this reason, when constructing the constraint that will be sent to the solver, a constraint that captures this domain of each parameter is also added.

Example. After the execution of the first usage scenario, we study its path constraint obtained from executing the if statement from Line 14, Listing 1.1: *which* = 1. In order to cover another execution path through the application we invert that constraint and obtain (*which* $\neq$ 1) and add the constraints inherent to the *which* property: *which* = 1 $\lor$ *which* = 2 $\lor$ *which* = 3. For these constraints the constraint solver obtains the result *which* = 3, and the new scenario $u_2 = \langle \langle \#fc, onmousedown \rangle, \{which : 3\} \rangle$ is generated. When we execute the usage scenario u_2 the resulting path constraint is *which* $\neq$ 1 $\land$ *which* $\neq$ 2, because both the condition of the if statement in Line 14, and the condition of the if statement in line 19 were evaluated to false. By inverting these constraints we obtain two constraints: $which \neq 1 \wedge which = 2$; and $which = 1$, and using the constraint solver we get two solutions: $which = 2$ and $which = 1$. The solution $which = 1$ is discarded since the scenario with the exact parameters already exists, and out of $which = 2$ we obtain a new scenario $u_3 = \langle \langle \#fc, onmousedown \rangle, \{ which : 2 \} \rangle$.

5.3   Generating Scenarios by Exploring the Event-Space

When generating scenarios by exploring the event-space the goal is to extend event chains, either with events newly registered during the execution of a scenario, or with already executed events that are still registered at the end of scenario execution. Algorithm 3 gives more detail about the whole process.

Algorithm 3. createByExtendingEvents(u, U, $executionInfo$)

1: **for all** e : getEventRegs($executionInfo$) **do**
2:      **if** wasInstanceExecuted(e, U) **then**
3:          **for all** e^p : getPreviousParametrizations(e, U) **do**
4:              **if** connectionExists($executionInfo$, e^p) **then**
5:                  $u_n \leftarrow$ createCopy(u)
6:                  $u_n \leftarrow$ appendEventToScenario(u_n, e^p)
7:                  $U \leftarrow$ appendScenario(U, u_n)
8:              **end if**
9:          **end for**
10:     **else**
11:         $u_n \leftarrow$ createCopy(u)
12:         $u_n \leftarrow$ appendEventToScenario(u_n, parametrizeWithDefaults(e))
13:         $U \leftarrow$ appendScenario(U, u_n)
14:     **end if**
15: **end for**

After the execution of a scenario the process traverses all events that are still registered at the end of the execution. If the event has already been executed (at least one parametrization of that event already exists in previously executed scenarios) then all execution logs of those events parametrizations are traversed. During the execution of each scenario we build a dependency graph [7] which captures the dependencies between code constructs that exist in a scenario. The insight that we use here is: there is a potential connection between an event and a scenario if the scenario modifies variables and/or objects on which the control-flow of the event, either directly, or indirectly, depends on (influences the branching conditions). If a connection exists between the execution info of the parametrized event and the execution info of the current scenario, then a new scenario is created by appending the parametrized event to the parametrized events from the current scenario. If the event has not yet been executed, then the process is similar to the process of generating initial usage scenarios – the newly registered event is parametrized with default parameters, and a new scenario is created by appending the parametrized event to the events from the current scenario.

Example. When analyzing the execution of the u_0 scenario, a new event, which has not been executed so far, is registered in Line 15, Listing 1.1 – $\langle \#fc, onmousemove \rangle$. This leads to the creation of a new usage scenario: $u_4 = \langle \langle \#fc, onmousedown, \{which: 1\} \rangle; \langle \#fc, onmousemove, \{pageX: 50, pageY: 50\} \rangle \rangle$. If we also study the process after the execution of $u_2 = \langle \langle \#fc, onmousedown, \{which: 2\} \rangle \rangle$ scenario, we can see that the event $\langle \#fc, onmousedown \rangle, \{which: 2\}$ writes to the variable *clicks*, created outside of the event context, at line 20, Listing 1.1. That same variable influences the control flow of the event (there exists a data dependency from the variable *clicks* to the if statement condition) – u_2 is dependent on itself – a new scenario u_5 is created: $u_5 = \langle \langle \#container, onmousedown, \{which: 2\} \rangle; \langle \#container, onmousedown, \{which: 2\} \rangle$.

5.4 Prioritizing Scenarios

The algorithms described in the previous sections create new usage scenarios by systematically exploring the event and value space of the application. This means that the number of generated scenarios considerably grows with application complexity. For this reason we determine the next scenario that will be executed and analyzed based on the following procedure: if there is a non-analyzed scenario created by exploring the value space, or a scenario whose last event has not so far been executed, the process selects it. If there are no such scenarios, i.e. only the scenarios created by extending the event chain with already executed events are available, then select the next scenario randomly with the following prioritization function:

$$P = 1 - \frac{\sum_{i=0}^{m} cov(e_i)}{m+1}$$

The formula is based on the intuition that executing scenarios with events that have already achieved high code coverage is likely to be less useful than executing scenarios with events with low coverage [2]. After the execution of every scenario, for every function visited during the evaluation of each event e, we recalculate the branch coverage achieved so far. We then use the prioritization function to guide the random selection of the next usage scenario that will be executed and analyzed. In the prioritization function: *cov* represents event branch coverage achieved so far.

6 Filtering Scenarios

In order to achieve high coverage, the process generates a number of scenarios. However, we are typically interested in obtaining a minimal number of scenarios that still achieve the same coverage. The main idea of this part of the process is to remove events that are not related to the UI controls that implement the feature (see Section 3.1), and to reduce the number of scenarios based on scenario coverage.

Algorithm 4. filterUsageScenarios(U, *selectors*)

1: **for all** $u_i \in U$ **do**
2:     **if** notRelatedToFeature(u_i, *selectors*) **then**
3:         $U \leftarrow$ removeScenario(U, u_i)
4:     **end if**
5: **end for**
6: *jointCoverage* $\leftarrow$ getJointCoverage(U)
7: **for all** $u \in$ sortDescendingByNoOfEvents(U) **do**
8:     **if** canScenarioBeRemoved(u, *jointCoverage*) **then**
9:         *jointCoverage* $\leftarrow$ removeScenarioCoverage(*jointCoverage*, u))
10:         $U \leftarrow$ removeScenario(U, u)
11:     **end if**
12: **end for**

For every executed scenario, the process checks whether the scenario is related to the specified UI controls (Section 3.1) – if it is not, the scenario is filtered away. The process then calculates joint scenario coverage, which is a map that shows, for each code expression, how many scenarios have executed that expression. Then, all scenarios are traversed in descending order, starting from the scenario with the longest event chain. For each scenario, the algorithm checks whether the joint coverage would remain the same if the expressions executed by the scenario would be removed. If so, the scenario is removed from the set of scenarios, and its coverage from *jointCoverage*.

Example. In the example application, the scenario generation phase has generated the following six scenarios:

- $u_0 = \langle\langle \#fc, onmousedown \rangle, \{which : 1\}\rangle; \ cov_0 = \{9 - 15, 25\}$
- $u_1 = \langle\langle \#sc, onclick \rangle, \{pageX : 50, pageY : 150\}\rangle; \ cov_1 = \{9 - 13, 25, 26\}$
- $u_2 = \langle\langle \#fc, onmousedown \rangle, \{which : 3\}\rangle; \ cov_2 = \{9 - 14, 19, 25\}$
- $u_3 = \langle\langle \ \#fc, onmousedown, \{which: 2\}\rangle\rangle; \ cov_3 = \{9 - 14, 19, 20, 21, 25\}$
- $u_4 = \langle\langle \ \#fc, onmousedown, \{which: 1\}\rangle; \langle \#fc, onmousemove, \{pageX: 50, pageY: 50\}\rangle\rangle; \ cov_4 = \{9 - 17, 25\}$
- $u_5 = \langle\langle \ \#fc, onmousedown, \{which: 2\}\rangle; \langle \#fc, onmousedown, \{which: 2\}\rangle; \ cov_5 = \{9 - 14, 19, 20, 21, 23, 25\}$

First all scenarios are traversed in order to remove the ones that do not contribute to the feature. In this case, this means the removal of scenario u_1 because it neither occurs on, nor does it modify the selected UI control ($\#fc$). Next, a joint coverage for the remaining scenarios is calculated. Here, we will discuss in terms of code lines, but the algorithm in general works on AST nodes. Joint coverage, from the perspective of executed lines, for the remaining scenarios

u_0, u_2, u_3, u_4, u_5 is: 9-14→5, 15→2, 16-17→1, 19→3, 20→2, 21→2, 23→1, 25→5. First we process the scenario u_5, which can not be removed from the set because it is the only scenario that executes line 23. Similarly, u_4 can not be removed because no other scenario executes lines 16 and 17. Scenario u_3 can be removed, because all of its lines are executed by at least one other scenario. After the removal of u_3 the joint coverage is: 9-14→4, 15→2, 16-17→1, 19→2, 20→1, 21→1, 23→1, 25→4. Similarly, u_2 and u_0 can also be removed.

7   Evaluation

We have performed two types of evaluation: *i)* on a case study application, where we study how the process is able to generate feature usage scenarios, and *ii)* on a suite of web applications, where we study the coverage the process was able to achieve when generating test cases. All results were obtained with the Firecrow tool[2] which implements the algorithms described in this paper.

7.1   Generating Feature Usage Scenarios – A Case Study

Consider the example application shown in Figure 3 which represents a tourist information application that enables the user to: *i)* toggle between different types of accommodation (by using the select menu marked with 1, or by pressing keyboard keys: e.g. A – Apartments, or H – hotels), *ii)* to select map locations (marked with 2) with mouse clicks which will change the information and photos displayed in the photos section (marked with 3); *iii)* to toggle between different photos (marked with 3) by clicking on buttons, or by pressing keyboard buttons (e.g. 1 for the first photo, 2 for the second photo); *iv)* to toggle between different county map zoom levels (marked with 4) by clicking on the county map; *v)* to automatically cycle between different event information (marked with 5).

The example application has three distinct high-level features: *i)* selecting the map location and viewing its information (sections marked with 1, 2, and 3); *ii)* toggling between different county map zoom levels (marked with 4); and *iii)* viewing event information (marked with 5). Even in the case of these relatively simple features, specifying usage scenarios with high coverage is a time-consuming activity that requires in-depth knowledge of application behavior and the understanding of the underlying implementation. For example, a developer who wants to specify a usage scenario that exercises the complete behavior of the first feature has to be aware of different ways the location can be selected (by mouse clicking on the location point in the map, by changing the type of displayed locations through the select box, or by pressing keyboard keys), and of different ways the photos (marked with 3) can be toggled (either with mouse clicks on different buttons, or with keyboard presses).

We have initialized the process for each of the features with the results shown in Table 1. For each feature, the process was able to achieve full coverage (in general this does not have to be the case), and it was successful in generating usage

---

[2] https://github.com/jomaras/Firecrow

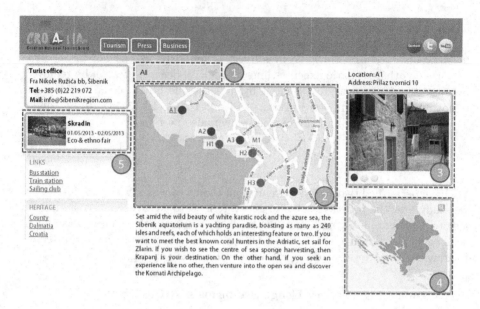

Fig. 3. Case study application

Table 1. A case study of generating feature usage scenarios

Feature	All Scenarios	Kept Scenarios	Gen. events	User events
Feature 1	25	12	12	12
Feature 2	25	1	2	2
Feature 3	25	1	1	1

scenarios that target specific UI controls. The table shows how many scenarios
the process generated in order to achieve full coverage (column All Scenarios),
how many scenarios were kept after the filtering process (Kept Scenarios), and
how many events in total the filtered scenarios have (Gen. events). The table
also shows the minimum number of events, we were able to find, to achieve full
coverage. In this application, the process was able to generate feature scenarios
which in total have the minimal number of events we were able to determine
by studying the application code. In general, since scenarios can be picked randomly from the set of generated scenarios, the generated sequences of events in
all analyzed scenarios are not necessarily minimal.

7.2 Generating Usage Scenarios for the Whole Page

For this experiment we have evaluated the approach by generating 100 tests for
a suite of web applications, most of them obtained from 10k and 1k JavaScript
challenges[3]. The code of all applications, and the generated scenarios can be

---

[3] http://10k.aneventapart.com/ and http://js1k.com/

obtained from: *www.fesb.hr/~jomaras/download/usageScenarioGenerator.zip*. Table 2 shows the results. For each application it shows the lines of code (LOC), statement coverage that can be achieved just by loading the page (L-Cov), coverage that can be achieved by executing the initially registered events with default parameters (I-Cov), coverage the process was able to achieve (A-Cov), and statement coverage that we were able to achieve by constructing event chains manually (M-Cov). The table also shows how many scenarios were kept after the filtering phase (Kept), and how many events have the final generated scenarios together. On average, the process is able to achieve additional 17,6% coverage when compared to the coverage achieved by loading the page and executing all registered events.

Table 2. Experiment results for generating 100 usage scenarios that target whole pages: LOC - Lines of Code, L-Cov – statement coverage on page load, I-Cov – statement coverage on executing initially registered events, A-Cov – Achieved Coverage, M-Cov – Maximum coverage we were manually able to achieve, Kept – Number of remaining scenarios after filtering, Gen. Events - total number of generated events.

App	LOC	L-Cov	I-Cov	A-Cov	M-Cov	Kept	Gen. Events
Snake	223	57,5%	63,7%	90%	98,36%	3	14
Prism	401	56,5%	70,5%	82,5%	94%	7	17
Jump	313	63,2%	65,8%	70,32%	98,23%	2	11
Agency	303	35,1%	57,4%	100%	100%	12	12
Slider	128	45,6%	71,7%	77,17%	86,41%	3	9
Minesweeper	175	59,1%	85,2%	93,91%	95,97%	6	7
3DMaker	385	18,9%	31%	42,59%	94,2%	2	8
floatwar	457	17,1%	45%	64,47%	93,7%	2	9
snowpar	352	19%	61,8%	81,5%	88,42%	19	22
3DModel	2567	17,8%	55,6%	81,8%	81,8%	24	24

8   Conclusion

Usage scenarios that execute application features with high coverage are used in many software engineering activities, such as testing, or reuse. Manually specifying these usage scenarios is a time-consuming activity, and automating it would bring considerable benefits. In this paper we have presented an automatic method for generating feature usage scenarios. The method works by systematically exploring the event and value space of the application. In order to create high-coverage scenarios we utilize techniques such as symbolic execution, and dependency tracking. In order to reduce the number of generated scenarios, we analyze the relationships between the scenarios and features, and remove all non-related scenarios. We also subsume scenarios based on their coverage. We have evaluated the method on a case study application, and the evaluation shows that the method is able to generate scenarios that target certain application features. We have also performed the evaluation on a suite of web applications, and the results show that an increase of code coverage, when compared to the initial coverage achieved simply by loading the page and executing all registered events, can be achieved.

For future work we plan to expand the usage scenario process to generate tests which take into account the server-side code, and we plan to perform the evaluation on a larger set of web applications. Since one motivation for developing this approach was to support the identification of feature code by automatically generating high-coverage usage scenarios, we plan to utilize this method in the development of an automatic feature identification process (by extending [7]).

References

1. Alshahwan, N., Harman, M.: Automated web application testing using search based software engineering. In: 26th International Conference on Automated Software Engineering, ASE 2011, pp. 3–12. IEEE Computer Society (2011)
2. Artzi, S., Dolby, J., Jensen, S.H., Møller, A., Tip, F.: A framework for automated testing of javascript web applications. In: 33rd International Conference on Software Engineering, ICSE 2011, pp. 571–580. ACM (2011)
3. Eisenbarth, T., Koschke, R., Simon, D.: Locating features in source code. IEEE Transactions on Software Engineering 29(3), 210–224 (2003)
4. Godefroid, P., Klarlund, N., Sen, K.: Dart: directed automated random testing. ACM Sigplan Notices 40, 213–223 (2005)
5. Godefroid, P., Levin, M.Y., Molnar, D.: Automated whitebox fuzz testing. NDSS (2008)
6. Jussien, N., Rochart, G., Lorca, X.: The choco constraint programming solver. In: CPAIOR 2008 Workshop on Open-Source Software for Integer and Contraint Programming (2008)
7. Maras, J., Carlson, J., Crnkovic, I.: Extracting client-side web application code. In: 21st International Conference on World Wide Web, WWW 2012, pp. 819–828. ACM (2012)
8. Mesbah, A., Bozdag, E., van Deursen, A.: Crawling ajax by inferring user interface state changes. In: Eighth International Conference on Web Engineering, ICWE 2008, pp. 122–134. IEEE (2008)
9. Mesbah, A., van Deursen, A., Roest, D.: Invariant-based automatic testing of modern web applications. IEEE Transactions on Software Engineering 38(1), 35–53 (2012)
10. Saxena, P., Akhawe, D., Hanna, S., Mao, F., McCamant, S., Song, D.: A symbolic execution framework for javascript. In: 2010 IEEE Symposium on Security and Privacy (SP), pp. 513–528. IEEE (2010)
11. Sen, K., Marinov, D., Agha, G.: CUTE: a concolic unit testing engine for C, vol. 30. ACM (2005)

Supporting Customized Views for Enforcing Access Control Constraints in Real-Time Collaborative Web Applications

Patrick Gaubatz[1], Waldemar Hummer[2], Uwe Zdun[1], and Mark Strembeck[3]

[1] Faculty of Computer Science, University of Vienna, Austria
{firstname.lastname}@univie.ac.at
[2] Distributed Systems Group, Vienna University of Technology, Austria
lastname@infosys.tuwien.ac.at
[3] Institute for Information Systems, WU Vienna, Austria
{firstname.lastname}@wu.ac.at

Abstract. Real-time collaborative Web applications allow multiple users to concurrently work on a shared document. In addition to popular use cases, such as collaborative text editing, they can also be used for form-based business applications that often require forms to be filled out by different stakeholders. In this context, different users typically need to fill in different parts of a form. Role-based access control and entailment constraints provide means for defining such restrictions. Major challenges in the context of integrating collaborative Web applications with access control restrictions are how to support changes of the configuration of access constrained UI elements at runtime, realizing acceptable performance and update behaviour, and an easy integration with existing Web applications. In this paper, we address these challenges through a novel approach supporting constrained and customized UI views that support runtime changes and integrate well with existing Web applications. Using a prototypical implementation, we show that the approach provides acceptable update behaviour and requires only a small performance overhead for the access control tasks with linear scalability.

1 Introduction

Real-time collaborative Web applications such as Google Docs[1], Etherpad[2], or Creately[3] aim to efficiently support the joint work of different team members, allowing them to collaboratively work on the same artifact at the same time. In addition to such popular examples, the real-time collaboration approach can also be used in typical business applications that often require multiple forms to be filled out by different stakeholders [7]. A crucial – though in the context of real-time collaborative Web applications often neglected – aspect of these business applications is access control.

---

[1] https://docs.google.com
[2] http://etherpad.org
[3] http://creately.com

F. Daniel, P. Dolog, and Q. Li (Eds.): ICWE 2013, LNCS 7977, pp. 201–215, 2013.

In recent years, role-based access control (RBAC) [14] emerged as a standard for access control in software systems. In RBAC, roles are used to model different job positions and scopes of duty within an information system. These roles are equipped with permissions to perform tasks. Human users (subjects) are assigned to roles according to their work profile [17]. For example, in an e-health application only a doctor shall be allowed to file a report. Moreover, a second doctor needs to check and sign the same report (four-eyes principle). In this example the role *doctor* is equipped with both permissions, i.e., filing and signing a report. To prevent a single subject from performing both tasks on the same report (thus undermining the four-eyes principle) we have to constrain these two tasks with an entailment constraint. *Entailment constraints* (see, e.g., [3,18,20]) provide means for placing restrictions on the subjects who can perform a task x given that a certain subject has performed another task y. *Mutual exclusion* and binding constraints are typical examples for entailment constraints. For instance, a *dynamic mutual exclusion* (DME) constraint defines that two subjects must not perform two mutually exclusive tasks in the same instance of a Web document. This means, that the permissions to perform two DME tasks can be assigned to the same subject or role, but for each instance of a particular Web document, we need two distinct individuals to perform both tasks. Binding constraints, on the other hand, can be seen as the opposite of mutual exclusion constraints. For example, *subject binding* defines that the subject who performed the first task must also perform the bound tasks.

Ideally, realizing form-based business applications with a real-time collaborative Web application approach would enable us to enforce RBAC and entailment constraints directly as the users collaboratively work on the forms, i.e., by constraining (e.g. by disabling, locking, or hiding) certain control elements in the user interfaces (UI) for certain subjects. However, so far this topic has – to the best of our knowledge – not been addressed in the existing literature. Major open challenges in this context are how to support changes of the configuration of access constrained UI elements at runtime, realizing acceptable performance and update behaviour, and the easy integration with existing Web applications.

In this paper, we address these challenges that are inherent to enforcing access control constraints in the context of real-time collaborative Web applications. The client-side part of our approach follows the Model-View-ViewModel pattern [15]. Additional server-side components complement our service-based architecture. The resulting architecture enables us to support runtime changes and facilitates the integration our approach with existing applications (see Section 6.2). Furthermore, we show that the approach provides acceptable update behaviour and requires only a small performance overhead for the access control tasks. In our experiments, it shows linear scalability (see Section 6.1). The remainder of this paper is structured as follows: An example scenario motivates our approach in Section 2. In Sections 3 and 4 we propose a novel approach supporting constrained and customized UI views. In Section 5, we describe a prototypical implementation and revisit the motivating example. After comparing to related work in Section 7 we conclude in Section 8.

2 Motivating Example and Challenges

As a motivating example, consider a Web-based application where patient health records are maintained using forms for data entry. The data entry procedure is typically included in a business process with well-defined roles and responsibilities (see, e.g., [9]). In previous work, we presented *CoCoForm* [7], a real-time collaborative Web application framework in which several users can concurrently fill out HTML forms.

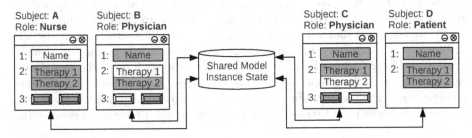

Fig. 1. Form-based Collaborative Web Application with Customized Views

Figure 1 shows a simplified example of using *CoCoForm* in the e-health domain. It includes four subjects with shared access to the health record of a patient. The subjects take different roles (nurse, physician, patient) which define their permissions within the application. The nurse enters the name and other personal data of the patient into a textfield (identified by "1"), physician B adds "Therapy 1" to the list of therapies (field "2"), and physician C suggests an additional specialized therapy "Therapy 2". The entire form record is then confirmed by both physicians (buttons "3"). To enforce the four-eyes principle (DME constraint), after physician B clicks the first submit button, the second button is deactivated for physician B, but remains active for physician C. Moreover, each physician can only modify his own therapy suggestions (subject-binding constraint). Finally, the patient should have read-only access to the data. To enforce these constraints, each user has a customized view with partial access to the collaboratively shared model. In Figure 1, white elements can be accessed and modified by the respective user, whereas elements with gray background are subject to access limitations (e.g., read-only but not editable).

A major challenge to realize such customized views for access control constraints is that the *configuration of constrained UI elements* must be *computed server-side* and *effected client-side*. Moreover, this *configuration* might *change dynamically at runtime*. Other challenges are related to *performance and update behaviour*: This means, we immediately need to deliver customized views to all UIs that access the same instance of a Web document (e.g., in the example the UIs need to be updated immediately after one of the subjects changes a document). Such an *immediate update* is required to prevent users from performing actions that were either already performed by another user or that are constrained by an entailment constraint (which may have a direct impact on the subjects who are allowed to fill in certain form field for example, see Section 1). In order to be applicable in real-world application scenarios, the approach should *efficiently handle large numbers of simultaneously connected users*. Finally, the approach should allow for an *easy integration with existing Web applications*.

3 Approach Synopsis

The aim of our approach is to support access control and customized views in real-time collaborative Web applications. The *View* of a Web application represents the UI with all visible and invisible elements, form input fields, interactive content, and more. The elements and associated interactions in the UI are subject to constraints (e.g., actions that require a certain permission) which are encoded in well-defined (RBAC) models. Our approach maps the model elements to configuration properties, and clients request the runtime values of these configurations from a *View Service*. The user-specific configurations computed by the server-side *View Service* are then applied to the *View* on the client-side.

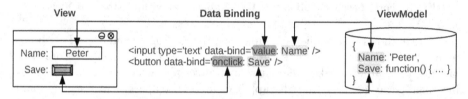

Fig. 2. Data Binding between View and ViewModel

As the basic binding concept between the *View* and the *Model*, our approach applies the *Model-View-ViewModel* (MVVM) pattern [15]. The MVVM is a specific version of the Presentation Model pattern (see [6]). It relies on the data binding concept, which ensures that the *View* and the state of its components are bound to properties of a *ViewModel*. This means that changes of the *ViewModel* are automatically reflected in the *View*. For instance, in Figure 2 we can see that the `value` attribute of the `<input>` field is bound to the property `Name` in the *ViewModel*. Secondly, the `onclick` handler of the `button` is bound to the *ViewModel*'s `Save` property. In general, the *ViewModel* acts as a mediator between the Model and the View by encapsulating all logic (e.g., formatting and data type conversion) needed to expose the properties and functionalities of the *Model* to the bound *View*. Additionally, it is in charge of reacting to user commands (e.g., a user fills out an input field) and reflecting them by performing the corresponding *Model* state changes. In general, the MVVM pattern makes it easy to realize the client-side part of the required *View Customization* functionality. In particular, we can customize a client's *View* just by configuring its *ViewModel* properties.

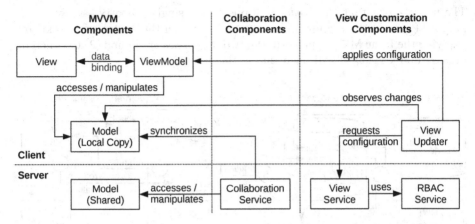

Fig. 3. Architectural Overview

Figure 3 provides an architectural overview of the components (i.e., both server-side and client-side) and interactions in our approach that are needed to realize the required *View Customization* functionality. The left-hand column of the figure depicts the core components of the MVVM architecture. In contrast to the classic MVVM architecture, in our approach the *ViewModel* does not directly access/manipulate the shared *Model* (i.e., the shared application state). Instead, it accesses/manipulates only a local copy of the shared *Model.* That is, a *Collaboration Service*, which is the cornerstone of a real-time collaborative Web application, ensures that the server-side shared *Model* is constantly kept in sync with all client-side copies of it. While the *Collaboration Service* allows us to let users collaboratively work on the same Web document, it certainly does not provide means for constraining (e.g., disabling, locking, or hiding) certain control elements in the UI for certain users. Consequently, the *View Service* uses the central *RBAC Service* to compute *ViewModel* configurations. Although these *ViewModel* configurations are computed server-side, they need to be effected client-side, i.e., to constrain UI elements in the *Views* of each client. To account for this, the client-side *View Updater* component of each client actively requests (i.e., pulls) the computed *ViewModel* configurations from the *View Service*. Eventually, these configurations are then applied to the *ViewModel,* which in turn – through data binding – effectively constrain the *Views* of each client.

4   Supporting Customized Views

This section details how the different components of the architecture outlined in Figure 3 enable us to enforce access control policies and entailment constraints directly as the users collaboratively work on a shared *Model,* i.e., by constraining certain control elements in the UI for certain subjects.

Firstly, we want to exemplify our UI customization approach using Figure 4. The figure is divided in two parts, the client-side part and the server-side part.

The figure shows that the *Model* contains only a single property `Name` which is mapped ① to both, a `value` and a `label` property in the *ViewModel*. Next, by applying the basic MVVM pattern, the two properties are bound ② to concrete `<label>` and `<input>` HTML elements in the *View*.

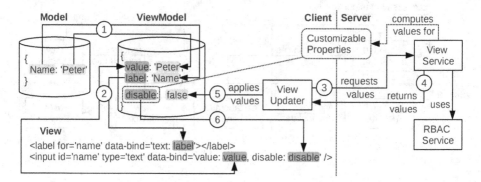

Fig. 4. View Customization Example

Next, we assume that the `<input>` field (and the associated action in the RBAC model) is constrained by some RBAC policy. To customize the `<input>` and dynamically make it enabled or disabled, we add the `disable` property to our *ViewModel*. The name of the property (`disable`) is added to the set of *Customizable Properties*. That is, we do not want the client to decide about the value of the `disable` property on its own. Instead, the server has to compute the values for each *Customizable Property*. Thus, the client requests ③ the values from the server-side View Service. The View Service uses the RBAC Service to determine the concrete value for the `disable` property (`true` if and only if the client is allowed to change the `Name` property of the *Model*). The View Service returns ④ the list of *Customizable Properties* together with their customized values to the client-side View Updater. Next, the View Updater applies ⑤ these customized values to the *ViewModel*. Finally, the property value is automatically reflected ⑥ in the *View*, as we have bound the `disable` property of the *ViewModel* to the `disabled` flag of our `<input>` field.

Abstracting from the example in Figure 4, the basic idea of our approach is that the core *ViewModel* is augmented with additional *Customizable Properties*. These properties are used to easily implement customizations in the *View* (e.g., enabling/disabling an `<input>` field). While the property names are defined and processed on the client-side, the actual values for these properties are computed for each user separately on the server side. In summary, the purpose of the *Customizable Properties* is twofold:

1. **Enablement.** At the client-side, these properties have an enabling character, i.e. they allow for realizing the customization of the *View*.
2. **Contract.** Additionally, they can be considered as a contract between the *ViewModel* and the server-side View Service. That is, the client-side *ViewModel* defines the set of *Customizable Properties* and the server-side View

Service provides the actual values for these properties. For instance, if the server returns a value of `true` for the `disable` property (see the example above), the client is responsible for actually disabling the `<input>` field in the client's *View*. Hence, the client and the server must have a common view of the semantics of each property.

4.1   Client-Side Updates of the ViewModel

The View Updater is in charge of requesting and applying *ViewModel* configurations from the View Service. We propose a simple request/response style of communication between these two components.

```
1   var subject, role,
2       viewModel = {
3           value: 'Peter', label: 'Name', // core properties
4           disable: false, visible: true // customizable properties
5       };
6
7   function requestView() {
8       var xhr = new XMLHttpRequest(),
9           uri = '/viewService?subject=' + encodeURI(subject) + '&role=' + encodeURI(role);
10      xhr.open('GET', uri);
11      xhr.onload = function() {
12          var configuration = JSON.parse(this.response); // e.g. {disable: true, visible: true}
13          for (var property in configuration) {
14              viewModel[property] = configuration[property];
15          }
16      };
17      xhr.send();
18  };
19
20  function onModelChange(property, value) { // called whenever the Model changes
21      requestView();
22      viewModel[property] = value;
23  };
```

Listing 1. A Simple View Updater Example

Listing 1 illustrates an excerpt of the corresponding exemplary client-side JavaScript code. After firing the request (line 17) we asynchronously process the response that contains the requested *ViewModel* configuration. In the example from Listing 1, the *Customizable Properties* consist of two properties `disable` and `visible` (line 4). Correspondingly, the *ViewModel* configuration returned by the View Service contains concrete values for these two properties, e.g., {`disable: true, visible: true`}. The next step is to apply this configuration to our *ViewModel*. To this end, the JSON-encoded result of the View Service is parsed, and each entry in the result is applied to the local `viewModel` variable (lines 12-15).

Having discussed how the View Updater requests and applies *ViewModel* configurations, we now draw our attention to the question when it should issue its requests. In general, we can say that this depends on the application's context. However, in our context, i.e., RBAC and entailment constraints, we can also say that *Views* need to be updated exclusively after a *Model* change has happened. Whenever a property is changed in the shared *Model* (i.e., the application state), all *Views* need to be re-computed and (potentially) updated. This circumstance is also reflected in Listing 1 (lines 20-23), where we can see that a new request is triggered for every *Model* change that happens (via the `onModelSync()` callback).

4.2   Server-Side Computation of ViewModel Configurations

The computation of *ViewModel* configurations is done server-side, i.e., by the View Service. Upon a request, the View Service returns a *ViewModel* configuration to the requesting client-side View Updater component.

```
1   function onRequest(subject, role) {
2       var property = 'Name', // there is just a single 'Name' property in our model
3           response = {
4               disable: !rbacService.canWrite(subject, role, property),
5               visible: rbacService.canRead(subject, role, property)
6           };
7       return response; // e.g. {disable: false, visible: true}
8   }
```

Listing 2. Basic View Service Example

For instance, in Listing 2 we can see an excerpt of the implementation of a very basic View Service[4] that is tailored to return a configuration for the set of *Customizable Properties* defined in the application code presented in Listing 1. In essence, the service has to compute values for the two *Customizable Properties*, i.e., `disable` and `visible`. As we can see (line 4), it "asks" the central RBAC Service if the provided `subject`/`role` combination has the permission to change (i.e., write) the application's *Model* property, i.e., `Name`. A positive answer (i.e., the user has the permission to change the *Model* property) is reflected with a `disable` value of `false`, which in turn enables the UI element and eventually allows this specific user to manipulate the *Model* property in her customized *View*. Similarly, the service uses the RBAC Service to determine a value for the `visible` property. Eventually, it returns the JSON-encoded configuration (line 7) to the requesting client. Note, that the required parameters of the service, i.e., `subject` and `role` could be supplied as URI parameters (as in line 9 in Listing 1).

5   Implementation – The CoCoForm Framework

This section discusses a prototype implementation of our approach, called Constrainable Collaborative Forms (CoCoForm)[5]. We used CoCoForm to implement and evaluate the e-health record case from Section 2.

---

[4] Note that we chose JavaScript solely for its well-known and concise syntax.

[5] A proof-of-concept demo is available at `http://demo.swa.univie.ac.at/cocoform2`

Our prototype is based on the OpenCoweb[6] framework, which consists of both, a Collaboration Service (as in Figure 3) and a (client-side) JavaScript API. The latter allows to subscribe to incoming *Model* change events, i.e., by registering a callback function which in turn enables us to trigger our View Updater component (as in Listing 1).

The View Updater issues simple XMLHttpRequests to obtain *ViewModel* configurations from the View Service. The View Service is implemented as a plain HTTP Service in Java, using the JAX-RS API[7], and the configurations are returned in JSON format. The central RBAC Service, which is utilized by the View Service, has been presented in previous work [7]. We use a model-driven approach for defining forms and securing them using access control constraints. Server-side we internally work with Ecore[8] model instances which are marshalled into JSON for the client-side JavaScript application.

Besides OpenCoweb's JavaScript API, we use the Knockout[9] library for realizing the MVVM pattern in the client-side application code. In particular, we also use Knockout's Mapping plugin which allows us to automatically transform the JSON-encoded *Model* into a *ViewModel*. The Mapping plugin also allows us to easily update the *ViewModel* whenever the *Model* changes. Additionally, we augment the *ViewModel* with additional `visible` and `editable` properties. We also use Knockout's template mechanism to (1) create the needed input fields and buttons on-the-fly and (2) establish data binding using corresponding `data-bind` attributes.

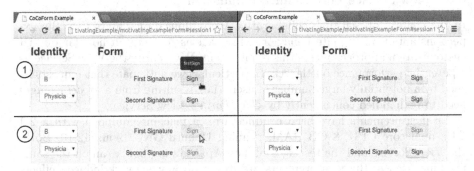

Fig. 5. Customized Views and Dynamic Mutual Exclusion with *CoCoForm*

Motivating Example Revisited. Now we want to revisit the dynamic mutual exclusion example from Section 2 and discuss a concrete implementation using *CoCoForm*. Figure 5 shows four screenshot excerpts of an example form with two dynamically mutual exclusive buttons. In particular, these buttons represent the first and the second signature on a patient record (as described in Section 2).

---

[6] OpenCoweb, `http://opencoweb.org`
[7] JAX-RS, `http://jax-rs-spec.java.net`
[8] Eclipse Modeling Framework, `http://www.eclipse.org/modeling/emf`
[9] Knockout, `http://knockoutjs.com`

Figure 5 is vertically split into two columns, i.e., the *View* of the first user (subject B) and the second user (subject C). Both subjects are concurrently working on this form. In the first row (indicated with ①) we can see that both buttons are available for both subjects. The mouse pointer in the upper left part indicates that subject B clicks the first signature button. This click results in a *Model* change which triggers the View Updater component of both clients. As a result, the View Updaters of both clients issue a request to the View Service, resulting in the updated Views in ②. While the first button has been disabled for both clients (which reflects the requirement that any form element can only be manipulated once), the second button is only disabled for subject B. This is due to the dynamic mutual exclusion constraint which demands that subject B, who has just clicked the first button, must be prevented from clicking the second button (see Section 2). However, subject C is still allowed to click the second button. In summary, this example illustrates how our approach enforces access control constraints in real-time collaborative Web applications by dynamically changing the UIs of each user at runtime.

6 Evaluation

In the following sections we discuss both, our lessons learned and the limitations of our approach and the findings of the conducted performance evaluation.

6.1 View Service Performance Evaluation

In the context of real-time collaborative Web applications, users typically expect instantaneous update behavior, which led us to study in how far our UI customization approach meets this requirement. We identify the View Service as a potential performance bottleneck. In particular, we anticipate that requests issued by a potentially large number of users (i.e., resulting from a *Model* change) need to be handled concurrently by *CoCoForm's* View Service.

All measurements have been conducted on a machine equipped with a 2.4 GHz dual core CPU, 8 GB RAM, running Ubuntu GNU/Linux 12.10. Both, the View Service and the testing tool, i.e., Apache's ab tool[10], ran on the same machine. Hence, the measurements are free from any network-induced effects such as latency, jitter and so on.

Figure 6 depicts the average response times of both, the actual View Service (solid line) and a "Null" (i.e., no computation at all) Service (dashed line), for a given number of concurrent requests. For instance, in the case of 600 concurrent requests, the average response time for all clients is roughly 200 ms while the response time of the Null Service is roughly 50 ms. This means, that in this case it takes roughly 150 ms to compute a single *ViewModel* configuration, while the rest of 50 ms accounts for the underlying communication and Web Service stack.

The evaluation results indicate that our View Service implementation has linear scalability. Even in the case of 2000 users working on the same form

---

[10] Apache ab tool, http://httpd.apache.org/docs/2.4/programs/ab.html

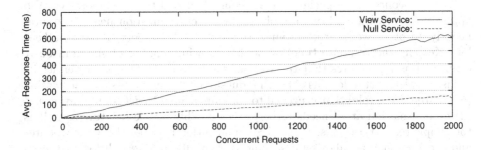

Fig. 6. View Service Response Times

document collaboratively, the average response time remains well below a second. In our experiment, the View Service's response times amount to approximately four times the response times of the Null Service. As the Null Service represents the theoretical minimum that is possible for the given Web Service framework, we consider the performance overhead acceptable.

6.2 Lessons Learned

We implemented the *CoCoForm* prototype (see Section 5) to demonstrate the feasibility of our approach (see Section 4). We showed that access control policies and entailment constraints in the context of real-time collaborative Web applications can effectively be enforced by dynamically constraining UI elements for certain subjects. In the following paragraphs we want to discuss our lessons learned and the limitations of our approach.

Our approach is complementary to currently available frameworks and solutions that support the development of real-time collaborative Web applications such as Apache Wave[11], ShareJS[12] and OpenCoweb (see Section 5). This is due to the fact that it is completely decoupled from the collaborative aspects of the application. In essence, supporting customized views using our approach merely requires the deployment of a single, dedicated and self-contained View Service as well as hooking-in the View Updater code into the client-side application code.

Although our approach is built upon the MVVM pattern, it does not exclude other approaches (e.g., the classic Model-View-Controller pattern). Instead, we argue that our approach can coexist with others. In that case, the *ViewModel* is solely used to realize the customizable parts of the *View*. Hence, it just contains the set of *Customizable Properties*. The only requirement is that the corresponding DOM nodes (e.g., <input> elements) are augmented with additional data binding attributes (e.g., data-bind). Note that this even works in the case of dynamically generated (i.e., generated using JavaScript code) DOM nodes, as long as it is possible to add the data binding attributes.

---

[11] Apache Wave, http://incubator.apache.org/wave
[12] ShareJS, http://sharejs.org

A major concern – especially in the context of real-time collaborative Web applications – is the ability to apply the View customization nearly instantaneously. In other words, the response times of the View Service must be kept low. Keeping the response time low with a growing number of simultaneously connected users, requires that the system is able to scale. Our View Service itself is completely stateless, as (1) each request contains all necessary information (e.g., subject and role) that is needed to compute a *ViewModel* configuration and (2) no information at all needs to be persisted. This stateless nature as well as the simple request/response style of communication between the View Updater and the View Service allows for scaling horizontally in a straightforward manner, i.e., the communication can be routed through a load-balancing proxy that distributes each request among multiple instances of the service.

However, the request/response communication style also comes with a couple of challenges. For example, there is the issue of "the needless request". This is the case when the View Service returns a *ViewModel* configuration that is not different from the currently active one. Hence, we could have saved both client-side and server-side computing resources (e.g., CPU time, network bandwidth, etc.) if we simply had not issued this "needless request" in the first place. This issue can be addressed using a push approach (instead of the presented pull approach). That is, the View Service would selectively push new *ViewModel* configurations to the clients only if it is necessary (i.e., at least one *ViewModel* property needs to be changed). However, this push approach introduces a certain amount of complexity to the View Service. For instance, it would require an explicit session handling, i.e., in a push scheme we have to maintain a list of connected clients to correctly update the corresponding *ViewModels*. Moreover, a push scheme would also require to keep track of each client's *ViewModel* to determine if we need to push a new *ViewModel* to a particular client. In summary, the push approach allows for avoiding "needless requests" (in fact, no requests are made at all) while the pull approach comes with a lower complexity, especially when scaling (i.e., when multiple instance of the View Service have to coordinate session with each client's *ViewModel* configuration). Another idea to – at least – mitigate this problem would be a more efficient client-side triggering logic. For instance, we could provide the clients with a list of *Model* properties that are not constrained by any access control constraint at all. Then, the clients would not need to request a new *ViewModel* configuration whenever a *Model* change event arrives that is contained in the list of unconstrained properties.

In our approach access control policies and entailment constraints are enforced client-side, i.e., by constraining UI elements. From a security perspective, however, we often cannot trust code that is executed on the client (i.e., the browser). The reason is that we can not prevent a potential attacker from modifying the code to be executed. For instance, an attacker might be able to change the *View-Model* configuration to gain access to a constrained UI element and eventually pass a *Model* change event (i.e., concerning a constrained *Model* property) to the Collaboration Service. However, we could contain the effects of such client-side code injections by preventing such unauthorized *Model* changes (1) from being applied to the server-side *Model* and (2) from being distributed to other session participants. This can be achieved by routing all incoming (i.e., coming from the clients) *Model* change events trough an enforcement proxy. This proxy uses the RBAC Service to decide if it should forward the event to the Collaboration Service (i.e., in case the client has the permission to change the *Model* property) or not. This guarantees that client-side code injections do not lead to server-side *Model* changes or impact session participants.

Finally, our approach assumes that the *Model* is being synchronized with all clients. That is, all clients "see" exactly the same *Model*. However, if this *Model* contains sensitive information, this might be an issue. We will address this problem as part of our ongoing research.

7   Related Work

In this section we discuss related work in the area of customized and shared application views, collaboration platforms as well as access control enforcement.

Customized and Shared Application Views. Similar to customized views in our approach, Koidl et al. [12] propose user-specific Web site rendering. However, their approach aims at user-centric personalization of Web experience, whereas the customized views in our approach result from RBAC policies and entailment constraints. An interesting aspect in their solution is that the personalization is cross-site, i.e., it spans the Web sites of multiple providers. Our approach currently does not implement cross-provider policies. However, we presented a related approach for cross-organizational access control in Web service based business processes in [9]. As part of our future work, we will integrate cross-site capabilities in our approach for real-time collaborative Web applications. Berry et al. [2] have applied role-based view control to desktop applications. Their approach captures the virtual framebuffer of application windows and applies blurring, highlighting, pixelizations, and other manipulations over the rendered view. Our approach benefits from the fact that manipulation of Web user interfaces is easier to achieve; using the path to the target DOM element, our client-side View Updater takes care of customized view manipulations.

Collaboration Platforms. The seminal work of Sun et al. [19] proposes the transparent adaptation (TA) approach to convert single-user applications into collaborative multi-user applications. The cornerstone of TA is operational transformation (OT) [4]. Our approach is orthogonal to OT: the RBAC policies and entailment constraints provide an application workflow with well-defined responsibilities, and we maintain document consistency by allowing only sequences of operations that comply with this workflow. Farwick et al. [5] discuss an architecture for Web-based collaborative metamodeling. Their framework allows multiple users to work on graphical meta-models collaboratively. Modifications of the (meta-)models are secured by basic access control measures, but in contrast to our work, they do not explicitly address customized views and dynamic updates resulting from the enforcement of RBAC entailment constraints. Heinrich et al. [8] present a generic collaboration infrastructure aimed at transforming existing single-user Web applications into collaborative multi-user Web applications by synchronizing DOM trees. In other words, their approach makes sure that the DOM trees of all clients in a collaborative session is constantly kept in sync. As we strive for customizing the DOM tree for each client, this approach is completely at odds with ours. Consequently, we require synchronization to take place at the model-level instead of the view-level (as in [8]).

Security and Access Control Enforcement. A plethora of approaches have been presented for integrating security and access control in Web applications. Joshi et al. [10] provide an early study on generic security models for Web-based applications. Starnberger et al. [16] use smart card based security and discuss a generic proxy architecture to enforce authorizations. In [1], Belchior and colleagues model RBAC policies using RDF triples and N3Logic rules. Mallouli et al. [13] use extended finite state machines (EFSM) to model systems with OrBAC [11] (Organization Based Access Control) security policies. However, none of these approaches addresses the enforcement of access control policies and entailment constraints in dynamic real-time Web applications.

8   Conclusion and Future Work

In this paper, we demonstrate that access control policies and constraints – in particular entailment constraints – in the context of real-time collaborative Web applications can effectively be enforced by dynamically constraining UI elements for certain subjects. We show that our service-based approach can be used to realize the corresponding UI view configuration functionality and we provide evidence that it is potentially capable of meeting the – especially in the context of real-time collaborative Web applications important – requirement of nearly instantaneous update behavior, even for a large number of simultaneously connected users. Although the client-side part of the UI view configuration functionality is built upon the MVVM pattern, we show that it can easily coexist with others.

As future work we will look into privacy issues (see Section 6.2) and apply our approach to other types of collaborative processes. In particular, we are interested in establishing the concept of entailment constraints in more dynamic processes (e.g., text editing or modeling) where we will have to deal with completely dynamic (i.e., changing at runtime) access control and constraint models.

References

1. Belchior, M., Schwabe, D., Silva Parreiras, F.: Role-based access control for model-driven web applications. In: Brambilla, M., Tokuda, T., Tolksdorf, R. (eds.) ICWE 2012. LNCS, vol. 7387, pp. 106–120. Springer, Heidelberg (2012)
2. Berry, L., Bartram, L., Booth, K.S.: Role-based control of shared application views. In: 18th ACM Symposium on User Interface Software and Technology (UIST), pp. 23–32 (2005)

3. Bertino, E., Ferraria, E., Atluri, V.: The specification and enforcement of authorization constraints in workflow management systems. ACM Transactions on Information and System Security 2(1), 65–104 (1999)
4. Ellis, C.A., Gibbs, S.J.: Concurrency control in groupware systems. SIGMOD Record 18(2), 399–407 (1989)
5. Farwick, M., Agreiter, B., White, J., Forster, S., Lanzanasto, N., Breu, R.: A web-based collaborative metamodeling environment with secure remote model access. In: Benatallah, B., Casati, F., Kappel, G., Rossi, G. (eds.) ICWE 2010. LNCS, vol. 6189, pp. 278–291. Springer, Heidelberg (2010)
6. Fowler, M.: Presentation model. Essay (July 2004)
7. Gaubatz, P., Zdun, U.: Supporting entailment constraints in the context of collaborative web applications. In: 28th Symposium on Applied Computing (2013)
8. Heinrich, M., Lehmann, F., Springer, T., Gaedke, M.: Exploiting single-user web applications for shared editing: a generic transformation approach. In: Proceedings of the 21st International Conference on World Wide Web, pp. 1057–1066 (2012)
9. Hummer, W., Gaubatz, P., Strembeck, M., Zdun, U., Dustdar, S.: An integrated approach for identity and access management in a SOA context. In: 16th ACM Symposium on Access Control Models and Technologies (SACMAT) (2011)
10. Joshi, J.B.D., Aref, W.G., Ghafoor, A., Spafford, E.H.: Security models for web-based applications. Communications of the ACM 44(2), 38–44 (2001)
11. Kalam, A.A.E., Benferhat, S., Miège, A., Baida, R.E., Cuppens, F., Saurel, C., Balbiani, P., Deswarte, Y., Trouessin, G.: Organization based access control. In: 4th IEEE Int. Workshop on Policies for Distributed Systems and Networks (2003)
12. Koidl, K., Conlan, O., Wade, V.: Towards user-centric cross-site personalisation. In: Auer, S., Díaz, O., Papadopoulos, G.A. (eds.) ICWE 2011. LNCS, vol. 6757, pp. 391–394. Springer, Heidelberg (2011)
13. Mallouli, W., Orset, J.M., Cavalli, A., Cuppens, N., Cuppens, F.: A formal approach for testing security rules. In: 12th ACM Symposium on Access Control Models and Technologies (SACMAT), pp. 127–132. ACM (2007)
14. Sandhu, R., Coyne, E., Feinstein, H., Youman, C.: Role- based access control models. Computer 29(2), 38–47 (1996)
15. Smith, J.: WPF apps with the Model-View-ViewModel design pattern. MSDN Magazine (2009)
16. Starnberger, G., Froihofer, L., Goeschka, K.M.: A generic proxy for secure smart card-enabled web applications. In: Benatallah, B., Casati, F., Kappel, G., Rossi, G. (eds.) ICWE 2010. LNCS, vol. 6189, pp. 370–384. Springer, Heidelberg (2010)
17. Strembeck, M.: Scenario-driven Role Engineering. IEEE Security & Privacy 8(1) (January/February 2010)
18. Strembeck, M., Mendling, J.: Generic algorithms for consistency checking of mutual-exclusion and binding constraints in a business process context. In: Meersman, R., Dillon, T.S., Herrero, P. (eds.) OTM 2010. LNCS, vol. 6426, pp. 204–221. Springer, Heidelberg (2010)
19. Sun, C., Xia, S., Sun, D., Chen, D., Shen, H., Cai, W.: Transparent adaptation of single-user applications for multi-user real-time collaboration. ACM Transactions on Computer-Human Interaction 13(4), 531–582 (2006)
20. Wainer, J., Barthelmes, P., Kumar, A.: W-RBAC - A Workflow Security Model Incorporating Controlled Overriding of Constraints. International Journal of Cooperative Information Systems (IJCIS) 12(4) (December 2003)

Towards Simulation-Based Similarity of End User Browsing Processes

Sudhir Agarwal[1] and Martin Junghans[2]

[1] Stanford Computer Science Department, Stanford University
353 Serra Mall, Stanford, CA-94301, USA
sudhir@cs.stanford.edu
[2] Institutes AIFB and KSRI, Karlsruhe Institute of Technology
Englerstr. 11, 76131 Karlsruhe, Germany
junghans@kit.edu

Abstract. For increasingly sophisticated use cases an end user needs to extract, combine, and aggregate information from various (often dynamic) web pages from different websites. Current search engines do not focus on combining information from various web pages in order to answer the overall information need of the user. Semantic Web and Linked Data usually take a static view on the data and rely on providers cooperation. Web automation scripts, initially developed for testing websites, allow end users to capture their browsing activities as executable processes and share them with other end users. A script can contain instructions for accessing, extracting and merging (dynamic) information from various websites for a particular purpose. Techniques for allowing users to search for scripts that satisfy complex constraints restrict to existing scripts in the repository, i.e. they do not deduce scripts that may satisfy the request as well. In this paper, we show how semantic descriptions of web sites can be derived from such scripts, and how such semantic descriptions of web sites along with usage information present in the scripts can be used to obtain new scripts with similar functionality.

1 Introduction

For many practical purposes end users need information that is scattered across multiple websites. Static websites can be reached and their content can be indexed by the crawlers of state of the art search engines. However, in many cases, end users still require to do a lot of manual work to compile together the required information. Consider for example an end user who is interested in knowing the names of the chairs of a particular track at the previous WWW conferences. As of today Google does not deliver satisfactory results for queries similar to "track chairs of all WWW conferences". Search engines focus on finding individual highly ranked web pages and not on providing the required information directly. Search engines results often contain links to web pages with similar content even though the information need of the user might require pages with complementary information. As a result, an end user needs to pose multiple queries to a search engine, browse through the hits, and aggregate the required information fragments outside of the found web pages. The case of dynamic websites to access the information in the Deep Web [1] is even more complex and still an open challenge

F. Daniel, P. Dolog, and Q. Li (Eds.): ICWE 2013, LNCS 7977, pp. 216–223, 2013.
© Springer-Verlag Berlin Heidelberg 2013

for search engines since it is hard for automatic crawlers to sensibly interact with the dynamic websites. Furthermore, indexing such information is not a suitable technique since the information underlying dynamic websites changes so rapidly that the index becomes quickly outdated.

In contrast to search engine crawlers, end users are able to reach the dynamic web pages. Information retrieval has focused on analyzing such click trails of millions of end users mainly for the purpose of improving web search results. Click trails can be used as endorsements to rank search results more effectively [2], trail destination pages can themselves be used as search results [3], and the concept of teleportation can be used to navigate directly to the desired page [4]. Similarly, large-scale studies of web page revisitation patterns [5] focus on how often users revisit the same page, while ignoring how people get there. The statistics based click analysis methods typically do not consider semantics of user queries and pages. As a result, a frequently used and thus recommended path may not necessarily satisfy the information need, and end users still require to figure out themselves which of the recommended web pages are actually relevant for them and which interactions are required with which web pages.

Semantic Web [6] has proposed the annotation of web pages in order to describe the information content of web pages. However, apart from the fact that still most of the web pages are not annotated, it is hard to build a server-sided semantic information search engines since a crawler will be unable to reach and index the semantic annotations within deep web pages. Linked Data [7] separates the structured data from the traditional web (and as a result also from the end users) completely. The Linked Data approach is primarily useful for application developers since end users cannot be expected to consume RDF directly. Therefore, end users still require human understandable applications to interact with. Semantic Web and Linked Data approaches (i) heavily rely on the availability of structured data, and (ii) providers are expected to provide access to their data through APIs, which is unlikely to happen for valuable data, and (iii) the data made accessible by a provider is often not semantically aligned that of other providers and its usage is restricted, e.g. for advertisement purposes only.

Approaches for searching navigational plans, e.g., [8] cannot compute navigational paths that consist of data flow between web pages, which are not connected in the web graph as well as require a mediated schema. In contrast, web scripts that combine different data sources can introduce and model additional links (like data exchange between different web pages).

Recently, browsing scripts, initially developed for the purpose of testing web sites, have drawn a lot of attention as they can be very useful for the end users as well, especially when end users share their scripts with other end users. In our previous work [9] we have shown how browsing processes satisfying complex user constraints can be efficiently retrieved from a repository of browsing processes. However, the search technique is limited to the directly known scripts as it does not deduce new scripts that may have the required functionality.

Our Approach: We aim at providing end users with a list of browsing processes such that each browsing process in the list will lead an end user to the required information. Our approach build on the idea of end users sharing their browsing processes with other end users so that a large number of browsing process are available for end users to choose from. Specifically in this paper our aim is to equip existing browsing process search with the ability to deduce new scripts. We achieve this by providing a technique for computing browsing processes similar to a given browsing process. We first show how user browsing processes (consisting of link selection, form inputs, and information extraction steps) can be formalized. Then we present a method to automatically derive semantic annotations of websites from the browsing processes. Then, we show how functionally similar browsing processes can be generated from the known browsing processes. The computation of the set of all similar browsing processes is done offline, i.e. prior to searching.

2   Formalization of End User Browsing Processes

In this section, we present how end user browsing processes can be described formally. The formalization enables generic automatic procedures such as for verification, testing, search and composition. Browsing processes capture users' interactions with websites and local operations. In order to be able to construct browsing processes for a given need we need a formal and semantic model of websites. In contrast to top-down semantics based approaches that require semantically annotated websites, we show how semantic annotations of websites can be derived from browsing processes.

An end user browsing process is a sequential process that coordinates the execution of multiple websites. An end user has a local knowledge base, and the browsing activities that an end user carries out can be categorized into input, output, and local (wrt. the end user knowledge base) actions. An input action causes addition of knowledge from a website into the knowledge base, the output activity emits (without deleting) knowledge from the knowledge base to a website, and a local action causes changes in the knowledge base independent of the websites such as deletion or alignment of knowledge. Such browsing processes can be easily modeled by a process algebra such as π-calculus [10] with the syntax $\mathbf{0} \mid c[\mathbf{x}].P \mid c\langle\mathbf{y}\rangle.P \mid \tau.P$, where $\mathbf{0}$ denotes the process that does nothing and used as termination symbol, $c[\mathbf{x}].P$ denotes a process that inputs some values along the channel c, binds them to $\mathbf{x}$, and then behaves like the process P, $c\langle\mathbf{y}\rangle.P$ denotes a process that outputs values $\mathbf{y}$ along the channel c, and then behaves like the process P, and finally $\tau.P$ denotes a process that performs a local action, and then behaves like the process P. A local action is an action performed by the end user in his/her local knowledge base in order to structure the knowledge as per user's needs. The set of local actions available to an end user depends on the data model of the knowledge base, e.g. a relational model will allow different operations than a graph based model.

In a pure process algebra such as the π-calculus the process resources and variable are seen as strings without any structure. As a result, it is hard for an end user to understand which values he or she should provide for the variables in order to get the desired result. We fill this gap by allowing process variables to have semantics with the help of a domain ontology O_D expressed in $\mathcal{ALC}$ (attributive concept language with complements) [11]. E.g., input parameters $\mathbf{x}$ and the communication channel c of an input activity are process resources and further described in O_D. With $\mathcal{ALC}$ we can describe not only the types of process variables but also their relationships with other process variables. For example, if an input activity has two parameters of type 'Person', we can also describe that the first person should be father of the second person. Precisely, the local knowledge modeled as ABox of $\mathcal{ALC}$ can be modified by adding or removing following types of axioms: (i) add sameAs relation between two individuals, (ii) add typeOf relation between an individual and a concept, (iii) domain specific relationships between two individuals (object properties), and (iv) relationships between an individual and a literal (data properties).

Example 1. The WWW 2013 conference website at URL www2013 contains a link to the call for research papers web page www2013/cfp that provides links of the form www2013/cfp/trackname for all the research tracks of the conference. Selecting one of the provided links returns the page about the track that lists topics, chairs, and PC members of the track. The second website is the DBLP at dblp that among other information on the entry page contains the web form dblp/search for searching for publications of an author. The form dblp/search takes the author name as single input value and returns a page with the list of publication of the author.

A researcher who is interested in submitting a research paper to the "Bridging Structured and Unstructured Data" track wishes to know more about the research background of the track chairs. For this purpose he wants to have a list of most recent 3 journal articles of the track chairs. For this purpose, the researcher performs the following navigation actions (i) visit www2013/cfp, (ii) click on www2013/cfp/bridging, (iii) extract the names $tc_1, \ldots, tc_k$ of the track chairs, (iv) visit dblp, (v) for each track chair tc_i enter tc_i in the form dblp/search and extract the publication of tc_i. In our formalism this browsing steps can be formalized as a process as:

$$\text{www2013/cfp}\langle\rangle.\text{www2013/cfp/bridging}\langle\rangle.$$
$$\text{www2013/cfp/bridging}[tc_1, tc_2].\text{dblp}\langle\rangle.$$
$$\text{dblp/search}\langle tc_1\rangle.\text{dblp/search}[p_1^1, p_1^2, p_1^3].$$
$$+\text{pubOf}(p_1^1, tc_1).+\text{pubOf}(p_1^2, tc_1).+\text{pubOf}(p_1^3, tc_1).$$
$$\text{dblp}\langle\rangle.\text{dblp/search}\langle tc_2\rangle.\text{dblp/search}[p_2^1, p_2^2, p_2^3].$$
$$+\text{pubOf}(p_2^1, tc_2).+\text{pubOf}(p_2^2, tc_2).+\text{pubOf}(p_2^3, tc_2).\mathbf{0}$$

As shown in the above example end users' actions for integrating the extracted knowledge with his/her local knowledge base are part of the browsing process. Note that an end user has direct incentives for keeping his/her knowledge base consistent since it makes it easier to query already visited information much faster and in structured way, e.g. with SPARQL. If the domain ontology used for structuring his/her knowledge base is a shared vocabulary among a group of end users, the web browsing processes become easily reusable within the group.

Definition 1. *In an expression of form $x[y].P$ the occurrence of y is a binding occurrence and in each case the scope of the occurrence is P. An occurrence of y in a browsing process is said to be free if it does not lie within the scope of a binding occurrence of y. The set of names occurring free in P is denoted by $fn(P)$.*

Definition 2. *For a set of atomic propositions P and a set of actions A, a labeled transition system (LTS) is a tuple (S, T, A, λ), where S is a finite set of states, $T \subseteq S \times A \times S$*

a set of labeled transitions between the states, and $\lambda : S \rightarrow 2^{AP}$ *a labeling function that maps each set* $s \in S$ *to the set of atomic propositions that are true in* s.

Formal semantics of a browsing process is defined by a mapping to an LTS that is a finite linear sequence of states connected by transitions. A state represents the content of the knowledge base at a point of time, and a transition an input, output, or local action. The mapping is done by applying the following three rules:

$$\frac{\overline{\quad}}{\tau.P \xrightarrow{\tau} P}, \quad \frac{\overline{\quad}}{x\langle y\rangle.P \xrightarrow{x\langle y\rangle} P}, \quad \text{and} \quad \frac{\overline{\quad}}{x[z].P \xrightarrow{x[w]} P\{w/z\}} \quad \text{with } w \notin \mathit{fn}(P).$$

The main idea for obtaining the LTS for a given process expression lies in viewing the process expressions as states and applying the rules on the states to obtain next states. E.g., the first rule states with the nominator − that a silent action does nor require any preconditions to fire, and with the denominator $\tau.P \xrightarrow{\tau} P$ that the process evolves from state $\tau.P$ to state P by performing the silent action. Analogous for the other two rules.

3   Computation of Similarity between Browsing Processes

Our overall aim is to find known and similar processes efficiently as well as rank them and to provide the ranked list of appropriate browsing processes to an end user in a same way search engines presents their results. For this purpose, we first compute semantic similar websites. A website usage in a browsing process can be replaced by the usage of a semantically similar website in order to obtain a new browsing process that provides the similar functionality. In this paper, we only deal with the problem of similarity computation.

3.1   Derivation of Semantic Description of Websites

A website can be seen as a sequential process. It outputs pages to and receives inputs from a user through her web browser. Similar to an end user performing local operations in her knowledge base, a web server can perform local operations, e.g., by invoking CGI scripts or servlets.

A web page is a message sent by a server. In addition to the information content, a web page offers a choice of links and forms. The links and the action URLs of the forms refer to external or internal locations wrt. the web server. Sometimes, a web page may contains an HTTP redirect instruction to redirect the browser to another URL. The output action of the server that produces a web page with URL u with l values $v_1, \ldots, v_l$, m, links $l_1, \ldots, l_m$ and n forms $f_1, \ldots, f_n$ is described as $u\langle v_1, \ldots, v_l, l_1, \ldots, l_m, f_1, \ldots, f_n\rangle.P$, where P denotes the web server process (may be simply 0) after outputting the web page.

Form submission and link selection are similarly modeled except that a user has the option of filling in values in the former case. We model the arguments of a link as classes and the values of the arguments as instances of the corresponding classes of the ontology associated with the website. The semantic annotation of the link arguments also allow specification of relationships of arguments with other arguments or other ontology elements. The input parameters of a form are described in a similar fashion. The name of the ontology class corresponding to the range of a value can be often derived from the id or label of the input field (see e.g. [12]). Note that we require only the existence of an id or a label. They ids and labels may or may not be semantically meaningful. Some form input types provide a set of predefined values from which one or more values may be selected. In these cases, the provided values are modeled as ontology instances, while the class representing the range of an input field as an enumeration class instead of a normal class. Execution semantics of the formalism for describing websites is defined by mapping its syntax to an LTS that is constructed by applying the rules of execution semantics [13]. The states of the LTS correspond to the knowledge of the process in that stage of the execution, and the transitions correspond to the atomic (input, output, or local) activities. There exists decidable reasoning procedures for LTSs in which the ABox of the ontology may change but the TBox of the ontology may not change during the execution [14].

Having the formal models of browsing processes and websites, we now present the derivation of semantic descriptions of websites from a given set of browsing processes. The main insight underlying such a derivation is that an output of a browsing process corresponds to an input of a web form, and an input of a browsing process corresponds to an output of a web form.

Algorithm 1. Derivation of Website Annotations

---

for all browsing processes $P \in \mathcal{P}$ do

Let $s_0, \ldots, s_n$ and $t_1, \ldots, t_n$ with $(s_{i-1}, t_i, s_i) \in T$ denote states and transitions of P

for all t_i do

if t_i is an output action with values $x_1, \ldots, x_n$ then

add the annotations of $x_1, \ldots, x_n$ from the state s_{i-1} to the annotations of input variables of the web form or the link

else if t_i is an input action with variables $v_1, \ldots, v_n$ then

add the annotations of $v_1, \ldots, v_n$ from the last state of the LTS, i.e. s_n, to the semantic annotations of the values on the web page.

Algorithm 1 describes the derivation of semantic annotations of websites from the information appearing in the browsing processes. Note that due to the chosen level of abstraction, link selections and form submissions are treated similarly and it is not possible to detect whether an output activity of a browsing process corresponds to a link selection or a form submission. However, this does not create any obstacles in our approach. If a distinction of links and forms is desired the browsing process language can be enhanced to add these information. A good heuristic could be to consider the output activities without arguments as as link selections.

3.2 Computing Similar Websites

From the generic description of websites, we compute the semantic similarity of websites as follows: A website w_1 simulates another website w_2, in short $w_1 \sim w_2$, if for every possible input i for w_2 if w_2 outputs o then w_1 also outputs o. In order to compute $w_1 \sim w_2$ we need to check (i) that w_1 accepts every input that w_2 accepts, and

(ii) that the output of w_1 has all the semantic annotations that the output of w_2 has. This means, the state of w_2 after input must be a model of the semantic annotations of input parameters of w_1, and the state of w_1 at the time of output must be a model of semantic annotations of output parameters of w_2. Both conditions can be checked by a DL reasoner that supports rules, e.g. HermiT [15] by modeling the states as ABoxes, the semantic annotations as queries, and checking if an ABox is an answer of the query.

3.3   Computing Similar Browsing Processes

We compute similar browsing processes of a given browsing process by replacing the usage of websites in the browsing process by the usage of websites that simulate the websites as shown in the Algorithm 2. The algorithm computes in each iteration of the **while** loop the set $sim(P)$ of browsing processes that are similar to a browsing process P. The termination of the algorithms is guaranteed since the number of browsing processes, the number of websites within a browsing process, and the number of websites to similar to a website are all finite, and the algorithm continues with the next iteration only when it can construct at least one new browsing process.

Algorithm 2. Compute similar browsing processes

---

changed := true
while changed = true **do**
    changed := false;
    Let the set of browsing processes be $\mathcal{P}$
    for all browsing processes $P \in \mathcal{P}$ **do**
        for all websites W that are used in P **do**
            for all websites V that simulate W **do**
                obtain P' by replacing W by V in P
                if $P' \notin \mathcal{P}$ **then**
                    add P' to $sim(P)$; changed := true;
    $\mathcal{P} := \mathcal{P} \cup sim(P)$

---

4   Conclusion and Outlook

In this paper, we targeted the problem of tediousness of information gathering from various websites from a bottom-up perspective that proposes capturing and sharing of end user browsing processes as opposed to the top-down approach that requires annotated websites in the first place. We have shown how an end user browsing process can be formalized without requiring extra manual effort for declarative semantic annotations, and how processes can be mapped to a labeled transition system. We have further shown how semantic annotations of the web browsing processes can be derived from end user actions. Existing techniques for searching and composing browsing processes could exploit the similarity of browsing processes to deduce new browsing processes and to gain performance respectively. Such an extension of the search technique presented in one our previous work [9] is planned as future work.

Acknowledgments. The authors acknowledge the support of the European Community's Seventh Framework Programme FP7-ICT-2011-7 (XLike, Grant 288342).

References

1. Bergman, M.K.: The deep web: Surfacing hidden value. The Journal of Electronic Publishing 7 (2001)
2. Bilenko, M., White, R.W.: Mining the search trails of surfing crowds: identifying relevant websites from user activity. In: Proceedings of the 17th International Conference on World Wide Web, WWW 2008, pp. 51–60. ACM (2008)
3. White, R.W., Huang, J.: Assessing the scenic route: measuring the value of search trails in web logs. In: Proceeding of the 33rd International ACM SIGIR Conference on Research and Development in Information Retrieval (SIGIR), pp. 587–594. ACM (2010)
4. Teevan, J., Alvarado, C., Ackerman, M.S., Karger, D.R.: The perfect search engine is not enough: a study of orienteering behavior in directed search. In: Dykstra-Erickson, E., Tscheligi, M. (eds.) CHI, pp. 415–422. ACM (2004)
5. Adar, E., Teevan, J., Dumais, S.T.: Large scale analysis of web revisitation patterns. In: Proceedings of the SIGCHI Conference on Human Factors in Computing Systems, CHI 2008, pp. 1197–1206. ACM (2008)
6. Berners-Lee, T., Hendler, J., Lassila, O.: The Semantic Web: a new form of Web content that is meaningful to computers will unleash a revolution of new possibilities. Scientific American 5, 34–43 (2001)
7. Bizer, C., Heath, T., Berners-Lee, T.: Linked data - the story so far. International Journal on Semantic Web and Information Systems 5, 1–22 (2009)
8. Friedman, M., Levy, A.Y., Millstein, T.D.: Navigational plans for data integration. In: Hendler, J., Subramanian, D. (eds.) AAAI/IAAI, pp. 67–73. AAAI Press / The MIT Press (1999)
9. Junghans, M., Agarwal, S.: Efficient search for web browsing recipes. In: Proceedings of the 20th International Conference on Web Service (ICWS 2013). IEEE (June 2013)
10. Milner, R., Parrow, J., Walker, D.: A Calculus of Mobile Processes, Parts I and II. Journal of Information and Computation 100, 1–77 (1992)
11. Schmidt-Schauß, M., Smolka, G.: Attributive concept descriptions with complements. Artif. Intell. 48, 1–26 (1991)
12. Madhavan, J., Ko, D., Kot, L., Ganapathy, V., Rasmussen, A., Halevy, A.: Google's deep web crawl. Proceedings of the VLDB Endowment Archive 1, 1241–1252 (2008)
13. Agarwal, S., Lamparter, S., Studer, R.: Making Web services tradable - A policy-based approach for specifying preferences on Web service properties. Web Semantics: Science, Services and Agents on the World Wide Web, Special Issue on Policies 7(1), 11–20 (2009)
14. Gabbay, D., Kurucz, A., Wolter, F., Zakharyaschev, M.: Many-dimensional modal logics: theory and applications. Studies in Logic, vol. 148. Elsevier Science (2003)
15. Motik, B., Shearer, R., Horrocks, I.: Hypertableau Reasoning for Description Logics. Journal of Artificial Intelligence Research 36, 165–228 (2009)

A Domain Specific Language for Orchestrating User Tasks Whilst Navigation Web Sites

Sérgio Firmenich[1,2], Gustavo Rossi[1,2], and Marco Winckler[3]

[1] LIFIA, Facultad de Informática
[2] Universidad Nacional de La Plata and Conicet Argentina
[3] IRIT, Université Paul Sabatier, France
{gustavo,sergio.firmenich}@lifia.info.unlp.edu.ar,
winckler@irit.fr

Abstract. In this paper we claim that there are a lot of processes over Web applications that require a high level of coordination between individuals and tasks featuring procedures. We propose hereafter a Domain Specific Language (DSL) for describing the asynchronous orchestration users' tasks including manual users' tasks (i.e. simple instructions that tell users what to do during the navigation) and automated tasks (i.e. tasks that can be partially or completely automated by client-side scripts). The approach is illustrated by examples and a case study showing the tools, for which an empiric evaluation is presented.

Keywords: task and process modeling, Web application, Web augmentation.

1   Introduction

Although Web navigation was regarded in the past as a solitary activity, nowadays, many users are engaged in repetitive and collaborative activities that are supported by uncountable Web applications [6]; for example booking a seat in a flight or explaining friends how to book a seat next yours in a flight... Moreover, many of these tasks involve dealing with different Web sites, which run independently with no support to the actual users' concern [4].

This lack of integration of different Web resources has motivated the development of mash-ups tools that are able merge into a specialized applications a set resources that are scattered among different Web sites [8]. The problem is that mash-up are used straightforward, when most of tasks users perform are volatile and do not really require the creation of a new an entirely new applications.

The integration of data across applications can also be done by Web augmentation artifacts, which perform interventions over Web applications DOMs. Some Web augmentation approaches [1][4] aim to support users task by adapting the Web pages visited accordingly.

In this paper we propose a Domain Specific Language (DSL) for describing *procedures* that are aimed to orchestrate user tasks over multiple Web sites. It supports flexible process modeling by allowing users to combine manual task and automated tasks from a repertoire of patterns of tasks performed over the Web. Whilst manual tasks can be regarded as simple instructions, automated tasks correspond to *Web*

F. Daniel, P. Dolog, and Q. Li (Eds.): ICWE 2013, LNCS 7977, pp. 224–232, 2013.

augmentation [4] tools (i.e. *augmenters*). The approach is duly illustrated by a case study describing a trip planning over the Web.

The rest of the paper is organized as follows: section 2 motivates and presents related works; section 3 introduces the approach. Section 4 present the DSL followed by the corresponding tool support (section 5). In section 5 we also present a comparative study using our tools; and lately section 6 presents the conclusions and future work.

2   Motivation and Related Work

Web Augmentation is not a new concept, and it is becoming really important from the point of view of users, who are expecting new kinds of mechanisms for personalizing their experience while navigating the Web. Large communities of scripting such as GreaseMokey prove the value of this technique. There are other similar approaches. Mashup tools, for instance, have the same final goal: improve the users' experience. Neither mash-ups nor existing Web augmentation techniques provide a definite and flexible solution for supporting users tasks. Here, we compare our approach with others DSL/tools for supporting users tasks.

Some approaches allow users to specify the steps involved in certain tasks in order to repeat these steps later. For example CoScripter [4] records the user interactions (based on DOM events) and then the user may reproduce the same steps automatically. Other approaches define DSLs that aim to help to automate tasks. For instance, ChickenFoot [1] extends JavaScript with new sentences (e.g. "click()", "enter()", etc.). In this way, to develop a script for automating Web use is easier. Both Chicken-Foot and CoScripter are powerful approaches but these do not contemplate changes in the process, since it is completely DOM-dependent. With the same philosophy we can mention Selenium [7], which can be used for this task automation, although it was originally defined for testing. While all these approaches may help users by allowing them to automate only primitive tasks, our approach mixes these with augmentation ones, which adapt Web pages accordingly to the current user tasks. It implies that not only repetitive processes may be defined but complex scenarios of adaptation. Besides that, the manual execution of certain tasks gives the control to users. In this way, sensitive tasks (for example payments, or sensible information use) are not performed by automatic tasks in which users may not trust.

3   Overview of Our Approach for Orchestration of Web Tasks

This section provides a view at glance of our approach and the type of users' tasks supported which include: *primitive* and *augmentation tasks.*

We refer as *primitive* tasks to a basic set of tasks that are already supported by the Web browser. These tasks include actions such as *"go to a Web page"*, *"fill in a form"*, etc. Primitive tasks used in our approach are heavily inspired by previous works that have already proposed a taxonomy for these user tasks [7].

For us, *augmentation* tasks are those ones that require advanced scripts programming (based on Web augmentation techniques) to be executed over the Web browser. Some of these tools are able to perform changes in DOM's changing Web pages on the client side. In previous work [4] we have developed a set of Web augmentation tools, called *augmenters,* using the CSN framework. The CSN framework is a tool that supports the development of scripts aimed to adapt Web sites accordingly to the actual users' concern. *Augmenter* are integrated into the Web browser via the framework. Once installed, augmenters are accessible to the user via a contextual menu. The framework has two main user roles: i) developers: are users with programming skills who can extend the framework by creating augmenters; ii) final users: who use augmenters to improve their performance whilst navigating the Web. For example, Figure 1 shows the activation of the augmenter *DataCollection* used to collect data from Web pages. The data collected is presented as a kind of floating post-it called *Pocket.* In the example the user is collecting point of interest under the name of *"PoI".* As we shall, the collection of Web page data requires an advanced script (i.e. an augmenter), it modifies the DOM page (by creating a floating DIV element) and extend what users can do over a Web page (i.e. create electronic post-its); so that when a user runs the *DataCollection* augmenter he in fact performing an *augmentation* task.

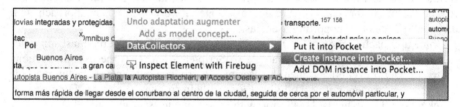

Fig. 1. Example of the use of the augmenter *DataCollection*

Augmenters can also be used in combination to create complex sequences of tasks. Figure 2 shows the combined execution of augmenters. In this example a user executes the augmenter *CreateGoogleMapsLink* from the *Pocket* element (2.a). This action adds an anchor to *GoogleMaps* next to each occurrence of the concept *"PoI"* (2.b) that can then navigated to the corresponding *GoogleMaps* web site (2.c).

Fig. 2.a. Triggering augmenter using *GoogleMapLink*   **Fig. 2.b.** Adaptation performed by the augmenter *GoogleMapLink*   **Fig. 2.c.** Navigation to GoogleMaps

3.1   Overview of the Approach

The goal is to allow users to create complex processes, called *procedures*, by composing *primitive* and *augmentation* tasks. The composition is a sequence of tasks formalized by a DSL and stored as a XML file. A dedicated tool parses that XML file and executes the procedures on the Web browser. Figure 3 provides a view at glance of the approach. As we shall see, the approach include three phases, as follows:

- Definition of tasks: it concerns the inclusion of task to be composed. This phase requires skilled Web developers who program augmenters. This is technically demanding, but the work should be done once and it will benefit all users. Nonetheless, the framework provides a large set of both primitive and augmentation tasks.
- During *Composition* phase, users create a sequence of tasks available in the *repository*, which is exported by the *factory* and defined by the means of a DSL describing all tasks in the procedure. This artifact, defined by the DSL, may be shared with other users in order to support them in the accomplishment of the same task.
- *Execution*: this phase features a player that is concerned by the execution of the procedure previously encoded by the DSL.

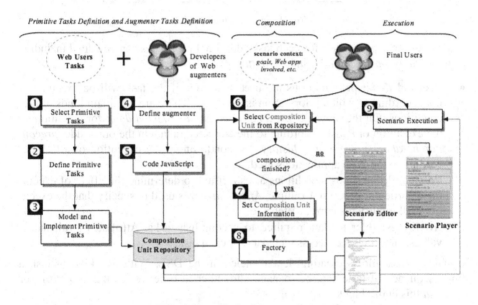

Fig. 3. Overview of the approach

4   A DSL for Web Task Composition

Procedures will be defined according with the DSL metamodel shown in Figure by a UML class model. This metamodel defines those elements contemplated by the DSL and their relations. Basically, the DSL defines a procedure as a XML file containing a list of tasks. Primitive tasks supported are based on [3]. The set of augmenters depends on what was developed by users. Composed tasks are used to group several tasks in a single block. Tasks have three main properties: *repetition* property for specifying if the task may be executed more than once. The *optional* property allows skipping the execution of the task. If *automatic* property is *true*, then the player automatically triggers the task.

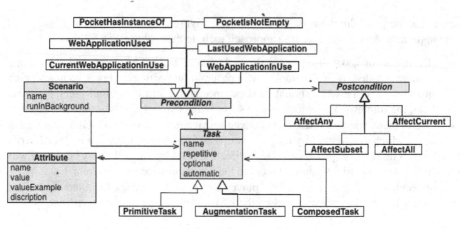

Fig. 4. The DSL metamodel

Besides these properties, for each task additional properties can be added including *preconditions*, *postconditions* and *attributes*:

- **Preconditions:** preconditions are used to decide if the task will be executed or not according to which information is available. There are two main kinds of preconditions. On the one side, *preconditions about collected data*: for conditioning the execution of a task according to the collected data. On the other side, *preconditions about navigational history*: for conditioning the execution of a task according to the Web applications used.

- **Post-conditions:** post-conditions are specified to determine the effect of executing a particular task. For example, *AffectCurrent* is used to specify that the execution will modify the current Web site.

- **Attributes:** refer to data required to accomplish tasks. Attributes (with name, values, etc.) are specified as metadata for each task.

ComposedTask allows creating dependencies in the DSL. With this kind of task a finite sequence of tasks can be manage altogether in order to mark as *repetitive* or *optional* this entire block.

In the example from Figure 3, we have used both pre and post conditions. For example in the augmentation task *IconifiedLink* we have specified the *AffectSubset* precondition with a regular expression that matches with all Wikipedia articles. In this way, when a new *"PoI"* is collected, all Wikipedia articles will be adapted by adding the corresponding link to Google Maps (the focused Wikipedia article and any other opened in non-focused Browser tabs). In order to show an example of precondition, we have used the *PocketHasInstanceOf* one in order to execute the augmenter only if an instance of *"PoI"* was collected.

5   Tool Support

We have developed two tools: an editor for creating procedures and a procedure player for parsing and executing procedures.

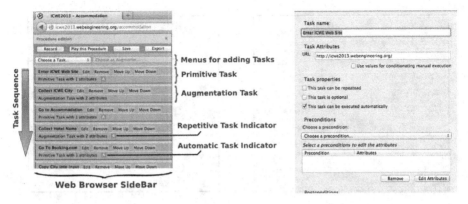

Fig 5.a. General view of the tool   **Fig. 5.b.** Edition of a single task

Figure 5.a shows the editor: a sidebar that allows users to specify tasks into the procedure while analyzing Web sites. The tool provides an assisted mode: users may *record* their interaction with the Web and the corresponding tasks will be added to the procedure automatically. This mode contemplates both primitive and augmentation tasks. Figure 5.b shows how to edit a task. It allows users to specify the name, pre- and post-conditions as well as values for both properties and attributes.

The Procedure Player is shown in Figure 6. When the user selects a procedure to be executed, this appears in the Procedure Player. Once it is running, the Procedure Player may execute automatically a task (if the tasks was marked as automatic). Those tasks that have been executed appear with different styles, in order to give visual feedback to users when a task was finished. For manual tasks the Procedure Player waits to the corresponding user interaction. When this happens the task state changes and the following task in the sequence is executed. When the procedure has finished, the user may share the procedure execution (which includes both tasks definition and data used in each task) for future executions or even for share with partners.

5.1 A Simple Case Study Using the Tools

Figure 6 shows the execution of a procedure for planning a trip to ICWE2013. The first task *"Enter ICWE Web Site"* is automatic and it loads the ICWE2013 Web site. Then the procedure waits a manual task, which require from users to collect a *City* into the Pocket. Once it is made, the procedure loads the accommodation page.

The task *"Collect Hotel name"* allows user to collect hotel names. After that, an automatic task opens the site booking.com for searching rooms. Figure 6.b shows the booking.com loaded with the "Destination" input filled with the city previously collected. The procedure follows with augmenters for highlighting the selected hotels.

Fig. 6.a. Task Execution: collecting accommodation

Fig. 6.b. Task Execution: looking for hotels rooms

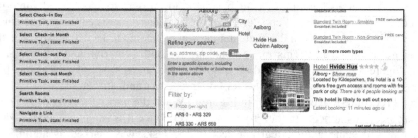

Fig. 7. Trip to ICWE procedure execution: searching and highlighting collected hotels

Figure 7 shows the procedure state once the user has finished several primitive tasks for searching for rooms. Once the results are shown, the hotel names collected are used by the task "*Highlight collected Hotels*" which adapt the current Web page for highlighting the relevant hotels. Once the hotel room payment is finished, the procedure gives the same support for buying flight tickets: it opens expedia.com, prefills the forms for search (it uses the geolocation component provided by the framework), etc. since some tasks are marked as automatic. Finally, it supports to the user in the task of filling forms with his personal data.

5.2   Evaluation

We have evaluated empirically the approach by performing the same task in different ways: manually, automatically with other tool (Selenium) and with procedures. We defined three procedures with different levels of automation: i) repeating the task structure but reentering all information, ii) repeating task structure and reusing information from previous execution, iii) fully automated. We assessed quantitatively the interactions made by the user using GOMS-Keystroke (KLM) model [6]. The GOMS-Keystroke (KLM) allows to simulate the performance of a trained user proposing the average time to perform basic action (for instance, *reach for mouse* takes 0,40 sec). Thus, provided a detailed scenario of user actions including low-level user actions, it is possible to estimate user performance (i.e. speed).

The task was *Planning a Trip to ICWE, which* implied to use three different Web sites: i) ICWE2013 home page to get information about the conference; ii) Expedia.com to buy flights tickets; and iii) boking.com to book a room in one of the conference hotel.

Table 1 summarizes the results obtained with each approach. The task was decomposed into smaller ones in order to show when the use of a tool makes the difference. A first task, *Create Artifact*, is only valid when a tool for automating tasks is used.

Table 1. Results of the evaluation

Task	Normal Use	Selenium	Procedures		
			Semi automatic	Semi automatic with data reutilization	Automatic
Create Artifact	-	9,5	-	472,2	-
Execute Artifact	-	-	9,5	9,5	9,5
Get information about the conference	12	9,5	14,2	14,2	0
Search Flights	35,9		1,7	1,7	0
Select Flights	5		6.3	6.3	0
Enter Passenger Information	25,5		25,5	0	0
Pay Flights	59,7	9,5	59,7	1,7	0
Search Room	19,9		3,6	3,6	0
Select Room	6,5		5,1	5,1	0
Enter Passenger Information	29,4		27,5	0	0
Pay Room	51,4	9,5	51	4,8	0
Total	245,3	28.5	202,8	46,9	9,5

Table also shows how much time was necessary with each approach. The most time consuming was *the normal use* (245,3s). Selenium consumed 28.5s. The automatic *procedure* was the fastest. However it can be counterproductive since users lose the control over task. Semi-automatic execution only reproduced automatically those aspects like prefilling forms, and opening URLs when the previous task is finished, etc. Semi-automatic execution with data reutilization implies more automation by reusing data used in previous executions of the procedure such as prefilling forms with passenger information, credit card information, etc. In this case each confirmation steps (i.e. clicking search buttons) were performed manually. Finally, the full-automated procedure performs even these last actions, but leaving the user unable to control the task. Defining the procedure took 472,2 sec. This time would be lower/higher accordingly to the automation level used. We only measured the case we thought was the best choice in our approach.

6   Conclusions and Future Work

We presented an approach and DSL for orchestrating user tasks over the Web. The approach allows easy integration of client-side scripts to build procedures that can be share with other users. The DSL provides a certain level of abstract that could be used to analyze the sequences of users' tasks used in procedures compositions. Each task may be pre-conditioned, and the data is not fixed a priori (the approach contemplates data collection as tasks); which gives flexibility. Manual tasks are contemplated too, in order to give control to users who may feel uncomfortable if the whole task is delegated in an automatic tool.

The case study presented shows that the tools are completely functional. An empiric evaluation shows how the approach improves the performance in the execution of complex tasks. However we need additional studies to explore the usability and potential of user adoption of such tools. In addition with user testing of the tools, future work will address the possibility of having synchronous communication between users performing procedures. Our ultimate goal is to allow users who create and share procedures with friends, be able to follow the execution of the procedures.

The approach opens up the way for potential collaboration between users. By sharing *procedures* or even synchronize users' *procedures* execution would allow users to collaborate in order to accomplish a task altogether or even to share a procedure execution with a partner.

References

1. Bolin, M., Webber, M., et al.: Automation and customization of rendered web pages. In: UIST 2005, pp. 163–172. ACM Press (2005)
2. Card, S., Moran, T., Newell, A.: The psychology of human-computer interaction, p. 448. Lawrence Erlbaum Associates, Hillsdale (1983)
3. Byrne, M.D., John, B., Wehrle, N., Crow, D.: The tangled Web we wove: a taskonomy of WWW use. In: Proc. of Conf. on Human factors in computing systems (CHI 1999), pp. 544–551. ACM, New York (1999)
4. Firmenich, S., Winckler, M., Rossi, G., Gordillo, S.: A Framework for Concern-Sensitive, Client-Side Adaptation. In: Auer, S., Díaz, O., Papadopoulos, G.A. (eds.) ICWE 2011. LNCS, vol. 6757, pp. 198–213. Springer, Heidelberg (2011)
5. Leshed, G., Haber, E., Matthews, T., Lau, T.: CoScripter: automating & sharing how-to knowledge in the enterprise. In: Proc. of ACM SIGCHI 2008, pp. 1719–1728. ACM Press (2008)
6. Morris, M.R.: A survey of collaborative web search practices. In: Proc. of ACM SIGCHI 2008, pp. 1657–1660. ACM Press (2008)
7. Selenium, http://jroller.com/selenium/ (last visit: February 26, 2013)
8. Yu, J., Benatallah, B., Casati, F., Daniel, F.: Understanding Mashup Development. IEEE Internet Computing 12, 44–52 (2008)

Tag Cloud Generation for Results of Multiple Keywords Queries

Martin Leginus, Peter Dolog, and Ricardo Gomez Lage

Department of Computer Science, Aalborg University,
Selma Lagerlofs Vej 300, 9220 Aalborg-East, Denmark
{mleginus,dolog,ricardo}@cs.aau.dk
http://iwis.cs.aau.dk/

Abstract. In this paper we study tag cloud generation for retrieved results of multiple keyword queries. It is motivated by many real world scenarios such as personalization tasks, surveillance systems and information retrieval tasks defined with multiple keywords. We adjust the state-of-the-art tag cloud generation techniques for multiple keywords query results. Consequently, we conduct the extensive evaluation on top of three distinct collaborative tagging systems. The graph-based methods perform significantly better for the Movielens and Bibsonomy datasets. Tag cloud generation based on maximal coverage is more suitable for the Delicious dataset because of the different statistical properties of the dataset.

1 Introduction

Tag cloud is an information retrieval interface that is commonly utilized by users of social tagging systems. It depicts a selection of terms used for resource annotations by the users. Tags of tag cloud are usually depicted with different colours and font-sizes. These visual aspects of tags express their popularity and importance within a system. A tag of the tag cloud links to a set of resources that are annotated and referenced with the given tag. Users can retrieve the set of resources by clicking on the relevant tag.

Tag clouds are usually studied as exploration interfaces depicting the most frequent tags of all resources in a system. In that sense, tag clouds provide a rough summary of resources and their topic distribution within the system. Therefore, the tag cloud is suitable for unspecific retrieval and exploration tasks and serves as a starting point for more specific keyword-based search [1].

In this paper we focus on tag cloud generation techniques for multiple keyword query results. In other words, as a user expresses his information goal with a combination of keywords a tag cloud is generated on top of all the related resources i.e., resources retrieved by the placed query. The tag cloud generation conditioned by multiple keyword query is motivated by several real-world scenarios.

Firstly, there is a need for query specific tag clouds due to the large amount of various resources within the recent collaborative tagging systems e.g., Flick

F. Daniel, P. Dolog, and Q. Li (Eds.): ICWE 2013, LNCS 7977, pp. 233–248, 2013.

(picture sharing site), Youtube (video repository) or Delicious (bookmark sharing system). The motivation for such tag clouds is:

– Underlying dataset contains a vast amount of data with diverse topics. Many of these topics are completely irrelevant for given users and the context of their work.
– Users would like to get an overview or follow dynamics of resources related to their interests or preferences (expressed in a query or in a user profile).

Secondly, the majority of information retrieval tasks are defined as a combination of several independent keywords. For instance, almost 67% of all placed queries in the USA are queries that consist of two or more keywords [3]. Similar statistics are reported for other countries. Therefore, there is a need for tag clouds generated with respect to multiple keywords queries.

In such scenarios, tag clouds present tags with respect to the query keywords entered by a user. This visual interface describes resources retrieved by the query that contain tags matching query keywords. Even though users can perform the same tasks as with most-frequent-tags tag clouds i.e., impression making, browsing or exploring resources, only a subset of resources related to the query term is considered for the tag cloud generation. Consequently, it results in an improved exploration of resources as it filters out irrelevant documents.

In this paper we propose a set of tag selection techniques to generate tag clouds from the results of multiple keyword queries. These techniques are extensions of existing methods that were introduced in [9] and [6]. The contribution with respect to our previous work [6] are as follows:

– Different encodings of prior probability distributions for stochastic restarts of random walk based algorithms. This was needed to achieve a better performance of graph based methods when multiple keyword queries are considered.
– A graph transformation is conducted on top of syntactically pre-clustered tag space. It results into higher coverage of the generated tag clouds as was shown in [7].
– The extended graph-based methods improve relevancy of tag clouds *with 45 % on Movielens* dataset and *21 % on Bibsonomy* in comparison to the state-of-the-art tag selection techniques.

We conclude through extensive experimental evaluations of three different datasets which method performs the best.

The structure of the paper is organized as follows; Section 2 positions our work with respect to related findings in the literature. Section 3 describes various tag selection techniques we have explored for the generation of tag clouds. Section 4 describes experimental set up and results which we gained from the experiments. Section 5 summarizes the paper achievements and roadmap to future work.

2 Related Work

Tag clouds are suitable for data-impression tasks within systems that contain annotated resources. The interface is generated from certain tag labels of system resources. Users exploit tag clouds for the better understanding of a topic's diversity of a large number of considered resources. Tag clouds are often utilized within social networks and blog monitoring, medical-surveilance and fraud-detection systems.

Many studies investigated various aspects of tag cloud's visualization [2]. Tag color, size and position are important properties that influence user decision during tag cloud exploration. Furthermore, tags can be sorted alphabetically or sementically grouped based on their co-occurences. [7] proposes to cluster syntatically similar tags to avoid redudancies in the tag cloud which improves the coverage of generated tag clouds.

[9] proposes a synthetic user model aimed for tag cloud evaluation. They introduce various synthetic metrics that measure the qualities of tag clouds such as coverage, overlap and balance. Moreover, [9] introduces 4 tags selection algorithms for tag cloud generation. The first method selects the most popular tags within a system. The other two algorithms choose tags based on term frequency-inverse document frequency (tf-idf). The last and the most promising algorithm maximizes the coverage of selected tags in a tag cloud. These selection algorithms only focus on specific properties and aspects of tag cloud as coverage, frequency, and diversity. In this work, we consider extensions of these tags selection methods for multiple keywords queries.

As we presented in [6], coverage and overlap are too general measures and might not be suitable for query conditioned tag clouds. In this work, we exploit extensions of a topic sensitive version of PageRank algorithm, personalized HITS and constrained version of Markov Chain algorithm described in [6, 10]. The extension for tag cloud generation of multiple keyword query results is that the prior probabilities have to be set differently than in the case of one keyword queries to achieve better performance.

3   Methods for Tag Clouds Generation with Respect to Multiple Keyword Queries

In this section, we present a set of methods for tag cloud generation with respect to multiple keyword queries. For convenience, from now on we refer to multiple keyword query simply as query. The general application of these methods can be summarized as follows:

1. Retrieve all system resources annotated or related to the entered query.
2. Perform tags selection method on top of the tag space of retrieved system resources.
3. The top-k most relevant tags are presented in the generated tag cloud to the end user.

The following methods explore all tags used for annotation of resources that were retrieved with respect to the query. The exploration involves an evaluation of different aspects of invidual tags. The first group of presented methods select tags based on their coverage or populatity of resources in the system. The second group of the methods transforms tags and their co-occurrence (a number of resources that are annotated with the same two tags) into a graph structure. The graph is then used as an input for different tag importance estimation algorithms.

3.1 Most Frequent Tags from Corpus (MFTC)

This method is the most common approach for generating tag clouds on top of the entire dataset. The entire tag space is sorted and orded according to the tag annotation frequency in descending order. The final tag cloud contains the top-k most frequent tags. The advantage is that the most frequent topics within the system are propagated to the tag cloud. On the other hand, the tag cloud does not cover other not so frequently represented topics which could be relevant for the user.

3.2 Most Frequent Tags from Query Result Set (POP)

The method is very similar to the previous one. The difference is that the set of resources is constrained to those resources that are annotated by at least one keyword from the query. The method creates tag clouds from top-k most popular tags of the documents (D_{T_q}) that are associated with the set of keywords of the query T_q. We assume that for each keyword exists the same tag in the system. The method was initially proposed by Venetis et al. [9] for single keyword queries. Drawbacks of this method are similar as with the MFTC technique.

3.3 Term Frequency - Inverse Document Frequency Selection (TFIDF)

The method ranks each tag t of the documents (D_{T_q}) that is associated with the query keywords T_q. The ranking function computes term frequency - inverse document frequency (tf-idf) for each tag and the document from the set of resources $D_t \cap D_{T_q}$ where D_t is the set of resources that are annotated by the tag t. These values are aggregated with the summation and are sorted in descending order. The top-k tags with the highest score are selected for the final tag cloud. The method was introduced by Venetis et al. [9] for single keyword queries tag cloud generation. The advantages and shortcommings of TFIDF based methods are similar to their advantages and disadvantages with respect to information retrieval tasks on top of traditional document repositories such as no consideration of semantic similarities between tags.

3.4 Max Coverage Selection (COV)

This selection explores a tag space of the documents (D_{T_q}) in the greedy fashion such that it tries to maximize a coverage of the selected tags. It iterates through the tag space and at each iteration step selects the tag that covers the highest number of uncovered documents. The method was proposed by Venetis et al.

[9] for single keyword queries. The advantage of the method is maximization of coverage and at the same time minimization of overlap between tag clouds tags. However, in our previous work [6], we pointed out that there are problems with tag cloud generation that maximizes coverage. The optimization of coverage might result into the generation of tag clouds that contain terms with high coverage but are irrelevant for the specific user's information retrieval goal.

3.5   Graph Based Methods

In the following subsections, we describe graph based tag cloud generation methods. Firstly, we introduce graph transformation of the tag space. Secondly, we describe three graph based methods. Finally, we propose a new adjustment of prior distribution for the random restarts of graph-based methods.

Graph Creation. The problem of a tag cloud generation with respect to specific query tags can be also transformed into estimating relative importance of other tags within underlying graph of tags with respect to the query. Firstly, an original tag space can be transformed into a graph structure where different aspects of tags relations can be captured.

In this work we utilize the following approach for graph creation. The graph creation is similar to our previous work [6], the difference is that the original tag space is syntactically pre-clustered. The syntactical clustering is presented in Section 3.10. First, we calculate a tag pair co-occurence using Jaccard similarity coefficient for all clustered tags, (see Formula 1) where $\mathrm{cocr}(t_i, t_j)$ represents co-occurence of two tags t_i, t_j i.e., the number of resources annotated by both tags t_i, t_j. Further, $\mathrm{f}(t_i)$ denotes a frequency of use of the particular tag in the system).

$$\mathrm{JAC}(t_i, t_j) = \frac{\mathrm{cocr}(t_i, t_j)}{\mathrm{f}(t_i) + \mathrm{f}(t_j) - \mathrm{cocr}(t_i, t_j)} \tag{1}$$

When the calculated similarity for a tag pair is greater than a predefined threshold α, we consider such tags as similar. Second, each similar tag pair is transformed into two directed edges $t_1 \to t_2$ and $t_2 \to t_1$. One could propose to construct only undirected graph, but in this context we construct directed graph in order to apply various graph based algorithms which are limited only to directed graph structures. Finally, we employ various graph-based algorithms to select the most relevant tags with respect to query tags.

In order to introduce different graph algorithms for relative importance of tags within the graph, we present preliminaries on graphs and their properties.

Graph preliminaries A directed graph $G = (V, E)$ consists of two sets: a set of nodes V and a set of edges E. In this context, each node corresponds to one particular tag from the underlying clustered tag space (the clustering is described in 3.10). Each edge e is defined as an ordered pair of nodes (u, v) for directed link from u to v. Therefore, an edge represents a relationship between two particular tags. A walk from u to v is a sequence of edges $(u, u_1), (u_1, u_2) \ldots (u_k, v)$. A walk is a path if no nodes are repeated. Various graph algorithms are based on a notion of k-short paths. It is a set of all paths shorter than k between u and v in the graph. Other algorithms use a number of outgoing and ingoing edges for deriving an importance of a particular node in the graph. Therefore, we define

- $s_{out}(u)$ as a set of distinct outgoing edges from u
- $s_{in}(u)$ as a set of distinct ingoing edges towards u
- $d_{in}(u) = |s_{in}(u)|$ and $d_{out}(u) = |s_{out}(u)|$

Graph Based Methods. We present three graph-based algorithms for estimating a relative importance I of each node in the graph with respect to the set of query keywords. These methods are originally introduced in [6] for the tag cloud generation conditioned by single keyword queries. The algorithms rank an importance of a tag t with respect to the query keywords T_q where $\{t, t_q\} \in G$ and $t_q \in T_q$. It is denoted as:

$$I(t|T_q)$$

Sorting tags according to their importance with respect to the tags from T_q yields ranked tags. Eventually, it is easy to proceed with a tag cloud generation when only top-k most relevant tags are selected for the final tag cloud.

There exist two distinct approaches for estimating a relative importance of tags.

1. **Distance based approach:** The intuition is that a node is more relevant to a particular node when a graph distance between these nodes is smaller. In this context, a tag t is less relevant to the set of query tags T_q when there are many intermediate tags on the graph path from t to tags from T_q.
2. **Stochastic approach:** The importance of a node is estimated with a stochastic process. A reader can imagine a token that is randomly traversing a graph. The token steps from one node u to another node v with a transition probability which is given by $d_{in}(v)$ and $d_{out}(v)$. The random traversal of the graph after a certain time converges. It means that the time of the token spent at a certain graph node become stable. The time spent by the token at each vertex expresses an importance of the particular vertex in the graph.

In this paper, we focus on the stochastic approach only. This is motivated by the finding from our previous work [6]. The distance based techniques are computionally expensive and directly dependent on the graph size.

Stochastic Approaches for Tag Cloud Generation. The technique of measuring importance of nodes in the graph is based on the simulation of stochastic process e.g., random traversal of the graph. For the tag cloud generation it can be conceived in the following way: There is a tag cloud creator that randomly explores the graph structure of tags. The tag cloud creator visits a particular node (tag) in the graph and then randomly hops to one from the tag neighbours of the current node. Each visit of the cloud creator at certain tag can be interpreted as the evaluation whether a given tag is important for the desired tag cloud. When this stochastic process lasts infinitely long time, a period that the tag cloud creator has spent at a certain tag can be perceived as its impor- tance. As imaginary tag cloud creator can stay within a particular part of the sub-graph too long a definition of a back probability needs to be included. The back probability influences how often the random traversal of graph should be restarted i.e., start a new random walk from one node that belongs to the query keywords set. The transition probability from a tag t_1 to t_2 is defined as

$$p(t_2|t_1) = \frac{1}{d_{out}(t_1)}$$

for all tags t_2 that have an ingoing edge from t_1. Otherwise, a transition prob- ability equals 0. This process can be classed as a first-order Markov Chain and there are various algorithms based on this process.

3.6   PageRank with Priors (PgRank)

This famous algorithm has been proposed in [8] and since then it has been used for relevance and importance ranking of web resources within the web graph. The PageRank reflects a behaviour of a random surfer where a certain set of similar web pages is browsed by the user. After some time, surfer randomly visits a different web page. Let us assume that the random surfer will browse and explore web pages forever, in such situation, a time that he spends at a particular site expresses also its importance in the web graph.

In this work, we focus on estimation of an importance of the tag t with respect to T_q. Therefore, we describe a topic sensitive PageRank as was introduced by [4]. A bias towards query tags is introduced with a vector of prior probabilities $p_r = \{p_1 \ldots p_{|V|}\}$. Sum of prior probabilities equals to 1. In this work we consider more query tags T_q, hence the prior probabilities are set only for these query nodes. The setting of prior probabilities is described in the following Section 3.9. A random restart of the random walk is achieved with a back probability β. It conditions how frequently a stochastic process returns back to the root nodes i.e., query tags from T_q. Consequently, we are able to define iterative stationary probability:

$$\pi(v)^{(i+1)} = (1 - \beta) \left(\sum_{u=1} d_{in}(v)p(v|u)\pi^{(i)}(u) \right) + \beta p_v \tag{2}$$

The resulting importance ranks biased towards T_q are considered as definition of importance after convergence i.e.;

$$I(t|T_q) = \pi(t) \tag{3}$$

The advantages of graph-based methods were presented in [6], where more rele- vant tag clouds were generated. However, the method requires to set up several parameters such as the back probability β and prior probabilities with respect to a specific dataset.

3.7   HITS with Priors (HITS)

In the similar way, we utilize HITS algorithm where a bias towards root query nodes is introduced through a vector p_r of prior probabilities.

Similarly, the setting of the prior distributions is described in Section 3.9. A random surfer is achieved with a back probability β - it determines how often we jump back to a root node. The iterative stationary distributions for authorities and hubs is defined in the following way:

$$a(v)^{(i+1)} = (1 - \beta) \left(\sum_{u=1} d_{in}(v) \frac{h^{(t)}(u)}{H^{(i)}} \right) + \beta p_v \qquad (4)$$

$$h(v)^{(i+1)} = (1 - \beta) \left(\sum_{u=1} d_{out}(v) \frac{a^{(t)}(u)}{A^{(i)}} \right) + \beta p_v \qquad (5)$$

where

$$H^i = \sum_{v=1}^{|V|}) \sum_{u=1} d_{in}(v) h^i(u) \qquad (6)$$

$$A^i = \sum_{v=1}^{|V|}) \sum_{u=1} d_{out}(v) a^i(u) \qquad (7)$$

The motivation is similar as with the topic sensitive PageRank algorithm only difference is that at each even step of the traversal only ingoing edges to the current node (tag) are considered and at each odd step only outgoing edges are considered as possible steps. The resulting importance ranks (stationary distribution of each node) biased towards T_q are considered as definition of importance after convergence i.e.;

$$I(v|T_q) = \pi(v) \qquad (8)$$

The algorithm has the similar properties as the PageRank with priors or the k-step Markov Chain methods. However, the setting of the prior distribution is more complicated. There is a need to encode prior probabilities for hubs and authorities in the graph.

3.8   k-step Markov Chain (k-MarkovCh)

The technique is different to the previous methods in the implementation of a random surfer model. It is achieved with a path length limitation. The step constraint determines how often a token jumps back to one query node from the query keyword set. The smaller the path length parameter is the more often a stochastic traversal of the graph restarts back to a node chosen according to the prior probabilities of nodes. We discuss this issue in the following Section 3.9. A bias to the root nodes is introduced through a vector p_r of prior probabilities.

The constructed graph can be represented as well with the transition matrix A which is constructed in the following way. If there is an directed edge from a node u to v, then we put a transition probability on row u, column v of the matrix A.

$$I(v|R) = [A \cdot p_R + A^2 \cdot p_R \ldots A^K \cdot p_R] \tag{9}$$

The resulting importance ranks (stationary distribution of each node) biased towards T_q are considered as definition of importance after convergence i.e.; The method depends on the proper setting of the number of steps the random walk is performed until the restart is performed. The tuning of this parameter might be complicated and vary for different datasets.

3.9 Adjustment of Prior Distribution for Stochastic Restarts of Random Walks

The prior probability for single keyword queries is defined in a simple, straight-forward way. The probability for the query tag t_q is set to 1 and for all other nodes it is set to 0 [6]. However, this approach does not work for multiple key-word queries. The naive extension would be to set a prior probability for each query tag t_q from the set of query tags T_q such that $p(t_q) = \frac{1}{|T_q|}$ However, this approach does not capture individual popularity of a query tag in the corpus. In other words, when a rarely used tag is chosen as a query tag t_q, such tag does not co-occure with many tags. Therefore, there are not many edges connecting this graph node with other nodes. Therefore, a random traversal of the graph initi-ated from the rarely used tag/node might reach not important/relevant nodes (tags). Consequently, it results into an inclusion of irrelevant tags into the tag cloud. We verified this assumption by series of preliminary evaluations. The naive approach of setting prior probabilities for multiple keywords queries suf-fers from the inclusion of irrelevant tags into the final tag cloud. Therefore, we

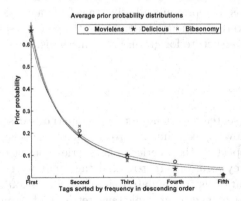

Fig. 1. Prior probability distributions and their corresponding exponential fit for Movielens, Delicious and Bibsonomy datasets when generating tag clouds for queries that consist of five keywords

propose a simple intuitive setting of prior probabilities which capture a relative popularity of the individual query tag t_q from the set of query tags T_q. The relative popularity for each query tag t_q is computed in the following way:

$$p(t_q) = \text{popularity}(t_q) = \frac{f(t_q)}{\sum_{t_{qi} \in T_q} f(t_{qi})}.$$

The sum of all popularities of tags from T_q equals to 1. Therefore, we set for each query tag t_q, the prior probability that equals to popularity(t_q). In this way, the more popular tags are more likely to be chosen after the restart of the random walk. To motivate the presented approach, we observed the frequency distribution of query tags, when the size of the query tags is set to 5. We randomly selected 30 different queries for each dataset, each query consists of a set of five query tags that are semantically similar (the selection process is more detailed in Section 4.2). Figure 1 presents an average distribution of relative popularities of query tags for each dataset. All three presented distributions and their corresponding exponential fits indicate a large differences in relative tags popularities among considered query tags. Therefore, it empirically proves our intuition about adjusting prior probabilities of query tags with respect to their relative popularity.

3.10   Syntactical Pre-clustering of Tags

All the presented techniques generate tag clouds from the syntactically clustered tag space. We compute Levenhstein edit distance for each tag pair from the initial tag space as it was succesfully utilized in our previous work [7]. Once, an edit distance is calculated, the tag space is split into clusters. Each cluster consists of tags where the Levenhstein distance is equal or lower than a defined threshold (a number of maximum changes to transform a tag from the tag pair into a second tag). Then, the most frequent tag for each cluster is selected and is used in all further computations. It represents all other tags from a considered cluster. This syntactical pre-clustering avoids redudancies in the generated tag clouds, results into a denser graph structure for graph based methods.

4   Experiments

To compare the presented tag cloud generation methods described in Section 3 we conduct the following experiments. We measure the relevance of generated tag clouds with respect to the queries. The queries consist of several (ranging from two till five keywords) context-related tags that were derived from user profiles. The motivation is to simulate different information retrieval scenarios such as retrieval goal defined by multiple tags, retrieval of resources similar to the selected resource which can be described by the set of assigned tags, and various surveilance tasks where an expert monitors occurrence of predefined terms in the system. The relevance of the generated clouds is measured on top of the

Movielens dataset,a snapshot of Bibsonomy dataset [5], and Delicious dataset. The Bibsonomy dataset contains 206589 distinct items and 51565 tags. The total number of tagging posts is 466818. The Movielens dataset contains 16518 unique tags and 7601 movies. The total number of tagging posts is 95580. The Delicious dataset represents all bookmarking activities on www.delicious.com from 8th till 16th of September 2009. It contains 187359 users, 185401 unique tags and 355525 bookmarks. The total number of tagging posts is 2046868.

The tag cloud selection techniques are implemented in Java 6 and source code together with all results are available on our Web site[1].

The rest of the evaluation section is organized as follows. Firstly, we define required evaluation metrics. Secondly, we describe a methodology of the conducted experiments. In the end, we present and analyze evaluation results.

4.1 Evaluation Metrics

In this paper we measure the *relevance* of generated tag clouds with respect to the queries that consist of several context-related tags. We do not measure *coverage*, as we showed in our previous work [6] as this synthetic metric might be misleading. The following paragraph introduce formally the *relevance* metric.

A set of exiting documents is denoted as D , the whole set of existing tags is denoted as T, and the set of documents assigned to a tag $t \in T$ is denoted as D_t. The generated tag clouds is a set of tags which is denoted as T_c. The relevance of T_c expresses how relevant the tags in T_c are with respect to the query keyword t_q. We compute a relevance of each tag t from T_c in the following fashion:

$$rel(T_c) = avg_{t \in T_c} \frac{|D_t \cap D_{T_q}|}{|D_t|}, \tag{10}$$

where $|D_t|$ is the number of documents assigned to a tag t and $|D_{t_q}|$ is the number of all documents that are associated with a query tag t_q. The metric ranges between 0 and 1. When the relevance for a particular tag t is close to 1, the majority of documents annotated with a tag t is covered by the documents from D_{t_q}. The more D_t and D_{t_q} overlap, the more related t is to t_q. When $D_t \subseteq D_{t_q}$, then t can be perceived as more specific sub-category of the original query t_q.

4.2 Evaluation Methodology

We randomly select 15 distinct users from each dataset. Each user profile is pruned such that it contains only context-related tags. In this evaluation, we define context-related tags as all the tags assigned by the user to the semantically similar resources. The intention is to avoid tag cloud generation for semantically different keywords in the query. For example, a tag cloud generated with respect to the query keywords like *Christianity* and *Ubuntu* is likely to not produce any relevant results to the users. Therefore, we concentrate only on tags which are topically similar e.g., *russian*, *dictionary* and *software*. We assume that all

---

[1] http://people.cs.aau.dk/$\sim$mleginus/icwe2013/

resources annotated by the given user are semantically similar when they share at least one tag. For each user, we iteratively change the size of the pruned user profile and measure the relevance of the generated tag clouds.

For each query set of tags T_q, where the size of T_q equals k, we perform the following evaluation:

1. Generate a tag cloud with respect to given query tags T_q utilizing specific tags selection method such that tag cloud contains at most n-tags.
2. Measure the *relevance* of the generated tag cloud.
3. Increase the size of tag cloud n. If maximum size is reached, increment the size of T_q.

The above-described evaluation is conducted for each datasets and all considered tags selection methods.

4.3   Graph-Based Techniques

Graph-based tag clouds generation consists of these two steps:

1. Perform syntactical clustering of the original tag space.
2. Make a graph transformation from the syntactically clustered tag space.
3. Make a tag selection utilizing graph-based relevancy ranking algorithms with respect to the set of query tags T_q.

Each phase requires a certain parameters setting which are presented in the following paragraphs.

Graph Creation from Tag Space. An important step of graph-based tag cloud generation is a proper graph transformation. The proposed approach is computing a tag pair co-occurence for all tags. When this measure for a tag pair is greater than a predefined threshold α, we consider such tags as similar. Eventually, each related tag pair is transformed into two directed edges $t_1 \rightarrow t_2$ and $t_2 \rightarrow t_1$. We have manually explored various similarity thresholds for both datasets and attained the best results with $\alpha = 0.035$ for Bibsonomy, $\alpha = 0.2$ for Movielens and $\alpha = 0.01$ for Delicious.

Parameters Setting of Graph-Based Techniques. The performance of *Pagerank (PgRank)*, *Hits* and *k-step Markov Chain (k-MarkovCh)* strongly depends on proper parameter settings. As the goal of this work is to identify the most relevant tags with respect to a given query tag t_q, we set the parameters in the following way:

- Prior probabilities for all algorithms are defined as relative ratio of frequency t_q with respect to the total frequency sum of all the tags of the query, and 0 for other tags.
- A back probability β for *Pagerank* and *Hits* is relatively high ($\beta = 0.9$) in order to introduce often restart of random walk from the query tag.
- For *k-step Markov Chain* method, we set a constant k to 6.

The majority of these parameters were the same as in [6, 10].

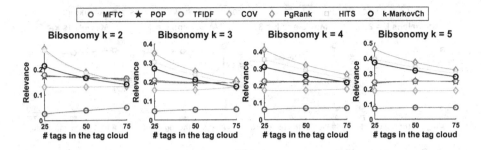

Fig. 2. Relevance on Bibsonomy dataset with different selection techniques and their corresponding logarithmic fit

4.4   Results

We conducted the evaluation for the presented datasets and the methods following the introduced methodology. We iteratively increased the number of tags in the tag cloud starting with 25 till 75 tags with the step 25. Moreover, we explored different query sizes, i.e., number of tags in the query, ranging from $k = 2$ till $k = 5$. The results for the Bibsonomy dataset are presented in Figure 2. The graph-based tags selection methods outperform all baseline techniques in almost all settings. The largest improvements can be observed for tag clouds with the size $n = 25$ and all query sizes. In these cases, the Relevance is improved about 0.21, 0.19, 0.15 and 0.18 for the query sizes 2, 3, 4 and 5 respectively. The MFTC method attains the worst results, similarly COV method perform worse than other compared methods. Obviously, tag cloud optimization with respect to the coverage results into inclusion of more irrelevant tags to the final tag cloud. The best graph based method is Pagerank algorithm. The performance of HITS algorithm decreases as the number of query tags increases. Similarly, k-Markov Chain attains lower Relevance as PageRank algorithm, because k constant is still the same for larger query sets. Therefore, the imaginary token may reach further from the query tags in the graph. However, this can be beneficial for cases where the goal is to deliver more diverse tag clouds as overlap is slightly lower than for Pagerank algorithm. Graph based methods attain the best results also for the Movielens dataset. The Relevance is improved about 0.40, 0.44, 0.45 and 0.3 for these query sizes 2, 3, 4 and 5 respectively (see Figure. 3). The TF-IDF methods does not attain such good results as there are many relevant tags which are used frequently on top of all resources in the dataset. The graph based methods perform very similarly. However, the methods attain lower relevance for large tag clouds.

On the contrary, the graph based methods attain similar or lower relevance for tag clouds generated from the Delicious dataset (see Figure 4). For tag clouds which contain 25 tags the best performing method is PageRank algorithm. On the other hand, for the tag clouds with more tags, the COV method outperforms other techniques. Decreased performance of the graph based methods is caused by the Delicious dataset data distribution. In particular, there are many very

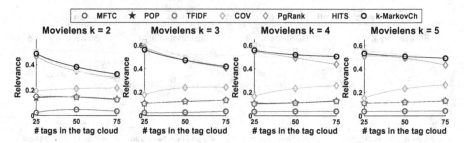

Fig. 3. Relevance on Movielens dataset with different selection techniques and their corresponding logarithmic fit

frequent tags in the dataset, i.e., almost 20 tags that were assigned at least 10000 times, almost 500 tags that were placed by users at least 1000 times. On the other hand, there are 172554 tags that were utilized for annotation less than 10 times. Consequently, the underlying co-occurrence graph links very frequent tags with very rarely used tags. It results into the inclusion of more frequent tags into tag clouds. Such inclusion causes lower relevance.

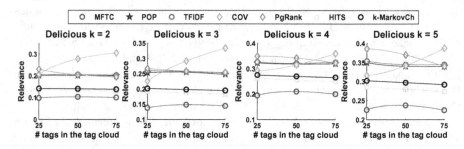

Fig. 4. Relevance on Delicious dataset with different selection techniques and their corresponding logarithmic fit

4.5 Discussions and Limitations

The presented results demonstrate that graph-based methods can be succesfully exploited for tag cloud generation tasks. The improvements are significant (in some cases almost tripled relevance such as for the Bibsonomy and Movielens dataset). The advantage of the graph-based methods is an ability to generate tag clouds with respect to the particular set of query tags. The methods allow you to predefine which tag from the query tags should be more preferred by adjusting prior distribution for stochastic restarts of Markov Chains. Moreover, these methods allow you to generate more diverse tag clouds with still relatively high relevance (the smaller back probability β is the more diverse final tag clouds are). Despite of these advantages, the methods do not perform that well on top of datasets with the long-tail distribution of tags. We consider datasets with the long-tail distribution of tags as those that contain very few tags which are frequently utilized within the system. Moreover, these datasets include a large number of infrequently used tags. The graph-based methods select tags utilizing co-occurrence graph which links more frequent tags with rarely used tags. Obviously, it results in the inclusion of more frequent tags into the final tag clouds. This bevahiour causes decreased relevance of the generated tag clouds.

5   Conclusions

We explored the set of tag cloud generation methods with respect to multiple keyword query. The graph-based methods perform the best at the Movielens and the Bibsonomy datasets. This is achieved due to the proposed extension of the setting of prior probabilities for the random walk based algorithms. On the other hand, the graph-based methods do not perform well for the Delicious dataset. The Delicious dataset has different distribution of tags with many very frequent tags which decreases performance for more specific queries. For future work, we plan to investigate how to build tag clouds based on user preferences. Moreover, we aim to define tag cloud generation methods that will capture diversity and novelty of the considered resources.

Acknowledgements. This work has been supported by FP7 ICT project M-Eco: Medical Ecosystem Personalized Event-Based Surveillance under grant No. 247829. Moreover, the author wish to thank Vicki Chapman for her help with the proofreading.

References

1. Aras, H., Siegel, S., Malaka, R.: Semantic cloud: an enhanced browsing interface for exploring resources in folksonomy systems. In: Workshop on Visual Interfaces to the Social and Semantic Web (VISSW2010), IUI 2010, Hong Kong, China, 2010 (February 7, 2009)
2. Bateman, S., Gutwin, C., Nacenta, M.: Seeing things in the clouds: the effect of visual features on tag cloud selections. In: Proceedings of the Nineteenth ACM Conference on Hypertext and Hypermedia, pp. 193–202. ACM (2008)
3. A.T. Company, Keyword and search engines statistics (2013)
4. Haveliwala, T.: Topic-sensitive pagerank: A context-sensitive ranking algorithm for web search. IEEE Transactions on Knowledge and Data Engineering 15(4), 784–796 (2003)
5. Knowledge and U. o. K. Data Engineering Group. Benchmark folksonomy data from bibsonomy, version of January 1, 2010 (2010)
6. Leginus, M., Dolog, P., Lage, R.: Graph based techniques for tag cloud generation. In: Proceedings of the 24th ACM Conference on Hypertext and Social Media. ACM (2013)
7. Leginus, M., Dolog, P., Lage, R., Durao, F.: Methodologies for improved tag cloud generation with clustering. In: Brambilla, M., Tokuda, T., Tolksdorf, R. (eds.) ICWE 2012. LNCS, vol. 7387, pp. 61–75. Springer, Heidelberg (2012)

8. Page, L., Brin, S., Motwani, R., Winograd, T.: The pagerank citation ranking: Bringing order to the web. Technical Report 1999-66, Stanford InfoLab, Previous number = SIDL-WP-1999-0120 (November 1999)

9. Venetis, P., Koutrika, G., Garcia-Molina, H.: On the selection of tags for tag clouds. In: Proceedings of the Fourth ACM International Conference on Web Search and Data Mining, WSDM 2011, pp. 835–844. ACM, New York (2011)

10. White, S., Smyth, P.: Algorithms for estimating relative importance in networks. In: Proceedings of the Ninth ACM SIGKDD International Conference on Knowledge Discovery and Data Mining, KDD 2003, pp. 266–275. ACM, New York (2003)

Summaries on the Fly: Query-Based Extraction of Structured Knowledge from Web Documents

Besnik Fetahu[1], Bernardo Pereira Nunes[1,2], and Stefan Dietze[1]

[1] L3S Research Center, Leibniz University Hannover, Germany
{fetahu,nunes,dietze}@L3S.de
[2] Department of Informatics - PUC-Rio - Rio de Janeiro, RJ - Brazil
bnunes@inf.puc-rio.br

Abstract. A large part of Web resources consists of unstructured textual content. Processing and retrieving relevant content for a particular information need is challenging for both machines and humans. While information retrieval techniques provide methods for detecting suitable resources for a particular query, information extraction techniques enable the extraction of structured data and text summarization allows the detection of important sentences. However, these techniques usually do not consider particular user interests and information needs. In this paper, we present a novel method to automatically generate structured summaries from user queries that uses POS patterns to identify relevant statements and entities in a certain context. Finally, we evaluate our work using the publicly available New York Times corpus, which shows the applicability of our method and the advantages over previous works.

Keywords: POS pattern analysis, knowledge extraction, text summarization, query-based summaries, entity recognition.

1 Introduction

The majority of Web resources consist of unstructured textual content. Due to the vast amount of information, filtering and adaptation of information to different user needs and contexts is crucial.

Information retrieval (IR) techniques facilitate the discovery and retrieval of relevant documents, often resulting in large sets of ranked documents shown to a user. When processing the retrieved documents, as part of such user queries, efficient methods are needed to enable users to quickly assess and judge the content of each document, in particular with respect to its relevance to the query.

Therefore, text summarization techniques aim at decomposing documents into its most important chunks like paragraphs, sentences, etc. Most prominent approaches on text summarization techniques rely on topic modeling methods [2], with each document belonging to one or more topics, and summarizing by detecting the importance of a sentence towards the defined topic. Despite the fact that text summarization approaches significantly reduce the amount of content,

F. Daniel, P. Dolog, and Q. Li (Eds.): ICWE 2013, LNCS 7977, pp. 249–264, 2013.

they are not focused on the user interests. Hence, it often generates a generic summary of a textual document that might not reflect the user interests. Furthermore, after processing and detecting the most relevant concepts in a document, common text summarization techniques do not take advantage of the concepts found for representing the summaries in a structured form, which would improve reasoning over the structured text [1,3,28].

Information extraction (IE) approaches, specifically Named Entity Recognition (NER) tools and environments (e.g. GATE [7], DBpedia Spotlight[1], Alchemy[2], AIDA[3] or Apache Stanbol[4]), automatically generate structured data such as entities and their relationships [18] from unstructured Web resources, which would assist the information retrieval process.

In order to provide relevant information focused on particular user needs, we introduce a novel query-driven summarization and knowledge extraction approach based on POS pattern analysis, topic modeling and NER. Concisely, our approach exploits POS co-occurrence frequency from documents retrieved given a user query to summarize the results that match most frequent POS pattern. Additionally, we use DBpedia[5] and Freebase[6] as background knowledge to enrich, structure and disambiguate the concepts of each retrieved document.

As main contributions of this paper, we introduce a novel POS pattern detection approach for relevance judgment of statements in unstructured texts; adapt techniques of text and data processing into a *query-based document summarization* approach; create a new conceptual entity type based on the co-occurrence of certain POS tags, such as *noun phrases*; and, finally, the incremental population of a knowledge base for further reasoning. To the best of our knowledge, this is the first work that extracts focused and structured summaries, which satisfy given user queries and information needs. From now on, we refer to this approach as *focused knowledge extraction.*

The paper is structured as follows: Section 2 presents the related work on summarization and Section 3 introduces concepts used and formalizes the problem of focused knowledge extraction. Section 4 presents an overview and the pre-processing steps of our approach and Section 5 introduces the focused knowledge extraction for generating query-based summaries. Finally, in Section 6 we show the evaluation and the results of our work followed by a brief discussion and conclusions in Section 7.

2   Related Work

Most of the approaches for text summarization and extraction rely on combined methods. For instance, natural language processing (NLP) and information extraction (IE) techniques are usually used to generate extraction patterns [9],

---

[1] http://spotlight.dbpedia.org
[2] http://www.alchemyapi.com
[3] http://adaptivedisclosure.org/aida/
[4] http://incubator.apache.org/stanbol
[5] http://dbpedia.org
[6] http://www.freebase.com

while Latent Semantic Analysis (LSA) is combined with clustering techniques, such as Latent Dirichlet Allocation (LDA), to select representative textual content from texts [26].

As for IE approaches, the extraction of important pieces of information from textual contents is mainly based on entities and entity relations [9,17,10], where they use static patterns along with semantic and lexical features to achieve higher precision. The extraction of relations and events are usually performed in large sets of Web pages or data streams, such as Twitter[7] [21]. The approach on generating patterns for extracting relations is similar to ours with the difference that in our case instead of using fixed set of patterns, they are automatically generated based on the evidence provided by the retrieved documents for a specific user query.

Additional work on summarization [4,22,27,13] attempt on incorporating user query interests. However, they rely on naive heuristics of counting specific terms and defining manually extraction rules.

The field of Natural Language Processing (NLP) is a clear direction on leveraging the unstructured textual content, where the methods exploit the syntactic and semantic structure of languages used in resources. Related works on co-reference resolution depict the importance of an entity or part of sentence that can be implied for a specific context [15,20] and to resolve disambiguation of specific sentence parts. Similarly to our pattern generation approach, Hovy et al. [14] uses "Tree Kernels" to encode different needs of detecting events, relations and timestamps by incorporating POS tags, semantic types and other terms of interest. Moreover, SUMMONS [19] a summarization tool that builds templates for filling-in necessary information, and generates natural language as concise summary representation of the filled template. In our approach, we use co-reference to resolve ambiguities in the text.

A notable effort in text summarization tasks was performed by Blei et al. introducing the Latent Dirichlet Allocation (LDA) approach [2], which is based on a generative probabilistic model for topic construction. Particularly, we use LDA for generating clusters of a set of related topics. Apart from this, LDA is often used as a tool for summarization.

Other approaches on document clustering and summarization [26] rely on constructing document-term and sentence-term matrices using Latent Semantic Analysis (LSA). In this case, most important sentences selected based on generated eigenvalues from a non-negative matrix factorization are chosen as a base for language models. In this way, meaningful representations of clusters as sentences are generated rather than terms.

Following the same direction using LSA, Wan [25] considers subtopic creation from the main topic narrative text. Thus, sentences are measured for their relationship to the subtopics and presented as summaries for a particular subtopic. Similarly, Gong and Liu [12] consider IR and LSA techniques for ranking and identifying most important sentences as a means to construct summaries with broad coverage for a set of textual resources.

---

[7] http://www.twitter.com

Recent efforts from the semantic Web community consider the task of summarization from unstructured content [5,3,6,1], which are mainly based on the previously mentioned methodologies. Briefly, the approaches aim at summarizing the content into structured format such as Linked Data or as part of Ontology construction.

The method presented in this paper goes beyond the creation of text summaries and aims to generate structured context-based summaries. Although, previous semantic-based methods have partially addressed this issue, we incorporate specific user needs into an automatic pattern generation approach to extract only the information that fits the user query context.

3   Background

3.1   Concepts and Fundamentals

For the sake of clarity and to avoid confusion, we introduce concepts that are used throughout this work. An **action** is defined as a verb phrase that indicates an activity involving one or more **entities** as *subject/object*, whereas **entity** is a less restrictive concept compared to traditional NER approaches, and is not necessarily required to belong to one of the types (*people, location, organization,* etc.) or a newly defined **entity** *type iMisc* in Section 5.2.

Additionally, the previous concepts **action, entity** are also contextually defined. An **action context** captures additional information like *subject/object* as **entities** found in a specific context, whereas **entity context** contains additional descriptive information such as *adjectives, quantities, etc.*

3.2   Problem Definition

Briefly, we formalize the task of generating contextualized summaries and present examples for illustration. Let $D = \{d_1, d_2, \ldots, d_m\}$ be a set of documents and $T = \{t_1, t_2, \ldots, t_n\}$ a set of topics, where a topic is defined as a representation of most important terms from the corpus in D, formally defined as $t_i = \{w_1, w_2, \ldots, w_k\}$. We then define matrix $D \times T = [x_{ij}]_{(mn)}$, such that, $x_{ij} = o(d_i, t_j)$, for $i = 1 \ldots m \wedge j = 1 \ldots n$, where $o(d_i, t_j)$ is defined by a binary relation B indicating whether a document is related to a topic or not.

Now, let $Q = \{q_1, q_2, \ldots, q_z\}$ be a set of queries where $q_k = \{e_1, \ldots, e_v\}$ is a list of query terms. For instance, the user query "European+Union" results in the singleton term $e_1 = $ "European Union". The result is a subset of matching documents $D' \subset D$ and the set of topics $T' \subset T$, where $\forall t \in T', \exists d \in D' \wedge o(d, t) \in B$. Note that, we also perform a query expansion step for each $q_k \in Q$, however, to preserve the clarity of the definition, we assume that the new terms introduced by the query expansion method are already considered in Q.

In what follows, we define the set σ as the union of POS tags from the terms in topic definitions from T' as $\rho = \cup_{(t \in T')} \omega(t)$ where $\omega \in \{NN, NNP, \ldots, VB, CD\}$ and the query terms from q_k as $\phi = \cup_{(e \in q_k)} e$, hence

$\sigma = \rho \cup \phi$. Elements in σ are used to construct a square matrix which are added as row and column entries. The co-occurrence of two elements (σ_i, σ_j), for $i, j = 1 \ldots l$, computed for the documents in $D', P = [\delta(i,j)]_{lxl}$, e.g. $\sigma = \{NN, VB, \ldots, \text{"European Union"}\}$.

Finally, a set of patterns $\Psi \in \{\psi_1, \ldots, \psi_y\}$ consists of a combination of elements from σ and a score assigned based on P. From documents in D' we define a set of sentences $S = \{s_{11}, \ldots s_{1v}, \ldots, s_{mv}\}$. As generated output from patterns in ψ and sentences in S, we define the focused summaries as $C = \{((s_{(i,j)}, \psi_k), (E, A))\}$ such that for $s_{(i,j)} \exists \psi_k \wedge f(s_{(i,j)}, \psi_k), f(s, \psi)$ is the match of sentence $s_{(i,j)}$ with pattern ψ. $E = \{e_1, \ldots, e_p\}$ and $A = \{a_1, \ldots, a_z\}$ are the set of **entities** and **actions** from sentence $s_{(i,j)}$ and $\forall e \in E, \exists e \in s$ and $\forall a \in A, \exists a \in s$.

4 Overview and Running Example

This section presents the overall workflow of our focused knowledge extraction approach based on a running example. Fig. 1 shows the whole process starting from the user query input. Indeed, the user plays a central role in the generation of the summary, since the resulting summary is based on the user query terms.

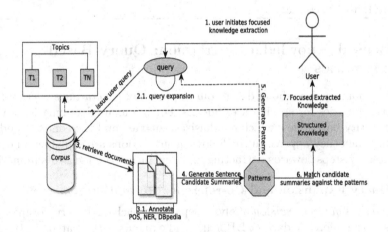

Fig. 1. Focused Knowledge Extraction Workflow

Let $q_1 = \{\text{"European Union"}\}$ be a query term where $q_1 \in Q$ issued by the user. Thus, the query term q_1 is processed and expanded using reference datasets, which results in new terms $q_k \in Q$. For instance, the query expansion for "European Union" results in $Q = \{\text{"European Union"}, \text{"European Union member economies"}, \text{"G20 nations"}, \ldots, \text{"International Organizations of Europe"}\}$.

The query expansion is performed for each query term provided by the user, where based on reference datasets, such as DBpedia and Freebase, related terms are automatically added to the list of user query terms Q. The terms added to the list Q are labels (rdfs:label) from the directly related **entities** in such reference datasets, explained in detail in Section 5.1. The query expansion aims at improving recall and might be useful to disambiguate a particular user query. The disambiguation occurs when the query has multiple terms, which facilitates the identification of the user context.

Once the query terms are expanded, a set of relevant documents is retrieved, according to these terms. Since the corpus is pre-processed, annotated with POS tags and co-reference resolution applied, the task is synthesized to generate a set of patterns scored for their likelihood of appearance on the set of the retrieved documents.

Thus, in the case of the query Q, the top patterns generated is $[JJ \rightarrow VB \rightarrow$ "European Union" $\rightarrow RB]$. The set of topics is defined by the 1000 most representative topic terms extracted from the corpus. The set of the topics are selected using a topic modeling tool based on LDA [2] and annotated with POS tags.

As a result, we obtain all the documents and topics that serve as input to generate the summaries focused on the extracted knowledge and based on user queries. The example below shows a generated summary for query "European Union", in blue color are shown the **entities**, while in red the **actions**.

Bulgaria $\rightarrow$ joined $\rightarrow$ European Union, on Monday $\rightarrow$ helping to end $\rightarrow$ geographic divisions $\rightarrow$ left $\rightarrow$ cold war $\rightarrow$ extending $\rightarrow$ borders of the now 27-member bloc eastward to the Black Sea.

5 Focused Knowledge Extraction: Query-Based Summaries

In this section, we describe in details our approach of generating structured and focused summaries for specific user queries. For the focused summaries we propose an entity-based view which emphasizes **entities** and the contexts and **actions** in which they appear. In the following subsections are explained in details the necessary steps towards extracting and generating the focused summaries.

5.1 Query Expansion and Co-reference Resolution

The process of *query expansion* analyzes separately each query term for matching entities in the reference dataset DBpedia, and expands with related entities that are directly connected from all properties and assigned to the original query term. Moreover, the related query terms are extracted from the related entities using their label (rdfs:label). For instance, the query term "European Union" is considered as a singleton term if it is indicated as a cunjunction of terms. Finally, the query is reformulated as the disjunction of the original terms and the ones found during *query expansion*. However, this step can be exploited in addition also as a *query refinement* process by considering the conjunction rather than the disjunction.

Whereas co-reference resolution aims at resolving ambiguities of terms e.g "the president of the European Union" can be resolved to "Herman Van Rompuy", using Stanford's NLP tool [15,20].

5.2 *iMisc* Entity Type Definition

Determining the entity *type* is important for our approach, thus for named entity recognition we rely on the approach in [11], which detect annotation types such as *person, location, organization, date.* However, in many cases detecting the entity type is not possible, hence we rely on a *term matrix* which computes co-occurrence term frequencies of noun phrases among a set of previously analyzed and annotated documents based on the approach in [24,23], and recognizes named **entities** of *type iMisc* to distinguish from the other *types.*

An entity of type *iMisc* consists of terms which co-occur and can be formalized as the following: $entity[iMisc] = \bigcup_{i=1}^{k} \text{co-occur}(term_i, term_{i+1})$, where, in our case the maximum value for k was found to be 3 (indicating 3 terms that co-occur).

5.3 Automated Pattern Generation

One of the main challenges on creating user-query based summaries, is the extraction of **entities** and **actions** relying on patterns that adapt automatically to the intent of a user and set of retrieved documents. A pattern consists of a combination of items from the set σ that co-occur in a set of retrieved documents (see Section 3.2), with POS tags extracted from the annotation of topic definition terms and query terms.

Note that the set of POS tags is limited only to the topic definition terms (as representative for the set of retrieved documents), and ignore other POS tags not related to the topic definition terms. Thus, for a set of pairs of POS tags and query terms (σ), all non-repetitive combinations are considered to construct patterns for a given user query.

The combinations are represented in a symmetric matrix $P = [\delta_{(i,j)}]_{l \times l}$ in Eq. 1, hence, as rows and columns items from the set σ. The matrix is computed for each issued query and each entry ($\delta_{(i,j)}$) of the matrix represents the conditional probabilities of two items from σ co-occurring in the set of retrieved documents D'.

For instance, consider again our running example with the query "European Union" (referred with the acronym **EU**), which after the *query expansion* step results in the set of query terms $Q = \{$ "European Union member economies", "G20 nations", ..., "International Organizations of Europe"$\}$. The resulting matrix is as follows:

$$
P = \begin{bmatrix}
 & CD & VBD & \cdots & NN & EU \\
CD & p(CD|CD) & p(VBD|CD) & \cdots & p(NN|CD) & p(EU|CD) \\
VBD & p(CD|VBD) & p(VBD|VBD) & \cdots & p(NN|VBD) & p(EU|VBD) \\
\vdots & \vdots & \vdots & \vdots & \vdots & \vdots \\
NN & p(CD|NN) & p(VBD|NN) & \cdots & p(NN|NN) & p(EU|NN) \\
EU & p(CD|EU) & p(VBD|EU) & \cdots & p(NN|EU) & p(EU|EU)
\end{bmatrix} \quad (1)
$$

Given the resulting matrix P in Eq 1, we compute all possible combinations of patterns, supported by evidence from the set of retrieved documents. The problem of automatically generating patterns is modeled as a *directed tree graph*, thus, a pattern represents a *path* from a **root node** to a **leaf node**.

From each element in σ for a query a *directed tree graph* is modeled with all possible combinations with other element in σ (when the conditional probability between the two elements is than zero in P). The transition probabilities from one node to another represent the likelihood of those elements from the document's text with a specific POS tag or query term appearing together. Therefore, each path from the **root node** to one of the **leaf nodes** represents a pattern of variable number of elements.

The pattern scores are computed for the path from the **root node** to one of the **leaf nodes**. The score of a pattern represents the marginal probability of the probability of two nodes in the path co-occurring in the retrieved documents.

In more details, for an σ_i considered as the root node ("European Union") of the *directed tree graph*, as shown in our example in Fig. 2. The score of the pattern having as a root node "European Union" is computed as in Eq. 2, where for the i-th row in matrix P probabilities for each parent/child node transition are multiplied. Finally, the higher the score of the pattern the more important the pattern is, conveying important information about the most representative syntactical and semantical structures of a document.

$$\forall \psi \in \Psi, \psi_{score} = p(\sigma_i) \cdot \prod_{j=1}^{l} p(\delta_{i,j}|\delta_{i,j-1}) \qquad (2)$$

To reduce the large number of detected patterns, we retain only the top-10 high scoring patterns as computed in Eq. 2.

Table 1 shows a small subset of patterns with highest scores generated for our running example. Using the generated patterns, individual sentences from the retrieved documents are *matched* against one of the patterns, and are further considered for generating focused summaries. A *match* is considered when a sentence contains an ordered set of terms having the same syntactical structure (ignoring POS tags that are not found in the topic definition terms) as a pattern, we consider the relaxation of a full match and look for partial matches thus increasing coverage of the summaries.

5.4   Contextual Structure of Extracted Knowledge

A necessary and important step after finding sentences decomposed from the retrieved documents is extraction of the knowledge as a pre-condition for generating focused summaries. As indicated in Section 5, our summaries provide an entity centric view, following the RDF schema visualized in Fig. 3.

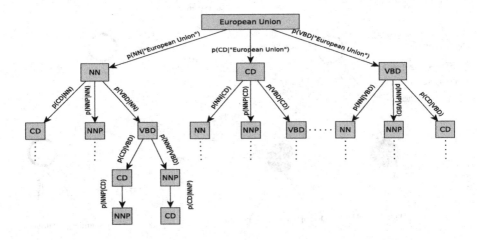

Fig. 2. Pattern Generation approach using directed tree graphs

Table 1. Automatically generated extraction patterns

Generated Patterns	Pattern Score ψ_{score}
$JJ \to VB \to$ "European Union" $\to RB$	$5.71E-09$
$JJ \to NN \to RB \to VB \to EU$	$4.63E-09$
$VB \to$ "European Union" $\to JJ \to RB$	$2.86E-09$
$VB \to$ "European Union" $\to JJ \to NN \to RB$	$1.16E-09$
"European Union" $\to JJ \to NN \to RB \to VB$	$6.99E-10$

In Fig. 3, similar as in [8] we consider several structures describing concepts introduced in Section 3.1. We separate the defined structures into two categories *global* and *local*, explained in more details below.

Global structures such as **entity** and **action** capture relevant information about these concepts, disregarding their context. Only the description and the *type* of an **entity** as defined using standard NER tools[8] and the defind *iMisc type*. While, for an **action** the *state* as the verb tense is extracted and used as an indicator of whether the *action* is completed or an ongoing/future activity. Additionally, **entities** are enriched using DBpedia Spotlight with reference datasets like DBpedia, and a link (`owl:sameAs`) is provided to the reference instance in DBpedia.

Local structures like **entity-context** and **action-context** capture *contextual* information about the two global structures **entity** and **action**. With respect to **entity-context**, attributes (terms of POS tag *adjective*) and features like quantifiers (terms of POS tag as *cardinal number*) are captured for an **entity** describing for a specific context. Whereas for **action-context** we consider

---

[8] http://nlp.stanford.edu/software/corenlp.shtml

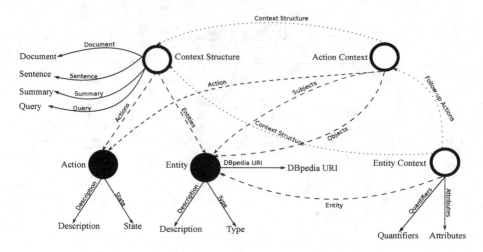

Fig. 3. Focused Knowledge Extraction RDF Schema

subject/object (**entities** belonging to the same context) as context specific information with which an **action** is linked. Finally, the *context structure* captures information about the source of information, matching pattern, along with the source document and user query.

The proposed RDF schema for representing and storing the focused summaries offers the functionality of viewing **entities** appearing in different context, showing the perspectives and their involvement for different queries. While additional information obtained after **entity** enrichment provides an interlinking mechanism to other data sources that lead to inferring of new knowledge for focused summaries.

Final aim of our *focused knowledge extraction* is constructing a publicly available knowledge base of summaries generated for different corpora and contexts over time, which will be incrementally populated and enriched. Access to the schema, the RDF dataset and other related tools and evaluation is available from a dedicated Website[9].

6   Evaluation and Results

In this section, we present a thorough evaluation of our approach followed by results and discussion. Concisely, the automatically generated summaries by our method are compared against abstractive manually created summaries. An "abstractive summary" is the summary that does not necessarily contain a similar syntactical structure as the original document, but covers its main concepts. The relevance of the automatically generated summaries for a given query against the original manually created summaries for each document in our corpus was assessed by humans and also using ROUGE [16].

---

[9] htttp://l3s.de/~fetahu/QueryBased_Summaries/

6.1   Dataset

As for the dataset, we used a subset of the New York Times (NYT) corpus, which contains $40,000$ articles and its manually generated abstractive summaries from 2007. The articles are manually annotated with **entities** such as persons, locations and organizations[10]. In general, the length of the summaries from the NYT corpus ranges from 1 to 3 sentences. These summaries are used as gold-standard to measure the coverage of the automatically and contextualized summaries generated by our approach.

6.2   Evaluation Process

The evaluation is divided into two steps: (1) focused-summary appropriateness to user queries; and (2) focused-summary coverage.

The evaluation of step (1) aims at measuring how well an automatically generated summary represents the query terms and concepts implied by the query. In this evaluation, we created a questionnaire where we showed to the participants the query terms used to retrieve the documents and the automatically generated summaries. The participant has also access to the original summary and the document content. For this evaluation, we had 17 participants in which they evaluated, in average, 20 summaries and chose whether the automatically generated summary is "relevant" or "not relevant" to a given query.

As for the second evaluation, we use ROUGE-n metric (Recall-Oriented Understudy Gisting Evaluation) [16] for computing the coverage of the automatically generated summaries against the manually created summaries in terms of a contiguous sequence of words (n-grams). For instance, $n = 1$ represents the unigram "European", while $n = 2$ represents the bigram "European Union". The coverage ratio of the contextualized summaries and the manually generated summaries for the length n is computed as follows:

$$ROUGE_n = \frac{\sum_{s \in S} \sum_{w_n \in s} |match(w_n)|}{\sum_{s \in S} \sum_{w_n \in s} |(w_n)|} \tag{3}$$

where $|match(w_n)|$ is the total number of the $n-grams$, represented as w_n, that are part of the automatically generated summary and the manually generated summaries, i.e. the reference summaries S. Obviously, ROUGE-n is a recall metric between a candidate summary and a set of reference summaries. Our evaluation was performed over 20 queries, which generated approximately 110 summaries on average per query. The manually created summaries extracted from the NYT corpus were used as reference summaries. Note that, the automatically generated summary and its reference summary correspond to the same document in the corpus.

---

[10] http://www.ldc.upenn.edu/Catalog/catalogEntry.jsp?catalogId=LDC2008T19

6.3   Results

The first evaluation used manual evaluators and aimed at assessing the relevance of a summary given a user query, 76% of the automatically generated summaries were marked as "relevant".

For the second evaluation, we used ROUGE-1 to compare the automatically generated summaries and the manually generated abstractive summaries. Fig. 4 summarizes the results obtained by a sample of user queries. Our method achieved 25% precision for the query "Super Bowl", which is a comparatively high precision value for such task. Furthermore, the query "Terrorist Attacks" obtained 32% in terms of recall. The F_1 measure ranged from 12% to 26%, which is comparable to traditional summarization techniques.

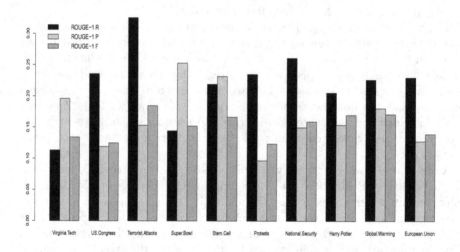

Fig. 4. Results for ROUGE-1 metric for different queries

Table 2. Generated focused summaries for different queries

Query	European Union	Super Bowl	US Congress	Virginia Tech	Stem Cell	Protest	Harry Potter	Global Warming	National Security	Terrorist Attacks
#Q.Terms	7	13	17	28	5	2	22	5	0	0
#Doc.	157	370	13	12	105	129	10	198	250	57
#Summ.	129	325	19	11	86	103	7	170	207	52

In Table 3 we show a small subset of generated summaries for the evaluation queries reported in Table 2. For readability reasons, we do not show all the information about **entities** and **actions**, and their contexts, however, we indicate the two different structures with colors in blue and red, respectively.

Table 3. Sample generated focused summaries from retrieved documents for the reported evaluation queries

Query: "European Union"	Query: "Super Bowl"
Bulgaria → joined → European Union European Union on Monday → helping to end → geographic divisions → left → cold war → extending → borders of the now 27-member bloc eastward to the Black Sea.	New York Giants → are to realize → Super Bowl they → held so firmly → beginning of the season → felt completely → implausible weekend they → have to win → three games on the road.
Georges Prtre → is → former music director of the Paris Opera → has conducted → most world → leading → symphony orchestras.	Philadelphia Eagles → have played → N.F.C. championship games in the past past years → reached → Super Bowl after the season → losing to → New England.
Query: "National Security'	**Query: "Virginia Tech"**
Kissinger Henry A (Dr) → was named → secretary of state in while → keeping → post as national security adviser.	Clemson University → try to start → new streak Wednesday University of Maryland → plays → host Carolina → lost to → unranked Virginia Tech on Saturday.
Republicans → forced to → Congressional sidelines for the first time in years → growing increasingly agitated → Democratic timetable.	Virginia → needed → mountain-sized comeback → topple → Georgia Tech in the Gator Bowl Louisville → took → advantage of some timely turnovers to → outlast → Wake Forest.
Query: "Stem Cell"	**Query: "Protest"**
Republicans → boasted → support for embryonic stem cell research as a way to → find → treatments for a wide range of diseases.	Students → clashed → police in this country last May attention → focused not just → demands → hold → elections without government meddling leaders → organizing → protests.
Democrats → applauded → Mr. Spitzer Eliot (Gov) calls → insure → 500000 children → lack → health insurance → enroll → 900000 adults → are → eligible Medicaid → enrolled → issue debt → pay → stem cell research.	Submarine → rammed → Japanese fishing vessel in waters off Hawaii → killing → nine people.
Query: "Global Warming"	**Query: "Harry Potter"**
Scientists over how to → describe → climate threat → is particularly → intense experts → work → final language in portions of the latest assessment of global warming by the Intergovernmental Panel on Climate Change.	Dresden → played → Blackthorne Paul Blackthorne Paul → is → Harry Potter → grown up to become → Columbo.
Scientists → shouting lately → global warming → is → human-caused catastrophe.	America → taking → children movies → has become → central cultural activity.
Query: "Terrorist Attacks"	**Query: "US Congress"**
Homeland Security Department → is essentially → first line of defense again terrorist attacks → is serving → nation.	Proposal → being considered → small businesses → allow write → larger part of they → go to → court → challenge → federal regulations.
Pentagon → has increased → domestic intelligence collection efforts → help ensure → American bases → are protected → potential terrorist attacks.	Bush George W (Pres) → has been → bit forthright things → have gone → Iraq Cheney Dick (Vice Pres) → spoke → enormous successes → refused to pay even → curled-lip service → consulting → Congress.

7 Conclusions and Future Work

Our approach addresses the task of focused knowledge extraction applied to the problem of generating focused entity-centric summaries for a given user query. We exploit POS pattern analysis and NER techniques to identify relevant statements and entities within a certain context to automatically generate query-based summaries. We also provide an RDF schema with the structured summaries for further reasoning in a publicly available knowledge base, which directly contributes to create a body of knowledge about entities and their appearance contexts over time. Furthermore, the techniques presented in this paper expand state of the art techniques on text summarization as well as information extraction.

We extensively evaluated our approach in order to validate that the automatically generated summaries address the user query needs and that it covers the main concepts of the documents. Indeed, our results showed that 76% of the summaries were relevant to the user queries and the concepts contained in the query. Moreover, our automatic evaluation proved to be comparable to state of the art techniques when assessed using the ROUGE-1 metric. In terms of the best performing queries, the results for precision, recall and F1 reached 25% of precision for the query "Super Bowl", 35% of recall and a F1 of 26% for the query "Terrorist Attacks". This shows that our approach extracted focused knowledge with high precision by incorporating the user interests through the query terms and it detected the importance of specific POS tags after a POS analysis of the terms in different topics.

As part of future work, we are working on reducing the number of patterns generated for a query. Since, it is a combinatorial problem when looking for patterns that involve many query terms. However, this problem could be circumvented by introducing a prior language analysis step to constrain the number of patterns that are appropriate. Moreover, we plan to apply this technique to several other domains.

References

1. Augenstein, I., Padó, S., Rudolph, S.: Lodifier: Generating linked data from unstructured text. In: Simperl, E., Cimiano, P., Polleres, A., Corcho, O., Presutti, V. (eds.) ESWC 2012. LNCS, vol. 7295, pp. 210–224. Springer, Heidelberg (2012)
2. Blei, D.M., Ng, A.Y., Jordan, M.I.: Latent dirichlet allocation. Journal of Machine Learning Research 3, 993–1022 (2003)
3. Bouayad-Agha, N., Casamayor, G., Wanner, L., Díez, F., López Hernández, S.: FootbOWL: Using a generic ontology of football competition for planning match summaries. In: Antoniou, G., Grobelnik, M., Simperl, E., Parsia, B., Plexousakis, D., De Leenheer, P., Pan, J. (eds.) ESWC 2011, Part I. LNCS, vol. 6643, pp. 230–244. Springer, Heidelberg (2011)
4. Brandow, R., Mitze, K., Rau, L.F.: Automatic condensation of electronic publications by sentence selection. Inf. Process. Manage. 31(5), 675–685 (1995)
5. Bryl, V., Giuliano, C., Serafini, L., Tymoshenko, K.: Supporting natural language processing with background knowledge: Coreference resolution case. In: Patel-Schneider, P.F., Pan, Y., Hitzler, P., Mika, P., Zhang, L., Pan, J.Z., Horrocks, I., Glimm, B. (eds.) ISWC 2010, Part I. LNCS, vol. 6496, pp. 80–95. Springer, Heidelberg (2010)
6. Cheng, G., Tran, T., Qu, Y.: Relin: Relatedness and informativeness-based centrality for entity summarization. In: Aroyo, L., Welty, C., Alani, H., Taylor, J., Bernstein, A., Kagal, L., Noy, N., Blomqvist, E. (eds.) ISWC 2011, Part I. LNCS, vol. 7031, pp. 114–129. Springer, Heidelberg (2011)
7. Cunningham, H., Maynard, D., Bontcheva, K., Tablan, V.: A framework and graphical development environment for robust nlp tools and applications. In: ACL, pp. 168–175 (2002)
8. Dietze, S., Maynard, D., Demidova, E., Risse, T., Peters, W., Doka, K., Stavrakas, Y.: Entity extraction and consolidation for social web content preservation. In: SDA, pp. 18–29 (2012)

9. Etzioni, O., Banko, M., Soderland, S., Weld, D.S.: Open information extraction from the web. Commun. ACM 51(12), 68–74 (2008)
10. Fader, A., Soderland, S., Etzioni, O.: Identifying relations for open information extraction. In: EMNLP, pp. 1535–1545 (2011)
11. Finkel, J.R., Grenager, T., Manning, C.D.: Incorporating non-local information into information extraction systems by gibbs sampling. In: ACL (2005)
12. Gong, Y., Liu, X.: Generic text summarization using relevance measure and latent semantic analysis. In: SIGIR, pp. 19–25 (2001)
13. Grefenstette, G.: Short query linguistic expansion techniques: Palliating one-word queries by providing intermediate structure to text. In: Pazienza, M.T. (ed.) SCIE 1997. LNCS, vol. 1299, pp. 97–114. Springer, Heidelberg (1997)
14. Hovy, D., Fan, J., Gliozzo, A.M., Patwardhan, S., Welty, C.A.: When did that happen? - linking events and relations to timestamps. In: EACL, pp. 185–193 (2012)
15. Lee, H., Peirsman, Y., Chang, A., Chambers, N., Surdeanu, M., Jurafsky, D.: Stanford's multi-pass sieve coreference resolution system at the conll-2011 shared task. In: Proceedings of the Fifteenth Conference on Computational Natural Language Learning: Shared Task, CONLL Shared Task 2011, Stroudsburg, PA, USA, pp. 28–34. Association for Computational Linguistics (2011)
16. Lin, C.-Y.: Rouge: A package for automatic evaluation of summaries. In: Marie-Francine Moens, S.S. (ed.) Text Summarization Branches Out: Proceedings of the ACL 2004 Workshop, Barcelona, Spain, pp. 74–81. Association for Computational Linguistics (2004)
17. Mausam, M., Schmitz, S., Soderland, R.: Bart, and O. Etzioni. Open language learning for information extraction. In: EMNLP-CoNLL, pp. 523–534 (2012)
18. Pereira Nunes, B., Kawase, R., Dietze, S., Taibi, D., Casanova, M.A., Nejdl, W.: Can entities be friends? In: Reggio, G., Astesiano, E., Tarlecki, A. (eds.) Abstract Data Types 1994 and COMPASS 1994. LNCS, vol. 906, pp. 45–57. Springer, Heidelberg (1995)
19. Radev, D.R., McKeown, K.: Generating natural language summaries from multiple on-line sources. Computational Linguistics 24(3), 469–500 (1998)
20. Raghunathan, K., Lee, H., Rangarajan, S., Chambers, N., Surdeanu, M., Jurafsky, D., Manning, C.D.: A multi-pass sieve for coreference resolution. In: EMNLP, pp. 492–501 (2010)
21. Ritter, A., Mausam, Etzioni, O., Clark, S.: Open domain event extraction from twitter. In: KDD, pp. 1104–1112 (2012)
22. Tombros, A., Sanderson, M.: Advantages of query biased summaries in information retrieval. In: SIGIR, pp. 2–10 (1998)
23. Toutanova, K., Klein, D., Manning, C.D., Singer, Y.: Feature-rich part-of-speech tagging with a cyclic dependency network. In: Proceedings of the 2003 Conference of the North American Chapter of the Association for Computational Linguistics on Human Language Technology, NAACL 2003, Stroudsburg, PA, USA, vol. 1, pp. 173–180. Association for Computational Linguistics (2003)
24. Toutanova, K., Manning, C.D.: Enriching the knowledge sources used in a maximum entropy part-of-speech tagger. In: Proceedings of the 2000 Joint SIGDAT Conference on Empirical Methods in Natural Language Processing and Very Large Corpora: Held in Conjunction with the 38th Annual Meeting of the Association for Computational Linguistics, EMNLP 2000, Stroudsburg, PA, USA, vol. 13, pp. 63–70. Association for Computational Linguistics (2000)

25. Wan, X.: Topic analysis for topic-focused multi-document summarization. In: CIKM, pp. 1609–1612 (2009)
26. Wang, D., Zhu, S., Li, T., Chi, Y., Gong, Y.: Integrating document clustering and multidocument summarization. TKDD 5(3), 14 (2011)
27. White, M., Korelsky, T.: Multidocument summarization via information extraction. In: Proceedings of the HLT Conference, pp. 263–269 (2001)
28. Zhou, Y., Guo, Z., Ren, P., Yu, Y.: Applying wikipedia-based explicit semantic analysis for query-biased document summarization. In: Huang, D.-S., Zhao, Z., Bevilacqua, V., Figueroa, J.C. (eds.) ICIC 2010. LNCS, vol. 6215, pp. 474–481. Springer, Heidelberg (2010)

Mining Taxonomies from Web Menus:
Rule-Based Concepts and Algorithms

Matthias Keller and Hannes Hartenstein

Steinbuch Centre for Computing, Karlsruhe Institute of Technology, D-76128 Karlsruhe,
Germany
{matthias.keller,hannes.hartenstein}@kit.edu

Abstract. The logical hierarchies of Web sites (i.e. Web site taxonomies) are
obvious to humans, because humans can distinguish different menu levels and
their relationships. But such accurate information about the logical structure is
not yet available to machines. Many applications would benefit if Web site taxonomies could be mined from menus, but it was an almost unsolvable problem
in the past. While a tag newly introduced in HTML5 and novel mining methods
allow to distinguish menus from other contents today, it has not yet been re-
searched, how the underlying taxonomies can be extracted, given the menus. In
this paper we present the first detailed analysis of the problem and introduce
rule-based concepts for addressing each identified sub problem. We report on a
large-scale study on mining hierarchical menus of 350 randomly selected domains. Our methods allow extracting Web site taxonomy information that was
not available before with high precision and high recall.

Keywords: Web site taxonomies, Web mining, Content hierarchies.

1   Introduction

What would a user do first to gain an overview over the information she can find on
the ICWE2013 conference Web site? Most likely she will scan the prominently
placed main menu at the top of the page. Maybe she is interested in the call for papers, so she would move the mouse pointer over the corresponding menu item to expand the child items. On the top level the contents of the site are organized hierarchically and the tree structure can be parsed unambiguously by users. This applies to
most other Web sites as well.

Web site taxonomies, understood as logical hierarchies, are obvious to users, but
not yet available to machines. Although nested lists can be modeled, HTML does not
include language features that allow marking the different menu levels, e.g. the root
menu of a Web site. There is a lot of previous work that focuses on extracting and
generating different kinds of hierarchies based on Web content, e.g. from the hyperlink structure, URL structure or from text features. These hierarchies are very useful
for many applications – but only because they approximate the real logical content
organization. Humans, in contrast, are able to decode the logical organization from
the menu structure and information architects, which are responsible for organizing

F. Daniel, P. Dolog, and Q. Li (Eds.): ICWE 2013, LNCS 7977, pp. 265–282, 2013.

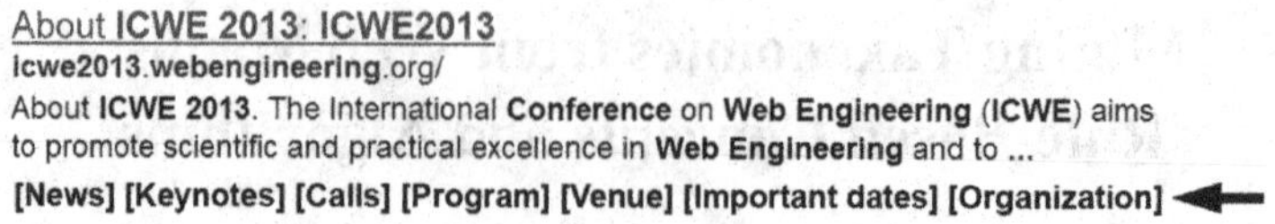

About **ICWE 2013**: **ICWE2013**
Icwe2013.webengineering.org/
About **ICWE 2013**. The International **Conference** on **Web Engineering** (**ICWE**) aims
to promote scientific and practical excellence in **Web Engineering** and to ...
[News] [Keynotes] [Calls] [Program] [Venue] [Important dates] [Organization] ◄——

Fig. 1. Integrating taxonomy information in the presentation of search results (mockup based on the search result presentation of google.com)[1]

and labeling information, express it in that way. Information architects emphasize the importance of well-designed taxonomies for usability (e.g. [1],[2]). If, based on menus, Web site taxonomies could be mined more accurately regarding human perception, all methods that rely on approximations of the logical hierarchy of Web sites would benefit, e.g. methods for automated sitemap generation [3], related entity finding [4], keyword enrichment [5] or Web site classification [6]. In addition, precise taxonomy information would allow whole new applications, in particular the integration of taxonomies in the presentation of search results (Fig. 1). The mockup illustrates that the first level of the Web site taxonomy provides useful information about the complete range of site content – information users cannot find in current search result summaries.

However, the seemingly simple problem of extracting taxonomies from menus appears to be a hard one at a closer look. Humans are able to decode visual features such as the position, size and layout of menus as well as color information for distinguishing different menu levels or menu types. These features carry semantics that are lost in the underlying markup code. But recent developments change the situation. The nav-tag introduced in HTML5 brings new possibilities for analyzing menus. Menus can be labeled as such and in turn machines are able to distinguish menus from other content. In addition, the MenuMiner-algorithm [7] presented recently allows identifying fixed menus independent from the underlying markup semantic.

In this paper we present the first thorough analysis of the problem of extracting logical taxonomies from hierarchical menus. We decompose the problem and present solutions for the different sub problems. We demonstrate that general design rules exist that allow solving each sub problem without analyzing visual features. In contrast to previous approaches, we focus on the real logical structure as perceived by humans. This requires an extensive evaluation, because no benchmark exists and the evaluation can only be conducted against the human perception.

The structure and the contributions of this paper are:

In Section 2 we define the central terms and *specify the problem statement* based on these definitions. In Section 3 we present the *first in-depth analysis of the problem* of extracting taxonomies based on menus. We identify three *sub problems that have not been described before* and propose *novel rule-based concepts* for solving each sub problem. We explain how the different levels within a menu can be distinguished, how active menu items can be determined and how Web site taxonomies can be assembled without analyzing visual features. Our concepts are generic because they rely

---

[1] Google provides shortcut links for some sites at a similar position that are based on ranking algorithms and that do not summarize the site content as the first level of a taxonomy does.

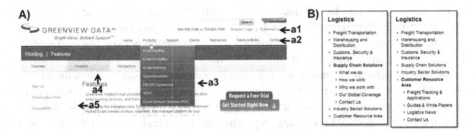

Fig. 2. Examples of different types of menus

on analyze the structure of the underlying HTML code only, but do not consider tag semantics. The methods consume little resources and do not require parsing Javascript or downloading presentational resources as images or CSS-files. In Section 4 we describe in more detail how the partial solutions are implemented and integrated into a single application. We introduce the novel *ListWalker-algorithm* that allows extracting taxonomies based on the order of the menu items only. In Section 5 we evaluate in a *large-scale study* how well the implementation performs. Correctness is evaluated against the human perception of the logical site structure. To our knowledge *no other taxonomy mining approach has been proven to extract the logical structure as perceived by humans with similar accuracy* regarding the identification of the first taxonomy level and, thus, the main content sections of sites. Finally, related work is presented in Section 6.

2   Problem Statement

In this paper the term *menu* denotes a user interface element of a Web site and its markup code. Menus have the single purpose of providing access to other resources (cf. Fig. 2). In other words, menus are implementations of navigation design patterns (e.g. [8]). A single menu can be part of multiple pages of a site. From the Web mining perspective the menu is defined by all its code snippets from all the pages it is presented on. The menu can occur in page-dependent variations with different *menu items* being expanded or collapsed (Fig. 2(B)). Thus, the code snippets of a single menu can differ. Different menu levels that are nested are considered as one menu if the underlying HTML code is continuous, e.g. in case of the menu shown in Fig. 2(B). In contrast, *a4* and *a5* in Fig. 2(A) are two separate menus.

In this paper the term *Web site taxonomy* describes a logical tree structure in which Web documents are arranged by information architects to facilitate access. Each node of the logical tree represents a document and has a label. Each node also represents a *site section* given by the subtree rooted at that node. Web site taxonomies are logical structures, not link structures. Taxonomies can also be distinguished from the design models representing them, e.g. whiteboard drawings, bullet lists or elaborated models part of Web engineering methods as WebML [9], OOHDM [10] or UWE [11]. To serve the purpose of facilitating human access, Web site taxonomies must be obvious to users. In particular, users must be able to decode the original tree structure. Since menus are the user interface elements that provide access to other resources, taxonomies are usually implemented as hierarchical menus. Humans are able to decode the tree structure based on visual and functional features unambiguously. For example, in Fig. 2(B) a visual feature is that the child nodes are indented. Functional features encoding hierarchical structures are, e.g., that a submenu is expanded when the mouse pointer is moved over the parent item (cf. Fig. 2(A)) or different sub trees are permanently expanded depending on the active page (cf. Fig. 2(B)). Multiple menus can have the same underlying taxonomy, e.g. when there is a main menu at the top and a second level menu at the left side of a page.

This paper addresses the problem of automatically retrieving the underlying taxonomies from Web site menus. Taxonomies are understood as the logical organization as it is perceived by humans. Because of the nav-tag newly introduced in HTML5 and novel mining methods [7] the menus itself can be separated from other content. It is also assumed that if a single menu appears on multiple pages, all of its code snippets can be identified as belonging together.

The mining method should be correct in such a way that the delivered taxonomies match human perception. It should be universal and not be limited to specific menu implementations.

In addition, a viable solution should fulfill the following requirements:

— To enable efficient execution, parsing or interpreting Javascript code should not be necessary. For the same reason HTML rendering or downloading additional resources such as CSS files or images should not be required as well.
— The method should not rely on the way the menus are implemented in HTML, e.g. whether lists or span-tags are used to model menu items.
— The method should be fault tolerant. Input snippets that do not represent hierarchical menus but other page elements, e.g. breadcrumbs, should not lead to incorrect results.

3   Decomposing the Problem

In this section we describe how the problem extracting Web site taxonomies from menus can be broken down into sub problems that can be solved without analyzing visual features, rendering HTML code or executing Javascript code.

Multiple levels of a Web site taxonomy can be implemented by a single menu. Thus, extracting intra-menu hierarchies is the first sub-problem. Pages can be logically arranged under a menu item, even if they are not linked from within a sub menu of that item. Assigning pages to menu items is the second sub problem. Because different levels of a single taxonomy can be implemented by separate menus, extracting inter-menu hierarchies is the third sub problem.

3.1   Intra-menu Hierarchies

Sub Problem: *Extracting taxonomy information from individual menus.* Single menus often represent multiple levels of the Web site taxonomy. Humans can decode the different levels by visual or functional features, but machines cannot interpret these features. The underlying HTML code does not reliably reflect the taxonomy. For example, Fig. 3 shows the logical structure of the menu snippet *a1* from Fig. 4. In the Web site taxonomy the node *p1* is a parent node of *p2*, but in the structure of the underlying HTML code *p1* and *p2* are siblings.

Solution: Menus that represent more than one level can be divided into two classes: (1) The first class are client menus for which the server always returns the same markup code on all pages. These menus only have a single snippet variant. Sub items are collapsed or expanded on the client-side via Javascript and CSS. (2) The second class are server menus with varying menu snippets depending on the active page (e.g. Fig. 2(B), Fig. 4). The menu state is generated on the server-side and not dynamically changed on the client side.

Client menus: In practice client menus are easier to deal with, since the original hierarchy can be derived by parsing the HTML tree using a simple page segmentation algorithm described in [7]². One reason is that usually each menu level has its own container element to switch it on or off. Additionally, since only client-side manipulation of the menu is involved, the logical structure of the menu must be available on client-side. Moreover, instead of proprietary scripts usually Javascript frameworks are used which render menus as nested lists as a kind of standard.

Server menus: Server menus display only fragments of the Web site taxonomy on each page. Fig. 3, for example, shows the logical structure of the menu snippets *a1* and *b1* from Fig. 4. Both menus use different patterns to generate the displayed taxonomy fragment: For the first menu all ancestors are rendered but not their siblings. In the second menu, the siblings of the ancestor p1 are also visible. In case of server menus the logical structure is often not preserved in the underlying HTML code. We found that instead of analyzing the HTML structure, other information can be utilized: There are general design rules almost all menus adhere to. They result from the three basic questions Web navigation has to answer: *"Where am I?"*, *"What's here?"* and *"Where can I go next?"* [2]. To indicate the current location and to allow users to navigate back to previous levels, the ancestors of the current node are always visible,

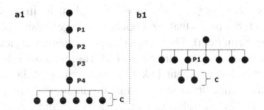

Fig. 3. Logical structure of the Web site taxonomy fragments represented by snippet *a1* and snippet *b1* of Fig. 4.

---

² A minor refinement of the algorithm described in [7] was made: ul-elements were always kept as containers and li-elements were always stripped.

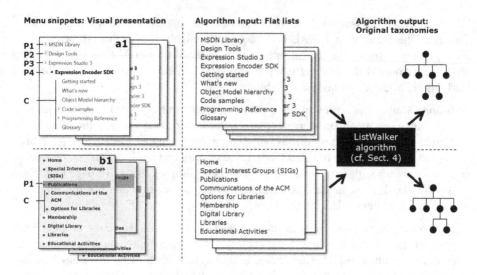

Fig. 4. The ListWalker algorithm processes the menu snippets as flat lists

even if the siblings of the ancestors are collapsed (cf. P1-P4 in snippet a1, Fig. 4). The ancestors appear in their logical order. Another design rule is that child nodes of the active node, if any, are always expanded to answer the question "Where can I go next?". All ancestors are usually presented prior to the child nodes. We found that given these general design rules the taxonomy can be extracted by processing all snippets of a menu as flat lists (Fig. 4), regardless depth or whether parent levels are expanded or not. The ListWalker-algorithm, presented in Section 4.2, extracts the taxonomy solely from the menu items that the snippets contain and their order. The underlying HTML structure and the semantics of the tags are ignored. The solution is very generic and can be applied to menus, regardless of whether tables, lists or other HTML elements are used.

3.2   Page Assignment

Sub Problem: *Assigning pages to site sections.* Each menu item corresponds to a site section, given by all the pages that are logically arranged under that item (at least the page linked by the menu item). There are often pages that are logically arranged under a certain menu item, even if they are not linked from within a sub menu of that item. For example, in Fig. 5 the content link L in the section "Asia" links a page that is clearly part of this section from the information architecture point of view. In such cases the parent-child relationship cannot be derived from intra-menu hierarchy information (cf. previous section) because there is no link to the child in the menu. In contrast to machines, humans are able to interpret complex visual features (e.g. that the item "Asia" is highlighted). Even if the item "Asia" would not be highlighted on the right-hand page, humans would attribute the page to this menu item, because of the link context and semantic knowledge.

Fig. 5. The page on the right is not linked by a menu item but by a link in the content area (L) only. It is still a child page of the active menu item "Asia" (A).

Solution: If the intra-menu structure is known, features can be extracted that allow to distinguish whether a page is arranged under a certain menu item or not. For example, in Fig. 5 the menu item "Asia" defines a site section and the linked page is part of this section. In order to extract distinguishing features for identifying other pages of this section, it is necessary to find examples of pages that are not part of this section. In general, pages linked by random other menu items cannot be used as negative examples for a section, because the menu items could as well be child nodes of the item defining the section. But if the intra-menu hierarchy is known, child nodes can be identified and excluded. For instance, the menu in Fig. 5 represents only a single level of the taxonomy and, based on this knowledge, all pages linked by other menu items can be used a negative examples for the section "Asia". The features we consider are (1) CSS classes that are assigned to the menu items and (2) URL directories of the linked pages.

(1) By analyzing the CSS classes, in many cases the active menu items can be detected without considering the actual visual presentation. Usually there are certain CSS classes that are used to highlight menu items and our method aims at determining these. Fig. 6 illustrates this approach. For example, the method assumes that the menu item "Europe" is highlighted on the page "Europe" but not on any other page linked in the same menu. If there are one or more CSS classes that are assigned to the menu item "Europe" if that page is active and, at the same time, these classes are not assigned to that menu item on any other page linked in the menu, it can be derived that these classes mark the item as active. Thus, if there are other pages of the site on which the same classes are assigned to the menu item "Europe", it can be concluded that these are child pages of the item as well.

(2) The second feature that can be used for page assignment is the hierarchical URL structure. Often the pages belonging to a site section, i.e. the child pages of a certain menu item, reside under the same directory. While the directory structure of a Web site may or may not reflect the logical structure, aligning it with menu items allows determining whether this is the case. Similar to the CSS feature it can be analyzed for all menu items whether they point to a directory that differs from the directory the other menu items point to. If menu items have child nodes, they can be considered additionally. Fig. 7 illustrates this approach. The URLs of the child nodes of the menu item "Audi Sport" have a common directory prefix that is exclusive in a way that no other pages linked by other menu items reside under this directory. All other pages of

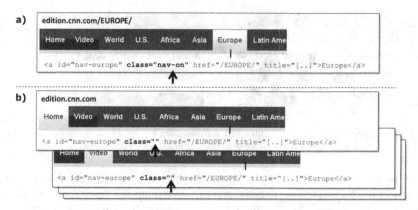

Fig. 6. When the linked page is active, the menu item "Europe" has a CSS class that is missing when another menu item is active, indicating that the class "nav-on" is used to mark the active menu item[3]

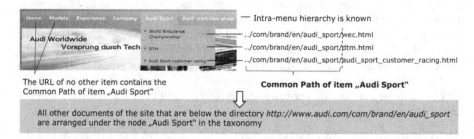

Fig. 7. The child nodes have a common directory and in turn all pages residing under this directory can be interpreted as child nodes of the menu item (source: http://www.audi.com)

the site that are not linked in the menu and are located below this directory can now be assigned as child nodes to the menu item "Audi Sport" as well.

3.3   Inter-menu Hierarchies

Sub Problem: Different levels of a Web site taxonomy are often implemented in separate menus. For example, a horizontal menu bar at the top represents the first level and a separate vertical menu at the left side represents the second level. These relations must be extracted in order to recover the original taxonomy. The menus representing taxonomy levels must also be distinguished from other menus, e.g. menus providing contextual links or navigation aids.

Solution: Menu-submenu relationships can be discovered based on the presented menu items. Fig. 8 illustrates the idea. If the items of a parent menu are traversed, the items of the child menu change with each page transition. The child menu will never have the same items for different active parents if a taxonomy is the underlying

---

[3] The CSS classes used to mark active items are often not assigned to the links, i.e. a-elements, but their parents (e.g. li-elements). This has to be considered in the implementation.

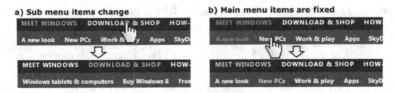

a) Sub menu items change   **b) Main menu items are fixed**

Fig. 8. The menu items of the lower menu change when the upper menu is traversed, while the upper menu is fixed if the lower menu is traversed. Thus, a menu-submenu relationship can be derived without analyzing presentational features (source: http://windows.microsoft.com).

structure. If, in contrast, the items of a sub menu are traversed, the menu items of the parent menu will not change. Despite promising preliminary results, the solution that is evaluated in Section 4 does not include this kind of analysis. In our evaluation runs we found that the task of discovering menu-submenu relationships is more challenging than we expected due to noise and irregularities. However, training a classifier on a large sample would be a solution but this is beyond the scope of this paper.

For distinguishing menus that represent levels of the taxonomy we first extract the intra-menu hierarchies and then try to arrange additional pages in this tree by applying the concepts presented in the previous section. This is done for all menus without testing in advance whether they really represent taxonomies or not. In the end, it is examined whether tree structures have been extracted, and if so, the most extensive is returned as Web site taxonomy (cf. Sect. 4).

4 Implementation

In this section we describe the implementation of the presented concepts in detail. We first describe how the concepts are integrated into a single solution based on the MenuMiner-algorithm [7]. Then, we introduce the ListWalker-algorithm that allows extracting intra-menu hierarchies based on flat lists.

4.1 Solution Overview

We implemented the rule-based methods described in Section 3 on top of the MenuMiner-algorithm [7] that delivers the boundaries of menus that are repeated on multiple pages (Fig. 9). In the example, two menus are found (Fig. 9(2)). Two variations

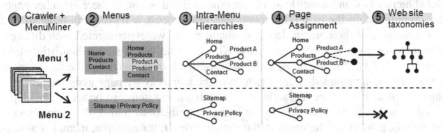

Fig. 9. (1) The MenuMiner-algorithm is used to extract menus. (2) By parsing the HTML structure and applying the ListWalker-algorithm intra-menu hierarchies are extracted. (3) The page assignment methods are applied to extend the hierarchies. (4) Heuristics are used to determine Web site taxonomies.

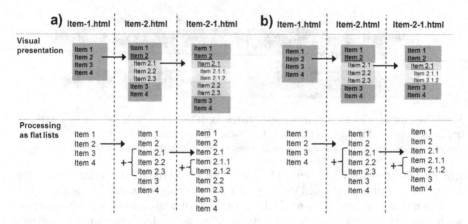

Fig. 10. On navigation paths descending the Web site taxonomy the child nodes are successively expanded. Thus, if the root state is known, the taxonomy can be extracted based on flat lists.

("menu states") of menu 1 are found on the site, one variant in which the child nodes of "Products" are collapsed and another one in which the child nodes are expanded. In the example, Menu 2 has only a single state. Instead of the MenuMiner-algorithm, the nav-tag introduced in HTML5 can be used for retrieving the menus of a site if it is widely applied in the future, because the methods can deal with noise, e.g. other navigation elements, such as breadcrumbs or paginations that not represent levels of the Web site taxonomy. Those elements will not deliver hierarchies and are ignored.

In the next step, HTML tree parsing for analyzing client menus and the ListWalker-algorithm (Section 4.2) for parsing server menus are applied (Fig. 9(3)). Both methods are used for each menu and if they both deliver hierarchy information, the most complete tree structure is kept for further processing. The overlap coefficient (cf. [12]) is used for handling noise, e.g. an additional hyperlink on one page that is missing on others, and deciding whether two slightly different snippets are considered as one and the same.

Then, the page assignment methods are applied (Fig. 9 (4)) and heuristics are used to determine the global taxonomy (Fig. 9 (5)). The implementation presented in this paper relies on first trying to discover hierarchical structures for all menus found individually and then judging which menu represents most likely the first level of the global hierarchy using a metric and other criteria listed below. If there are other pages that do not contain the menu, the menu selection process is repeated in order to find all taxonomies of the domain. In our evaluation runs we experimented with different ways of computing the selection metric K_i and found that a simple heuristic works best: $K_i = A_i / P_i$. The metric A_i is the average depth of the pages in the hierarchy of menu i, including pages that are arranged in the hierarchy by page assignment. If the page is neither part of the hierarchy nor an active menu item can be found, the depth is considered to be 0. The other factor influencing the detection of the main menu is the average position of the menu in the source code. If, for example, menu i is always the first menu in the source code of all pages it is contained, P_i has the value 1. In addition, we discard menus if one of the following boundary conditions is not met: (A) The menu has less than 15 items, (B) not more than 30% of the text content appears in average before the menu (to exclude footer menus), and (C) no other menu with a lower average position P_i appears on more pages.

4.2   ListWalker-Algorithm

As argued in Section 3.1 the underlying HTML code does usually not reflect the logical structure of the taxonomy fragments rendered on different pages in case of server menus. However, there are two general design rules: (1) All ancestors of the active page are expanded and displayed above the active page (to allow ascending to parent levels). The ancestors appear in their logical order. Sibling of the ancestors may or may not be expanded. (2) If the active page has child nodes theses are always expanded (to allow further descending the hierarchy). The child nodes appear below the active page.

Algorithm 1. ListWalker

Input: $W = \{1,2,\dots,m\}$ – the m pages of the site

$\quad\quad N_i = \{n_{i,1}, n_{i,2} \dots n_{i,l_i}\} \subseteq W$, $i \in W$ – the l_i Menu Items of Page i

Output: G – the edges of the hierarchy

1.   // init
2. $G := \{\}; R := \{\}$
3.   for each $\left(N_i \text{ with } n_{i,1} = i\right)$
4.   for each $\left(n_{i,j} \in N_i \text{ with } j > 1\right)$
5. $R := R \cup \left(N_i, N_j\right)$
6.   // main loop
7.   while $(|R| > 0)$
8.   Randomly select $\left(N_i, N_j\right) \in R$;
9. $R := R \setminus \left(N_i, N_j\right)$;
10. $k := 0$;
11.   while $(k < |N_i|)$
12.   If $\left(\left(k{=}0 \text{ OR } n_{j,k-1}{=}j\right) \text{ AND } \left(\text{notContains}(N_j, n_{j,k})\right)\right)$
13.   break;
14. $k := k + 1$
15.   while $\left(k < |N_j| \text{ AND notContains}(N_i, n_{j,k})\right)$
16. $G := G \cup \left(j, n_{j,k}\right)$
17. $R := R \cup \left(N_j, N_{n_{j,k}}\right)$
18. $k := k + 1$

The ListWalker algorithm presented in this section allows extracting the hierarchy by processing the menu snippets ("menu states") as flat lists based on these design rules. Fig. 10 illustrates the fundamental approach. The figure shows the menu behavior when a user descends the taxonomy starting from the root. Example *a* shows an implementation in which the parent levels, the current level and the children of the active item are expanded. In example *b* the intermediate level is collapsed. The child nodes can be easily derived based on the flat list representation because they are successively expanded. For example, the child nodes of Item-2 in example *a* can be retrieved taking the menu items of page *Item-2.html* and subtracting the items of the previous state (state of *Item-1.html*), leaving Item 2.1, Item 2.2 and Item 2.3. This approach works for example *b* as well. Child nodes cannot be retrieved by subtracting the items of random states. Instead a valid reference state is necessary that is either a parent or sibling. If, e.g., in example *b* the menu state of *Item-2-1.html* would be used as reference to compute the children of *Item-2.html*, Item 2.2 and Item 2.3 would be wrongly assigned as children to that page. The reference state problem can be narrowed down to finding a root page that has no parent. The root page is a reference state for all its menu items. Thus, for each menu item the child nodes can be determined – and each menu item is again a reference state for its children and so on.

Algorithm 1 is the skeleton of the ListWalker algorithm. The pages W of the site are numbered from 1 to m. For page $w \in W$ the menu state is modeled as $N_w = \{n_{w,1}, n_{w,2}, ...\} \subseteq W$, the ordered list of pages linked in the menu. The algorithm computes G, the edges of the taxonomy as illustrated in Fig. 9. Because of the two design rules, there is usually a state with $n_{i,1} = i$, which is a state of a page that contains a link to itself at the first position (for example the states of *Item-1.html* in Fig. 10). Such a state will be referred to as first item state (FIS) in the following. The FIS can be determined easily and in case of a top level menu, the FIS is usually the homepage. Since a FIS belongs to the first level of the hierarchy and has no parent, it is always a root state and can be used as initial reference state for its siblings. There might be multiple FIS, because the extracted states of a menu can encompass multiple separated trees, e.g. sub sites in different languages.

In Algorithm 1, R holds tuples of reference states and unprocessed states. R is initially filled by iterating the menu items of the FISs, which are either children or siblings (lines 03-05). In the main loop a random tuple is taken from R (line 08) until R is empty. The loop starting at line 11 traverses the items of the menu state under examination until the first child page, which can be identified by being absent in the reference state. As additional condition the position is considered. Child pages are usually placed directly after their parent, but we also found implementations where a sub menu is positioned above or below the parent menu (line 12). The loop starting at line 15 iterates the child pages until a menu item is reached that is contained in the reference state, denoting the end of the sub menu. The edges from the parent to the child pages are added to G (line 16) and the active state is added as reference state for each child page to R for further processing.

In addition to the basic algorithm, a few extensions must be included to make it applicable for real world Web sites:

- Algorithm 1 delivers valid reference states recursively for all states except the FISs. As listed, the algorithm does not discover their child pages. A reference state for a FIS can be found by searching for extracted menu states whose items are a subset of the FIS.
- Real world menus often contain items that are redirections to pages that are placed somewhere else in the tree. If not considering these crosslinks, wrong reference states will result in faulty edges. Thus a tuple (N_j, N_d) with $d = n_{j,k}$ that represent a crosslink must not be added to R in line 17. Crosslinks can be

identified by testing if $\{n_{d,1}, n_{d,2} \dots d\} \subseteq \{n_{j,1}, n_{j,2} \dots d\}$ is not fulfilled. That is, the predecessors of the active item must also be predecessors of that item in the reference state.

5   Evaluation

The MenuMiner-algorithm scales very well [7] and the methods presented in this paper are little resource consuming. The operations including analyzing the crawled pages have linear-time complexity. In relation to the number of pages the number of menus grows sublinear and thus processing the menus is uncritical. Since runtime performance is not an issue and due to space limitations we focus on evaluating the correctness.

5.1   Methodology

For evaluating the method a data set was constructed by crawling 350 domains. The domain list was the result of a first crawl seeded with yahoo.com. The crawler was configured to discover new domains in a depth-first manner. In order to spread the samples, the next 25 discovered domains were skipped each time a domain was added to the list. Finally the 350 domains were crawled separately. A crawl was stopped if all pages were retrieved or 100 pages were processed by the MenuMiner algorithm, which means that all linked pages were downloaded, too. All in all 259,525 pages were crawled. One page from each domain was randomly selected and the main menu, the active menu item, the second menu level and its active item were labeled if existing.[4] In this paper the term main menu refers to a menu that implements the first level of the Web site taxonomy. We labeled menus as main menus if

- The menu is indispensable for site navigation
- The menu items represent the main content sections
- At least three menu items are links to pages of the same site
- No other menu fulfills the previous conditions

By using these conditions for most of the samples either the main menu could be identified clearly or the absence of a main menu could be determined. However, some samples could not be labeled with reasonably certainty and were excluded from the evaluation. These were pages in languages with non-latin alphabets and pages that seem to contain multiple main menus according to the above definitions. The active menu item was labeled as well and if existing, the second level and the active second level menu item were labeled as well. The active menu items were tagged not only if highlighted, but also if they could be determined otherwise, e.g. by an additional breadcrumb navigation. Similar to the main menu, the second level menus that could not be labeled with certainty were excluded (2.9% of the samples).

---

[4] The labeled data set is available from:
http://dsn.tm.kit.edu/download/icwe2013/data.zip

The method was evaluated as a binary classification task. A positive classification means that the method delivers a menu or a menu item respectively. For evaluating the correctness the URLs were compared. If all menu items of a mined menu are contained in the labeled menu, it is considered as true positive (TP), otherwise as false positive (FP). On the other hand, additional menu items in the labeled menu are allowed, because the mined menu items represent the global menu while additional items may appear on certain pages. However, for 76.4% of the samples, the number of labeled items equals the number of mined items, and for the other samples, on average 74.6% of the items were mined. If no menu or menu item respectively was mined and if none was labeled it counts as true negative (TN), otherwise as false negative (FN).We were evaluating Precision as TP/(TP+FP) and Recall as TP/(TP+FN) for the task of detecting the main menu, the active main menu item, the secondary menu and the active secondary menu item (Table 1). In the evaluation of correctness of the active menu items only pages were included for which the menu itself was detected correctly. Four different configurations were evaluated: Configuration A using CSS selectors for page assignment (cf. Section 3.1), configuration B using URL prefixes, configuration AB using both methods and A_{res}, a more restrictive version of A, delivering only menus if they contain a submenu. Similarly, only the TPs from the main menu detection were included in the evaluation of the secondary menu.

5.2   Results

Fig. 11 and Table 1 show that the configurations A, B and AB detect the first Taxonomy level with a Precision around 0.9 and Recall around 0.75. Method A is a very accurate solution for detecting active menu items, with a Precision close to 0.97. Because the active menu items indicate different site sections, the method delivers precise topical segmentations of sites that were not available previously. Method B has a higher Recall but reduced Precision. The combined method performs well with a Precision of 0.89 and Recall of 0.8. For detecting the secondary menu, the configurations succeed with good Precision values above 0.85. Menu items that are no hyperlinks seem to be the main reason for errors here. However, Recall is low, because only secondary menus that are nested within the main menu can be found yet.

We believe that Precision is fundamental for the applicability of a hierarchy mining method in most scenarios. Since no comparable methods exist, even a low Recall is an improvement. The results show that there is room for increasing Precision at the cost of Recall. Thus we implemented method A_{res} which only delivers global menus that contain a second level, based on the idea that if a nested secondary menu was found, the main menu is identified correctly with high probability. As expected, Recall is significantly reduced, but Precision is almost perfect.

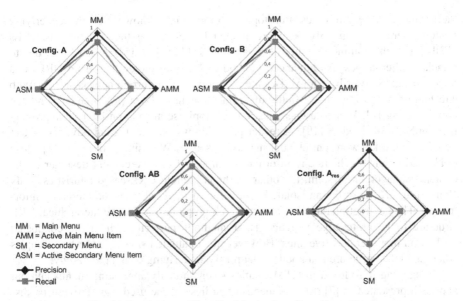

Fig. 11. Precision and Recall of the evaluated configurations

Table 1.

	Config. A	Config. B	Config. AB	Con. A$_{res}$
Main Menu				
Precision	0.903	0.898	0.893	0.986
Recall	0.756	0.755	0.754	0.278
TP/FP/TN/FN	177/19/44/57	176/20/44/57	175/21/44/57	70/1/44/182
Active Main Menu Item				
Precision	0.968	0.882	0.894	0.96
Recall	0.555	0.714	0.8	0.511
TP/FP/TN/FN	61/2/65/49	75/10/61/30	84/10/60/21	24/1/22/23
Secondary Menu				
Precision	0.864	0.857	0.857	0.857
Recall	0.373	0.471	0.471	0.529
TP/FP/TN/FN	19/3/123/32	24/4/121/27	24/4/120/27	18/3/33/16
Active Secondary Menu Item				
Precision	0.933	0.9	0.9	0.933
Recall	1	1	1	1
TP/FP/TN/FN	14/1/4/0	18/2/4/0	18/2/4/0	14/1/3/0

6   Related Work

In this paper, we use the term taxonomy mining to denote the process of extracting hierarchies that are pre-designed by information architects and that are obvious to humans because of the visual presentation. Thus, works that generate new hierarchies based on textual or structural information (e.g. [13]) are not considered in this section as well as works on extracting non-hierarchical structures (e.g. [14]) or recovering application models (e.g. [15]). Yang et al. [16] state that the extraction of Web site hierarchies is a very new research topic. Although it is known, that the underlying content hierarchy can only be approximated by analyzing the structure of URLs [17][4], it is the common method (e.g. used in [17],[16],[18],[5]) up until now due to a lack of alternatives. An advanced method of learning hierarchies from URLs and query strings is described in [5]. Despite the limitation of current approaches for Web site hierarchy mining, many fields of application have been proposed, e.g. related entity finding [4], Web site classification [6], topic segmentation [17] or improving recommendation models [19]. A recent paper shows that contextual advertising can benefit from a keyword enrichment method based on Web site taxonomies [5]. Bose et al. [19] obtain the hierarchy information directly from the content designer or the content management system, the other methods include URL-based heuristics. Only Yang et al. [16] describe an isolated evaluation of the quality of the hierarchy information. They extract hierarchies from the Web graph but utilize the hierarchical URL structure to generate edge weights. Their methods perform well in the conducted evaluation that includes five sites. However, the evaluated sites seem to be examples where the URL structure is a good model for the underlying content hierarchy.

The nav-tag introduced in HTML5 allows semantically annotating menus and our approach presented in [7] delivers menus regardless of the used tags. Previously, discerning menus from other content was an unsolved problem. Few other works included the task of mining menus or link lists, but consider it as side issued not evaluated separately. An exception is the method described in [20] that discovers ranked lists of menus and navigation aids ("key information"). The Precision seems to be not very high, since in an evaluation of five sites only for two sites the best ranked block really contains key information. Liu et al. [21] report an average Precision of 0.92 for detection of "navigation link sets" on five news sites but it is not clear if these are equivalent to the main navigation. However that is a very good result compared to our experience with using this kind of features [22].

7   Conclusion

In this paper we demonstrated that Web site taxonomies can be accurately mined based on menus. Our rule-based approach succeeds without resource-consuming HTML rendering and is not bound to the semantics of specific tags. We evaluated the method on 350 randomly selected real-world Web sites. The method was able to detect the first level of the Web site taxonomy correctly with Precision above 0.9 at high Recall and the secondary menu with Precision above 0.86. Page assignment is possible with Precision around 0.97. Thus, the method delivers a very accurate topical segmentation. Such precise information about the logical organization of Web sites was not available before and cannot be extracted from the Web graph or the URL structure. One tested configuration delivers the first menu level with almost perfect precision, but, currently, at the expense of reduced Recall.

However, the methods can be further adjusted based on the labeled data set generated for evaluation and we expect that perfect Precision with a much higher Recall is possible in the future. The combination of separated menus into a single taxonomy was beyond the scope of this paper and needs more research.

Web site taxonomy information has been used in many fields and thus, many applications can benefit from the more accurate mining methods presented in this paper. Also, the extracted taxonomy information can be used for whole new applications, e.g. to enhance the presentation of search results.

References

1. Morville, P., Rosenfeld, L.: Information architecture for the World Wide Web. O'Reilly, Sebastopol (2006)
2. Kalbach, J.: Designing Web navigation. O'Reilly, Sebastopol (2007)
3. Lin, S.-H., Chu, K.-P., Chiu, C.-M.: Automatic sitemaps generation: Exploring website structures using block extraction and hyperlink analysis. Expert Systems with Applications 38, 3944–3958 (2011)
4. Yang, Q., Jiang, P., Zhang, C., Niu, Z.: Reconstruct Logical Hierarchical Sitemap for Related Entity Finding. In: Voorhees, E.M., Buckland, L.P. (eds.) The Nineteenth Text Retrieval Conf (TREC 2010). National Institute of Standards and Technology, NIST (2010)
5. Pavan Kumar, G.M., Leela, K.P., Parsana, M., Garg, S.: Learning website hierarchies for keyword enrichment in contextual advertising. In: Proceedings of the Fourth ACM International Conference on Web Search and Data Mining, pp. 425–434. ACM, Hong Kong (2011)
6. Amitay, E., Carmel, D., Darlow, A., Lempel, R., Soffer, A.: The connectivity sonar: detecting site functionality by structural patterns. In: Proceedings of the Fourteenth ACM Conference on Hypertext and Hypermedia, pp. 38–47. ACM, Nottingham (2003)
7. Keller, M., Nussbaumer, M.: MenuMiner: revealing the information architecture of large web sites by analyzing maximal cliques. In: Proceedings of the 21st Int'l. Conf. Companion on World Wide Web, pp. 1025–1034. ACM, Lyon (2012)
8. Rossi, G., Schwabe, D., Lyardet, O., Puc-rio, D.D.I., MarquêS, R., Vicente, S.: Improving Web information systems with navigational patterns. Computer Networks 31 (1999)
9. Ceri, S., Fraternali, P., Bongio, A.: Web Modeling Language (WebML): a modeling language for designing Web sites. Computer Networks 33, 137–157 (2000)
10. Schwabe, D., Rossi, G., Barbosa, S.D.J.: Systematic hypermedia application design with OOHDM. In: Proc. of the the Seventh ACM Conf. on Hypertext, pp. 116–128. ACM, Bethesda (1996)
11. Koch, N., Knapp, A., Zhang, G., Baumeister, H.: Uml-Based Web Engineering. In: Rossi, G., Pastor, O., Schwabe, D., Olsina, L. (eds.) Web Engineering: Modelling and Implementing Web Applications, pp. 157–191. Springer London, London (2008)
12. Jones, W.P., Furnas, G.W.: Pictures of relevance: a geometric analysis of similarity measures. J. Am. Soc. Inf. Sci. 38, 420–442 (1987)
13. Ho, Q., Eisenstein, J., Xing, E.P.: Document hierarchies from text and links. In: Proceedings of the 21st International Conference on World Wide Web, pp. 739–748. ACM, Lyon (2012)
14. Zheng, X., Gu, Y., Li, Y.: Data extraction from web pages based on structural-semantic entropy. In: Proc. of the 21st Int'l. Conf. Companion on World Wide Web, pp. 93–102. ACM, Lyon (2012)

15. Bernardi, M., Di Lucca, G., Distante, D.: The RE-UWA approach to recover user centered conceptual models from Web applications. International Journal on Software Tools for Technology Transfer 11, 485–501 (2009)
16. Yang, C.C., Liu, N.: Web site topic-hierarchy generation based on link structure. J. Am. Soc. Inf. Sci. Technol. 60, 495–508 (2009)
17. Kumar, R., Punera, K., Tomkins, A.: Hierarchical topic segmentation of websites. In: Proceedings of the 12th ACM SIGKDD International Conference on Knowledge Discovery and Data Mining, pp. 257–266. ACM, Philadelphia (2006)
18. Cheung, W.K., Sun, Y.: Identifying a hierarchy of bipartite subgraphs for web site abstraction. Web Intelli. and Agent Sys. 5, 343–355 (2007)
19. Bose, A., Beemanapalli, K., Srivastava, J., Sahar, S.: Incorporating concept hierarchies into usage mining based recommendations. In: Nasraoui, O., Spiliopoulou, M., Srivastava, J., Mobasher, B., Masand, B. (eds.) WebKDD 2006. LNCS (LNAI), vol. 4811, pp. 110–126. Springer, Heidelberg (2007)
20. Wang, C., Lu, J., Zhang, G.: Mining key information of web pages: A method and its application. Expert Syst. Appl. 33, 425–433 (2007)
21. Liu, Z., Ng, W.K., Lim, E.-P.: An Automated Algorithm for Extracting Website Skeleton. In: Lee, Y., Li, J., Whang, K.-Y., Lee, D. (eds.) DASFAA 2004. LNCS, vol. 2973, pp. 799–811. Springer, Heidelberg (2004)
22. Keller, M., Nussbaumer, M.: Beyond the Web Graph: Mining the Information Architecture of the WWW with Navigation Structure Graphs. In: Proc. of the 2011 Int'l. Conf. on Emerging Intelligent Data and Web Technologies, pp. 99–106. IEEE Computer Society, Tirana (2011)

Evaluation of Personalized Social Ranking Functions of Information Retrieval

Mohamed Reda Bouadjenek[1,*], Amyn Bennamane[2,*],
Hakim Hacid[3,*], and Mokrane Bouzeghoub[1]

[1] PRiSM Laboratory, Versailles University
{mrb,mok}@prism.uvsq.fr
[2] Dell Innovation House, Dublin, Ireland
amyn_bennamane@dell.com
[3] SideTrade, Boulogne-Billancourt, France
hhacid@sidetrade.com

Abstract. There is currently a number of interesting research works performed in the area of bridging the gap between Social Networks and Information Retrieval (IR). This is mainly done by enhancing the IR process with social information. Hence, many approaches have been proposed to improve the ranking process by personalizing it using social features. In this paper, we review some of these ranking functions.

1 Introduction

The Web 2.0 has introduced a new freedom for the user in his relation with the Web through social platforms, which are commonly used as means to interact. Hence, users are more active in generating content, which is one of the most important factors for the increasingly growing quantity of data. From the research perspective, this brings important and interesting challenges for many research fields like Information Retrieval (IR), which is the focus of this paper.

IR is performed every day in an obvious way over the Web, typically under a search engine. However, finding relevant information remains challenging for end-users. In existing IR systems, queries are usually interpreted and processed using document indexes and/or ontologies, which are hidden for users. The resulting documents[1] are not necessarily relevant from an end-user perspective, in spite of the ranking. To improve the IR process and reduce the amount of irrelevant documents, there are mainly three possible improvement tracks: (i) query reformulation, (ii) improvement of the IR model, and (iii) post filtering or re-ranking of the retrieved documents. In this last track, many approaches has been proposed to improve the ranking process by personalizing it using social features. In this paper, we propose to review some of these personalized social ranking functions that rely on social annotations as source of social information. These annotations are associated to documents in social bookmarking systems. In this paper, we try to mainly answer the following questions: *What are these*

---

* This work has been mainly done when authors was at Bell Labs France, Villarceaux.
[1] We also refer to documents as web pages or resources.

F. Daniel, P. Dolog, and Q. Li (Eds.): ICWE 2013, LNCS 7977, pp. 283–290, 2013.

functions and how do they work? What is the context where each function is more efficient? What is the best ranking function?

The main contributions of this work can be summarized as follows:

1. We propose a deep study of the state of the art in social ranking functions.
2. We propose a deep analysis of the performances of these personalized social ranking functions and a comparison with non-personalized social approaches.
3. Finally, we propose a discussion on the effectiveness, the weakness and the performance of each approach in different contexts.

The rest of this paper is organized as follows: in Section 2, we introduce the main concepts used throughout this paper. In Section 3, we review the personalized ranking functions studied. Section 4 presents the dataset we used, and the evaluation methodology. The evaluations are presented and discussed in Section 5. Finally, Section 6 concludes this paper.

2   Background

In this section, we formally define the basic concepts that we use in this paper. Then, we formally define the problem of personalized ranking.

2.1   Background and Notation

Social bookmarking systems are based on the techniques of *social tagging*. The principle is to provide the user with a mean to freely annotate resources on the Web with tags, e.g. URIs in *delicious*. These annotations can be shared with others. This unstructured approach to classification is often referred to as a *folksonomy*. A folksonomy is based on the notion of bookmark defined as follows:

Definition 1. *Let U, T, R be respectively the set of Users, Tags and Resources. A bookmark is a triplet (u,t,r) such as $u \in U, t \in T, r \in R$, which represents the fact that the user u has annotated the resource r with the tag t.*

Then, a folksonomy is formally defined as follows:

Definition 2. *Let U, T, R be respectively the set of Users, Tags and Resources. A folksonomy $\mathbb{F}(U, T, R)$ is a subset of the Cartesian product $U \times T \times R$ such that each triple $(u, t, r) \in \mathbb{F}$ is a bookmark.*

In this paper we use the notation summarized in Table 1.

2.2   Problem Definition

Let consider a folksonomy $\mathbb{F}(U, T, R)$ whose a user $u \in U$ submits a query q to a search engine. We would like to re-rank the set of resources $R_q \subseteq R$ (or documents) that match q, such that relevant resources for u are highlighted and pushed to the top for maximizing his satisfaction and personalizing the search results. The ranking follows an ordering $\tau = [r_1 \geq r_2 \geq \cdots \geq r_k]$ in which $r_k \in R$ and the ordering relation is defined by $r_i \geq r_j \Leftrightarrow Rank(r_i, u, q) \geq Rank(r_j, u, q)$, where $Rank(r, u, q)$ is a ranking function that quantify similarity between the query and the resource w.r.t the user [7].

Table 1. Paper's Notation Overview

Variable	Description
u, d, t	Respectively a user u, a document d and a tag t.
U, D, T	Respectively a set of users, documents and tags.
$\mid A \mid$	The number of element in the set A.
$T_u, T_d, T_{u,d}$	Respectively the set of tags used by u, tags used to annotate d, and tags used by u to annotate d.
$D_u, D_t, D_{u,t}$	Respectively the set of docs tagged by u, docs tagged with t, and docs tagged by u with t.
$U_t, U_d, U_{t,d}$	Respectively the set of users that use t, users that annotate d, and users that used t to annotate d.
$Cos(\boldsymbol{A}, \boldsymbol{B})$	The cosine similarity measure between two vectors.
$\overrightarrow{p_u}$	The vector of the profile of the user u, estimated by its social annotations weighted using the tf-idf.

3   Personalized Ranking Functions Based on Folksonomies

In this Section, we formally define the different personalized ranking functions studied in this paper. We each time present the ranking score of a document d for a query q issued by a user u denoted $Rank(d, q, u)$.

3.1   Profile Based Personalization (Xu08)

The approach presented by Xu et al. [9] assumes the ranking score of a document d is decided by two aspects: (i) a textual matching between q and d, and (ii) a user interest matching between u and d. Hence, following our notation in Table 1, their approach can be defined as follows:

$$Rank(d, q, u) = \gamma \times Cos(\overrightarrow{p_u}, \overrightarrow{T_d}) + (1 - \gamma) \times Sim(\overrightarrow{q}, \overrightarrow{d}) \qquad (1)$$

where, γ is a weight that satisfies $0 \le \gamma \le 1$, and $Sim(\overrightarrow{q}, \overrightarrow{d})$ denotes the textual matching score between d and q.

3.2   Topics Based Personalization (LDA-P)

We present here a topics-based approach. This approach is based on Latent Dirichlet Allocation (LDA) [3]. LDA-P relies on the fact that the set of tags can be used to represent web pages and as input for LDA to construct a model. Then, for each document that matches a query, LDA-P computes a similarity between its topic and the topic of the user profile using the cosine measure (inferred using the previous constructed LDA model). The obtained similarity value is merged with the textual ranking score to provide a final ranking score for a document that matches a query w.r.t the query issuer as follows:

$$Rank(d, q, u) = \gamma \times Cos(\overrightarrow{u_{topic}}, \overrightarrow{d_{topic}}) + (1 - \gamma) \times Sim(\overrightarrow{q}, \overrightarrow{d}) \qquad (2)$$

where, $0 \le \gamma \le 1$, $\overrightarrow{u_{topic}}$ and $\overrightarrow{d_{topic}}$ are respectively the vectors that model the user and the document topics based on the constructed LDA model.

3.3   Social Context Based Personalization (SoPRa)

The approach proposed by Bouadjenek et al. [4] is similar to [9]. However, the authors propose to enhance the ranking process by considering a new aspect, which is the social matching score. This approach takes into account the entire social context that surround both users and documents and is called SoPRa. Following our notation, SoPRa can be defined as follows (β is set to 0.5):

$$Rank(d, q, u) = \gamma \times Cos(\vec{p_u}, \vec{T_d}) + (1 - \gamma) \times \left[\beta \times Cos(\vec{q}, \vec{T_d}) + (1 - \beta) \times Sim(\vec{q}, \vec{d})\right] \tag{3}$$

3.4   Scalar Tag Frequency Based Personalization (Noll07)

The approach presented by Noll and Meinel [6] considers only a user interest matching between u and d. This approach does not make use of the user and document length normalization factors, and only uses the user tag frequency. The authors normalize all document tag frequencies to 1, since they want to give more importance to the user profile. Following the notation given in Table 1, their ranking function can be defined as follows:

$$Rank(d, q, u) = \sum_{t \in T_u \land t \in T_d} |D_{u,t}| \tag{4}$$

3.5   Scalar tf-if Based Personalization (tf-if)

Vallet et al. [7] proposed to improve the Noll07 approach above by including a weighting scheme based on an adaptation of the *tf-idf* as follows:

$$Rank(d, q, u) = \sum_{t \in T_u \land t \in T_d} (tf_u(t) \times iuf(t) \times tf_d(t) \times idf(t)) \tag{5}$$

3.6   Affinity Based Personalization

Bender et al. [1] proposed several personalized ranking functions based on relations in a folksonomy. More precisely, we study in this paper the following two ranking functions that we consider as relevant to this survey:

1. Semantic Search: This approach ranks documents by considering users that hold similar content to the query, i.e., users who used at least one of the query terms in describing their content.
2. Social Search: This approach ranks documents by considering friends of the query issuer who used at least one of the query terms for tagging.

We refer the reader to the original paper for their definition. In the next sections, we describe the evaluations we have performed on these functions.

4   Dataset and Evaluation Methodology

In this section, we describe the dataset we used and the evaluation methodology.

4.1 Dataset

To evaluate our approach, we have selected a *delicious* dataset, which is public, described and analyzed in [8]. Before the experiments, we performed four data preprocessing tasks: (1) We remove annotations that are too personal or meaningless, e.g. "toread", "Imported IE Fa-vorites", etc. (2) The list of terms undergoes a stemming by means of the Porter's algorithm in such a way to eliminate the differences between terms having the same root. (3) We downloaded all the available web pages while removing those which are no longer available using the *cURL* command line tool. (4) Finally, we removed all the non-english web pages. Table 2 gives a description of the resulted dataset:

Table 2. Details of the delicious dataset

Bookmarks	Users	Tags	Web pages	Unique terms
9 675 294	318 769	425 183	1 321 039	12 015 123

4.2 Evaluation Methodology

Making evaluations for personalized search is a challenge since relevance judgments can only be assessed by end-users [2]. This is difficult to achieve at a large scale. However, different efforts [2,5] state that the tagging behavior of a user of a folksonomy closely reflects his behavior of search on the Web. In other words, if a user tags a document d with a tag t, he will choose to access the document d if it appears in the result obtained by submitting t as query to the search engine. Thus, we can easily state that any bookmark (u, t, r) that represents a user u who tagged a document d with tag t, can be used as a test query for evaluations. The main idea of these experiments is based on the following assumption:

For a query $q = \{t\}$ issued by u with query term t, relevant documents are those tagged by u with t.

Hence, for each evaluation, we randomly select 2000 pairs (u, t), which are considered to form a personalized query set. For each corresponding pair (u, t), we remove all the bookmarks $(u, t, r) \in \mathbb{F}, \forall r \in R$ in order to not promote the resource r (or document) in the results obtained by submitting t as a query in our algorithm and the considered baselines. By removing these bookmarks, the results should not be biased in favor of documents that simply are tagged with query terms and making comparisons to the baseline uniformly. Hence, for each pair, the user u sends the query $q = \{t\}$ to the system. Then, we retrieve and rank all the documents that match this query using a specific baseline, where documents are indexed based on their textual content using the *Apache Lucene*. Finally, according to the previous assumption, we compute the Mean Average Precision (MAP) and the Mean Reciprocal Rank (MRR) over the 2000 queries.

5 Results and Discussion

In this section, we conduct several experiments, which intend to address the following questions:

1. What is the effectiveness of these personalized ranking functions on users with different profile lengths?
2. Can these personalized ranking functions achieve good performance even if users have no bookmarks?
3. Are these personalized ranking functions efficient for large datasets?
4. What is the best personalized ranking function?

In the following, Section 5.1 addresses question 1 and 2, Section 5.2 shows the analysis of question 3, and lastly, Section 5.3 tackles question 4.

5.1   Performance on Different Users

Here, we try to study the ability of the personalized ranking approaches to achieve good performance for users that have different profile length, i.e. users that used few terms in their tagging actions. Hence, we propose to compare these approaches using the evaluation process described in Section 4.2. We select 2000 query pairs (u, t) based on the number of tags the users used in their tagging actions. The query pairs are grouped into 6 classes: "0", 1-5", "6-10", "11-15", "16-20", and "21-30", denoting how many tags users have used in their tagging actions, e.g. class "1-5" is composed with users who have a profile length between 1 and 5. Note that we fixed γ to 0.5 for all the approaches. The experimental results are shown in Figure 1.

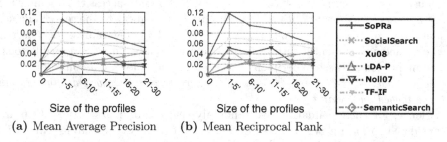

(a) Mean Average Precision   (b) Mean Reciprocal Rank

Fig. 1. Performance comparison on different queries, while fixing $\gamma = 0.5$

The results show that the performance of all the profile based approaches decrease for users with high profile length, i.e. SoPRa, Xu08, LDA-P, Noll07, tf-if. This is certainly due to the fact that these approaches fail to determine the user expectations, if he expressed his interest in different fields. However, the affinity based personalization approaches increase their performance for users with high profile length. These approaches are based on other user experiences with common tastes and affinities with the query issuer. Hence, we believe that modeling a user profile with simply his tags is not enough to generate satisfactory search results, especially for active users on social networks. We must go beyond that by considering their social relatives for ranking purpose.

Finally, we note that many personalized ranking functions are not able to provide a suitable ranking of documents for users with no tags. Currently, all

Table 3. Summary of the analysis

	General Performance[a]	Time Complexity[b]	Cold Start[c]	Adaptability[d]	Effectiveness[e]
Xu08	★★	$O(\mid \vec{p_u} \mid + \mid \vec{q} \mid)$	+	+	-
LDA-P	★	$O(n+ \mid \vec{q} \mid)$	+	-	-
SoPRa	★★★	$O(\mid \vec{p_u} \mid +2\times \mid \vec{q} \mid)$	+	+	-
Noll07	★	$O(\mid T_u \mid)$	-	+	-
tf-if	★	$O(\mid T_u \mid)$	-	+	-
SemanticSearch	★★	$O(\mid q \mid \times \mid U_t \mid)$	+	+	+
SocialSearch	★★	$O(\mid q \mid \times \mid U_t \mid \times \mid \vec{p_u} \mid)$	-	+	+

[a] The general retrieval performances. ★★★ : very effective; ★★ : effective; ★ : not effective.

[c] The cold start is a potential problem of a system to effectively handle new entities, e.g. users, items, or tags. In other words, it concerns the issue that the system cannot draw any inferences for users or items about which it hasn't information. + : can cope with cold start problem; - : cannot cope with cold start problem.

[b] The complexity is given for computing the ranking score of one document.

[d] Adaptability refers to the ability of approaches to consider new data and to quickly update their model. Considering new data is a key problem for these ranking functions since they are based on social networks, which are growing quickly. + : can easily update the model; - : cannot easily adapt the model.

[e] The effectiveness of the approaches for different profile lengths. + : effective for users with high profiles lengths; - : not effective for users with high profiles lengths.

the approaches, which are able to rank documents for users with no tags relay on the Lucene naive score for dealing with cold start problem.

5.2 Efficiency Analysis

We compare here the algorithms from the point of view of complexity. If we look at the complexity of each algorithm, we can distinguish 3 categories of algorithms, upon which we find common properties in term of computing complexity. These categories are the following: (i) Xu08, LDA-P and SoPRa algorithms, (ii) follow the Noll07 and tf-if algorithms, and (iii) the two last Affinity-based algorithms. The second category of algorithms is the most efficient with a complexity borned by the profile size of the user. Xu08-based algorithms come second in complexity, keeping the user profile size linearity and adding to it the query length. Finally, the third category is the affinity-based algorithms, which are the slowest ones, because they grow with at least the product of the profile size and the query size. This complexity analysis is summarized in Table 3.

5.3 Summary

Table 3 summarizes the personalized ranking functions studied from different point of views. This table is built upon our appreciation of the approaches.

As a conclusion, we believe that SoPRa offers the best trade off between retrieval performance, time complexity, cold start problem, and adaptability. However, the retrieval performance of this approach decreases for users with high profile length. We believe that we can tackle this issue by extending this ranking function by leveraging the social relatives of the query issuer.

6   Conclusion

This paper discusses a contribution to the area of Social Information Retrieval, which bridges the gap between traditional Information Retrieval and Social Networks. In this context, many approaches have been proposed to improve the ranking process by personalizing it using social features. We reviewed many of these personalized functions by proposing: (i) a deep study of the state of the art of ranking functions in social collaborative setting, (ii) a deep analysis of the performances of these personalized social ranking functions, and (iii) a discussion on the effectiveness, the weakness and the performance of each approaches in different contexts.

References

1. Bender, M., Crecelius, T., Kacimi, M., Michel, S., Neumann, T., Parreira, J.X., Schenkel, R., Weikum, G.: Exploiting social relations for query expansion and result ranking. In: ICDE Workshops (2008)
2. Bischoff, K., Firan, C.S., Nejdl, W., Paiu, R.: Can all tags be used for search? In: CIKM (2008)
3. Blei, D.M., Ng, A.Y., Jordan, M.I.: Latent dirichlet allocation. J. Mach. Learn. Res. 3, 993–1022 (2003)
4. Bouadjenek, M.R., Hacid, H., Bouzeghoub, M.: Sopra: A new social personalized ranking function for improving web search. In: SIGIR (2013)
5. Krause, B., Hotho, A., Stumme, G.: A comparison of social bookmarking with traditional search. In: Macdonald, C., Ounis, I., Plachouras, V., Ruthven, I., White, R.W. (eds.) ECIR 2008. LNCS, vol. 4956, pp. 101–113. Springer, Heidelberg (2008)
6. Noll, M.G., Meinel, C.: Web search personalization via social bookmarking and tagging. In: Aberer, K., et al. (eds.) ASWC 2007 and ISWC 2007. LNCS, vol. 4825, pp. 367–380. Springer, Heidelberg (2007)
7. Vallet, D., Cantador, I., Jose, J.M.: Personalizing web search with folksonomy-based user and document profiles. In: Gurrin, C., He, Y., Kazai, G., Kruschwitz, U., Little, S., Roelleke, T., Rüger, S., van Rijsbergen, K. (eds.) ECIR 2010. LNCS, vol. 5993, pp. 420–431. Springer, Heidelberg (2010)
8. Wetzker, R., Zimmermann, C., Bauckhage, C.: Analyzing social bookmarking systems: A del.icio.us cookbook. In: ECAI (2008)
9. Xu, S., Bao, S., Fei, B., Su, Z., Yu, Y.: Exploring folksonomy for personalized search. In: SIGIR (2008)

Building Rich Internet Applications Models: Example of a Better Strategy

Suryakant Choudhary[1], Mustafa Emre Dincturk[1], Seyed M. Mirtaheri[1],
Guy-Vincent Jourdan[1,2], Gregor v. Bochmann[1,2], and Iosif Viorel Onut[3,4]

[1] EECS - University of Ottawa
[2] Fellow of IBM Canada CAS Research, Canada
[3] Research and Development, IBM® Security AppScan®, Security Systems
[4] IBM Canada Software Lab, Canada
{schou062,mdinc075,smirt016}@uottawa.ca,
{gvj,bochmann}@eecs.uottawa.ca,
vioonut@ca.ibm.com

Abstract. Crawling "classical" web applications is a problem that has
been addressed more than a decode ago. Efficient crawling of web applications that use advanced technologies such as AJAX (called Rich
Internet Applications, RIAs) is still an open problem. Crawling is important not only for indexing content, but also for building models of
the applications, which is necessary for automated testing, automated
security and accessibility assessments and in general for using software
engineering tools. This paper presents a new strategy to crawl RIAs. It
uses the concept of Model-Based Crawling (MBC) first introduced in [1],
and introduces a new model, the "menu model", which we show to be
much simpler than previous models for MBC and more effective at building models than previously published methods. This method and others
are compared against a set of experimental and real RIAs.

Keywords: Crawling, RIAs, AJAX, Modeling.

1 Introduction

The ability to automatically extract a model of a website is important for several
reasons. The most obvious one is to index the content of the sites, which is
done through "crawling". Indexing is obviously a central feature of the Web,
but not the only reason why inferring models is important. We also require
models for tasks related to good software engineering: models are needed as input
for automated testing of applications ("model-based testing"), models are also
needed for automated security assessments, for automated usability assessments,
or simply as a way to better understand the structure of the website.

Nearly two and a half decades of research in the area of model extraction and
crawling has produced a large body of work with many powerful solutions [2].
The majority of the studies, however, focus on traditional web applications,
where the HTML view of the page is generated on the server side. In this model,

F. Daniel, P. Dolog, and Q. Li (Eds.): ICWE 2013, LNCS 7977, pp. 291–305, 2013.

there is a one-to-one relation between the URL of the page and the state of its *Document Object Model* (DOM) [3]. Thus, many of the proposed web crawlers use the URL to identify the state of the DOM. Such assumption reduces the basic task of crawling the Web to the task of finding all the valid and reachable URLs from a set of seed URLs.

However, the so-called *Rich Internet Applications* (RIAs) break the one-to-one relationship between the URL and the state of the DOM. In RIAs, DOMs are partially updated by client-side script execution (such as JavaScript®), and asynchronous calls to the server are done through technologies such as AJAX [4]. Such sophisticated client-side applications create a one-to-many relation between the URL and the reachable DOM states associated with that URL.

This evolution is positive, but comes at a cost which has been underestimated: the crawling techniques developed for traditional web applications just do not work on RIAs. We have lost our ability to crawl and model web applications as they are typically created today[1]. Even simple websites are not immune to the problem since common tools to create and maintain website content are increasingly adding AJAX-like scripts to the page. We need to address this issue, which means to develop web crawlers that do not rely solely on the URL to uniquely identify the state of the application, but also take into consideration the DOM structure and its properties to identify different states of the application. There is some work being done in that domain (see [5] for an overview), but more must be done. This paper is one step in this direction.

Crawling RIAs is much more complex than crawling traditional web applications. The one-to-many relation between a URL and states of the DOM can be modeled as a directed graph referred to as the *application graph*. In the application graph, each state of the DOM is a node, and each JavaScript event is a directed edge. To construct such a graph, one must differentiate between different states of the DOM, which is a challenge in itself, but outside the scope of this paper (see e.g. [6] for a discussion on the topic). In this model, taking an edge from a node means executing a JavaScript event from the DOM that the node represents.

After defining the application graph, the task of crawling a RIA is reduced to the task of discovering every state in the application graph. The state that is reached when a given URL is loaded is called the "initial state of the URL". For a crawler to ensure that all states reachable from a given URL are discovered, the crawler has to start from the initial state of the URL, take every possible transition, and do this for every newly discovered state recursively. This often takes a long time. It is thus interesting for a crawler to discover as many states as possible during early stages of the crawl, and postpone executing events that most probably lead to visited states.

To this end, we have introduced a general approach called *model-based* crawling [1], where a crawling strategy aims at discovering the states of the application

---

[1] See e.g. `https://developers.google.com/webmasters/ajax-crawling/docs/getting-started`, in which Google suggests to create static URLs to index the pages that will not be reached by the crawler because of AJAX.

as soon as possible by making predictions based on an anticipated model for the application. In this paper, we propose a new strategy, called the Menu strategy, using the model-based crawling approach. This new algorithm is simpler and more efficient to discover all reachable DOM states in a RIA than the other known strategies.

The rest of this paper is organized as follows: in Section 2, we give an overview of model-based crawling. In Section 3, we explain the proposed strategy in details. Section 4 presents the experimental study. In Section 5, a summary of related works is presented. In Section 6, we conclude the paper.

2   Overview

Building a model of a RIA is potentially a very lengthy process, because of the large number of states and transitions involved. Because of this, many of the existing strategies do not try to build a complete model of the application being crawled. Our approach is different: we insist that under some assumptions, given enough time the strategy should produce a complete model of the RIA. On the other hand, we acknowledge that, most of the time, we will not have enough time to complete the crawl. Thus, our first goal is to produce a complete model as efficiently as possible, which means that we want to minimize the number of events we need to execute to produce such a model. Our second goal is that, as we produce this model, we should discover as many states as possible, as early as possible during the crawl. Because, in most cases, it is more important to find the states than it is to find the transitions. If we are not going to run the crawl to the end, we want to ensure that the partial model being built will contain as much states as possible.

When we crawl a website, we make the following assumptions: we assume that, if user inputs are involved, we have access to a collection of sample inputs that are good enough to build the model. We do not address here the question of how to generate such inputs. The second assumption is that the RIA being crawled is deterministic from the point of view of the crawler. This means that, from the same state, the same action will always produce the same result (go to the same state). Although this assumption is fairly commonly made in the literature, we recognize that it is a very limiting assumption and that more work will have to be done to relax it in the future. Finally, we assume that we can always "reset" the RIA by reloading the URL, and thus the underlying application graph is strongly connected.

In general, it is not possible to devise a strategy that would be efficient at finding the states early, since the underlying graph could be any graph. We have introduced model-based crawling as a solution to this problem [1]. With model-based crawling, we initially assume that application will follow a particular behavioral model referred to as *meta-model*. It is anticipated that the model of the application will be an instance of this meta-model. An efficient (ideally, optimal) strategy is designed based on this anticipation. However, it is not strictly assumed that the RIA being crawled will actually follow the meta-model. During the crawl, each time we see a difference between the anticipated behavior and the actual behavior, we adapt the strategy accordingly.

A model-based strategy usually consists of two phases:

1. **State exploration phase** where the objective is to discover all the application states as predicted by the meta-model of the strategy.
2. **Transition exploration phase** where the objective is to execute all remaining events, to complete the model.

It is possible that, during the second phase, new states are discovered, in which case we will switch back to the first phase. Thus, a model-based crawling strategy may alternate between these two phases multiple times before finishing the crawl. The strategy finishes the crawl when it has executed all the events in the application, which guarantees to have discovered all the states of the application.

The first model-based crawling strategy is the "Hypercube" strategy where the application is anticipated to have a hypercube structure [1]. The Hypercube strategy is an optimal strategy for the RIAs that fully follow the hypercube meta-model. However, in practice, few RIAs follow this model, and the algorithms involved are rather complex. Even though the results were better than other strategies even for RIAs that do not follow this model, we present here a new strategy that is better still, much easier to understand and is based on a meta-model more commonly found in RIAs.

3   Menu Model

The proposed crawling strategy is based on the idea that some events will always lead the application to the same resulting state, regardless of the source state from which the event is executed. These kind of events are referred to as the "menu events".

We called this new model *menu model* because our menu events are often the intended model behind application menus. Such behavior is realized by the menu items present in a web application such as *home, help, about us* etc.

Once an event is identified as a menu event, we can use it to anticipate some part of the application graph, and use this anticipated graph to build an efficient strategy. Thus, the core of the strategy is to identify these menu events, and then execute the events that are not menu events sooner than the menu events (since menu events are anticipated to produce known states). In practice, we prioritize the events based on the execution history:

1. **Globally unexecuted events**: This category represents the events that have not yet been executed at any state discovered so far. Events in this category have the highest priority.
2. **Locally unexecuted events**: This category represents the events that have been executed at some discovered state but have not been executed at the current state of the application. Events in this category are further divided into the following subcategories:

(a) **Non-classified events**: Events in this subcategory has been executed only once globally. A second execution is necessary to classify the event. Events in this subcategory have the second highest priority next to the globally unexecuted events.

(b) **Menu events**: Events in this subcategory follow the menu model hypothesis when the first two executions are considered: their executions from two different states have led to the same state. They have the lowest priority.

(c) **Self-Loop events**: Events in this subcategory have not changed the state of the application in their first two executions. They have the same priority as the menu events.

(d) **Other events**: All the remaining events belong to this category. These are the events that have shown neither menu nor self-loop behavior in their first two executions. These events have the same priority as non-classified events.

Since the events in the menu and self-loop categories are not expected to lead to a new state, they have the lowest priority.

The categorization of the events is done throughout the crawl. The priority sets are updated as new events are found in newly discovered states and as more information about results of the execution instances of the events become available.

3.1   State Exploration Phase

The primary goal of the state exploration phase is to discover all the states of the application as soon as possible. To do so, the strategy constructs and maintains a graph model of the application. The application graph is a weighted directed graph, $G = (V, E)$ where V represents the states discovered and E represents the edges. An edge may be an executed event, a *reset*, or a *predicted* transition. A reset is the action of resetting the application to its initial state by reloading the URL. For simplicity, we assume each event to have the same unit cost, but the cost of reset is different and it depends on the application being crawled. A predicted edge corresponds to a non-classified event or a menu event that is not executed in the source state (for the purpose of predicting transitions, all non-classified events are assumed to be menu events). In the case of a non-classified event, the predicted resulting state is the state which was reached on the first execution of the event, and in the case of a menu event it is the resulting state of the menu event. A self-loop predicted edge correspond to an unexecuted self-loop event. In this case, the predicted resulting state is the starting state of the self-loop edge. Figure 1 shows an instance of G.

The state exploration phase starts by categorizing the events (initially, the crawler only knows the events on the initial state; but, as the crawl progresses, previously unseen events can be found on newly discovered states). Each event initially belongs to the globally unexecuted category. Unexecuted events are then picked according to the priority sets. All the instances of the events from a higher

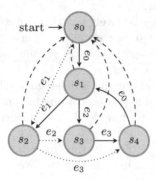

Fig. 1. An example of application graph G under construction: solid lines are executed transitions, dashed lines are resets, dotted lines are predicted transitions

priority set are exhausted before executing an event from a lower priority set. Among the events with the same priority, the priority is given to any event which is closer to the current state than the others (closeness is in terms of number of transitions that needs to be taken to reach a state where the event is enabled and unexecuted), otherwise one is chosen at random. During the state exploration phase, we execute all the unexecuted events in the application, except for categorized menu and self-loop events.

Once an event is picked for execution, the strategy always uses the shortest known path from the current state s_{curr} to the state s_{next} where the event is going to be executed. This calculated shortest path may contain predicted transitions. A predicted transition may of course be wrong, and the application may end up in a state that is not the predicted one. During the execution of the path, the strategy verifies, after each predicted transition, that the state reached is the one predicted. When this is not the case, the crawled RIA contradicts the menu model (at least from that state, and for this event). To adapt to such a violation, the strategy discards the current path and looks for the next unexecuted event from the state reached.

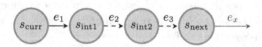

Fig. 2. Path from the current state to state s_{next} where the next event can be executed. Solid lines represent known transitions, and dotted lines represent predicted transitions.

For instance, considering the execution of the example path shown in Figure 2, let us assume that there is a violation when the predicted transition e_2 (originating from s_{int1}) is taken. As Figure 3 shows, after executing event e_2 on s_{int1}, we reach state s' instead of s_{int2}. Due to this violation, the menu strategy ignores the rest of the path segments, and builds a new path from the current state (s') to a next state with an unexecuted event.

During the execution of a path, each predicted transition leads to the execution of an event that had not been executed from that state before, which permits the categorization of that event if it is not already categorized.

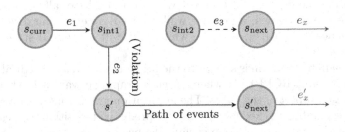

Fig. 3. Example of a violation for the path in Figure 2

3.2   Transition Exploration Phase

The state exploration phase executes all the events discovered during that phase, except for the events in the menu and the self-loop categories. Once the state exploration phase is over, the menu strategy moves to the transition exploration phase. The transition exploration phase verifies the validity of the assumptions made at the state exploration phase by executing all these remaining events. In an application that follows the menu model, all the states of the application are found by the end of the state exploration phase. Any violating menu or self-loop events, however, may lead to the discovery of a new state.

During the transition exploration phase, the strategy tries to find the least costly path to execute all the remaining events in the application. The cost of this path is measured in terms of the total number of events and resets required.

If we define *a walk of the graph* as a sequence of adjacent edges, the transition exploration problem can be mapped to the problem of finding the least costly walk of the graph that traverses all the edges representing the unexecuted events at least once. During the transition exploration phase, should the execution of any unexecuted event lead to the discovery of a new state, the strategy switches back to the state exploration phase. This mechanism expedites finding new states. Thus, the menu strategy might alternate between the state and transition exploration phases many times before it finishes the crawl of the application.

Graph Walk. The transition exploration phase uses a walk generator function to calculate a walk that covers all of the unexecuted events. During the calculation of the graph walk, the application graph includes predicted transitions.

Hence, executing the event sequence in the walk might not result in the expected state. In fact, a single violation can make the event sequence invalid. To avoid this, a step-wise approach in construction of the whole walk is taken. The walk generator function splits the event sequence into multiple walk segments. Each walk segment may start with a reset, may be followed by zero or more already executed events, and ends with an unexecuted event.

Considering the example in Figure 1 where the results of all the unexecuted events have been assumed, a possible walk that covers every unexecuted event is the sequence $< e_1, e_3, e_0, e_1, e_2 >$, which starts at the initial state, s_0, and terminates at s_3.

Our immediate situation is similar to the problem known as the Rural Chinese Postman Problem (RCPP) [7], where given a graph we want a least cost tour covering only a subset of the edges. The application graph contains known transitions corresponding to executed events and predicted transitions corresponding to unexecuted menu and self-loop events. We need a least cost tour to execute all the remaining unexecuted events.

Unfortunately, the RCPP is an NP-complete problem, so we do not attempt to solve this problem. Instead, we use the Chinese Postman Problem (CPP). In CPP, given a graph we want a least cost tour of all the edges. Unlike the RCPP, there are polynomial algorithms for the CPP. However, this is not a perfect analogy to our situation: in the current graph, we have both executed and predicted transitions, and we only want to execute the predicted ones. If we consider the subgraph containing only the predicted transitions, this subgraph may not be connected, and a tour may not exist. To address this problem, we augment this subgraph with a few of the known transitions (including resets if necessary), until the graph is strongly connected again. We then use CPP to create a tour that goes over every transitions. This solution gives reasonably good results (although clearly non optimal) at a small computational cost.

Violation and Strategy Adaptation. When going over the tour, each predicted transition may lead to a violation of the assumption, and the application can end up in a state that is not the one predicted. There are two cases to handle:

1. **Wrong known state:** This is the case where the resulting state has been discovered previously, but it is not the expected state. When this happens, the predicted edge is removed from the graph, replaced with the newly executed transition. At this point, we end up in the wrong state in the tour. Instead of recomputing a tour, we have opted for a simpler solution: the strategy keeps the original walk, and brings the application back to the state that was expected to be reached initially. To do this, we simply find the shortest known path that does not contain any predicted edges from the current state to that next state, and execute it first.
2. **New state:** Should a violation lead to the discovery of a new state, the crawling strategy switches back immediately to the state exploration phase. However, we do not discard the calculated CPP walk, which is reused later when the strategy reaches the transition exploration phase again. At this

point, the existing CPP is augmented to include any additional discovered
unexecuted events.

Due to space constraints, we do not include more details which can be found
in [8].

4 Implementation and Evaluation

In this section, we present our experimental results, comparing the efficiency of
the Menu strategy against many other existing crawling strategies on several
AJAX-based RIAs.

4.1 Measuring the Efficiency of a Strategy

As explained before, our definition of an efficient strategy is a strategy that builds
the entire model quickly, while finding all the states as early as possible in the
process. In order to measure speed, instead of measuring time, we measure the
number of event executions and the number of resets required by each strategy
to complete both tasks (find all the states, find the complete model). This is
reasonable since the time spent for event executions and resets dominates the
crawling time and the numbers depend only on the decisions of the strategy.
And this way, the results do not depend on the hardware that is used to run
the experiments and are not affected by the network delays which can vary in
different runs.

We combine these numbers to define a cost unit as follows. We measure for
each application the following two values. $t(e)_{avg}$: the average event execution
time obtained by measuring the time for executing each event in a randomly
selected set of events in the application and taking the average, and $t(r)_{avg}$: the
average time to perform a reset. For simplicity, we consider each event execution
to take $t(e)_{avg}$ and take this as a cost unit. Then, we calculate "the cost of reset":
$c_r = t(r)_{avg}/t(e)_{avg}$. Finally, the cost that is spent by a strategy to find all the
states of an application is calculated by $n_e + n_r \times c_r$ where n_e and n_r are the
total number of events executed and resets used by the strategy to find all the
states, respectively[2].

4.2 Crawling Strategies Used for Comparison

- Optimized Standard Crawling Strategies: The standard crawling strategies
  are Breadth-First and Depth-First. We use "optimized" versions of these
  strategies, meaning that when there is a need to move from the current state
  to another known state, the shortest known path from the current state to

---

[2] We measure the value of c_r before crawling an application and give this value as a
parameter to each strategy. A strategy, knowing how costly a reset is compared to
an average event execution, can decide whether to reset or not when moving from
current state to another known state.

the desired state is used. This is in contrast to using systematic resets. The results presented here with the optimized versions are much better than the ones obtained using the standard, non-optimized Breadth-First and Depth-First strategies.

- Greedy Strategy [9]: This is a simple strategy that prefers to explore an event from the current state, if there is one. Otherwise, it chooses an event from a state that is closest to the current state.
- Other Model-based Crawling Strategies: We also compare with other existing model-based strategies: The Hypercube strategy [1] is based on the anticipation that the application has a hypercube model. The Probability Strategy [10] prioritizes the events by estimating their probabilities of discovering a new state based on their previous explorations.
- The Optimal Cost: We also present the optimal cost of discovering all the states for each application. This cost is calculated once the model is known (after the application is crawled first with one of the strategies). Finding an optimal path that visits every state in a known model is possible by solving an Asymmetric Traveling Salesman Problem (ATSP). We use an exact ATSP solver [11] to find this path. This gives us an idea of how far from the optimal speed each strategy is (for the first phase, find all the states). Of course, this optimal is not a strategy on its own, and can only be calculated once the entire model is known.

4.3   Subject Applications

We are comparing the strategies using two test RIAs and four real RIAs[3]. This number is not as large as we would like, but we are limited by the tools that are available to us. Each new RIA requires a significant amount of work before we can crawl it[4]. With the increasing exposure to this problem, better tools will be made available, and we will be able to test our solutions on a much broader test set.

- Bebop: This is an AJAX-based interface to browse a list of publications. We have used an instance that contains 5 publications. It has 1,800 states and 145,811 transitions. The measured cost of reset is 2.

---

[3] http://ssrg.eecs.uottawa.ca/testbeds.html

[4] We stress that the work in question is not related to the strategy described here, but to the limitation of the available tools. One approach to implement a RIA crawler is to control an external browser using an API such as Selenium WebDriver (as Crawljax [12] does). The main drawback of this approach is the inability to detect automatically all the events in a page since the DOM interface does not have a method to check if an element has an event registered dynamically (using addEventListener method in JavaScript). So, the user needs to specify the elements that should be interacted with in an application. Our approach is to implement a browser as part of the crawler. Thus, our crawler has more control over the application and can detect automatically all the events in a page. However, this requires more work since we need to make sure that our browser supports all the functionality required by the RIA.

- jQuery FileTree: This is an AJAX-based file explorer. For this study, we used an instance that allows browsing Python source code. It has 214 states, 8,428 transitions. The measured cost of reset is 2.
- Periodic Table: This is an AJAX-based periodic table. It has 240 states, 29,034 transitions. The measured cost of reset is 8.
- Clipmarks: This was a AJAX-based social network. We have used a partial local copy of this website for the experimental study. It has 129 states, 10,580 transitions. The measured cost of reset is 18.
- Altoro Mutual: This is an AJAX version of a demo website in the form of a fictional banking site. It has 45 states, 1,210 transitions. The measured cost of reset is 2.
- TestRIA: This is a AJAX test application in the form of a generic homepage. It has 39 states, 305 transitions. The measured cost of reset is 2.

4.4 Experimental Setup

We have implemented all the mentioned crawling strategies in a prototype of IBM® Security AppScan® Enterprise[5]. Each strategy is implemented as a separate class in the same code base, so they use the same DOM equivalence mechanism, the same event identification mechanism, and the same embedded browser. For this reason, each strategy extracts the same model for an application.

We crawl each application with each strategy ten times and present the average of these crawls. In each crawl, the events of each state are randomly shuffled before they are passed to the strategy. The aim here is to eliminate influence caused by exploring the events of a state in a certain order since the strategy may not define an exploration priority for the events on a state.

4.5 Costs of Discovering States (Strategy Efficiency)

The box plots in Figure 4 show the results. For each application and for each strategy, the figure contains a box plot. A box plot consists of a line and a box on the line. The minimum point of the line shows the cost of discovering the first state (always equal to the cost of reset for the application). The lower edge, the line in the middle and the higher edge of the box show the cost of discovering 25%, 50% and 75% of the states, respectively. The maximum point of the line shows the cost of discovering all the states. The plots are drawn in logarithmic scale for better visualization. Each horizontal dotted line shows the optimal cost for the corresponding application.

The results show that for all applications the Greedy strategy and the model-based strategies are significantly more efficient than Breadth-First and Depth-First. It can also be seen that the Menu strategy has the best performance to discover all the states except for the Bebop where it is very close to the best. In

---

[5] Details are available at http://ssrg.eecs.uottawa.ca/docs/prototype.pdf Since our crawler is built on top of the architecture of a commercial product, we are not able to provide open-source implementations of the strategies currently.

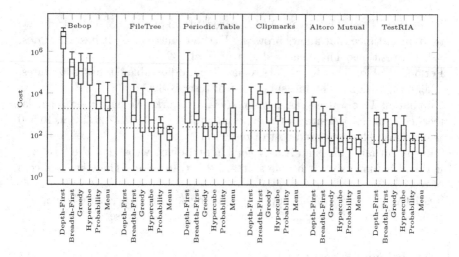

Fig. 4. Costs of Discovering the States (Strategy Efficiency), in logarithmic scale. Each horizontal dotted line shows the optimal cost for the corresponding application.

4 out of 6 cases, it was the first to discover the 75% of the states. In addition, the Menu strategy was the first to discover the 50% and the 25% of the states in all cases, except for Clipmarks where it is very close to the best. This is particularly important if one assumes that the crawl will not be run to the end and that in most cases it will be cut short. It shows that the Menu is the strategy that will provide the most information after the least amount of time.

4.6 Costs of Complete Crawl

The previous results show the costs of discovering all the states. However, the crawl does not end at this point since a crawler cannot know all states are discovered until all the events are explored from each state (in other words, we could provide this information only because we have run the tests to the end). In Table 1, the total number of events and the total number of resets during the crawl are shown as well as the costs calculated based on these numbers.

It can be seen that the model-based strategies and the Greedy strategy finish crawling with a significantly less cost compared with Breadth-First and Depth-First. The Menu is in the same ballpark as the other model-based strategies, but not better. However, the complete crawl is not as important a factor as finding all the states, as explained before.

5   Related Works

A survey of traditional crawling techniques is presented in [2]. For RIA crawling, a recent survey is presented in [5]. Except for [1, 10, 13] which present other

Table 1. Total Costs of Crawling

	Bebop			FileTree			Periodic Table			Clipmarks			Altoro Mutual			TestRIA		
	Events	Resets	Cost	Events	Resets	Cost	Events	Resets	Cost	Events	Resets	Cost	Events	Resets	Cost	Events	Resets	Cost
Depth-First	13,386,210	27	13,386,264	99,336	13	99,362	897,358	236	899,246	19,569	72	20,868	6,876	34	6,944	1,433	1	1,435
Breadth-First	943,001	8,732	960,466	26,375	1,639	29,652	64,850	14,633	181,916	15,342	926	32,015	3,074	334	3,742	1,216	55	1,326
Greedy	826,914	27	826,968	20,721	13	20,747	29,926	236	31,814	11,396	56	12,398	2,508	34	2,576	1,001	1	1,003
Hypercube	816,142	27	816,196	19,865	13	19,891	29,921	236	31,809	11,350	56	12,356	2,489	34	2,557	994	1	996
Probability	816,922	27	816,976	19,331	13	19,357	29,548	236	31,436	11,456	62	12,563	2,451	34	2,520	972	1	974
Menu	814,220	27	814,274	19,708	13	19,734	37,489	236	39,377	11,769	71	13,043	2,457	35	2,527	974	1	976

model-based crawling strategies and [9] which presents the Greedy strategy, the published research uses Breadth-First or Depth-First strategies for crawling RIAs. As we have seen, Breadth-First and Depth-First strategies are less efficient than the Greedy and the model-based strategies.

[14] and [15] suggest algorithms to index a RIA. [15] offers an early attempt in crawling AJAX applications based on user events and building the model of the application. The application model is constructed as a graph using the Breadth-First strategy. [14] introduces an AJAX-aware search engine for indexing the contents of RIAs. In this model components are adapted to handle RIAs. The crawler identifies JavaScript events and runs a standard Breadth-First search on them. [16] offers an algorithm, called *AjaxRank*, similar to *PageRank* [17] tailored to RIAs, to give weight to different states based on the connectivity.

[18–20] seek to automate regression and other testing of a RIA. *Crawljax* [12, 21] constructs a state-flow graph of the application by exercising client-side code and identifying the events that change the state of the application. Crawljax differentiates states using Levenshtein distance method [22], and uses a Depth-First strategy. [23] describes the derivation of test sequences from the application model obtained by crawling. [24] is similar, but takes a white-box testing approach where the program fragments of the states are analyzed.

Several other tools exist to create an FSM model of the application. *RE-RIA* [25] uses execution traces to create the FSM model of the application. As an improvement to *RE-RIA*, *CrawlRIA* [26] generates the execution traces by running a Depth-First strategy. *CreRIA* facilitate reverse engineering of a RIA for dynamic analysis. *DynaRIA* offers a tool to comprehend a RIA better for testing and other purposes. It also helps to visualize the run-time behavior of the application.

6   Conclusion

A new model-based crawling algorithm was introduced: the Menu model. The proposed architecture models the web application based on the JavaScript events in each state of the DOM. It makes assumptions about the category of events in order to derive a strategy, then learns, and adapt its categories as the crawling proceeds. A prototype of the system is implemented and the results are evaluated against several other model-based crawling algorithms. We have shown empirically that Menu strategy is better than other known strategies when it comes to finding all the states of the application being modeled.

Acknowledgments. This work is partially supported by the IBM Center for Advanced Studies, and the Natural Sciences and Engineering Research Council of Canada (NSERC).

The views expressed in this article are the sole responsibility of the authors and do not necessarily reflect those of IBM.

Trademarks: IBM and AppScan are trademarks or registered trademarks of International Business Machines Corp., registered in many jurisdictions worldwide. Other product and service names might be trademarks of IBM or other companies. A current list of IBM trademarks is available on the Web at *Copyright and trademark information* at www.ibm.com/legal/copytrade.shtml. Java and all Java-based trademarks and logos are trademarks or registered trademarks of Oracle and/or its affiliates.

References

1. Benjamin, K., von Bochmann, G., Dincturk, M.E., Jourdan, G.-V., Onut, I.V.: A strategy for efficient crawling of rich internet applications. In: Auer, S., Díaz, O., Papadopoulos, G.A. (eds.) ICWE 2011. LNCS, vol. 6757, pp. 74–89. Springer, Heidelberg (2011)
2. Olston, C., Najork, M.: Web crawling. Found. Trends Inf. Retr. 4(3), 175–246 (2010)
3. World Wide Web Consortium (W3C): Document Object Model (DOM) (2005), http://www.w3.org/DOM/
4. Garrett, J.J.: Ajax: A new approach to web applications (2005), http://www.adaptivepath.com/publications/essays/archives/000385.php
5. Choudhary, S., Dincturk, M.E., Mirtaheri, S.M., Moosavi, A., von Bochmann, G., Jourdan, G.V., Onut, I.V.: Crawling rich internet applications: the state of the art. In: Proceedings of the 2012 Conference of the Center for Advanced Studies on Collaborative Research, CASCON 2012, pp. 146–160 (2012)
6. Choudhary, S., Dincturk, M.E., Bochmann, G.V., Jourdan, G.V., Onut, I.V., Ionescu, P.: Solving some modeling challenges when testing rich internet applications for security. In: 2012 International Conference on Software Testing, Verification, and Validation, pp. 850–857 (2012)
7. Eiselt, H.A., Gendreau, M., Laporte, G.: Arc routing problems, part ii: The rural postman problem. Operations Research 43(3), 399–414 (1995)
8. Choudhary, S.: M-crawler: Crawling rich internet applications using menu metamodel. Master's thesis, EECS - University of Ottawa (2012), http://ssrg.site.uottawa.ca/docs/Surya-Thesis.pdf
9. Peng, Z., He, N., Jiang, C., Li, Z., Xu, L., Li, Y., Ren, Y.: Graph-based ajax crawl: Mining data from rich internet applications. In: 2012 International Conference on Computer Science and Electronics Engineering (ICCSEE), vol. 3, pp. 590–594 (March 2012)
10. Dincturk, M.E., Choudhary, S., von Bochmann, G., Jourdan, G.-V., Onut, I.V.: A statistical approach for efficient crawling of rich internet applications. In: Brambilla, M., Tokuda, T., Tolksdorf, R. (eds.) ICWE 2012. LNCS, vol. 7387, pp. 362–369. Springer, Heidelberg (2012)
11. Carpaneto, G., Dell'Amico, M., Toth, P.: Exact solution of large-scale, asymmetric traveling salesman problems. ACM Trans. Math. Softw. 21(4), 394–409 (1995)

12. Mesbah, A., van Deursen, A., Lenselink, S.: Crawling ajax-based web applications through dynamic analysis of user interface state changes. TWEB 6(1), 3 (2012)
13. Benjamin, K., Bochmann, G.V., Jourdan, G.V., Onut, I.V.: Some modeling challenges when testing rich internet applications for security. In: Proceedings of the 2010 Third International Conference on Software Testing, Verification, and Validation Workshops, ICSTW 2010, pp. 403–409. IEEE Computer Society, Washington, DC (2010)
14. Duda, C., Frey, G., Kossmann, D., Zhou, C.: Ajaxsearch: crawling, indexing and searching web 2.0 applications. Proc. VLDB Endow. 1(2), 1440–1443 (2008)
15. Duda, C., Frey, G., Kossmann, D., Matter, R., Zhou, C.: Ajax crawl: Making ajax applications searchable. In: Proceedings of the 2009 IEEE International Conference on Data Engineering, ICDE 2009, pp. 78–89. IEEE Computer Society, Washington, DC (2009)
16. Frey, G.: Indexing ajax web applications. Master's thesis, ETH Zurich (2007), http://e-collection.library.ethz.ch/eserv/eth:30111/eth-30111-01.pdf
17. Page, L., Brin, S., Motwani, R., Winograd, T.: The pagerank citation ranking: Bringing order to the web, Standford University, Technical Report (1998)
18. Roest, D., Mesbah, A., van Deursen, A.: Regression testing ajax applications: Coping with dynamism. In: ICST, pp. 127–136. IEEE Computer Society (2010)
19. Bezemer, C.P., Mesbah, A., van Deursen, A.: Automated security testing of web widget interactions. In: Proceedings of the the the 7th Joint Meeting of the European Software Engineering Conference and the ACM SIGSOFT Symposium on The Foundations of Software Engineering, ESEC/FSE 2009, pp. 81–90. ACM, New York (2009)
20. Mesbah, A., van Deursen, A.: Invariant-based automatic testing of ajax user interfaces. In: IEEE 31st International Conference on Software Engineering, ICSE 2009, pp. 210–220 (May 2009)
21. Mesbah, A., Bozdag, E., Deursen, A.V.: Crawling ajax by inferring user interface state changes. In: Proceedings of the 2008 Eighth International Conference on Web Engineering, ICWE 2008, pp. 122–134. IEEE Computer Society, Washington, DC (2008)
22. Levenshtein, V.: Binary Codes Capable of Correcting Deletions, Insertions and Reversals. Soviet Physics Doklady 10, 707 (1966)
23. Marchetto, A., Tonella, P., Ricca, F.: State-based testing of ajax web applications. In: Proceedings of the 2008 International Conference on Software Testing, Verification, and Validation, ICST 2008, pp. 121–130. IEEE Computer Society, Washington, DC (2008)
24. Artzi, S., Dolby, J., Jensen, S.H., Møller, A., Tip, F.: A framework for automated testing of JavaScript web applications. In: Proc. 33rd International Conference on Software Engineering (ICSE) (May 2011)
25. Amalfitano, D., Fasolino, A.R., Tramontana, P.: Reverse engineering finite state machines from rich internet applications. In: Proceedings of the 2008 15th Working Conference on Reverse Engineering, WCRE 2008, pp. 69–73. IEEE Computer Society, Washington, DC (2008)
26. Amalfitano, D., Fasolino, A.R., Tramontana, P.: Rich internet application testing using execution trace data. In: Proceedings of the 2010 Third International Conference on Software Testing, Verification, and Validation Workshops, ICSTW 2010, pp. 274–283. IEEE Computer Society, Washington, DC (2010)

Intelligent and Adaptive Crawling
of Web Applications for Web Archiving

Muhammad Faheem[1] and Pierre Senellart[1,2]

[1] Institut Mines–Télécom, Télécom ParisTech, CNRS LTCI, Paris, France
[2] The University of Hong Kong, Hong Kong
firstname.lastname@telecom.paristech.fr

Abstract. Web sites are dynamic in nature with content and structure changing overtime. Many pages on the Web are produced by content management systems (CMSs) such as WordPress, vBulletin, or phpBB. Tools currently used by Web archivists to preserve the content of the Web blindly crawl and store Web pages, disregarding the CMS the site is based on (leading to suboptimal crawling strategies) and whatever structured content is contained in Web pages (resulting in page-level archives whose content is hard to exploit). We present in this paper an *application-aware helper* (AAH) that fits into an archiving crawl processing chain to perform intelligent and adaptive crawling of Web applications (e.g., the pages served by a CMS). Because the AAH is aware of the Web application currently crawled, it is able to refine the list of URLs to process and to extend the archive with semantic information about extracted content. To deal with possible changes in structure of Web applications, our AAH includes an adaptation module that makes crawling resilient to small changes in the structure of Web site. We show the value of our approach by comparing the output and efficiency of the AAH with respect to regular Web crawlers, also in the presence of structure change.

1   Introduction

Social Web Archiving. The World Wide Web has become an active publishing system and is a rich source of information, thanks to contributions of hundreds of millions of Web users. Part of this public expression is carried out on social networking and social sharing sites (Twitter, Facebook, Youtube, etc.), part of it on independent Web sites powered by content management systems (CMSs, including blogs, wikis, news sites with comment systems, Web forums). Content published on this range of *Web applications* includes information that is newsworthy today or valuable to tomorrow's historians. Barack Obama thus first announced his 2012 reelection as US president on Twitter [1]; blogs are more and more used by politicians both to advertise their political platform and to listen to citizens' feedback [2]; Web forums have become a common way for political dissidents to discuss their agenda [3]; user-contributed wikis such as Wikipedia contain quality information to the level of traditional reference materials [4].

F. Daniel, P. Dolog, and Q. Li (Eds.): ICWE 2013, LNCS 7977, pp. 306–322, 2013.

Because Web content is distributed, perpetually changing, often stored in proprietary platforms without any long-term access guarantee, it is critical to preserve this valuable material for historians, journalists, or social scientists of future generations. This is the objective of *Web archiving* [5], which deals with discovering, crawling, storing, and ensuring long-term access to Web data.

Application-Aware Archiving. Current archival crawlers, such as Internet Archive's Heritrix [6], function in a conceptually simple manner. They start from a *seed* list of URLs to be stored in a queue. Web pages are then fetched from this queue one after the other (respecting crawling ethics, limiting the number of requests per server), stored as is, and links are extracted from them. If these links point to resources in the scope of the archiving task, they are added to the queue. This process ends after a specified time or when no new relevant URL can be found.

This approach does not confront the challenges of modern Web application crawling: the nature of the Web application crawled is not taken into account to decide the crawling strategy or the content to be stored; Web applications with dynamic content (e.g., Web forums, blogs, etc.) may be crawled inefficiently, in terms of the number of HTTP requests required to archive a given site; content stored in the archive may be redundant, and typically does not have any structure (it consists of flat HTML files), which makes access to the archive cumbersome.

The aim of this work is to address this challenge by introducing a new *application-aware* approach to archival Web crawling. Our system, the *application-aware helper* (AAH for short) relies on a knowledge base of known Web applications. A *Web application* is any HTTP-based application that utilizes the Web and Web browser technologies to publish information using a specific template. We focus in particular on social aspects of the Web, which are heavily based on user-generated content, social interaction, and networking, as can be found for instance in Web forums, blogs, or on social networking sites. Our proposed AAH only harvests the important content of a Web application (i.e., the content that will be valuable in a Web archive) and avoids duplicates, uninteresting URLs and templates that just serve a presentational purpose. In addition the application-aware helper extracts from Web pages individual items of information (such as blog post content, author, timestamp).

To illustrate, consider the example of a Web forum, say, powered by a content management system such as vBulletin. On the server side, forum threads and posts are stored in a database; when a user requests a given Web page, the response page is automatically generated from this database content, using a predefined template. Frequently, access to two different URLs will end up presenting the same or overlapping content. For instance, a given user's posts can be accessed both through the classical threaded view of forum posts or through the list of all his or her post displayed on the user profile. This redundancy means that an archive built by a classical Web crawler will contain duplicated information, and that many requests to the server do not result in novel pieces of content. In extreme cases, the crawler can fall into a *spider trap* because it has infinitely many links to crawl. There are also several noisy links such as to a print-friendly page or advertisement, etc., which would be better to avoid during the constitution of the archive. On the contrary, a Web crawler that is aware of the information to be crawled can determine an optimal path to crawl all posts of a forum, without any useless requests, and can store individual posts, together with their authors and timestamps, in a structured form that archivists and archive users can benefit of.

Template Change. Web applications are dynamic in nature; not only their content changes over time, but their structure and template does as well. Content management systems provide several templates that one can use for generating wiki articles, blog posts, forum messages, etc. These systems usually provide a way for changing the template without altering the informational content, to adapt to the requirements of a specific site. The layout may also change as a new version of the CMS is installed. All these layout changes result in possible changes in the DOM tree of the Web page, usually minor. This makes it more challenging to recognize and process in an intelligent manner all instances of a given content management systems, as it is hopeless to hope to manually describe all possible variations of the template in a Web application knowledge base. Another goal of this work is an intelligent crawling approach that is resilient to minor template changes, and, especially, automatically adapts to these changes, updating its knowledge of CMSs in the process. Our adaptation technique relies on both relaxing the crawling and extraction patterns present in the knowledge base, and on comparing successive versions of the same Web page.

Outline. After presenting the related work (Sect. 2) and giving some preliminary definitions (Sect. 3), we describe our knowledge base of Web applications in Sect. 4. The methodology that our application-aware helper implements is then presented in Sect. 5. We discuss the specific problem of adaptation to template changes in Sect. 6 before covering implementation issues and explaining how the AAH fits into a crawl processing chain in Sect. 7. We finally compare the efficiency and effectiveness of our AAH with respect to classical crawling approach in crawling blogs and Web forums in Sect. 8. Initial ideas leading to this work were presented as a PhD workshop article in [7]; the description of the algorithms and system, adaptation to template change, experimental results, are fully novel.

2   Related Work

Web Crawling. Web crawling is a well-studied problem with still ongoing challenges. A survey of the field of Web archiving and archival Web crawling is available in [5]. A *focused*, or *goal-directed*, crawler, crawls the Web according to a predefined set of topics [8], and thus influences the crawler behavior not based on the structure of Web applications as is our aim, but on the content of Web pages. Our approach does not have the same purpose as focused crawling: it aims at better archiving of known Web applications. Both strategies for are thus complementary.

Content in Web applications or *content management systems* is arranged with respect to a template (which may include left or right sidebar of the Web page, navigation bar, header and footer, main content, etc.). Among the various works on template extraction, Gibson et al. [9] have performed an analysis of the extent of template-based content on the Web. They have found that 40–50% of the Web content (in 2005) is template-based (i.e., part of some Web application), which is growing at the rate of 6–8% per year. This research is a strong hint at the benefit of handling Web application crawling in a specific manner.

Forum Crawling. Though application-aware crawling in general has not yet been addressed, there have been some efforts on content extraction from Web forums. One such approach [10], dubbed Board Forum Crawling (BFC), leverages the organized structure of Web forums and simulates user behavior in the extraction process. BFC deals with the problem effectively, but is still confronted to limitations as it is based on simple rules and can only deal with forums with some specific organized structure.

Another technique [11], however, does not depend on the specific structure of the Web forum. The iRobot system assists the extraction process by providing the sitemap of the Web application being crawled. The sitemap is constructed by randomly crawling a few pages from the Web application. After sitemap generation, iRobot obtains the structure of the Web forum in the form of a directed graph consisting of vertices (Web pages) and directed arcs (links between different Web pages). Furthermore a path analysis is performed to provide an optimal traversal path which leads the extraction process in order to avoid duplicate and invalid pages. A later effort [12] identified a few drawbacks in iRobot and improved the original system in a number of way: a better minimum spanning tree discovery technique [13], a better measure of the cost of an edge in the crawling process as an estimation of its approximate depth in the site, and a refinement of the detection of duplicate pages. iRobot [11,12] is probably the work closest to ours. In contrast with that system, the AAH we propose is applicable to any kind of Web application, as long as it is described in our knowledge base. Also differently from [11,12], where the analysis of the structure of a forum has to be done independently for each site, the AAH exploits the fact that several sites may share the same content management system. Our system also extracts structured and semantic information from the Web pages, where iRobot stores plain HTML files and leaves the extraction for future work. We finally give in Sect. 8 a comparison of the performance of iRobot vs AAH to highlight the superior efficiency of our approach. On the other hand, iRobot aims at a fully automatic means of crawling a Web forum, while the AAH relies on a knowledge base (manually constructed but automatically maintained) of known Web applications or content management systems.

Web Application Detection. As we shall explain, our approach relies on a generic mechanism for detecting the kind of Web application currently crawled. Again there has been some work in the particular cases of blogs or forums. In particular, [14] uses support vector machines (SVM) to detect whether a given page is a blog page. In [14], SVMs are trained using various traditional feature vectors formed of the content's bag of words or bag of n-grams, and some new features for blog detection are introduced such as the bag of linked URLs and the bag of anchors. Relative entropy is used for feature selection.

Wrapper Adaptation. Wrapper adaptation, the problem of adapting a Web information extractor to (minor) changes in the structure of considered Web pages or Web sites, has received quite some attention in the research community. An early work is that of Kushmerick [15] who proposed an approach to analyze Web pages and already extracted information, so as to detect changes in structure. A "wrapper verification" method is introduced that checks whether a wrapper stops extracting data; if so, a human supervisor is notified so as to retrain the wrapper. Chidlovskii [16] introduced some grammatical and logic-based rules to automate the maintenance of wrappers, assuming only slight changes in the structure of Web pages. Meng, Hu, and Li [17] suggested a schema-guided wrapper maintenance approach called SG-WRAM for wrapper adaptation. Lerman, Minton, and Knoblock [18] developed a machine learning system for repairing wrapper for small markup changes. Their proposed system first verifies the extraction from Web pages, and if the extraction fails then it relaunches the wrapper induction for data extraction.

Our template adaptation technique is inspired by the previously cited works: we check whether patterns of our wrapper fail, and if so, we try fixing them assuming minor changes in Web pages, and possibly using previously crawled content on this site. One main difference with existing work is that our approach is also applicable to completely new Web sites, never crawled before, that just share the same content management system and a similar template.

Data Extraction from Blogs, Forums, etc. A number of works [19,20,21] aim at automatic wrapper extraction from CMS-generated Web pages, looking for repeated structure and typically using tree alignment or tree matching techniques. This is out of scope of our approach, where we assume that we have a preexisting knowledge base of Web applications. Gulhane et al. [22] introduced the Vertex wrapper induction system. Vertex detects site changes by monitoring a few sample pages per site. Any structural change can result in changes in page

$\langle \text{expr} \rangle$ $::= \langle \text{step} \rangle \mid \langle \text{step} \rangle$ `"/"` $\langle \text{expr} \rangle$
                              $\langle \text{step} \rangle$ `"//"` $\langle \text{expr} \rangle$
$\langle \text{step} \rangle$ $::= \langle \text{nodetest} \rangle \mid \langle \text{step} \rangle$ `"["` $\langle \text{predicate} \rangle$ `"]"`
$\langle \text{nodetest} \rangle$ $::= tag \mid$ `"@"` $tag \mid$ `"*"` $\mid$ `"@*"` $\mid$ `"text()"`
$\langle \text{predicate} \rangle$ $::=$ `"contains("` $\langle \text{value} \rangle$ `","` $string$ `")"` $\mid$
                              $\langle \text{value} \rangle$ `"="` $string \mid integer \mid$ `"last()"`
$\langle \text{value} \rangle$ $::= tag \mid$ `"@"` tag

Fig. 1. BNF syntax of the XPath fragment used. The following tokens are used: *tag* is a valid XML identifier; *string* is a single- or double-quote encoded XPath character string; *integer* is any positive integer.

shingle vectors that may render learned rules inapplicable. In our system, we do not monitor sampled Web pages but dynamically adapt to pages as we crawl them. The AAH also applies adaptation to different versions of a content management system found on different Web sites, rather than to just a specific Web page type.

3   Preliminaries

This section introduce some definitions that we will use throughout this paper. A *Web application* is any application or Web site that uses Web standards such as HTML and HTTP to publish information on the Web in a specific template, in a way that is accessible by Web browsers. Examples include Web forums, social networking sites, geolocation services, etc. A *Web application type* is the content-management system or server-side technology stack (e.g., vBulletin, WordPress, the proprietary CMS of Flickr, etc.) that powers this Web application and provides interaction with it. Several different Web applications can share the same Web application type (all vBulletin forums use vBulletin), but some Web application types can be specific to a given Web application (e.g., the CMS powering Twitter is specific to that site).

We use a simple subset of the XPath expression language to describe *patterns* in the DOM of Web pages that serve either to identify a Web application type, or to determine navigation or extraction *actions* to apply to that Web page. A grammar for the subset we consider is given in Fig. 1. Basically, we only allow downwards axes and very simple predicates that perform string comparisons. The semantics of these expressions is the standard one. In the following, an *XPath expression* is always one of this sublanguage.

A *detection pattern* is a rule for detecting Web application types and Web application, based on the content of a Web page, HTTP metadata, URL components. It is implemented as an XPath expression over a virtual document that contains the HTML Web page as well as all other HTTP metadata.

A *crawling action* is an XPath expression over an HTML document that indicates which action to perform on a given Web page. Crawling actions can be of two kinds: *navigation actions* point to URLs to be added to the crawling queue; *extraction actions* point to individual semantic objects to be extracted from the Web page (e.g., timestamp, blog post, comment). For instance, `div[contains( @class, 'post')]//h2[@class='post-message']//a/@href` is a navigation action to follow certain types of links.

The application-aware helper distinguishes two main kinds of Web application *levels*: *intermediate* pages, such as lists of forums, lists of threads, can only be associated with navigation actions; *terminal pages*, such as the individual posts in a forum thread, can be associated with both navigation and extraction actions. For intelligent crawling, our AAH needs not only to distinguish among Web application types, but among the different kinds of Web pages that can be produced by a given Web application type. The idea is that the crawler will navigate intermediate pages until a terminal page is found, and only content from this terminal page is extracted; the terminal page may also be navigated, e.g., in the presence of paging.

Given an XPath expression e, a *relaxed expression* for e is one where one or several of the following transformations has been performed:

- a predicate has been removed;
- a *tag* or *string* token has been replaced with another such token.

A *best-case relaxed expression* for e is one where at most one of these transformations has been performed for every step of e. A *worst-case relaxed expression* for e is one where potentially multiple transformations have been performed on any given step of e.

To illustrate, consider e =div[contains(@class,'post')]//h2[@class='post-message']. Examples of best-case relaxed expressions are div[contains(@class,'post')]//h2 or div[contains(@class,'post')]//h2[@id='post-content']; on the other hand, div[contains(@class,'message')]//div[@id='post-content'] is an example worst-case relaxed expression.

4   Knowledge Base

The AAH is assisted by a *knowledge base* of Web application types. This knowledge base specifies how to detect specific Web applications and which crawling actions should be executed. Types are arranged in a hierarchical manner, from general categorizations to specific instances (Web sites) of this Web application. The knowledge base also describes the different levels under a Web application type and then, based on this, different crawling actions that should be executed against this specific page level. The knowledge base is specified in a declarative language, so as to be easily shared and updated, hopefully maintained by non-programmers, and also possibly automatically learned from examples. The W3C has normalized a Web Application Description Language (WADL) [23] for describing resources of HTTP-based applications. WADL does not satisfy all our needs: in particular, there is no place for the description of Web application recognition patterns. Consequently, our knowledge-based is described in a custom XML format.

For each Web application type, and for each level, the knowledge base contains a set of detection patterns that allows to recognize whether a given page is of that type or that level. The vBulletin Web forum CMS can for instance be identified by searching for a reference to a specific script with the detection pattern: script [contains(@src,'vbulletin_global.js')]. Pages of the "list of forums" type are identified[1] when they match the pattern a[@class="forum"]/@href.

Similarly, for each Web application type and level, a set of navigation and extraction actions (for the latter, only in the case of terminal levels) is provided.

---

[1] The example is simplified for the sake of presentation; in reality we have to deal with several different layouts that vBulletin can produce.

5   Application-Aware Helper (AAH)

Our main claim is that different crawling techniques should be applied to different types of Web applications. This means having different crawling strategies for different forms of social Web sites (blogs, wikis, social networks, social bookmarks, microblogs, music networks, Web forums, photo networks, video networks, etc.), for specific content management systems (e.g., WordPress, phpBB), and for specific sites (e.g., Twitter, Facebook). Our proposed approach will detect the type of Web application (general type, content management system, or site) currently processed by the crawler, and the kind of Web pages inside this Web application (e.g., a user profile on a social network) and decide on further crawling actions (following a link, extracting structured content) accordingly. The proposed crawler is intelligent enough to crawl and store all comments related to a given blog post in one place, even if comments stays on several Web pages.

The AAH detects the Web application and Web page type before deciding which crawling strategy is appropriate for the given Web application. More precisely, the AAH works in the following order:

1. it detects the Web application type;
2. it detects the Web application level;
3. it executes the relevant crawling actions: extracting the outcome of extraction actions, and adding the outcome of navigation actions to the URL queue.

The AAH loads the Web application type detection patterns from the knowledge base and executes them against the given Web application. If the Web application type is detected, the system executes all the possible Web application level detection patterns until it gets a match.

The number of detection patterns for detecting Web application type and level will grow with the addition of knowledge about new Web applications. In order to optimize this detection, the system needs to maintain an index of these patterns. To this aim, we have integrated the YFilter system [24] (an NFA-based filtering system for XPath expressions) with slight changes according to our requirements, for efficient indexing of detection patterns, in order to quickly find the relevant Web application types and levels. YFilter is developed as part of a publish–subscribe system that allows users to submit a set of queries that are to be executed against streaming XML pages. By compiling the queries into an automaton to index all provided patterns, the system is able to efficiently find the list of all users who submitted a query that matches the current document. In our integrated version of YFilter, the detection patterns (either for Web application type or level) will be submitted as queries; when a document satisfy a query, the system will stop processing the document against all remaining queries (in contrast to the standard behavior of YFilter), as we do not need more than one match. In addition, to deal with predicates that are present in our language but that YFilter does not support, we modify the system so that additional filters can be tested before validating a match.

Input: a URL u, sets of detection patterns D and crawling actions A
if $alreadyCrawled(u)$ **then**
    if $hasChanged(u)$ **then**
        $markedActions \leftarrow detectAndMarkStructuralChanges(u, A)$;
        $newActions \leftarrow alignCrawlingActions(u, D, markedActions)$;
        $addToKnowledgeBase(newActions)$;

Algorithm 1. Adaptation to template change (recrawl of a Web application)

6 Adaptation to Template Change

We describe here how the AAH adapts to changes in the structure of Web applications. Structural changes w.r.t. the knowledge base may come from varying versions of the content management system, or from alternative templates proposed by the CMS or developed for specific Web applications. The AAH determines when a change has occurred and tries adapting patterns and actions.

We deal with two different cases of adaptation: first, when (part of) a Web application has been crawled before the template change and a recrawl is carried out after that (a common situation in real-world crawl campaigns); second, when crawling a new Web application that matches the Web application type detection patterns but for which (some of) the actions are inapplicable.

Recrawl of a Web Application. We first consider the case when part of a Web application has been crawled successfully using the patterns and actions of the knowledge base. The template of this Web application then changes (because of an update of the content management system, or a redesign of the site) and it is recrawled. Our core adaptation technique relearns appropriate crawling actions for each crawlable object; the knowledge base is then updated by adding newly relearned actions to it.

As later described in Sect. 7, crawled Web pages with their Web objects and metadata are stored in the form of RDF triples into a RDF store. Our proposed system detects structural changes for already crawled Web applications by looking for the content (stored in the RDF store) in the Web pages with the crawling actions used during the previous crawl. If the system fails to extract the same content with these actions, the structure of the Web site has changed.

Algorithm 1 gives a high-level view of the template adaptation mechanism in the case of a recrawl. It first checks whether a given URL has already been crawled by calling the *alreadyCrawled* Boolean function, which just looks for the existence of the URL in the RDF store. An already crawled Web page will then be checked for structured changes with the *hasChanged* Boolean function.

Structural changes are detected by searching for already crawled content (URLs corresponding to navigation actions, Web objects, etc.) in a Web page by using the existing and already learned crawling actions (if any) for the corresponding Web application level. The *hasChanged* function takes care of the fact that failure to extract deleted information should not be considered as a

Input: a URL u and a sets of crawling actions A
if *not alreadyCrawled(u)* **then**
    for $a \in A$ **do**
        if *hasExtractionFailed(u, a)* **then**
            relaxedExpressions ← *getRelaxedExpressions(a)*;
            for *candidate* ∈ *relaxedExpressions* **do**
                if *not hasExtractionFailed(u, candidate)* **then**
                    addToKnowledgeBase(candidate);
                    break;

Algorithm 2. Adaptation to template change (new Web application)

structural change. For instance, a Web object such as a Web forum's *comment* that was crawled before may not exist anymore.

In the presence of structural changes, the system calls the *detectAndMark-StructuralChanges* function which detects inapplicable crawling actions and mark them as "failed". All crawling actions which are marked as failed will be aligned according to structural changes. The *alignCrawlingActions* function will relearn the failed crawling actions.

Crawl of a New Web Application. We are now in the case where we crawl a completely new Web applications whose template is (slightly) different from that present in the knowledge base. We assume that the Web application type detection patterns fired, but either the application level detection patterns or the crawling actions do not work on this specific Web application.

Let us first consider the case where the Web application level detection pattern works. Recall that there are two classes of Web application levels: intermediate and terminal. We make the assumption that on intermediate levels, crawling actions (that are solely navigation actions) do not fail – on that level, navigations actions are usually fairly simple (they typically are simple extensions of the application level detection patterns, e.g., //div[contains(@class, 'post')] for the detection pattern and //div[contains(@class, 'post')]//a/@href for the navigation action). In our experiments we never needed to adapt them. We leave the case where they might fail to future work. On the other hand, we consider that both navigation actions and extraction actions from terminal pages may need to be adapted. The main steps of the adaptation algorithm are described in Algorithm 2. *getRelaxedExpressions* creates two set of relaxed expression (for best-case and worst-case). For each set, different variations of crawling action will be generated by relaxing predicates and tag names, enumerated by the number of relaxation needed (simple relaxations come first). Tag names are replaced with existing tag names of the DOM tree so that the relaxed expression matches. When relaxing an attribute name inside a predicate, the AAH only suggests candidates that would make the predicate true; to do that, the AAH first collects all possible attributes and their values from the page. We favor relaxations that use parts from crawling actions in the knowledge base for other Web application types of the same general category (e.g., Web forum). The system orders expressions by the number of required relaxations (best-case ones first). Any expression which succeeds in the extraction will still be tested with a few more pages of the same Web application level before being added to the knowledge base for future crawling.

If the system does not detect the Web application level, then the crawling strategy cannot be initiated. First, the system tries adapting the detection pattern before fixing crawling actions. The idea is here the same as in the previous part: the system collect all candidate attributes, values, tag names from the knowledge base for the detected Web application type (e.g., WordPress) and then creates all possible combinations of relaxed expressions, ordered by the amount of relaxation, and test them one by one until one that works is found. To illustrate, assume that the candidate set of attributes and values are: @class='post', @id='forum', @class='blog' with candidate set of names article, div, etc. The set of relaxed expression will be generated by trying out each possible combination: // article [contains(@class, 'post')], // article [contains(@id, 'forum')], // article [contains(@class, 'blog')], etc.

7   System

The application-aware helper is implemented in Java. On startup, the system first loads the knowledge base and indexes detection patterns using a YFilter [24] implementation adapted from the one available at http://yfilter.cs.umass.edu/. Once the system receives a crawling request, it first makes a lookup to the YFilter index to detect the Web application type and level. If the Web application type is not detected, the AAH applies the adaptation strategy to find a relaxed match as previously described. If no match is found (i.e., if the Web application is unknown), a generic extraction of links is performed.

When the Web application is successfully detected, the AAH loads the corresponding crawling strategy from the knowledge base and crawls the Web application accordingly, possibly using the adaptation strategy. Crawled Web pages are stored in the form of WARC [25] files – the standard preservation format for Web archiving – whereas structured content (individual Web objects with their semantic metadata) is stored in an RDF store. The knowledge base is potentially updated with new detection patterns or crawling actions.

The AAH is integrated with Heritrix [6], the open-source crawler[2] developed by the Internet Archive. In the crawl processing chain, the AAH replaces the conventional link extraction module. Crawling actions determined by the AAH are fed back into the URL queue of Heritrix.

The open-source AAH code and the list of all sites in our experimental dataset are available at http://perso.telecom-paristech.fr/~faheem/aah.html.

---

[2] http://crawler.archive.org/

8   Experiments

We present in this section experimental performance of our proposed system on its own and with respect to a baseline crawler, GNU wget[3] (since the scope of the crawl is quite simple – complete crawling of specific domain names – wget is as good as Heritrix here).

Experiment Setup. To evaluate the performance of our system, we have crawled 100 Web applications (totaling nearly 3.3 millions Web pages) of two forms of social Web sites (Web forum and blog), for three specific content management system (vBulletin, phpBB, and WordPress). The Web applications of type WordPress (33 Web applications, 1.1 million of Web pages), vBulletin (33 Web applications, 1.2 million of Web pages) and phpBB (34 Web applications, 1 million Web pages) were randomly selected from three different sources:

1. http://rankings.big-boards.com/, a database of popular Web forums.
2. A dataset related to European financial crisis.
3. A dataset related to the *Rock am Ring* music festival in Germany.

The second and third datasets were collected in the framework of the AR-COMEM project[4]. In these real-world datasets corresponding to specific archival tasks, 68% of the seed URLs of Web forum type belongs to either vBulletin or phpBB, which explains while we target these two CMSs. WordPress is also a prevalent CMS: the Web as a whole has over 61 million Wordpress sites [26] out of a number of blogs indexed by Technorati [27] of around 133 million. Moreover, Wordpress has a 48% market share of the top 100 blogs [28]. All 100 Web applications were both crawled using wget and the AAH. Both crawlers are configured to retrieve only HTML documents, disregarding scripts, stylesheets, media files, etc.

The knowledge base is populated with detection patterns and crawling actions for one specific version of the three considered CMSs (other versions will be handled by the adaptation module). Adding a new Web application type to the knowledge base takes a crawl engineer of the order of 30 minutes.

Performance Metrics. The performance of the AAH will be mainly measured by evaluating the number of HTTP requests made by both systems vs the amount of *useful* content retrieved. Evaluating the number of HTTP requests is easy to perform by simply counting requests made by both crawlers. Coverage of useful content is more subjective and we use the following proxies:

1. Counting the amount of textual content that has been retrieved. For that, we compare the proportion of 2-grams (sequences of two consecutive words) in the crawl result of both systems, for every Web application.
2. Counting the number of external links (i.e., hyperlinks to another domain) found in the two crawls. The idea is that external links are a particularly important part of the content of a Web site.

---

[3] http://www.gnu.org/software/wget/
[4] http://www.arcomem.eu/

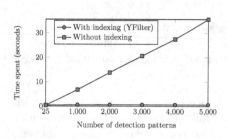

Fig. 2. Performance of the detection module

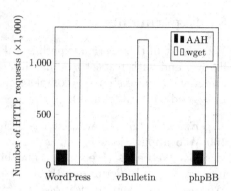

Fig. 3. Total number of HTTP requests used to crawl the dataset

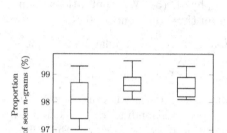

Fig. 4. Box chart of the proportion of seen *n*-grams for the three considered CMSs. We show in each case the minimum and maximum values (whiskers), first and third quartiles (box) and median (horizontal rule).

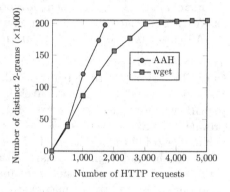

Fig. 5.   Crawling   `http://www.rockamring-blog.de/`

Efficiency of Detection Patterns. We first briefly discuss the use of YFilter to speed up the indexing of detection patterns. In Fig. 2 we show the time required to determine Web application type in a synthetically generated knowledge base as the number of Web application types grows up to 5,000, with or without using YFilter indexing. The system takes a time linear in the number of detection patterns when indexing is turned off, taking up to several dozens of seconds. On the other hand, detection time is essentially constant with YFilter activated.

Crawl Efficiency. We compare the number of HTTP requests required by both crawlers to crawl each set of Web applications of the same type in Fig. 3. Notice how the application-aware helper makes much fewer requests (on average 7 times fewer) than a regular blind crawl. Indeed, for blog-like Web sites, a regular crawler make redundant HTTP requests for the same Web content, accessing to a post by tag, author, year, chronological order, etc. In a Web forum, many requests end up being search boxes, edit areas, print view of a post, areas protected by authentication, etc.

Table 1. Coverage of external links in the dataset crawled by the AAH

CMS	External links	External links (w/o boilerplate)
WordPress	92.7%	99.8%
vBulletin	90.5%	99.5%
phpBB	92.1%	99.6%

Crawl Effectiveness. The crawling results, in terms of coverage of useful content, are summarized in Fig. 4 and in Table 1. Figure 4 presents the distribution of the proportion of n-grams crawled by the AAH with respect to those of the full crawl. Not only are the numbers are generally very high (for the three types, the median is greater than 98%), but the results are also very stable, with a very low variance: the worst coverage score on our whole dataset is greater than 97% (typically, lower scores are achieved for small Web sites where the amount of boilerplate text such as menus or terms of use remains non negligible). This hints at the statistical significance of the results.

The proportion of external links covered by the AAH is given in Table 1. The application-aware helper has ignored nearly 10 percent of external links since every page may use widgets, such as those of Facebook, Amazon, etc., with URLs varying from one page to another. Once we have excluded boilerplate with defined set of patters, we see that more than 99.5% of the external links are present in the content crawled by the AAH.

To reach a better understanding of how an application-aware crawl enfolds, we plot in Fig. 5 the number of distinct 2-grams discovered by the AAH and wget during one crawl (in this particular case, of a given WordPress blog), as the number of requests increase. We see that the AAH directly targets the interesting part of the Web application, with a number of newly discovered 2-grams that grows linearly with the number of requests made, to reach a final level of 98% 2-gram coverage after 1,705 requests. On the other hand, wget discovers new content with a lower rate, and, especially, spends the last 2/5 of its requests discovering very few new 2-grams.

Comparison to iRobot. The iRobot system [11] that we discussed in Sect. 2 is not available for testing because of intellectual property reasons. The experiments of [11] are somewhat limited in scope, since only 50,000 Web pages are considered, over 10 different forum Web sites (to compare with our evaluation, on 3.3 million Web pages, over 100 different forum or blog Web sites). To compare the AAH to iRobot, we have crawled one of the same Web forum used in [11]: http://forums.asp.net/ (over 50,000 Web pages). The completeness of content of the AAH (in terms of both 2-grams and external links, boilerplate excluded) is over 99 percent; iRobot has a coverage of *valuable pages* (as evaluated by a human being) of 93 percent on the same Web application. The number of HTTP requests for iRobot is claimed in [11] to be 1.73 times less than a

Table 2. Examples of structural pattern changes: desktop vs mobile version of http://www.androidpolice.com/

Desktop version	Mobile version
div[@class='post_title']/h3/a	div[@class='post_title']/h2/a
div[@class='post_info']	div[@class='post_author']
div[@class='post_content']	div[@class='content']

regular Web crawler; on the http://forums.asp.net/ Web application, the AAH makes 10 times fewer requests than wget does.

Adaptation When Recrawling a Web Application. To test our adaptation technique in the case of a recrawl of a Web application in a realistic environment (without having to wait for Web sites actually to change), we have considered sites that have both a desktop and mobile version with different HTML content. These sites use two different templates to present what is essentially the same content. We simulated a recrawl by first crawling the Web site with a User-Agent: HTTP header indicating a regular Web spider (the desktop version is then served) and then recrawling the mobile version using a mobile browser User-Agent:.

Our system was not only able to detect the structural changes from one version to another, but also, using already crawled content, to fix the failed crawling actions. Table 2 presents one exemplary Web application that has both a desktop and mobile versions, with a partial list of the structural changes in the patterns across the two versions. Our system was able to automatically correct these structure changes in both navigation and extraction, reaching a perfect agreement between the content extracted by the two crawls.

Adaptation for a New Web Application. As stated earlier, we have experimented our system with 100 Web applications, starting from a straightforward knowledge base containing information about one specific version of the three considered content management systems. Among the 100 applications, 77 did not require any adaptation, which illustrates that many Web applications share common templates. The 23 remaining ones had a structure that did not match the crawling actions in the knowledge base; the AAH has applied adaptation successfully to these 23 cases. Most of the adaptation consisted in relaxing the class or id attribute rather than replacing the tag name of an element. When there was a tag name change, it was most often from span to div to article or vice versa, which is fairly straightforward to adapt. There was no case in the dataset when more than one relaxation for a given step of an XPath expression was needed; in other words, only best-case relaxed expressions were used. In 2 cases, the AAH was unable to adapt all extraction actions, but navigation actions still worked or could be adapted, which means the Web site could still be crawled, but some structured content was missing.

9   Conclusions

In Web archiving, scarce resources are bandwidth, crawling time, and storage space rather than computation time [5]. We have shown how application-aware crawling can help reduce bandwidth, time, and storage (by requiring less HTTP requests to crawl an entire Web application, avoiding duplicates) using limited computational resources in the process (to apply crawling actions on Web pages). Application-aware crawling also helps adding semantics to Web archives, increasing their value to users.

Our work can be extended in several ways, that we shall explore in future work. First, we can enrich the pattern language we use to allow for more complex detection and extraction rules, moving to a full support of XPath or even more powerful Web navigation languages allowing to crawl complex Web applications making use of AJAX or Web forms. There is a trade-off, however, between the expressive power of the language and the simplicity of template adaptations. Second, we want to move towards an automatically constructed knowledge base of Web applications, either by asking a human being to automatically annotate the part of a Web application to extract or crawl, using semi-supervised machine learning techniques, or even by discovering in an unsupervised manner new Web application types by comparing the structure of different Web sites, determining the optimal way to crawl them by sampling, in the spirit of iRobot [11].

Acknowledgment. This work was funded by the European Union's Seventh Framework Program (FP7/2007–2013) under grant agreement 270239 (AR-COMEM).

References

1. Jupp, E.: Obama's victory tweet 'four more years' makes history. The Independent (November 2012), http://ind.pn/RF5Q60
2. Coleman, S.: Blogs and the new politics of listening. The Political Quarterly 76(2) (2008)
3. Mulvenon, J.C., Chase, M.: You've Got Dissent! Chinese Dissident Use of the Internet and Beijing's Counter Strategies. Rand Publishing (2002)
4. Giles, J.: Internet encyclopaedias go head to head. Nature 438 (2005)
5. Masanès, J.: Web archiving. Springer (2006)
6. Sigurðsson, K.: Incremental crawling with Heritrix. In: IWAW (2005)
7. Faheem, M.: Intelligent crawling of Web applications for Web archiving. In: WWW PhD Symposium (2012)
8. Chakrabarti, S., van den Berg, M., Dom, B.: Focused crawling: A new approach to topic-specific Web resource discovery. Comp. Networks 31(11-16) (1999)
9. Gibson, D., Punera, K., Tomkins, A.: The volume and evolution of Web page templates. In: WWW (2005)
10. Guo, Y., Li, K., Zhang, K., Zhang, G.: Board forum crawling: A Web crawling method for Web forums. In: Web Intelligence (2006)
11. Cai, R., Yang, J.M., Lai, W., Wang, Y., Zhang, L.: iRobot: An intelligent crawler for Web forums. In: WWW (2008)

12. Ying, H.M., Thing, V.: An enhanced intelligent forum crawler. In: CISDA (2012)
13. Edmonds, J.: Optimum branchings. J. Res. Nat. Bureau Standards 71B (1967)
14. Kolari, P., Finin, T., Joshi, A.: SVMs for the blogosphere: Blog identification and splog detection. In: AAAI (2006)
15. Kushmerick, N.: Regression testing for wrapper maintenance. In: AAAI (1999)
16. Chidlovskii, B.: Automatic repairing of Web wrappers. In: WIDM (2001)
17. Meng, X., Hu, D., Li, C.: Schema-guided wrapper maintenance for Web-data extraction. In: WIDM (2003)
18. Lerman, K., Minton, S.N., Knoblock, C.A.: Wrapper maintenance: A machine learning approach. J. A. I. Res. (2003)
19. Lim, S.J., Ng, Y.K.: An automated change-detection algorithm for HTML documents based on semantic hierarchies. In: ICDE (2001)
20. Artail, H., Fawaz, K.: A fast HTML Web page change detection approach based on hashing and reducing the number of similarity computations. Data Knowl. Eng. (2008)
21. Ferrara, E., Baumgartner, R.: Automatic wrapper adaptation by tree edit distance matching. In: Hatzilygeroudis, I., Prentzas, J. (eds.) Combinations of Intelligent Methods and Applications. SIST, vol. 8, pp. 41–54. Springer, Heidelberg (2011)
22. Gulhane, P., Madaan, A., Mehta, R., Ramamirtham, J., Rastogi, R., Satpal, S., Sengamedu, S.H., Tengli, A., Tiwari, C.: Web-scale information extraction with vertex. In: ICDE (2011)
23. W3C: Web application description language (2009), http://www.w3.org/Submission/wadl/
24. Diao, Y., Altinel, M., Franklin, M.J., Zhang, H., Fischer, P.: Path sharing and predicate evaluation for high-performance XML filtering. ACM TODS (2003)
25. ISO: ISO 28500:2009, Information and documentation – WARC file format
26. WordPress: WordPress sites in the world (2012), http://en.wordpress.com/stats/
27. The Future Buzz: Social media, Web 2.0 and internet stats (2009), http://goo.gl/HOFNF
28. Royal Pingdom: WordPress completely dominates top 100 blogs (2012), http://goo.gl/eifRJ

Enhancing Web Revisitation
by Contextual Keywords

Tangjian Deng, Liang Zhao, and Ling Feng

Tsinghua National Laboratory for Information Science and Technology
Dept. of Computer Science and Technology, Tsinghua University, Beijing, China
{dtj08,jing-zhao11}@mails.tsinghua.edu.cn, fengling@tsinghua.edu.cn

Abstract. Web revisitation is a common behavior supported by many web history tools. Taking advantages of access context (like time, location, concurrent activity), context-based search of previously accessed web pages is also being investigated, due to the fact that context under which information is accessed tends to be more easily to remember than content. To mimic users' memory recall, we present a way to automatically capture user's access context from user's concurrent computer programs, and manage it in a probabilistic context tree for each accessed web page in a life cycle. An algorithm for contextual keyword search of accessed web pages, together with a revisitation feedback mechanism, are also given. We evaluate the proposed method on synthetic data and through a 6-week user study. The comparisons of revisit precision and recall show our method outperforms the existing contextual search method *YouPivot*. In the user study, our method can also work as effectively as popular methods (like bookmark, browse history) in recall rate (over 90%), while with less average time cost (16.25 seconds) than that (38.66 seconds) of those methods to complete a web revisitation task.

Keywords: Web revisitation, context memory, contextual keyword search, revisitation feedback.

1 Introduction

Web Revisitation Support. The web is playing a significant role in people's daily activities in delivering information to one's fingertips. Among the common web behavior, revisitation of previously browsed web pages constitutes an important web access portion [5,2,21]. According to [17], over 58% of web pages accessed by 23 users within a 6-week period were revisited ones. The analysis of a 1-year web search by 114 users also revealed that around 40% of queries belong to revisitation requests [19]. To support web revisitation, a number of web history techniques and tools have been developed [14,1,10,22,3].

Bookmark. Manual bookmark of favorite web pages embedded in web browser is a traditional way to enable users to re-locate the visited pages. Users can also mark a specific part within a visited web page by the *Landmark* tool [13]. The *SearchBar* [15] allows users to organize their search keywords and clicked pages under different topics for easy navigation.

F. Daniel, P. Dolog, and Q. Li (Eds.): ICWE 2013, LNCS 7977, pp. 323–337, 2013.

History Tools. Web browsers maintain users' accessed URLs according to visit time (*e.g., today, yesterday, last week, etc.*). *Google Web History*[1] keeps users' search keywords and clicked pages, then puts them into different categories like image, news, normal page, and so on. Users can either navigate or search the history by keywords from accessed page titles/contents. The *Contextual Web History* [22] improves the visual appearance of web browser history by combining thumbnails of web sites and snippets of contents, assisting users to easily browse or search the history by time. The dynamic browser toolbar [11] can further recommend relevant visited pages according to the currently viewed page.

Re:Search Engine. The *Re:Search* system [18] can support simultaneous finding and re-finding on the web. When a user's query is similar to a previous query, *Re:Search* obtains the current results from an existing search engine, and fetches relevant previously viewed results from its cache. The newly available results are then merged with the previously viewed results to create a list that supports intuitive re-finding and contains new information.

Contextual Search. Access context is also exploited for web revisitation, due to the fact that context under which information is accessed sometimes is more easily to remember than content itself [4,20]. [9] developed a *YouPivot* system, which allows users to search the context they remember, so that users can see what was going on under that context. User's web activities are logged via the Chrome Extension and sent to *YouPivot*, which also pulls LastFM and Twitter data and retrieves calendar data via public ICS files. Also, the user can time-mark a moment worth remembering, and provide a description on it for contextual recall in *YouPivot*. [6,7] also developed a *ReFinder* system to allow users to manually annotate such access context as time, location, and concurrent activity for the visited web pages or local files, with which the users can pose structured re-find requests to the previously accessed web pages or files.

YouPivot and *ReFinder* are two closely related work of this study, with the following differences.

- Instead of prompting users to manually annotate access context as done by *ReFinder*, this paper proposes a method to automatically capture the access context through users' computer programs running before and after the access event. Historical access context is managed in probabilistic context trees, each linked to an accessed web page URL. Later users can revisit the web pages by contextual keywords. This is different from the *ReFinder* system which only supports structured context-based re-search.
- Unlike *YouPivot* which keeps context persistently, this study considers progressive evolution of historical access context trees, since along with human memory fade, the past context for recall will also degrade gradually. Revisitation requests can thus be more realistically interpreted and fast executed.
- To tailor to different users' revisitation habits, we incorporate a feedback mechanism during users' web revisitation to dynamically adjust historical context memory and relevant result ranking. This is not discussed in either *YouPivot* or *ReFinder*.

---

[1] http://www.google.com/history

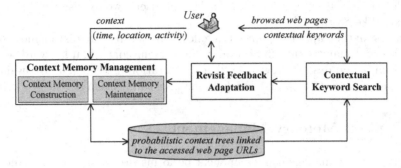

Fig. 1. Our web revisitation framework

Our Work. Fig. 1 outlines the basic idea and framework of our contextual keywords based web revisitation, consisting of three components: *context memory management, contextual keyword search,* and *revisit feedback adaptation.*

1) *Context Memory Management.* It captures and represents each access context as a *probabilistic context tree*, bounded with the corresponding accessed web page URL. The tree is comprised of contextual keywords, inferred automatically from user's running computer programs. The probability assigned to each keyword node reflects how likely the user will use the keywords for later revisit. The probabilistic context trees are organized as a context memory, evolving along with the elapsing time. The keyword nodes are measured by retention strengths, which will decrease as they age, leading to the circumstance that the contextual keywords may become from specific to general. Meanwhile, the keyword nodes' probabilities will decrease gradually due to memory decay.

2) *Contextual Keyword Search.* Since the mappings between web pages and probabilistic context trees have been built, we take the contextual keywords as input, and produce a list of web pages as output. For a contextual keyword search, we find out all the match trees with non-zero probabilities, where the trees are ranked based on their probabilities from high to low. Then the visited web pages linked by the trees are returned straightforwardly.

3) *Revisit Feedback Adaptation.* From the user's actions of web revisitation by contextual keywords, the revisited web pages and the revisit conditions (the match contexts) are recorded as user's revisit feedbacks, which are then used to guide the adjustments on context memory construction and maintenance.

We evaluate our approach by conducting two sets of experiments with synthetic data and through a 6-week user study. In the synthetic data experiment, we simulate the contextual search method *YouPivot* and use it as a baseline. The comparisons of revisit precision and recall show our method outperforms *YouPivot,* as our method can adapt to the user's revisitation habit. In the user study, the revisit recall rate of our revisit prototype is over 90%. On average, 16.25 seconds are needed to complete a web revisitation task with our method and 38.66 seconds with popular methods like bookmark, browse history, search engines, *etc.* The experimental results show that our prototype provides a complementary effective solution in facilitating user's web revisitation through contextual keywords.

The rest of the paper is organized as follows. We address context memory construction and maintenance in Section 2. We present contextual keyword search in Section 3, and describe revisit feedback adaptation in Section 4. We evaluate our approach in Section 5 and conclude the paper in Section 6.

2   Context Memory Management

Context memory management component performs two tasks, *i.e.*, construction of context memory, followed by dynamic maintenance of the context memory.

2.1   Context Memory Construction

Three kinds of user's access context, *i.e.*, *access time*, *access location*, and *concurrent activity*, are considered in this study. *Access time* is determinate. *Access location* is obtained based on the IP address of user's computing device or his/her possible GPS information if available. We infer user's *concurrent activity* from his/her computer programs running before and after the page access as follows.

We continuously monitors the change of the current focus program window during the user's interacting with his/her computer. Each focus object held by the program window can be either a web page or not like a word document, a friend with whom the user is chatting online, *etc.* A focus window possesses a start time, an end time, and a focus time length.

Definition 1. *The user's computer activities is a sequence of focus windows, denoted as $\mathcal{O} = \langle O_1, O_2, \ldots \rangle$, where O_i ($i \geq 1$) denotes a quadruple (t_{begin}, t_{end}, t_{focus}, object) representing the start time, the end time, the focus time length and the focus object respectively. For any $1 \leq i < j$,*

(1) $O_i(t_{begin}) \leq O_j(t_{begin})$;

(2) $O_i(t_{focus}) \leq Length(O_i(t_{end}) - O_i(t_{begin}))$;

(3) if $O_i(object) = O_j(object)$, then $Length(O_j(t_{begin}) - O_i(t_{end})) > \tau_{gap}$.

Table 1. An example of the user's computer activities

No.	Start Time	End Time	Focus Time (sec)	Window Object
1	*2012/8/9 10:04:24*	*2012/8/9 10:09:47*	96	*MSN - Lily*
2	*2012/8/9 10:05:38*	*2012/8/9 10:16:38*	128	*eBay - jeans*
3	*2012/8/9 10:06:07*	*2012/8/9 10:06:20*	13	*eBay - shoes*
4	*2012/8/9 10:06:51*	*2012/8/9 10:13:03*	199	*eBay - shirt*
...	...	...	...	...

If the objects of any two focus windows are the same and the time gap between them is less than a threshold τ_{gap} (10 minutes), they will be merged together as one window. Table 1 demonstrates an example of the user's computer activities. In this study, if the focus time length of a browsed web page is greater than a threshold $\tau_{wf} = 30$ seconds, we consider it as a to-be-revisited web page. Note that τ_{wf} will adjust based on user's revisit feedback.

Definition 2. *Let w_p be a to-be-revisited web page, a time window $\mathcal{T}_W$ $(w_p(t_{begin}) - \Delta t_b, w_p(t_{end}) + \Delta t_e)$, a threshold of focus time length τ_{cf}. For every $O_c \in \mathcal{O}$ (the sequence of focus windows) overlaps with $\mathcal{T}_W$, namely, $O_c(t_{begin}) < (w_p(t_{end}) + \Delta t_e)$ and $O_c(t_{end}) > (w_p(t_{begin}) - \Delta t_b)$, if $O_c(t_{focus}) \geq \tau_{cf}$, then O_c is considered as an **associated context** for w_p.*

The associated contexts for w_p depend on the 3 parameters Δt_b, Δt_e and τ_{cf}. Initially, we set $\Delta t_b = \Delta t_e = 10$ minutes, $\tau_{cf} = 90$ seconds. They will adjust to the user's revisit feedbacks, and the details are described in Section 4.

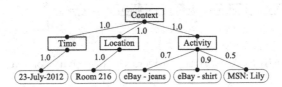

Fig. 2. Example of a probabilistic context tree

Consider the uncertain characteristic of user's memory, the obtained associated contexts are formulated into a probabilistic context tree. An example of context tree is shown in Fig. 2. Besides access time and location, each context extracted from user computer activities forms a leaf node of the context tree. The edge linking a child node to a parent node in the context tree has a probability in $[0, 1]$. It reflects the likelihood that the child node is used as a contextual recall cue. For simplicity, all the edges are set as probability 1.0, except the ones linking the activity leaf nodes and their parent nodes. We use the association probability between an activity context O_c and the to-be-revisited web page w_p as the probability of the edge linking O_c and its parent node. To compute the association probability, we consider four features: 1) the focus time length of O_c; 2) the appearing times of O_c; 3) the time distance between O_c and w_p; and 4) the content similarity between O_c and w_p, $sim(O_c, w_p) = \frac{TermCount(O_c \wedge w_p)}{TermCount(O_c)}$. We normalize the four values within the same context tree, denoted as f_1, f_2, f_3 and f_4, respectively, where $0 \leq f_i \leq 1$ ($i = 1, 2, 3, 4$). Taking the four features into account, the initial association probability pr_0 between O_c and w_p is computed:

$$pr_0 = (f_1 + (1 - f_2) + (1 - f_3) + f_4)/4 \qquad (1)$$

Intuitively, the longer the focus time length of the context and the more similar the context to the web page, the larger association probability between them, while the appearing times of the context and the time distance between the context and the web page lead to the opposite case.

2.2   Context Memory Maintenance

Probabilistic context trees in the context memory evolves dynamically in life cycles to reflect the gradual degradation of human's context memorization as well as the contextual keywords that human users will use for recall. For each leaf node in a probabilistic context tree, both its value and its association probability will progressively decay with time.

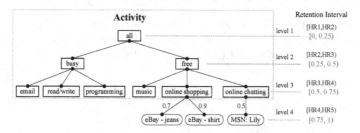

Fig. 3. An abstraction hierarchy of activity context

Taking the *actitivity* context type for example, we build an n-leveled abstraction hierarchy H, where lower-leveled activity values are more precise than upper-leveled ones, as shown in Fig. 3. The captured "*eBay-jeans*" activity value is initially located at the bottom level n. It will climb upwards along H, and finally disappear when reaching the top level 1. In order to quantitatively measure such a context value degradation process, we introduce and compute the *retention strength* $R \in [0, 1]$ of a context value v, based on which we determine its locating level in the hierarchy. Assume each hierarchical level has a reference retention interval $[HR_i, HR_{i+1})$ $(1 \le i \le n)$, which is evenly distributed in $[0, 1]$ in this study. If v's retention strength R falls into $[HR_i, HR_{i+1})$, then the context value belongs to level i. According to the psychology studies [16], we define the retention strength of a context value in its context hierarchy as a function of the exponential in the square root of time.

For context value v captured and assigned web page association probability pr_0. It initially situates at the bottom level n of its n-leveled context hierarchy H. Let $[HR_i, HR_{i+1})$ be the retention interval of the i-th hierarchical level in H. At v's age t, the **retention strength** of v is defined as:

$$R(t) = r_0 \cdot e^{-\lambda \sqrt{t}} \tag{2}$$

where λ is the context memory decay rate, and r_0 is the initial retention strength of v, computed as: $r_0 = HR_n + (HR_{n+1} - HR_n) \cdot pr_0 \quad \in [HR_n, HR_{n+1})$.

Intuitively, the larger v's web page association probability pr_0 is, the better the context value v is remembered. Thus, pr_0 affects r_0 positively.

Assume after age $t_{01} \in [T_{min}, T_{max}]$, v will start to degrade from the bottom level n to its upper level n-1, where

$$t_{01} = T_{min} + (T_{max} - T_{min}) \cdot pr_0 \qquad (3)$$

and T_{min} and T_{max} are user-dependent, and initially set to 14 days and 21 days in this study. The revisitation feedback mechanism will adjust the two settings based on user's revisitation requests and result ranking.

Putting HR_n and t_{01} into Equation 2, we get

$$\lambda = \frac{1}{\sqrt{t_{01}}} \ln \frac{r_0}{HR_n} = \frac{1}{\sqrt{T_{min} + (T_{max} - T_{min}) \cdot pr_0}} \ln \frac{r_0}{HR_n} \qquad (4)$$

With r_0 and λ, we can compute the retention strength $R(t)$ of v at age t according to Equation 2. If it falls in the range of $[HR_i, HR_{i+1})$, then context value v degraded to the i-th level of H.

In a similar fashion, the web page association probability pr_0 of context value v also evolves along with the elapsing time.

$$Pr(t) = pr_0 \cdot e^{-\lambda \sqrt{t}} \qquad (5)$$

After each degradation computation, the decay rate λ is adjusted to $\lambda = \frac{1}{\sqrt{T_{min} + (T_{max} - T_{min}) \cdot Pr(t)}} \ln \frac{r_0}{HR_n}$.

3   Contextual Keyword Search

Given a set of contextual keywords as a user's revisit request $Q = \{k_1, k_2, \ldots, k_n\}$, we evaluate it over the context memory, and returns a ranked list of the match probabilistic context trees with their linked web pages as the final result. Evaluation of Q proceeds in two steps. Nodes containing contextual keywords are first identified. Their contribution to the final tree ranking is then computed.

We apply the Dewey encoding scheme to probabilistic context trees based on [8,23,12]. In our probabilistic context trees, the Dewey number of the root is actually the tree id. For each node v in a probabilistic context tree, we build an index according to its keywords. The mapping between the node and its all probabilities (from the root to it) is also kept, denoted as $\varphi : v \to PrLink$, e.g., the node "eBay - jeans" $\to \langle 1.0, 0.7 \rangle$ as shown in Fig. 2. Through scanning the keyword inverted node lists, the match nodes are identified. The relationship between a node v and its local probabilistic keyword distributions $dist$ w.r.t. Q is maintained, denoted as $\mu : v \to dist$. Assume $PNode \leadsto \{CNode_1, CNode_2, \ldots, CNode_m\}$, where $CNode_i$ is a relevant child node of $PNode$ against Q, $1 \le i \le m$. The computation of $PNode$'s keyword distributions is as follows: for each $1 \le i \le m$, $\mu : CNode_i \to dist$ is promoted by multiplying $Pr_{rev}(PNode \leadsto CNode_i)$ (the probability of the edge) and the part $0 \to \mu_0$ is set to $1 - Pr_{rev}(PNode \rightsquigarrow CNode_i)$. Then $\mu : PNode \rightarrow dist$ is merged using a set of bitwise **OR** operations with $\mu : CNode_i \rightarrow dist$, i.e., multiply $\mu : PNode$ with each part of $\mu : CNode_i$ and then add the product to the corresponding part (based on the bitwise **OR** operation) of $\mu : PNode$.

Since the tree id can be easily got from the Dewey code of a node, based on the match nodes, we can easily get the match context trees, whose probabilities of matching the revisit request Q can be computed accordingly. Assume there are m match nodes $v_1, ..., v_m$ in a context tree, p be the lowest common ancestor of the m match nodes. We compute, promote and merge the keyword distributions of the m match nodes into that of the p node, denoted as $S = \{v_1, ..., v_m\} \rightarrow S = \{p\}$. During the promotion process, especially, for $\forall v \in S$, if $\nexists c \in S$ satisfying that c is a descendent of v, then v can be promoted to its parent v_p. The keyword distributions of v_p are created or updated at the same time. Then v is removed from S, while v_p is put into S if $v_p \notin S$. Let $Pr(path_p)$ be the product of the probabilities from the root to p, $p.\mu_{2^n-1}$ be the distribution $(2^n - 1) \rightarrow \mu_{2^n-1}$, then the probability that the context tree matches Q equals $Pr(path_p) \cdot p.\mu_{2^n-1}$.

Algorithm 1. Context-Based Revisit Algorithm

---

input:
    a revisit request $Q = \{k_1, ..., k_n\}$ and a set of probabilistic context trees
output:
    a ranked list of context trees $\mathcal{R}$ that match request Q
1: load node list $L = \{L_i\}$, $1 \le i \le n$, $\varphi : v \rightarrow PrLink$, determine the match context
    trees $T = \{ct_1, ct_2, ...\}$ based on L, create and update $\mu : v \rightarrow dist$;
2: **for** each $ct \in T$ **do**
3:    divide the match nodes of ct into $S = \{S_i\}$, $1 \le i \le \mathcal{L}$, $S.num = \sum |S_i|$;
4:    **for** $i = \mathcal{L}$; $i \ge 1$; $--i$ **do**
5:      **if** $|S_i| = 0$ **then**
6:        **continue;**
7:      **for** each $v \in S_i$ **do**
8:        **if** $S.num = 1$ **then**
9:          $ct.prob = \text{ComputeProb}(v \rightarrow dist, v \rightarrow PrLink)$;
10:         **if** $ct.prob > 0$ **then**
11:           insert ct into $\mathcal{R}$ according to $ct.prob$;
12:          $i = 0$; **break;**
13:        let p be the parent of v;
14:        **if** $p \notin S_{i-1}$ **then**
15:          create $p \rightarrow PrLink$ and $p \rightarrow dist$, put p into S_{i-1};
16:        **else**
17:          update $p \rightarrow PrLink$ and $p \rightarrow dist$, decrease $S.num$ by 1;
18:        remove v from S_i;
19: **return** $\mathcal{R}$;

Example 1.   Consider the context tree shown in Fig. 2 w.r.t. a revisit request $\{eBay, jeans\}$. *Two match nodes "eBay - jeans" and "eBay - shirt" are got. The* *first node with distributions {'11'→1, '10'→0, '01'→0, '00'→0} and the second node with distributions {'11'→0, '10'→1, '01'→0, '00'→0} need to promote to their parent node "Activity", whose distributions is computed as {'11'→0.7, '10'→0.27, '01'→0, '00'→0.03}. Hence, the probability of the context tree matching the revisit request is $1.0 \cdot 0.7 = 0.7$.*

The algorithm for finding the match context trees and computing their probabilities is illustrated in Algorithm 1. It scans the keyword inverted node lists once and determines the elementary match context trees based on the match nodes. To compute the probability of a match context tree, it firstly divides the match nodes into different sets based on their hierarchical levels, and then promotes and merges the nodes one by one starting from the lowest level set. It stops the promotion process if there remains only one node, which is no other than the lowest common ancestor of the match nodes. The match context tree will be inserted into the result list at the right position if its probability *w.r.t.* the revisit request is larger than zero.

Complexity Analysis: (1) *Time.* Identifying the match context trees T (Line 1) takes $O(n \cdot |T|)$. Dividing the match nodes into different sets (Line 3) takes $O(\sum_{i=1}^{\mathcal{L}} |\mathcal{S}_i|)$. Promoting and merging the match nodes (Line 4 - 18) takes $O(\mathcal{L} \cdot \sum_{i=1}^{\mathcal{L}} |\mathcal{S}_i|)$. Thus, the total time cost is $O(n \cdot |T|) + O(|T| \cdot \mathcal{L} \cdot \sum_{i=1}^{\mathcal{L}} |\mathcal{S}_i|)$ $= O(|T| \cdot \mathcal{L} \cdot \sum_{i=1}^{\mathcal{L}} |\mathcal{S}_i|)$. Clearly, it depends on the number of match context trees, the depth of the context tree and the number of the match nodes. (2) *Space.* In computing the rankings of the match context trees, we need to store the match nodes temporally. So the additional space cost is $\sum_{i=1}^{\mathcal{L}} \beta \cdot |\mathcal{S}_i| \cdot T$, where β is the cost for storing a match node, T is the number of match context trees and $|\mathcal{S}_i|$ is the number of match nodes in the ith level of a context tree.

4   Revisit Feedback Adaptation

As the outcome of context memory construction and maintenance will directly impact the actions of the user's web revisitation by contextual keywords, the user's revisit feedbacks should be taken into account in the on-going management of context memory, so as to provide more suitable contexts for the user to search.

The user's revisit feedbacks, denoted as $\mathcal{F} = (\mathcal{W}_R, \mathcal{C}_R)$, are comprised of a set of true revisit web pages $\mathcal{W}_R$ and a set of the corresponding revisit conditions (match contexts) $\mathcal{C}_R$, obtained from the user's revisit actions. Based on $\mathcal{F}$, some useful information depicting the user's revisit habit can be got, *e.g.*, the focus time lengths of the revisited web pages and the match contexts, as well as the time distance between them, *etc*. Besides, if the match contexts are at the second lowest hierarchical level, their current ages are recorded.

For convenient reference, we denote $\mathcal{H} = (W_F, C_F, \Delta T_B, \Delta T_E, D\tau)$ as the parameters characterizing the user's web revisitation habit, where W_F is the set of the focus time lengths of $\mathcal{W}_R$, C_F is the set of the focus time lengths of $\mathcal{C}_R$, ΔT_B and ΔT_E are the sets of the lengths of $(\mathcal{W}_R(t_{begin}) - \mathcal{C}_R(t_{end}))$ and $(\mathcal{W}_R(t_{end}) - \mathcal{C}_R(t_{begin}))$ respectively, and $D\tau$ is the set of ages at which $\mathcal{C}_R$ decay from the bottom level to the next upper level.

Assumption 1. *The parameters W_F, C_F, ΔT_B and ΔT_E of the user's revisit habit satisfy a normal distribution separately, namely, $W_F \sim \mathcal{N}(\mu_1, \sigma_1^2)$, $C_F \sim \mathcal{N}(\mu_2, \sigma_2^2)$, $\Delta T_B \sim \mathcal{N}(\mu_3, \sigma_3^2)$, and $\Delta T_E \sim \mathcal{N}(\mu_4, \sigma_4^2)$.*

Upon the user's revisit actions, the mean values and standard deviations $W_F(\mu_1, \sigma_2)$, $C_F(\mu_2, \sigma_2)$, $\Delta T_B(\mu_3, \sigma_3)$, $\Delta T_E(\mu_4, \sigma_4)$ and the minimum and maximum values T_{min}, T_{max} of $D\tau$ will be updated accordingly.

Adjustments. The revisit feedback adaptation over context memory management refers to the adjustments of several key parameters: (1) $\tau_{wf} = \mu_1 - 2\sigma_1$; (2) $\tau_{cf} = \mu_2 - 2\sigma_2$; (3) $\Delta t_b = \mu_3 + 2\sigma_3$; (4) $\Delta t_e = \mu_4 + 2\sigma_4$; (5) $T_{min} = \min\{D\tau\}$; and (6) $T_{max} = \max\{D\tau\}$. The objectives of these adjustments are to capture the to-be-revisited web pages and the to-be-employed contexts as far as possible, and to maintain the context memory at more appropriate decay rates.

Reinforcement. Because the recall actions can often refresh the user's memory, during the evolution process, certain parts of the context memory are reinforced due to the user's revisit actions. Thus, we set the current time as the new born time of the involving contexts, and reset the decay rate $\lambda = \frac{1}{\sqrt{T_{min} + (T_{max} - T_{min}) \cdot pr_0}} \ln \frac{r_0}{HR_n}$ based on Equation 4.

5   Evaluation

To evaluate our approach, we implemented a prototype called $\mathcal{RE}\mathcal{V}$isit and conducted two sets of experiments: with synthetic data and through a user study. The two experiments focus on two measurements: 1) revisit result quality (precision, recall and ranking); and 2) revisit response time. $\mathcal{RE}\mathcal{V}$isit is implemented in $C\#$. The first experiment with synthetic data is conducted on a PC with 2.2 GHz Intel Core 2 Duo CPU, and 2 GB memory on Windows 7 OS.

5.1   Experiment on Synthetic Data

Design: We first build two extra components: 1) *data simulator*, to simulate the generation of a user's computer activities; and 2) *user simulator*, to simulate the user's memory over the generated data and the user's revisit actions, acts as a "real user". *Data simulator* generates 3-month data comprising of 7 activity types: *email, browsing, programming, read/write, music, online shopping* and *online chatting*. It separately generate a set of phrases (2 to 5 words) for each activity type. For a data item, the time span ($t_{end} - t_{begin}$) is a random value from 30 seconds to 15 minutes, the focus time (t_{focus}) is from 5 seconds to half of the time span, the activity type is randomly selected and the keywords are generated from the corresponding set of phrases, where the keywords' repetition rate is 3%, and the data type is also set randomly to be web page or not. In total, 27,824 data items are generated, where the web pages occupy about 57%.

For each generated web page, if $t_{focus} \geq 30$ seconds, it will be stored as a candidate revisit target by *user simulator*, which will identify a set of associated contexts based on its own $\Delta t_b = 5$ minutes, $\Delta t_e = 15$ minutes, $\tau_{cf} = 60$

seconds, $T_{min} = 10$ days and $T_{max} = 28$ days. Every *period* (7 days), *user simulator* will randomly select a part of the the candidate revisit targets as the true to-be-revisited web pages. For each of them, it chooses 2 keywords from the corresponding stored contexts with higher association probabilities as a revisit request. Then the revisit requests are submitted to $\mathcal{R}EVisit$. Meanwhile, $\mathcal{R}EVisit$ identifies each generated web page, and then build a probabilistic context tree for the possible to-be-revisited one, based on its own $\Delta t_b = \Delta t_e = 10$ minutes, $\tau_{cf} = 90$ seconds, $T_{min} = 14$ days and $T_{max} = 21$ days. Every *period*, $\mathcal{R}EVisit$ processes the revisit requests from *user simulator*, and then the relevant parameters are updated according to the revisit feedbacks.

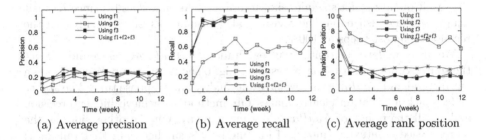

(a) Average precision   (b) Average recall   (c) Average rank position

Fig. 4. Results on synthetic data using different features in memory construction

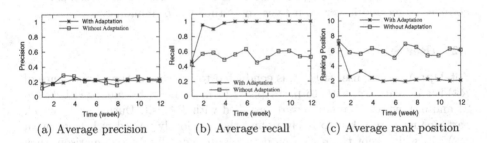

(a) Average precision   (b) Average recall   (c) Average rank position

Fig. 5. Results on synthetic data with/without revisit feedback adaptation

Results: The average precision, recall and ranking position of the revisit results are studied under different settings of context memory management, including applying various features in computing the association probabilities between the contexts and the targets, and with or without revisit feedback adaptation. Clearly, the adopted features will impact the revisit result quality, as demonstrated in Fig. 4. Note that the influence of the f_4 feature is not shown since the content similarity is very minimal in the synthetic data. Consider the feedback adaptation, as $\mathcal{R}EVisit$ at first does not grasp the revisit habit of the "real user" and probably not capture the most associated contexts for later revisit,

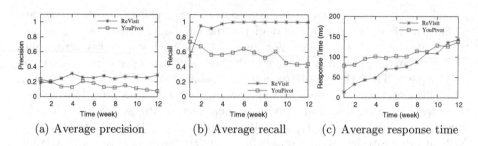

(a) Average precision   (b) Average recall   (c) Average response time

Fig. 6. Comparison results between $\mathcal{RE}$Visit and *YouPivot* on synthetic data

the result quality is not so good, shown in Fig. 5. As time goes by, since $\mathcal{RE}$Visit adapts to the revisit habit, the revisit quality become better, especially that the recall rate almost keeps at 100%.

We also simulate the contextual search method *YouPivot* (as we did not get the source code) and use it as a baseline. Fig. 6 shows the comparisons between our method and *YouPivot* on revisit result quality and response time. The ability of feedback adaptation clearly makes our method to achieve higher precision and recall than that of *YouPivot* as time goes by. On the other side, as the search space (context memory) of our method is smaller than that (all data) of *YouPivot*, it takes less time cost for our method than *YouPivot* to perform revisit actions. As the generated data is continuously growing, more and more possible to-be-revisited web pages are recorded, and the context memory size becomes larger and larger, so it takes more time to do re-finding.

5.2   User Study

Set-Up: A 6-week user study was conducted to investigate the performance of $\mathcal{RE}$Visit in real case, with 16 participants (8 male and 8 female, aged between 21 and 37), whose computers were installed with $\mathcal{RE}$Visit. During that period, participants were asked to freely re-find the previously visited web pages with $\mathcal{RE}$Visit, which kept the re-finding details automatically. For comparison, they were also asked to re-find the same web pages by popular methods like browsing or searching history list, using search engine, bookmark, *etc.* and meanwhile record the details in the re-finding process, such as revisit method, input-keywords, the response time, *etc.* The user study with $\mathcal{RE}$Visit gathered 864 web revisitation records in total, 54 records per participant in average.

Results: The participants used time, time + activity, activity as re-finding contextual cues at the percentage of 3.97%, 6.29% and 89.74%, respectively. It indicates that users tend to remember activity more often than time. Note that place was not referred to in the user study, the reason is probably that participants did the experiment with IP-fixed computers. Fig. 7 shows the result quality of $\mathcal{RE}$Visit by using different contexts as revisit requests. Since users tend to forget time more easily than activity, using time only to revisit works poorer than the other cases. While activity works quite well as re-finding cues, since richer

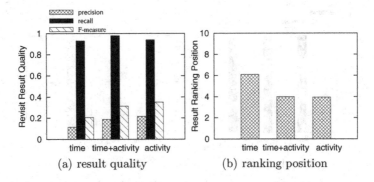

Fig. 7. The result quality of using *time, time+activity* and *activity* with $\mathcal{REV}$isit

information makes it more easily to be remembered and distinguished. For the ranking positions of the revisited targets, time-only also works poorer than the other two cases. Participants were more likely to use less than 3 contextual keywords in a revisit request, where 1-keyword occupies 55.87%, 2-keyword occupies 31.28%, 3-keyword occupies 8.66%, and the remainder is occupied by more than 3 keywords. The result quality of using different number of contextual keywords with $\mathcal{REV}$isit is shown in Fig. 8. It is interesting to discover that the precision is not proportional to keyword number. The reason is that the 4- and 5-keyword revisit requests often contain time, which can not play well in revisitation.

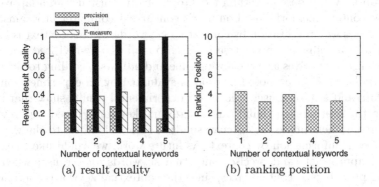

Fig. 8. The result quality of using different number of keywords with $\mathcal{REV}$isit

The overall performance comparison between $\mathcal{REV}$isit and popular methods is shown in Fig. 9. The precision rate of $\mathcal{REV}$isit is lower than that of searching history. It is mainly because $\mathcal{REV}$isit supports general matching, and participants tended to revisit by general contextual keywords like music, shopping, chatting and so on, and thus the result list returned by $\mathcal{REV}$isit was sometimes longer. The average time cost for a revisit request shows that $\mathcal{REV}$isit outperforms the traditional methods. The reason includes several aspects. The long history list

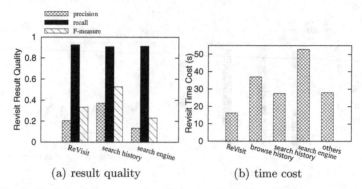

(a) result quality   (b) time cost

Fig. 9. Performance comparison between $\mathcal{R}E\mathcal{V}$isit and popular methods

often required users to spend a bit more time to re-locate the desire targets, and participants sometimes even gave up browsing when they could not find the target after several minutes. Searching history needs exact match, and participants had to try a few more times if they could not remember the keywords very well. While the query results and their rankings are frequently updated within the search engine, participants sometimes felt difficult to get the targets.

6   Conclusion

In this work, we propose a method to automatically construct an adaptive and evolutive context memory based on user's concurrent computer programs, supporting user's web revisitation by contextual keywords. Access context is formulated as a probabilistic context tree for each possible to-be-revisited web page. Context memory evolves as the elapsing time and adjusts according to the user's revisit feedbacks. The proposed method is evaluated by an experiment on synthetic data and a 6-week user study. Our experimental results show that it can adapt to the user's revisit habit, and contextual keywords based web revisitation offers another simple yet effective solution since it is closer to the way that human recalls information by context. As future work, we would like to explore the more appropriate and precise contextual keywords for the user when constructing probabilistic context trees, since the contextual keywords contained in the context trees directly influence the user's web revisitation action. Also, the preferable contexts would be explored based on the user's revisit activities.

Acknowledgments. The work is supported by National Natural Science Foundation of China (60773156, 61073004), Chinese Major State Basic Research Development 973 Program (2011C B302203-2), Important National Science & Technology Specific Program (2011ZX0 1042-001-002-2), and research fund of Tsinghua-Tencent Joint Laboratory for Internet Innovation Technology.

References

1. Abrams, D., Baecker, R., Chignell, M.: Information archiving with bookmarks: personal webspace construction and organization. In: CHI, pp. 41–48 (1998)
2. Adar, E., Teevan, J., Dumais, S.T.: Large scale analysis of web revisitation patterns. In: CHI, pp. 1197–1206 (2008)
3. Capra, R., Perez-Quinones, M.A.: Using web search engines to find and refind information. IEEE Computer 38(10), 36–42 (2005)
4. Chen, Y., Jones, G.: Integrating memory context into personal information refinding. In: The 2nd Symposium on Future Directions in Info. Access (2008)
5. Cockburn, A., Greenberg, S., Jones, S., Mckenzie, B., Moyle, M.: Improving web page revisitation: analysis, design and evaluation. IT & Society 1(3), 159–183 (2003)
6. Deng, T., Zhao, L., Feng, L., Xue, W.: Information re-finding by context: a brain memory inspired approach. In: CIKM, pp. 1553–1558 (2011)
7. Deng, T., Zhao, L., Wang, H., Liu, Q., Feng, L.: Refinder: a context-based information re-finding system. IEEE TKDE (August 14, 2012) (preprint)
8. Guo, L., Shao, F., Botev, C., Shanmugasundaram, J.: Xrank: ranked keyword search over xml documents. In: SIGMOD, pp. 16–27 (2003)
9. Hailpern, J., Jitkoff, N., Warr, A., Karahalios, K., Sesek, R., Shkrob, N.: Youpivot: improving recall with contextual search. In: CHI, pp. 1521–1530 (2011)
10. Jones, W., Bruce, H., Dumais, S.: Keeping found things found on the web. In: CIKM, pp. 119–126 (2001)
11. Kawase, R., Papadakis, G., Herder, E., Nejdl, W.: Beyond the usual suspects: context-aware revisitation support. In: ACM Conference on Hypertext and Hypermedia, pp. 27–36 (2011)
12. Li, J., Liu, C., Zhou, R., Wang, W.: Top-k keyword search over probabilistic xml data. In: ICDE, pp. 673–684 (2011)
13. MacKay, B., Kellar, M., Watters, C.: An evaluation of landmarks for re-finding information on the web. In: CHI 2005 Extended Abstracts, pp. 1609–1612 (2005)
14. Mayer, M.: Web history tools and revisitation support: a survey of existing approaches and directions. Foundations and Trends in HCI 2(3), 173–278 (2009)
15. Morris, D., Morris, M.R., Venolia, G.: Searchbar: a search-centric web history for task resumption and information re-finding. In: CHI, pp. 1207–1216 (2008)
16. Rubin, D.C., Wenzel, A.E.: One hundred years of forgetting: a quantitative description of retention. Psychological Review 103(4), 734–760 (1996)
17. Tauscher, L., Greenberg, S.: How people revisit web pages: empirical findings and implications for the design of history systems. International Journal of Human Computer Studies 47, 97–137 (1997)
18. Teevan, J.: The re:search engine: simultaneous support for finding and re-finding. In: UIST, pp. 23–32 (2007)
19. Teevan, J., Adar, E., Jones, R., Potts, M.: Information re-retrieval: repeat queries in yahoo's logs. In: SIGIR, pp. 151–158 (2007)
20. Tulving, E.: What is episodic memory? Current Directions in Psychological Science 2(3), 67–70 (1993)
21. Tyler, S., Teevan, J.: Large scale query log analysis of re-finding. In: WSDM, pp. 191–200 (2010)
22. Won, S.S., Jin, J., Hong, J.I.: Contextual web history: using visual and contextual cues to improve web browser history. In: CHI, pp. 1457–1466 (2009)
23. Xu, Y., Papakonstantinou, Y.: Efficient keyword search for smallest lcas in xml databases. In: SIGMOD, pp. 527–538 (2005)

A Linear and Monotonic Strategy to Keyword Search over RDF Data

Roberto De Virgilio[1], Antonio Maccioni[1], and Paolo Cappellari[2]

[1] Università Roma Tre, Rome, Italy
{dvr,maccioni}@dia.uniroma3.it
[2] Dublin City University, Dublin, Ireland
pcappellari@computing.dcu.ie

Abstract. Keyword-based search over (semi)structured data is today considered an essential feature of modern information management systems and has become an hot topic in database research and development. Most of the recent approaches to this problem refer to a general scenario where: (i) the data source is represented as a graph, (ii) answers to queries are sub-graphs of the source containing keywords from queries, and (iii) solutions are ranked according to a relevance criteria. In this paper, we illustrate a novel approach to keyword search over semantic data that combines a solution building algorithm and a ranking technique to generate the best results in the first answers generated. We show that our approach is monotonic and has a linear computational complexity, greatly reducing the complexity of the overall process. Finally, experiments demonstrate that our approach exhibits very good efficiency and effectiveness, especially with respect to competing approaches.

1 Introduction

The amount of data in the Semantic Web is exponentially increasing due to organizations that are opening up data in the form of *linked data* and, on the other side, to users that are interested in using them. In general, to access (semantic) data users must know how data is organized (e.g., Web ontologies) and the syntax of a specific query language (e.g., SPARQL). Clearly, this is an obstacle to information access and retrieval. For this reason Keyword Search (KS) systems are increasingly capturing the attention of researchers and industry, since they provide an effective facilitation to non-expert users. Let us consider the example in Fig. 1. Graph G_1 is a sample RDF version of the DBLP dataset (a database about scientific publications). Vertices in ovals represent entities, such as *aut1* and *aut2*, or concepts, such as *Conference* and *Publication*. Vertices in rectangles are literal values, such as *Bernstein* and *Buneman*. Edges describe connections between vertices. For instance, entity *aut1* is a *Researcher* of name *Bernstein*. Typically, given a keyword search query, a generic approach would: i) identify the vertices of the RDF graph holding the data matching the input keywords, ii) traverse the edges to discover the connections (i.e. trees or sub-graphs) between them that build n candidate solutions (with $n > k$), and iii) rank solutions

F. Daniel, P. Dolog, and Q. Li (Eds.): ICWE 2013, LNCS 7977, pp. 338–353, 2013.

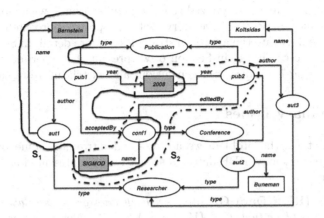

Fig. 1. An RDF graph G_1 from DBLP

according to a relevance criteria to return the top relevant k. Intrinsically, this process generates (or computes) more solutions than required (an overset of the most relevant answers), whereas it would be ideal to generate exactly the best k. For instance, if one is interested in the top-2 answers for the query $Q_1 = \{$Bernstein, SIGMOD, 2008$\}$ over G_1 in Fig. 1, then only S_1 (i.e. articles of *Bernstein* published in *SIGMOD 2008*) and S_2 (i.e. articles of *Buneman* published in *SIGMOD 2008*) shall be computed. Intuitively, S_1 is more relevant than S_2 because it includes more keywords and it should be retrieved as the first answer. Note that ranking functions consider more elaborated criteria to evaluate the relevance of an answer. It turns out however, that the relevance of answers is highly dependent on both the construction of candidates and their ranking. For this reason, the tasks of searching and of ranking are strongly correlated.

In this paper, we present a novel keyword based search technique over RDF graph-shaped data that builds the best k results in the first k solutions generated. This technique is inspired by a previous work [4]. The work in [4] builds top-k solutions in an approximate and sequential way focusing exclusively on the quality of the results. Differently, in this paper we address efficiency and scalability, beyond effectiveness, providing new algorithms to optimize the complexity of finding the best answers. To validate our approach, we have developed a system for keyword-based search over RDF data that implements the techniques described in this paper. Experiments over widely used benchmarks (Coffman et al. [3]) shows very good results with respect to other approaches, in terms of both effectiveness and efficiency. Specifically, we propose two different strategies for our framework. The first presents a linear computational cost and enables the search to scale seamlessly with the size of the input. The second, inspired by the Threshold Algorithm proposed by Fagin et al. [6], guarantees the monotonicity of the output as we show that the first k solutions generated are indeed the top-k. Referring the example in Fig. 1 with k = 2, that strategy builds solutions S_1 and S_2 in this order.

The rest of the paper is organized as follows. In Section 2, we introduce some preliminary issues. In Section 3 we overview the proposed approach to KS, while in Section 4 we illustrate the approach strategies in more detail. In Section 5, we discuss related research and in Section 6, we present the experimental results. Finally, in Section 7, we draw our conclusions and sketch future research.

2   Preliminary Issues

This section states the problem we address and introduces some preliminary notions and terminology. RDF datasets are naturally represented as labeled directed graphs.

Definition 1 (RDF Data Graph). *An RDF data graph is a labeled directed graph G composed by a tuple $G = \{V, E, \Sigma_V, \Sigma_E, L_G\}$ where V is a set of vertices and $E \subseteq V \times V$ is a set of ordered pairs of vertices, called edges. Σ_V and Σ_E are the sets of vertices and edge labels, respectively. The labeling function L_G associates an element of V to an element of Σ_V and an element of E to an element of Σ_E.*

Intuitively, the problem of KS over RDF is addressed by exploring the dataset to find sub-graphs holding information relevant to the query. We follow the traditional Information Retrieval approach to value matching adopted in full-text search for semantic query expansion. This involves syntactic and semantic similarities to support an imprecise matching. Since this is not a contribution of our work, we will not discuss it further. We define a path as the sequence of vertices and edges from a source to a sink. The *sources* of a graph are those nodes with no in-going edges and the *sinks* are the nodes with no out-going edges.

Definition 2 (Path). *Given a graph $G = \{V, E, \Sigma_V, \Sigma_E, L_G\}$, a path is a sequence $pt = l_{v_1} - l_{e_1} - l_{v_2} - l_{e_2} - \ldots - l_{e_{n-1}} - l_{v_f}$ where $v_i \in V$, $e_i \in E$, $l_{v_i} = L_G(v_i)$, $l_{e_i} = L_G(e_i)$, and v_1 is a source and v_f is a sink.*

If a source is not present, a fictitious one can be added. For instance, the graph in Fig. 1 has two sources: *pub1* and *pub2*. An example path is $p_i =$ pub1-author-aut1-name-Bernstein. Obviously, at running time we are interested in the paths relevant to the query, that is, the paths containing at least one vertex matching a keyword of the query. In particular, as assumed in [12], users enter keywords corresponding to attribute values, that are necessarily within the sink's labels. Under this assumption, we do not search URIs: this is not a limitation because nodes labeled by URIs are usually linked to literals, which represent verbose descriptions of such URIs. We index all paths starting from a source and ending with a sink. In a path, the sequence of edge labels describes the corresponding structure. To some extent, such a structure describes a schema for the values on vertices that share the same connection type. While we cannot advocate the presence of a schema, we can say that such a sequence is a *template* for the path. Therefore, given a path p, its template t_p results from the path where each vertex label is replaced with the wildcard #. In the example again using Fig. 1, the template t_{p_2} associated to p_2 is #-author-#-name-#. We say that p_2 satisfies t_{p_2}, denoted with $p_2 \approx t_{p_2}$. Multiple paths that share the same template can be considered as homogeneous. When two paths p_i and p_j share a common node, we say that there is an intersection between p_i and p_j and we indicate it with $p_i \leftrightarrow p_j$. Finally, a solution S to Q over G is a set of paths forming a connected components, i.e. a directed labeled sub-graph of G where the paths present pairwise intersections as defined below.

Definition 3 (Solution). *A solution S is a set of paths $p_1, p_2, \ldots, p_n$ where $\forall p_a, p_b \in S$ there exists a sequence $[p_a, p_{w_1}, \ldots, p_{w_m}, p_b]$, with $m < n$, such that $p_{w_i} \in S$, $p_a \leftrightarrow p_{w_1}$, $p_b \leftrightarrow p_{w_m}$, and $\forall i \in [1, m\text{-}1] : p_{w_i} \leftrightarrow p_{w_{i+1}}$.*

Ranking and Monotonicity. Given the query Q_1 over the graph illustrated in Fig. 1, the solutions are represented by $S_1 = \{p_1, p_2, p_3\}$ and $S_2 = \{p_4, p_5\}$. Intuitively, S_1 is more relevant than S_2 because it includes more terms from the input query. To assess the relevance of a solution S for a query Q, a scoring function $score(S, Q)$ is adopted. It returns a number that is greater when the solution is more relevant. Then, the ranking is given by ordering the solutions according to their relevance. We say that a ranking is monotonic if the i-th solution is more relevant than the $i + 1$-th solution. Consequently, a query answering process is monotonic if it generates the solutions respecting a monotonic ranking (i.e. the solution of the i-th step is always more relevant than that of the $i + 1$-th step). In the following sections, we will use the notation $score(p, Q)$ and $score(S, Q)$ to evaluate the relevance of a path p and of a solution S with respect to the query Q, respectively. We remark that, unlike all current approaches, we are independent from the scoring function. In fact, we do not impose a monotonic, aggregative nor an "ad-hoc for the case" scoring function. Without giving further details, for the running example and for the experiments we used the scoring function presented in [4].

Problem Definition. Given a labeled directed graph G and a keyword search based query $Q = \{q_1, q_2, \ldots, q_n\}$, where each q_i is a keyword, we aim at finding the top-k ranked answers $S_1, S_2, \ldots, S_k$ to Q.

3 Keyword Search over RDF

This section overviews our approach to keyword search over RDF and discusses the conditions under which the solution generation process exhibits a monotonic behavior with respect to the score of the solutions.

Overview. Let G be an RDF data graph and Q a KS query over it. Our approach provides two main phases: the *indexing* (done off-line), in which all the paths of G are indexed, and the *query processing* (done on-the-fly), where the query evaluation takes place. The first task is described in more detail in [2]. In the second phase, all paths P relevant for Q (i.e. all paths whose sinks match

$cl_1[\#\text{-year-}\#]$:
$$\begin{pmatrix} p_1 : \text{pub1-year-2008} \\ p_4 : \text{pub2-year-2008} \end{pmatrix}$$

$cl_2[\#\text{-author-}\#\text{-name-}\#]$:
$$(p_2 : \text{pub1-author-aut1-name-Bernstein})$$

$cl_3[\#\text{-acceptedBy-}\#\text{-name-}\#]$:
$$(p_3 : \text{pub1-acceptedBy-conf1-name-SIGMOD})$$

$cl_4[\#\text{-editedBy-}\#\text{-name-}\#]$:
$$(p_5 : \text{pub2-editedBy-conf1-name-SIGMOD})$$

Fig. 2. Clustering of paths

at least one keyword of Q) are retrieved in G by exploiting the index and the best solutions are generated from P. An important feature of this phase is the use of the scoring function while computing the solutions. This phase is performed by the following two main tasks:

Clustering. In this task we group the paths of P into clusters cl_i according to their template, and we return the set $\mathcal{CL}$ of all clusters. As an example, given the query Q_1 and the data graph G_1 of Fig. 1, we obtain the clusters shown in Fig. 2. In this case clusters cl_1, cl_2, cl_3 and cl_4 correspond to the different templates extracted from P. Before the insertion of a path p in the cluster, we evaluate its score. The paths in a clusters are ordered according to their score with the greater coming first, i.e. $score(p_1, Q_1) \geq score(p_4, Q_1)$. It is straightforward to demonstrate that the time complexity of the clustering is $O(|P|)$: we must only execute $|P|$ insertions into $\mathcal{CL}$ at most.

Building. The last task aims at generating the most relevant solutions by combining the paths in the clusters built in the previous step. This is done by picking and combining the paths with greatest score from each cluster, i.e. the most promising paths. Note that by building solutions with paths from different clusters we diversify the solution content since we do not include homogeneous data, i.e. from the same cluster. The combination of paths is led by a strategy that decides whether a path has to be inserted in a final solution or not. In particular, two different strategies are exploited as follows.

1. *Linear strategy*: guarantees a linear time complexity with respect to the size of the input. Basically, the final solutions are the connected components of the most relevant paths of the clusters.
2. *Monotonic strategy*: generates the solutions in order according to their relevance in a quadratic time complexity with respect to the size of the input. As the linear strategy, it computes the connected components from the most relevant paths in the clusters. Unlike the previous strategy, the path interconnection is not the only criterion to form a solution. At this point every connected components is locally analyzed to check if it fulfills the monotonicity, i.e. we check if the solution we are generating is the optimum. This check is supported by the so called τ-*test*, which is explained in the next Section 3. Furthermore, we derived a variant of this strategy that, reducing a bit the quality of the results, is able to optimize the analysis guaranteeing the execution in linear time w.r.t. the size of the input.

Monotonic Generation. Monotonicity when building the result set represents a significant challenge in keyword search systems. This means returning the optimum solution at each generation step instead of enduring the processing of blocks of candidate solutions and then selecting the optimum. The second strategy relies on the Theorem 1 to guarantee the monotonicity of the building. It requires to verify the two following properties, i.e. Property 1 and Property 2, on the scoring function. Our strategy is independent from such implementation: it works with any scoring function as long as it satisfies the properties below. Furthermore, the two properties are very general and in fact, they are fulfilled by the most common IR based functions. It is possible to prove that the *pivoted normalization weighting method* (SIM) [11], which inspired most of the IR scoring functions, satisfy Properties 1 and 2. For the sake of simplicity, we discuss the properties by referring to the data structures used in this paper.

Property 1. *Given a query Q and a path p, $score(p, Q) = score(\{p\}, Q)$.*

This property states that the score of a path p is equal to the score of the solution S containing only that same path (i.e. $\{p\}$). It means that every path must be evaluated as the solution containing exactly that path. Consequently we have that, if $score(p_1, Q) > score(p_2, Q)$ then $score(\{p_1\}, Q) > score(\{p_2\}, Q)$. Analogously, extending Property 1 we provide the following.

Property 2. *Given a query Q, a set of paths P in which p_β is the more relevant path (i.e. $\forall p_j \in P$ we have that $score(p_\beta, Q) \geqslant score(p_j, Q)$) and P^* is its power set, we have $score(S = P_i, Q) \leq score(S = \{p_\beta\}, Q) \; \forall P_i \subseteq P^*$.*

In other words, given the set P containing the candidate paths to be included in the solution, the scores of all possible solutions generated from P (i.e. P^*) are bounded by the score of the most relevant path p_β of P. This property is coherent and generalizes the Threshold Algorithm (TA) [6]. Contrarily to TA, we do not use an aggregative function, nor we assume the aggregation to be monotone. TA introduces a mechanism to optimize the number of steps n to compute the best k objects (where it could be n > k), while our framework produces k optima solutions in k steps. To verify the monotonicity we apply a so-called τ-*test* to determine which paths of a connected component cc should be inserted into an optimum solution $optS \subset cc$. The τ-test is supported by Theorem 1. Firstly, we have to take into consideration the paths that can be used to form more solutions in the next iterations of the process. In our framework they are still within the set of clusters $\mathcal{CL}$. Then, let us consider the path p_s with the highest score in $\mathcal{CL}$ and the path p_y with the highest score in $cc \setminus optS$. Then we define the threshold τ as $\tau = max\{score(p_s, Q), score(p_y, Q)\}$. The threshold τ can be considered as the upper bound score for the potential solutions to generate in the next iterations of the algorithm. Now, we provide the following:

Theorem 1. *Given a query Q, a scoring function satisfying* PROPERTY 1 *and* PROPERTY 2, *a connected component cc, a subset $optS \subset cc$ representing an optimum solution and a candidate path $p_x \in cc \setminus optS$, $S = optS \cup \{p_x\}$ is still optimum iff $score(S, Q) \geq \tau$.*

Necessary condition. Let us assume that $S = optS \cup \{p_x\}$ is an optimum solution. We must verify if the score of this solution is still greater than τ. Reminding to the definition of τ, we can have two cases:

- $\tau = score(p_s, Q) > score(p_y, Q)$.

  In this case $score(p_s, Q)$ represents the upper bound for the scoring of the possible solutions to generate in the next steps. Recalling the PROPERTY 1, we have $score(p_s, Q) = score(S' = \{p_s\}, Q)$. Referring to the PROPERTY 2, the possible solutions to generate will present a score less than $score(S' = \{p_s\}, Q)$: $S = optS \cup \{p_x\}$ is optimum. Therefore, $score(S = optS \cup \{p_x\}) \geq \tau$.

- $\tau = score(p_y, Q) > score(p_s, Q)$.

  In a similar way, $score(S = optS \cup \{p_x\}, Q) \geq \tau$.

Sufficient condition. Let us consider $score(S = optS \cup \{p_x\}, Q) \geq \tau$. We must verify if $S = optS \cup \{p_x\}$ is an optimum solution. From the assumption, $score(S = optS \cup \{p_x\}, Q)$ is greater than both $score(p_s, Q)$ and $score(p_y, Q)$. Recalling again the properties of the scoring function, the possible solutions to generate will present a score less than both $score(S' = \{p_s\}, Q)$ and $score(S' = \{p_y\}, Q)$. Therefore, $S = optS \cup \{p_x\}$ is an optimum solution. $\square$

4   Building Strategies

Given the query Q and the set P of paths matching the query Q, we compose those paths to generate the top-k solutions. As said in the previous section, we organize such paths into clusters. In the following we discusses two strategies to compose the paths organized in the set $\mathcal{CL}$ of clusters.

4.1   The Linear Strategy

Given the set of clusters $\mathcal{CL}$, the building of solutions is performed by generating the connected components cc from the most promising paths in $\mathcal{CL}$ as shown in Algorithm 1.

Algorithm 1. Building solutions in linear time

    Input   : The map $\mathcal{CL}$, a number k.
    Output: A list S of k solutions.

```
 1  S ← ∅;
 2  while |S| < k and CL is not empty do
 3  │   first_cl ← ∅;
 4  │   cc ← ∅;
 5  │   foreach cl ∈ CL do
 6  │   │   first_cl ← first_cl ∪ cl.DequeueTop() ;
 7  │   cc ← FindCC(first_cl );
 8  │   s ← ∅;
 9  │   foreach cc ∈ cc do
10  │   │   s.Enqueue(cc);
11  │   S.InsertAll(s.DequeueTop(k-|S |)) ;
12  return S;
```

The algorithm iterates k times at most to produce the best k solutions (i.e. a list $\mathcal{S}$). At each iteration, we initialize a set first_cl with the best paths from each cluster, that is the paths with the highest score (lines [3-6]). DequeueTop retrieves the top paths from cl, i.e. all paths having the same (top) score. Referring again to the example of Fig. 1, in the first iteration we have first_cl $= \{p_1, p_2, p_3, p_5\}$. Out of first_cl we compute the connected components cc (line [7]), each of which represents a solution. For the example, $\{p_1, p_2, p_3, p_5\}$ represents a single connected component cc_1. At the second iteration, we have first_cl $= \{p_4\}$ and thus, $cc_2 = \{p_4\}$. Then, all generated connected components are included into a priority queue s, in order with respect to the score. Finally, through a variant of DequeueTop, we insert the top n elements (i.e. n = k -$|\mathcal{S}|$) of s into $\mathcal{S}$ (line [11]). The execution concludes when k solutions are produced (i.e $|\mathcal{S}| <$ k) or $\mathcal{CL}$ becomes empty.

Computational Complexity. Algorithm 1 produces the best-k solutions in linear time with respect to the number I of paths matching the input query Q: it is in $O(k \times I) \in O(I)$. In the worst case, the algorithm iterates k times. The execution in lines [4-5] is $O(|(CL)|) \in O(I)$. Then we have to execute FindCC that is $O(I)$ since each path knows which are the other intersecting paths. Finally, both the executions in lines [9-11] and line [12] are in $O(I)$ (i.e. at most we have to make I insertions). Therefore, the entire sequence of operations in Algorithm 1 is in $O(k \times I) \in O(I)$.

Ranking. Observing the solutions of the running example, S_1 contains the unnecessary p_5, while S_2 is partially incomplete (i.e. it should include p_5). Such strategy tends to produce solutions *exhaustive* but not optimally *specific*, that is to include all relevant information matching the query but not optimally limiting the irrelevant ones. Moreover the solution generated at each step may not be the optimum solution, i.e. the strategy is not monotonic. In fact, it may happen a generation of a sequence of two solutions S_i and S_{i+1} where $score(S_{i+1}, Q) > score(S_i, Q)$. The next section discusses the conditions under which the solution generation process exhibits a monotonic behavior with respect to the score of the solutions.

4.2   The Monotonic Strategy

To generate the top-k solutions guaranteeing monotonicity, differently from Algorithm 1, the building algorithm (Algorithm 2) introduces an exploration procedure to analyze the connected components of the most relevant paths (line [9]).
    The function MonotonicityExploration (Algorithm 3) finds the best solutions CCOpt in cc by launching the analysis over each connected component cc.

Monotonicity Analysis. Algorithm 4 checks if the solution we are generating is (still) optimum, thus, preserves the monotonicity. It is a recursive function that generates the set OptSols of all solutions (candidate to be optimum) by

---

Algorithm 2. Monotonic Building of top-k solutions

    Input   : A list CL of clusters, a number k.
    Output: A List S of k solutions.

```
 1  while |S| < k do
 2      first_cl ← ∅;
 3      cc ← ∅;
 4      foreach cl ∈ CL do
 5          first_cl ← first_cl ∪ cl.DequeueTop() ;

 6      cc ← FindCC(first_cl );
 7      if CL is not empty then
 8          p_s ← getTopPath(CL );
 9          BSols ← MonotonicityExploration(cc, CL, p_s);
10          S.InsertAll(BSols ) ;

11      else
12          foreach cc ∈ cc do
13              sol ← newSolution(cc);
14              ccSols.Enqueue(sol );

15          S.InsertAll(ccSols.DequeueTop(k-|S |)) ;

16  return S;
```

Algorithm 3. Monotonicity Exploration

    Input   : A set cc of connected components, a list CL of clusters, a path p_s.
    Output: A list of solutions BSols.

```
1  CCOpt ← ∅;
2  foreach cc ∈ cc do
3      CCOpt.Enqueue( MonotonicityAnalysis(cc, ∅, p_s));

4  BSols.InsertAll(CCOpt.DequeueTop());
5  InsertPathsInClusters(CCOpt, CL );
6  return BSols ;
```

---

combining the paths in a connected component cc. At the end it returns a solution optS given by the maximal and optimum subset of paths in cc. It takes as input the connected component cc, the current optimum solution optS and the top path p_s contained in CL.

If cc is empty, we return optS as it is (lines [1-2]). Otherwise, we analyse all paths $p_x \in cc$ that present an intersection with a path p_i of optS ($p_x \leftrightarrow p_i$). If there is not any intersection then optS is the final optimum solution (lines [6-7]). Otherwise, for each p_x, we calculate τ (line [9]), through the function getTau, and then execute the τ-test on each new solution optS', that is optS $\cup \{p_x\}$. If optS' satisfies the τ-test (line [11]), then it represents the new optimum solution: we insert it into OptSols and we invoke the recursion on optS' (line [12]). Otherwise, we keep optS as optimum solution and skip p_x (line [14]). At the finish, we want the optimal solution that is not a subset of any other. This is done by selecting the best and maximal solution optS from OptSols by using TakeMaximal (line [15]). Let us consider our running example. As with the linear strategy, in the first iteration of the algorithm we start from first_cl = $\{p_1, p_2, p_3, p_5\}$. By using the scoring function in [4], the paths of first_cl have scores 2.05, 1.63, 1.6 and 1.49 respectively. Now the exploration considers all possible combinations of these paths to find the optimum solution(s). Therefore, at the beginning

---

Algorithm 4. Monotonicity Analysis

Input : A set of paths cc, a solution optS, a path p_s.
Output: The new (in case) optimum solution optS.

```
1  if cc is empty then
2  │  return optS;

3  else
4  │  OptSols ← ∅;
5  │  foreach pₓ ∈ cc do
6  │  │  if (∄pᵢ ∈ optS : pₓ ↔ pᵢ) and optS is not empty then
7  │  │  │  OptSols ← OptSols ∪ optS ;

8  │  │  else
9  │  │  │  optS' ← optS ∪ {pₓ};
10 │  │  │  τ ← getTau(cc - {pₓ }, pₛ );
11 │  │  │  if score(optS', Q) ≥ τ then
12 │  │  │  │  OptSols ← OptSols ∪ MonotonicityAnalysis(cc - {pₓ }, optS', pₛ);

13 │  │  │  else
14 │  │  │  │  OptSols ← OptSols ∪ optS ;

15 │  optS ← TakeMaximal(OptSols ) ;
16 │  return optS;
```

---

we have $optS = \{p_1\}$, since p_1 has the highest score, and p_s is p_4. The value of τ is 1.86. The algorithm will then retrieve the following admissible optima solutions: $S'_1 = \{p_1, p_2, p_3\}$, $S'_2 = \{p_1, p_3\}$, and $S'_3 = \{p_1, p_2, p_5\}$. These solutions are admissible because they satisfy the τ-test and corresponding paths present pairwise intersections. During computation, the analysis skips solutions $S'_4 = \{p_1, p_2, p_3, p_5\}$ and $S'_5 = \{p_1, p_3, p_5\}$ because they do not satisfy the τ-test: the scores of S'_4 and S'_5 are 1.55 and 1.26 respectively, as they are both less than τ. Finally, the function TakeMaximal will select S'_1 as the final first optimum solution S_1 since it has more paths and the highest score. Following a similar process, at the second round, the algorithm will return $S_2 = \{p_4, p_5\}$ with a lesser score than S_1.

Computational Complexity. Although this analysis achieves our goal, the computational complexity of the result generation process is in $O(I^2)$. As for Algorithm 1, in the worst case the computation iterates k times. In lines [2-6] we follow the same strategy as with Algorithm 1. Therefore, the executions in lines [4-5] and line [6] are in $O(|\mathcal{CL}|) \in O(I)$ and $O(I)$ respectively. Then we have a conditional instruction: if the condition is true, we execute the monotonicity exploration (lines [8-10]), otherwise we consider each connected component $cc \in$ cc as a solution to insert into S (lines [12-15]). As in Algorithm 1, the execution in lines [12-15] is in $O(I)$. In lines [8-10] we call the function MonotonicityExploration, that executes the analysis of monotonicity at most I times. This analysis is performed by the recursive function MonotonicityAnalysis: in Algorithm 4 the main executions are in lines [9-12] and line [15]. In both the execution is in $O(I)$, since we have I elements to analyze at the most. Since in Algorithm 3 both the operations in line [4] and in line [5] are in $O(I)$, the complexity of the monotonicity exploration is $O(I^2)$. Therefore we conclude that the monotonic strategy is in $O(I^2)$.

Linear Monotonic Strategy. To reduce the complexity of the monotonic strategy, we provide a variant of the monotonicity analysis (i.e. LinearMonotonicityAnalysis) that reaches a linear time complexity of the overall process. Without showing the pseudo-code, we can say that this strategy directly selects the best path p_x in cc having an intersection with a path of optS. It stops the recursion as soon as the best path does not have intersection with a path in optS. In the worst case optS is the initial cc. LinearMonotonicityAnalysis recurses I times and each execution is $O(1)$, therefore the whole strategy is in $O(I)$. Nevertheless, with respect to the building using Algorithm 4, we can generate more specific solutions and (possibly) less exhaustive, since we compose each solution starting from the most relevant path (i.e. we favor keywords that are more closely connected in graph terms).

Correctness, Complexity and Quality of Results. Our discussion is supported by three measures proposed recently [10]: *exhaustivity* ($\mathcal{EX}$), *specificity* ($\mathcal{SP}$) and *overlap*. Exhaustivity measures the relevance of a solution in terms of the number of contained keywords. Specificity measures the precision of a solution in terms of the number of contained keywords with respect to other irrelevant occurring terms. Overlap measures the redundancy of the information content among the solutions. Clearly, the ideal ranking process balances exhaustivity and specificity while reducing overlap. The linear strategy focuses on maximizing the number of keywords in a solution, and consequently the number of paths, privileging $\mathcal{EX}$ to the detriment of $\mathcal{SP}$. On the other hand, the monotonic strategy tries to balance the number of keywords and the number of paths (i.e. maximizing the former and minimizing the latter); therefore $\mathcal{EX}$ and $\mathcal{SP}$ are perfectly balanced. The linear variant of the monotonic strategy is quite similar, but it privileges $\mathcal{SP}$ to the detriment of $\mathcal{EX}$, focusing only on minimizing the number of paths. Finally, all strategies do not generate overlapping solutions since $\forall cl_i, cl_j \in \mathcal{CL}$, with $i \neq j$, we have that $cl_i \cap cl_j = \emptyset$. It means that a path cannot belong to more than one cluster and moreover, we combine paths from different clusters that gather a different kind of information content. As we will demonstrate experimentally in Section 6, state-of-the-art approaches mainly focus on finding the most exhaustive solutions at the cost of a high level of overlapping. In terms of precision and recall, other approaches tend to privilege the recall (finding the best matches with the query) to the detriment of the precision (i.e. introducing a large number of irrelevant matches, that is *noise* in the result set). Demonstrating the correctness of our approach is straightforward. First of all, our algorithm always terminates. Indeed, (i) the clustering groups a finite set of paths (at most all the data graph G), (ii) the building strategies implement recursive functions to traverse finite sets of paths (clusters or connected components). They also employ sets of visited paths to avoid loops on the analysis. Second, our framework returns a match S in G for Q: all paths in S are paths in G that match at least a keyword of Q. Finally, if there exists a match S in G over Q, our framework is able to discover S. In fact, if there exists S for Q over G, then there exists a set of paths in S matching Q. Since our framework indexes all paths in G, we retrieve with Q those paths. If S is also a top-k solution, then we generate it.

5   Related Work

The most prominent work in the area of keyword search concerns the relational databases. Here, answers are usually trees composed of joined tuples, so-called *joined tuples trees* (JTTs). They can be classified in *schema-based* or *schema-free* approaches (see [13] for survey). Schema-based approaches (e.g., [8]) implement a middleware layer that makes use of schema information in order to interpret the query and produce a (possible large) number of relational queries. This inter- pretation is an NP-complete problem [8] and all the SQL statements produced must be executed but some (could) return empty results, leading to inefficiency, which is likely to worsen with the size of the dataset. Schema-free approaches (e.g., [1,9,7]) are more general as they search, on arbitrary graph-shaped data, the *(minimal) Steiner trees*. In all of these approaches a relevant drawback is that finding a (minimal) Steiner tree is known as an NP-Hard problem. Therefore the algorithms rely on (rather) complex sub-routines or heuristics to calculate approximations of Steiner trees. In the best case, such proposals have polynomial complexity in time. The relational approaches are not suitable to work well on RDF data and therefore new approaches have been proposed [12,14,5]. The work in [12] proposes a semi-automatic system to interpret the query into a set of can- didate conjunctive queries. Users can refine the search by selecting the computed candidate queries that best represent information need. Candidate queries are computed exploring the top-k sub-graphs matching the keywords. The approach in [14] relies on a RDFS domain knowledge to convert keywords in query-guides that help users to incrementally build the desired semantic query. While unnec- essary queries are not built (thus not executed), there is a strict dependency on user feedback. The work in [5] employs a ranking model based on IR and statistical methods.

6   Experimental Results

We implemented our approach in YAANII, a Java system for keyword search over RDF graphs. In our experiments, we used the benchmark provided by Coff- man et al. [3] which provides a standardized evaluation using three datasets of different size and complexity. It employs two well-know datasets, IMDB and WIKIPEDIA, and an ideal contrast due to its smaller size, MONDIAL. We used the RDF versions of all three datasets: the *Linked IMDb* and *Wikipedia3*, while for MONDIAL we converted the SQL dump into RDF ourselves. For each dataset, we run the set of 50 queries provided in [3] (see the paper for details and statistics). Experiments were conducted on a dual core 2.66GHz Intel Xeon, running Linux RedHat, with 4 GB of memory, 6 MB cache, and a 2-disk 1Tbyte striped RAID array, and we used Oracle 11g v2 to manage our index, as described in [2].

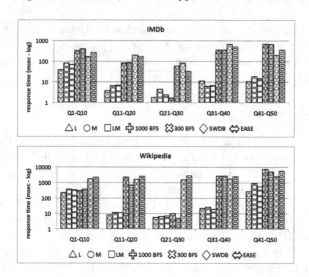

Fig. 3. Response Times on IMDB and WIKIPEDIA

Performance and Scalability. For query execution evaluation, we compared
the different strategies of our system (i.e. linear $\mathcal{L}$, monotonic $\mathcal{M}$ and the variant linear/monotonic $\mathcal{LM}$), with the most related approaches: SEARCHWEBDB
($\mathcal{SWDB}$) [12], EASE ($\mathcal{EASE}$) [9], and the best performing techniques based
on graph indexing, i.e. 1000 $\mathcal{BFS}$ and 300 $\mathcal{BFS}$ that are two configurations of
BLINKS [7]. For each dataset, we grouped the queries into five sets (i.e. ten
queries per set): each set is homogeneous with respect to the complexity of the
queries (e.g., number of keywords, number of results and so on). For each set, we
ran the queries ten times and measured the average response time. The total response time of each query is the time required for computing the top-10 answers.
We performed *cold-cache* experiments: we cleared all caches before restarting the
various systems and running the queries. The query response times are shown
in Fig. 3 (in *ms* and logarithmic scale). Due to space constraints, we report
times only on IMDB and WIKIPEDIA, since their much larger size poses more
challenges. However the performance on MONDIAL follows a similar trend. In
general EASE and SWDB are comparable with BLINKS. Our system performs
consistently better (in any strategy) for most of the queries, significantly outperforming the others in some cases (e.g., sets Q21-Q30 or Q31-Q40). This is due
to the greatly reduced (time) complexity of the overall process with respect to
those that spend a lot of time traversing the graph and computing candidates to
be (possible) solutions. An evaluation of the scalability of our system is reported
in Fig. 4.(a). In particular, we report the scalability of YAANII on IMDB. Our
system provides a similar behavior on WIKIPEDIA. The figure shows the scalability with respect to the size of the input, that is the number I of paths. Moreover
we enriched such experiment by introducing also scalability with respect to the
the average size of the query (i.e. $|Q|$), that is the number of keywords, as shown
in Fig. 4.(b). In particular we evaluate the impact of the number of keywords

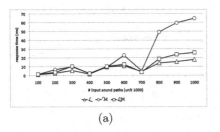
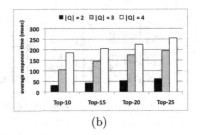

| (a) | (b) |

Fig. 4. (a) Scalability w.r.t. #paths on IMDB and (b) w.r.t. the size of Q

to find the top-k (i.e. k $\in \{10, 15, 20, 25\}$) solutions. Also in this case the time grows linearly. The impact of query length is relevant with a higher k.

Effectiveness. We have also evaluated the effectiveness of results. The first measure we used is the reciprocal rank (RR). For a query, RR is the ratio between 1 and the rank at which the first correct answer is returned; or 0 if no correct answer is returned. Fig. 5.(a) shows the mean reciprocal rank of the queries for each system in any dataset. Due to the small size, all systems show comparable performance on the MONDIAL dataset. Conversely, we have different results using IMDB and WIKIPEDIA. As expected, BLINKS and EASE performs poorly on this task since they implement a proximity search strategy where the ranking is unable to distinguish solutions containing a single node. SWDB performs well in average because it exploits an IR ranking strategy: usually IR-style search systems prefer larger results supporting the disambiguation of search terms. Our linear strategy $\mathcal{L}$ is comparable with SWDB. This strategy confirms the problems discussed in Section 3: $\mathcal{L}$ favors exhaustive solutions introducing *noise* in the final results (i.e. unnecessary information). On the other hand, the monotonic strategy $\mathcal{M}$ significantly outperforms all others: this strategy is able to return the best result for first (i.e. RR = 1) for all cases. In other words, it demonstrates how much $\mathcal{M}$ balances solutions between being exhaustive and specific. The linear/monotonic strategy $\mathcal{LM}$ shows a similar trend too. We then measured the interpolation between precision and recall to find the top-10 solutions, for each strategy on the queries on all datasets, that is for each standard level r_j of recall (i.e. 0.1, ..., 1.0) we calculate the average max precision of queries in $[r_j, r_{j+1}]$, i.e. $P(r_j) = max_{r_j \leq r \leq r_{j+1}} P(r)$. We repeated this procedure for each strategy. Similarly we calculate the top-10 interpolated precision curve averaged over the systems: Fig. 5.(b) shows the results. As expected, the precision of the other systems decreases dramatically for large values of recall. On the contrary our strategies keeps values within the range [0.6,0.9]. In particular, the monotonic strategy $\mathcal{M}$ presents the highest quality (i.e. a precision in the range [0.8,1]). $\mathcal{LM}$ and $\mathcal{L}$ also present good quality in results.

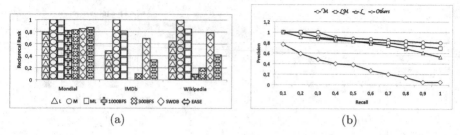

Fig. 5. (a) RR measures for all frameworks and (b) Effectiveness of YAANII

7 Conclusions and Future Work

In this paper, we presented a novel approach to keyword search query over large RDF datasets, by providing two strategies for top-k query answering. The linear strategy enables the search to scale seamlessly with the size of the input, while the monotonic strategy guarantees the monotonicity of the output. In the worst case, the two strategies present a linear and a quadratic computational cost respectively, whereas other approaches show these results as lower bounds (i.e. best or average cases). Furthermore, we described a variant of the second strategy that reaches both monotonicity and linear complexity. Experimental results confirmed our algorithms and the advantage over other approaches.

This work now opens several directions of further research. From a theoretical point of view, we are investigating algorithms to keyword search over distributed environments, retaining the results achieved in this paper. From a practical point of view, we are widening a more synthetic catalogue to index information (e.g., NoSQL technology), optimization techniques to speed-up the index creation and update (mainly DBMS independent) and compression mechanisms.

References

1. Bhalotia, G., Hulgeri, A., Nakhe, C., Chakrabarti, S., Sudarshan, S.: Keyword searching and browsing in databases using banks. In: ICDE, pp. 431–440 (2002)
2. Cappellari, P., De Virgilio, R., Maccioni, A., Roantree, M.: A path-oriented rdf index for keyword search query processing. In: Hameurlain, A., Liddle, S.W., Schewe, K.-D., Zhou, X. (eds.) DEXA 2011, Part II. LNCS, vol. 6861, pp. 366–380. Springer, Heidelberg (2011)
3. Coffman, J., Weaver, A.: An empirical performance evaluation of relational keyword search techniques. TKDE 99 1 (2012) (preprints)
4. De Virgilio, R., Cappellari, P., Miscione, M.: Cluster-based exploration for effective keyword search over semantic datasets. In: Laender, A.H.F., Castano, S., Dayal, U., Casati, F., de Oliveira, J.P.M. (eds.) ER 2009. LNCS, vol. 5829, pp. 205–218. Springer, Heidelberg (2009)
5. Elbassuoni, S., Blanco, R.: Keyword search over rdf graphs. In: CIKM, pp. 237–242 (2011)

6. Fagin, R., Lotem, A., Naor, M.: Optimal aggregation algorithms for middleware. In: PODS, pp. 102–113 (2001)
7. He, H., Wang, H., Yang, J., Yu, P.S.: Blinks: ranked keyword searches on graphs. In: SIGMOD (2007)
8. Hristidis, V., Papakonstantinou, Y.: Discover: Keyword search in relational databases. In: VLDB, pp. 670–681 (2002)
9. Li, G., Ooi, B.C., Feng, J., Wang, J., Zhou, L.: Ease: an effective 3-in-1 keyword search method for unstructured, semi-structured and structured data. In: SIGMOD (2008)
10. Piwowarski, B., Dupret, G.: Evaluation in (xml) information retrieval: expected precision-recall with user modelling (eprum). In: SIGIR, pp. 260–267 (2006)
11. Singhal, A., Buckley, C., Mitra, M.: Pivoted document length normalization. In: SIGIR, pp. 21–29 (1996)
12. Tran, T., Wang, H., Rudolph, S., Cimiano, P.: Top-k exploration of query candidates for efficient keyword search on graph-shaped (rdf) data. In: ICDE, pp. 405–416 (2009)
13. Yu, J.X., Qin, L., Chang, L.: Keyword Search in Relational Databases: A Survey. Data(base) Engineering Bulletin 33(1), 67–78 (2010)
14. Zenz, G., Zhou, X., Minack, E., Siberski, W., Nejdl, W.: From keywords to semantic queries - incremental query construction on the semantic web. Journal of Web Semantics 7(3), 166–176 (2009)

Identifying Candidate Datasets
for Data Interlinking

Luiz André P. Paes Leme[1], Giseli Rabello Lopes[2], Bernardo Pereira Nunes[2,3],
Marco Antonio Casanova[2], and Stefan Dietze[3]

[1] Computer Science Institute, Fluminense Federal University,
Niterói/RJ – Brazil, CEP 24210-240
`lapaesleme@ic.uff.br`
[2] Department of Informatics, Pontifical Catholic University of Rio de Janeiro,
Rio de Janeiro/RJ – Brazil, CEP 22451-900
`{grlopes,bnunes,casanova}@inf.puc-rio.br`
[3] L3S Research Center, Leibniz University Hannover, Appelstr. 9a, 30167 Hannover,
Germany
`{nunes,dietze}@l3s.de`

Abstract. One of the design principles that can stimulate the growth
and increase the usefulness of the Web of data is URIs linkage. However,
the related URIs are typically in different datasets managed by different
publishers. Hence, the designer of a new dataset must be aware of the
existing datasets and inspect their content to define *sameAs* links. This
paper proposes a technique based on probabilistic classifiers that, given
a datasets S to be published and a set T of known published datasets,
ranks each $T_i \in T$ according to the probability that links between S and
T_i can be found by inspecting the most relevant datasets. Results from
our technique show that the search space can be reduced up to 85%,
thereby greatly decreasing the computational effort.

Keywords: Linked Data, datasets recommendation, Bayesian classifier,
data interlinking.

1 Introduction

Over the past years there has been a considerable movement toward publishing
data on the Web following the Linked Data principles [1]. This huge effort has
resulted in the creation of catalogs of Linked Data datasets, such as *the Data
Hub*[1], to mainly make data findable and reusable. However, despite the fact that
extensive list of open datasets are available in these catalogs, most of the data
publishers still connects their datasets to other popular datasets, such as DB-
pedia[2], Freebase [3] and Geonames[4]. Although the linkage with popular datasets

---

[1] `http://datahub.io/`
[2] `http://dbpedia.org/`
[3] `http://www.freebase.com/`
[4] `http://www.geonames.org/`

F. Daniel, P. Dolog, and Q. Li (Eds.): ICWE 2013, LNCS 7977, pp. 354–366, 2013.
© Springer-Verlag Berlin Heidelberg 2013

would allow us to explore external resources, it would fail to cover highly specialized information. Basically, as described in [2], linkage with popular datasets is favoured because of two main reasons: (i) the difficulty in finding related open datasets; and (ii) the strenuous task of discovering instance mappings between different datasets.

Catalogues of linked data describe the content of datasets in terms of the update periodicity, authors, SPARQL endpoints, linksets with other datasets, amongst others, as recommended by *W3C Void Vocabulary* [3]. However, catalogues by themselves do not provide any explicit information to help the URI linkage process. Therefore, due to the lack of information or of an heuristic for selecting datasets, the search for links should be done almost by an exhaustive search of all datasets in the catalogues, which is rather unfeasible. On the other hand, catalogues may provide data for algorithms which would reduce the number of datasets to inspect.

This paper proposes a probabilistic classifier based on Bayesian theory that, given a dataset S to be published and a set T of known published datasets, ranks each $T_i \in T$ according to the probability that it will be possible to define links between URIs of S and T_i, so that most of the links, if not all, could be found by inspecting the most relevant datasets in the ranking. We refer to this technique as *dataset recommendation*.

The rest of the paper is organized as follows. Section 2 presents the most relevant related work in the area. Section 3 introduces our proposed technique based on probabilistic classifiers. Section 4 presents the experiments that we have conducted to test our technique. Section 5 presents some performance analysis. Finally, section 6 presents conclusions and future work.

2   Related Work

The recommendation for the interlinking of datasets in the Linked Data domain is a research area still initial but in expansion. Many recommendation systems have been studied and published, nevertheless most of them have been applied to e-commerce [4], social networks [5], professional jobs [6], amongst others, but they rarely have been applied to linked data recommendation. There are few approaches developed specifically for this purpose. The most related works are described in this section.

In general, the approaches to construct recommendation systems can be classified according to the filtering technique, as collaborative, content-based and hybrid [7, 8]. The first approach collect evidences for recommendation from similar behavior, for instance, if a group of users are interested in buying science fiction books, then recommend buying science fiction books for every one similar to them. The content-based approach is based on the preferences of users, for example, if a user has a collection of classical songs, then songs of the same genre are suggested. The hybrid approach combine the previous two to take advantage of their benefits.

In Open Innovation (OI) scenarios, where companies outsource tasks to a network of collaborators, Damljanovic et al. [9] present a Linked Data-based concept recommendation method for topic discovery that is used to match innovation problems and experts. Their approach exploits reference datasets to find direct or laterally related data from the user and problem descriptions. Although they tackle the problem of recommending experts to open innovation problems, their work is similar to ours since we focus on recommending the most relevant datasets to a data publisher.

Nikolov et al. [10, 2] propose an approach to identify relevant datasets for data linking. Their approach has two main steps: (i) searching for potential relevant entities in other datasets using as keywords a subset of labels in the new published dataset; and (ii) filtering out irrelevant datasets by measuring semantic concept similarities obtained by applying ontology matching techniques. The focus of their work is recommendation for the linking process. Thus, in the filtering step, they consider only the most relevant datasets based on their semantic similarity.

Lóscio et al. [11] propose the recommendation of relevant datasets for specific applications, i.e., sources that contribute to answering queries posed to the applications. The authors argue that a dataset may contribute to answering application queries, but the response may not be according to the user requirements. Thus, they propose the discovery of relevant datasets in a specific domain using information quality (IQ) as multidimensional criteria. Their recommendation function estimates a degree of relevance of a given dataset based on the IQ criteria of correctness, schema completeness and data completeness.

Oliveira et al. [12] use application queries and user feedback to the discover relevant datasets in Linked Data. The applications queries help filter datasets that are potentially strong candidates to be relevant and the user feedback helps analyze the relevance of such candidates. They argue that, by considering both aspects, one obtains better recommendations. While the works by Lóscio and Oliveira aim at recommending datasets with respect to user queries, Nikolov focuses on the recommendation for the linking process, which is closer to our approach.

Finally, Kuznetsov [13] presents a description of a data integration system for the Linked Open Space. In his work, he describes a modular architecture consisting mainly of a "linking system" responsible for (i) discovering relevant datasets for a given dataset and (ii) creating instance level linkage. Relevant datasets are discovered by using the *referer* attribute available in HTTP message header as described in [14] and ontology matching techniques are used to reduce the number of pairwise comparisons for instance matching. However, the work does not present any practical experiment to test the techniques. Although the approach described in this paper addresses the first step of the linking system described, we addressed (ii) in previous works [15–17].

Most of the related work presented in this section use techniques as keyword-based search, schema matching and ontology matching, while others adopt user feedback and information quality as criteria of relevance. By contrast, our approach considers the interlinking amongst data sources as a "high" level information, and does not perform analysis at the instance or schema levels. We do not explicitly consider a user query, and our recommendation function aims at recommending datasets that are candidates to be interlinked with a new dataset being published in the Web of Data. The inputs of our approach are the previous linkages of the candidates and some known linkage of the new dataset. For the generation of recommendation ranking, we propose a collaborative approach which uses Naive Bayes assumptions. To the best of our knowledge there is no previous work in this sense.

3   Proposed Technique

Instead of providing a restricted list of recommendations, we define the task of recommending datasets as a task of ranking existing datasets according to its relevance to URI linkage. Thus, it is at the user's discretion to decide how far he/she goes into the ranking in search for links. More precisely, the problem we address is:

> Given a dataset S, calculate a rank score for each dataset T_i $(i = 1, ..., m)$ in a known set T of datasets. The rank score should favor those datasets with the highest chance of containing resources that could be linked to resources of S.

We used metadata about connections between datasets available in catalogues as the source of evidences of relevance. The interconnection of datasets can be modeled as a directed graph $G = \{V, E\}$ where the nodes V are the datasets in T and there is an edge from A to B in E if and only if there is an RDF triple $t = (s, p, o) \in A$ whose subject s is a resource of A and whose object o is a resource of B; we say that t is a *link* from A to B. Furthermore, if there is an edge from A to B in E then we say that A is *connected* to B. Note that there can be only one edge from A to B, even if there are multiple distinct RDF triples linking A to B.

The actual evidences of relevance are extracted from the correlation between connections. For example, if datasets connected to DBLP, ACM and CiteSeer are very often connected to OAI (Open Archives Initiative) then suggest OAI for those datasets which are connected to DBLP, ACM and CiteSeer but not to OAI. Intuitively, a high degree of correlation between the sets of connections {DBLP, ACM and CiteSeer} and {OAI} may indicate that OAI is relevant for any dataset which is connected to DBLP, ACM and CiteSeer.

One can argue, at this point, that such correlation can be sometimes obvious inside a specific community, for example, datasets such as DBLP, ACM, Cite-Seer, IEEE, RAE, PubMed, etc. can be frequently correlated in the bibliographic domain. Moreover, generic datasets, such as DBPedia and Geonames, are correlated with quite a few datasets, as they provide generic resources and act as hubs for most datasets. However, as the Linked Data Web grows, the familiarity with the available datasets of specific domains can decrease and the generic datasets can become exceptions. Therefore, we believe that the correlation between connections, the basis of our recommendation technique, is an appropriate approach to the problem.

One can define the rank score function as a conditional probability:

$$score(T_i, S) = P(T_i|S). \tag{1}$$

where S is the event of selecting S as the dataset one wants to make recommendations to and T_i is the event of containing URIs in T_i that could be linked to URIs of S. As required, this score function favors those datasets with the highest probabilities of record linkage with S.

One can rewrite the above expression using Bayes's rule as follows:

$$score(T_i, S) = \frac{P(S|T_i)}{P(S)} P(T_i). \tag{2}$$

As in Bayesian classifiers [18, 19], one can represent S as a bag of features $F = \{f_1, ..., f_n\}$ and rewrite once more the above expression:

$$score(T_i, S) = \frac{P(\{f_1, ..., f_n\}|T_i)}{P(\{f_1, ..., f_n\})} P(T_i). \tag{3}$$

By the naive Bayes assumptions [18, 19] $P(\{f_1, f_2, ...,, f_n\}|T_i)$ can be calculated by multiplying probabilities. Moreover, because $P(S)$ is the same for every T_i and to make the computation simpler, the score function can be rewritten again:

$$score(T_i, S) = \left(\prod_{j=1..n} P(f_j|T_i) \right) P(T_i). \tag{4}$$

$$score(T_i, S) = \left(\sum_{j=1..n} log(P(f_j|T_i)) \right) + log(P(T_i)). \tag{5}$$

where we define that $\sum_{j=1..n} log(P(f_j|T_i)) = 0$, for $n = 0$, i.e., when S does not have any feature, the score function takes into account only the probability of connections to T_i. In this case, the most popular datasets , such as DBPedia, Geonames, etc. will be favored by the score at the expense of the more highly appropriate datasets. We are aware that the recommendation may not be quite accurate in such borderline cases, but we believe that a popularity-based ranking is preferable to no ranking at all, when nothing is known about S.

Equation 5, therefore, defines the final score function that induces the ranking of the datasets.

By using the maximum likelihood estimate of the probabilities [19] in a training dataset, the above probabilities can be calculated by the following ratios.

$$P(f_j|T_i) = \frac{count(f_j, T_i)}{\sum_{j=1}^{n} count(f_j, T_i)}. \tag{6}$$

$$P(T_i) = \frac{count(T_i)}{\sum_{i=1}^{m} count(T_i)}. \tag{7}$$

where $count(f_j, T_i)$ is the number of occurrences in the training set where datasets containing feature f_j are connected to a dataset T_i, $count(T_i)$ is the number of datasets connected to T_i in T disregarding the feature set. So, for any new dataset S represented by a set of features F, possibly empty, the rank position of each one of the existing datasets can be computed by equation (5).

So far we have used a generic set of features $F = \{f_1, ..., f_n\}$ of S without indicating how to apply it to the intuition that correlated datasets provide evidences on the degree of relevance of a dataset T_i to S. In the experiments of section 4, we used known connections of S as the feature set. In section 4, we also avoided the borderline case where no feature is known in order to analyze the effects of knowing some connections of S on the recommendations.

The maximum likelihood estimate can be computed in a training dataset as follows. Let,

- $Conn$ be a set of ordered pairs (T_j, T_i) indicating that a dataset T_j is connected to a dataset T_i in a training dataset.
- $Corr$ be a set of ordered triples (w, f_j, T_i) indicating that if a dataset w is connected to f_j then it is connected to T_i as well in the training dataset.

Fragments of $Conn$ and $Corr$ are depicted in Table 1.a and 1.b. Note that $Corr$ can be created from $Conn$ by making all possible combinations two by two of the connections of each distinct T_j.

Note that $count(f_j, T_i)$ in equation (6) can be computed from $Corr$ by counting distinct occurrences of pairs (f_j, T_i) and that $count(T_i)$ in equation (7) can be computed by counting distinct pairs (w, T_i). Equations (6) and (7) are then straightforward computed from these values.

4   Experiments

We tested the recommendation method with data available in the Data Hub catalogue[5], a repository of metadata of open datasets, in the style of Wikipedia. The Data Hub catalogue stores metadata of the datasets present in the Linking Open Data (LOD) cloud diagram [20]. It is openly editable and is running a data

---

[5] http://datahub.io

Table 1. Fragment of the existing connections of the Association for Computing Machinery (ACM) dataset in the Data Hub catalogue (*left side*) and simultaneous connections of ACM based on *Conn* and *Corr*

	Conn		Corr		
T_j	T_i		w	f_j	T_i
acm	dblp		acm	dblp	citeseer
acm	citeseer		acm	ieee	citeseer
acm	ieee		acm	citeseer	dblp
			acm	ieee	dblp
			acm	dblp	ieee
			acm	citeseer	ieee

(a)   (b)

cataloguing software (CKAN)[6] maintained by the Open Knowledge Foundation[7].

A multivalued property named *relationships*, available in the catalogue vocabulary and exposed by the REST API[8] of the catalogue, whose domain is the complete set of catalogued datasets, allows one to assert that a dataset T_j is connected to a dataset T_i by adding the assertions $T_j[relationships] = \_node$ and $\_node[object] = T_i$ to the catalogue data. We used the property *relationships* to extract the relation $Conn = (T_j, T_i)$.

To evaluate the technique, we adopted the 10-fold cross validation approach. The *Conn* relation is split into training and testing sets in ten different ways. Testing partitions contain datasets with known connections which are used as feature sets and ground truth connections for assessment of the ranking. Training partitions contain datasets to compute the probabilities in equations (6) and (7). The overall performance is taken as the average of the performances in the testing partitions. We stress that the references between datasets were extracted from existing metadata (property *relationships*) in the Data Hub catalogue.

In order to define a performance measure, recall that the technique aims at reducing the search space for defining links by ranking existing datasets. Without an appropriate ranking of datasets, the discovery of new connections to a dataset S requires the search for links possibly in all known datasets, which is unfeasible. With the appropriate ranking, datasets more likely to contain connections from S will be better positioned in the ranking and the search could be concentrated on those datasets at the top of the ranking. It is clear, however, that the reduction in effort will only be good if one can search only a small portion of the ranking. As we are going to show later, the results indicate that, on the average, only 15% of the ranking was needed to find all connections of S.

---

[6] http://ckan.org
[7] http://okfn.org
[8] http://datahub.io/api/rest/dataset/[datasetid]

From the above, we defined a performance measure based on the ranking positions of the discovered connections of datasets in the testing partitions. Intuitively, for example, if the less relevant discovered connection of a dataset was in the tenth position in a rank of one hundred datasets, it would mean that the search space for links could be reduced to 10% of the complete set of datasets, since no more connections would be found further down the ranking.

More formally, we define the performance measure as follows. Let,

- S be a dataset in a test partition
- C be the set of connections of S in the test partition
- $\{F, R\}$ be a partition of C
- F be the set of connection chosen as features of S
- R be the set of connections to be found

Table 2, shows the connections (a) of the Association for Computing Machinery (ACM) extracted from the Data Hub catalogue at http://datahub.io/api/rest/dataset/rkb-explorer-acm, and two different choices of feature sets F_1 (b) and F_2 (c). For each set of features, one wants to find the remaining connections of the ACM dataset.

Table 2. Existing connections of the Association for Computing Machinery (ACM) in the Data Hub catalogue (a), two sets of features of ACM (b and c)

C			
budapest	citeseer	cordis	courseware
curriculum	dblp	dbpedia	deepblue
dog-food	dotac	ecs-eprints	eprints
epsrc	eurecom	freebase	ft
ibm	ieee	irit	kisti
laas	newcastle	nsf	oai
pisa	rae2001	resex	risks
roma	southampton	ulm	wiki

F_1
deepblue
eurecom
nsf
resex

F_2
dblp
ecs-eprints
laas
rae2001

(a)   (b)   (c)

Start by computing the ranking $score(T_i, S)$ of all datasets T_i in the training partition for S represented by F_j, ($j = 1, 2$) and let P_j be the position furthest down in the ranking among all the positions of the datasets in $R_j = C - F_j$. The rankings for both feature sets are shown in Table 3.a and 3.b respectively.

Let P be the number of datasets that must be inspected, if one wants to find all connections of S following the ranking. Let M be the total number of distinct datasets in the training partition, then $P' = P/M$ is the proportion of datasets necessary to find all connections of S. The smaller the proportion is, the better the ranking will be. If one repeats the above process for each S in a testing partition and for each different partition $\{F, R\}$ of S, one can calculate the arithmetic mean of P' in a test partition p, denoted by $\overline{P'_p}$. If we repeat the process for all test partitions one can take the arithmetic mean of $\overline{P'_p}$, denoted by $\overline{\overline{P'_p}}$, as the overall performance.

In our running example, we have that $M = 768$. The result for the set F_1 shows that the worst dataset is in thirty-sixth place and, therefore, the performance in this case is calculated as $36/768 = 4,69\%$. On the other hand, if we take the feature set F_2, the performance is $128/768 = 16,67\%$.

Table 3. Fragment of the recommendation ranking given that ACM was represented by the set of features F_1 (a) and fragment of a second ranking given the set of features F_2 (b)

Fragment of ranking 1		Fragment of ranking 2	
position	dataset	position	dataset
4	freebase	6	wiki
5	ecs-eprints	7	eprints
6	kisti	8	oai
7	southampton	9	dotac
9	roma	10	citeseer
10	wiki	12	southampton
11	dblp	15	ieee
14	budapest	17	budapest
20	oai	25	curriculum
22	citeseer	29	ibm
27	ibm	58	eurecom
29	ieee	60	dbpedia
32	risks	67	risks
33	epsrc	127	deepblue
36	dbpedia	128	freebase

(a)   (b)

5   Performance Analysis

Recall from the previous section that

- S is a dataset in a test partition
- F is the set of connection chosen as features of S
- R is the set of connections to be found
- P is the number of datasets that must be inspected, if one wants to find all connections of S following the ranking
- P' is the proportion of datasets necessary to find all connections of S
- $\overline{P'_p}$ is the arithmetic mean of P' in a test partition p
- $\overline{\overline{P'_p}}$ is the the arithmetic mean of $\overline{P'_p}$ over all test partitions

- $\overline{P_p}$ is the arithmetic mean of P in a test partition p
- $\overline{\overline{P_p}}$ is the the arithmetic mean of $\overline{P_p}$ over all test partitions

Also recall that, given a dataset S, the purpose of the technique is to produce a ranking of datasets such that the closer a dataset S' is to the top, the higher the chances that S' contains resources that could be linked to resources of S.

In this section, we analyze the followings aspects of the recommendation technique:

Q1 Given a ranking of recommended datasets, how far down the ranking a dataset must be to contribute with new links? That is, what is the ranking efficiency?

Q2 What is the effect of the size of the feature set on the ranking efficiency. Would a bigger feature set lead to more precise rankings?

Q3 What is the effect of increasing the number of datasets to be found (or recommended)? If the number of irrelevant datasets increased relatively to what had to be found, then the method would be less efficient for large volumes of recommendations.

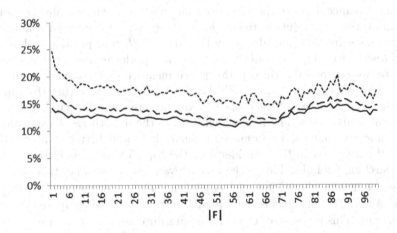

Fig. 1. Performance function $\overline{\overline{P'_p}}(|F|)$, where $|F|$ is the size of the feature set: (a) *dotted line*: Performance computed with rank positions of all datasets in R; (b) *dashed line*: Performance computed by discarding the worst rank position of the datasets in R; (c) *solid line*: Performance computed by discarding the two worst rank positions of the datasets in R

To answer the first two questions, we computed the average performance, $\overline{\overline{P'_p}}$, as a function of the size of the feature set $|F|$ (shown as *dotted line* in Fig. 1). One can see that the efficiency of the ranking is approximately 20%, no matter what is the size of the feature set $|F|$. Hence, the user may consider only the top 20% datasets in the ranking when searching for links.

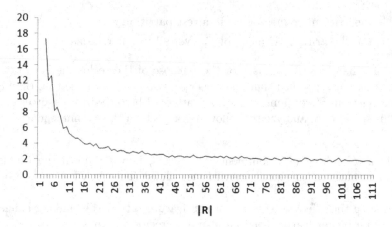

Fig. 2. Performance function $\overline{\overline{P_p}}(|R|)/|R|$, where $|R|$ is the size of the set of connections to be found. P is used instead of P' to compute the arithmetic means.

However, we realized that outliers caused by insufficient data distorted the average performance. Indeed, the size of training partitions was not always enough to compute the probabilities. Hence, for each set R, we computed a new performance measure that considers only the $(|R| - 1)th$ best positions (shown in *dashed line* in Fig. 1)). To confirm that the first performance curve was really disparate, we computed a third performance measure that considered only the $(|R| - 2)th$ best positions (shown as *solid line* in Fig. 1)). Note that the gap between the dotted curve and the dashed curve is greater than the gap between the dashed curve and the solid curve, which justifies the hypothesis. To summarize, Fig. 1 indicates that the performance measure is indeed better at about 15%, that is, the user may in fact consider only the top 15% datasets in the ranking when searching for links. This is the first relevant contribution of this paper.

To answer the third question, we analyzed the behavior of the ratio $\overline{\overline{P_p}}(|R|)/|R|$ (shown in Fig. 2). Note that here we used P instead of P' to compute the arithmetic means. This is because $|R|$ is also an absolute number of datasets. Therefore, $\overline{\overline{P_p}}(|R|)$ denotes the average worst position to find a total of $|R|$ datasets. It does not restrict the number of features of S. Actually, to compute $\overline{\overline{P_p}}(|R|)$ we considered datasets with any number of features. For instance, to compute $\overline{\overline{P_p}}(5)$ we selected all S in the testing partitions with $|C| > 5$ and for all partitions $\{F, R\}$ of each S where $|R| = 5$ we computed P. After that, we computed $\overline{\overline{P_p}}(5)$.

Note that $\overline{\overline{P_p}}(|R|)/|R|$ tends to be approximately equal to 2, which means that the number of datasets that should be inspected is twice the number of connections that have to be found. This result shows that the computational effort to find connections depends exclusively on the number of connections to be found in a proportion of 2:1. We stress that it is not an intuitive conclusion. We expected that, as the number of datasets to discover grew, the proportion of irrelevant datasets amongst the relevant ones would increase faster. This would negatively impact the recommendation algorithm. Unlike our expectation the number of irrelevant datasets increased in the same proportion. This is the second and last relevant contribution of this paper.

6 Conclusions

Aligned with the Linked Data recommendations [1], and the W3C VoID Vocabulary [3] we proposed a ranking technique that can be used to recommend datasets and that can dramatically reduce the computational effort to find connections amongst datasets. The technique proved to reduce about 85% of the search space and to make the computational effort of finding datasets proportional to the number of datasets to be found.

As future work, we plan to explore how to improve the results by taking into account the information domain of the datasets. Given a dataset S, the other datasets could be clustered by information domain and valued proportionally to the information domains of S. To achieve this, one would have to add a preliminary classification step to find all possible information domains of S.

References

1. Berners-Lee, T.: Linked Data. In: Design Issues. W3C (2006)
2. Nikolov, A., d'Aquin, M., Motta, E.: What Should I Link to? Identifying Relevant Sources and Classes for Data Linking. In: Proceedings of the Joint International Semantic Technology Conference (JIST), pp. 284–299. Springer, Heidelberg (2012)
3. Alexander, K., Cyganiak, R., Hausenblas, M., Zhao, J.: Describing Linked Datasets with the VoID Vocabulary. W3C (March 2011)
4. Schafer, J.B., Konstan, J., Riedi, J.: Recommender systems in e-commerce. In: Proceedings of the 1st ACM Conference on Electronic Commerce (EC), pp. 158–166 (1999)
5. Konstas, I., Stathopoulos, V., Jose, J.M.: On social networks and collaborative recommendation. In: Proceedings of the 32nd International ACM Conference on Research and Development in Information Retrieval (SIGIR), pp. 195–202 (2009)
6. Malinowski, J., Keim, T., Wendt, O., Weitzel, T.: Matching People and Jobs: A Bilateral Recommendation Approach. In: Proceedings of the 39th Annual Hawaii International Conference on Print (HICSS), p. 137c (2006)
7. Ricci, F., Rokach, L., Shapira, B., Kantor, P.B.: Recommender Systems Handbook. Springer (2011)
8. Jannach, D., Zanker, M., Felfernig, A., Friedrich, G.: Recommender systems: an introduction. Cambridge University Press, New York (2011)
9. Damljanovic, D., Stankovic, M., Laublet, P.: Linked Data-Based Concept Recommendation: Comparison of Different Methods in Open Innovation Scenario. In: Simperl, E., Cimiano, P., Polleres, A., Corcho, O., Presutti, V. (eds.) ESWC 2012. LNCS, vol. 7295, pp. 24–38. Springer, Heidelberg (2012)
10. Nikolov, A., d'Aquin, M.: Identifying Relevant Sources for Data Linking using a Semantic Web Index. In: Proceedings of the 4th Linked Data on the Web Workshop (LDOW) (2011)

11. Lóscio, B.F., Batista, M., Souza, D.: Using information quality for the identification of relevant web data sources. In: Proceedings of the 14th International Conference on Information Integration and Web-based Applications & Services, pp. 36–44 (2012)
12. de Oliveira, H.R., Tavares, A.T., Lóscio, B.F.: Feedback-based data set recommendation for building linked data applications. In: Proceedings of the 8th International Conference on Semantic Systems (I-SEMANTICS), pp. 49–55 (2012)
13. Kuznetsov, K.A.: Scientific data integration system in the linked open data space. Programming and Computer Software 39(1), 43–48 (2013)
14. Mühleisen, H., Jentzsch, A.: Augmenting the Web of Data using Referers. In: Proceedings of the 4th Linked Data on the Web Workshop (LDOW) (2011)
15. Leme, L.A.P.P., Casanova, M.A., Breitman, K.K., Furtado, A.L.: Instance-based OWL schema matching. In: Filipe, J., Cordeiro, J. (eds.) ICEIS. LNBIP, vol. 24, pp. 14–26. Springer, Heidelberg (2009)
16. Leme, L.A.P., Brauner, D.F., Breitman, K.K., Casanova, M.A., Gazola, A.: Matching object catalogues. Innovations in Systems and Software Engineering 4(4), 315–328 (2008)
17. Nunes, B.P., Mera, A., Casanova, M.A., Breitman, K.K., Leme, L.A.P.P.: Complex Matching of RDF Datatype Properties. Technical Report MCC12/11 (December 2011)
18. Witten, I.H., Frank, E., Hall, M.A.: Data Mining: Practical Machine Learning Tools and Techniques. Morgan Kaufmann (January 2011)
19. Manning, C.D., Schütze, H.: Foundations of Statistical Natural Language Processing. The MIT Press (2002)
20. Cyganiak, R., Jentzsch, A.: (Linking Open Data cloud diagram)

Discovering Links between Political Debates and Media

Damir Juric[1,3], Laura Hollink[2], and Geert-Jan Houben[1]

[1] Delft University of Technology
[2] VU University Amsterdam
[3] FER University of Zagreb

Abstract. Politics and media are heavily intertwined and both play a role in the discussion on policy proposals and current affairs. However, a dataset that allows a joint analysis of the two does not yet exist. In this paper we take the first step by discovering links between parliamentary debates in a political dataset and newspaper articles in a media dataset. Our approach consists of 3 steps. We first discover topics discussed in the debates. Second, we query a newspaper archive for relevant articles using a combination of debate elements: dates, actors, topics, and named entities of the debates. Finally, we discover links, represent them in RDF, and make them available for download. An evaluation of various versions of this approach shows that the topic detection adds to the quality of the discovered links, as well as the use of the semantic structure of the debate, such as headers and a division into smaller events.

Keywords: RDF, parliamentary debates, NER, topic modeling, linking.

1 Introduction

In this paper we present our work on the linking of political debates to media articles. We present the design choices for a model in which we capture parliamentary debates, including how they are covered by various media, and we describe the method for automatic linking between the speeches inside the debates and various media articles.

To make comparisons between different types of media outlets, links between datasets would need to be produced. Such links could, for example, support researchers that want to know how political debates are represented in the media and how the representation of topics and people change over time. We aim to facilitate this kind of analysis by providing links between datasets of political debate events and media data.

The presented method for link discovery aims to connect debate content on a speech level with relevant articles that contain not just the mentions of speakers but also mentions of speakers in a context of topics that politicians tackled in their speech in parliament. This goal made task much harder, because context of the consequential speeches is often very similar (politicians are speaking about same general topic of the day). We had to extract enough semantics from each particular speech so that we could retrieve more articles reporting on the particularities of politician's speech and

F. Daniel, P. Dolog, and Q. Li (Eds.): ICWE 2013, LNCS 7977, pp. 367–375, 2013.

not just mentioning his name in the context of general topics of the debate (which is also often the case). We used semantic and information retrieval techniques to generate automatic queries that contain the context of the parliamentary speeches and to search newspaper dataset for the connections between speeches and newspaper articles that are covering them. Since the debate transcripts that we use as a source posses structural elements such as debate and conversation descriptions, we wanted to explore if using these elements will help us in our goal of creating the debate-media dataset.

This paper is organized as follows. First, we describe the PoliMedia project in which this work is carried out. In Section 2 we present our method for discovering links between speeches and the media articles. In Section 3 we evaluate the method on a randomly generated dataset, and finally in Section 4 we conclude our work.

1.1   Related Work

We draw on previous work from various domains: other projects using parliamentary debate data, event modeling, relatedness discovery, topic modeling, and entity linking.

[1] presents an approach that extends existing metadata enrichment processes with a method to discover historical events. In [2], the authors put events as the central elements in the representation of data from domains such as history, cultural heritage, multimedia and geography. The Simple Event Model (SEM) is created to model events in these various domains, without making assumptions about the domain-specific vocabularies used. In [3] the authors describe a real life problem using SEM. The problem of link discovery is tackled in [4]: it presents a validation approach of detected alignment links between dialog transcript and discussed documents, in the context of a multimodal document alignment framework of multimedia events (meetings and lectures). In [5] the authors present a function that discovers relatedness between news articles across four aspects: relevance, novelty, connection clarity, and transition smoothness. Although, our work does not perform the same task (we do not have a knowledge base, and we are interested in topics and not just in the named entities), this field of work is related to ours. In [6] authors describe the system that disambiguate entity mentions in text and link them to a knowledge base. They approach readily ports to knowledge bases other than Wikipedia. The Text Analytics Conference on Knowledge Base Population (TAC-KBP) included the task of entity linking [7]. Some of the examples include the use of information retrieval techniques for retrieving the correct knowledge base entry, such as query expansion [8], and generative clustering models for entities in text based on knowledge base entries [9]. In [10] authors presented algorithm for linking between two different archives, the news archive as a source and multimedia archive as target. Although the problem is similar to ours, in this task target archive is heavily annotated by human annotators. Domain experts extracted entities and topics manually, which is different from our case. In [11] retrieval techniques are used to link between four different encyclopedias. They report 40% precision at 100% recall. In our case, we do not have the similar or same type of articles (like encyclopedia articles) but noisy spoken text and concise newspaper articles.

2   Linking Speeches from the Debates to Media Articles

Our PoliMedia method consists of three steps. First, we enrich the existing debate metadata with topics. Second, for each speech, we search the archive for candidate articles based on when they were published (7 days after the debate) and occurrence of the name of the speaker of the speech. Finally, we rank these candidate articles based on similarity to the query (automatically created from speech text) by comparing vectors of topics and named entities. We create links between a speech and an article if the similarity score is above a threshold t.

2.1   Topic Modeling

For each speech inside a debate segment (called *PartOfDebate* in our method) we extract ten words that represent one topic discussed inside the speech. Also all speeches contained inside one debate segment are concatenated into one text and the set of ten words that represent one topic of the debate segment as a whole is then extracted from that text. Debate is queried for all *PartOfDebate* identifiers, which represents a number of different topics that are being discussed in this particular debate. The *PartOfDebate* identifiers contain properties that lead to the actual speeches and their descriptions (*DebateContext*). At this point we create two vectors that are populated with named entity values (those values are objects in statements '*DebateContext mentions NEs$_{context}$*' and '*Speech mentions NEs$_{speech}$*'). The objects of the *hasSpokenText* and *hasText* properties are taken and sent for preprocessing. In the preprocessing step text we remove all the words that have high frequency but bring a small amount of information. In [12] it is stated that probabilistic topic models are a popular tool for the unsupervised analysis of text, providing both a predictive model of future text and a latent topic representation of the corpus, and that it can be used to check models, summarize the corpus, and guide exploration of its contents. Topic models lead to semantically meaningful decompositions of text because they tend to place high probability on words that represent concepts, and documents are represented as expressions of those concepts. We used a Java-based package for statistical natural language processing, document classification, clustering, topic modeling, information extraction, etc., called Mallet [13]. Mallet uses a fast and highly scalable implementation of Gibbs sampling. [14].

2.2   Search for Candidate Articles and Ranking

In the second step, we preselect data by fetching all available media from secondary datasets by using the Search and Retrieve protocol (SRU). Preselected data contains only those articles in which the name of the speaker from the debate can be found in a time span of seven days after the speech has been spoken in the parliament.

In the third step, the transcript of the parliamentary debate (in XML format) is used as a primary source for the task of finding links between the speeches that the debate consists of and the media articles. Each debate contains some basic metadata that depicts a debate as a whole (it should be noticed that one debate can actually contain more than one part with different topics (spoken on a same day) that we call *part of the debate* in this article), of which the date when the speeches were spoken in the Dutch parliament is the most important one. Each part of the debate (collection of speeches that are all about single theme) has its description that consists of an unstructured text. Each article is treated as a document D for which we calculate the similarity with the previously automatically created query Q_{exp} (that should represent the context of the debate). We pose our task of finding relevant newspaper articles for a speech in a debate as an information retrieval problem using the vector space model, where we consider the speech as the query Q and the newspaper article as the document D. Fetched candidate articles are tokenized, stripped of stop words, and indexed. Each article D is represented as a term vector $\vec{d}$ of length n, where n is the length of the total number of terms in our corpus of candidate articles. The elements of $\vec{d}$ are term frequency–inverse document frequency (TF-IDF) scores. We create vectors for each speech in the debate, made up of topic sets as discussed in Section 2.1 and named entities (NEs) that are associated to the speeches with the *polivoc:mentions* property. Similarly, we create vectors for topic sets and NEs derived from the *debateContext* of the speech. Element *debateContext* is a short description of the subjects that will be addressed in the forthcoming debate segment, that is read by the chairman (*voorzitter*) of the debate. Given the *debateContext*, we detect topic sets from the text of all speeches that fall under the same *debateContext*. We select NEs mentioned in the introductory text of the *debateContext*. In this way, the semantic structure of the debate enables us to treat the speeches not as isolated pieces of text but as part of a broader conversation.

In total, this process results in 4 vectors for each speech: NEs_{speech}, $NEs_{context}$, $Topics_{speech}$, $Topics_{context}$.

For each speech, we measure similarity between the article vectors of the candidate articles and the four debate speech vectors that represent the speech. We use two state-of-the-art measures: the cosine similarity measure and the BM25 similarity measure. Standard cosine similarity is used because it is proven to work best for this type of comparisons [4]. Both measures produce similar matches but with different rankings. Since ranking is not our primary concern (our goal is to populate the dataset with relevant documents, regardless of their ranking) we choose the cosine similarity measure because it suits better to our needs. Because cosine similarity values range between 0 and 1 it was easier to find a threshold for what we take as a relevant document, then with BM25. Articles with a score above a threshold (0.01) are linked to the speech with the *polivoc:coveredIn* property. We exclude articles where only one (or few) vector contributes to the high similarity score by means of an overlap measure. The overlap coefficient is related to the Jaccard index that computes the overlap between two sets. The method pipeline is presented in Fig. 1. The debate transcript serves as an entry point.

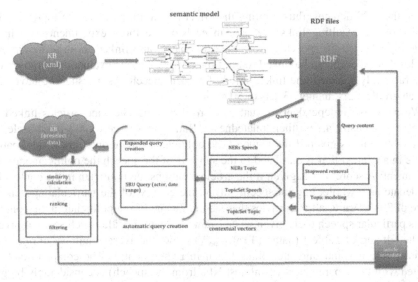

Fig. 1. Method pipeline

3 Experiments

To gain insight into the quality and added value of the various steps of the linking method described in the previous section, we have performed experiments with three versions of the method. Specifically, we have varied which information is used to rank the candidate articles (named entities (NEs), topics) and whether the *partOf* relations between speeches and larger parts of debates are used to also include information associated to these larger parts (debate segments).

Experiment 1: NEs in speech In the most simple form of our method, we rank articles only based on the NEs found in the speech.

Experiment 2: NEs + topics in speech Here, we include not only NEs but also topics detected for the speech.

Experiment 3: NEs + topics in speech and context Finally, we include not just NEs and topics extracted from the speech itself but combine those with NEs extracted from the debate context and topics extracted from all speeches in this context.

The method to query the media archive and select candidate articles is kept constant: we query the archive for articles that mention the name of the speaker and were published within 7 days after the date of the debate. The value 7 is based on our own estimation of the time media takes to write about political debates. Since it is kept constant, a potential suboptimal value will not affect the results. In the future, we intend to investigate what is the optimal value to produce the highest quality of links.

For the experiments, we have randomly selected 20 debates from our dataset of 10,924 debates. The subjects of those debates ranged from fraud in the social system to the European elections. In all three experiments we have linked speeches from within these 20 debates, thus limiting the effect of variations in debate topics on the quality of the resulting links. Second, in each of the three experiments, we have randomly selected 50 speeches from the 20 debates, and linked these to newspaper articles. One speech can be linked to multiple articles, but for evaluation purposes we have randomly selected one linked article for each speech. As a result, we have 150 speech-article pairs, namely 3 sets of 50 each.

We used two independent evaluators to read the speeches and articles linked to them and manually assess their relatedness. Rating was done on a 3-point scale. A score of *0* score is given if the name of the politician is mentioned in the newspaper article in a context that is unrelated to the subjects of the speech the politician gave in parliament; A score of *1* is given if the article mentions the politician in the context of the debate as a whole, but not specifically in the context of the particular speech; A score of *2* is given to all the articles that mention name of the politician in the context of his particular speech (X is given when evaluators can't decide which score to give).

The left part of Table 1 (dataset $Eval_{NESpeech}$) shows the average number of relevant, partially relevant and unrelated links found in Experiment 1. The complete dataset created with these parameters (using just NEs from the speech) is considerably bigger than other two datasets, as a result of using the least specific query (the whole dataset contains 5887 linked articles). Also, for the same reason this dataset contains a large number of unrelated articles. In [15], the authors stated that NEs play an important role in news documents. They wanted to exploit that characteristic by considering them as the only distinguishing features of the documents. In our experiments we found out that using just NEs is not enough to distinguish between newspaper articles. For that reason we included an additional element, the topics from the speech. Results of the evaluation of our method with that additional parameter can be seen in the middle part of Table 1 (dataset $Eval_{NESpeechTSpeech}$). It is visible that the second dataset represents an improvement over the first dataset in terms of quality (this dataset contained 4449 linked articles in total).

Table 1. Evaluation of produced links based on NEs from speech and on NEs and topics from speech speech and debate description element

$Eval_N$ $ESpeech$	Eval1	Eval2	$Eval_{NESpeechTSpeech}$	Eval1	Eval2	$Eval_{All}$	Eval 1	Eval 2
0	20/40%	18/36%	0	10/20%	13/26%	0	3/ 6%	9/18%
1	13/26%	16/32%	1	16/32%	20/40%	1	17/34%	19/38%
2	11/22%	8/16%	2	15/30%	11/22%	2	24/48%	20/40%
X	6/12%	8/16%	X	9/18%	6/12%	X	6/12%	2/ 4%

Finally, we produced the third dataset by harvesting the debate structure. We used NEs and topics from debate descriptions to create a query that is more specific than both previous queries. In $Eval_{All}$ we can see that the resulting dataset has the best quality (for our purpose that means the biggest number of relevant links, with scores 1 or 2). This dataset contained 3804 linked articles in total. Evaluator agreement (Cohen's Kappa) was 0.5207, which represents a moderate agreement.

Table 2. Evaluation of produced links based on speech and debate description element

Recall - To calculate recall we had to conduct a different kind of evaluation. Since for each speech we have a different query, only way to calculate meaningful recall was to analyze the speech, create the query manually and then search the library portal in the same time span as our algorithm. Evaluator task was to analyze five arbitrarily chosen speeches and to manually create a query that should retrieve all articles containing those terms in the given context. Then evaluator had to analyze articles retrieved from using the manual queries (115 newspaper articles) and to decide how many of them are relevant to the particular speech. With settings as in experiment nr.3 recall was 62% with precision 75% (using the same threshold as for previous evaluation). Lowering the threshold didn't change our recall but precision fall to 72% (Fig. 2ab, exp 3). We discovered that the only way to make the recall higher is to remove vector with NEs from debate description from the system. This vector is used as a control of topic drift, so without that vector we got highest recall but with low precision of 50% (Fig. 2ab, exp4). Since we aim to have more quality than quantity in our final dataset we decided to use the vector with NEs from debate descriptions. With settings as from experiments nr.1 and nr.2 we got again lower precision but higher recall in some cases (Fig. 2ab).

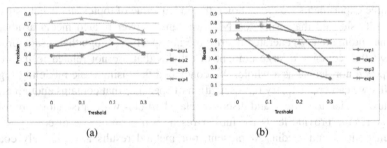

(a)   (b)

Fig. 2. Precision and relative recall

After this evaluation we can conclude that the query representation of the speech as a combination of named entities (from speech itself and debate descriptions) and topics (from speech itself and the whole conversation) in combination with used similarity measures works best for our goal of discovering media articles that covers the topics from the parliament. The structural elements contained in the transcripts (like possibility to distinguish segments of the debates that represents one conversation between many actors) played important part in formalizing a speech into a complex query. Also, great deal of help was the metadata available from the transcripts, which allowed us to preselect newspaper archive using predefined time span. Evaluation showed what we expected, that treating particular speech as a part of the bigger context (conversation) and creating a query that is a mixture of elements from both structures will retrieve higher number or relevant articles, because the newspaper articles from this domain are usually written in a form of report, where general subject discussed in the debate are mentioned intertwined with topics from particular speeches. Extracting topics from the speech was crucial for producing better recall and using just named entities from the speech produces very low precision. But extracting additional topics from collection of speeches contained under one description and additional extracting named entities from that description, gave us enough semantics to retrieve articles connected to the speech with reasonable precision and recall.

4   Conclusion and Next Steps

In this paper we have studied the creation of links between a dataset of political debates and a media archive. We have presented a linking method that takes advantage of metadata associated to the debates, NEs mentioned in the debate, topics detected in the debates, and the semantic *partOf* structure of the debates. We succeeded to create a pipeline for linking two very different types of text: debate transcripts containing spoken language full of digressions and different entities, and short and concise newspapers. We analyzed each parliamentary speech as a part of a bigger debate, i.e. taking into account the structure of the debate. The links we produced are of a different nature than those produced by e.g. ontology alignment tools.

In three experiments we have shown the added value of topics and debate structure. The results showed that using the NEs we can discover related media articles, but since the automatically generated queries are not specific enough their usage produces a dataset that contains a large amount of articles that are not related to the context from speech nor debate as a whole. We concluded that using topic modeling together with NEs we can create query representation of speeches that contains enough amount of context needed to retrieve and discover related articles with satisfactory precision.

These results provide leads for further research into automatic discovery of links between politics and media. At present, our method results are relatively coarsely typed links; we are able to discover that a speech and an article are linked, but we remain unclear about the nature and strength of the link. While it would be easy for us to *represent* a finer distinction of link types in RDF, the interpretation and usefulness of various types of links requires further study and will necessarily be an interdisciplinary effort. In future work, we aim to look into the direction of the links – whether politics influences media, or media influences politics – and the strength of the links, including how the strength varies as more time passes between the date of the political event and the publication of the media article.

While the presented method is designed to use the specific structure of the data and metadata at hand, the general idea of combining *who* (actors), *what* (named entities and topics) and *when* (dates) to find documents related to an event is applicable also outside the domain of Dutch parliamentary data. Future work includes generalization of the linking method to other (political) topics and other media collections such as televised news and radio bulletins (for which the first experiments look promising).

A virtual research environment will be built that allows the exploration of the debate topics and media coverage thereof via search and browsing. Next to the use of standard information retrieval libraries (Lucene), navigation options will be implemented that will allow users to browse through the linked datasets of debates and different types of media (newspapers, radio and video content).

References

1. van Erp, Marieke, et al.: Automatic Heritage Metadata Enrichment with Historic Events. In: Trant, J., Bearman, D. (eds.) Museums and the Web 2011: Proceedings. Archives & Museum Informatics, Toronto (2011)
2. van Hage, W., Malaisé, V., Segers, R., Hollink, L., Schreiber, G.: Design and use of the Simple Event Model (SEM). J. Web Semantics (2011)
3. van Hage, W.R., Malaisé, V., de Vries, G., Schreiber, G., van Someren, M.: Combining Ship Trajectories and Semantics with the Simple Event Model (SEM). In: Proceedings of the 1st ACM International Workshop on Events in Multimedia, pp. 73–80 (2009)
4. Mekhaldi, D., Lalanne, D.: Multimodal Document Alignment: Feature-based Validation to Strengthen Thematic Links. JMPT 1(1), 30–46 (2010)
5. Lv, Y., Moon, T., Kolari, P., Zheng, Z., Wang, X., Chang, Y.: Learning to model relatedness for news recommendation. In: WWW (2011)
6. Rao, D., McNamee, P., Dreze, M.: Entity Linking: Finding Extracted Entities in a Knowledge Base. Springer Lecture Notes in Computer Science: Multisource, Multilingual Information Extraction and Summarization (2011)
7. Gottipati, S., Jiang, J.: SMU-SIS at TAC 2010 - KBP Track Entity Linking. In: Proceedings of Text Analysis Conference (TAC 2010) Workshop (2010)
8. Gottipati, S., Jiang, J.: Linking entities to a knowledge base with query expansion. Empirical Methods in Natural Language Processing, EMNLP (2011)
9. Han, X., Sun, L.: A generative entity-mention model for linking entities with knowledge base. Association for Computational Linguistics (2011)
10. Bron, M., Huurnink, B., de Rijke, M.: Linking Archives Using Document Enrichment and Term Selection. In: Gradmann, S., Borri, F., Meghini, C., Schuldt, H. (eds.) TPDL 2011. LNCS, vol. 6966, pp. 360–371. Springer, Heidelberg (2011)
11. Kern, R., Granitzer, M.: German encyclopedia alignment based on information retrieval techniques. In: Lalmas, M., Jose, J., Rauber, A., Sebastiani, F., Frommholz, I. (eds.) ECDL 2010. LNCS, vol. 6273, pp. 315–326. Springer, Heidelberg (2010)
12. Chang, J., Boyd-Graber, J.L., Gerrish, S., Wang, C., Blei, D.M.: Reading Tea Leaves: How Humans Interpret Topic Models. In: Advances in Neural Information Processing Systems 22: 23rd Annual Conference on Neural Information Processing Systems (2009)
13. McCallum, Andrew Kachites: MALLET: A Machine Learning for Language Toolkit (2002), http://mallet.cs.umass.edu
14. Darling, W.M.: A Theoretical and Practical Implementation Tutorial on Topic Modeling and Gibbs Sampling (2011)
15. Montalvo, S., Martínez, R., Casillas, A., Fresno, V.: Bilingual news clustering using named entities and fuzzy similarity. In: Matoušek, V., Mautner, P. (eds.) TSD 2007. LNCS (LNAI), vol. 4629, pp. 107–114. Springer, Heidelberg (2007)

Assisting User Browsing over Linked Data: Requirements Elicitation with a User Study

Dhavalkumar Thakker, Vania Dimitrova, Lydia Lau, Fan Yang-Turner,
and Dimoklis Despotakis

University of Leeds, Leeds LS2 9JT, UK
{D.Thakker,V.G.Dimitrova,L.M.S.Lau,
F.Yang-Turner,scdd}@leeds.ac.uk

Abstract. There are growing arguments that linked data technologies can be utilised to enable user-oriented exploratory search systems for the future Internet. Recently, search over linked data has been studied in different domains and contexts. However, there is still limited insight into how conventional semantic browsers over linked data can be extended to empower exploratory search, which is open-ended, multi-faceted and iterative in nature. Empirical user studies in representative domains can identify problems and elicit requirements for innovative functionality to assist user exploration. This paper presents such an approach – a user study with a uni-focal semantic data browser over several datasets linked via domain ontologies is used to inform what intelligent features are needed in order to assist exploratory search through linked data. We report main problems experienced by users while conducting exploratory search tasks, based on which requirements for algorithmic support to address the observed issues are elicited. A semantic signposting approach for extending a semantic data browser is proposed as a way to address the derived requirements.

Keywords: Linked Data, Exploratory Search, Requirements Elicitation.

1   Introduction

Linked Data technologies have received wider acceptance, both in industry and academia. One of the major factors for this success has been the availability of large amount of semantic data in various formats and domains. In parallel with engineering solutions for seamless generation of semantic data, efforts have been made to facilitate user interaction with such data. There are growing arguments that Linked Data technologies can be utilised to enable user-oriented exploratory search systems for the future Internet [1]. In contrast to regular search, exploratory search is open-ended, multi-faceted, and iterative in nature, and is commonly used in scientific discovery, learning, and sense making [2].

There are a wide range of tools available for offering exploratory search using semantic web technologies (state of the art in [3] and [4]). However, exploratory search over linked data is still insufficiently studied. As pointed in a recent keynote focusing on interaction with Linked Data[5], although the technological platforms for

F. Daniel, P. Dolog, and Q. Li (Eds.): ICWE 2013, LNCS 7977, pp. 376–383, 2013.

exploring linked data are growing, enabling citizen users to explore inter-connectable links associated with structured data is still a key challenge. This calls for an urgent attention by researchers and technology developers to identify major issues with user exploration of linked data, derive requirements for new methods, and engineer solutions to implement these methods utilising semantic technologies and tools. Experimental studies with existing systems in domains well-presented in linked data can be used to elicit requirements for engineering new methods for user exploration.

The work presented in this paper follows the above arguments, and specifically focuses on *providing intelligent functionality embedded in a data browser to assist users in their exploratory search tasks over linked data*. This is part of an ongoing research examining intelligent interfaces for interactive sensemaking over linked data, conducted in the framework of the EU project Dicode (http://www.dicode-project.eu). We have built a fairly traditional semantic data browser – Pinta - which provides a base line for identifying key issues users face with conventional uni-focal exploratory search interfaces over linked data. An instantiation of Pinta in the Music domain is used in an experimental study with users to elicit requirements for intelligent assistance based on observations of challenges users face while interacting with MusicPinta; and suggesting a way to address them by adding signposting features.

Section 2 will present the base line system. A user study with MusicPinta is presented in Section 3. Section 4 reports observations of main interaction issues faced by users, based on which requirements for adding intelligent functionality are elicited. Following the requirements, a signposting approach for adding intelligent assistance is proposed. The paper concludes by pointing at future work.

2   Baseline System for Browsing through Semantic Data

In this section, we present a traditional semantic data browser called Pinta, which provides a uni-focal interface for browsing through several linked semantic datasets.

2.1   Pinta: A Generic Uni-focal Semantic Browser Shell

The main goal of Pinta is to enable users to easily tap into resources built from the Web and, in particular, exploring the use of the Linked Data paradigm. Figure 1 depicts three-layer architecture for Pinta which comprises: (i) Data Layer, including knowledge sources and content, (ii) Processing Layer, including modules for semantic augmentation and query, and (iii) Presentation Layer for content browsing. The **Data Layer** contains domain specific *ontological knowledge sources* and *content* assembled from the Web (Linked Data and other domain specific sources). The knowledge sources consist of graphs of ontological concepts relevant to the domain of interest. They provide the foundation for semantic augmentation of the content in the Processing Layer, and the structure for semantic trajectories for browsing in the Presentation Layer. The **Processing Layer** has two main services: (i) semantic augmentation of the assembled content designed using GATE and (ii) semantic queries to retrieve content for the Presentation Layer. The **Presentation Layer** provides a front-end for the output of semantic queries from the Processing Layer.

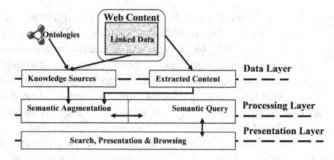

Fig. 1. Architecture of the generic uni-focal semantic data browser Pinta

The interface layout includes three main facets and a description (at the top) extracted from the knowledge datasets for the *focus entity (being currently explored)*: (i) Facet 1 includes facts about the focus entity; (ii) Facet 2 includes terms related to the focus entity; and (iii) Facet 3 shows related content.

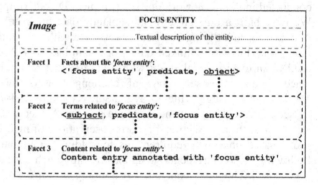

Fig. 2. A faceted-layout template for presenting a focus (currently explored) entity in Pinta

2.2   MusicPinta: An Instantiation of Pinta in the Music Domain

The Music domain has been selected for an instantiation of Pinta and has been used as a testbed to observe exploratory search and derive requirements for intelligent support. The Web of data is rich in music-related datasets and content. As of 2011, there were at least 13 datasets identified, with a diverse range of concepts and ambiguous entities covering instruments, performances/events, artists, and music genres. The data sets used for MusicPinta comprise the following resources.

DBpedia: for musical instruments and artists. This dataset is extracted from dbpedia SPARQL endpoint using CONSTRUCT queries. **DBTune**(http://dbtune.org/): for music-related structured data made available by the DBTune.org in linked data fashion. Among the datasets on DBTune.org we utilise: (i) **Jamendo -** a large repository of Creative Commons licensed music; (ii) **Megatune -** an independent music label; and (iii) **MusicBrainz** - a community-maintained open source encyclopaedia of music information.   **Amazon reviews** for musical instruments shown in Pinta. All datasets, except the reviews, were available as RDF datasets and the **Music ontology** (http://musicontology.com/) was used as schema to interlink them. The Amazon reviews were converted in RDF using Pinta's semantic augmentation of textual content in the Processing Layer. MusicPinta is available at: http://imash.leeds.ac.uk/services/pinta/musicpinta/.

3   User Study and Interaction with MusicPinta

To observe user exploratory search behaviour and elicit requirements for adding intelligent functionality in uni-focal semantic browsers over linked data, we conducted an exploratory study with MusicPinta.

The study involved 12 participants recruited on voluntary basis. All participants had IT background, good experience in web search. Each participant attended an individual session, conducted and observed by an experimenter for an hour: (i) using a Pre-study questionnaire [5 min] for collecting information about the user and test his/her domain awareness; (ii) introducing MusicPinta [10 min]; (iii) conducting Task 1 [15 min] aiming at identifying distinctive characteristics of the musical instrument "bouzouki"; (iv) conducting Task 2 [15 min] for identifying usage and features of the musical instrument "electric guitar"; (v) a Post-study questionnaire [10 min] for testing again the participant's domain awareness and gathering usability feedback; and, (vi) briefly interviewing [5 min] for eliciting the overall impression of using MusicPinta for exploratory search. After each task, the users were asked to fill-out a short questionnaire to assess cognitive load using the NASA-TLX questionnaire[6].

Table 1. User tasks in the experimental study

Task 1: Characteristics of a musical instrument [bozouki]	Task 2: Usage and features of a musical instrument [electrical guitar]
The music shop is extending its collection of instruments with international musical instruments. You work in an advertising agency which has been asked to prepare an advertisement script for some of the new instruments that will appear in the shop. A key part of the preparation of the advertisement script is the research of the product.	The music shop wants to increase the sales of its traditional musical instruments, such as electrical guitars. It intends to do this by adding links to creative commons album recordings with electric guitars, together with some interesting information about these albums to inspire customers to play/buy electric guitars or other musical instruments.
You have been asked to conduct a research of one of the new instruments, called bouzouki, using the information available in MusicPinta. You have to identify: • the main characteristics of bouzouki; • up to five similar instruments to bouzouki; • features that make bouzouki distinctive from the similar ones you have chosen. Go to 'Semantic Search' in MusicPinta and type bouzouki. Browse the content and follow links. Complete the provided form.	Furthermore, when displaying its electric guitar items, the shop wants to highlight key features people look for when purchasing electric guitars. You are asked is to conduct the research to address the above requirements by using information provided in MusicPinta. You have to review the information about electric guitar and identify: • three interesting album recordings that include electric guitars and specify what is interesting; • key features that people look for when purchasing an electric guitar. Go to 'Semantic Search' in MusicPinta and type electric guitar. Browse the content and follow links. Complete the provided form.

The study required participants to complete two tasks related to exploring musical instruments and was positioned within an advertising scenario for a fictitious UK music shop (see Table 1). In both tasks, the participants were given an entry point for browsing and asked to fill in their answers in a provided template. The tasks exhibit the characteristics of exploratory search tasks summarised in [7]: the main goal is learning and/or investigation of a musical instrument; there is a low level of specificity about the information needed and how to find it; search is open ended, requires finding several items and involves a degree of uncertainty; tasks are 'not too easy' and include multiple facets.

4   Requirements for Assisting User Browsing over Linked Data

Two musical instrument experts (one for Bouzouki, one for Electric guitar) have marked the outcome of participants for the two tasks. The marking is to measure how successful the participants have been in completing the tasks using MusicPinta. Participant achieved 70% average score for the task 1 and 48% for the task 2. The detailed analysis on the task performance and learning outcome in the user study is covered in our recent publication[8]. In this paper, we have only focused on the observations related to the task outcome and browsing behaviour that allow us to elicit requirements for supporting exploratory environments.

Observation 1: Abstraction Conundrum. While browsing specific instruments (e.g. Bouzouki), performances and performers, two participants clicked on abstract concepts, such as instrument, performance and performer, from the Music Ontology. In both cases, the participants were looking for concrete information (e.g. participant-12 clicked on instrument in task 1 when seeking for more detail about a musical instrument, while participant-05 clicked on performer and performance in task 2 when seeking more detail about an album). The aggregated datasets in MusicPinta have large number of instances for the abstract concepts (which is typical of linked datasets), which led to confusion as the result was a long list of performers, performance and instruments, and the participants quickly pressed back button.

Requirement 1: Offering Semantic Links at an Appropriate Level of Abstraction. The above observation motivates consideration on identifying what can be algorithmically offered as the right level of abstraction on various browsing junctures. This is important when the abstract concepts have large amount of concrete instantiations.

Observation 2: Exploring Entities/Content with Insufficient Information. Another interesting case is the high number of 'empty clicks' - the user clicks on a link and is taken to a page with no information, sees that this link is not helpful and quickly returns to the previous page. In task 1, such clicks concerned similar instruments, e.g. there was no information about bajitar, xalam, rebab. In task 2 such clicks concerned performances (music albums) and happened quite often. 'Empty clicks' leading to pages with no information was seen as one of the main reasons for user's frustration. At the same time, may be due to their experience of links that lead to dead ends, some links were perceived as empty without exploring them further and the users missed to click on important for the tasks information. With linked datasets, it is typical to find entities that do not have much explanation or links to other entities.

Similar issues were observed with content (Amazon Reviews in our user study). Users clicked to view some of the Amazon reviews to find out more information about an instrument and its review. However some of the reviews were deemed to have insufficient information to be useful. This observation is in line with relevant research conducted which concludes that not all reviews are equally helpful (for example, [9]).

Requirement 2: Reduce Entity Link Options. Avoid showing entity links that do not lead to any new information. Reduce number of entity links shown to the user based on their browsing value; allowing reduction of clutter and confusion. The challenge here is to define what 'browsing value' is and how to calculate it for an entity with respect to other entities from the same entity page.

Requirement 3: Reduce Content Link Options. Avoid showing content links that do not lead to any new information. Reduce number of content links shown to the user based on their helpfulness/usefulness.

Observation 3. Varied Selection Strategies while Facing Too Many Choices. Both tasks (deliberately) put the users in situations where they had too many choices. This means that the users had a large number of links to review while on a focus entity page. For example, the bouzouki page included 12 different links in the facts facet and 51 links in the terms. This is a typical situation with the datasets from linked data. For example, for the DBpedia dataset, which has 3.5M entities and 627M triples, on average, a user might have to review 192 links while exploring a focus entity.

We observed users following different strategies when presented with too many choices in the browsing interface: (i)clicking on the nearest classification link from the 'facts facet' (e.g. plucked string instruments or string instruments) to see general characteristics in the case of bouzouki as part of task 1. However, users rarely clicked on links from the facts facet as part of the task 2, as the task did not require this; (ii) clicking on instruments mentioned in the 'related terms facet'– (e.g. lute and mandolin mainly in task2; (iii) clicking on something (e.g. 'an instrument') that 'sounds familiar' (e.g. sitar, banjo, pipa in task 1); (iv) click on something (e.g. 'an instrument or an album') that sounds interesting or unusual (e.g. oud, xalam in task 1 and noticing a women artist or something interesting in the album name in task 2); (v) clicking on something that looks important (e.g. an artist has several albums in task 2); and, (vi) clicking randomly (after exhausting other strategies).

This observation is in line with the latest research in search engines and HCI; increasing numbers of options can make designers and users feel less confident when deciding and less happy with the results[10]. To support varied level of selection strategies, following requirement is derived.

Requirement 4. Take into Account Context to Cater for Interests and Importance. People when faced with many choices do select what they find useful/familiar/interesting/unusual/important. Hence, there is a merit in making it easier for users to decide/spot easily these values. The challenge here is how to measure and decide these values from the available options for a specific user or holistically.

5   Semantic Signposting to Assist Exploratory Search

The identified requirements from the study indicated the need for further algorithmic support to realise the exploratory search potential of semantic data browsers. One possible approach to address these requirements is **semantic signposting**.

In uni-focal exploration, a user focuses on one entity at a time represented on a page. This entity page contains links to various descriptions, image and links to other entities. Such entity page can be treated as a juncture in journey where the explorer has to make few choices. Some of the requirements elicited can be addressed by providing *signposts* guiding the explorer in making a choice about paths she can take.

Only showing 'important' links which are a subset of all possible links for the user to review as part of next path he/she can take.   Let us call *'candidate entities' all the* links possible to navigate from a focus entity page.   Importance of each candidate entity can be computed based on density parameters such as – number of further entities available from a candidate entity (i.e. number of directly connected entities to the candidate entity), number of potentially reachable entities from this entity (i.e. number of entities connected to candidate entity via directly connected entities) and type and weight of the connection (e.g. semantic relationship between candidate entities and it's directly connected entities). The judgement of creating subset of links can be implemented using density metrics for the semantic graphs[11], where density function shall allow comparing how dense/informative each of the path is originating from a candidate entity. The subset of links to be shown to the user in this case will be based on the density value of each link (i.e., candidate entity).

For more creative tasks (such as task 2 in our study) which require browsing through a large amount of content, the study appeared to provide indication that it will *not be very beneficial to limit the user entity choices*, as this can affect the free content exploration. Instead, signposting can include some *indicators about the 'importance' or 'value' of a content item*, e.g. if there is any description (or any multimedia content), its source of the content (e.g. DBpedia), if further semantic links are available in the content (e.g. albums with several musical instruments) to facilitate user choices. There can be some ordering based on the value. Again the judgement of importance can be implemented using density metrics for the semantic graphs.

Adaptive Signposts. One of the other parameters to consider while judging importance of links is consideration of user's prior knowledge, e.g. does user already know about a particular entity or class of entity? Such consideration in creation of signposts (i.e. reducing number of links shown to the user) can allow users to decide what is useful/familiar/interesting/unsual/important(R4). A possible way to 'sense' previous knowledge is to analyse the user clicks on the low classification level links – clicking on an instrument can indicate some familiarity with its most specific classification category (e.g. in the study, users familiar with Russian musical instruments clicked on Balalaika and users familiar with Chinese musical instruments clicked on Pipa). The necessary techniques to address such requirements can benefit from the research in the user modelling, adaptation and personalisation.   Such solution can allow creating signposts that include familiar and new knowledge together. Putting familiar and new items together in such a way can deepen the learning by association[12].

6   Conclusions

We have presented a study with a traditional uni-focal semantic data browser to observe browsing behaviour of users while interacting with several linked semantic datasets aiming at deriving requirements to inject intelligent features. We have found several intricate challenges that are applicable to typical interaction over linked semantic datasets. For example, disparity of the options available while browsing from an entity. In some cases large number of links available from an entity, hence posing too many options for the user to choose from and in other cases no links or information available making users frustrated.   We have also observed and reported varied levels of selection strategies when a user is faced with too many options.

Acknowledgements. The research reported in this paper is supported by the EU 7th Framework Programme under grant agreement ICT 257184 (DICODE project).

References

1. Waitelonis, J., Knuth, M., Wolf, L., Hercher, J., Sack, H.: The Path is the Destination–Enabling a New Search Paradigm with Linked Data. In: Linked Data in the Future Internet at the Future Internet Assembly (2010)
2. Marchionini, G.: Exploratory search: from finding to understanding. Communications of the ACM 49, 41–46 (2006)
3. Ferré, S., Hermann, A.: Semantic Search: Reconciling Expressive Querying and Exploratory Search. In: Aroyo, L., Welty, C., Alani, H., Taylor, J., Bernstein, A., Kagal, L., Noy, N., Blomqvist, E. (eds.) ISWC 2011, Part I. LNCS, vol. 7031, pp. 177–192. Springer, Heidelberg (2011)
4. Popov, I.O., Schraefel, M.C., Hall, W., Shadbolt, N.: Connecting the Dots: A Multi-pivot Approach to Data Exploration. In: Aroyo, L., Welty, C., Alani, H., Taylor, J., Bernstein, A., Kagal, L., Noy, N., Blomqvist, E. (eds.) ISWC 2011, Part I. LNCS, vol. 7031, pp. 553–568. Springer, Heidelberg (2011)
5. schraefel, m.: What does It Look Like, Really? Imagining how Citizens might Effectively, Usefully and Easily Find, Explore, Query and Re-present Open/Linked Data. In: Patel-Schneider, P.F., Pan, Y., Hitzler, P., Mika, P., Zhang, L., Pan, J.Z., Horrocks, I., Glimm, B. (eds.) ISWC 2010, Part II. LNCS, vol. 6497, pp. 356–369. Springer, Heidelberg (2010)
6. Hart, S.G., Staveland, L.E.: Development of NASA-TLX (Task Load Index): Results of empirical and theoretical research. I. J. Human Mental Workload 11, 139–183 (1988)
7. Wildemuth, B.M., Freund, L.: Assigning search tasks designed to elicit exploratory search behaviors. In: Proceedings of the Symposium on Human-Computer Interaction and Information Retrieval, HCIR 2012, pp. 1–10 (2012)
8. Dimitrova, V., Lau, L., Thakker, D., Yang-turner, F., Despotakis, D.: Exploring Exploratory Search: A User Study with Linked Semantic Data. In: ACM Workshop on Intelligent Exsploration of Semantic Data (IESD 2013), pp. 9–16 (2013)
9. Mudambi, S.M., Schuff, D.: What Makes a Helpful Online Review? A Study of Customer Reviews on Amazon.com. MIS Quarterly 34, 185–200 (2010)
10. Oulasvirta, A., Hukkinen, J., Schwartz, B.: When More Is Less: The Paradox of Choice in Search Engine Use. J. Evaluation, 1–7 (2009)
11. Alani, H., Brewster, C.: Ontology Ranking based on the Analysis of Concept Structures. In: Proceedings of the 3rd International Conference on Knowledge Capture (2005)
12. Roschelle, J.: Learning in Interactive Environments: Prior Knowledge and New Experience. Knowledge Creation Diffusion Utilization, American Association of Museums, 37–51 (1995)

A Framework for Migrating Web Applications to Web Services

Asil A. Almonaies, Manar H. Alalfi, James R. Cordy, and Thomas R. Dean

School of Computing, Queens University
Kingston, Ontario, Canada
{asil,alalfi,cordy,dean}@cs.queensu.ca

Abstract. In this paper, we present a framework for semi-automatically migrating monolithic legacy web applications to service oriented architecture (SOA) by separating potentially reusable features as web services. Software design recovery and source transformation techniques are used to automatically analyze and reprogram web application code to migrate existing web-based systems to support inter-business services and interactions. Such modernization helps make web applications more flexible, allowing them to more easily integrate functionality with other systems and respond to rapidly changing business needs. While the problem of migrating other kinds of legacy software systems to an SOA environment has been well studied in the literature, approaches to migrating legacy web applications to web services are lacking. We demonstrate our framework on the analysis and automated restructuring of an existing PHP web application, by migrating integrated internal features to independent, reusable web services.

1 Introduction

Service Oriented Architecture (SOA) is an increasingly important software architecture, designed to flexibly interconnect software components in response to rapid changes in the business environment. In SOA, applications are split into separate software services that can be maintained independently and easily reused. In order to provide the advantages of SOA in the context of the world wide web, Web Services are used as an enabling technology, allowing web-based business functionalities to interconnect in an object-model-neutral manner.

At present the vast majority of production web applications use a monolithic stand-alone software style. These applications are designed largely without clear modularity, which makes their maintenance and enhancement in response to rapidly changing business requirements a difficult task. Rather than re-implement the business functionality of these applications as services from scratch for the new world of interoperation and reuse, web providers would prefer to preserve their investment by migrating their existing web application functionality to web services. These dynamic legacy web applications are simply too important to be discarded, and thus they must be reused.

Several modernization approaches to move legacy systems to SOA environments have been described in the literature. However, to our knowledge only a few research studies have attempted to address the problem of automatically moving monolithic legacy dynamic web applications to SOA. Moreover, the work that is done in this area [1, 2, 3] is very general, discussing the benefits leveraging existing web applications in

F. Daniel, P. Dolog, and Q. Li (Eds.): ICWE 2013, LNCS 7977, pp. 384–399, 2013.
© Springer-Verlag Berlin Heidelberg 2013

moving to web services, without proposing any practical framework for actually implementing the change.

The nature of monolithic dynamic web applications, often with mixed paradigms and multi-lingual code, makes analysis and refactoring for the purpose of migration to SOA a challenging and error-prone problem. Automation of the migration process reduces human intervention, which reduces the time and cost and increases the consistency of the migrated code.

In this paper we present a framework and tool set that largely automates the migration from monolithic PHP web applications to SOA. Software design recovery and source transformation techniques are used to assist in automating the migration from legacy web applications to service-oriented web services. The result can be considered to be a service-oriented web application that implements the endpoints of a Web Service. The framework can also be used to combine different sets of services from two or more different web applications to construct a new web service application which behaves like the two original applications together.

The contributions of this paper are:

- A framework using an iterative process of incremental steps to analyze and reprogram existing web applications to web services based on the Service Component Architecture (SCA) web services standard.
- An automatic extraction process to extract and separate identified business features in dynamically-typed scripting languages as object-oriented classes.
- An automatic process for inferring the types of parameter values in dynamically–typed scripting languages using instrumentation and coverage testing.
- An automatic process for converting an object-oriented class into an SCA service component.
- A prototype set of tools using source analysis and transformation to automate the reprogramming of web applications written in PHP to extract and separate identified business features as web services.
- A demonstration of the framework and tool set in extracting web services from SCARF, a monolithic web application for a conference and research paper discussion forum, and automatically reprogramming it to use these services.

The rest of this paper is organized as follows: Section 2 gives an overview of our framework for SOA migration, and Section 3 details the steps of our automated iterative migration process. Section 4 presents a case study using our framework and automated process in practice. Section 5 relates our work to other work in SOA migration, and finally Section 6 summarizes our conclusions and outlines our future work.

2   A Web Application to SOA Migration Framework

Our proposed framework uses a new approach to the problem of legacy system migration to service-oriented architecture. It is one of the first approaches to explore the area of moving a monolithic web application to SOA with significant levels of automation. The proposed framework (Figure 1) consists of two main steps, Service Identification and Service Migration, to produce a new application using web services.

2.1 Service Identification

While our work concentrates on the service migration aspect of the problem, one of the main challenges in modernizing a web legacy system is the identification of potential service functionality that may have business value. Our approach does not attempt to solve the identification of services, rather we leverage the results of other research such as the work done by Asuncion et al.[4], which uses goal-based, model-driven and service-oriented approaches to identify business rules in the application.

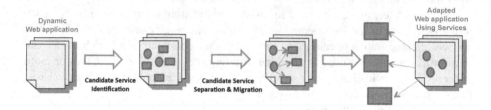

Fig. 1. A Migration Framework

In our framework, the output of the service identification step is a marked-up version of the web application source code in which sections of code with the desired business functionality have been identified as the operations of a candidate service. This tagged candidate service is then the input to our automated migration process.

In this paper we carried out the identification process manually. Based on the functionalities that we wanted to extract from the adapted web application, we identified each potential operation of the candidate service using XML markup of the application source. In our identification notation, each candidate service operation is marked up using a *<service function = function-name>* tag, where *function-name* is a user-suggested name for the candidate service operation (Figure 2).

2.2 Service Separation and Migration

Candidate service migration is the process of separating each identified candidate service into a separate class , extracting it from the original application code, converting the created class into a separate independent service, and adapting the original application code to use the separated service. Once extracted and migrated to a separate service, the extracted service is used by the adapted original application as a client, and can also be easily used by other web applications.

Legacy web applications are generally implemented using scripting languages such as PHP [5] or Python [6]. These languages are dynamically typed, reflexive and support dynamic changes to the code. The nature of monolithic dynamic web applications, often with mixed programming paradigms, makes the analysis and refactoring of web application source code challenging. Thus the process of separation & migration of candidate services is time consuming, technically complex and error-prone.

While there are a number of different approaches to migrating various kinds of legacy software systems to a service oriented architecture in the literature [7, 8, 9], approaches

```
<?php
include ("welcome.html");

$fname = "John";

<service function = Reverse>
    $name = strrev ($fname);
</service>

echo "My name is".$name;
?>
```

Fig. 2. Example Marked Candidate Service Operation

to migrating web applications to web services are lacking [10]. This lack of other approaches, and the clear need for automation to assist in web application migration is the focus of the work of this paper. The concrete goal of our research is to to automate the separation and migration of identified candidate services in PHP-based web applications to web services using IBM's Service Component Architecture (SCA) standard. While our work concentrates on PHP in this paper, the same process and strategy can be easily adapted to other web application languages and technologies.

3   Automating Service Migration

Our process for automating service separation and migration consists of several steps, each implemented using a TXL [11] source transformation of the PHP web application code. The five steps of our process are (Figure 3) :

1. Candidate Service Refactoring
2. Candidate Service Separation
3. Parameter Type Inference
4. Service Component Conversion
5. Database Refactoring

The following sections describe each of these steps in detail.

3.1 Candidate Service Refactoring

The input for the first step is the marked up source code of the web application which identifies PHP code sections as potential operations of the candidate service. In the simple example of Figure 2, a PHP code section is marked as the candidate service operation "Reverse".

The refactoring step automatically creates a PHP function for each of the marked up candidate code sections, and wraps them in a new class for the candidate service. Parameters and results of the functions are inferred from the dependencies of the code sections on their context, and the original code sections are replaced by parameterized calls to the functions of the new candidate service class.

When this step is complete, the application has been refactored to separate the original marked code sections into functions of the separate class (Figure 4). The user provides a name for the new class, in this case "Example".

3.2   Candidate Service Separation

In the next step, we automatically separate the new candidate service class into a separate PHP class file and generate the appropriate PHP code necessary for the original program to use it, including include directives for the separated class file and creation of an instance object for use in the original code.

As part of the separation, we create a constructor class for each of the operations wrapped in class, called the *return class*, which acts as a dictionary to contain the returned values of the operation. The results of the candidate service separation step on our simple example candidate class are shown in Figure 5.

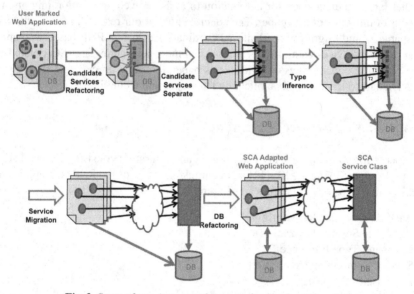

Fig. 3. Steps of our Automated Process for Service Migration

```
class Example {
    function Reverse ($name, $fname) {
        $name = strrev ($fname);
        return new Reverse_return ($name);
    }
}
```

Fig. 4. Example Class Generated by the Refactoring Step

3.3   Parameter Type Inference

Like most web application languages, PHP is a dynamically typed language, and types of function parameters are not normally specified. A parameter simply has whatever type it takes on at run time. Parameters to service operations, by contrast, must be specified as part of the service description.

Thus in this step we first instrument each function of the refactored and separated candidate service class to dynamically capture parameter types, and then run the instrumented application to cover execution of every candidate service operation function. The instrumentation stores in a file a table of each function annotated with the types of the parameters it receives when actually run. In some cases, parameters end up with a NULL type, if the corresponding variable has not been set when the function is called. In this case we delete the NULL values as they do not affect the output.

The type table file is then used to explicitly annotate the parameters of the service operation functions of the candidate service class with their expected types. These parameter types are required in the Service Component Conversion step (Section 3.4) both for creating the Web Services Description Language (WSDL) service description of the new service, and for creating SCA parameter annotations for the operations of the new service. The result of the parameter type inference step is a fully typed version of the separated candidate class file (Figure 6).

```php
<?php
include ("welcome.html");

include_once "Example_return.php";
include_once "Example.php";
$Example_obj = new Example ();

$fname = "John";

$Reverse_return_obj = $Example_obj -> Reverse ($name, $fname);
$name = $Reverse_return_obj -> name;

echo "My name is".$name;
?>
```

(a) Refactored Original Code after Candidate Service Class Separation

```php
<?php

include_once "Example_return.php";

class Example {
    function Reverse ($name, $fname) {
        $name = strrev ($fname);
        return new Reverse_return ($name);
    }
}
?>
```

(b) Separated Candidate Service Class

```php
<?php
class Reverse_return {
    public $name;
    public function __construct ($name) {
        $this -> name = $name;
    }
}
?>
```

(c) Return Value Constructor Class for Reverse Operation of Separated Candidate Service Class

Fig. 5. Example Refactored and Separated Candidate Service Class

```
<?php
include_once "Example_return.php";

class Example {
    function Reverse (NULL $name, string $fname) {
        $name = strrev ($fname);
        return new Reverse_return($name);
    }
}
?>
```

Fig. 6. Example Refactored and Separated Service Class after Type Inference

3.4   Service Component Conversion

After inferring parameter types of the separated candidate service class operation functions, we are ready to reprogram the class into a real service component. In this step we convert the separated candidate service class file into an SCA service component, by adding the required SCA annotations to the class and each of its operation functions specifying the name, number and types of the expected service operation message parameters. As part of this conversion, the Web Service Description Language (WSDL) service description file is created automatically by the SCA technology.

```
<?php
include ("welcome.html");

include_once "Example_return.php";
include_once ("SCA/SCA.php");
$Example_obj = SCA :: getService ("Example.wsdl");

$fname = "John";

$Reverse_return_objStr = $Example_obj -> Reverse ($name, $fname);
$Reverse_return_obj = unserialize ($Reverse_return_objStr);
$name = $Reverse_return_obj -> name;

echo "My name is".$name;
?>
```

(a) Converted Original Application as SCA Client

```
<?php
include_once "Example_return.php";
include "SCA/SCA.php";

/**
 * @service
 * @binding.soap
 */
class Example {
    /**
     * @param string $fname
     * @return string
     */
    function Reverse (string $fname) {
        $name = strrev ($fname);
        return serialize (new Reverse_return ($name));
    }
}
?>
```

(b) Converted Candidate Service Class as SCA Service

Fig. 7. Example Converted to a Web Service-based Application

In order to create an SCA component several steps are required. SCA service type annotations must be added to each of the service operation functions of the candidate service class to specify the types of parameters and return values of the operation. The SCA interface and SCA service annotations must be generated for the candidate service class to specify the service and its service binding (in the case of our conversions, the SOAP messaging protocol). And finally, the original adapted web application must be converted to a service client of the WSDL service description and SCA protocol.

Figure 7 shows the result of applying these transformations to the candidate service class file and refactored original application to create an SCA-based client/server relationship using the new web service.

3.5 Database Refactoring

In the final step of our migration, the original application database is refactored to separate those tables used only by the new separated service into a separate database, and remove them from the original application database. This allows the new web service to be used by other applications independently of the original. In our current implementation of the framework, this final step is done manually when required.

4   A Case Study: SCARF

In the previous sections we have outlined our framework for automatic migration of web applications to SOA using a sequence of source transformations that take identified potential service operations in the application code to separate reusable SCA web services. Our running example has demonstrated the application of the process to a small but representative toy web application.

Thus far we have used our framework on two real web applications, the Moodle course management system [12], a large production web application used by thousands of students and instructors worldwide, and SCARF, the Stanford conference and research forum, a research discussion forum application [13]. Due to space limitations, in this paper we only show the use of our framework in separating and migrating the paper management functionality of SCARF to a web service.

4.1 The SCARF Paper Management Subsystem

SCARF [13] is a PHP-based web application designed to help researchers and conference administrators create and maintain discussion forums for their research papers. In SCARF, papers are uploaded and stored in a database where users can view, comment and edit them, as well as organize them into sessions. SCARF is intended to support interactive conferences such as SIGCOMM, for which it was originally developed.

4.2 Step 1: Paper Management Service Identification

Our plan is to identify and separate a new web service for the research paper management aspects of SCARF, separating it from the user interface code of the web application so that it can be accessed and reused by other applications. The paper management system in SCARF supports several operations. For example, users can download a specific paper, edit the content of a paper, and add a new paper to the forum.

We begin by analyzing the SCARF source to identify the functionalities related to paper management. The business logic of the paper management functionality is spread over five PHP pages:

- *editpaper.php*: Logic to enable an authenticated user to add a new paper to the forum or edit the information of existing papers.
- *showpaper.php*: Logic to access specific paper details, such as name, authors, abstract, comments, the paper document and auxiliary files.
- *showsession.php*: Logic to show all papers available in a specific session with information about them.
- *getpaper.php*: Logic to download a paper.
- *getfile.php*: Logic to download an auxiliary file associated with a paper.

Each of these pages contains sections of code that provide particular discrete operations that we can identify as part of our candidate paper management service class, interspersed with user interface code to present and interact with the page. Figure 8 shows the tagged candidate service operation code sections for the paper management functionality of SCARF in the *editpaper.php* page.

4.3   Step 2: Refactoring

While candidate service operations are often contained in a single PHP source file, in the case of the SCARF paper management functionality, the code is spread over several different PHP source of the application. To handle this we use our refactoring transformation to generate several candidate service classes for the operations, one from each PHP page, and merge the results into a single unified candidate service class (Figure 9) before conversion to an SCA service.

We run our refactoring transformation in turn on each of the five tagged source pages, generating a new separate candidate service class for each one, while adapting the original page to use the new service. By specifying to the refactoring process that the new candidate service classes should each have the same name, in this case *papers*, we prepare them for merging.

When the refactoring step is complete, we have five generated candidate service classes, each with the same name, and each with its own set of candidate service operations. We then merge the candidate service operation functions from the five different classes into one single class file containing all of the candidate service operations, as shown in Figure 9. If the different generated candidate service classes have two operations with the same name and functionality, then we merge them by hand into a single operation function. If their functionality is different, then we must rename one of them and its corresponding calls in the adapted page file.

As part of the refactoring transformation, the results required by each candidate service operation are analyzed and a result value class generated for each candidate service operation. These classes do not require merging since each is a unique separate class, but the files containing them are merged into one, simply by concatenating them.

```php
<?php
include_once("functions.php");
<markIncludes/>
include_once("header.php");
//////////// (... 10 lines elided ...) ////////////
if (isset($_GET['paper_id'])) {
    $id = (int) $_GET['paper_id'];
    <service function=getPaperDetails>
    $result = query("SELECT title, abstract, session_id, pdf, pdfname FROM papers WHERE paper_id='".$id."'");
    $title = $result[0]["title"];
    $abstract = $result[0]["abstract"];
    $session_id = $result[0]["session_id"];
    $pdf = $result[0]["pdf"];
    $pdfname = $result[0]["pdfname"];
    $result = query("SELECT user_id FROM authors WHERE paper_id='".$id."' ORDER BY 'order'");
    $authors = Array();
    if ($result){
        foreach($result as $row) {
            $authors[] = $row;
        }
    }
    </service>
}
//////////// (... 60 lines elided ...) ////////////
    include("editform3.php");
    <service function=getFileEdit>
    $result = query("SELECT name, data FROM files WHERE paper_id='".$id."'");
    </service>
//////////// (... 75 lines elided ...) ////////////
    if (!isset($_POST['paper_id'])) {
        // new paper
        <service function=addPaper>
        $row = query ("SELECT MAX( 'order' ) as max FROM 'papers' WHERE session_id = '".$session."'");
        $order = (int) $row[0] + 1;
        query ("INSERT INTO papers (title, abstract, pdf, pdfname, session_id, 'order') VALUES ('".$title."', '".$
            abstract."', '".$pdf."', '".$pdfname."', '".$session."', '".$order."')");
        $row = query ("SELECT paper_id FROM papers WHERE title='".$title."' AND abstract='".$abstract."' AND pdfname
            ='".$pdfname."' AND session_id='".$session."' ORDER BY paper_id DESC");
        $id = $row[0]['paper_id'];;
        </service>
    } else {
        // updated paper paper
        if (!empty($filename)) {
            $pdfSetString = "pdf='$pdf', pdfname='$pdfname',";
        } else {
            $pdfSetString = "";
        }
        <service function=updatePaper>
        query("UPDATE papers SET title='".$title."', abstract='".$abstract."', ".$pdfSetString." session_id='".$
            session."' WHERE paper_id='".$id."'");
        $id = (int) $_POST['paper_id'];
        query("DELETE FROM authors WHERE paper_id='".$id."'");
        </service>
    }
//////////// (... 50 lines elided ...) ////////////
    $num = 0;
    <service function=addAuthors>
    foreach ($_POST['authors'] as $author) {
        if (! empty($author)) {
            query ("INSERT INTO authors ('paper_id', 'user_id', 'order') VALUES ('".$id."', '" .
                mysql_real_escape_string($author) . "', '".$num."')");
        }
        $num++;
    }
    </service>
    if (!isset($_POST['paper_id'])) {
        print "Paper added successfully";
    } else {
        print "Paper updated successfully";
    }
    print ". View <a href='showpaper.php?paper_id=$id'>the paper</a>";
}
include_once("footer.php");
?>
```

Fig. 8. Paper Management Operation Markup in the SCARF *editpaper.php* page

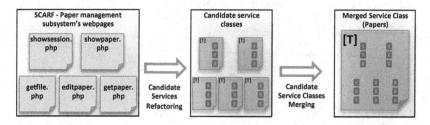

Fig. 9. Generating and Merging Candidate Service Operations from Multiple Application Pages

4.4   Step 3: Type Inference

Once the generated candidate service classes for each page have been merged into a single merged candidate service class, the remaining steps of the process simply proceed as for a single page. We use the the dynamic type inference technique of Section 3.3 to infer the types of the operation parameters of the new merged candidate service class by instrumenting and running the class with the adapted application pages to gather and store dynamic type information, and then use the type merging transformation to add the inferred types to the merged candidate service class operation functions.

Figure 10 shows the merged SCARF paper management candidate service after the instrumentation transformation, with instrumentation code highlighted. This temporary instrumented version of the merged candidate service class is exercised by running the SCARF application with the adapted application pages, exploring all of the paper management related links from the SCARF user interface until all of the candidate service operation functions have been called at least once.

The output of this step is an instrumentation file containing type signatures for all of the parameters of all fourteen of the candidate service operation functions (Figure 11), which are then merged into the candidate service class using the typing transformation described in Section 3.3 to yield the fully typed merged candidate service class.

4.5   Step 4: Conversion to SCA

In the final stage of the automated migration, conversion to an SCA service component, we use the transformations of Section 3.4 to turn the SCARF candidate service class into an SCA-based web service, and modify the pages of the adapted SCARF web application to use the new service as a client.

1. The typed candidate service class is automatically transformed to remove NULL parameters, to insert code to unserialize parameters that are of type object or array, and to serialize the result object of each operation.
2. The SCA annotation transformation of Section 3.4 is applied to the serialized candidate service class to yield an SCA service component. We add an include statement for the SCA library, and SCA annotations for the class and methods. These include @*service* and @*binding.soap* annotations for the class, and parameter and result type annotations for each operation function. This enables the class as a service.

```
<?php
include_once ("functions.php");
include_once "papers_return.php";

class papers {
    function addAuthors ($_POST, $author, $id, $num) {
        $FileHandle = fopen ("/tmp/papers.merge.php", 'a');
        fwrite ($FileHandle, "class papers\n function addAuthors(");
        fwrite ($FileHandle, gettype ($_POST).' $_POST');
        fwrite ($FileHandle, ",");
        fwrite ($FileHandle, gettype ($author).' $author');
        fwrite ($FileHandle, ",");
        fwrite ($FileHandle, gettype ($id).' $id');
        fwrite ($FileHandle, ",");
        fwrite ($FileHandle, gettype ($num).' $num');
        fwrite ($FileHandle, ") {\n");
        fwrite ($FileHandle, " }\n}\n");
        fclose ($FileHandle);
        foreach ($_POST ['authors'] as $author) {
            if (! empty ($author)) {
                query ("INSERT INTO authors ('paper_id', 'user_id', 'order') VALUES ('".$id."', '".
                    mysql_real_escape_string ($author)."', '".$num."')");
            }
            $num ++;
        }
        return new addAuthors_return ();
    }

    function updateFile ($id, $oldname, $name, $ext, $type, $data) {
        $FileHandle = fopen ("/tmp/papers.merge.php", 'a');
        fwrite ($FileHandle, "class papers\n function updateFile(");
        fwrite ($FileHandle, gettype ($id).' $id');
        fwrite ($FileHandle, ",");
        fwrite ($FileHandle, gettype ($oldname).' $oldname');
        fwrite ($FileHandle, ",");
        fwrite ($FileHandle, gettype ($name).' $name');
        fwrite ($FileHandle, ",");
        fwrite ($FileHandle, gettype ($ext).' $ext');
        fwrite ($FileHandle, ",");
        fwrite ($FileHandle, gettype ($type).' $type');
        fwrite ($FileHandle, ",");
        fwrite ($FileHandle, gettype ($data).' $data');
        fwrite ($FileHandle, ") {\n");
        fwrite ($FileHandle, " }\n}\n");
        fclose ($FileHandle);
        query ("DELETE FROM files WHERE paper_id='".$id."' AND name='".$oldname."'");
        query ("INSERT INTO files (paper_id, name, ext, type, data) VALUES ('".$id."$', '".$name."', '".$ext."',
            '".$type."', '".$data."')");
        return new updateFile_return ();
    }

    //////////// (12 more instrumented candidate service operation functions) ////////////
}
?>
```

Fig. 10. Instrumented Merged Candidate Service Class for SCARF Paper Management

3. Invoking the converted service class using the SCA WSDL generation URL $http : //hostname/path/papers.php?wsdl$ causes the SCA platform to generate the WSDL service description for the new service from the SCA annotations.

4. In the final transformation, the adapted source pages of the SCARF web application are converted to be an SCA client of the new web service. We add the include statement for the SCA library, create an instance of the proxy object for the service, and update each service operation call to use it.

Figure 12 shows the final SCARF paper management service class after conversion to an SCA service. Each of the adapted SCARF application pages from which the service operations were extracted are converted to SCA WSDL clients of the service using the final transformation of Section 3.4, and the migration is complete.

```
<?php
class papers{
    function getPaperDetails(array $result,integer $id,string $title,string $abstract,NULL $session_id,string $pdf,
        string $pdfname,NULL $authors,array $row) { }
    function getFileEdit(array $result,integer $id) { }
    function updatePaper2(string $newname,integer $id,string $oldname) { }
    function addPaper(array $row,integer $session,NULL $order,string $title,string $abstract,string $pdf,string $
        pdfname,integer $id) { }
    function updateFile(string $id,string $oldname,string $name,string $ext,string $type,string $data) { }
    function updatePaper(string $title,string $abstract,string $pdfSetString,integer $session,integer $id,array $_POST
        ) { }
    function deletePaper(integer $id,string $oldname) { }
    function addAuthors(array $_POST,NULL $author,integer $id,integer $num) { }
    function getFile(NULL $id,array $_GET,NULL $name,string $result) { }
    function getpaper(NULL $id,array $_GET,NULL $result) { }
    function getPaperAttribs(integer $id,array $_GET,array $result,NULL $title,NULL $abstract) { }
    function getFileInfo(NULL $result2,string $id) { }
    function paperTitle(NULL $result2,array $row) { }
    function paperAuthor(array $result3,array $row2) { }
}
?>
```

Fig. 11. Type Instrumentation Output of the SCARF Candidate Service Class

4.6 SCARF / SOA: Testing the Result

We validated the conversion of the SCARF paper management subsystem into a web service by testing the migrated SCARF web application in two ways.

First, we already knew how to cover all of the new web service operations from the SCARF browser interface, because we already had to test all of the operations of the candidate service class from the web interface as part of the type inference instrumentation step. To test the migrated SCARF, we exercised all of the same links in the SCARF user interface to cover all of the operations of the new paper management web service, and verified that the behaviour and output of each of the pages was the same for these tests in both the original and the migrated web application.

Second, to be certain that we had not changed any hidden behaviour, we logged the values of PHP variables before and after each tagged candidate service operation code segment in the original application, and compared those values to the same variables before and after the calls to the corresponding web service operations of the new extracted SCARF paper management web service.

5   Related Work

Our approach does not attempt to solve the identification of services, rather we leverage the results of other research such as the work done by Asuncion et al. [4], which uses a goal-based, model-driven approach to identify business rules in the application.

There has been a lot of work on migration of traditional legacy systems to SOA. Lewis et al.'s [8] SMART process provides a set of guidelines to identify the context, current system and target SOA system states and the gaps between them, and suggests the steps required to create a migration strategy. O'Brien et al. [14] describe a strategy for architecture reconstruction in legacy systems by identifying and reusing legacy components as services. Zhang and Yang introduce the use of cluster analysis [15], and Dwivedi and Kulkarni present a model-driven approach for service identification which utilizes process maps and service hierarchies [16]. Other approaches are presented by Chen et al. [17] and Aversano et al. [18].

```php
<?php
include_once ("functions.php");
include_once "papers_return.php";
include "SCA/SCA.php";

/**
 * @service
 * @binding.soap
 */
class papers {
    /**
     * @param string $_POSTStr
     * @param integer $id
     * @param integer $num
     * @return string
     */
    function addAuthors (string $_POSTStr, integer $id, integer $num) {
        $_POST = unserialize ($_POSTStr);
        foreach ($_POST ['authors'] as $author) {
            if (! empty ($author)) {
                query ("INSERT INTO authors ('paper_id', 'user_id', 'order') VALUES ('".$id."', '".
                    mysql_real_escape_string ($author)."')'".$num."')");
            }
            $num ++;
        }
        return serialize (new addAuthors_return ());
    }
    /**
     * @param string $id
     * @param string $oldname
     * @param string $name
     * @param string $ext
     * @param string $type
     * @param string $data
     * @return string
     */
    function updateFile (string $id, string $oldname, string $name, string $ext, string $type, string $data) {
        query ("DELETE FROM files WHERE paper_id='".$id."' AND name='".$oldname."'");
        query ("INSERT INTO files (paper_id, name, ext, type, data) VALUES ('".$id."'$', '".$name."', '".$ext."', '".$
            type."', '".$data."')");
        return serialize (new updateFile_return ());
    }
    /**
     * @param string $newname
     * @param integer $id
     * @param string $oldname
     * @return string
     */
    function updatePaper2 (string $newname, integer $id, string $oldname) {
        query ("UPDATE files SET name='".$newname."' WHERE paper_id='".$id."' AND name='".$oldname."'");
        return serialize (new updatePaper2_return ());
    }
    /**
     * @param integer $id
     * @param string $oldname
     * @return string
     */
    function deletePaper (integer $id, string $oldname) {
        query ("DELETE FROM files WHERE paper_id='".$id."' AND name='".$oldname."'");
        return serialize (new deletePaper_return ());
    }

    ////////// (10 more service operations) //////////
}
?>
```

Fig. 12. Final Migrated SCARF Paper Management Service Class

Much less work has been done in the area of migrating web applications to SOA. Tatsubori and Takashi's H2W framework [19] constructs web service wrappers for existing multi-paged web applications, and Dezhgosha and Angara [20] discuss how web services can be used to leverage existing web applications in a similar way. Vijaya and Rajan [21] focus on exploring the benefits of converting to web services, and Ajlan and Zedan [22] have worked on exposing the assignment module of Moodle as a web service, using a UML collaboration diagram to analyze and capture the necessary features.

In contrast, our work proposes a concrete generic framework of iterative steps for the migration of identified functionality to web services. Our goal is automation, and we have implemented our framework as a source transformation-based toolset that largely automates the migration of identified service operations in legacy PHP web applications to SCA-based web services.

6 Conclusions and Future Work

In this paper we have presented a framework and tool prototype that automates the migration of monolithic PHP web applications to web services in an SOA environment. The framework represents a new approach to the problem of migrating legacy systems to service-oriented architecture. It is one of the first approaches to explore the area of moving monolithic web applications to SOA, and the first to describe a complete detailed process with significant levels of automation.

Our framework consists of several automated steps: candidate service refactoring, candidate service separation, parameter type inference, service component conversion, and database refactoring. The result of applying our process is a new web application in which identified business operations have been separated into web services that both serve the original web application and can be reused by other applications.

At present our prototype implementation does not handle every feature of the PHP language. In particular, the refactoring step does not always detect all modifications or uses of variables in the tagged candidate service code fragments, in particular when variables appear inside strings. As a result the inferred parameters and return classes may in some unusual cases be incomplete. However, this is a well understood problem and it is relatively straightforward to extend the implementation. Due to the use of the TXL source transformation engine and its PHP grammar, at present our source transformations do not retain PHP comments from the original code. This is a known difficulty with source transformation tools, and can be addressed using the techniques described in Malton et al. [23].

There are several future lines of research for our work. While our migration process presently uses serialization to transfer non primitive data types, further analysis of the client application and the candidate service class could provide automated assistance for the migration of core data structures to Service Data Objects (SDO-DAS-XML) [24]. Currently every identified code segment in the original application is converted into a separate service operation. Clone detection techniques could identify similar operations and merge them into a single operation. While we have illustrated the automation of our process on the PHP language, our framework and its steps are not specific to any particular language. Extending our prototype automated migration tools to other web application languages such as Python is another area for future research.

References

[1] Tatsubori, M., Takahashi, K.: Decomposition and abstraction of web applications for web service extraction and composition. In: ICWS, pp. 859–868 (2006)

[2] Rajan, A., Otieno, J.: Leveraging traditional distributed applications to web services for e-learning applications. In: DEXA, pp. 430–435 (2004)

[3] Dezhgosha, K., Angara, S.: Web services for designing small-scale web applications. In: EIT, 4 p. (2005)

[4] Asuncion, C.H., Iacob, M.E., van Sinderen, M.: Towards a flexible service integration through separation of business rules. In: EDOC, pp. 184–193 (2010)

[5] Achour, M., Betz, F., Dovgal, A., Loopes, N., Magnusson, H., Richter, G., Seguy, D., Vrana, J.: PHP Manual, http://www.php.net/manual/en/index.php (last accessed August 2011)

[6] Van Rossum, G.: Python programming language, http://www.python.org/ (last accessed August 2011)

[7] Smith, D.: Migration of legacy assets to service-oriented architecture environments. In: ICSE, pp. 174–175 (2007)

[8] Lewis, G., Morris, E., O'Brien, L., Smith, D., Wrage, L.: SMART: The service-oriented migration and reuse technique. In: STEP, pp. 222–229 (2005)

[9] Sneed, H.M., Sneed, S.H.: Creating web services from legacy host programs. In: WSE, pp. 59–65 (2003)

[10] Almonaies, A., Cordy, J.R., Dean, T.R.: Legacy System Evolution towards Service- Oriented Architecture. In: SOAME, pp. 53–62 (2010)

[11] Cordy, J.R.: The TXL source transformation language. Sci. Comput. Program. 61, 190–210 (2006)

[12] Moodle Trust: Moodle, http://Moodle.org (last accessed October 2010)

[13] Tarjan, P., McKeown, N.: The Stanford Conference and Research Forum, http://scarf.sourceforge.net/ (last accessed March 2013)

[14] O'Brien, L., Smith, D.B., Lewis, G.A.: Supporting migration to services using software architecture reconstruction. In: STEP, pp. 81–91 (2005)

[15] Zhang, Z., Yang, H.: Incubating services in legacy systems for architectural migration. In: APSEC, pp. 196–203 (2004)

[16] Dwivedi, V., Kulkarni, N.: A model driven service identification approach for process centric systems. In: Congress on Services Part II, SERVICES-2, pp. 65–72 (2008)

[17] Chen, F., Li, S., Chu, W.C.C.: Feature analysis for service-oriented reengineering. In: APSEC, pp. 201–208. IEEE Computer Society (2005)

[18] Aversano, L., Cerulo, L., Palumbo, C.: Mining candidate web services from legacy code. In: WSE, pp. 37–40 (2008)

[19] Tatsubori, M., Takashi, K.: Decomposition and abstraction of web applications for web service extraction and composition. In: ICWS, pp. 859–868 (2006)

[20] Dezhgosha, K., Angara, S.: Web services for designing small-scale Web applications. In: International Conference on Electro Information Technology, 4 p. (2005)

[21] Rajan, A.V.S., Otieno, J.: Leveraging traditional distributed applications to web services for e-learning applications. In: 15th Intl. Workshop on Database and Expert Systems Applications, pp. 430–435 (2004)

[22] Ajlan, A., Zedan, H.: E-learning (MOODLE) Based on Service Oriented Architecture. In: The EADTU's 20th Anniversary Conference, pp. 62–70 (2007)

[23] Malton, A.J., Schneider, K.A., Cordy, J.R., Dean, T.R., Dousineau, D., Reynolds, J.: Processing software source text in automated design recovery and transformation. In: IWPC, pp. 127–134 (2001)

[24] Charters, G., Peters, M., Maynard, C., Srinivas, A.: An introduction to Service Data Objects for PHP, http://www.ibm.com/developerworks/library/os-sdophp/ (last accessed July 2011)

Automatic Refinement of Service Compositions*

Umberto S. Costa[1],**, Mirian Halfeld Ferrari[2],
Martin A. Musicante[1], and Sophie Robert[2]

[1] Universidade Federal do Rio Grande do Norte, DIMAp, Natal, Brazil
{umberto,mam}@dimap.ufrn.br
[2] Université d'Orléans, LIFO, Orléans, France
{mirian,sophie.robert}@univ-orleans.fr

Abstract. We propose a method for the automatic refinement of web service compositions: given a composite web service specification over *abstract* modules, our method generates lower-level versions of this composition. The refinement process is based on query rewriting techniques extended to take into account not only functional and non-functional requirements but also semantic information. Experimental results illustrate the performance and scalability of the method.

Keywords: Web Services, Service Compositions, Automatic Refinement.

1 Introduction

The composition of web services is a central task in Service-Oriented Software Development [1]. This task consists in combining pre-existing services in order to achieve new functionalities. The selection of services is based on the requirements of the compound service as well as on the descriptions of individual services. Services from different providers may not agree on the representation of data or functionality. The successful combination of services depends on the correct matching between their interfaces. In this scenario, the composition designer is in charge of providing mechanisms to find suitable services and to adapt their interfaces as required by the composition. A number of initiatives were proposed to tackle the problem of automatically composing web services. Approaches include the adaptation of techniques from areas such as Databases [2] or AI Planning [3].

In this paper we propose a mechanism for the automatic refinement of web service specifications, using semantic information. The Semantic Web can help to broaden the choice of services. Ontologies [4] may be used to align the representation of concepts, as well as to describe the relationships between services. The developer can describe a compound application in terms of semantic descriptions (*abstract services*). Each abstract service may correspond to one or

---

* This work was partly supported by the National Institute of Science and Technology for Software Engineering (INES), funded by CNPq (Brazil) 573964/2008-4; CAPES/UdelaR (Brazil) 021/2010; CAPES/STIC-AmSud (Brazil) 020/2010; ANR project ExaviZ.
** Bolsista da CAPES - Brasília/Brasil.

F. Daniel, P. Dolog, and Q. Li (Eds.): ICWE 2013, LNCS 7977, pp. 400–407, 2013.
© Springer-Verlag Berlin Heidelberg 2013

more concrete services, as published by individual providers. We assume that the construction of a composition of concrete services is based on a software development process formed by *Specification, Refinement, Evaluation* and *Coding* steps. This paper focuses on the *Refinement* step and presents an algorithm to automatically refine high-level specifications of service compositions into lower-level ones. Our method is based on the MiniCon algorithm [5] for query rewriting, known in the database domain. We begin with a higher-level composition specification expressed over abstract services and quality constraints. Our approach generates several translations of this specification into compositions over concrete services. The solutions produced will be ranked (*Evaluation*) and coded into concrete orchestrations. These two steps are beyond the scope of our work.

This paper is organised as follows: Section 2 describes our method; Section 3 presents some experiments; Section 4 concludes the paper.

2 Rewriting Compositions

Our algorithm for refining specifications of abstract compositions is structured in two main phases. In the first one, each concrete service definition is scanned in order to identify what parts of the specification it covers. The second phase of our algorithm combines concrete services, in order to cover the whole specification.

Both the abstract composition and concrete services are defined in the same way, by using the syntax: $C(\bar{t}) \equiv_{def} A_1(\bar{t_1}), \ldots, A_n(\bar{t_n}), Q_1(\bar{t_1'}), \ldots, Q_m(\bar{t_m'})$. The elements of the tuple $\bar{t}$ on the left-hand side of a definition are the formal parameters. These parameters represent input (marked with "?") or output (marked with "!") data. The right-hand side of the definition consists of abstract service calls and quality constraints. The same decorations are used for the parameters of these items. Additionally, optional parameters of abstract services inside the definition of concrete services are marked with "*". Quality constraints $Q_i(\bar{t})$ are of the form $(X\ op\ Y)$, $(X\ op\ a)$ or $(X \in C)$ where X and Y are variables, a is constant, $op \in \{<, >, \leq, \geq, =\}$ and C is a set of constants.

The first phase of our method consists in matching the specification of each concrete service with parts of the abstract composition. Each concrete service may be used to implement parts of the composition. Given the abstract composition $C(\ldots) \equiv_{def} A_1(\ldots), \ldots, A_n(\ldots), Q_1(\ldots), \ldots, Q_m(\ldots)$ and each concrete service $S_i(\ldots) \equiv_{def} A_i(\ldots), \ldots, A_j(\ldots), Q_k(\ldots), \ldots, Q_l(\ldots)$, our algorithm tries to match some abstract services on the right-hand side of the definition of S_i with the same services on the right-hand side of the definition of C. This matching consists in a (semantic) mapping to make their parameters compatible. For each possible matching, a tuple containing the mapping information is produced. Each of these tuples is called a PCD (*Partial Coverage Descriptor*).

A Partial Coverage Descriptor D for a concrete service S and a composition C is a tuple $\langle S, h, \varphi, G, Def, has\_opt \rangle$, where:

- S is the name of the concrete service involved in the matching.
- φ is a partial mapping from $Terms(C)$ to $h(Terms(S))$. This mapping defines the correspondence between the terms appearing on the abstract composition and terms that appear on the concrete service definition.

- h is a mapping from $Terms(S)$ to $Terms(S)$. For every term x that is not a parameter of S, $h(x) = x$. For terms x and y that are parameters of S, h may be such that $h(x) = h(y)$, where for every parameter x we have that $h(x) = h(h(x))$. This mapping is the head homomorphism in [5].
- G is the set of abstract service names and quality constraints covered by S.
- Def is a set of quality constraints of the abstract composition. Intuitively, this set will contain those conditions that cannot be guaranteed by S alone.
- has_opt is a boolean flag used to indicate that some abstract service in the definition of S has been used in G and has an optional parameter.   □

Roughly speaking, a PCD D indicates *(i)* which part of the abstract composition is covered by a concrete service S and *(ii)* how to relate the data processed by the composition with the parameters of the concrete service.

Example 1. Let $C(x?, y!) \equiv_{def} A_1(x?, x?), A_2(x?, y!)$ be an abstract composition. Let $S(a?, b?) \equiv_{def} A_1(a?, b?), A_3(a?)$ be the specification of a concrete service. Let us consider the abstract service call $A_1(x?, x?)$ in C. We can use the definition of S to cover part of the composition. Indeed, it is possible to obtain the PCD $D = \langle S, \varphi, h, \{A_1\}, \emptyset, \textbf{false} \rangle$ where $h(a) = a$, $h(b) = a$ and $\varphi(x) = h(a)$.   □

The algorithm below builds a set of PCDs, given an abstract composition C and a set of concrete service specifications $\mathcal{S}$.

Algorithm 1. (Build PCDs)

```
procedure build PCDs(C, S)                                              1
   PCDs := ∅;                                                           2
   for each abstract service A in the definition of C do                3
      for each concrete service S∈ S do                                4
         if there are mappings h and φ for A in the definitions of C and S then   5
            G := {A};                                                   6
            Def := ∅;                                                   7
            PCD := ⟨ S, h, φ, G, Def, has_opt ⟩;                       8
            AS := {A' | A' is an abstract service or quality constraints in C sharing   9
                       parameters with A or with other elements of AS}  10
            PCD_OK := true;                                             11
            while AS≠ ∅ and PCD_OK do                                  12
               A' := choose an abstract service from AS;                13
               if h, φ can be extended to cover A' then                14
                  Update PCD w.r.t. h, φ, G, Def, has_opt              15
                  AS := AS − A';                                       16
               else PCD_OK := false;                                   17
            if PCD_OK then PCDs := PCDs ∪ PCD;                         18
```

In the mappings for the abstract service A (line 5), parameters appearing on the left-hand side of C should only be mapped to parameters appearing on the left-hand side of concrete service definitions or optional ones. Then, Algorithm 1 looks for other abstract services or quality constraints connected to A. The set AS contains all abstract services or quality constraints of C that *(i)* have a data dependency to A and *(ii)* are not mapped by φ to parameters of S (line 9).

Example 2. Let $C(y!) \equiv_{def} A_1(x?, y!), A_2(x!), x \geq 10, y \in \{5, 4, 3\}$ be an abstract composition. Let us suppose $S(b!) \equiv_{def} A_1(a?, b!), A_2(a!), a = 10$. We will obtain a PCD covering not only the abstract service call $A_1(x?, y!)$, but, due to the mapping of x (on the composition) to a on S (*i.e.*, $\varphi(x) = a$), the PCD must also cover the abstract service call $A_2(x!)$ and the condition $x \geq 10$. This matching is possible because service S may cover A_2 and specifies that $a = 10$. □

One important difference between our algorithm and MiniCon [5], is that our method supports the notion of optional parameters in the specification of a concrete services, *i.e.*, parameters that can be ignored. The information about optional parameters is supposed to be provided by the vendor of the service as part of its specification. This situation is described in the next example.

Example 3. Let $C(u?, x!) \equiv_{def} A_1(u?, v!, w!), A_2(v?, w?, x!)$ be an abstract composition and $S(a?, c!) \equiv_{def} A_1(a?, *b!, c!)$ a concrete service specification where b is an optional parameter. Algorithm 1 builds the PCD $D = \langle S, h, \varphi, \{A_1\}, \emptyset, \mathbf{true} \rangle$ where h is the identity function; $\varphi(u) = a$, $\varphi(v) = b$, $\varphi(w) = c$. There are two data dependencies between A_1 and A_2, given by the parameters v and w on both service calls. None of these data dependencies is taken into account when the set AS is built at line 9 of Algorithm 1: *(i)* the variable v is mapped to the optional parameter b on the specification of S and *(ii)* the variable w is mapped by φ to c, which is a parameter of S. Notice that this PCD is marked as having optional parameters (last component of the tuple is **true**). This information will be used in the algorithm of the second phase to restrict combinations of PCDs. □

Our second phase algorithm combines PCDs to produce compositions over concrete services. To this end, it takes the set of PCDs produced by Algorithm 1 and looks for combinations of these PCDs to cover the right-hand side of the abstract service composition C. This procedure is described by Algorithm 2.

Algorithm 2. (Combine PCDs)

```
procedure Combine PCDs(C, PCDs)                                                1
    Given C = C(t̄) ≡_def A_1(...),...,A_n(...),Q_1(...),...,Q_m(...) and        2
        PCDs = {...,⟨S_i, h_i, φ_i, G_i, Def_i, has_opt_i⟩,...};               3
    for each combination {PCD_1,...,PCD_k}⊆ PCDs such that                     4
        (a) {A_1(...),...,A_n(...)} ⊆ G_1 ∪ ··· ∪ G_k;                         5
        (b) ∀ i,j . G_i ∩ G_j ⊆ Def_i ∩ Def_j;                                6
        (c) All deferred constraints in Def_1 ... Def_k hold;                  7
        (d) Input and output optional parameters should match.                8
    do Pre := ∅; Pos := ∅;                                                     9
        for each variable x ∈ Q_i such that Q_i ∉ G_1 ∪ ··· ∪ G_k do          10
            if x is an input parameter of C then Pre := Pre ∪ Q_i end if;     11
            if x is an output parameter of C then Pos := Pos ∪ Q_i end if;    12
        publish ⟨ Pre ⟩ C'(EC(t̄)) ≡_def S_1(t̄_1),...,S_k(t̄_k) ⟨ Pos ⟩;      13
```

Algorithm 2 tries to cover the definition of the abstract composition C by searching all subsets of PCDs such that: *(a)* they cover all the abstract services

$A_1, \ldots, A_n$ of C (line 5); *(b)* there is no overlapping of the abstract services covered by these PCDs, except for deferred quality constraints (line 6); *(c)* the deferred quality constraints of the PCDs must hold when their variables are instantiated using the mappings of the PCDs (line 7); *(d)* each term in C mapped to an optional output parameter (in the definition of S_i) can only be mapped to optional input parameters (in the definition of any concrete service) (line 8).

For each combination of PCDs satisfying the conditions above, one concrete composition is produced. The refined composition is published in line 13, with its pre- and post-conditions. These conditions are properties of the abstract composition that cannot be statically verified. Each concrete composition $C'(EC(\bar{t})) \equiv_{def} S_1(\bar{t_1}), \ldots, S_k(\bar{t_k})$ has a parameter tuple obtained by applying the function $EC(\bar{t})$ to the parameters of the abstract composition. This function expresses an equivalence class of parameters. The function $EC(\bar{t})$ permits to equate parameters that are different on the abstract composition but that are mapped to the same term on a concrete service as shown in Example 4.

Example 4. Let $C(x?, y?, z!) \equiv_{def} A_1(x?, y?, w!), A_2(w?, z!)$ be an abstract composition, $S_1(a?, r!) \equiv_{def} A_1(a?, a?, r!)$ and $S_2(c?, d!) \equiv_{def} A_2(c?, d!)$ be the specifications of concrete services. Algorithm 1 builds the following PCDs: $D_1 = \langle S_1, h_1, \varphi_1, \{A_1\}, \emptyset, \textbf{false} \rangle$, where h_1 is the identity, $\varphi_1(x) = a$, $\varphi_1(y) = a$ and $\varphi_1(w) = r$; $D_2 = \langle S_2, h_2, \varphi_2, \{A_2\}, \emptyset, \textbf{false} \rangle$ where h_2 is the identity, $\varphi_2(w) = c$ and $\varphi_2(z) = d$. In D_1, both x and y are mapped by φ_1 to a and thus define the equivalence class $\{x, y\}$. So, x and y correspond to the same parameter. Each occurrence of a must be replaced with the representative term of the equivalence class $\{x, y\}$. Thus, we can generate the concrete composition C' by using the terms in $EC(\langle x, y, z \rangle)$, as follows: $C'(x?, x?, z!) \equiv_{def} S_1(x?, w!), S_2(w?, z!)$. $\square$

The parameters of $S_1(\bar{t_1}), \ldots, S_k(\bar{t_k})$ in the concrete composition (Algorithm 2, line 13) are represented by the tuples $\bar{t_i}$. The terms in these tuples are obtained as $\bar{t_i} = f_i^{-1} \circ EC \circ \psi_i \circ h_i(\bar{t_i'})$, such that: *(i)* $\bar{t_i'}$ are the parameters of S_i; *(ii)* the mappings ψ_i rename the variables of the service S_i into the corresponding variables of the abstract composition; and *(iii)* the conversion functions f_i are provided by a set of ontologies. For each $t_j' \in h_i(\bar{t'})$, $\psi_i(t_j') = t_j$, if $\varphi_i(t_j) = f_i \circ h_i(t_j')$, and t_j' otherwise. As usual, conversion functions are bijective. In the case of the same representation of data, conversion functions are the identity.

It can be proved that the concrete service compositions produced by the combination of Algorithms 1 and 2 meet the requirements of the abstract composition, in functional terms. This is described by the following property:

Property 1 (Correctness). Given an abstract composition C, for each concrete composition C' obtained by our algorithm, the following property holds: $\forall \bar{t}, \bar{t'} \, . \, C'(\bar{t}?, \bar{t'}!) \Rightarrow C(\bar{t}?, \bar{t'}!)$. $\square$

Property 1 ensures that the solutions obtained by our method are functionally correct. Notice that the functionality implemented by the refined compositions may not cover all the cases considered by the abstract composition. The compositions obtained by our method depend on the available concrete services. The available services may not match all the cases of the specification.

3   Experiments

We have implemented a prototype of our method in Java on the basis of the MiniCon program. In the second phase of our method, all combinations of PCDs are considered, which implies an exponential time complexity (in the number of PCDs generated by the first phase of the method)[1]. This is due to the combinatorial nature of the problem, which is also faced by the MiniCon Algorithm. Figures 1 and 2 show the average time from 10 executions on a Dual Core 2.83GHz processor, 4GB RAM machine running Debian 6.

In Figure 1 we show the runtime for a composition with 10 abstract services and a varying number of concrete services (with two left-hand side parameters) defined by 10 abstract services. In these experiments each concrete service responds to the composition requirements with: (A) no quality constraint; (B) five quality constraints added to each definition; (C) MiniCon without quality constraints but with an optimization procedure. We have used an optimization to avoid the combinatorial explosion of the MiniCon approach, since each service can respond alone to composition requirements. The linear growth shown in Figure 1 is due to this optimization. The overhead introduced by the quality constraints in case (B) varies from 11% to 23% when compared to case (A).

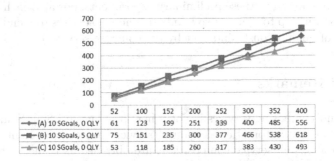

	52	100	152	200	252	300	352	400
(A) 10 SGoals, 0 QLY	61	123	199	251	339	400	485	556
(B) 10 SGoals, 5 QLY	75	151	235	300	377	466	538	618
(C) 10 SGoals, 0 QLY	53	118	185	260	317	383	430	493

Fig. 1. # Services × Time (ms)

In Figure 2, we show the runtime for an abstract composition formed by six abstract services and one quality constraint. The number of concrete services taken into account varies from 96 to 228. This is shown on the X-axis. For each number of concrete services, we varied the proportion of them that satisfies the quality constraints of the abstract composition. Percentages range from 0% to 100%. This is shown on the Z-axis of the picture. The Y-axis of the picture corresponds to the average execution time of the program.

We observe that for a reduced percentage of services that complies with the quality constraint, the first phase of the algorithm will produce a reduced number

---

[1] The first phase of our method is $O(m.n^2)$, where m is the number of concrete services and n is the number of abstract services invoked by the abstract composition and concrete service definitions.

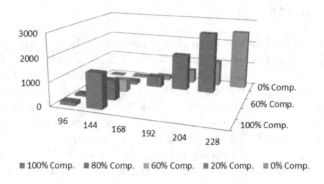

Fig. 2. # Services × Qly Compliance × Time (ms)

of PCDs, allowing the second phase to work with a fewer combinations. As the number of services that meet the quality restriction increases, the second phase of the algorithm shows its combinatorial nature, making it difficult to deal with more than about 150 concrete services. We should notice that on usual situations, the number of available concrete services is not expected to be that many. According to these preliminary experiments, our approach is feasible for problems with up to almost two hundred concrete services (depending on the proportion of quality constraints met by the concrete services).

4   Final Remarks

Selecting and composing services is not a new problem [6,7,8,9]: Some authors [10,11] consider an automatic selection of services, from the semantic point of view. To others, web service compositions are obtained as refinements of more abstract specifications [8,12]. Query Rewriting techniques [13,2,5] have been considered for generating compositions from abstract specifications. Recently, researchers have started to apply this technique in the context of web semantics and web service composition [7,8,9]. Our work is inserted in this context, where we use non-functional properties for fine-tuning the selection of services.

Our work adapts and extends the query rewriting method MiniCon to service composition. In this new context, it is important to remark that the definition of a composition or a service is not seen as a database query and, thus, is not imposed to the same restrictions. Besides this adaptation (that, for instance, makes useless the notion of safe rules required in [5]), the original method has been expanded to deal with optional parameters and quality constraints.

The advantages of our approach are significant: it eases the user's work, deferring technical details to further steps; takes into account both functional and non-functional requirements; offers different solutions that can be used latter when dealing with service evolution in runtime; allows the use of domain ontology information to perform data transformations (*i.e.*, in practice, our algorithm is capable of automatically performing data conversions in order to use services whose parameters do not match exactly).

Experiments using our prototype implementation show that our approach is feasible on real-life applications, where distinct concrete services rarely respond to the same non-functional requirements (restricting the possible choices during the rewriting). As a future direction, we are aware of the need of establishing theoretical properties of our approach. We are currently working on the classification of solutions according to an user profile.

Acknowledgements. Special thanks to Prof. R. Pottinger, who kindly made available the code of MiniCon, and to S. Munier for implementing a prototype of our method.

References

1. Marks, E., Bell, M.: Service-Oriented Architecture: A Planning and Implementation Guide for Business and Technology. Wiley (2006)
2. Levy, A.Y.: Logic-Based Techniques in Data Integration. In: Minker, J. (ed.) Logic-Based Artificial Intelligence, pp. 575–595. Kluwer, USA (2000)
3. Rao, J., Su, X.: A survey of automated web service composition methods. In: Cardoso, J., Sheth, A.P. (eds.) SWSWPC 2004. LNCS, vol. 3387, pp. 43–54. Springer, Heidelberg (2005)
4. Dobson, G., Sanchez-Macian, A.: Towards Unified QoS/SLA Ontologies. In: Proceedings of the IEEE Services Computing Workshops, SCW 2006, pp. 169–174. IEEE Computer Society, Washington, DC (2006)
5. Pottinger, R., Halevy, A.Y.: Minicon: A scalable algorithm for answering queries using views. VLDB J. 10(2-3), 182–198 (2001)
6. Alrifai, M., Risse, T.: Combining Global Optimization with Local Selection for Efficient QoS-aware Service Composition. In: Proc. of the 18th International Conference on World Wide Web, WWW 2009, pp. 881–890. ACM, New York (2009)
7. Barhamgi, M., Benslimane, D., Medjahed, B.: A query rewriting approach for web service composition. IEEE Trans. Serv. Comput. 3(3), 206–222 (2010)
8. Thakkar, S., Ambite, J.L., Knoblock, C.A.: A data integration approach to automatically composing and optimizing web services. In: Proc. of the ICAPS Workshop on Planning and Scheduling for Web and Grid Services (2004)
9. Zhao, W., Liu, C., Chen, J.: Automatic composition of information-providing web services based on query rewriting. Science China Information Sciences, 1–17 (2011)
10. Berardi, D., Calvanese, D., Giacomo, G.D., Lenzerini, M., Mecella, M.: Automatic composition of e-services. Technical Report 22-2003, Dipartimento di Informatica e Sistemistica, Universita di Roma La Sapienza, Roma, Italy (2003)
11. Izquierdo, D., Vidal, M.-E., Bonet, B.: An expressive and efficient solution to the service selection problem. In: Patel-Schneider, P.F., Pan, Y., Hitzler, P., Mika, P., Zhang, L., Pan, J.Z., Horrocks, I., Glimm, B. (eds.) ISWC 2010, Part I. LNCS, vol. 6496, pp. 386–401. Springer, Heidelberg (2010)
12. Mesmoudi, A., Mrissa, M., Hacid, M.S.: Combining configuration and query rewriting for Web service composition. Technical Report RR-LIRIS-2010-015, LIRIS UMR 5205 CNRS/INSA Lyon/U. Lyon 1/U. Lyon 2/EC Lyon (July 2010)
13. Duschka, O.M.: Query Planning and Optimization in Information Integration. PhD thesis, Department of Computer Science, Stanford University (December 1997)

A Generative Approach for the Adaptive Monitoring of SLA in Service Choreographies

Antonia Bertolino, Antonello Calabrò, and Guglielmo De Angelis

CNR–ISTI, Pisa, Italy
{antonia.bertolino,antonello.calabro,guglielmo.deangelis}@isti.cnr.it

Abstract. Monitoring is an essential means in the management of service-oriented applications. Here, event correlation results crucial when monitoring rules aim at checking the exposed levels of Quality of Service against the Service Level Agreements established among the choreography participants. However, when choreographies are enacted over distributed networks or clouds, the relevant monitoring rules might not be completely defined a-priori, as they may need to be adapted to the specific infrastructure and to the evolution of events. This paper presents an adaptive multi-source monitoring architecture synthesizing instances of rules at run-time and shows examples of use on a demonstration scenario from the European Project CHOReOS.

Keywords: Monitoring, Choreographies, Complex Event Processor, SOA, SLA, QoS.

1 Introduction

Service choreographies specify the intended interaction protocol among a set of cooperating services at the application business level [1]. With services becoming more and more pervasive and critical in everyday life and business, increasing importance assumes the quality exposed by those interactions. The agreed levels of Quality of Service (QoS) between the involved parties form the Service Level Agreements (SLAs). Hence, service choreographies are often augmented with notations expressing the non-functional properties that the choreographed service should abide by [2]. As a consequence, SLA monitoring and assessment become essential assets of any environment supporting choreography enactment.

Within the context of SOA, in order to effectively detect unexpected or undesirable behaviors of services, locate the origin of the issue, or even predict potential failures it is generally necessary to track, combine, and analyze events occurring at different abstraction levels. Therefore, in contrast with the use of more monitors operating in separate contexts, a promising strategy that is investigated in the literature is to architect SLA monitoring solutions able to reveal or predict run-time anomalies due to the combination of phenomena originated from sources operating at different levels [3]. We have recently developed [4] a monitoring architecture supporting the SLA monitoring of service

F. Daniel, P. Dolog, and Q. Li (Eds.): ICWE 2013, LNCS 7977, pp. 408–415, 2013.

choreographies from multiple sources, namely the infrastructure and the business layers, within the scope of the CHOReOS project[1].

The above mentioned multi-source monitoring solution, though, had not been conceived to deal with the continuous dynamic evolution that is typical of service compositions. In a context in which services may dynamically appear and disappear and are dynamically bound, it is reasonable to assume that the same SLA requirements to be monitored may also evolve, even as a reaction to some occurring event or situation that cannot be a-priori known. Moreover, the deployment and the execution of applications on highly dynamic Cloud infrastructures introduce further requirements of adaptability with respect to monitoring. Such requirements must be directly addressed by developers, providers, and maintainers of the choreography-based applications [5].

In this paper we present a monitoring infrastructure that improves on [4] by supporting the dynamic evolution of SLA monitoring rules. Specifically, our contribution is a *generative approach for the adaptive multi-source monitoring of SLAs in service choreographies*.

The rest of the paper is structured as follows: Section 2 introduces our adaptive multi-source monitoring framework including a generative module for the monitoring rules making the architecture adaptable at run-time; Section 3 reports about a case study demonstrating the application of the approach; finally Section 4 draws the conclusions.

2 Adaptive SLA Monitoring

In [4] we presented a monitoring architecture based on Glimpse [6] that supported the SLA monitoring of service choreographies from multiple sources. In the following we refer to such starting configuration as a Multi-source Monitoring Framework.

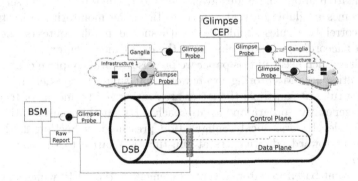

Fig. 1. Multi-source Monitoring Architecture

---

[1] See at http://www.choreos.eu

As shown in Figure 1, the configuration relies on a Distributed Service Bus (DSB) sharing distributed communication channels among the choreographed services. The DSB distinguishes between a set of channels on which both co-ordination and application messages flow (i.e. `Data Plane`), and another set dedicated to the monitoring activities (i.e., `Control Plane`). The data passing through the latter, can be correlated and analyzed by means of a Complex Event Processor (CEP).

Via the DSB, the Multi-source Monitoring Framework integrates three different monitoring facilities, each relative to a specific data source:

Infrastructure Monitor (IM): focuses on the status of the environment, providing support for the monitoring of resources, both in terms of their utilization and health status.

Business Service-Oriented Monitor (BSM): is responsible for monitoring the co-ordination messages that the choreographed services exchange with each other on the Data Plane channels of the DSB, by means of distributed interceptors. Then, BSM analyzes the temporal sequence of those events, checks the compliance of the SLA in the choreography specification, and, if any violation is found, it notify over the Control Plane.

Event Monitor (EM): refers to a generic event-based monitoring infrastructure able to bridge the notifications coming from the other two sources. Specifically at this level the other two kind of sources are wrapped by means of Glimpse Probes that forward notifications to the Glimpse CEP where they are processed and correlated.

Let us now refer to a scenario, such as the one that is emerging within the context of the Cloud paradigm, in which a solution that relies on the off-line definition of the monitoring rules appears not effective, as it is not thinkable to foresee a-priori the actual instantiation of the configurations. In fact, in the Cloud computing model enterprises provide infrastructures (e.g. machines) on-demand by allocating the exact amount of resources the customers need to use. Therefore, the information about the nodes available, and the mapping of the services on them becomes available only at run-time. Both the monitoring infrastructure and the correlation rules should deal with such dynamic contexts and adapt themselves according to the evolution of the deployment context.

To address such need, in this paper we propose a novel adaptive configuration of the Multi-source Monitoring Framework that supports the definition of the monitoring rules at run-time: the latter are synthesized by means of techniques based on generative programming approaches [7]. In this sense, with respect to the high-level hierarchical configuration presented in Section 2, the main improvement toward adaptiveness at run-time is relative to the source Event Monitoring.

In any event-based monitor, a central element is the CEP, which is the rule engine that analyzes the primitive events, generated from some kind of probes, in order to infer complex events matching the consumer requests. There exist several rule engines that can be used for this task (like Drools Fusion, RuleML), and for the sake of space we do not focus on traditional aspects of a CEP [6].

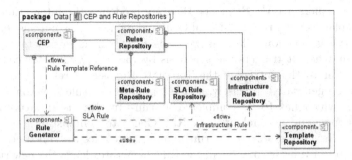

Fig. 2. Main Components of the CEP for the Adaptive Monitor

We focus instead on the specific components that support adaptiveness: as depicted in Figure 2, we have extended the CEP in its functionalities by including the sub-components: the Rules Repository, the Rule Generator, and the Template Repository.

The component Rules Repository abstracts the definition of three kind of repositories, each linking a dedicated kind of rule-set. Specifically, there is a repository storing the rules matching infrastructure events; a repository storing event rules about the SLA agreed among the choreographed business services; finally an additional repository storing the meta-rules enabling the run-time adaptation by means of generative procedures. A meta-rule is a special rule whose body implements the run-time synthesis procedure for populating both the SLA Rule Repository, and the Infrastructure Rule Repository.

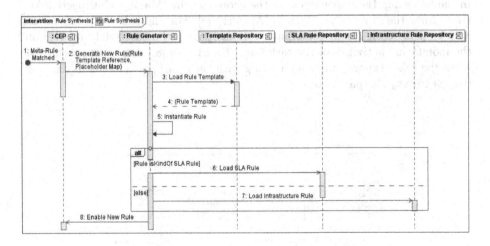

Fig. 3. Diagram of Interactions during Rule Synthesis

Figure 3 depicts a UML Sequence Diagram modeling the interaction schema that takes place among the traditional CEP and its new sub-components. Specifically, the rule generation is done in two steps. First, whenever a meta-rule within the CEP matches, it triggers the synthesis by the Rule Generator component. This will refer to the entries of the Template Repository relative to the kind of rules to be generated: precisely, a rule template is a rule skeleton, the specification of which has to be completed at run-time by instantiating a set of template-dependent placeholders. The Rule Generator will instantiate the latter with appropriate values inferred at run-time. Second, once the run-time synthesis of the new set of rules is completed, the Rule Generator loads the new rules into their corresponding repository (either SLA Rule Repository or Infrastructure Rule Repository) and enables them by refreshing the CEP's rule engine.

For the sake of completeness, we remark that both the SLA Rule Repository, and the Infrastructure Rule Repository can obviously also include sets of static rules that do not depend on the generative process discussed above.

3   Demonstration Scenario

The presented monitoring framework provides the facilities to adaptively detect and correlate events generated by different layers. In this section we show how this can help problems detection on a scenario referred by a choreography developed within the CHOReOS Project.

3.1   Scenario Description

In the following, the paper refers to the choreography "Manage Unexpected Arrival" from the "Passenger-Friendly Airport" [8]. For the sake of presentation with respect to the main contribution of the paper, the case study focuses on the monitoring activities of the task Book Amenities [8], and more specifically when the role Airport starts interacting with the other participants in the task (e.g. Security Company, etc.).

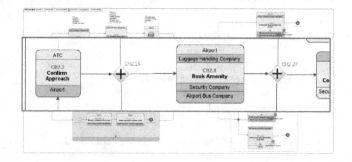

Fig. 4. The Passenger-Friendly Airport Use Case

Specifically, with respect to the interactions between the `Airport`, and the `Security Company`, the paper reports how to combine the run-time assessment of the QoS by the BSM with the information provided by the IM referring to the status of the nodes hosting the services.

Within the configuration of the scenario the infrastructural nodes were equipped on-purpose with means (i.e. "Load Knob") for injecting artificial disruptions by overloading them.

The components of the Multi-source Monitoring framework were distributedly deployed on dedicated nodes (i.e. hosting the DSB, the CEP, and the BSM). According to the configuration presented in Section 2, the scenario included a set of probes (i.e. Glimpse Probes) notifying either violations of SLAs at business service level, or information about the status of the nodes in the cloud hosting the services.

In addition, the BSM has been configured to intercept events on the `Data Plane`, while the CEP and the Glimpse Probe were bound to the `Control Plane`. Finally, an SLA regulating the latency of the interactions between the participants `Airport`, and `Security Company` has been loaded and activated within the BSM.

3.2   Execution and Adaptation

Within this case study we assumed that the rule knowledge base of the CEP has been instructed with a meta-rule specifying the action/countermeasure to activate if an SLA violation message occurs. We are assuming that the action depends on the specific machine where the violation occurred, and moreover it varies for the two different configurations about the monitored notifications: 1) SLA violation && node overload; 2) SLA violation && node not overloaded.

When the BSM reveals that an SLA violation has occurred, its associated Glimpse Probe sends a warning to the CEP. According to the generative process described in Section 2, the CEP first interacts with an internal registry associated with the `Data Plane` of the DSB in other to identify the IP address of the machine running the specific instance of the service that violated the SLA; then, its Rule Generator component synthesizes and enables a new rule looking for issues on the node hosting that service.

Listing 1 reports the auto-generated rule after an SLA violation of the service `Security Company` is raised to the CEP.

The generated rule is composed by two parts: the first begins at line 7, where the `$aEvent` represents the SLA Alert event sent by the BSM to the CEP. It is identified by the timestamp, a parameter checking if the event has been already managed by the CEP (i.e. `isConsumed`), and the name of the event. The second part begins at line 8, and represents the infrastructure event the Multi-source Monitoring framework looks for matching. Notably, this second part specifies a parameter called `getMachineIP` containing the IP address of the node that generated the infrastructure-level notification, which would be matched with the IP address retrieved from the SLA notification during the generation of the rule. In addition, such a declaration refers to a filter on the window frame within which the correlation should be considered valid (see at line: 8). Specifically Listing 1 specifies that two events can be correlated if **$bEvent** occurred within a 10 seconds interval after **$aEvent**.

```
1   <ComplexEventRuleActionList xmlns="http://labse.isti.cnr.it/glimpse/xml/ComplexEventRule"...>
2     <Insert RuleType="drools"><RuleName>
          SLA_violation_overload_Autogenerated_SecutiryCompanyService</RuleName>
3     <RuleBody>
4     rule "SecurityCompanyService_ INFRASTRUCTUREVIOLATION"
5         ...  ...
6     when
7       $aEvent : GlimpseBaseEventChoreos( this.isConsumed == true, this.getTimeStamp == 1360752708858,
          this.getEventName == "SLA Alert − SecurityCompanyService");
8       $bEvent : GlimpseBaseEventChoreos(this.isConsumed == false, this.getEventName == "load_one",
          this.getMachineIP == "67.215.65.132", this after[0,10s] $aEvent);
9     then
10      $bEvent.setConsumed(true); update($bEvent);
11      ResponseDispatcher.LogViolation("...","auto_generated_rule", "\nSLA and Infrastructure violation by
          service: SecurityCompanyService" + "\npossibly due to an overload on machine: " + $bEvent.
          getMachineIP());
12      retract($aEvent); retract($bEvent);
13    end
14    </RuleBody>
15    </Insert>
16  </ComplexEventRuleActionList>
```

Listing 1. Generated Rule : SLA violation due to the overload of the hosting node

In the simulation case that no artificial overload is injected, the rule at Listing 1 applies, and a notification is dispatched to the service provider/administrator as potentially the violation may be due to the service itself. On the other hand, by querying the "Load Knob" on the node hosting the **Security Company** service , it is possible to inject some artificial disruption at the infrastructure level. In this case, when both the SLA violation on **Security Company** and a notification of an overload peak from the machine hosting it occur, the rule at Listing 1 matches. The assigned countermeasure is to dispatch a notification for redistributing some of the services active on that specific node onto some others nodes of the cluster.

4   Conclusion and Future Work

Adaptability is a key problem in the distributed and dynamic environments subsumed by the paradigm of the service choreographies. Specifically, as choreographies are abstract specifications, they may include interaction schema that can evolve after the design phase, so that unexpected events or scenarios may actually take place at run-time.

In addition, adaptability is a crucial asset for monitoring infrastructures correlating phenomena originated from sources operating at different abstraction layers; for example trying to understand the causes of run-time anomalies such as the SLA violations among participants of a choreography. In these contexts the dynamicity is even more evident when the participants are executing in a distributed cloud-based infrastructure.

In this work we extended the Multi-source Monitoring framework originally introduced in [4] with features supporting the adaptive generation of the monitoring rules at run-time. Other works already exist, e.g. [3], and [5], arguing that SOA monitoring cannot address separately layer-specific issues. Moreover, the authors of both [9], and [10] previously considered that the monitoring activity can be enhanced with adaptation. On the one hand, these frameworks mainly refer to orchestrated service compositions while we focused on decentralized and message-oriented scenarios that are typical of service choreographies. On the other hand, our architecture refers to "adaptiveness" as a mean to deal with configurations/scenarios that cannot be completely specified either at design, or deployment time. The work and the application case study have been developed as part of the demonstrators of the CHOReOS project.

An interesting aspect of [9] that our work did not consider yet concerns the verification of the consistency between the run-time generated rules and the ones already loaded within the CEP. We are interested in supporting means ensuring such kind of consistency for the Multi-source Monitoring framework.

Acknowledgments. This work is part of the European Project FP7 IP 257178: CHOReOS. We thank the colleagues from Linagora and University of São Paulo for their contribution to some components of the Multi-source Monitoring Framework.

References

1. Barker, A., Walton, C.D., Robertson, D.: Choreographing Web Services. IEEE T. Services Computing 2(2), 152–166 (2009)
2. Bartolini, C., Bertolino, A., Ciancone, A., De Angelis, G., Mirandola, R.: Non-Functional Analysis of Service Choreographies. In: Proc. of the Workshop on Principles of Engineering Service Oriented Systems. IEEE-CS (June 2012)
3. Guinea, S., Kecskemeti, G., Marconi, A., Wetzstein, B.: Multi-layered Monitoring and Adaptation. In: Kappel, G., Maamar, Z., Motahari-Nezhad, H.R. (eds.) ICSOC 2012. LNCS, vol. 7084, pp. 359–373. Springer, Heidelberg (2011)
4. Ben Hamida, A., Bertolino, A., Calabrò, A., De Angelis, G., Lago, N., Lesbegueries, J.: Monitoring service choreographies from multiple sources. In: Avgeriou, P. (ed.) SERENE 2012. LNCS, vol. 7527, pp. 134–149. Springer, Heidelberg (2012)
5. Katsaros, G., Kousiouris, G., Gogouvitis, S.V., Kyriazis, D., Menychtas, A., Varvarigou, T.: A Self-adaptive hierarchical monitoring mechanism for Clouds. JSS 85(5), 1029–1041 (2012)
6. Bertolino, A., Calabrò, A., Lonetti, F., Di Marco, A., Sabetta, A.: Towards a Model-Driven Infrastructure for Runtime Monitoring. In: Troubitsyna, E.A. (ed.) SERENE 2011. LNCS, vol. 6968, pp. 130–144. Springer, Heidelberg (2011)
7. Czarnecki, K., Eisenecker, U.W.: Generative programming - methods, tools and applications. Addison-Wesley (2000)
8. Chatel, P., Vincent, H. (eds.): Passenger Friendly Airport Services Choreographies Design. Number Del. D6.2. The CHOReOS Consortium (2012)
9. Contreras, R., Zisman, A., Marconi, A., Pistore, M.: PRadapt: A framework for dynamic monitoring of adaptable service-based systems. In: Proc. of the Workshop on Principles of Engineering Service Oriented Systems, pp. 50–56 (June 2012)
10. Wetzstein, B., Karastoyanova, D., Kopp, O., Leymann, F., Zwink, D.: Cross-organizational process monitoring based on service choreographies. In: Proc. of the Symposium on Applied Computing, pp. 2485–2490. ACM (2010)

Detecting Occasional Reputation Attacks
on Cloud Services

Talal H. Noor, Quan Z. Sheng, and Abdullah Alfazi

School of Computer Science
The University of Adelaide, Adelaide SA 5005, Australia
{talal,qsheng,abdullah}@cs.adelaide.edu.au

Abstract. Cloud service consumers' feedback is a good source to assess
the trustworthiness of cloud services. However, it is not unusual that a
trust management system experiences malicious behaviors from its users.
Although several techniques have been proposed to address trust management in cloud environments, the issue of how to detect occasional reputation attacks on cloud services is still largely overlooked. In this paper,
we introduce an occasional attacks detection model that recognizes misleading trust feedbacks from occasional collusion and Sybil attacks and
adjusts trust results for cloud services that have been affected by these
malicious behaviors. We have collected a large collection of consumer's
trust feedbacks given on real-world cloud services (over ten thousand
records) to evaluate and demonstrate the applicability of our approach
and show the capability of detecting such malicious behaviors.

Keywords: Trust Management, Cloud Computing, Occasional Attacks,
Attacks Detection.

1 Introduction

The highly dynamic, distributed, and non-transparent nature of cloud services
makes trust management in cloud environments a challenging problem [10,6,8].
Several techniques have been proposed to assess and manage trust based on
feedback collected from participants [6,5,1]. However, not much attention has
been given to detect *occasional* and *periodic* reputation attacks on cloud services.
The main goal of our work is to detect occasional and periodic reputation attacks
on cloud services[1]. Unfortunately, this is not an easy task due to some unique
characteristics of cloud environments: i) consumers are dynamic and may have
multiple accounts for a particular service (e.g., owning multiple email accounts in
Gmail) which makes it difficult for a Trust Management Service (TMS) to detect
whether a Sybil attack is performed; ii) the occasional way that these attacks
occur, as described in [10], which makes the detection of such malicious behaviors
a significant challenge and significantly affects the performance of TMS. TMS

---

[1] Other techniques for detecting attacks on different distributions over an extended
period of time are previously proposed. Interested readers are referred to [9,8] for
more technical details.

F. Daniel, P. Dolog, and Q. Li (Eds.): ICWE 2013, LNCS 7977, pp. 416–423, 2013.
© Springer-Verlag Berlin Heidelberg 2013

should be able to efficiently detect such attacks and thus dilute the influence of those misleading feedbacks to enable more robust trust calculations.

In this paper, we overview the design and implementation of the occasional attacks detection model. This model allows TMS to detect misleading feedbacks from collusion and Sybil attacks and helps to have robust trust calculations. In a nutshell, the salient features of the model are i) *Occasional Collusion Attacks Detection Metric*: this metric distinguishes between misleading and credible feedbacks by detecting the occasional collusion attacks (i.e., attackers who intend to manipulate the trust results by giving multiple trust feedbacks to a certain cloud service in a short period of time [3]); ii) *Occasional Sybil Attacks Detection Metric*: this metric allows TMS to identify misleading trust feedbacks from Sybil attacks and detect occasional Sybil attacks (i.e., attackers who create multiple identities and leave misleading trust feedbacks in a short period of time to trick cloud service consumers into trusting cloud services that are not trustworthy [4]); iii) *Adaptivity and Flexibility*: the model is adaptive and flexible in the sense that it is possible to tweak the metrics according to the trust evaluation needs (e.g., to detect the collusion attacks only or to detect both attacks).

The remainder of the paper is organized as follows. Section 2 details the trust management service including the trust feedback collection and assessment and briefly describes the identity management service. Section 3 describes the details of our occasional attacks detection model. Section 4 reports the implementation and several experimental evaluations. Finally, Section 5 discusses the related work and provides some concluding remarks.

2   Trust Management Service (TMS)

In a typical reputation-based TMS, consumers either give feedback regarding the trustworthiness of a particular cloud service or request trust assessment for the service[2]. From consumers' feedback, the trust behavior of a cloud service is represented by a tuple $\mathcal{H} = (\mathcal{C}, \mathcal{S}, \mathcal{F}, \mathcal{T}_f)$, where $\mathcal{C}$ is the consumer's primary identity, $\mathcal{S}$ is the cloud service's identity, and $\mathcal{F}$ is a set of feedbacks (i.e., based on several Quality of Service (QoS) parameters including availability, security, response time, etc.). Each feedback in $\mathcal{F}$ is represented in numerical form with the range of $[0, 1]$, where 0, 1, and 0.5 means *negative*, *positive*, and *neutral* feedback respectively. $\mathcal{T}_f$ is the timestamps when feedbacks are given. TMS calculates the trust result, denoted as $\mathcal{T}_r(s)$, from the collected feedbacks as follows:

$$\mathcal{T}_r(s) = \frac{\sum_{c=1}^{|\mathcal{V}(s)|} \mathcal{F}(c, s) * \mathcal{O}_a(s, t_0, t)}{|\mathcal{V}(s)|} + \chi * \mathcal{C}_t(s, t_0, t) \qquad (1)$$

where $\mathcal{V}(s)$ denotes feedbacks given to the cloud service s and $|\mathcal{V}(s)|$ represents the total number of trust feedbacks. $\mathcal{F}(c, s)$ are feedbacks from the cth consumer weighted by the occasional attacks detection factors $\mathcal{O}_a(s, t_0, t)$ to allow TMS to dilute the influence of misleading feedbacks. $\mathcal{F}(c, s)$ is held in the invocation

---

[2] We assume a transaction-based feedback where all feedbacks are held in the TMS.

history record h and updated in TMS. $C_t(s, t_0, t)$ is the change rate of trust results in a period of time that allows TMS to adjust trust results for cloud services that have been affected by malicious behaviors. χ is the normalized weight factor for the change rate of trust results which increase the adaptivity where the higher χ is, the more the cloud service is rewarded and *vice versa*. More details on how to calculate $O_a(s, t_0, t)$ and $C_t(s, t_0, t)$ are described in Section 3.

Since trust and identification are closely related [2], the Identity Management Service (IdM) can facilitate TMS in the detection of occasional Sybil attacks against cloud services without breaching the privacy of consumers. When consumers attempt to use TMS for the first time, they are required to register their credentials at the trust identity registry in IdM to establish their identities. The trust identity registry stores an identity record represented by a tuple $\mathcal{I} = (\mathcal{C}, \mathcal{C}_a, \mathcal{T}_i)$ for each consumer. $\mathcal{C}$ is the consumer's primary identity. $\mathcal{C}_a$ represents a set of credentials' attributes (e.g., passwords, IP address, etc.) and $\mathcal{T}_i$ represents the consumer's registration time in TMS. More details on the detection of occasional Sybil attacks can be found in Section 3.

3   Occasional Attacks Detection Model

Occasional Collusion Attacks Detection Metric. We consider *time* in detecting occasional and periodic collusion attacks (i.e., periodicity). In other words, we consider the total number of feedbacks $|\mathcal{V}(s)|$ given to cloud service s during a period of time $[t_0, t]$. The sudden change in the feedback behavior indicates an occasional feedback collusion. To detect such behaviors, we measure the percentage of occasional and periodic change in the total number of trust feedbacks among the whole feedback behavior (i.e., consumers' behavior in giving feedbacks for a certain cloud service). The occasional feedback collusion factor $O_f(s, t_0, t)$ of cloud service s in a period of time $[t_0, t]$, is calculated as follows:

$$O_f(s, t_0, t) = 1 - \left(\frac{\left(\int_{t_0}^{t} |\mathcal{V}(s, t)| \, dt \right) - \left(\int_{t_0}^{t} \Delta_f(s, t) dt \right)}{\int_{t_0}^{t} |\mathcal{V}(s, t)| \, dt} \right)$$

$$where \, \Delta_f(s, t) = \begin{cases} C\mu\left(|\mathcal{V}(s, t)|\right) & if \, |\mathcal{V}(s, t)| \geq \\ & C\mu\left(|\mathcal{V}(s, t)|\right) \\ |\mathcal{V}(s, t)| & otherwise \end{cases} \tag{2}$$

where the first part of the numerator represents the whole area under the curve which represents the feedback behavior for cloud service s. The second part of the numerator represents the intersection between the area under the curve and the area under the cumulative mean of the total number of feedbacks $C\mu\left(|\mathcal{V}(s, t)|\right)$ (i.e., which represents the mean of all points in the total number of feedbacks and up to the last element because the mean is dynamic and changes from time to time). The denominator represents the whole area under the curve. As a result, the higher the occasional change in the total number of feedbacks, the more likely that the cloud service has been affected by occasional collusions.

Occasional Sybil Attacks Detection Metric. Malicious users may manipulate trust results to disadvantage particular cloud services by creating multiple accounts and giving misleading feedbacks in a short period of time (i.e., Sybil attacks). To overcome the occasional Sybil attacks, we consider the total number of established identities $|\mathcal{I}(s)|$ for consumers who gave feedbacks to cloud service s during a period of time $[t_0, t]$. The sudden changes in the total number of established identities is an indicator for an occasional Sybil attack. To detect such behavior, we measure the percentage of occasional and periodic change in the total number of established identities among the whole identity behavior (i.e., all established identities for consumers who gave feedbacks to a particular cloud service). The higher the change in the total number of established identities, the more likely that the cloud service has been attacked by an occasional Sybil attack. Similarly, the occasional Sybil attacks factor $\mathcal{O}_i(s, t_0, t)$ of a certain cloud service s in a period of time $[t_0, t]$, is calculated as follows:

$$\mathcal{O}_i(s, t_0, t) = 1 - \left(\frac{\left(\int_{t_0}^{t} |\mathcal{I}(s,t)| \, \mathrm{d}t \right) - \left(\int_{t_0}^{t} \Delta_i(s,t) \mathrm{d}t \right)}{\int_{t_0}^{t} |\mathcal{I}(s,t)| \, \mathrm{d}t} \right)$$

$$where \Delta_i(s,t) = \begin{cases} \mathcal{C}\mu\left(|\mathcal{I}(s,t)|\right) & if \ |\mathcal{I}(s,t)| \geq \\ & \mathcal{C}\mu\left(|\mathcal{I}(s,t)|\right) \\ |\mathcal{I}(s,t)| & otherwise \end{cases}$$

(3)

Based on the proposed occasional attacks detection metrics, TMS dilutes the influence of those misleading feedbacks by assigning the occasional attacks detection aggregated weights $\mathcal{O}_a(s, t_0, t)$ to each trust feedback as shown in Equation 1. $\mathcal{O}_a(s, t_0, t)$ is calculated as follows:

$$\mathcal{O}_a(s, t_0, t) = \frac{\phi * \mathcal{O}_f(s, t_0, t) + \iota * \mathcal{O}_i(s, t_0, t)}{\lambda}$$

(4)

where ϕ and $\mathcal{O}_f(s, t_0, t)$ denote the normalized weight of the occasional collusion attacks detection factor and the factor's value respectively. The second part of the equation represents the occasional Sybil attacks detection factor where ι denotes the factor's normalized weight and $\mathcal{O}_i(s, t_0, t)$ denotes the factor's value. λ represents the number of factors used to calculate $\mathcal{O}_a(s, t_0, t)$. For example, if we only consider the occasional collusion attacks detection factor, $\lambda = 1$; if we consider both the occasional collusion attacks detection factor and the occasional Sybil attacks detection factor, $\lambda = 2$.

Change Rate of Trust Metric. To allow TMS to adjust and tweak trust results for cloud services that have been affected by occasional reputation attacks we introduce the change rate of trust factor. The idea behind this factor is to compensate the affected cloud services by the same percentage of damage in the trust results. Given $Con(s, t_0)$ the conventional model (i.e., calculating the trust results without considering the proposed approach) for a cloud service s in a previous time instance, $Con(s, t)$ the conventional model for the same cloud service calculated in a more recent time instance, $\mathcal{O}_a(s, t_0, t)$ the occasional attacks detection aggregated weights, and $e_{\mathcal{O}a}$ the occasional attacks percentage threshold. The change rate of trust results factor $\mathcal{C}_t(s, t_0, t)$ is calculated as follows:

$$\mathcal{O}_t(s, t_0, t) = \begin{cases} \left(\frac{Con(s, t_0)}{Con(s, t)} \right) - 1 & if \ Con(s, t) < Con(s, t_0) \\ & and \ 1 - \mathcal{O}_a(s, t_0, t) \geq e_{\mathcal{O}a} \\ \\ 0 & otherwise \end{cases} \quad (5)$$

where $\left(\frac{Con(s, t_0)}{Con(s, t)} \right) - 1$ represents the change rate of trust results for cloud service s during a period of time $[t_0, t]$. The change rate of trust results will only be used if the conventional model in the more recent time instance is less than the conventional model in the previous time instance and the occasional attacks percentage during the same period of time $[t_0, t]$ (i.e., $1 - \mathcal{O}_a(s, t_0, t)$) is larger or equal to the occasional attacks percentage threshold. For instance, even if the conventional model in the current time for the cloud service a is less than the conventional model 10 days ago, the cloud service a will not be rewarded because the occasional attacks percentage is less than the occasional attacks percentage threshold (e.g., $1 - \mathcal{O}_a(a, t_0, t) = 20\%$ and $e_{\mathcal{O}a} = 30\%$). The change rate of trust results is designed to limit the rewards to cloud services that are affected by slandering attacks [4] (i.e., cloud services that have decreased trust results) because TMS can dilute the increased trust results from self-promoting attacks [3] using the occasional attacks detection factors (i.e., $\mathcal{O}_a(s, t_0, t)$). The adaptive change rate of trust results factor can be used to assign different weights using χ the normalized weight factor as shown in Equation 1.

4   Implementation and Experimental Evaluation

System Architecture. The architecture consists of several layers including: i) *Trust Data Provisioning* for collecting cloud services and trust information where the *Cloud Services Crawler* module is developed based on the Open Source Web Crawler for Java (crawler4j[3]) and extended to allow TMS to automatically discover cloud services on the Internet and the *Trust Feedbacks Collector* module is developed to collect feedbacks directly from consumers and stores them in the *Trust Feedbacks Database*. Moreover, an IdM is developed to allow consumers to establish their identities before using TMS through registering their credentials at the *Trust Identity Registry* where the total number of established identities is collected using the *Identity Info Collector*. ii) *Trust Assessment Function* for handling trust assessment requests from users where the *Factors Calculator* is developed to calculate the occasional attacks detection factors and the *Trust Assessor* to calculate the trust of cloud services by assigning the factors weights to feedbacks and store them in the *Trust Results and Factors Weights Storage*.

---

[3] http://code.google.com/p/crawler4j/

Experimental Design and Setup. In order to validate our approach, we collected real world trust feedbacks on cloud services by crawling review websites such as `CloudHostingReviewer.com` and `cloud-computing.findthebest.com` where consumers usually give their feedback on cloud services that they have used. The collected data is represented in a tuple $\mathcal{H}$ where the feedback represents several QoS parameters as aforementioned and a set of credentials are augmented for each corresponding consumer. We managed to collect 10,076 feedbacks given by 6,982 consumers to 113 real-world cloud services. The collected data is divided into 2 groups of cloud services, one is used to validate our model against occasional collusion attacks and the other is used to validate the model against occasional Sybil attacks. Each cloud service group represents a *Peaks* behavior model. We conducted several experiments to validate the proposed occasional attacks detection model and to demonstrate its robustness against occasional collusion and Sybil attacks. We use two experimental settings: i) measuring the robustness of our model with a conventional model $Con(s, t_0, t)$ (i.e., turning $\mathcal{O}_a(s, t_0, t)$ to 1 for all feedbacks), and ii) measuring the performance of our model using two measures namely *precision* (i.e., to know how well TMS did in detecting attacks) and *recall* (i.e., to know how many detected attacks are actual attacks). In our experiments, TMS starts rewarding cloud services that have been affected by malicious behaviors when the occasional attacks percentage reaches 25% (i.e., $e_{\mathcal{O}a} = 25\%$), so the rewarding process will occur only when there is a significant damage in the trust result.

Robustness Against Occasional Collusion Attacks. In occasional collusion attacks experiments, we simulated malicious users to increase trust results of cloud services (i.e., self-promoting attack [3]) by giving multiple feedbacks with the range of [0.8, 1.0]. From Figure 1, we note that results when considering to calculate the trust with our model decrease quickly after a short period of time and the responsible metric for this detection is the occasional collusion attacks detection metric. In addition, we can see that our model achieves 0.508 in precision and scores 0.689 in recall. Overall there is a fair degree in recall which indicates that most of the detected attacks are actual attacks. This means that our model can successfully detect occasional attacks and TMS diluted the increased trust results from self-promoting attacks using the proposed factors.

Robustness Against Occasional Sybil Attacks. In occasional Sybil attacks experiments, we simulated malicious users to decrease trust results of cloud services (i.e., slandering attack [4]) by establishing multiple identities and giving feedbacks with the range of [0, 0.2]. From Figure 2 we can see that trust results when considering to calculate the trust with our model response effectively where 5 peaks in trust results appear (i.e., Figure 2(a)). This is true because the cloud service was rewarded when the occasional attacks occurred. Moreover, we note that the overall precision of our model is 0.435, while the overall recall is 0.652 (See Figure 2(b)). This means that our model can successfully detect occasional Sybil attacks and reward affected cloud services using the change rate of trust factor.

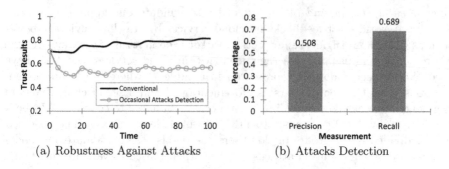

(a) Robustness Against Attacks   (b) Attacks Detection

Fig. 1. Occasional Collusion Attacks Experiments

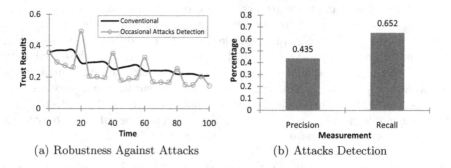

(a) Robustness Against Attacks   (b) Attacks Detection

Fig. 2. Occasional Sybil Attacks Experiments

5 Discussions and Conclusion

Over the past few years, trust management has been one of the hot topics especially in the area of cloud computing. Some of the research works use policy-based trust management techniques. For example, Ko et al. [7] proposed TrustCloud framework for accountability and trust in cloud computing which consists of five layers including workflow, data, system, policies and laws, and regulations layers to address accountability in the cloud environment from all aspects. Brandic et al. [1] proposed a novel approach for compliance management in cloud environments to establish trust where the approach is developed using a centralized architecture and uses compliant management technique to establish trust. Unlike previous works that use policy-based techniques, we evaluate the trustworthiness of a cloud service using reputation-based trust management techniques.

Other research works use reputation-based trust management techniques. For instance, Habib et al. [5] proposed a multi-faceted Trust Management (TM) system architecture which models uncertainty of trust information collected from multiple sources using a set of Quality of Service (QoS) attributes such as security, latency, availability, and customer support. Hwang et al. [6] proposed a security-aware cloud architecture where trust negotiation and data coloring techniques are used to support cloud providers and the trust-overlay networks to support consumers. Unlike previous works, we propose an occasional attacks detection model that not only detects misleading trust feedbacks from collusion and Sybil attacks, but also has the ability to adaptively adjust the trust results for cloud services that have been affected by occasional malicious behaviors.

Our work presented in this paper is one of the first few that focuses on the detection of occasional reputation attacks on cloud services. We present several techniques enabling the detection of such attacks. In particular, we introduce an occasional attacks detection model that detects misleading feedbacks from collusion and Sybil attacks. Our model has the capability to adjust trust results for cloud services that have been affected by such malicious behaviors. We also have collected a large collection of consumer's trust feedbacks given on real-world cloud services to evaluate and demonstrate the applicability of our approach.

Acknowledgments. Talal H. Noor and Abdullah Alfazi's work has been supported by King Abdullah's Postgraduate Scholarships, the Ministry of Higher Education, Kingdom of Saudi Arabia.

References

1. Brandic, I., et al.: Compliant Cloud Computing (C3): Architecture and Language Support for User-Driven Compliance Management in Clouds. In: Proc. of CLOUD 2010 (2010)
2. David, O., Jaquet, C.: Trust and Identification in the Light of Virtual Persons (June 2009),
   http://www.fidis.net/resources/deliverables/identity-of-identity/
   (accessed March 10, 2011)
3. Douceur, J.R.: The Sybil Attack. In: Druschel, P., Kaashoek, M.F., Rowstron, A. (eds.) IPTPS 2002. LNCS, vol. 2429, pp. 251–260. Springer, Heidelberg (2002)
4. Friedman, E., et al.: Manipulation-Resistant Reputation Systems. In: Algorithmic Game Theory, chap, pp. 677–697. Cambridge University Press, New York (2007)
5. Habib, S., et al.: Towards a Trust Management System for Cloud Computing. In: Proc. of TrustCom 2011 (2011)
6. Hwang, K., Li, D.: Trusted Cloud Computing with Secure Resources and Data Coloring. IEEE Internet Computing 14(5), 14–22 (2010)
7. Ko, R., et al.: TrustCloud: A Framework for Accountability and Trust in Cloud Computing. In: Proc. of SERVICES 2011 (2011)
8. Noor, T.H., Sheng, Q.Z.: Credibility-Based Trust Management for Services in Cloud Environments. In: Kappel, G., Maamar, Z., Motahari-Nezhad, H.R. (eds.) ICSOC 2011. LNCS, vol. 7084, pp. 328–343. Springer, Heidelberg (2011)
9. Noor, T.H., Sheng, Q.Z.: Trust as a Service: A Framework for Trust Management in Cloud Environments. In: Bouguettaya, A., Hauswirth, M., Liu, L. (eds.) WISE 2011. LNCS, vol. 6997, pp. 314–321. Springer, Heidelberg (2011)
10. Ren, K., et al.: Security Challenges for the Public Cloud. IEEE Internet Computing 16(1), 69–73 (2012)

Multi-tenancy Performance Benchmark
for Web Application Platforms

Rouven Krebs, Alexander Wert, and Samuel Kounev

SAP AG, Applied Research,
Dietmar-Hopp-Allee 16, 69190 Walldorf, Germany
{rouven.krebs}@sap.com
Karlsruhe Institute of Technology, IPD,
Kaiserstrasse 12, 76131 Karlsruhe, Germany
{alexander.wert,kounev}@kit.edu

Abstract. Cloud environments reduce data center operating costs through resource sharing and economies of scale. Infrastructure-as-a-Service is one example that leverages virtualization to share infrastructure resources. However, virtualization is often insufficient to provide Software-as-a-Service applications due to the need to replicate the operating system, middleware and application components for each customer. To overcome this problem, multi-tenancy has emerged as an architectural style that allows to share a single Web application instance among multiple independent customers, thereby significantly improving the efficiency of Software-as-a-Service offerings. A number of platforms are available today that support the development and hosting of multi-tenant applications by encapsulating multi-tenancy specific functionality. Although a lack of performance guarantees is one of the major obstacles to the adoption of cloud computing, in general, and multi-tenant applications, in particular, these kinds of applications and platforms have so far not been in the focus of the performance and benchmarking community. In this paper, we present an extended version of an existing and widely accepted application benchmark adding support for multi-tenant platform features. The benchmark is focused on evaluating the maximum throughput and the amount of tenants that can be served by a platform. We present a case study comparing virtualization and multi-tenancy. The results demonstrate the practical usability of the proposed benchmark in evaluating multi-tenant platforms and gives insights that help to decide for one sharing approach.

Keywords: Platform, SaaS, Multi-tenancy, Benchmark.

1 Introduction

Cloud Computing enables ubiquitous and convenient on demand access to computing resources over network [2]. Cloud users benefit from the lower costs and increased flexibility, in an efficient and scalable manner, the elimination of an upfront commitment, and payment on a short-term pay per use basis [2].

F. Daniel, P. Dolog, and Q. Li (Eds.): ICWE 2013, LNCS 7977, pp. 424–438, 2013.

The National Institute of Standards and Technology [19] defines three service models for cloud computing. The Infrastructure-as-a-Service (IaaS) model allows to provide and share hardware resources using virtualization technology. The Platform-as-a-Service (PaaS) model allows to deploy and develop applications of different customers within a shared cloud middleware environment. Finally, the Software-as-a-Service (SaaS) model provides hosted applications accessed remotely via the Internet.

Multi-tenancy is an architectural style in SaaS scenarios that enables the sharing a single application instance among multiple independent customers. This style increases efficiency by sharing not only the hardware but also the operating system, the middleware and the application components themselves. The term tenant refers to a group of users sharing the same view on an application. This view includes the data they access, the application configuration, the user management, particular functionalities and related non-functional properties [18]. According to the Gartner's hype cycle from 2011 [24] [21], multi-tenancy is estimated to become mainstream in 2-5 years.

Implementing the functionality to share a single application instance among several tenants is a complex task [11][20] that has to be performed for every developed application. Therefore, the best approach for realizing multi-tenancy is to employ a middleware platform or a PaaS environment that natively supports the development by encapsulating basic functionality such as for example the management and identification of tenants. Google App Engine [10], SAP NetWeaver Application Server and force.com [28] support the developer with predefined interfaces and implicit functionality reducing the development effort for creating a multi-tenant application.

While Cloud Computing provides many advantages as described above, it still fails to provide high availability and response time guarantees required for running mission-critical applications. Various reports [22] [4] indicate that performance is still one of the major obstacles for the adoption of the cloud paradigm. To gain insight into the performance provided by cloud platforms, representative application benchmarks and metrics are needed. Various benchmarks and metrics with focus on cloud environments were developed in the last view years. However, such benchmarks are usually focused on specific aspects of cloud services like persistence or features like infrastructure elasticity.

To the best of our knowledge, no benchmark that explicitly supports the evaluation of multi-tenant platforms exists so far. To fill this gap, in this paper we propose an extended version of an existing benchmark to support multi-tenancy. This benchmark can be used to evaluate the performance of an on premise middleware system or a PaaS environment supporting multi-tenant applications.

The selected case study to evaluate the usability of the benchmark is motivated by our former publication [20]. In this paper, we present an estimation approach to balance the increasing development costs for developing a multi-tenant application (MTA) with the decreasing operating costs resulting from the improvements in resource efficiency. Furthermore, given that, running multiple copies of an application in separate virtual machines (VM), each customized for a given tenant, is often considered as an alternative to adopting a multi-tenant architecture, we decided to evaluate the two approaches in terms of the performance they provide. Our approach allows to find the point at which multi-tenancy is more efficient with respect to resource utilization in a given application scenario.

In summary, the contribution of this paper is twofold: We present an extended version of an established benchmark to support multi-tenancy. Furthermore, we present a comparison of virtualization and multi-tenancy which helps to estimate the efficiency of the approaches.

The remainder of the paper is structured as follows. In Section 2, we outline important and common design aspects of multi-tenant systems. Section 3 presents our extensions of the TPC-W benchmark based on the outcomes of the previous section. Furthermore, we give an insight into our implementation. Section 4 presents our case study investigating the efficiency of multi-tenant systems compared to virtualization. Section 5, surveys related work and Section 6 concludes the paper.

2   General Design Concerns in Multi-tenant Architectures

To ensure isolation in a multi-tenant application (MTA) one has to make a number of architectural decisions. Furthermore, PaaS scenarios raise some additional requirements concerning the actual implementation. In this section, we give a short overview of the most important architectural aspects related to our work and the impact of multi-tenancy on potential benchmarks and metrics.

2.1   Tenant Identification

When a request arrives at a MTA not only the specific user has to be identified, but also the tenant it belongs to. Various approaches exist to identify the tenant. One solution is to attach the tenant specific information to the user identification. However, this approach requires an authentication of the user and duplicate user names in different tenants are not possible, thus, violating isolation. Another widely used approach (e.g., Google App Engine [10]) is to use the host name as a basis for the tenant identification. In this scenario, various host aliases point to the same application instance/IP address. Thus, a tenant identification is possible without requiring a login and duplicate user names are supported. A common approach to transfer the tenant's identifier along the execution path leverages the thread context to which the relevant information is attached.

2.2   Database

In general, we distinguish three major approaches to separate a tenants data from the data persisted by other tenants (Wang et al. [27] and Chong et al. [6]). The dedicated database system provides a separate dedicated database for each tenant and has the best isolation at the cost of the highest overhead. In a dedicated table/schema approach, every tenant uses the same database management system, but separate tables or schemas. This scenario enables at least a partial sharing. However, some mutual performance influences between tenants are now possible. The highest degree of sharing, respectively efficiency, is established by sharing the same tables and schemas. To differentiate the data, a column with the tenant id is added to each table. This approach also has the largest consequences on the application or platform. An application has to take care of the tenant id in every database statement. If the platform provides an abstraction of the database, it might handle the additional tenant id in a transparent way (e.g., EclipseLink [8]).

2.3 Tenant Meta-Data

Koziolek [17] presents a high level architecture for MTAs based on observations he made about existing offerings. In general, this architecture reflects a Web Application Architecture with an additional meta data storage for the tenant specific information (e.g., customization, database id, tenant name, SLAs). Another element is the meta-data manager which enables access to the meta-data and adjusts the application according to the information stored in the meta-data. The variability of information stored in the meta data is high. However, we can assume that at least an id for the tenant, a display name for the tenant and a database identifier is available. Depending on the employed data management approach, the latter may refer to an tenant specific id or database connection. Platforms with multi-tenancy support usually provide access to the tenant meta-data.

2.4 Security

Normally either the implemented persistency APIs of the platforms or the application developer has to ensure the separation of data by using SQL statements with tenant id as aforementioned. In addition, tenant specific caches might be required. The identification of a tenant might base on an identity management system as part of the meta-data manager. However, the access to the application might allow to run attacks against other tenants with extended privileges. This has to be reflected by special measures like SQL encoding and stack overflow prevention.

2.5 Metrics for a Multi-tenant Benchmark

In traditional benchmarks, usually one or several performance metrics are observed in relation to the amount of simulated users, the request rate, and sometimes price (e.g., [1]). Based on this information, a quality metric of the system is derived.

In a multi-tenant system, we can also incorporate the amount of tenants, for example, considering the throughput and response time in relation to the amount of tenants. This metric might be of interest when the per tenant overhead and the total amount of tenants a platform could serve is relevant. Furthermore, it might answer the question about the optimal amount of tenants for one application server. Another metric might define a fixed number of tenants by observing the QoS based on the amount of users for each.

It is worth to mention that real applications serve tenants with different amounts of users and various database sizes and consequently various resource demands. If these factors are known for the scenario under investigation the benchmark might reflect this.

2.6   PaaS Persistence

We consider traditional middleware and PaaS environments with multi-tenancy support. Existing PaaS environments provide an application runtime container and various embedded services accessed via an API (e.g., Google App Engine, SAP NetWeaver Cloud). Persistence services are of major importance. Existing offerings provide SQL or key value stores. However, in the majority of cases, the access to the storage is only permitted within the application runtime container. Even in cases where a user interface to manipulate individual data records exists, it is normally impossible to directly load high amounts of data.

3   Multi-tenant Benchmark

In this section, we present our extensions of the TPC-W benchmark [1] based on the implementation provided in [5] and focus on our modifications for cloud environments with multi-tenancy support. TPC-W was already used successfully in the field of multi-tenancy [26] and already satisfies some of the requirements for a cloud benchmark [3] .

3.1   TPC-W

The Transaction Processing Performance Council (TPC) developed a transactional Web e-commerce benchmark (TPC-W) [1]. Its focus is on business oriented transactional Web servers. The workload models an Internet commerce environment emulating an online bookshop. The benchmark emulates multiple on-line browser sessions by accessing dynamically generated Web pages. The benchmark provides three workload profiles that differ in their the browse-to-buy request ratio resulting in different proportions of database reads or inserts/updates: primarily shopping, browsing and Web-based ordering. The load can be varied by the amount of emulated browsers (EB) sending requests to the system. One EB corresponds to one user calling various Web transactions in a closed workload. To ensure portability, TPC does not require the use of a specific implementation. Instead a detailed specification of the functionality that must be provided by an implementation is published.

3.2   Multi-tenant TPC-W Specification

We extended the specification of TPC-W in several points to cover the relevant conceptual aspects of multi-tenant systems described in Section 2. The PaaS persistence related concerns (cf. Section 2.6) do not directly relate to the specification of the benchmark and will be discussed in Section 3.3.

The Tenant Meta Data Manager (cf. Section 2.3) provided by a platform is used to render the tenant's display name as part of various Web pages (Home Page, Customer Registration Page, Buy Confirm Page). In one the pages (Buy Confirm) the tenant's identifier is also rendered.

For environments with a native connection to one schema on one database server, a `tenantId` column is added to every table (cf. Section 2.2). Consequently, the primary key has to be a combination of the `tenantId` and the entity specific id field. In addition to the TPC-W standard the `tenantId`, retrived from the meta-data manager, is added to every SQL request from the application to ensure data isolation and thus privacy of the data. In addition, we recommend to encode all SQL parameters for security reasons. TPC-W does not specify application internal caches; thus, we do not have to provide a tenant specific access mechanism.

Several database management systems do not support the auto generation of combined primary keys. Thus, an application based key generation mechanism is applied to generate the primary keys. To ensure portability, we specify the usage of a key-value table with segment support to reduce overhead. This solution consists of a database table which provides a key counter for each table and each tenant. To avoid overhead, the key-value table is accessed via an application local cache. This cache increases the counter by a count of 1000 and thus it could return 1000 ids before the next update of the key table. It has to be ensured that increasing the database key counter by several application instances does not result in unresolved conflicts. This key counter mechanism is used to generate the primary keys. It is worth mentioning, that the `tenantId` part of the key must not be generated, as this is a value derived by the request that triggered the database update.

For environments with a native connection to various SQL servers or schemas for each tenant the auto generation for the keys can be reused and the additional column for the tenant id becomes obsolete. In such situations we assume that the database connection/schema is either provided in a transparent way by the platform or is stored in an application specific configuration where it is mapped to the tenant. In the latter case, for every SQL request, the appropriate connection must be selected based on the tenants id returned by the tenant meta-data manager.

For environments with an API based access to the persistence layer, where the data isolation aspect is transparent to the application the above methods might be irrelevant. However, if the data isolation aspect is not transparent the described solutions have to be considered.

The load driver has to support the platform specific tenant identification mechanism (cf. Section 2.1). As every tenant accesses the same application, we assume similar workload profiles.

The relevant metrics and the exact setup concerning the number of users for each tenant depends on the goals of the benchmarking scenario. For our case study, we defined static workload profiles for each tenant with an increasing amount of tenants.

3.3 Implementation

The basis of our version [5] provides a Java Servlet based application that accesses the database with the help of one central class using a JDBC connection. Figure 1 shows an overview of the elements used in our version of the TPC-W benchmark. In the following, we briefly describe the functionality of the various elements and how they are related to each other.

TPCW_home_interaction is one example of 14 servlets used in our implementation. The servlets render the html pages and implement the expected work flow. Every servlet has a reference to the *TenantMetaDataAccess* and uses an implementation of the interface *ITPCW_Tenant* to access the meta-data for the tenant that owns the current thread.

TPCW_Database implements the JDBC-based communication with the database, which is implemented as described in Section 3.1. It also encapsulates the key generator.

The *TenantMetaDataAccess* class implements the access to the platform's tenant meta-data. It hides the platform specific implementation for accessing information about the tenants. Thus, it is possible to port the implementation to another platform by changing the implementation of this class. The *TenantMeta-DataAccess* provides a platform specific implementation of the *ITPCW_Tenant* interface.

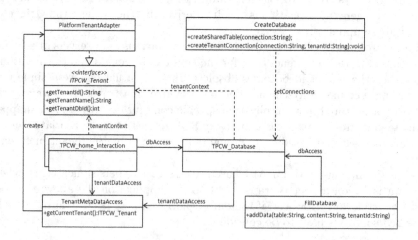

Fig. 1. Overview of the Multi-Tenant TPC-W Benchmark

ITPCW_Tenant defines the interface that represents a concrete tenant encapsulating the communication with the meta-data manager to provide tenant specific information.

CreateDatabase extends *HttpServlet* and is a proxy to create the required schema in the platform environment when no direct access is available. The method *createSharedTable* creates a shared schema in the database. Method *createTenantConnection* creates a schema without tenant id for each tenant. The corresponding connection and type of database multi-tenancy is then set in the *TPCW_Database*. Thus, using *createTenantConnection* enables separate schema and separate databases to be used. If the platform provides the tenant specific connections in a transparent way, one has to modify *TPCW_Database*.

FillDatabase is a proxy extending *HttpServlet* to initialize the databases data for the benchmark run using *TPCW_Database*.

The *Load Driver* is provided in [5]. The target platform in our case differentiates tenants by the host name. Therefore, we created one instance of the load driver for each tenant with a tenant specific hostname as a target.

4 Case Study

In this section, we apply our extended version of the TPC-W benchmark in a case study demonstrating its use for performance evaluation. In addition, we present a comparison of virtualization and multi-tenancy which helps to estimate the efficiency of the approaches.

4.1 Goals

The main goal of the presented case study is to compare an application-based multi-tenancy approach with a pure virtualization-based approach in terms of performance. In particular, we investigate the following main question: *Given a certain setup, under which conditions is an application-based multi-tenancy approach more efficient than a virtualization-based approach, and vice versa?*

In order to address this question, we investigate the following research questions for each of the two scenarios:

- **RQ1:** What is the maximum throughput that can be achieved with the corresponding sharing approach depending on the tenants-size.
- **RQ2:** Under which relationship between the tenant size and number of tenants is a multi-tenant architecture more efficient?

4.2 Experimental Setup

In order to address the research questions mentioned above, we perform a series of experiments.

Figure 2 shows the experimental setups for the virtualization-based scenario (Figure 2a) and the multi-tenancy scenario (Figure 2a). In both cases, the experimental setup comprises three physical servers: The *Load Server* is used for

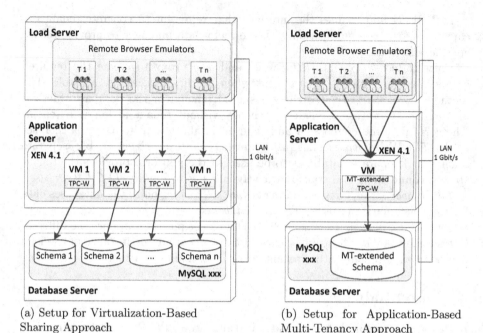

(a) Setup for Virtualization-Based
Sharing Approach

(b) Setup for Application-Based
Multi-Tenancy Approach

Fig. 2. Experimental Setup

user emulation, the *Application Server* hosts the application logic part of the
benchmark and the *Database Server* serves as the persistence layer. These three
physical machines have the same characteristics. In particular, each of them has
a processing power of 16 x 2,13 GHz, a memory capacity of 16 GB, and SUSE
Enterprise 11 as operating system. The machines are connected by a 1 Gbit/s
LAN. For our experiments, we assume there are n equal-sized tenants T1...Tn
each comprising m users (cf. Section 3.2) emulated by means of Remote Browser
Emulators (RBE) (cf. [1]) running on the Load Server. The browsing workload
mix defined by [1] is used to generate load.

In the following, we explain the differences in the two scenarios.

Scenario I: Virtualization-Based Approach. In this scenario, the customer contexts are separated by means of separate VMs and separate database
schemata (cf. Figure 2a). Thus, for each customer context the Application Server
hosts a VM on top of a common XEN 4.1 hypervisor. Each VM is running a separate application instance of TPC-W within an SAP-specific customized version
of Apache Tomcat. Given that TPC-W is an I/O-intensive application, compared to the Database Server, the CPU consumption on the Application Server
is relatively small. Thus, given that the focus of our comparison is on the Application Server tier, it is reasonable to pin the cores of all VM to one physical
core to avoid the database from being the bottleneck. The available memory

capacity is equally distributed among the VM and the host operating system. Similarly to the application layer, the separation on the persistence layer is realized by means of a separate database schemata. Thus, each TPC-W instance uses its own, dedicated database schema. However, all database schemata are hosted within a common MySQL 5.1 process executed on the Database Server.

Scenario II: Multi-tenancy Approach. In the multi-tenant scenario, the tenants are separated by the notion of separate tenant contexts at the application layer and an extended database schema which allows for accessing tenant-specific data. Correspondingly, the experimental setup for Scenario II comprises only one VM and only one database schema (cf. Figure 2b). The single VM hosts the multi-tenant version of TPC-W (cf. Section 3.2) deployed on the extended Apache Tomcat. The Tomcat instance provides a Tenant Meta Data Manager (cf. Section 2.1). Based on the tenant-specific meta-data, the benchmark accesses the extended database schema. Similarly to the setup of Scenario I, the virtual processing unit of the single VM is pinned to a single physical CPU core.

Testing Methodology. We performed 10 experiment series in total, five for each scenario. For every series, the size of each tenant was fixed to 250, 500, 750, 1000 or 1500 users. We are interested in the maximum throughput of the system. Thus, we started each experiment series with one active tenant and increased the amount of tenants stepwise until the application started to throw time out exceptions. To ensure equal conditions the databases were newly created, and filled with data before every run. Afterwards, the database management system and the VMs were restarted prior to starting the load driver. In the multi-tenancy scenario we restarted the VM as well. The warm-up phase was set to 10 minutes and the measurement period was 30 minutes.

4.3   Results

In this section we present the results of our measurements. Figure 3 presents a general overview of the most important data gathered, whereas the specific research questions **RQ1** and **RQ2** are addressed by Figure 4a and Figure 4b. The confidence intervals in all measurements were negligibly small and are thus omitted for compactness.

In Figure 3, the number of tenants is shown on the x-axis and the throughput in transactions/second on the y-axis. The various curves represent measurements with the multi-tenancy and virtualization-based sharing approach for various amounts of users per tenant. In general the CPU utilization became a bottleneck and prevented the system to achieve higher throughputs. In the virtualization scenario with a tenant size of 250 users, the amount of guest domains was limited to 12 due to a lack of memory which resulted in memory exceptions when the server was lunched. Although the systems CPU was underutilized with only 12 domains. The measurement with 250 users and multi-tenancy were stopped at 20 tenants due to time limitations for further experiments and the already existing

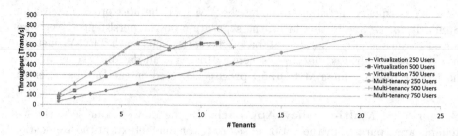

Fig. 3. Throughput Dependent on the Amount of Tenants

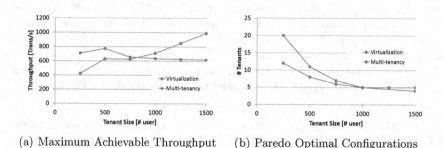

(a) Maximum Achievable Throughput   (b) Paredo Optimal Configurations

Fig. 4. Maximum Throughput and Paredo Based Decision Support

data to answer our research questions. We assume unused potential concerning the amount of tenants because of very low response times and a CPU utilization of around 70%. The figure also shows that the advantage of multi-tenancy is less for the 500 users scenario and even lower for 750 users. In similar measurements for 1000 and 1500, users we observed lower maximum throughputs in the multi-tenancy case.

Figure 4a focuses on **RQ1**. The maximum overall throughput of all tenants is shown on the y-axis. The x-axis presents the number of users for each tenant. By increasing the number of tenants for each tenant size, the maximum throughput was determined. The maximum throughput decreases with lower values for the tenant size in the case of virtualization whereas in the case of multi-tenancy throughput remains stable.

Figure 4b shows the tenant size on the x-axis and the amount of tenants at which the maximum throughput was achieved on the y-axis. Thus it presents paredo optimal configurations in terms of the maximum throughput for the virtualization and multi-tenancy scenario. It shows, that multi-tenancy is less efficient in situations with more than 1000 users as there the amount of served tenants and the throughput is below the capabilities of virtualization. In the range between 250 and 1000 users per tenant, virtualization is a usable model, for the given hardware configuration, if the amount of tenants to be served is below the curve for virtualization. Nevertheless, multi-tenancy is able to serve more tenants with a higher total throughput by using the same hardware in these boundaries. The benefits of multi-tenancy becomes more significant in scenarios with 250 users or less. At these, the total throughput for virtualization was not longer limited by the CPU, instead the memory become the bottleneck. Multi-tenancy uses memory resources very efficiently as it avoids to allocate static memory for the application, application server and OS. Consequently multi-tenancy can still achieve a high throughput and good utilization of the CPU in these cases. Thus, this figure addresses **RQ2**.

Especially for stateless web applications with low memory demands the CPU is the primary bottleneck, beside I/O which is not subject of this discussion. Based on our results we can conclude that virtualization produces additional overhead on the CPU with an increasing amount of VMs hosted on one server, thus the throughput was limited. Nevertheless, these drawbacks are widely negligibly. The most important observation is the inefficient usage of the memory when virtualization is used to serve one application for several customers. Consequently, the primary factor for selecting one of the solutions should be the memory. If an application requests a high amount of memory the overheads for the OS and application server may also become less important. Especially in stateless applications with small memory demands multi-tenancy outperforms virtualization for small tenants as here the static memory allocations of the runtime environment become the limiting factor. Furthermore, multi-tenancy allows to over commit memory, which is not possible using Xen.

5   Related Work

Performance is of major interest in cloud computing [2] [4]. Conventional middleware benchmarks for classical platforms (e.g., SPECjEnterprise [25]) do not support essential cloud features like multi-tenancy. Therefore, several new benchmarks have emerged in the last years to support the performance evaluation of cloud platforms. Most activities focus IaaS and cloud-specific features like elasticity [14]. Others focus on cloud specific services like persistence [7] [13].

Virtualization enables sharing at the infrastructure level. Thus, it is a key enabler for IaaS clouds and it has been widely used over the past years in data centers. A number of benchmarks have been developed in the past years for evaluating virtualization platforms.

One example is VMmark [12], a benchmark developed by VMware. VMmark defines a tile as a set of VMs serving different predefined applications (e.g., SPECweb2005). The benchmark score is based on a normalized overall throughput of the applications as a function of the amount of deployed tiles. The total throughput increases as long as the system is not saturated. As part of the benchmark results VMware publishes the maximum throughput and the number of tiles. This approach is similar to our approach, where we consider the overall system throughput depending on the amount of tenants.

Binnig et al. [3] discuss characteristics of cloud services and derive a list of requirements for a cloud benchmark. Afterwards, they analyze the existing TPC-W benchmark, discuss why the TPC-W benchmark satisfies requirements for cloud benchmarking and discuss some initial ideas for a new benchmark that overcomes some shortcomings of the TPC-W benchmark. Major shortcomings reported are the requirement of ACID properties for data operations and invalid metrics for adaptable and scalable systems in terms of elasticity. However, we observe a trend in PaaS environments to support the ACID properties (e.g., SAP NetWeaver Cloud[23]) for complex Web applications. Furthermore, a PaaS provider or customer usually has the opportunity to control the elasticity mechanisms as required for a performance test. Finally, our focus is on multi-tenancy features that were not considered in [3].

The authors of [26] present a method for resource demand estimation on a per tenants base. Furthermore, they provide a mechanism to ensure performance isolation. For the evaluation, they used an implementation of TPC-W. However, they did not report any extensions for data isolation nor any usage of platform provided multi-tenancy services.

MulTe [15] is a framework that helps building and running existing database benchmarks to evaluate various performance metrics of multi-tenant database management systems. However, our definition of multi-tenancy assumes a shared application instance, as opposed to merely a shared DBMS used by several applications. Therefore, MulTe goals defer from our own.

Regarding the tradeoff decisions several papers present approaches to increase the efficiency of multi-tenant systems (e.g., [29], [9]). However, they do not help to come to a tradeoff decision for various resource sharing approaches.

In [27], various sharing options for implementing multi-tenant persistence are discussed. The authors evaluate their non-functional behavior including performance aspects. Given that our focus is on the application tier the database was not a bottleneck in our scenario.

6   Conclusion

Performance concerns are one of the major obstacles for potential cloud customers. We analyzed the most important concepts of multi-tenant applications and identified features provided by platforms to support multi-tenancy. To support the performance engineering process this paper proposes an extension of the TPC-W benchmark for platforms that support the identified multi-tenancy features. This includes various multi-tenant persistence models, tenant identification mechanisms and access to tenant specific meta-data. We evaluated the usability of the proposed benchmark in a case study where the maximum throughput of a multi-tenancy supporting platform based on the amount of tenants and users per tenant was evaluated. Furthermore, we leveraged the benchmark to compare a virtualization based with a multi-tenancy based sharing approach.

Multi-tenancy shows only a moderate benefit as long as additional virtual machines can be started to handle new tenants. Once the lack of memory start limiting the capability to lunch further virtual machines, multi-tenancy shows significant advantages as it still serves and increasing amount of tenants with good performance. Overall, multi-tenancy exhibits significantly higher efficiency for a high amount of tenants with low usage, because it avoids a high static memory allocation. In our case study, we observed that memory was the primary limitation of virtualization. As long as CPU is the bottleneck the advantages of MTAs are less.

In our future research, we will leverage this benchmark for the evaluation of performance isolation between different tenants. Furthermore, we are interested in the efficiency of mutual utilized resources when load profiles underlie fluctuations and the impact of various load profiles for different tenants.

Acknowledgements. The research leading to these results has received funding from the European Union's Seventh Framework Programme (FP7/2007-2013) under grant agreement № 258862 and was supported by the German Research Foundation (DFG), grant RE 1674/6-1 (Transfer project KIT-SAP).

References

1. TPC Benchmark W, Transaction Processing Performance Council (2002)
2. Armbrust, M., Fox, A., Griffith, R., Joseph, A.D., Katz, R.H., Konwinski, A., Lee, G., Patterson, D.A., Rabkin, A., Stoica, I., Zaharia, M.: Above the clouds: A berkeley view of cloud computing. Tech. Rep. UCB/EECS-2009-28, EECS Department, University of California, Berkeley (February 2009)
3. Binnig, C., Kossmann, D., Kraska, T., Loesing, S.: How is the weather tomorrow?: towards a benchmark for the cloud. In: Proceedings of the Second International Workshop on Testing Database Systems (2009)
4. Bitcurrent. Bitcurrent cloud computing survey 2011. Tech. rep., bitcurrent (2011)
5. Cain, H.W., Rajwar, R., Marden, M., Lipasti, M.H.: An architectural evaluation of Java TPC-W. In: Proceedings of the Seventh International Symposium on High-Performance Computer Architecture (2001)
6. Chong, F., Carraro, G., Wolter, R.: Multi-tenant data architecture (June 2006)
7. Cooper, B.F., Silberstein, A., Tam, E., Ramakrishnan, R., Sears, R.: Benchmarking cloud serving systems with ycsb. In: Proceedings of the 1st ACM Symposium on Cloud Computing, SoCC 2010, New York, NY, USA (2010)
8. Eclipse Foundation. Eclipselink/development/indigo/multi-tenancy (October 2012)
9. Fehling, C., Leymann, F., Mietzner, R.: A framework for optimized distribution of tenants in cloud applications. In: 2010 IEEE 3rd International Conference on Cloud Computing, CLOUD (2010)
10. Google. Google Cloud Platform (November 2012), https://cloud.google.com/index
11. Guo, C.J., Sun, W., Huang, Y., Wang, Z.H., Gao, B.: A framework for native multi-tenancy application development and management. In: E-Commerce Technology and the 4th IEEE International Conference on Enterprise Computing, E-Commerce, and E-Services (2007)
12. Herndon, B., Smith, P., Roderick, L., Zamost, E., Anderson, J., Makhija, V., Herndon, B., Smith, P., Zamost, E., Anderson, J.: Vmmark: A scalable benchmark for virtualized systems. Tech. rep., VMware (2006)

13. Huang, S., Huang, J., Dai, J., Xie, T., Huang, B.: The hibench benchmark suite: Characterization of the mapreduce-based data analysis. In: ICDE Workshops (2010)
14. Islam, S., Lee, K., Fekete, A., Liu, A.: How a consumer can measure elasticity for cloud platforms. In: Proceedings of the Third Joint WOSP/SIPEW International Conference on Performance Engineering, New York, NY, USA (2012)
15. Kiefer, T., Schlegel, B., Lehner, W.: MulTe: A multi-tenancy database benchmark framework. In: Nambiar, R., Poess, M. (eds.) TPCTC 2012. LNCS, vol. 7755, pp. 92–107. Springer, Heidelberg (2013)
16. Koziolek, H.: Towards an architectural style for multi-tenant software applications. In: Proc. Software Engineering (SE 2010). LNI, vol. 159 (February 2010)
17. Koziolek, H.: The sposad architectural style for multi-tenant software applications. In: Proc. 9th Working IEEE/IFIP Conf. on Software Architecture (WICSA 2011), Workshop on Architecting Cloud Computing Applications and Systems (July 2011)
18. Krebs, R., Momm, C., Kounev, S.: Architectural Concerns in Multi-Tenant SaaS Applications. In: Proceedings of the 2nd International Conference on Cloud Computing and Services Science, CLOSER 2012 (2012)
19. Mell, P., Grance, T.: The NIST definition of cloud computing. digital (2011)
20. Momm, C., Krebs, R.: A Qualitative Discussion of Different Approaches for Implementing Multi-Tenant SaaS Offerings. In: Proceedings of Software Engineering 2011 (SE 2011), Workshop (ESoSyM 2011) (2011)
21. Natis, Y.: Gartner reference model for elasticity and multitenancy. Gartner report, Gartner (June 2012)
22. Packman, E., Taylor, P., Rachitsky, L., Rejali, S., Power, S., Rae, I., Koffler, D.: Bitcurrent: Cloud comuting performance. Tech. rep., bitcurrent (June 2010)
23. SAP AG. SAP NetWeaver Cloud (November 2012), https://netweaver.ondemand.com
24. Smith, D.: Hype cycle for cloud computing. Tech. rep., Gartner, ID Number: G00214915 (July 2011)
25. Spec. Specjenterprise2010, (November 2012), http://www.spec.org/jEnterprise2010/
26. Wang, W., Huang, X., Qin, X., Zhang, W., Wei, J., Zhong, H.: Application-level cpu consumption estimation: Towards performance isolation of multi-tenancy web applications. In: IEEE CLOUD (2012)
27. Wang, Z.H., Guo, C.J., Gao, B., Sun, W., Zhang, Z., An, W.H.: A study and performance evaluation of the multi-tenant data tier design patterns for service oriented computing. In: IEEE International Conference on e-Business Engineering, ICEBE 2008 (2008)
28. Weissman, C.D., Bobrowski, S.: The design of the force.com multitenant Internet application development platform. In: Proceedings of the 35th SIGMOD International Conference on Management of Data, SIGMOD 2009. ACM (2009)
29. Zhang, Y., Wang, Z., Gao, B., Guo, C., Sun, W., Li, X.: An effective heuristic for on-line tenant placement problem in saas. In: IEEE International Conference on Web Services (2010)

Agile Software Development with Open Source Software in a Hospital Environment – Case Study of an eCRF-System for Orthopaedical Studies

Tünay Özcan[1,2], Semra Kocak[1], and Philipp Brune[2]

[1] Orthopädische Studienzentrale des Universitätsklinikums
Oberer Eselsberg 45, D-89081 Ulm
[2] Hochschule Neu-Ulm
Wileystraße 1, D-89231 Neu-Ulm
tuenay_oezcan@yahoo.com,
semra.kocak@rku.de,
philipp.brune@hs-neu-ulm.de

Abstract. In recent years, agile development of web-based applications as well as open-source software (OSS) have been subject to research and practical application in many domains. For the healthcare sector, the use of OSS has been studied in the literature with contradicting findings. Regarding OSS in clinical applications, mainly case studies from hospital-wide IS have been reported. Agile methods have been examined merely in the context of healthcare software product development. However, the development of web-based applications in clinical departments using agile methods and OSS has not been studied so far. Thus, in this paper the feasibility of such an approach is examined for an electronic case report form (eCRF) application for orthopaedical studies. It is demonstrated how OSS-based web engineering projects may be successfully accomplished in highly specialized environments like clinical departments by properly taking into account their specific requirements.

Keywords: Web Application Engineering, Open Source Software, Agile Software Development, Healthcare IS, Clinical Studies.

1 Introduction

The healthcare sector in general and especially clinical centers in the western world are currently facing increasing economical pressure due to medical progress and demographic change. The lack of financial and personal resources forces healthcare providers to strongly optimize their processes in order to cope with these changes. However, all optimizations need to take into account the high quality standards required for medical treatment [5]. Therefore, information systems (IS) play an important role, i.e. electronic patient record (ePR) systems [5].

F. Daniel, P. Dolog, and Q. Li (Eds.): ICWE 2013, LNCS 7977, pp. 439–451, 2013.

The German federal association for healthcare IT (Bundesverband Gesund-heits-IT) in 2011/2012 conducted a survey among stakeholders in hospitals to identify IS trends and measure user satisfaction. On the question "which in-tranet/internet application would become increasingly important within the next 5 years" for them, 82 of 100 interviewed physicians answered that state-of-the-art medical knowledge will become more and more important. To collect and distribute this knowledge by scientific publications, clinical studies are required.

Clinical studies require to collect and store the underlying empirical data in a structured and persistent form. Therefore, information technology plays an im-portant role. eCRF applications allow to perform patient surveys in electronic form and support the related data management and administrative tasks. During the development of an eCRF application it is especially important to focus on the user requirements, in particular those of the patients and physicians, to ensure an efficient process support and a high user acceptance of the resulting software. Thus, in the present case a web-based eCRF application for orthopaedical clin-ical studies was developed individually by and for the center for orthopaedical studies (Orthopädische Studienzentrale) of the Ulm university hospital. Due to the close interaction with the relevant stakeholders (in particular physicians) and the unclear detail requirements at project start, an agile method based on Scrum was chosen for the project [7,24,32].

To ensure long-time support and operation, an application also needs to ad-here to the standards and requirements of the IT organization. Therefore, beside the selection of an appropriate development method, the application architecture and the proper choice of its technical components are crucial for the application's success [27]. Here, open source software (OSS) provides a possible alternative to commercially available solutions. Besides the savings of the licence fees, OSS usu-ally offers good transparency, extendability and the support of open standards [13]. In the literature, agile software development of web-based applications not only for but in a clinical department in combination with OSS has not been studied so far [3]. Thus, this paper analyses the feasibility of such an approach by examining the proof-of-concept implementation of the real eCRF system Or-thoClinical. In addition, the usability of OSS components as a basis for designing the software architecture of web-based applications is analysed in this context.

The rest of this paper is organized as follows: In section 2 the related work is reviewed and section 3 describes the project context of the proof-of-concept im-plementation of OrthoClinical. Section 4 illustrates the selection and customiza-tion of the agile concepts used, and in section 5 the application architecture including the selected OSS components is presented. In section 6 the results of the evaluation of the proof-of-concept prototype are discussed in detail. We conclude with a summary of our findings.

2   Related Work

Since the introduction of Extreme Programming (XP) [6] and the declaration of the agile manifesto [7], agile methods have been intensively discussed in research and practice [12]. Popular agile methods today include the Crystal family [1] and in particular Scrum [32]. All these methods more or less form a set of best practices, which have to be customized according to the requirements of each project [2].

Reasons for the success of Scrum and other agile methods have been studied by various authors [29,10,25]. In [12], 36 studies regarding agile methods are examined, mainly related to XP, which is found to be inadequate for larger organizations. Hence, agile methods show to be most effective with smaller teams and social factors being the most important influence on project success [12].

One example reported for the use of Scrum in the healthcare sector is a pilot project related to imaging diagnostic systems conducted by GE Healthcare corporation [3]. In the context of critical systems development in general, agile methods and OSS have been also examined, but not explicitly with respect to the healthcare sector [15].

In recent years, the use of OSS in the healthcare sector has been studied by different publications. Most of the authors focus on the general economical, organizational and technical advantages and disadvantages of OSS, with heterogeneous findings [11,27,13,28]. Especially in Europe, a limited acceptance of OSS in the healthcare sector is observed [13]. The majority of the examined clinical OSS projects were not completed due to inactivity already in early stages. However, these projects mainly were related to the development of hospital information systems (HIS) and imaging diagnostics [16].

Various authors report case studies on individual OSS projects, i.e. the redesign of the Irish Beaumont hospital's IT infrstructure [14], the Decentralized Hospital Computer Program (DHCP) system [8] and its successor VistA [9,20], clinical decision support systems [34,31], the Mediboard system in Mali [4], a private cloud platform for healthcare data in India [17], or the MyHealthService project [35]. In addition, there exist some projects related to imaging diagnostics based on OSS, i.e. an approach for image processing based on the Digital Imaging and Communications in Medicine (DICOM) standard [18]. Another example is PrivacyGuard, a tool supporting the anonymization of clinical image data [30].

However, the literature on applications in the clinical research domain is sparse. With respect to eCRF systems, only the project PHPSurveyor was studied. Originally developed for a special disease pattern, it may be also used in other contexts due to its modular design [23]. Regarding the orthopaedic domain, Shah et al. have analyzed the existing Electronic Data Capture (EDC) systems available commercially or as OSS [33]. They state that the majority of the clinical departments still is using inefficient spreadsheet applications to support clinical studies, which is considered inflexible, insecure and inefficient with respect to process support. Also the data is stored that way in a non-standard and poorly structured form, thus prohibiting data exchange from the beginning. In addition, it is observed that some physicians are still not willing to share their data with others, despite the medical benefits of such data collections. Reasons are considered to be a lack of physicians' resources and missing IT support in form of adequate EDC systems. Therefore, the authors recommend the data collection on the level of individual institutions by means of databases in combination with intuitive and user-friendly front-end systems [33].

Thus, it can be concluded that the use of agile methods in combination with OSS in the healthcare sector has rarely been studied in the literature. In particular, projects implementing individual web-based applications in the domain of clinical research and their integration with the hospital-wide IT organization have not been reported so far at all. In addition, only very few case studies from the German or European regions even about partial aspects of the mentioned topics exist. Thus, in the present work it is examined by studying the implementation of the OrthoClinical eCRF system at the Ulm university hospital, how:

- agile methods may be adapted to the clinical domain to enable rapid development of efficient applications,
- a web-based orthopaedical eCRF system with integrated study management module may be developed based on OSS, and which OSS components may be selected for its architecture in order to fulfill the requirements regarding cost efficiency, interoperability, rapid development and standard conformance.

3 Project Context

The RKU - Universitäts- und Rehabilitationskliniken Ulm (University and Rehabilitation Clinics Ulm) are maximum care clinics focussing on orthopaedics and neurology. Founded in 1969 by the Ulm university hospital, today the clinics offer acute care and subsequent medical and professional rehabilitation of orthopaedic and neurological patients. In addition, the clinics support teaching and research at the university hospital. Therefore, some of the physicians working at RKU are directly employed by the university hospital. In total, RKU has a staff of 500, including 60 employees in medical service and 176 in nursing.

The orthopaedical department founded the center for orthopaedical studies in 2011 to support the research activities of the physicians. It supports the data collection, extraction and analysis for clinical studies among ambulant patients. Located at RKU, the center organizationally belongs directly to the university hospital. So far, the data for clinical studies was collected by means of paper-based questionnaires handed out to the ambulant patients. Then, the filled-out questionnaires were manually recorded in a spreadsheet application and subsequently analyzed with standard statistics software tools. To enable more efficient research, the implementation of an adequate software solution for electronic data collection and processing was necessary. In a first step, this system should be only used by the center for orthopaedical studies and primarily help to reduce the workload of the physicians with respect to the extension of the clinical study database.

This paper describes the development of a first prototype of this application, called OrthoClinical. For an easy access by different types of client devices (mobile and stationary), OrthoClinical was designed as web-based application.

The prototype was required to support at least the design and administration of electronic questionnaires and the electronic execution of patient surveys (i.e. in the patients' waiting area by means of a tablet computer). Later, it should be extended to a full-featured eCRF system supporting retrospective as well as prospective studies.

4   Agile Methodology

The selection of an adequate project methodology was performed by means of the decision matrix proposed by Cockburn [1]. The priorities of the project were considered to be productivity and tolerance, since first results should be available at an early stage, which the team atmosphere should enable. Thus, the productivity and tolerance grid was chosen as basis for the decision (see Fig. 1).

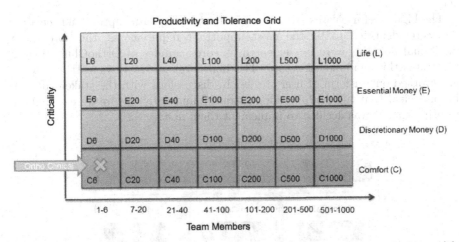

Fig. 1. Decision matrix for project methodology selection according to Cockburn [1]

The project's criticality was classified as "Comfort", since the system only reduces the workload of the users. The development team consisted of 3 persons. Thus, according to Cockburn it is a C6 project requiring cost-effective development, since no direct financial benefits are expected, frequent delivery of working software and a high demand for communication between the team and other stakeholders.

To meet this requirements a combination of the agile methods Crystal Clear and Scrum was chosen. Usually Scrum is considered to requires an experienced team with good technical skills in the development environment used. Additionally, a close interaction with the customer representatives is needed, i.e. for testing the delivered software after each sprint [10]. However, these requirements were not completely met by the project. Neither experienced developers were available, nor the customer representatives (physicians) were able to perform a regular quality assurance after each sprint due to their tight schedules and shifted working times.

According to Crystal Clear, the "Exploratory 360" strategy was used at project start [2]. Thereby, the items business value, requirements, technology plan, team make up and working conventions were analyzed and defined. The category domain model was integrated into the working conventions and not considered separately.

First, together with the stakeholders the business value definition was worked out [2]. Therefore, interviews with the assistant medical director, physicians, medical documentation officers and MD students were done to estimate the system's expected value for the orthopaedical department. It became obvious that the system should not only improve the efficiency of the processes but also increase the transparency about the research activities at RKU. For a cost-efficient implementation it was decided to develop the application based in OSS. To support different client devices, the implementation as a web-based application was chosen.

The high-level use cases related to administration, data capture and scheduling were identified to be the most important requirements, therefore these functional domains were implemented as core modules of OrthoClinic. Fig. 2 illustrates this modular structure. The high-level use cases were then refined and worked out in form of user stories. In discussions with the stakeholders it become clear that the modules administration and data capture were of highest priority, thus it was decided to implement them first.

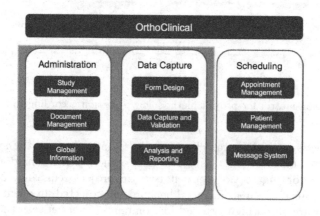

Fig. 2. Functional modules of OrthoClinical

Crystal Clear defines the project roles executive sponsor, expert user, lead designer, designer-programmer and coordinator, the latter being responsible for project management. In smaller teams it is necessary for the members to take multiple of these roles [2]. Therefore, during the team make-up of the OrthoClinical project the roles sponsor, coordinator, lead designer, designer-programmer

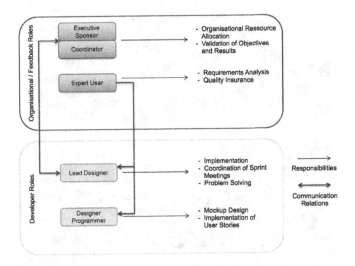

Fig. 3. Project roles according to Crystal Clear with the respective communication relations and responsibilities

and expert user were assigned. The role of the expert user was taken first by a medical specialist, and second by a staff member of the center for orthopaedical studies. Fig. 3 illustrates the assigned project roles with their respective communication relations and tasks within the project.

Working conventions help to organize the daily work of the team. Therefore, Crystal Clear defines seven categories, namely frequent delivery, reflective improvement, osmotic communication, personal safety, focus, easy access to expert user und technical environment. Osmotic communication and easy access to expert user proved to be especially challenging in the present project context.

Osmotic communication should allow the developers to take part directly or indirectly in every development-related communication process. However, since in the present scenario not all developers were able to work at the same time at the project, an indirect form of osmotic communication was established by means of an information board (see Fig. 4). Here, i.e. coding standards or informations about development items were put on visible to all team members. Also problems or impediments could be noted and discussed on the board by all developers. Thereby it was possible to discuss ideas or solutions without the need for all team members to be physically present all the time.

The easy access to an expert user also proved to be a challenge to the project. Crystal Clear requires the expert user to be continuously involved in the development process as close as possible to ensure that deviations between the current implementation and the requirements are identified quickly. However, in the present case this principle needed to be adapted. At project start a physician was denoted as the expert user. However, due to the tight schedules and shifted working times of the physicians this proved not to be feasible. Instead, the role of the expert user was additionally taken by a medical documentation officer, who

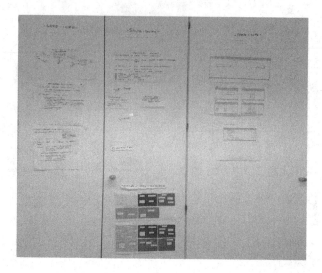

Fig. 4. Snapshot of the information board used for communication between the team members

was also involved in the development himself. Thus, no continuous independent quality assurance could be guaranteed.

The actual development work was organized using Scrum. Before the start of the first iteration (sprint) already all major requirements needed to be identified. First, since the physician serving as the expert user was not available during the rest of the project, and second because it is required for software projects at RKU to deliver a detailed IT security and privacy concept at project start.

The functional requirements were specified as user stories collected in interviews with selected physicians and medical documentation officers. To further involve the other physicians and obtain their feedback, the collected user stories were distributed to all of them in written form. In total, 22 user stories were identified and put into the product backlog. According to Scrum, the user stories in the product backlog should be prioritized by the product owner. The role of the product owner in the project was taken by different persons, first by the project sponsor, then for pragmatic reasons by the expert user and the lead programmer.

So far, three sprints were performed, each lasting for one week. Sprint meetings were scheduled on demand and after each sprint. Due to time limitations not all user stories could be implemented as planned during these sprints. After the first sprint the prioritization and number of relevant user stories was adjusted. Scrum requires to involve the users in the testing and approval of the implemented user stories after each sprint. This proved not to be feasible in the clinical context. In the future, the regular early morning status meetings of the physicians might be used for testing individual functionalities and for general information about the project progress. This would not only allow a better individual feedback by the physicians, but also provide an environment for broader discussions with the users.

5   Application Architecture and OSS Components

OrthoClinical was realized as a web-based application with a standard three-tier architecture, composed of the database, business logic and presentation layers. Therefore, in general different OSS platforms may be considered, in particular the frequently used PHP and Java Enterprise Edition (EE) environments [22], since for the latter also different open source implementations exist. Criteria for the selection of the used components were license fees, initial skill adaptation effort, interoperability, a high productivity within short development cycles and support for open standards. From these, the initial skill adaptation effort strongly depends on the experience and knowledge of the team members. Thus, no general statement for other projects is possible here.

Both Java EE and PHP fulfill the selection criteria license fees, interoperability and high productivity. PHPSurveyor, the only OSS-based eCRF web application documented in the literature so far, was developed using PHP [23]. However, for OrthoClinical some significant disadvantages of PHP were identified: First, the initial skill adaptation effort would have been higher for PHP, since the team members already had Java EE but little PHP development experience. Second, PHP in contrast to Java EE does not provide a dedicated support for business logic implementation by a built-in component architecture. Due to the lack of type safety, for PHP also a higher testing effort was expected. In contrast, Java EE with its Enterprise Java Beans (EJB) component architecture provides a solid foundation for implementing business logic. With Eclipse and Netbeans IDE [21] also powerful development environments exist for Java EE.

Thus, Java EE and Java ServerFaces (JSF) 2.0 were selected as the development platform [22]. The standard JSF framework was extended for OrthoClinical by the Primefaces library. Using JSF and the Primefaces UI library [26] enabled the developers to create a professional web user interface by combining visual components. The communities of both frameworks are very active and questions could be discussed with members in various forums. JSF is well documented. In contrast, Primefaces indeed offers many realistic examples, but lacks a comprehensive open online documentation.

Enterprise Java Beans (EJB) like JSF is a standardized technology. This is an advantage regarding extendability and maintainability. The data access layer was implemented using Java Persistence API (JPA) and EclipseLink for object-relational mapping (ORM) [22]. The database layer was realized by the popular database management system (DBMS) MySQL 5.2.

NetBeans 7.2 with its integrated GlassFish application server was used as development environment. It provides i.e. a powerful scaffolding functionality for automatically generating business logic classes (EJB) and JSF pages from a relational database model [21]. For the creation of this database model and the administration of the underlying DBMS the MySQL Workbench software was used. The scaffolding functionality of NetBeans IDE proved to be extremely useful. A disadvantage was the instability of the integrated GlassFish server. As a workaround, the server subsequently was installed and administrated separately from NetBeans.

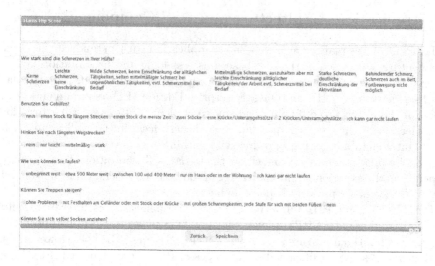

Fig. 5. Screenshot of a questionnaire form (Harris Hip Score, in German language) in OrthoClinical

Fig. 5 shows a screenshot of a patient questionnaire form (Harris Hip Score) in the resulting OrthoClinical web application developed this way.

6   Prototype Evaluation

In retrospect, the developers consider the selected OSS implementation of the Java EE technology stack and development tools as mature and effective means to build user-friendly and reliable web-based applications. In particular the scaffolding functionality of Netbeans IDE for generating skeleton JSF pages and presentation and business layer Java Beans in combination with the Primefaces UI library strongly supported the rapid development of working increments of the software during the sprints.

To validate the practical usability of OrthoClinical for patient surveys, an empirical usability test was performed. Therefore, 14 randomly selected patients in the orthopaedical department were asked to fill out the questionnaire for the so-called Harris Hip Score in OrthoClinical (see Fig. 5) using a tablet PC. All participants were asked to perform a representative and identical task in OrthoClinical, namely to "fill out the Harris Hip Score questionnaire for the hip body region". They did not receive any special training on how to use OrthoClinical before. The objective was to measure the usability criteria effectiveness, efficiency and user satisfaction. Effectiveness indicates if the users are able to perform a certain task successfully, efficiency measures the effort necessary for it. User satisfaction indicates the subjective perception of the usability by the test persons. The last criteria is only meaningful with respect to the average user satisfaction of the respective peer group [19]. During the tests the patients were observed and the durations to complete the test task were measured. A successful completion of the test task required the participants to perform the following steps: 1. selection of the patient region in OrthoClinical, 2. fill out the questionnaire, 3. save the results. After the test, the participants were interviewed to measure the usability criteria. The results are shown table 1.

Table 1. Results of the usability test of OrthoClinical from the patients' perspective

Age	Effectiveness	Efficiency	User Satisfaction
25 – 45	Yes, without support	3.5 min.	High
45 – 65	Yes, with support	4.5 min.	Medium
65 – 75	No, despite support	< 8 min.	Low

The results show that older patients in general had problems using electronic client devices, regardless of the user-friendly web-based frontend. Two patients even refused to take part in the test because they never had used such devices in their everyday life. Some participants also criticised the current way how questionnaires are displayed in OrthoClinical (all question on one web page). They suggested that there should be a separate page for answering each question. On the positive side, the overall GUI layout of the web pages was considered well structured.

Participants between 25 and 35 years were able to perform the task without support in an average of 3.5 minutes. The 45 to 55 year old patients partially needed help, i.e. regarding the scrolling of the questionnaire page. The user satisfaction in this user group was medium. The test persons older then 65 years had significant problems using OrthoClinical. Despite personal assistance they were not able to successfully complete the task. As a reason for this an overall lack of computer skills was mentioned.

7 Conclusion

In conclusion, the project demonstrated that it is in general possible to use agile methods for web-based application development in a clinical environment. However, these methods need to be customized and extended with respect to the identified specific requirements. Due to the required quality insurance measures at project start it was not possible to use agility during all phases of the development process. To get an approval for the project by the IT administration it was i.e. necessary to create an technical specification and IT security document in advance, which already defined key functionalities, the software architecture, and the data model. Nevertheless it was possible for the rest of the project to design and use a tailored agile methodology combining elements of Scrum and Crystal Clear.

The OSS components used developing the OrthoClinical web application proved to provide an efficient alternative to commercially available products. Originally, the main reason for the clinics administration to use OSS was the savings of license fees. However, during the project also further advantages like extendability and vendor independence became apparent.

However, further research is necessary to evaluate the presented approach more extensively for a longer duration, and also in various similar project contexts.

References

1. Cockburn, A.: Selecting a projects methodology. IEEE Software 4, 64–71 (2000)
2. Cockburn, A.: Crystal Clear - A human powered methodology for small teams. Addison-Wesley (2005)
3. Deitsch, A., Hughes, R.: Ge healthcare goes agile. Information Week, 59–63 (2010)
4. Bagayoko, C.: Selection of secure single sign-on solutions for heterogeneous computing environments. BMC Medical Informatics and Decision Making 10(22), 1–13 (2010)
5. Bärwolff, H., Hüsken, V., Victor, F.: IT-Systeme in der Medizin IT- Entscheidungshilfe für den Medizinbereich - Konzepte, Standards und optimierte Prozesse. Vieweg+Teubner Verlag, Wiesbaden (2006)
6. Beck, K.: Extreme Programming eXplained - Embrace Change. Addison-Wesley (2000)
7. Beck, K., et al.: Principles behind the agile manifesto (2001), http://agilemanifesto.org/principles.html
8. Brown, S., et al.: Vista u.s. department of veteran affairs national scale his. International Journal of Medical Informatics 69, 135–156 (2003)
9. Byrne, C., et al.: The value from investments in health information technology at the u.s. department of veteran affairs. Health Affairs 29(4), 1–13 (2010)
10. Cesar, A., et al.: An empirical study on the relationship between use of agile practices and the sucess of scrum projects. In: Proc. of the 2010 ACM-IEE International Symposium on Empirical Software Engineering and Measurment (ESEM 2010), vol. 10 (2010)
11. Dinevski, D., Inchingolo, P., Krajnc, I., Kokol, P.: Open source in health care and open three example. In: IEEE International Symposium on Combuter Based Medicine (2007)
12. Dyba, T., Dingsor, T.: Empirical studies of agile software development: A systematic review. Information and Software Technology 50, 833–859 (2010)
13. Murray, P., et al.: Open source and healthcare in europe time to put leading edge ideas into practice. Medical Informatics in a United and Healthy Europe (2009)
14. Fitzgerald, B., Kenny, T.: Open source software in the trenches: Lessons from a large-scale oss implementation. In: 24th International Conference on Information Systems (ICIS), pp. 316–326 (2003)
15. Gary, K.: Agile methods for open source safety critical software. Software Practice and Experience, 943–962 (2011)
16. Hogarth, M., Turner, S.: A study of clinilally related open source software projects. In: AMIA Annu. Symp. Proc., pp. 330–334 (2005)

17. Lakshimi, M., Malar, J.D.: An open source private cloud solution for rural health-care. In: International Conference on Signal Processing Communication Comouting and Networking (2011)
18. Marcheschi, P., Mazzarisi, A., Benassi, A., Ferdeghini, E.: An open source based radiological information system to support a clinical cardiology depearment. In: Computer in Cardiology, pp. 363–366 (2003)
19. Hartmann, M.: Usability Untersuchungen eines Internetauftrittes nach DIN EN ISO 9242 Am Praxisbeispiel der Firma MAFI Transport Systeme GmbH. Diplom-ica Verlag GmbH (2008)
20. Molin, J.D.: Open innovation; transforming health systems trough open and evi-dence based healthcare ict innovation. Communication & Strategy 3, 17–35 (2011)
21. Netbeans: The netbeans e-commerce tutorial (2012), http://netbeans.org/kb/docs/javaee/ecommerce/entity-session.html
22. Oracle: The java persictence api a simpler programming model for entity persis-tence (2012), http://www.oracle.com/technetwork/articles/javaee/jpa-137156.html
23. Orr, S., Straus, S., Holyrod-Leduc, J.: Development and example of a web based open source clinical tool. In: AMIA 2005 Symposium, pp. 330–334 (2005)
24. Pichler, R.: Scrum agiles Projektmanagement erfolgreich einsetzen. Dpunkt Verlag (2008)
25. Pries-Heje, L., Pries-Heje, J.: Agile and distributed project management: A case study revealing why scrum is useful. In: ECIS 2011 Proceedings, vol. 217 (2011)
26. Primefaces: Ultimate jsf component suite (2012), http://www.primefaces.org
27. Ralston, B.: Open source expected to improve innovation. Health Management Technology 30(8), 12–13 (2011)
28. Reynolds, C., Wyatt, J.: Open source, open standards and health care information systems. J. Med. 13(1) (2011)
29. Rising, L., Janoff, N.: The scrum software development process for small teams. IEEE Softw. 17(4), 26–32 (2000)
30. Rodrigez, D.G., Carpenter, T., van Hemert, J., Wardlaw, J.: An open source toolkit for medical imaging de-identification. Eur. Radiol., 1896–1903 (2010)
31. Sackett, D.: Implementing an integrative mulitagent clinical decision support sys-tem with open source software. J. Med. Sys. 36(1), 123–137 (2012)
32. Schwaber, K.: Scrum alliance - scrum guide (2009), http://www.scrum.org/Scrum-Guides
33. Shah, J.: Electronic data captuare for registries and clinical trails in orthopaedic surgery: Open source versus comercial systems. Clin. Orthop. Relat. Res. 468(10), 2664–2671 (2010)
34. Shirabad, S.: Implementing an intergrative multi-agent clinical decision support system with open source software. J. Med. Syst., 123–127 (2010)
35. Vognild, L., Fernandez, L., Burkow, T.: The myhealth service approach for chronic disease management based on free open source software und low cost components. In: 31st Annual International Conference of the IEEE EMBS, pp. 1234–1237 (2009)

USTO.RE: A Private Cloud Storage Software System

Frederico Durão[1], Rodrigo Assad[2], Anderson Fonseca[3], José Fernando[3,4],
Vinícius Garcia[3], and Fernando Trinta[5]

[1] Federal University of Bahia, Computer Science Department
Av. Adhemar de Barros, Salvador - Bahia, Brazil
freddurao@dcc.ufba.br
[2] Federal Rural University of Pernambuco
Recife - Pernambuco, Brazil
assad@deinfo.br,assad@usto.re
[3] Federal University of Pernambuco
Recife - Pernambuco Brazil
{afs8,jfsc,vcg}@cin.ufpe.br
[4] University Center of João Pessoa - UNIPÊ
João Pessoa - Paraiba, Brazil
gentio@gmail.com
[5] Federal University of Ceará
Fortaleza - Ceará, Brazil
fernando.trinta@lia.ufc.br

Abstract. Cloud computing is a computing model where hardware,
platforms and software are seen as services; viz. Infrastructure as a Service, Platform as a Service, and Software as a Service, respectively. Data
as a Service (DaaS) is based on the concept that the product, data in this
case, can be provided on demand to the user, regardless of geographic or
organizational separation between provider and consumer. DaaS applications are for the most part based on excessive data replication in order
to guarantee data availability, which means excessive costs in hardware
investments. This white paper presents the specification, implementation and evaluation of a system called **USTO.RE** which aims to be
an effective and low-cost alternative for storing data, thereby mitigating
the problem of excessive data replication and thus allows itself to be
considered a reliable platform from the perspective of data availability.
Evaluation scenarios and the results achieved in our experiments to evaluate the system as well as possible lines for future development will be
presented.

1 Introduction

Recent CISCO report[1] on predictions about mobile data traffic, show that they
currently achieve a flow of approximately 0.6 *exabytes* of mobile data per month.

---

[1] Cisco Visual Networking Index: Global Mobile Data Traffic Forecast Update, 2011
– 2016, URL: http://bit.ly/x5V50B, last access on 05/03/2012.

F. Daniel, P. Dolog, and Q. Li (Eds.): ICWE 2013, LNCS 7977, pp. 452–466, 2013.
© Springer-Verlag Berlin Heidelberg 2013

This report states that the flow of mobile data will be multiplied by a factor larger than 10 by 2016, based on the fact that the speeds will be multiplied by similar values. The considerable increase in the amount of information produced by users associated with the need to access data in a ubiquitous manner led to the emergence of data storage systems in the cloud [8].

Cloud Storage Systems appear quite attractive to home users, by providing them with the ability to access, retrieve and store their files from anywhere at anytime. Studies show that in 2010, the amount of data produced was greater than the storage capacity [2]. Thus, we can infer that the tendency is for this disparity to grow increasingly, corroborating the report submitted by CISCO. The applications of cloud storage based on the principles of Cloud Computing, in which users pay for what they consume and can access data from anywhere with growth in storage resources, are done on demand. Because of this relationship, a service model commonly used for the applications of cloud storage is the cloud storage of Data as a Service (DaaS).

There are a number of platforms in the cloud data storage [8], most of which have common features: i) the need to assemble a dedicated infrastructure to ensure the availability of data when the user requests access; or ii) the lack of reliability from the standpoint of ensuring the availability of data, which can be clearly identified from the analysis of contracts of service providers.

In the context of these issues, the project **USTO.RE** proposes the reduction of costs associated with the need for a dedicated infrastructure of cloud storage systems through an approach based on the Peer to Peer (P2P) network. This approach significantly reduces the *CAPEX*, which encompasses capital expenditure or investments on acquisition for companies to build their own data storage environment. The main advantage of **USTO.RE** is that it opportunistically benefits from opportunistic storage resources and idle disks of computers in the existing infrastructure of the company.

The remainder of this paper describes the architecture and results of tests conducted with **USTO.RE**. Section 2 reviews other works related to our proposal, and Section 3 introduces the system and provides an overview of its architecture. Section 4 describes the project use case, testing scenarios and their achievements. Finally, Section 5 draws the main conclusions and outlines future lines of investigation.

2   Related Work

There are several existing solutions for data storage in the cloud DaaS model. In general, these solutions are proprietary and closed, which therefore prevents a more detailed technical analysis on each proposal. Looking at some of the major existing solutions, such as *Amazon S3, Megastore, MSFSS* and *Hadoop Distributed File System* (HDFS), we note that they invariably utilize all a common strategy based on replication of data across multiple servers, where the number of servers involved in replication, ranges from 3 to 7 depending on the solution. This forced replication is done because there is no automation in the processes of replication that can guarantee 99.9999999% availability [8].

Amazon S3 (*Simple Storage Service*) [2] is the storage system behind many of the services of Amazon.com known as Dynamo [8], which recently had its SQL-database launched under the name DynamoDB [8]. The DynamoDB has a backup policy where at least three copies of the same data are made, and two are made in one and the same zone on a third outer zone, so as to increase the availability of the information. According to 2009 data, the system stored about 40 billion files of 400,000 customers. Their challenges include ensuring availability and fault management.

Megastore, is a system developed with a focus on online interactive services [3]. It was developed and is used by Google for a long time and handles more than 3 billion written and 20 billion read transactions daily. It also stores a value close to a petabytes of raw data in their datacenters spread globally.

MSFSS is a distributed file system highly scalable and flexible, designed to store a large amount of small files [18]. Its architecture is divided into three main components: *single master, storage nodes* and *metadata servers*. Every file stored in the system receives a 128-bit identifier (*FID - File ID*) generated after its storage. These files are stored in the local file system of each node storage. Further, MSFSS supports data replication, which ensures consistency between replicas and performs rapid synchronization to identify obsolete ones. The FSI (*File System Interface*) library provides access to the system for external clients and allocates a large amount of FIDs processes in *batch* and leaves stored in local memory for later use [18]. By default, MSFSS replicates the files twice although this value can be configured to ensure greater availability and reliability. During the reading process, any replica can be considered, on the other hand, in the process of writing, all replicas must be updated automatically. To minimize latency, the data is stored near the user and the replicas close to each other. It separates groups by regions and creates 3 to 5 replicas for data centers.

Wuala[2] is an online cloud file storage that unlike the majority of online file storage services like Dropbox and Box.com, which offer paid plans only as a means to expand storage. Wuala offers the option to gain additional online storage in exchange for some of the user's unused local disk space to commit to the network. Similarly to our approach, uploads are encrypted automatically, anything that is sent to backup is given a high-grade file encryption to prevent hackers and other nefarious evildoers from messing with the cache of files. Also similarly as our approach, Wuala offers a simple, yet capable, mobile app for Android and iOS devices, making file access easy and accessible from anywhere. An interesting feature about Wuala is the possibility of adjusting the bandwidth so that one can easily cap the amount of upstream and downstream net traffic that available to Wuala. Unlike our approach, after installing Wuala, it will mount WualaDrive on the computer as a network drive, where one can directly access all files and even save files directly there. A key feature is the possibility of building groups and share files with distinct collections of users.

---

[2] www.wuala.com/en

Worth mentioning that every uploaded files in a group will be counted against storage quota for every group members. Tagging mechanism is allowed. Unlike our approach Wuala doesn't keep files versioned with date. Instead they will keep your files for up to 10 versions.

Symform[3] is a also an online cloud backup service that encrypts, shreds, and globally distributes data. Similarly as Wuala, Symform's customers join the Symform network by contributing excess local drive space and, in exchange, receive free cloud backup. Symform is basically a folder synchronization product. One can only select folders that wants to synchronize with the cloud. There is not option of selecting individual files or file types for backup. Once a folder is selected, all sub-folders in that tree are included. Similarly as our approach, Symform encrypts the data and chops it up into fragments. The ideal size for a folder is 64 MB and that block of data is broken into 64 1 MB fragments. To that data, 32 parity fragments are added and all 96 fragments are distributed to 96 member devices (contribution nodes) out in the cloud. The algorithm for adding parity is actually a RAID algorithm. Every piece of data sent to backup is monitored by a Cloud Control metadata where Symform keeps track of where each fragment is sent. Symform constantly monitors the performance and availability of contribution nodes. If a member's device becomes unavailable, Symform sends an email notifying them, and can recreate the data from the unavailable device (from other data and parity) to send to another contribution node. Data is geographically dispersed, which increases data security. According to Symform, member contribution nodes are located in 150 countries.

Freenet[4] is a free P2P software designed for anonymous file sharing. Indeed, the Freednet is targeted at those who want to exercise free speech without fear of censorship or retribution. Unlike most of file sharing discussed in this paper is the single one which allows one to publish websites and take part in online bulletin boards obviously only accessible to those who use the software. Unlike our approach, the Freenet network is decentralized without any central hub. The shared files are stored encrypted in different computers around the world. The size of the default folder where shared files are stored is determined by the user during installation and it can go from a few Megabytes up to dozens of Gigabytes. Because all the stored data is encrypted Freenet users do not know what they are sharing and have no saying on what is being shared, this allows for denial of knowledge. A particular feature is that files in Freenet are kept or deleted depending on popularity, if something isn't downloaded for some days, Freednet wil delete them.

AeroFS[5] is on software for file sharing on the Web and is nearly as seamless and simple Dropbox, but with the added security that comes from keeping data (and data transfers) confined to local computers rather than on someone else's server. The level of OS integration present and its ease of configuration make it a very promising "personal cloud" solution. As to the security, data is fully

---

[3] http://www.symform.com/

[4] https://freenetproject.org/

[5] https://aerofs.com/

encrypted before being transferred to other computers, preventing it from being intercepted and decoded in transit. Installing the AeroFS software creates a folder in the user profile, much like Dropbox does, and this can be changed from the default location as desired. Aside from the security advantages, AeroFS frees users from the limited amount of storage space provided by other cloud service vendors. The size of a "personal cloud" is limited only by the amount of disk space on your various computers. Limiting download and upload bandwidth is also possible, which is especially desirable if the syncing is occurring between multiple clients. The versioning system in AeroFS keep older versions stored as long as there is sufficient free local disk space; if one's disk gets too full, it will begin silently deleting the very oldest items to make more room. AeroFS' versioning system keeps old versions until it runs out of space, and then begins deleting the oldest copies of files to make more room. Our approach does not implement this feature, rather we let the users take care of this own files. Conflict management is the a concern, file conflicts are not solved properly if problems occurs. And finally, the AeroFS's biggest shortcoming, which is lack of access from Web browsers or mobile devices. Dropbox (and, for that matter, Google Drive, SugarSync, Box.com, and most of the other major players in this field) offers apps for iOS and Android as well as a robust Web client that can be used to access your files while on public computers.

The HDFS is a file system used by Hadoop [14] and its related projects. Hadoop is a framework for analysis and processing of large amounts of data using *MapReduce* [7]. One of the main features of Hadoop is the partitioning of data and computation thereof using thousands of hosts. For instance, the *cluster* Hadoop at Yahoo! reached 25,000 servers (with cluster up to 3,500 servers) and stored 25 *Petabytes* of data [14].

The abovementioned works have in common excessive replication of information. This fact has to do with the need to ensure high data availability, increase reliability, and performance of information retrieval. However, the use of replicas does not only bring benefits. It creates an extra data traffic on the network, which can be so excessive to the point of becoming the main bottleneck for an application, and may generate a cost so high that the band can make the application unfeasible [17].

These solutions infer the need to purchase infrastructure in order to provide a dedicated service and to guarantee a replica of the data. In order to improve this scenario, the goal of **USTO.RE** is to allow for the creation of a cloud data storage using P2P technology that is based on the availability of each peer to dynamically create federations and set the amount of replications for the *chunk*[6] of each file. This approach is allowed in environments where peers have increased availability (low failure rate) with one minor replication, and in the case of a more dynamic environment as company Intranet, it has further replication. In the next section, our proposal will be explained in detail.

---

[6] Chunk is a piece of information, i.e. a "small" part of a file stored. Files are divided into chunks, which in turn are replicated storage points in cloud infrastructure.

3   The USTO.RE System

The architecture of **USTO.RE** was specified with the target of achieving a set of quality attributes peculiar to distributed storage systems that met the main benefits offered by P2P applications, namely

Scalability: Given the possibility of exploring hardware resources of a large number of (hosts) machines connected to the network, this is done mainly through the rational use of idle resources in large corporations..

Optimization Iterations (messaging): The distance between the peers interacting in the system has an impact on overall performance in the latency of individual interactions, so the load network traffic also suffers from a negative impact on this latency. In this context, the choice of using the strategy is aimed at federation grouping related peers and to reduce this latency.

Availability: P2P systems are based on free computers that join the system at any time. Furthermore, the connections are not managed by the system or some authority that ensures connectivity and quality of service. In this context, a strategy for ensuring service availability should be implemented considering the basic characteristics of a storage system with high availability and the restrictions imposed on a P2P network.

Data Security: When it comes to data storage, protection and security policies should be effectively adopted to ensure user privacy and system data consistency.

Figure 1 overviews the **USTO.RE** architecture, its major components, dependencies and relationships. The architecture comprises a set of five components structured in three layers. They are: i) *Super Peers Rendezvous Relay* or simply *Super Peers*, ii) *Servers* iii) *proxies*, iv) Relational SQL and Non-Sql Databases and v) Simple Peers. These components have different functions and interact as a decentralized distributed and hybrid system, similar to a P2P network, where each node performs both functions as a server and clients. The components are grouped dynamically as associations of data, where the groups are assembled so as to minimize the messaging system.

The organization of this system architecture enables a multi-layered distribution of processing, since the components are physically distributed. However, because it is a hybrid P2P architecture that is structured and multi-layered, the system has a horizontal distribution. In this horizontal distribution in a P2P network, a client or a server can be physically divided into pieces that are logically equivalent, where each operates on its own portion of the data that provides a balanced load. In the following, we present the components of the **USTO.RE** architecture.

3.1   Super Peers

The *Super Peers* act as reference points for other components of the architecture, being the gateway to the participation of servers, proxies and simple peers. The role of a *Super Peer* is to set up federations when each data peer requests the

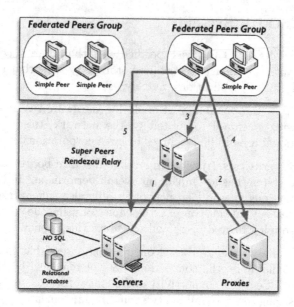

Fig. 1. USTO.RE Architecture

network connection. For this, *Super Peers* must have its location previously known by all other peers through a pre-configuration. Consequently, they are the first components to be initialized to the correct functioning of **USTO.RE**. Also as a result, a *Super Peer* keeps information on all servers, *Proxies* and *Simple Peers*, grouping them dynamically according to the profile of each peer, to be explained below.

It is also the role of this type of *peer*, to dynamically choose peers and federations of servers based on a proximity algorithm [9]. The federation grouping allows elastic growth and ensures system scalability, because there is a limit to the number of associations that can be created. By definition, elastic growth is the characteristic of the system grow or decrease, in terms of capacity and resource consumption of dynamic and non-intrusive way. The peers communicate with the network through the P2P JXTA protocol [16] and can optionally offer a service interface REST [16] to allow for interoperability with other applications.

3.2   Servers

The *Server Peers* offer a list of services and must be executed immediately after the startup of *Super Peers* (Step 1 in Figure 1). *Super Peers* establish a synchronization scheme, thus ensuring that the list of servers in each of them would be updated as the input or output of a *Sever Peer*.

The definition of *peers* with specific functionality in the network differs from some proposals for P2P systems, where which each *peer* should be able to play all the roles, thus promoting the idea of a DHT (*Distributed Hash Table*) [13,11]. However, the implementation using a DHT in its essence is quite costly and difficult to scale [12]. Therefore, **USTO.RE** adopted the creation of hierarchical levels that implement well-defined services and that can grow horizontally. Among the available services via the servers, we can mention.

1. **Authentication:** used for each peer to get authenticated;
2. **Availability:** allows one to check the availability of each peer;
3. **Chunk:** used to monitor the chunks storage;
4. **Error:** allows servers to monitor eventual errors;
5. **Output Control:** controls the voluntary withdrawal of a peer when it disconnects from the network voluntarily;
6. **Management Directories:** used for storage and retrieval of entire directories;
7. **Manages File:** used for file storage and retrieval;
8. **Search Peers:** search for a set of peers that comply with Service-Level Agreement (SLA) for file storage;
9. **tree** Directories: used to preview entire directories;
10. **Access Security:** controls the access permission to the chunks;
11. **Trace:** maintains a list of users and files being accessed when a file is requested to be recovered.

As shown in Figure 1, the *Server Peers* access two types of database to maintain consistency of the system. A traditional relational database contains data from users of the system, and a non-SQL database [5] which allows horizontal growth and faster recovery of information related to the files and *chunks* saved. The choice of this separation is given by the issues related to system performance, since with increasing volume and file *chunks* saved the management system database try to become a bottleneck point, and using a distributed system enables natively become a viable and scalable solution [5].

All information regarding authentication and the SLA peers are saved in a relational database because of the relational integrity assurance provided by this type of database. Already, the service of *FileTracker*, which allows for the identification of which peer has pieces of the file to be recovered, is used in a SQL database that allows for its horizontal growth. Instances of banks, whether they be relational or non-sql, can be shared between more than one server. A *Server Peer* can provide one or more network services; therefore, the same as creating federations of data, one can start peer and server proxies with increasing demand scalability and resilience of the system.

3.3 Proxy

After initialization of *Super Peers* and *Server Peers*, the third component that needs to be executed is the *Proxy*. Each proxy acts as a catalog, a location service for services running on different **USTO.RE** servers. A *Proxy* when announcing a *Super Peer* (Step 2 in Figure 1), receives the list of registered servers. In addition, a *Proxy* gets the information of what services are available on each server. Thus, when a peer requests information about a particular service, a *Proxy* provide a reference to a server that meets this requirement. Thus, a *Proxy* establishes a bridge between service consumers, typically the *Simple Peers*, and providers of a service, in this case, the *Server Peers*.

3.4 Simple Peers

Simple Peers are responsible for storing the files chunks. In fact, these machines provide storage space to be shared among multiple users. Each *Simple Peer* has a profile that defines its availability in the network. This availability is related to the time period in which the peer is available to share data. As an example, a peer that is in a corporate Intranet can have on one's profile: availability assigned at "8:00 to 12:00 and 14:00 to 18:00". Thus, when a *Simple Peer* connects to the network, it receives from the *Super Peer* the list of proxies available in the network (Step 3 in Figure 1). From this list, the proxy searches for a specific service and gets the reference over which servers proffer a particular service (Step 4 in Figure 1). A *Server Peer* is chosen randomly, and *Simple Peers* request the desired service (Step 5 in Figure 1). If a service is not met for any reason, such as a timeout, the proxy can provide a new *Server Peer* to the *Simple Peer*.

Each peer has a REST service interface [16] that allows user authentication, storage, retrieval and deletion of data saved. This feature presents a key advantage in terms of the possibility of harmonizing the system with other existing interfaces, such as Amazon's S3. In the current architecture, data storage service can be modified to work with other alternatives (i.e. Megastore, MSFSS or S3).

To ensure each balanced chunk is scattered in the network, each peer must periodically report their current state in order to maintain the SLA to date. Figure 2 (a) shows the *peer* (PL $_1$) workflow from the moment he announces his profile to the established communication with other peers through the server (PS $_1$). Periodically every peer sends a message to servers as *"keep-alive"* stating that he is online. This way, the server knows that the *peer* is complying with the agreed profile (SLA) and becomes eligible for receiving *chunks* at the specified time. Still, every *peer* checks with other existing peers whether its own chunks are replicated in the minimum amount of *peers* obeying the criterion of availability required [9]. Otherwise, it replicates the chunk(s) in other available peer. When the *peer* owner of this *chunk* re-connects to the network, it will be notified that there is *chunk* excess, thereby excluding it.

Figure 2 (b) shows the workflow between peers and servers from the login of the peer in the network until the file is stored. After the *peer* (PL$_1$) is connected to the P2P network$_1$, the Super Peer indicates a Server Peer to authenticate it. Once authentication succeeds, the process of identifying pairs to form federations takes place. With federation (group of *peers*) established, the system is able to receive files. By receiving a file (*"arq1.zip"*), the *peer* PL$_1$ informs the need to store it in the system, it is made to a segmentation of the file (in *chunks*) and these segments are sent to be saved in the P2P network$_1$. Then, to make the save, there is a routine analysis to measure the reliability of the state peers and hence the availability of segments of the network file, and if there is a combination of peers that meets the SLA for storage, the segments of the file are sent to these

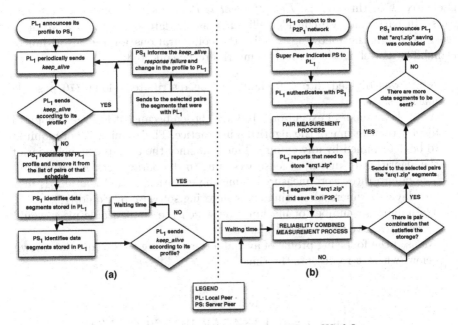

Fig. 2. a) Peer Workflow b) Server Proxy Workflow

peers. If there are no more segments of files to be saved, the PS_1 peer server communicates to the PL_1 *peer*, which requested the file saving, that it was saved successfully.

4 Experimental Evaluation

For assessing the project with regard to performance and scalability, a pilot project was planned and carried out addressing three different scenarios. The methodology *Goal - Question - Metric* (GQM) [4] guided the evaluation by establishing the purpose of the study, the questions to be answered, and the metrics used to interpret the answers.

Three scenarios were assessed using **USTO.RE**. The first two were designed to test the feasibility of peer selection algorithm and performance of the proposed solution, thus validating the system in a corporate Intranet. The third scenario validation was performed with the system implemented. In the latter case, there is the scalability of the solution by adding peers gradually until it reaches 40 P2P clients with maximum 5Gb storage, and two servers providing interfaces for accessing REST nodes.

4.1 Scenario 1

As described earlier, this scenario aims at analyzing the algorithm of peer selection in order to assess its performance within a corporate Intranet. The question associated with this goal is: *How efficient is the algorithm for the selection of peers?* In particular, we consider efficiency as the latency of the algorithm to select peers. In the following, we list the configurations for the algorithm of availability as well as the respective metrics to be collected:

- A file was divided into 100 chunks to be distributed along 376 possible machines;
- As to the number of executions, 100 was chosen because it is large enough to display the runtime of the algorithm in practice. This number is not required to be determined by any empirical method since the asymptotic behavior of the algorithm is known, at least according to the parameters of Cormen [6].
- The failure rates were measured using the empirical model Garden [1] in a 296-day experiment of continuous monitoring software by Squid [15];
- The minimum number of machines on which the configurable piece would necessarily have to be placed was 5;
- We used the following profile of availability according to the equation shown below, where t represents the time:

$$f(t) = \begin{cases} & \text{Reliability} \\ 0, se\ t = \{0,1,2,3,4,5,6,7, 18,19,20,21,22, 23\} \\ 0.50, & \text{if}\ t = \{12,13\} \\ 0.99 & \text{else} \end{cases}$$

The result of the executions was arranged in three separate sheets, measuring: i) runtime; ii) mean number of machines where the same chunk was sent, and iii) average chunks per machine. As a result, the algorithm has proven to be quite satisfactory in terms of execution time, achieving the arithmetic mean time of 1.92 ms with a maximum time of 34 ms, and a minimum of less than 1 ms. As will be seen in the results of Scenario 3, this time is the same as the time spent to access files on the *Windows Netbios* network.

4.2   Scenario 2

Following the GQM methodology, the goal for this scenario is to analyze the **USTO.RE** efficiency in terms of user within a corporate Intranet and the related question is: *How fast is the USTO.RE in use?*. We consider speed-related performance of **USTO.RE** as the basic system features.

As a natural behavior, the **USTO.RE** performance depends on the amount of messages exchanged by its internal components. This amount of messages in turn is directly related to the size of chunks and the size of queues of chunks that form these messages. In this context, the performance was evaluated in terms of variation in the size of chunks and the queue, thereby examining the impact of these variables on time data transmission. The objective of this test is therefore to identify what is needed to perform specific settings when the system is running in LAN environments where throughput is high and WAN environments where throughput is lower and more varied.

For this particular test execution, 20 machines were utilized, and all had the same configuration, Pentium IV with 2GB of RAM and a 100Mbps network card, i.e. old desktops that are compliant with cloud computing features and efficient use of computing resources. Fifteen (15) out of 20 were utilized to send data whereas five (5) were used for storage with 10TB of storage space. The machines sent 1Gb of data, as follows:

- 3 machines sending 2000 files of 500 Kb;
- 6 machines sending 500 files of 5 Mb;
- 3 machines sending 50 files of 50 Mb;
- 3 machines sending 5 files of 200 Mb.

Table 1 presents the results obtained for the data transmission system in terms of Chunks and Queue. In the leftmost column are the values of the chunk size and the amount of the queue in terms of chunks. That is, for the first case, each system message has one queue comprising 10 chunks of 128Kb.

Table 1. Average Delivery Time of Chunks per Queue

Chunks/Queue	Time	Chunks/Queue	Time
128/10	00:03:20	32/10	00:12:03
128/8	00:03:08	32/8	00:14:53
128/6	00:04:54	32/6	00:18:50
128/4	00:06:22	32/4	00:22:59
128/2	00:13:15	32/2	00:59:19
64/10	00:05:46	16/10	00:23:17
64/8	00:07:32	16/8	00:30:00
64/6	00:10:15	16/6	00:32:15
64/4	00:12:02	16/4	00:47:49
64/2	00:30:31	16/2	02:03:10

As can be seen, there is a significant impact on system performance when there are variations in the parameters analyzed. This impact is higher when there is variation in the size of the chunk. This occurs because there is an augment in the number of messages to be sent in order for a file to be saved. This same rationale applies to the variation of the queue, but is not as significant for the final performance of the system.

Considering that the queue size was not a significant factor in the performance of the system, we opted to use chunks of 128Kb and queues in size 10 for LAN and WAN environments.

In this scenario, we also examined the issues related to the performance of the machines. It was observed that the machines receiving data reached their full storage capacity, i.e. 100% CPU usage, 2GB of memory consumption and

20Mbps of traffic in this situation. Comparing the transmission rate obtained with the results reported by *Google File System (GFS)* in the Session *Micro Test*[10], we can observe that **USTO.RE** has reached about 40% of the processing capacity of the GFS. Taking into account the difference between the real-world and test environments, the **USTO.RE** used an *HUB* and not a *switch*, as well as cheaper network cards that limit the transmission capacity. In addition, the chunks were 128KB instead of 4MB as in SFM. However, these results indicate that it is possible to overcome the results of GFS. With regard to the machines that were spreading data, they consumed little recourse, i.e. 128MB of RAM, nearly half the CPU consumption.

4.3   Scenario 3

For the latter scenario, the scalability of the system is tested. The goal therefore is to evaluate **USTO.RE** potential from the user-centric standpoint within a corporate Intranet, and the related question is: *How functional is the USTO.RE to the user?* We consider the functional potential through *USTO.RE* scalability and performance in relation to the environment that exists today on corporate Intranets for storing and sharing data.

In the latter assessment, we utilized a performatic access control tool to validate the **USTO.RE** scalability and performance of file transfer. In the test scenario the goal was to assess the system's growth capacity, both vertically and horizontally. For this, we used two servers providing REST service interfaces that connected to the P2P network, performed the download the file and stored in the P2P network. During the test, as a) interfaces services began to become bottleneck point, others were added as needed; and b) as more nodes were needed for the P2P network, they also were added thus allowing the growth of the system.

In this test scenario, all peers were 100% available, i.e. 24 hour, making each *chunk* replicated by 2-3 machines according to the algorithm described in [9].

As a result, the tests for reading files (with an average size of 11Mb), the waiting time to get it was on average 28 seconds (to measure this average, each file was restored three times and the average time obtained corresponds to this result). As to downloading files via the REST service interface, the average time was 31 seconds, thus demonstrating the efficiency of the proposed architecture with the service Filetracker (measurement performed with the same procedure as above). These test results showed that in comparison to other network storage solutions, the system can produce an acceptable performance. Figure displays the screen with some system files saved.

5   Conclusion

This paper presented **USTO.RE**, a cloud storage system at a low cost with high reliability. This tool consists of peers in a P2P network and an algorithm that allows to dynamically calculate how many nodes a *chunk* should be replicated so that when files are requested to be restored, the system ensures its availability. Evaluations were performed in order to validate the algorithm that supports the proposal, as well as the feasibility of the solution, achieving satisfactory results. In addition, new test scenarios are being validated to investigate the solution's degree of scalability. Future works include the calculation of optimal storage size per peer in order to increase storage efficiency. Further, we also aim at researching the utilization or adaptation of an algorithm that allows to group more efficiently the peers in federations, thus improving the storage efficiency as well as its replication.

Acknowledgments. Authors would like to thank the University Center of João Pessoa - UNIPÊ for financing the publication of this article.

References

1. Abd-El-barr, M.: Design and Analysis of Reliable and Fault-tolerant Computer Systems. Imperial College Press, London (2006)
2. Amazon. Amazon Simple Storage Service (Amazon S3) (March 2012), http://aws.amazon.com/pt/s3/ (last access March 5, 2012)
3. Baker, J., Bond, C., Corbett, J., Furman, J.J., Khorlin, A., Larson, J., Leon, J.-M., Li, Y., Lloyd, A., Yushprakh, V.: Megastore: Providing scalable, highly available storage for interactive services. In: CIDR 2011, pp. 223–234 (2011)
4. Basili, V.R., Caldiera, G., Rombach, D.: The Goal Question Metrics Approach, vol. I, pp. 528–532. John Wiley & Sons (February 1994)
5. Chang, F., Dean, J., Ghemawat, S., Hsieh, W.C., Wallach, D.A., Burrows, M., Chandra, T., Fikes, A., Gruber, R.E.: Bigtable: a distributed storage system for structured data. In: Proceedings of the 7th USENIX Symposium on Operating Systems Design and Implementation, vol. 7, p. 15. USENIX Association (2006)
6. Cormen, T.H., Leiserson, C.E., Rivest, R.L., Stein, C.: Introduction to Algorithms, 3rd edn. MIT Press (2009)
7. Dean, J., Ghemawat, S.: Mapreduce: simplified data processing on large clusters. Commun. ACM 51, 107–113 (2008)
8. DeCandia, G., Hastorun, D., Jampani, M., Kakulapati, G., Lakshman, A., Pilchin, A., Sivasubramanian, S., Vosshall, P., Vogels, W.: Dynamo: amazon's highly available key-value store. SIGOPS Oper. Syst. Rev. 41, 205–220 (2007)
9. Duarte, M.: Um algoritmo de disponibilidade em sistemas de backup distribuído seguro usando a plataforma peer-to-peer. Dissertação de mestrado, Centro de Informática, Universidade Federal de Pernambuco, Recife-PE, Brazil (2010)
10. Ghemawat, S., Gobioff, H., Leung, S.-T.: The google file system. SIGOPS Oper. Syst. Rev. 37(5), 29–43 (2003)
11. Loest, S.R., Madruga, M.C., Maziero, C.A., Lung, L.C.: Backupit: An intrusion-tolerant cooperative backup system. In: Proceedings of the 2009 Eigth IEEE/ACIS International Conference on Computer and Information Science, pp. 724–729. IEEE Computer Society (2009)
12. Nocentini, C., Crescenzi, P., Lanzi, L.: Performance evaluation of a chord-based jxta implementation. In: Proceedings of the 2009 First International Conference on Advances in P2P Systems, pp. 7–12. IEEE Computer Society (2009)

13. Oliveira, M.: Ourbackup: A p2p backup solution based on social networks. M.sc. dissertation, Universidade Federal de Campina Grande, Campina Grande – PB, Brazil (2007)
14. Shvachko, K., Kuang, H., Radia, S., Chansler, R.: The hadoop distributed file system. In: Proceedings of the 2010 IEEE 26th Symposium on Mass Storage Systems and Technologies (MSST), pp. 1–10. IEEE Computer Society (2010)
15. Squid. Squid: Optimising web delivery (2012), http://www.squid-cache.org/ (last access March 5, 2012)
16. Webber, J., Parastatidis, S., Robinson, I.: REST in Practice: Hypermedia and Systems Architecture. O'Reilly Media (2010)
17. Yang, Q., Xiao, W., Ren, J.: Prins: Optimizing performance of reliable internet storages. In: Proceedings of the 26th IEEE International Conference on Distributed Computing Systems, p. 32. IEEE Computer Society (2006)
18. Yu, L., Chen, G., Wang, W., Dong, J.: Msfss: A storage system for mass small files. In: Shen, W., Yang, Y., Yong, J., Hawryszkiewycz, I., Lin, Z., Barthes, J.-P.A., Maher, M.L., Hao, Q., Tran, M.H. (eds.) 11th International Conference on Computer Supported Cooperative Work in Design (CSCWD), Los Alamitos, CA, USA, pp. 1087–1092. IEEE Computer Society Press (April 2007)

Market Intelligence: Linked Data-driven Entity Resolution for Customer and Competitor Analysis

Ulli Waltinger[1], Dan Tecuci[2], Florin Picioroaga[3], Cosmin Grigoras[3], and Sean Sullivan[4]

[1] Siemens AG Corporate Technology, Munich, Germany
[2] Siemens Corporation, Corporate Technology Princeton, NJ, USA
[3] Siemens AG Corporate Technology, Brasov, Romania
[4] Siemens Energy Inc. Orlando, USA
{ulli.waltinger,dan.tecuci,florin.picioroaga,
cosmin.grigoras,sean.sullivan}@siemens.com
http://www.siemens.com/

Abstract. In this paper, we present a linked data-driven method for named entity recognition and disambiguation which is applied within an industry customer and competitor analysis application. The proposed algorithm primarily targets the domain of geoparsing and geocoding, but it can easily be adapted to other problems such duplicate detection. The contributions of this paper are three fold: First, we want to give an overview of *Market Intelligence*, a customer and competitor analysis application developed for Siemens Energy, which allows users to pose questions and queries on regularly crawled websites, emails and RSS feeds, to detect and respond to competitor, customer, and market trends more effectively. Second, we describe the UIMA-based processing architecture that builds the framework for analyzing and converting unstructured heterogeneous documents into a structured and semantically-enhanced knowledge representation. Third, we propose a novel algorithm that is used within the framework for content analysis and entity disambiguation. The performed evaluation shows with an accuracy of up to 91.69% that the proposed method for named entity recognition and disambiguation is very effective, while at the same time relying on Linked Data only.

Keywords: Named Entity Recognition, Named Entity Disambiguation, Word Sense Disambiguation, GeoParsing, GeoCoding, Market Intelligence.

1 Introduction

Today enterprises deal with decisions that involve the analysis of information from various heterogeneous sources on a massively scale. In this context, an effective information access and analysis can be seen as one of the fundamental building blocks within the decision making process and in the process of

F. Daniel, P. Dolog, and Q. Li (Eds.): ICWE 2013, LNCS 7977, pp. 467–481, 2013.

enabling an cost-effective customer service [1]. The amount of available information nowadays grows at an amazing speed, which raises several challenges. More precisely, it is assumed that enterprise data will grow by 800 percent in the next five years, whereas 80 percent of it exists by means of documents, files or other unstructured data [1]. That is, most of the data and resources available lack of meta data or being semantically augmented, which support an efficient and well-defined data exploration and analysis for market intelligence applications. In this context information extraction and retrieval techniques, such as Named Entity Recognition (NER) and Disambiguation (NERD) [2, 3], are an important part for obtaining and automatically analyzing such information hidden in unstructured, machine-readable documents. Especially in the area of customer and competitor analysis applications, plays the automatic identification and resolution of entities, such as company names, their location and connected profiles a significant role. These applications aim to provide information about business opportunities, strengths and weaknesses of customers/competitors that are primarily distributed across various unstructured sources. In the setup of *Market Intelligence*, a project of Siemens Corporation, Corporate Technologies and Siemens Energy, we aim to identify customer and competitor information from unstructured documents to enable answers such as: What are the service units of company X that are located around Clive and Jupiter?, Which units on the East Coast remain open? or Is there a company X that has installed component Y? In this context, the automatic extraction and disambiguation of context-specific entities and its geo-related references [4] are in the center of the project scope. That is, in this paper, we do not focus on the aspect of natural language question answering, but targeting the challenge of not only extracting business relevant information out of regularly crawled websites, emails and RSS feeds, but also applying a context-specific disambiguation, of the extracted information. As an example:

"The units located in **Jupiter** [↦Jupiter, Florida] and **Princeton** [↦Princeton, British Columbia] (Canada) [↦Canada] will remain open."

"**Princeton** [↦Princeton, New Jersey] (US) [↦United States], the city **New York** [↦New York City] and the state **New York** [↦New York] need to be notified."

In this example, one can identify that the surface form of the geo-related entities entities are often ambiguous. That is, taken out of context, the same name (e.g. *Princeton, Jupiter,* or *New York*) may have multiple meanings (i.e. refer to different entities). There are three main contributions of this paper: In Section 2, we give an overview of *Market Intelligence*, the customer and competitor analysis application developed for Siemens Energy, in which the described components are integrated. Section 3 reviews related work. Thereupon in Section 4, we describe the UIMA-based processing architecture that builds the framework for analyzing and converting unstructured heterogeneous documents into a structured and semantically-enhanced knowledge representation. In Section

5, we propose a NERD algorithm that is used within the framework for content analysis and entity disambiguation targeting the domain of geoparsing and geocoding. In Section 6, we present the evaluation of the entity disambiguation algorithm that is applied on two different datasets. Finally, Section 7 concludes this paper.

2   Overview of Market Intelligence

Information about business opportunities, new regulations, competitor and customer news is massive and scattered across an ever growing number of sources. Hidden in publicly available news, internal bulletins, market reports or documents it is difficult to keep track of latest developments and get a global picture of the market situation. The goal of the *Market Intelligence* application is to aggregate and analyze such data and extract actionable knowledge from it. Currently we focus on the following functionalities: automated classification of incoming information into business relevant categories, automatic identification of named entities from a catalog of entities of interest, instant notification based on custom-made rules that use the result of classification and entity recognition, and collaboration (sharing and commenting). The data that is analyzed comes from a set of publicly available websites identified by the business as being of interest. Among the named entities identified, geolocations are of great importance. Figure 1 shows a map representation of a set of selected news and Figure 2 shows an individual piece of news with its corresponding annotations.

The application is being developed for Siemens Energy Service.

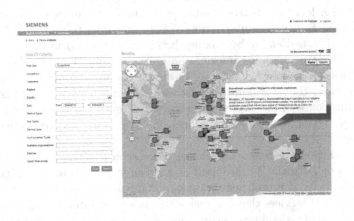

Fig. 1. Screenshot of the Market Intelligence application

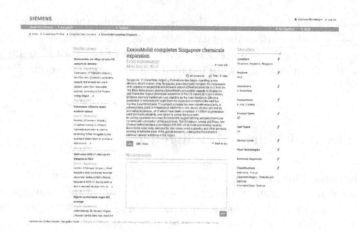

Fig. 2. Metadata annotations in Market Intelligence web application

3   Related Work

Documents, articles and other comprised resources contain named entities of different flavor, as for example locations, products or people, but also weapons or organizations, which play a significant role in automatic data analytic (e.g. product and relationship mining, location detection, sentiment analysis). Named Entity Recognition (NER) has been extensively addressed in different research fields [5, 6, 3], and can be seen as one of the fundamental components of current information extraction and retrieval sytems. This task focuses on the identification of proper nouns, which are further classified into a predefined set of entity categories (e.g. location, persons, numeric or time). As an extension of it, the task of Named Entity Disambiguation (NED), attempts to additionally disambiguate the classified entity by linking the entity to real world object identifier (e.g. URI). That is, mapping information units to explicitly and uniquely mentioned entities in a knowledge base. As one of the most prominent comprised knowledge base, the *Wikipedia* data set was heavily used for this task lately [7, 6]. In this context, numerous approaches have been published using concept similarity [8–11] or relatedness measures [6, 12] to rank the respective object candidates.

Most recently, RDF-based knowledge bases such as *Freebase*[1], *GeoNames*[2], *YAGO* [13], or *DBpedia* [14] are used as a resource for web-based entity identifier [15, 16]. For an comprehensive overview and comparison of current (publicly available) NERD services that leverage RDF-based repositories as a resource see [3]. The domain of geocoding or geoparsing [4], can be seen as a geospatial extension of NER(D). This research field is concerned with the automatically mapping of locations specifically, referred to as the processing of textually-encoded spatial

---

[1] www.freebase.com

[2] www.geonames.org

data [17]. Note that we see geoparsing as the task of location-based extraction from text (NER), and gecoding as the NED complement, the mapping of references to real-world counterparts [17]. Similar to current NER approaches, we can identify three different branches of methods [4]: Gazetteer-based lookup methods [18], Rule-based approaches (e.g. GATEs ANNIE module [19]) by using a set of symbolic rules to encode the decision procedure (Definite Clause Grammars via Prolog) [20]. The third branch uses machine learning-based approaches. Most commonly using a sliding window, which is introduced in order to extract a set of classification properties and features (e.g. context, length, string surface) [21]. In this work, we are using for the NER component, the Gazetteer-based approach as a stimulus for the learning-based entity classification. With regards to NED, we are focusing on meta data via *DBpedia* only. In this context, the approaches of [10] and [16] are most related to our approach in the sense of putting the textual context of an entity in the center for the task of candidate ranking. However, different to others, our approach does not rely on any training cycle for graph construction or edge weighting, but operates entirely on the RDF-metadata only. In addition, the method proposed in this paper allows to incorporate the (initial) named entity category as an stimulus and part of the evidence strategy for disambiguation.

4   Information Processing Architecture

The overall processing architecture of the *Market Intelligence* application can be divided into two interconnect pipelines: the data management pipeline, which leads the data workflow between the different processing components, and the UIMA pipeline that bears the content extraction and analysis procedures.

4.1   Data Management Pipeline

The process of data transformation consists of the following components (see Figure 3):

1. **Content Dispatcher:** This components collects the heterogeneous data from various sources (RSS, E-Mails, crawled web pages) via custom adapters.
2. **Content Transformer:** The aggregated data collection gets pre-processed via processing templates (i.e. extracting the only the text from the incoming data).
3. **Content Storage:** The extracted content fragments are stored to a relational database storage.
4. **Message Broker:** Each content fragment is further sent out as a message to a message broker.
5. **UIMA Connector:** The message from the message broker is consumed by a component (pipeline connector) responsible for transforming the received data to a data structure (Common Analysis Structure) accepted by the UIMA framework.

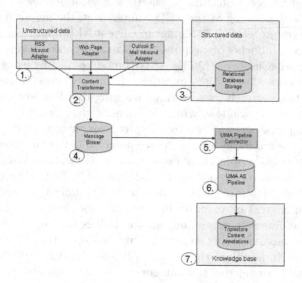

Fig. 3. Overview of the general processing work flow of the Marketing Intelligence pipeline

6. **UIMA Pipeline:** UIMA pipeline runs the analysis engines on the given data and extracts the information specific to each engine. We will call this information annotation.
7. **Annotation Storage:** The extracted annotations are stored in a knowledge base as triple statements.

4.2   UIMA Pipeline

The *UIMA framework*[3] has been used for analyzing the text message and extracting the information required. More precisely, the framework consists of a set of text analyzing engines that are grouped in a single processing pipeline. The analyzing engines are refereed to as *annotators*. The results of these *annotators* are defined as *annotations*. All these *annotations* are then persisted by a special component called *consumer*. The *Market Intelligence* project incorporates the following UIMA components:

1. **LocationAnnotator** that recognizes the geographical locations (cities, countries) that occur in the respective content fragments. This component additionally resolves each entity by its unique URI representation (see Section 5).
2. **OrganizationAnnotator** that recognizes customers and competitors entities. It utilizes the gazetteer component as available within *GATE*[4].

---

[3] http://uima.apache.org/
[4] http://gate.ac.uk/

3. **ClassifierAnnotator** that recognizes domain-specific meta-information, such as *fuel type, business segmentation, joint venture* etc. using Support Vector Machines.

4. **RegularExpressionAnnotator** that is used for matching meta-information, based on a set of regular expressions.

5. **RDFCASConsumer** is used to store the annotations in the RDF-based triple format.

Subsequently, all annotations produced by components within the UIMA pipeline can be viewed and further processed (deleted or adding new ones) within the Market Intelligence web application.

5   Evidence-Based Entity Disambiguation

As described in the previous section, the UIMA pipeline integrates several entity annotators and an entity disambiguation annotator that focuses on geo-related references. The work flow of this evidence-based component is depicted in Figure 4, and can be subdivided into three consecutive components. At first, the recognition task that combines a state-of-the-art NER library with domain-specific gazetteer induction. Second, the disambiguation task which utilizes *DBpedia* as an resource for entity disambiguation and URI identifier assignment. Finally, the connector to the MI application, which makes use of the data set of *GeoNames* to construct SPARQL queries based on prior templates. In the following, we describe each individual component in more detail.

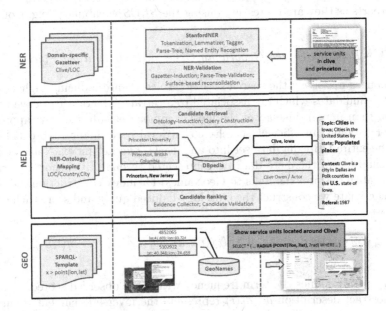

Fig. 4. Overview of the work flow of the evidence-based geospatial named entity recognition and disambiguation

5.1 NER - Named Entity Recognition

The NER phase focuses on the identification and tagging of single nouns and phrases using *StanfordNER* ([21]). That is, each input document is preprocessed by applying tokenization, lemmatization, part-of-speech-tagging, parse-tree extraction and (default) named entity recognition. Subsequently, a NER validation is applied that enhances and corrects the default token representation as generated by *StanfordNER*. This component utilizes domain-specific gazetteers (e.g. clive may also refer to a city) to re-annotate those text segments, which could not be identified within the pre-processing phase. In addition, multi-word units (e.g. jupiter, florida), which are missed by *StanfordNER* will be concatenated by reconciliation the surface- and the parse-tree representation. The resultant *StanfordNER*-enhanced object representation is further used as an input for the NED component.

5.2 NED - Named Entity Disambiguation

The NED components can be subdivided into the candidate retrieval and the candidate ranking module.

Candidate Retrieval. The candidate retrieval module utilizes the *DBpedia* data set not only to retrieve a a list of object identifier, but also uses the ontology[5] to typify and validate the search strategy. That is, we incorporate a mapping between the entity category (e.g. LOC for location) and the respective *DBpedia* counterparts as they are represented using the *SKOS* vocabulary (e.g. Country, City, ...).

$$LOC \mapsto PopulatedPlace; Geography; CelestialBody; NaturalPlace; \cdots \quad (1)$$

This changes massively the search strategy, since we are inducing higher confidence to candidates which are associated to a certain category (e.g. clive rather location than name), instead of the most common "eat-all-you-can" approach. In order to allow an efficient search-and-retrieval performance, we decided to parse the entire DBpedia data set into an *Apache Lucene*[6] index. Note, we used only a snapshot of the meta data (as represented through title, short abstracts, articles categories and the links to GeoNames) for index construction. For each entity candidate we construct the Ontology-induced query and score each entity as follows:

$$score_{can}(q, d) = \log_{10}(\sum_{t \in q}(tf(t \in d) \cdot idf(t)^2 \cdot t_b \cdot norm(t, d))) \quad (2)$$

where $tf(t \in d)$ defines the term frequency within the observed scored DBpedia short abstract description d; $idf(t)$ represents the inverse document frequency

---

[5] http://wiki.dbpedia.org/Ontology
[6] http://lucene.apache.org

applied to the DBpedia summary description representation. t_b is the search time boost of term t in the query q. $norm(t, s)$ encapsulates a few (indexing time) boosts and length factors with reference to *Lucene's* document and field boost property [22]. Note, we collect only the 100 best entity candidates which are further passed to the ranking component.

Candidate Ranking: The candidate ranking can be subdivided into the evidence collection and the evidence validation phase. More precisely, at first, we collect a number of evidences that consider the confidence and the probability that a candidate refers to a proper entity instance, in order to, subsequently, rank and validate the most likely referred instances of a given candidate. The evidence collector utilizes the following measures:

Popularity-Based Evidence: This measure follows the rational that given an surface form of an token there exist a prior assumption of which entity might be meant. As for instance, just given the context *"We live in New York"*, the majority of people would think of the city rather than the state of *New York*. This prior stimulus can be deduced from the number of referels (or backlinks), which are interlinked to a certain entity. That is, the number of pointing hyperlinks, established by human, operates as a *common sense* amplifier for a certain entity, as proposed by [23]. Though, we define the popularity-based evidence score as follows:

$$evi_{pop}(u) = n \cdot \log_{10}(\log_{10}(b_u)) \tag{3}$$

where b_u refers to the number of incoming links to a certain DBpedia entity u. That is, we use the double logarithmic normalized backlink score as an (probability-based) evidence for the most popular referenced DBpedia instance for a given surface form (e.g. *Princeton (New Jersey)*: 0.51 v.s. *Princeton (British Columbia)*: 0.30)

Surface-Based Evidence: The surface-based evidence refers to quotient between the intersection and the union of the pairwise compared term features among the input entity, e, and the current observed DBpedia entity u (e.g. Princeton $\mapsto$ Princeton (New Jersey))

$$evi_{sur}(e, u) = \frac{tf_{e,u}}{tf_{e,u} + tf_e + tf_u} \tag{4}$$

That is, this score collects evidences for the term overlap on its surface form. While the surface-based evidence is a good indicator for a successful mapping, there exist a lot of false positive examples for it. For example: surface form of *Aspen* $\mapsto$ *Aspen* within *DBpedia* (evi_{sur} : 1.0), though the article *Aspen* describes not *Aspen, Colorado* but a certain tree species.

Context-Based Evidence: The context-based score collects evidence from the description of each *DBpedia* entity. The rational behind this evidence score is that each (surface form) of an entity is primarily instantiated through its context.

We define context as the surrounding terms co-occur (left/right) with the entity within a word window of size m.

$$evi_{con}(c,u) = \frac{\sum\limits_{i=1}^{n} c_i \times u_i}{\sqrt{\sum\limits_{i=1}^{n} (c_i)^2} \times \sqrt{\sum\limits_{i=1}^{n} (u_i)^2}} \qquad (5)$$

That is, we apply the standard cosine measure to obtain the similarity between the context of the input entity (c) using m word features left and right from the observed token by means of its sentence representation, and the context of the entity candidate as given by its short summary value (u). Note that we applied the normalized term frequency for input vector construction utilizing nouns and ner entities only.

Topic-Based Evidence: The topic-based evidence measures the correlation from the initial mapped named entity category and the respective *DBpedia* category associated to the candidate. More precisely, since we are able to traverse the category taxonomy within *DBpedia* by means of its graph-based representation (e.g. *Princeton (New Jersey)* $\mapsto$ *University towns in the United States* $\mapsto$ *Cities in the United States*), we are able to score the normalized graph-path distance, between the initial mapping category uc and the respective category candidate note nc by:

$$evi_{top}(uc,nc) = 1/|dis(uc,nc)| \qquad (6)$$

The rational behind this approach is to allow to adjust the confidence of an entity candidate by its assigned category even if the latter was not part of the initial ontology mapping process (e.g. LOC $\mapsto$ Country, City,...). Note, we allowed also a substring match of nodes to score the distance (e.g. *City* $\mapsto$ *Cities in the United States*).

Mutual Evidence Confidence: In this NED phase, the k evidences are accumulated to a mutual confidence score defined as

$$conf_{evi}(d) = \frac{score_{can} + \sum\limits_{i=1}^{k} (\lambda \cdot evi_i) + \phi}{k+2} \qquad (7)$$

$$d_{max} = \arg\max_{d \in D} conf_{evi}(d) \qquad (8)$$

where ϕ represents the redirect amplifier as an indicator whether an respective redirect instance was used for the calculation (e.g. *NYC* $\mapsto$ *New York City*). λ is defined as a weighting parameter (evaluation setup $\lambda = 2$). In a final step, all entity candidates, $d \in D$ are ranked by its $conf_{evi}$ score, and the final entity instance is selected by means of $d_{max} > \mu$. That is, we allow the disambiguation assignment only for those entities with a sufficient mutual evidence confidence $(\mu = 0.3)$.

5.3 GEO - Geospatial Analysis

The final component in the processing pipeline is the geospatial analysis. Here, the newly assign *DBpedia* URI is mapped to it *GeoNames* URI counterpart. For this task, we use the already available triples linking within the *DBpedia* data set. Having successfully assigned a given *GeoNames* URI, we apply different *SPARQL* template queries to collect the information need for the MI applications. As for example to infer from a *city* $\mapsto$ *country*, or it's *geographic coordinates* as: $Clive_{raw} \mapsto Clive, UnitedStates_{nerd} \mapsto 4852065_{geo} \mapsto (lat : 41.60304; lon : -93.72411_{geo}) \mapsto State : Iowa_{geo} \mapsto Country : UnitedStates_{geo}$

The set of inferred geographical information is finally stored within the RDF-based triple store component, and subsequently get interlinked to the *GeoNames* dataset, and to business-related entities. The business entities are imported from the database by use of a translator importer, which requires the hidden semantics of the tabular form information to be declared up front and will be used for clusters of same type information.

6 Experiments

We conducted two different experiments, in order to evaluate the proposed evidence-based method to named entity recognition and disambiguation for the domain of geoparsing and geocoding. We decided to use two different data sets, not only to allow a generic comparison to other state-of-the-art approaches, but also to evaluate *both sides* of the targeted application. More precisely, since the algorithm is part of the pre-processing component of the MI application, it is used to facilitate both, not only the annotation process for the unstructured document collection, but also for the analysis of the questions and queries as posed by the users against MI application. Therefore, we decided to use for the evaluation of the backend side, a standard data set - the *CoNLL* task data set [24] - since multiple approaches have already been evaluated. The second data set, targets the user perspective of the application and is part of an entity-biased question-answering corpus collection [25]. Both data sets have already been manually annotated and build therefore the reference plain and bench mark for our evaluation. In the following, we describe the respective corpus properties in more detail.

6.1 Dataset

The *CoNLL* dataset was created by [16] based on the *CoNLL 2003* data [24]. It consists of 1.393 news article, which were manually annotated by means of corresponding *YAGO*[7] entities. Each of the total 34,956 mentions was disambiguated by two students, with an overall distribution of 25 entities per article on average. For the experiment, we have used both, the test set with 4,458 entities, refereed to as *CoNLL-TestA* and the training set with 27,790 entities, denoted

---

[7] http://www.mpi-inf.mpg.de/yago-naga/yago/

as *CoNLL-TestB*. Note, since our approach does not rely on the existence of a training corpus, we used both within our experiments. For a detail description on the used corpus see [16]. The *QA* data set[8] consists of 5,500 questions initially created by [26] in the context of question classification. This question collection has been additionally processed by [25] comprising a training set of 5000 and a test set of 500 questions. For each question, the named entities were annotated and classified by means of the standard categories person, location and organization. For the experiments, we extracted only those question, which refer to location-based entities and manually assigned and validated their corresponding *DBpedia* URI's.

6.2 Results

The results of the backend evaluation (CoNLL) are shown in Table 1. We have used the results published by [16] and [11] as our reference base line. As we can identify the performance of the location based disambiguation performs, with an accuracy of over 91%, equally well on both datasets. The overall macro precision is slightly under the best performing system, the micro precision however is outperforming the benchmark results. Though, with regards to the disambiguation of organizations, we could identify the limitations of our algorithm. Given just the entity candidate *Barcelona*, our method classifies it as an location, and subsequently disambiguates the candidate to the city *Barcelona* rather than to the soccer team *F. C. Barcelona*, which potentially could be identified by the broader context of the entire document. Note that we used a sentence-based context window for the experiments.

Table 1. Result of test set B [16] using 1392 documents and 4458 entities. (Organization which are tagged as locations e.g Barcelona but it is F.C. Barcelona;) with Competitor Results.

	NERD TestA (4458).	NERD TestB (27790).	ML-Ref [16]	Kulk [11]
Acc - LOC	**91.69**	**91.50**		
Acc - PER	78.6	86.7		
Acc - ORG	43.8/76.5	60.7/78.6		
MicroPrec	73.1	**84.1**	81.82	72.87
MacroPrec	71.3	79.6	81.91	76.74

The results of the second experiments are shown at Table 2. As a reference baseline, we have used the results published by [25] and the results of *Nlp-Geo*[9] [27]. Even though, the second data set is with a size of 200 annotated questions rather small, our systems performs, with an accuracy of 83%, very well on the task of location-based entity recognition and disambiguation.

---

[8] Accessible at `https://qa.l2f.inesc-id.pt/wiki/index.php/Resources`
[9] `http://code.google.com/p/nlp-geo/`

Table 2. Result of NERQ data set as provided by [25] using 200 questions ((Geo-Precision)85.04 (Geo-Recall)62.43)

	NERD QA (200)	Geo-NLP[27]	Supervised [25]
Acc - LOC	83,91	75,11	59,43

6.3 Discussion

Overall, the result of both experiments show that our evidence-based method performs on a very satisfying basis on both sides of the application pipeline. Analyzing the individual errors of the evaluation more closely, we can identify some systematic issues using the evidence-based method: First, using a sentence-based context window allows a sufficient level for most of the test cases, though, it does not consider the topic of entire documents. As for example, the occurrence of *cyprus* is correctly identified as an entity, but mapped to *Cyprus* as the country instead of *Cyprus_national_football_team*, which the article referred to. Similar examples, *New_Zealand* as the country instead of *New_Zealand_national_rugby_union_team*, or *Birmingham* as the country instead of *Birmingham_City_F.C.* Second, synonymous entities (in terms of redirects) have not been separately evaluated or resolved. That is, even if the redirects within *DBpedia* map *World Wide Web* to *Internet* or *Islam* ↦ *Muslim*, we treated the assignment of *World Wide Web* as an error, if in the test set the entity *Internet* was used. Third, the algorithms makes use of the actual entity category as a stimulus for the disambiguation task. More precisely, different to other approaches, our method doe not disregard the entity category (e.g. LOC) during the disambiguation phase. However, wrongly classified entity information is passed on to the NED component, influencing the candidate retrieval and the topic-based evidence score. From the perspective of the access to the comprised Linked Data resources, for performance reasons, we decided to index the RDF-dataset of *DBpedia* in an offline mode. That is, we used a snapshot of selected metdata information to allow an efficient search-and-retrieval process. Though, this task could be also achieved using an endpoint service only, as it is deployed for the task of the *GeoNames* mapping.

7 Conclusion

In this paper, we gave an overview of the customer and competitor analysis application *Market Intelligence* for *Siemens Energy*. This system allows users to pose questions and queries on regularly crawled document repositories, to detect and respond to competitor, customer, and market trends more effectively. We described the overall UIMA-based processing architecture that builds the framework for analyzing and converting unstructured heterogeneous documents into a structured and semantically-enhanced knowledge representation. Finally, we presented a multiple evidence-based method for named entity recognition and disambiguation which is applied within the industry-based analysis application.

The proposed algorithm primarily targeted the domain of geoparsing, though, it's application was also evaluated for the domain of person and organization resolution. The performed evaluation shows with an accuracy of up to 91.69% that the proposed method for named entity recognition and disambiguation is very effective, while at the same time relying on *Linked Data* only.

References

1. IBM-Whitepaper, I.: Leveraging content integration for improved customer service. Technical report (2010)
2. Collins, M., Singer, Y.: Unsupervised models for named entity classification. In: Proceedings of the Joint SIGDAT Conference on Empirical Methods in Natural Language Processing and Very Large Corpora, pp. 100–110 (1999)
3. Rizzo, G., Troncy, R., Hellmann, S., Bruemmer, M.: NERD meets NIF: Lifting NLP extraction results to the linked data cloud. In: 5th Workshop on Linked Data on the Web, LDOW, Lyon, France (April 16, 2012)
4. Hill, L.L.: Georeferencing: The Geographic Associations of Information. Digital Libraries and Electronic Publishing (2006)
5. Extracting company names from text. In: Proceedings of the Seventh IEEE Conference on Artificial Intelligence Applications, vol. i (1991)
6. Milne, D.N., Witten, I.H.: Learning to link with wikipedia. In: Proceedings of the 17th ACM Conference on Information and Knowledge Management, CIKM 2008, Napa Valley, California, USA, October 26-30, pp. 509–518 (2008)
7. Bunescu, R., Pasca, M.: Using Encyclopedic Knowledge for Named Entity Disambiguation. In: Proceedings of the 11th Conference of the European Chapter of the Association for Computational Linguistics (EACL 2006) (2006)
8. Cucerzan, S.: Large-scale named entity disambiguation based on wikipedia data. In: Proceedings of the EMNLP-CoNLL, Prague, Czech Republic, June 28-30, pp. 708–716 (2007)
9. Nguyen, H.T., Cao, T.H.: Named entity disambiguation on an ontology enriched by Wikipedia. In: RIVF, pp. 247–254. IEEE (2008)
10. Waltinger, U., Mehler, A.: Who is it? context sensitive named entity and instance recognition by means of wikipedia. In: 2008 IEEE / WIC / ACM International Conference on Web Intelligence, WI 2008, Sydney, NSW, Australia, December 9-12. Main Conference Proceedings, pp. 381–384 (2008)
11. Kulkarni, S., Singh, A., Ramakrishnan, G., Chakrabarti, S.: Collective annotation of wikipedia entities in web text. In: Proceedings of the 15th ACM SIGKDD, KDD 2009, pp. 457–466. ACM, New York (2009)
12. Waltinger, U., Mehler, A.: Social semantics and its evaluation by means of semantic relatedness and open topic models. In: 2009 IEEE/WIC/ACM International Conference on Web Intelligence, WI 2009, Milan, Italy, September 15-18. Main Conference Proceedings, pp. 42–49 (2009)
13. Suchanek, F.M., Kasneci, G., Weikum, G.: Yago: a core of semantic knowledge. In: Proceedings of the 16th International Conference on World Wide Web, WWW 2007, pp. 697–706. ACM, New York (2007)
14. Auer, S., Bizer, C., Kobilarov, G., Lehmann, J., Cyganiak, R., Ives, Z.: DBpedia: A Nucleus for a Web of Open Data. In: Aberer, K., et al. (eds.) ASWC 2007 and ISWC 2007. LNCS, vol. 4825, pp. 722–735. Springer, Heidelberg (2007)

15. Mendes, P.N., Jakob, M., García-Silva, A., Bizer, C.: Dbpedia spotlight: shedding light on the web of documents. In: Proceedings of the 7th International Conference on Semantic Systems, I-Semantics 2011, pp. 1–8. ACM, New York (2011)
16. Hoffart, J., Yosef, M.A., Bordino, I., Fürstenau, H., Pinkal, M., Spaniol, M., Taneva, B., Thater, S., Weikum, G.: Robust disambiguation of named entities in text. In: Conference on EMNLP 2011, Edinburgh, Scotland, United Kingdom, pp. 782–792 (2011)
17. Leidner, J.L., Lieberman, M.D.: Detecting geographical references in the form of place names and associated spatial natural language. SIGSPATIAL Special 3(2), 5–11 (2011)
18. Tobin, R., Grover, C., Byrne, K., Reid, J., Walsh, J.: Evaluation of georeferencing. In: Proceedings of the 6th Workshop on Geographic Information Retrieval, GIR 2010, pp. 7:1–7:8. ACM, New York (2010)
19. Cunningham, H., Maynard, D., Bontcheva, K., Tablan, V.: GATE: A Framework and Graphical Development Environment for Robust NLP Tools and Applications. In: Proceedings of the 40th Anniversary Meeting of the Association for Computational Linguistics (ACL 2002) (2002)
20. Bilhaut, F., Charnois, T., Enjalbert, P., Mathet, Y.: Geographic reference analysis for geographic document querying. In: Proceedings of the HLT-NAACL 2003 Workshop on Analysis of Geographic References, HLT-NAACL-GEOREF 2003, Stroudsburg, PA, USA, vol. 1, pp. 55–62. Association for Computational Linguistics (2003)
21. Finkel, J.R., Grenager, T., Manning, C.: Incorporating non-local information into information extraction systems by gibbs sampling. In: Proceedings of the 43rd Annual Meeting on Association for Computational Linguistics, ACL 2005, Stroudsburg, PA, USA, pp. 363–370. Association for Computational Linguistics (2005)
22. Hatcher, E., Gospodnetic, O., McCandless, M.: Lucene in Action, 2nd revised edn. Manning (2010)
23. Waltinger, U., Breuing, A., Wachsmuth, I.: Interfacing virtual agents with collaborative knowledge: Open domain question answering using wikipedia-based topic models. In: Proceedings of the 22nd International Joint Conference on Artificial Intelligence, IJCAI 2011, Barcelona, Catalonia, Spain, July 16-22, pp. 1896–1902 (2011)
24. Tjong Kim Sang, E.F., De Meulder, F.: Introduction to the conll-2003 shared task: language-independent named entity recognition. In: Proceedings of the HLT-NAACL 2003, CONLL 2003, Stroudsburg, PA, USA, vol. 4, pp. 142–147. Association for Computational Linguistics (2003)
25. Ana Cristina Mendes, L.C., Lobo, P.V.: Named entity recognition in questions: Towards a golden collection. In: Calzolari, N. (ConferenceChair) Choukri, K., Maegaard, B., Mariani, J., Odjik, J., Piperidis, S., Rosner, M., Tapias, D. (eds.) Proceedings of the LREC 2010, Valletta, Malta. European Language Resources Association (ELRA) (May 2010)
26. Li, X., Roth, D.: Learning question classifiers: the role of semantic information. Nat. Lang. Eng. 12(3), 229–249 (2006)
27. Benefico, S.: Geo-related Information Extraction from natural language using YAGO. Technical report (2012)

GAwI: A Comprehensive Workspace Awareness Library for Collaborative Web Applications

Matthias Heinrich[1], Franz Josef Grüneberger[1], Thomas Springer[2],
Philipp Hauer[3], and Martin Gaedke[3]

[1] SAP AG, Germany
{matthias.heinrich,franz.josef.grueneberger}@sap.com
[2] Dresden University of Technology, Germany
thomas.springer@tu-dresden.de
[3] Chemnitz University of Technology, Germany
{philipp.hauer,martin.gaedke}@cs.tu-chemnitz.de

Abstract. In the light of the Web 2.0 movement, the rise of collaborative web applications like Google Docs lead to an enormous end-user adoption largely due to their advanced multi-user capabilities (i.e. document synchronization in real-time and sophisticated workspace awareness support). Nevertheless, the development of collaborative web applications, in particular, the implementation of workspace awareness widgets such as telepointers, radar views, etc., is costly since there are no comprehensive libraries promoting widget reuse. Therefore, we introduce the enhanced Generic Awareness Infrastructure (GAwI) allowing for an efficient development of collaborative web applications. Efficiency is fostered through GAwI's reusable set of widgets and its non-invasive integration. In this paper, we expose GAwI's enhanced widget set, verify GAwI's comprehensiveness in terms of workspace awareness and demo the GAwI integration and GAwI widgets in two widespread open-source editors.

1 Introduction

Collaborative web applications like Google Docs allow multiple users to change the very same document simultaneously. Besides document synchronization and conflict resolution, collaborative real-time applications require a third distinctive multi-user capability, namely, workspace awareness, which is commonly exposed through awareness widgets such as participant lists, telepointers, radar views, etc. In essence, Workspace Awareness (WA) supports collaborators to understand the actions and intentions of others [1]. For example, participant lists allow understanding who is in the shared workspace or creation coloring widgets indicate who authored new content.

Nevertheless, even though collaborative web applications necessitate WA capabilities to efficiently support joint work [2], modern collaboration frameworks targeting the web (e.g. Apache Wave [3], beWeeVee [4] or CEFX [5]) do not offer WA features at all. Consequently, the traditional from-scratch implementation of WA functionality for collaborative web applications results in time-consuming and costly development projects neglecting WA widget reuse.

F. Daniel, P. Dolog, and Q. Li (Eds.): ICWE 2013, LNCS 7977, pp. 482–485, 2013.
© Springer-Verlag Berlin Heidelberg 2013

Therefore, we introduced the Generic Awareness Infrastructure (GAwI) in [6] advocating non-invasive WA incorporation and WA widget reuse. In this paper, we present an enhanced set of reusable awareness widgets including a telepointer, radar view, artifact marking and telecaret widget. Moreover, we validate the comprehensiveness of the resulting WA library and showcase the enhanced awareness widget set in a dedicated screencast that is available at http://vsr.informatik.tu-chemnitz.de/demo/GAwI/.

2   GAwI Overview

The collaboration system architecture including GAwI components is shown in Figure 1(a) and consists of a server and an arbitrary number of clients. In detail, the depicted collaboration system comprises the abstract web editor stack (including Editor UI, Editor API, W3C APIs and the DOM), the concurrency control system (including the Generic Sync Adapter and the server-side DOM Sync Service) and the Generic Awareness Infrastructure. While the generic concurrency control, which is discussed in [7], synchronizes DOM changes and resolves editing conflicts, GAwI captures, distributes and provides input for WA widgets [6]. The generic nature of GAwI is promoted by relying exclusively on standardized W3C APIs instead of editor-specific ones that would entail an extra WA adapter implementation for each supported web editor.

Nevertheless, the GAwI presented in [6] accommodates only two awareness widgets (participant list and creation coloring) and thus, lacks WA support in a comprehensive and holistic manner. Gutwin et al. introduced the 10 WA elements [2] listed in Figure 1(b) (presence, identity, etc.) that have to be covered by a *comprehensive* WA library. Currently, the spider chart in Figure 1(b) gives a rough estimation to what extent WA elements are covered by GAwI [6]. On the one side, the participant list reflects if collaborators are present and reveals their identity; on the other hand, the creation coloring widget discloses who carried out what action and which artifacts were affected. In particular, the *where-elements* location, gaze, view and reach are not sufficiently supported.

3   GAwI Enhancements

To enhance GAwI's existing set of WA widgets and to effectively support all 10 WA elements, we implemented 4 extra awareness widgets depicted in Figure 1(c). In the following, we discuss implementation details that allow for reuse.

Telepointer: To be aware of the mouse cursor of other participants, the telepointer mimics the cursor movements remotely. Our implementation built on top of standardized W3C APIs starts capturing local mouse cursor changes when the DOM Core mousemove event is fired. Since participants' viewports may differ in various aspects (e.g. size, zoom level or resolution), the x and y window coordinates cannot be exploited. Instead, we leverage the underlying DOM node (e.g. a text node representing a heading or an SVG node visualizing a circle) as

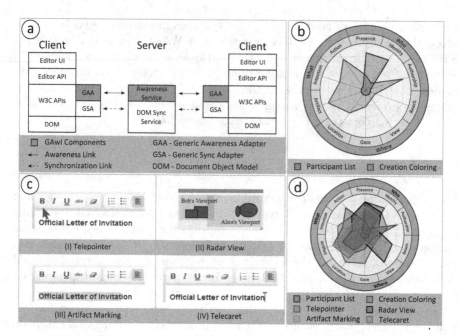

Fig. 1. (a) The GAwI architecture [6] (b) WA elements [2] and their as-is coverage (c) Set of added awareness widgets (d) Comprehensiveness analysis of WA support

the reference point for positioning calculations which results in more accurate positions in heterogeneous environments. The telepointer shape is drawn on a HTML5 canvas layer that spans the entire shared workspace. Adopting a pixel-based canvas is essential since SVG-based solutions may impair performance.

Radar View: To highlight where participants are working, the radar view exposes a miniaturized view including all document artifacts and semi-transparent viewports. Miniaturizing HTML documents is not trivial since HTML consists of a variety of different media objects that cannot be scaled in a uniform manner (e.g. scaling fonts differs from scaling images). Hence, we used the html2canvas JavaScript library to generate a pixel-based representation from the DOM view that can be uniformly scaled to a miniature view. However, taking a snapshot of the DOM view is costly and thus, the radar view is only updated if a fixed time interval elapsed and not if document artifacts are changed.

Artifact Marking: Local artifact selections are highlighted remotely by the artifact marking widget and thus provide means to focus the attention of collaborators on a specific object. The capturing phase is triggered by mouse events (e.g. `click`) and has to ensure that the selection area is properly calculated. Absolute coordinates are once again not an option due to heterogeneous window sizes, zoom levels, etc. The HTML5 Editing API provides so called `Range` objects that allow specifying continuous selection parts based on content rather than on coordinates. These range objects are exploited to draw a properly dimensioned, semi-transparent `<div>` node on top of selected document artifacts.

Telecaret: Communicating the local text cursor position to teammates is the task of the telecaret. Thereby, DOM keyboard events (e.g. `keydown`) are used to initiate the telecaret re-positioning. Analog to calculating artifact marking areas, the range object also enables telecaret positioning whereas range objects with the same start and end point are adopted. The visualization is materialized through an extra `<div>` element inheriting the participant list's color code.

Besides providing details about the application-agnostic implementation, Figure 1(d) depicts an assessment of the individual widgets regarding their support for the 10 WA elements. Even though this expert estimate is coarse-grained and an end-user study could detail the results, the trend becomes apparent that the sum of all widgets can comprehensively cover all WA elements. However, the support for gaze, reach and intention leaves room for improvement.

4 GAwI Demonstration and Conclusions

In this demo (cf. `http://vsr.informatik.tu-chemnitz.de/demo/GAwI/`), we leverage two web-based open-source editors, namely, CKEditor [8] and SVG-edit [9], to showcase GAwI capabilities. First, we show the non-invasive integration of GAwI in the prominent CKEditor, i.e. the integration entails no source code changes to the editor's JavaScript code. Second, we demo WA widgets in a word processor application (CKEditor) and third, we employ a graphics application (SVG-edit) to again present the generic WA widgets.

In essence, in this paper, we discussed a set of AW widgets that drive development efficiency for collaborative web applications due to their generic nature and non-invasive incorporation into existing web applications. In a next step, we will conduct a user study adopting the collaborative CKEditor and the multi-user SVG-edit to thoroughly assess the functionality and usability of GAwI widgets.

Acknowledgments. This work was partially supported by funds from the European Commission (project OMELETTE, contract number 257635).

References

1. Dourish, P., Bellotti, V.: Awareness and Coordination in Shared Workspaces. In: CSCW, pp. 107–114 (1992)
2. Gutwin, C., Greenberg, S.: A Descriptive Framework of Workspace Awareness for Real-Time Groupware. Computer Supported Cooperative Work 11, 411–446 (2002)
3. ASF: Apache Wave, `http://incubator.apache.org/wave/` (2013)
4. Corvalius: beWeeVee, `http://www.beweevee.com` (2013)
5. Gerlicher, A.: CEFX (2013), `http://sourceforge.net/projects/cefx/`
6. Heinrich, M., Grüneberger, F.J., Springer, T., Gaedke, M.: Reusable Awareness Widgets for Collaborative Web Applications - A Non-invasive Approach. In: Brambilla, M., Tokuda, T., Tolksdorf, R. (eds.) ICWE 2012. LNCS, vol. 7387, pp. 1–15. Springer, Heidelberg (2012)
7. Heinrich, M., Lehmann, F., Springer, T., Gaedke, M.: Exploiting Single-User Web Applications for Shared Editing: A Generic Transformation Approach. In: WWW, pp. 1057–1066 (2012)
8. CKSource: CKEditor (2013), `http://ckeditor.com/`
9. Schiller, J., Rusnak, P.: SVG-edit (2013), `http://code.google.com/p/svg-edit/`

On Weighted Hybrid Track Recommendations

Simon Franz[1], Thomas Hornung[1], Cai-Nicolas Ziegler[2],
Martin Przyjaciel-Zablocki[1], Alexander Schätzle[1], and Georg Lausen[1]

[1] Institute of Computer Science, Albert-Ludwigs-Universität Freiburg, Germany
{franzs,hornungt,zablocki,schaetzl,lausen}@informatik.uni-freiburg.de
[2] American Express, PAYBACK GmbH, München, Germany
cai-nicolas.ziegler@payback.net

Abstract. Music is a highly subjective domain, which makes it a challenging research area for recommender systems. In this paper, we present our TRecS (Track Recommender System) prototype, a hybrid recommender that blends three different recommender techniques into one score. Since traceability is an important issue for the acceptance of recommender systems by users, we have implemented a detailed explanation feature that supports transparency about the contribution of each sub-recommender for the overall result. To avoid overspecialization, TRecS peppers the result list with recommendations that are based on a serendipity metric. This way, users can benefit from both recommendations aligned with their current taste while gaining some diversification.

1 Introduction

While e-commerce has embraced the benefits of using recommender systems early on, the music domain has long been influenced by offline radio stations, where static playlists based on track popularity and expert preselections are broadcast to every listener. With the advent of music streaming platforms, such as Last.fm[1] or Spotify[2], the balance has shifted and users can now create their own private radio stations. As a downside, users now have to curate their own playlists and are less likely to discover new music. For this, a music recommender system is an elegant supplement, which can make use of both the wisdom of the crowds and the user's past listening history.

In this paper, we present our TRecS prototype that combines multiple metrics into one comprehensive prediction score: the similarity of tracks is computed based on the listening history of Last.fm users (*track similarity*), the tags that are associated with tracks (*tag similarity*), and the temporal listening profile of individual tracks (*time similarity*). While these metrics assure recommendations that share characteristics with music a user has liked so far, we have additionally implemented a serendipity measure [1] that includes complementary music to the list of recommended tracks. TRecS is a weighted hybrid recommender [2], where the weights for each metric are adjustable, and the system supports an

---

[1] http://www.last.fm
[2] http://www.spotify.com

F. Daniel, P. Dolog, and Q. Li (Eds.): ICWE 2013, LNCS 7977, pp. 486–489, 2013.
© Springer-Verlag Berlin Heidelberg 2013

explanation for each recommended track with respect to the contribution of each sub-recommender to the overall prediction score. A study with over 140 participants has shown that the perceived quality of recommendations gradually improves with the number of rated recommendation lists.

2   TRecS Architecture and Design

TRecS relies on one collaborative metric and two content-based metrics (cf. Section 2.1) [3]. The overall architecture of the system is shown in Figure 1. Our crawled data set from Last.fm is first preprocessed (e.g. data cleansing and disambiguation) and reduced to 50,000 tracks while maintaining key characteristics of the original data set. Afterwards, for each metric the similarity between all songs is precomputed and stored in the knowledge base. At runtime, when a user requests a new recommendation list, the user's context, i.e. the tracks rated so far, is used to compute the next recommendations based on a weighted score of the three sub-recommenders. Before the result list is returned, it is peppered with additional serendipitous tracks (cf. Section 2.4).

The TRecS prototype is available online with an introductory tutorial at:

http://trecs.informatik.uni-freiburg.de

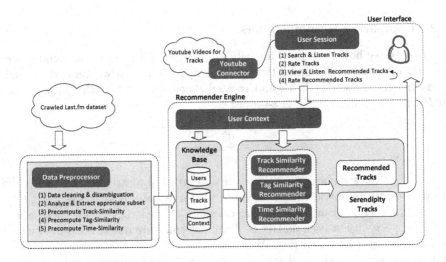

Fig. 1. TRecS system architecture

For computing similarities, each track is represented as a vector of *features*. The similarity between each track can now be determined with some distance metric between these vectors. Thus, it is sufficient to describe for each recommender *how* features are represented for each track and *which* distance metric is used.

2.1 Similarity Metrics

TRecS puts three different recommender systems to use, each based on its own similarity metric:

1. **Track similarity.** Each track is represented as a vector $\alpha_i = (c_1, \ldots, c_n)$, where c_j represents the number of times the user $j \in U$ has listened to this track, and $|U| = n$ is the number of all users. The similarity is determined by the *Pearson product-moment correlation* (see, e.g., [4]).
2. **Tag similarity.** With tag similarity, each track is represented as a vector $\beta_i = (l_1, \ldots, l_m)$, where $l_j \in [0, 100]$ represents the score to what extent the tag $l_j \in L$ "describes" this track, where $|L| = m$ is the number of all used tags. Since for tags we do not need to care for user-specific scales, the similarity is determined by the *cosine similarity measure* [4].
3. **Time similarity.** Every season has its music, e.g. there are typical songs for Valentine's day or Christmas. To capture this behavior, each track is represented as a vector $\gamma_i = (w_1, \ldots, w_{52})$, where w_j is the number of times the track has been listened to in the jth week of the year, accumulated over all users. Similar to tag similarity, the *cosine similarity* is computed.

Every recommender generates a track-track similarity matrix $A^k, k \in \{1, 2, 3\}$. These are used for generating predictions for the active user.

2.2 Comparing Recommenders

In order to see how close the similarity estimates of all three recommenders are to each other, we implemented the following approach: First we iterated through every matrix $A^k, k \in \{1, 2, 3\}$, and created a new matrix B^k, where the entries of B^k, i.e., $b_{i,j}^k$, are defined as z-scores:

$$b_{i,j}^k = \frac{a_{i,j}^k - \overline{a}^k}{\sigma^k}, \tag{1}$$

where σ^k is the standard deviation over all entries of matrix A^k, and $\overline{a}^k$ is the mean over all its entries. Now we build all three pairs of matrices $\{B^x, B^y\}$, where $x, y \in \{1, 2, 3\}$ and $x \neq y$, and calculate the matrix C^{xy} for each, where $c_{i,j}^{xy} = |b_{i,j}^x - b_{i,j}^y|$. For each matrix C^{xy} we now calculate one scalar value, which is the mean over all its entries. We denote this scalar by $\overline{c}^{xy}$ and it gives us an indication how close the similarity matrices produced by recommender x versus y are. The lower the value, the closer they are to each other.

The results show that the track and tag recommender are *closest* to each other ($\overline{c}^{12} = 0.93$), while the time recommender produces more deviating results from both the track ($\overline{c}^{13} = 1.33$) and the tag recommender ($\overline{c}^{23} = 1.67$). This well aligns with our conjectures before conducting this test.

2.3   Prediction Generation

The prediction score $p(u, t_{new})$ of a track t_{new}, which user u has so far not rated yet, is computed based on a linear combination of the similarity scores of the three recommenders, denoted as $sim(t_{new}, t)$:

$$p(u, t_{new}) = \frac{\sum\limits_{t \in Tracks} sim(t_{new}, t) \cdot r(u, t)}{\sum\limits_{t \in Tracks} sim(t_{new}, t)} \qquad (2)$$

The so far rated songs of a user are considered by $r(u, t)$, reflecting a rating of user u for track t. If a user has only rated tracks of a few different artists so far, the majority of the recommendations might be from only one artist. To alleviate this undesirable behavior, for each artist at most two tracks are recommended to the user, working as a simple diversification means [5].

The weights of the three recommenders can be adjusted in the prototype and are set to equal weighting by default.

2.4   Adding Serendipity

For recommending serendipitous tracks, the last five positively rated tracks of the user are investigated. For *each* of these tracks, the last five users having listened to this track are selected, yielding (at most) 25 candidate users U_{cand}. The intersection of tracks the users in U_{cand} have listened to is computed and the tracks with the highest overlap are chosen.

If there are tracks with the same overlap, the number of times the track has been listened to by *all* users gives the final rank. The tracks are inserted in the result list, with the constraint that the serendipity ranking's order is preserved.

The ratio of serendipitous to similarity-based tracks is set to 30% vs. 70% by default.

References

1. Zhang, Y.C., Séaghdha, D.Ó., Quercia, D., Jambor, T.: Auralist: Introducing Serendipity Into Music Recommendation. In: Adar, E., Teevan, J., Agichtein, E., Maarek, Y. (eds.) WSDM, pp. 13–22. ACM (2012)
2. Burke, R.: Hybrid Web Recommender Systems. In: Brusilovsky, P., Kobsa, A., Nejdl, W. (eds.) Adaptive Web 2007. LNCS, vol. 4321, pp. 377–408. Springer, Heidelberg (2007)
3. Adomavicius, G., Tuzhilin, A.: Toward the Next Generation of Recommender Systems: A Survey of the State-of-the-Art and Possible Extensions. IEEE Trans. Knowl. Data Eng. 17(6), 734–749 (2005)
4. Baeza-Yates, R.A., Ribeiro-Neto, B.A.: Modern Information Retrieval - The Concepts and Technology Behind Search, 2nd edn. Pearson Education Ltd., Harlow (2011)
5. Ziegler, C.N., McNee, S., Konstan, J., Lausen, G.: Improving Recommendation Lists Through Topic Diversification. In: Proceedings of the 14th International World Wide Web Conference, Chiba, Japan. ACM Press (May 2005)

A Hybrid B2B App Recommender System

Alexandru Oprea[1], Thomas Hornung[2], Cai-Nicolas Ziegler[3],
Holger Eggs[1], and Georg Lausen[2]

[1] SAP Commercial Platform, St. Leon-Rot & SAP Research, Darmstadt, Germany
{alexandru.dorin.oprea,holger.eggs}@sap.com
[2] Institute of Computer Science, Albert-Ludwigs-Universität Freiburg, Germany
{hornungt,lausen}@informatik.uni-freiburg.de
[3] American Express, PAYBACK GmbH, München, Germany
cai-nicolas.ziegler@payback.net

Abstract. Recommender systems are integral to B2C e-commerce, with little use so far in B2B. We present a live recommender system that operates in a domain where users are companies and the products being recommended B2B apps. Besides operating in an entire new domain, the SAP Store recommender is based on a weighted hybrid design, making use of a novel confidence-based weighting scheme for combining ratings. Evaluations have shown that our system performs significantly better than a top-seller recommender benchmark.

1 Introduction and Motivation

The SAP Store caters to SME companies that aim to drive their business via B2B apps, e.g., for customer relation management or compliance. Many of these apps are geared towards specific industries and their needs. As the number of partners producing them is growing, so is the number of apps in the store itself and thus the complexity for the user (who represents a company) to actually *find* what he is looking for.

To actively help the user, we propose a hybrid recommender system that addresses exactly the needs of this specific B2B scenario. The system puts to use both knowledge-based, collaborative, and content-based sub-recommenders. Moreover, we present a novel hybrid weighting scheme [1] that incorporates *confidence scoring* for the predictions produced, so that sub-recommenders contribute for recommendations according to their confidence weight.

The system is live and can be used by logged-in users[1]. We have conducted empirical evaluations via hold-out testing that show that the recommender outperforms the non-personalized top-seller recommender.

2 Recommender System Architecture

The architecture of the recommender is depicted in Figure 1. Overall, we have three different information sources for generating new recommendations: the

---

[1] See http://store.sap.com

F. Daniel, P. Dolog, and Q. Li (Eds.): ICWE 2013, LNCS 7977, pp. 490–493, 2013.
© Springer-Verlag Berlin Heidelberg 2013

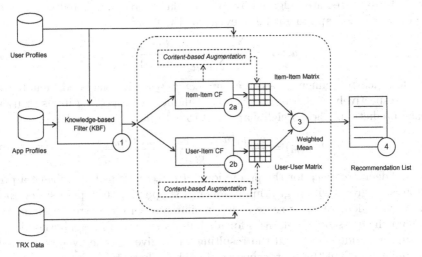

Fig. 1. SAP Store recommender system architecture

user profiles (e.g., company size, industry, country), the app profiles (e.g, supported industries, business areas), and the transactional customer data (e.g., sales orders, downloads).

Initially, the knowledge-based component filters the list of relevant apps by a set of plausibility rules resulting in an unsorted set of candidate apps (1). These are fed to an item-item (2a) and user-item collaborative filter (CF), see (2b) [2].

To deal with the cold-start problem in cases where only sparse ratings are available for apps, a content-based augmentation scheme computes similarities based on the *cosine similarity measure* [3] between properties of the apps. For users that are new to the system, the similarity can be determined by comparing their profiles to other users based on their cosine similarity. This way, the two matrices will contain meaningful entries for all users and apps known to the system, and recommendations get more personalized once more context data is available. The scores of the two CF algorithms are combined by a *weighted mean* (cf. Section 2.1), and a sorted top-k recommendation list is returned.

The calculation of the matrices is done off-line as the computation is quadratic in the number of users or apps, respectively.

2.1   Weighting by Confidence Scores

The score of a recommended app is based on a weighted mean of the constituent item-item and user-item scores. Each of these gives an estimate of how much a user might like an app; e.g., Eq. 1 shows how a prediction score for the item-item case is determined for app a_m for user u: The ratings $r_u(b)$ of u for apps $b \in R_u$

he has already rated are weighted by their similarity to a_m, denoted $s(b, a_m)$, as an indicator if this app might be relevant for the user[2].

$$p_i(u, a_m) = \frac{\sum_{b \in R_u} s(a_m, b) \cdot r_u(b)}{\sum_{b \in R_u} s(a_m, b)} \qquad (1)$$

Now, for each recommender score a *confidence score* is calculated, denoted c_i and c_u respectively, which is based on the number of supporting items or users of each prediction. These weights are used to determine the overall score p:

$$p(u, a_m) = \frac{c_i \cdot p_i(u, a_m) + c_u \cdot p_u(u, a_m)}{c_i + c_u} \qquad (2)$$

The confidence score c_u for the prediction $p_u(u, a_m)$ tells us how *reliable* a prediction is. It grows with a growing number of supporting data points: For each user u_i, we calculate the z-score of his similarity with our current user u. We now sum these z-score similarities for all k users in user u's neighborhood [2]. The sum is divided by k and the resulting value gives us the average normalized similarity of all the users whose ratings have been taken into account for $p_u(u, a_m)$. The same is done for the item-based case.

Since we are making use of standard z-scores, the linear combination shown in Eq. 2 based on the two confidence weights is sound. The confidence scheme represents a powerful means to adjust the hybrid recommender's weighting according to the predicted reliability of each of the two sub-recommenders.

3 Performance Evaluation

In order to test the performance of the presented hybrid recommender using our novel confidence-based weighting scheme, we conducted an empirical evaluation with real-world data of 5,233 users (e.g., companies registered for and using the SAP Store) having purchased or expressed interest in 615 app solutions.

The frequency distribution in Fig. 2(a) shows leads per app, i.e., how many companies have purchased or expressed interest in each app, sorted in descending order. The log-log plotted graph exhibits a power-law distribution, so a small number of apps attracts a high number of leads. This is confirmed by Fig. 2(b), showing that the top-5 apps accumulate 29% of all leads, and top-100 capture 90%. We thus conjecture that a non-personalized top-seller recommender, which only recommends the top-N most popular apps, will perform very well.

We adopted a hold-out cross-validation approach for testing, where one rating r_v of a user is withheld and all others are used to define his profile and calculate predictions, aiming to recommend exactly r_v. For baselining, we compared our recommender's performance with that of the top-seller recommender. The evaluation task for each of the two recommenders was to produce a list of top-N recommendations and count in how many cases the produced list contained r_v.

The evaluation is shown in Tab. 1. All results exhibit statistical significance at the $p < .05$ level, so we see the hybrid approach outperforms the top-seller.

---

[2] The score p_u for the user-item case is computed in an analogous way, with additional consideration of the user's average rating to level the effect of subjective ratings.

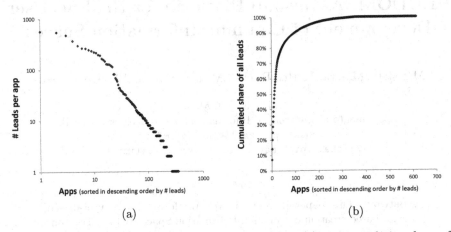

Fig. 2. Log-log frequency distribution of leads per app (a) and cumulative share of leads by number of apps (b)

Table 1. Performance benchmark results

	Top-1	Top-3	Top-5	Top-10
Hybrid recommender	10.9%	24.4%	33.5%	51.2%
Top-seller	6.6%	18.9%	27.6%	43.4%

4 Conclusion and Outlook

We have presented our recommender for the new domain of B2B apps, making use of a novel hybrid weighted scheme based on confidence scoring. Our first evaluations have shown very promising results and the system has gone live into operational use at SAP. In the future, we want to tune the recommending algorithms further and aim at doing the matrix calculations in real-time, using HANA [4], SAP's new high-performance in-memory database.

References

1. Burke, R.: Hybrid Web Recommender Systems. In: Brusilovsky, P., Kobsa, A., Nejdl, W. (eds.) Adaptive Web 2007. LNCS, vol. 4321, pp. 377–408. Springer, Heidelberg (2007)
2. Adomavicius, G., Tuzhilin, A.: Toward the Next Generation of Recommender Systems: A Survey of the State-of-the-Art and Possible Extensions. IEEE Trans. Knowl. Data Eng. 17(6), 734–749 (2005)
3. Baeza-Yates, R.A., Ribeiro-Neto, B.A.: Modern Information Retrieval - The Concepts and Technology Behind Search, 2nd edn. Pearson Education Ltd., Harlow (2011)
4. Färber, F., May, N., Lehner, W., Große, P., Müller, I., Rauhe, H., Dees, J.: The SAP HANA Database – An Architecture Overview. IEEE Data Eng. Bull. 35(1), 28–33 (2012)

PEUDOM: A Mashup Platform for the End User Development of Common Information Spaces

Maristella Matera, Matteo Picozzi, Michele Pini, and Marco Tonazzo

Politecnico di Milano
Dipartimento di Elettronica, Informazione e Bioingegneria - DEIB
{matera,picozzi}@elet.polimi.it,
{michele.pini,marco.tonazzo}@mail.polimi.it

Abstract. This paper presents a Web platform for the user-driven, service-based creation of Common Information Spaces (CISs). Two composition environments, characterized by intuitive visual notations, enable i) the integration of services to create UI-rich components and ii) the synchronization of components into interactive workspaces. Collaborative features allow multiple users to collaborate, synchronously and asynchronously, to share and co-create CISs.

Keywords: Collaborative Mashups, End User Development, Common Information Spaces.

1 Introduction

Web 2.0 has accelerated the evolution of the Web, becoming a driver of innovation. End users are now involved in the process of content creation, and this opportunity raised the users' will to become active creators of applications, thus promoting the *mashup* phenomenon. So far, mashups have been conceived as Personal Information Spaces (PISs), i.e., vertical applications solving situational needs, assembled by the end users by integrating ready-to-use resources. Mashups, however, have a great potential to accommodate the sharing and co-creation of knowledge [1]. While collaboration has been extensively investigated in the CSCW (Computer Supported Cooperative Work) area, the co-creation of web-based Common Information Spaces (CISs), especially by means of web mashups approaches, is still scarcely explored. Recent works highlight the need for collaboration [2], but the proposed solutions only cover specific aspects (e.g., awareness in synchronous editing), while they do not offer comprehensive approaches ranging different forms of synchronous and asynchronous collaboration.

1.1 Demo Organization

This demo presents the main ingredients of our approach for the collaborative construction of CISs. We illustrate the collaborative mechanisms introduced in PEUDOM, a platform for the end user development of mashups that

F. Daniel, P. Dolog, and Q. Li (Eds.): ICWE 2013, LNCS 7977, pp. 494–497, 2013.

offers visual paradigms for the creation of UI-rich components and the synchronization of such components to create orchestrated information spaces. The demo introduces the web environments supporting the visual composition of PISs, and the collaborative mechanisms that allow users to make PISs evolve into CISs. The demo also illustrates the models underlying the composition paradigms, the techniques for the automatic generation of application schemas, the pervasive execution of the resulting mashups on different devices to facilitate sharing, and the mechanisms for schema co-evolution in collaborative scenarios. The rest of this paper describes some basic ingredients of our approach that will be also illustrated during the demo. More details on the composition paradigm and the underlying models can be found in [3,4]. A video demonstrating the use of PEUDOM for CIS co-creation is available at http://home.dei.polimi.it/picozzi/peudom/demoICWE.html.

2   Models and Tools for PIS Composition

In our mashup platform, component integration complies with an *event-driven, publish-subscribe* paradigm that enables the synchronization of *components'* behaviors. Components wrap (remote or local) services and expose *events* and *operations*. The coupling of components within an integrated workspace is based on the subscription of *operations*, which become *listeners*, for *events* exposed by other components. Subscriptions are expressed in a *composition schema* represented in an XML-based domain specific language [3], which is then used to govern the execution of the PIS, i.e., the synchronization of the different components according to the defined listeners. As shown in Figure 1, a web environment, the *Mashup Dashboard*, enables the creation of PIS schemas. An *Event Handler* on the client-side intercepts the visual composition actions executed by the end-user, and automatically translates them into elements, i.e., listeners and property values, of the PIS schema. Based on the so created schema, the *Mashup Engine* acts as an event bus: it listens to and handles the events raised by the interaction with each single components, and activates the subscribed operations as prescribed by the listeners in the composition schema. A relevant characteristic of our approach is the interleaving of the design and execution phases [3]: users immediately experience the effect of their composition actions (i.e., the composition schema is immediately interpreted and executed); thus they can iteratively and interactively refine the resulting applications.

The platform also provides a web environment for the creation of components (*Component Editor* in Figure 1). Through the *Service Manager* module, it offers support for querying REST services, displaying the retrieved results in a visual format, and visually defining selection and projection queries over such results. A *visual mapping* process indeed allows the user to select data attributes and associate them to user interface elements playing the role of *data collectors*. The association of data from multiple services to a same UI data collector also defines integration queries [4]. The editor, through the *Visual Mapping Manager*, translates the visual actions into an XML-based component schema. The execution of

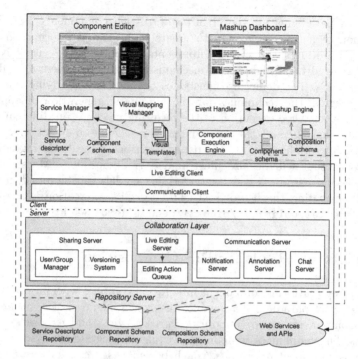

Fig. 1. Platform Architecture

the so created component is then possible within the Mashup Dashboard, as well as standalone apps on different devices where execution engines, coded according to the target technology, interpret and instantiate the component schema.

3   From PIS Composition to CIS Co-Creation

PEUDOM exploits a "lightweight" execution paradigm, hosting all the modules for composing and executing the composite information spaces at the client-side. As highlighted in Figure 1, server side modules instead manage the sharing of resources by multiple users and the synchronous and asynchronous communication. A schema versioning, an annotation system and an activity log system support synchronous communication. Instant messaging and live editing then enable synchronous collaboration. For example, if a user performs an action on a client that modifies locally a shared PIS (i.e., a CIS), this action is propagated (through the *Live Editing Client*) to a *Live Editing Server* in charge of updating the composition schema on each listening client. The server maintains a representation of all the distributed editing actions: every editing session on a CIS is associated with an *Editing Action Queue* from which messages are broadcasted to all the active CIS instances, except the one where the modification originated. On a client listening to modification actions, the Live Editing Client interprets the received actions and actuates the changes on the local schema.

The server-side management of the editing action queue ensures the synchronized evolution of all the active PIS instances. With respect to the paradigm adopted for PIS construction, the CIS composition schema is now enriched with *status meta-data* (e.g., parameter values to query single components, items selected in a given data set), so that each CIS instance is synchronized not only with respect to the composition structure (i.e., components and listeners), but also with respect to behavioral aspects, e.g., the displayed data set filtered out by different actions of concurrent users. Therefore, the composite application is now long-lasting and stateful: both structure and state variables are maintained across different sessions.

4   Conclusions

Collaboration in mashup-based development can be beneficial in *collective intelligence* scenarios [5], where teams of people co-create knowledge by sharing integrated information spaces with professional peers, in *meta-design environments* [6], where end-users shape up their tools in collaboration with expert developers, or in scenarios where people, not able to develop by themselves their own applications, ask for help and advice from experts within reference communities in a kind of *crowdsourced Web Engineering* [7]. This demo illustrate our solution for the *collaborative development* of CISs. The proposed techniques have been experimented by extending our Web platform for mashup development, but they address elements, such as *services, components, composition schemas,* that are recurrent in the majority of mashup platforms. Also due to the component-based nature of the collaborative modules, and the customizability of their event-driven logic, we believe the proposed techniques and their supportive software modules can be easily adapted and exploited in the context of other approaches.

References

1. Ardito, C., Costabile, M.F., Desolda, G., Matera, M., Piccinno, A., Picozzi, M.: Composition of situational interactive spaces by end users: a case for cultural heritage. In: Proc. of NordiChi 2012, pp. 79–88. ACM (2012)
2. Heinrich, M., Grüneberger, F.J., Springer, T., Gaedke, M.: Reusable awareness widgets for collaborative web applications - a non-invasive approach. In: Brambilla, M., Tokuda, T., Tolksdorf, R. (eds.) ICWE 2012. LNCS, vol. 7387, pp. 1–15. Springer, Heidelberg (2012)
3. Cappiello, C., Matera, M., Picozzi, M., Sprega, G., Barbagallo, D., Francalanci, C.: Dashmash: A mashup environment for end user development. In: Auer, S., Díaz, O., Papadopoulos, G.A. (eds.) ICWE 2011. LNCS, vol. 6757, pp. 152–166. Springer, Heidelberg (2011)
4. Cappiello, C., Matera, M., Picozzi, M.: End User Development of Mashups. In: Proc. of CHI International. LNCS, Springer (in print, 2013)
5. Grasso, A., Convertino, G.: Collective intelligence in organizations: Tools and studies - introduction. CSCW 21(4-5), 357–369 (2012)
6. Fischer, G., Giaccardi, E., Ye, Y., Sutcliffe, A.G., Mehandjiev, N.: Meta-design: a manifesto for end-user development. Commun. ACM 47(9), 33–37 (2004)
7. Nebeling, M., Leone, S., Norrie, M.C.: Crowdsourced web engineering and design. In: Brambilla, M., Tokuda, T., Tolksdorf, R. (eds.) ICWE 2012. LNCS, vol. 7387, pp. 31–45. Springer, Heidelberg (2012)

Customized Views on Profiles in WebID-Based Distributed Social Networks

Stefan Wild, Olexiy Chudnovskyy, Sebastian Heil, and Martin Gaedke

Chemnitz University of Technology, Germany
{firstname.lastname}@informatik.tu-chemnitz.de

Abstract. WebID as an extensible and distributed identification approach enables users to globally authenticate themselves, connect to each other and manage their identity data at a self-defined place. Identity data stored in WebID profile documents can be protected from unauthorized access using appropriate access control methods. While existing methods are primarily about securing resources, they lack providing adequate mechanisms for controlling access to specific data *within* profiles.

This paper presents our approach to create customized views on profiles in WebID-based distributed social networks. We introduce fine-grained personalized filters based on SPARQL templates and demonstrate their integration into an existing identity management platform.

Keywords: Social Web, Semantic Web, WebID, Access Control.

1 Introduction

Centralized social networks such as Facebook, Google+ or LinkedIn provide varied possibilities for personal information exchange, but try to bind users within their own domains [6]. Avoiding data silos and enabling users to remain in control of their data asks for a distributed social network (DSN). A DSN can be implemented on the basis of W3C's WebID specification [4]. WebID as a universal identification mechanism enables authentication through a client certificate that includes an URI, called WebID, referring to a resource containing the identity owner's data, called WebID profile. WebID profiles are extensible and machine-readable through RDF and domain specific vocabularies like FOAF. It is in the user's interest to consolidate personal data at one place and publish it in a uniform way to enable data reuse across different services and Web applications.

Unprotected WebID profiles, however, are potential information sources for known and wanted, but also for unknown and unwanted requesters. Authenticating via WebID requires a publicly accessible profile as it contains the profile owner's public keys, i.e., also data irrelevant to authentication per se could be retrieved [2]. Existing mechanisms only provide coarse access control and require outsourcing profile data to be protected as separate resources. There is a clear need for fine-grained and user-defined access control of WebID profile data.

We identified 3 requirements a solution has to fulfill: First, identity owners must be enabled to express fine-grained views on WebID profiles targeting different requesting agents. Second, view definitions must be portable to other systems

F. Daniel, P. Dolog, and Q. Li (Eds.): ICWE 2013, LNCS 7977, pp. 498–501, 2013.

without making major adjustments. Third, views on profiles must be standard compliant to ease maintenance, ensure traceability and reliable processing.

This paper addresses these requirements by the following contributions: First, we propose a flexible approach to customize views on WebID profiles using fine-grained filters. Second, we present an RDF-based filter language using SPARQL. Third, we demonstrate the integration of view customization facilities into an existing WebID identity provider and profile management platform.

The rest of this paper is organized as follows: We analyze related work in Section 2, present our solution in Section 3, and conclude the paper in Section 4.

2   Related Work

Web Access Control (WAC) enables access control to resources at the document level and supports assigning access rights to agents identified by WebIDs [2]. Access control lists specified by WAC are machine-readable through RDF and can be stored as self-contained resources independently from the resources they control access to. While WAC is well-suited for scenarios with many resources to be protected, it lacks possibilities to secure specific data within resources [1]. A fine-grained control requires outsourcing specific profile parts as separate resources and defining corresponding ACLs, which entails declining portability.

Similar to WAC, the Access Control Ontology (ACO) can only control access to resources [3]. ACO is more flexible than WAC, as it additionally supports defining roles and enables to directly map permissions to HTTP verbs.

The approach proposed in [5] enables manipulating profile data for specific requesting agents. Relevant profile data is addressed through URIs or RDF triple elements and logic defined by a custom vocabulary is interpreted to establish diverse views on profiles for specific requesting agents. Using a custom vocabulary limits expressiveness and portability. View definitions offer alternative information sources relative to existing WebID profile data. This requires further processing to merge or replace specific triples. Like ACO and WAC, treating particular profile data independently requires outsourcing as separate resources.

In contrast to the presented techniques, our approach enables filtering at the level of identity attributes while avoiding to distribute profile data.

3   Customized Views on WebID Profiles

To create customized views on WebID profiles, our solution automatically selects a filter specified for the requesting agent. If no filter specification is available, an identity fallback function retrieves the most appropriate filter. The entire WebID profile is converted via a graph-to-graph transformation into a filtered profile containing only data satisfying the visibility constraints defined for the requesting agent. For the transformation, we use SPARQL CONSTRUCT statements to apply a whitelisting to particular WebID profile data. The representation of the filtered profile is then sent back to the requesting party. Figure 1 illustrates this approach. Filters are created by WebID profile owners and stored in a machine-readable way within the profiles. As an RDF-based language using

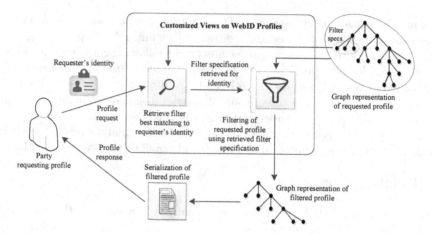

Fig. 1. Approach to Customized Views on WebID Profiles

SPARQL, the proposed *WebID Profile Filter Language (WPFL)* defines such filter specifications consisting of `filter:entity`, i.e., the requesting agent, and `filter:command`, i.e., the filter logic specified in SPARQL. WPFL also connects the filter specification with the WebID profile and is exemplarily shown below:

```
<WebID> filter:specification [
   filter:entity ENTITY;
   filter:command COMMAND ] .
```

We implement the approach using Sociddea - a WebID identity provider and management platform. Sociddea facilitates creating and editing views via a GUI, as shown in Figure 2. While the GUI targets unskilled users and is less expressive, Sociddea also allows to directly input SPARQL statements, which is more powerful but requires basic knowledge of Semantic Web technologies.

As all filter specifications are consolidated in the identity owner's WebID profile, this solution represents a portable approach. Using SPARQL as a well-established and proven language increases maintainability and flexibility, e.g., it also enables handling new identity attributes and conditional filtering.

Demonstration. In the demo session, we will show the creation WebID profiles using Sociddea. We present how users can define profile views via GUI and SPARQL queries. Finally, we demonstrate the filter selection and application depending on different requesting agents. Further information and a prototype is available at `http://vsr.informatik.tu-chemnitz.de/demo/sociddea/`.

4   Conclusion

By enabling identity owners to control the way their profile data is exposed to others, we made a significant step towards privacy in WebID-based DSNs. Filtering of WebID profile data allows identity owners to keep control about

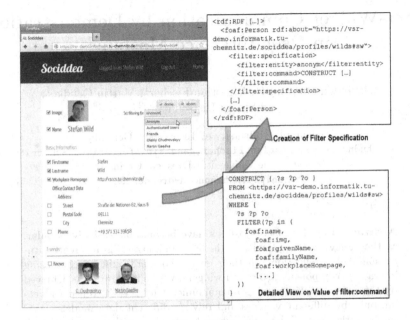

Fig. 2. Creation of Filter Specification based on User Selection

amount and nature of personal data being presented to entities requesting their profile data. In future work, we will analyze an extension of the filtering towards capabilities for dynamically adding and replacing profile data. We also plan to research the topic of reusing filters by sharing them between users of a DSN.

Acknowledgment. This work was funded by the European Commission (project OMELETTE, contract 257635).

References

1. Chudnovskyy, O., Wild, S., Gebhardt, H., Gaedke, M.: Data Portability Using WebComposition/Data Grid Service. International Journal on Advances in Internet Technology 4(3 & 4), 123–132 (2012)
2. Hackett, M., Hawkey, K.: Security, Privacy and Usability Requirements for Federated Identity (2012)
3. Tomaszuk, D., Gaedke, M., Gebhardt, H.: WebID+ACO: A distributed identification mechanism for social web (2011)
4. Tramp, S., Frischmuth, P., Ermilov, T., Shekarpour, S.: An Architecture of a Distributed Semantic Social Network. Semantic Web (2012)
5. Tramp, S., Story, H., Sambra, A., Frischmuth, P., Martin, M., Auer, S.: Extending the WebID Protocol with Access Delegation. In: Proceedings of the Third International Workshop on Consuming Linked Data (COLD 2012) (2012)
6. Yeung, C.M.A., Liccardi, I., Lu, K., Seneviratne, O., Berners-Lee, T.: Decentralization: The future of online social networking. In: W3C Workshop on the Future of Social Networking Position Papers 2 (2009)

Inter-Widget Communication by Demonstration in User Interface Mashups

Olexiy Chudnovskyy[1], Christian Fischer[1], Martin Gaedke[1],
and Stefan Pietschmann[2]

[1] Chemnitz University of Technology, Germany
{olexiy.chudnovskyy,christian.fischer,gaedke}@informatik.tu-chemnitz.de
[2] Technische Universität Dresden, Germany
stefan.pietschmann@tu-dresden.de

Abstract. User Interface Mashups have become increasingly popular, as they allow end users with little programming skills to create situational Web applications on their own. Those are built by composing interactive components, so-called widgets, whose integration is achieved by the means of "inter-widget communication" (IWC). Since widgets are built by different vendors and rely on different data models, IWC rarely works "out of the box", which leaves users with the tedious task of manual wiring and limited functionality.

This paper presents a semi-automatic, end-user friendly approach to extend widgets with IWC capabilities by employing the programming by demonstration paradigm. The solution is demonstrated using an extension of Apache Rave, an open-source widget composition platform.

Keywords: mashup, inter-widget communication, programming by demonstration.

1   Introduction

User Interface Mashups (UI Mashups) facilitate the aggregation of several widgets on a canvas or "workspace" to create situational applications. The integration of functionality and data offered by widgets is achieved by the so-called *Inter-Widget Communication* (IWC). The corresponding messaging infrastructure provided by many platforms allows for synchronization and message transfer between widgets which lets them act as one integrated solution with significantly improved user experience [3,4,2]. Many of the widgets currently available on the Web do not make use of IWC. Some of them are simply not designed to be used in compositions. Others rely on component models unaware of IWC mechanisms, such as W3C widgets. Finally, IWC-enabled widgets developed by different parties suffer from compatibility problems with regard to communication models and data formats. As result, users often have to input the same data multiple times and synchronize views manually.

In prior work [1] we have proposed a semi-automatic context-independent approach for extending widgets with IWC capabilities. It is targeted at domain

F. Daniel, P. Dolog, and Q. Li (Eds.): ICWE 2013, LNCS 7977, pp. 502–505, 2013.

experts and skilled users, as a basic understand of data types is required. The work presented here addresses users with little or no programming skills and provides the following major contributions: First, we show how Web-based widgets can be extended towards IWC capabilities on the graphical user interface (GUI) level automatically; Second, we demonstrate how IWC configuration can be done using the *programming by demonstration* (PBD) technique; Finally, we demonstrate how this approach has been integrated and tested with several open source projects.

The rest of the paper is structured as follows. After giving an overview of related works in the next section, Sect. 3 presents the proposed solution for end-user friendly IWC configuration. Finally, Sect. 4 concludes the paper and gives an outlook on future work.

2   Related Work

Building mashups by demonstration has been explored in the Karma project [6]. The project focused on so called data mashups, i.e. ones, which extract, integrate and display data from different sources. Users apply PBD technique to specify, how data from Web pages is extracted, normalized and combined together. In contrast, the focus of this work lies on widget-based mashups and thus requires further techniques to configure GUI-level IWC between widgets.

Geppeto project introduced the idea of programming on the GUI level and applied it the context of widget-based dashboards [5]. Using several special-purpose widgets and the PBD technique users are able to define workflows consisting of multiple GUI actions across different widgets. However, the recorded workflows can only be triggered by user or by pre-defined system events and not by widgets themselves.

Several research projects have focused on end-user friendly IWC configuration. Within the CRUISE project [4] users can establish connections between widgets by means of the drag&drop technique. However, widgets need to be designed this way and rely on semantically compatible data types. The solution presented in this paper is more generic, as widgets do not need to be IWC aware or to comply with any particular interface.

3   End-User Friendly IWC Configuration

The proposed concept is applied in the context of so-called choreographed UI mashups [7]. Therein, communication emerges without an explicit data flow definition: Widgets send and receive messages based on the publish-subscribe (pub/sub) messaging pattern. To be semantically compatible they utilize a reference ontology describing the data concepts shared. Widgets themselves are treated as black boxes with public interfaces exposing publications and subscriptions to certain topics and the data types involved.

Implementations of this model predominantly support application-level events and operations. GUI changes and interactions are usually not communicated via pub/sub. Naturally, if widgets do not expose application-level interfaces or the concepts are incompatible (e.g., by not using a common reference ontology), IWC becomes impossible. Our approach addresses this problem by enriching the widget interface with events and operations at the presentation layer. These can be employed to orchestrate widget GUIs – guided by the user – thereby establishing connections between widgets.

To enrich widgets with the new interface we have extended the widget containers Apache Wookie[1] and Shindig[2] so that DOM-event listeners are automatically added to the source code of instantiated widgets, e. g., for HTML inputs, select boxes, buttons, and anchors. These extension mechanisms allow for an easy monitoring and invocation of state changes for the above-mentioned elements. To establish a "connection" between widgets, users perform GUI actions in one widget, which should *lead* to the message transfer, and actions in another widget, which should be executed *after* the message transfer. A learning system then detects correlations in recorded action sequences indicating possible data flow. One correlation currently supported in our prototype is the reoccurance of text in different HTML input elements. If a user searches for "London" in a weather forecast widget and right after that selects the same city in a map widget, the platform will detect this repeated input and derive a "connection" between the GUI elements. Fig. 1 illustrates this example workflow.

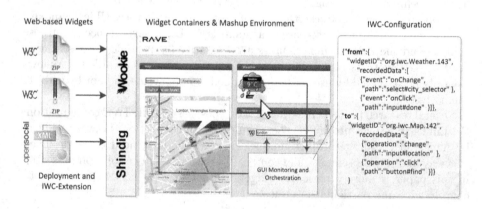

Fig. 1. Configuration of IWC using Programming by Demonstration

From then on, whenever a user starts a similar interaction with the source widget, the system will automatically complete the corresponding interaction in the target widget with the help of the automatically integrated code. The configuration is stored per workspace and user so that widgets can be reused in different contexts without prior source code modifications.

In the demo session we plan to showcase the above-mentioned trip planning scenario. First, we demonstrate how a map, a weather forecast, and a Wikipedia

---

[1] http://wookie.apache.org/

[2] http://shindig.apache.org

widget can be automatically extended towards IWC capabilities. Then, we show how the desired data flow can be configured by simply interacting with the aggregated widgets. Finally, we present the derived IWC configuration and automatic re-execution of the recorded actions.

A screencast of the planned demonstration and a running prototype based on Apache Rave[3] are available at http://vsr.cs.tu-chemnitz.de/demo/iwc-pbd.

4 Conclusions

This paper describes an approach to extend stand-alone widgets with IWC functionality in an end-user friendly fashion. To achieve this, widgets are automatically equipped with GUI-level observers, which allow for the deduction of logical connections by monitoring user interactions. As a result, widget integration does not require any programming skills. Users apply the same techniques as they do while naturally interacting with their Web applications.

The approach is currently limited to simple patterns of user interactions with a focus on Web-based forms. Future work will explore how to detect and transfer complex data between widgets. Further, we plan to conduct a user study to improve on the usability and scrutability of the approach.

Acknowledgment. This work was supported by the European Commission (project OMELETTE, contract 257635).

References

1. Chudnovskyy, O., Müller, S., Gaedke, M.: Extending web standards-based widgets towards inter-widget communication. In: 4th Intl. Workshop on Lightweight Integration on the Web, pp. 93–96 (2012)
2. Chudnovskyy, O., Nestler, T., Gaedke, M., Daniel, F., Ignacio, J.: End-User-Oriented Telco Mashups: The OMELETTE Approach. In: WWW 2012 Companion Volume, pp. 235–238 (2012)
3. Lizcano, D., Soriano, J., Reyes, M., Hierro, J.J.: Ezweb/fast: Reporting on a successful mashup-based solution for developing and deploying composite applications in the upcoming ubiquitous soa. In: Proc. of the 2nd Intl. Conf. on Mobile Ubiquitous Computing Systems, Services and Technologies, pp. 488–495. IEEE (September 2008)
4. Pietschmann, S., Voigt, M., Meißner, K.: Rich communication patterns for mashups. In: Brambilla, M., Tokuda, T., Tolksdorf, R. (eds.) ICWE 2012. LNCS, vol. 7387, pp. 315–322. Springer, Heidelberg (2012)
5. Skrobo, D.: Widget-Oriented Consumer Programming. AUTOMATIKA: Journal for Control, Measurement, Electronics, Computing and Communications 50(3-4), 252–264 (2009)
6. Tuchinda, R., Knoblock, C.A., Szekely, P.: Building Mashups by Demonstration. ACM Transactions on the Web 5(3), 1–45 (2011)
7. Wilson, S., Daniel, F., Jugel, U., Soi, S.: Orchestrated User Interface Mashups Using W3C Widgets. In: Harth, A., Koch, N. (eds.) ICWE 2011. LNCS, vol. 7059, pp. 49–61. Springer, Heidelberg (2012)

---

[3] http://rave.apache.org

A Linked Data Perspective for Effective Exploration of Web APIs Repositories

Devis Bianchini, Valeria De Antonellis, and Michele Melchiori

Dept. of Information Engineering University of Brescia
Via Branze, 38 - 25123 Brescia (Italy)
{bianchin,deantone,melchior}@ing.unibs.it

Abstract. In this paper, we propose a novel approach to provide a comprehensive cross-repositories view of the available Web APIs information, in order to enhance effective multi-perspective Web APIs search for fast development of web mashups. The approach is based on Linked Data principles to identify and use semantic links across repositories for search purposes. Specifically, the paper considers Web APIs search across the popular ProgrammableWeb and Mashape repositories by combining their distinctive Web API descriptions.

1 Approach Overview

The problem of searching Web APIs to be aggregated for fast web mashup development necessarily comes up against the fact that Web APIs are shared by providers across different public repositories, which focus on distinct aspects that are considered for Web API search. In this paper, we propose a novel approach to provide a comprehensive cross-repositories view of the available Web APIs information, in order to enhance effective multi-perspective Web APIs search. Specifically, we consider Web APIs search on the `ProgrammableWeb`[1] (PW) and `Mashape`[2] (MP) repositories by combining their distinctive Web API descriptions. With respect to related approaches on Linked Web services and Linked Web APIs [1,2], we rely on information stored within public available repositories without forcing the web designers to perform semantic annotation of Web APIs.

An overview of our approach is shown in Figure 1. The approach is based on Linked Data principles: (i) the contents of repositories are formally represented (based on RDF), to make them machine processable and enable access through non-proprietary tools (e.g., SPARQL endpoints); (ii) metrics and criteria to automatically identify semantic links between RDF elements (e.g., Web APIs, developers' profile) across different vocabularies are defined; (iii) identified links are also published as open data to be properly exploited for Web API search. Starting from the PW and MP repositories, RDF vocabularies which represent their contents are designed using the main concepts in this domain of

---

[1] http://www.programmableweb.com/
[2] https://www.mashape.com/

F. Daniel, P. Dolog, and Q. Li (Eds.): ICWE 2013, LNCS 7977, pp. 506–509, 2013.

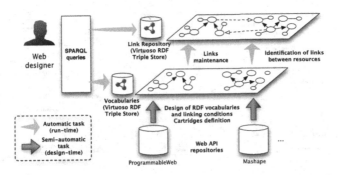

Fig. 1. Overview of the methodology for Linked Web API publication and search

interest: categories, tags, web mashups and actors involved in Web API sharing, namely providers and web mashup developers. Vocabularies are stored within the RDF Triple Store of the Virtuoso Universal Server, on which the approach is implemented. Links across different vocabularies are also stored in a *Link Repository*, built upon the Virtuoso Triple Store. Web API search strategies, based on RDF vocabularies and cross-repositories, are then applied, inspired by [3]. Such strategies are implemented through SPARQL queries issued on the Virtuoso Universal Server to query the contents of different repositories in a combined way. Due to the dynamic nature of Web API repositories, a link maintenance mechanism has been also implemented.

2   Linked Web API RDF Vocabulary Definition

The RDF representation of PW and MP vocabularies, together with cross-repositories links (dashed arrows) are shown in Figure 2. Class modeling should rely on external vocabularies or ontologies, when available [4]. For instance, we modeled actors involved in Web API sharing within the two vocabularies in Figure 2 using the FOAF (Friend of a Friend) ontology.

The relevant classes of resources which have been included in the PW and MP vocabularies reflect the distinctive features of the two repositories for Web API description. The PW repository focuses on the Web APIs, the way they are aggregated into mashups, developers who may be the owners of mashups or providers of Web APIs. On the other hand, the MP repository is a cloud API hub focusing on people involved in Web API sharing, denoted as *mashapers* in the repository, distinguishing among three roles, namely Web API providers, consumers (who used the Web API in one of their own mashups) and followers (who declare their interest on the Web API). This perspective is further enriched through relationships between mashapers.

Semantic links between resources across different repositories are identified, as well as the conditions to be verified to set the links. Formally, we represent a semantic link $\mathcal{L}$ as follows: $\mathcal{L} = \langle \text{type}, s\_URI, t\_URI, \text{conf}, [\text{when}] \rangle$, where

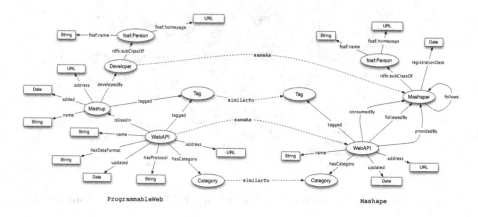

Fig. 2. Linked Web API vocabulary

s_URI and t_URI are the URIs of the source and target resources of the link, respectively, `conf` is the confidence to set the link (obtained through similarity metrics depending on the link type) and the optional element `when` denotes when the link has been established and threrefore stored within the Link Repository. With reference to the vocabularies shown in Figure 2, the following link types have been identified:

- `sameAs` link between Web APIs, to denote that two APIs registered in the repositories refer to the same component;
- `similarTo` link between categories and tags used to classify Web APIs;
- `sameAs` link between developers' profiles, to denote that a developer within the `ProgrammableWeb` repository corresponds to a mashaper registered within `Mashape`.

3   Link Exploitation and Maintenance

Contents of the Link Repository can be exposed as open data and used to browse Web API information across PW and MP repositories. A query is formally defined as $Q = \langle C_Q, T_Q, F_Q, M_Q \rangle$, where C_Q is the set of categories, T_Q is the set of tags, F_Q (optional) is a set of pairs $\langle$`tech_feature=value`$\rangle$ and M_Q (optional) is a mashup (that is, a set of Web APIs) which the Web API to search for will be aggregated in. A search interface supports designers that are not confident with SPARQL in query formulation.

When the query Q is formulated, the Link Repository is inspected to expand the set of categories and tags specified in the query. The expanded set of categories and tags are used to retrieve Web APIs from the PW and MP repositories. Pairs of retrieved Web APIs (one from PW and one from MP) are compared: if a `sameAs` link between Web APIs is already stored within the Link Repository, the Web APIs are reconcilied, otherwise the link is checked to be established. At the same time, the Link Repository is updated with the new links. Links oldest than a predefined set of days in the Link Repository are never considered to check semantic links across repositories and are periodically deleted by the system. The last search steps concern filtering and ranking of search results. Retrieved Web APIs are filtered out according to the set of required features $\mathcal{F}_Q$ if specified in $\mathcal{Q}$. Finally, search results are ranked according to their appropriateness with respect to the target mashup $\mathcal{M}_Q$ if specified in $\mathcal{Q}$ and according to their popularity. Specifically, we define the similarity between two mashups $\mathcal{M}_1$ and $\mathcal{M}_2$ (as sets of Web APIs) using the following formula:

$$MashupSim(\mathcal{M}_1, \mathcal{M}_2) = \frac{2 \cdot |\mathcal{M}_1 \cap \mathcal{M}_2|}{|\mathcal{M}_1| + |\mathcal{M}_2|} \tag{1}$$

where $|\mathcal{M}_1 \cap \mathcal{M}_2|$ denotes the number of common Web APIs in the two mashups and $|\mathcal{M}_i|$ the number of Web APIs in the mashup $\mathcal{M}_i$. Given the set M_W of mashups of a Web API W among search results, the appropriateness of W with respect to the mashup $\mathcal{M}_Q$ is given by $max_j \{MashupSim(\mathcal{M}_Q, \mathcal{M}_j)\}$, where $\mathcal{M}_j \in M_W$. Popularity of a result is measured as the number of developers who used that Web API in their own mashups.

4   Concluding Remarks

In [3,5] we demonstrated the usefulness of considering multi-perspective Web API description for searching purposes on the `ProgrammableWeb` repository, leaving to the Web API consumers the task of adding information about their profile and the way they used Web APIs in their mashups. On the basis of those results, we moved to the development of a novel approach based on Linked Data principles to provide a comprehensive cross-repositories view of the available Web APIs information. In this paper, we presented the approach by considering Web APIs search on the ProgrammableWeb and Mashape repositories and combining their distinctive Web API descriptions.

References

1. Taheriyan, M., Knoblock, C., Szekely, P., Ambite, J.: Semi-Automatically Modeling Web APIs to Create Linked APIs. In: Proc. of the ESWC 2012 Workshop on Linked APIs (2012)
2. Pedrinaci, C., Liu, D., Maleshkova, M., Lambert, D., Kopecky, J., Domingue, J.: iServe: a Linked Services Publishing Platform. In: Proc. of ESWC Ontology Repositories and Editors for the Semantic Web (2010)
3. Bianchini, D., De Antonellis, V., Melchiori, M.: Semantic Collaborative Tagging for Web APIs Sharing and Reuse. In: Brambilla, M., Tokuda, T., Tolksdorf, R. (eds.) ICWE 2012. LNCS, vol. 7387, pp. 76–90. Springer, Heidelberg (2012)
4. Villazón-Terrazas, B., Vilches, L., Corcho, O., Gómez-Pérez, A.: Methodological Guidelines for Publishing Government Linked Data. Springer (2011)
5. Bianchini, D., De Antonellis, V., Melchiori, M.: A Multi-perspective Framework for Web API Search in Enterprise Mashup Design. In: Salinesi, C., Norrie, M.C., Pastor, Ó. (eds.) CAiSE 2013. LNCS, vol. 7908, pp. 353–368. Springer, Heidelberg (2013)

Responsive Design and Development: Methods, Technologies and Current Issues

Michael Nebeling and Moira C. Norrie

Institute of Information Systems, ETH Zurich
CH-8092 Zurich, Switzerland
{nebeling,norrie}@inf.ethz.ch

Abstract. Responsive design is a major trend in web development to cater for the diversity of devices used for web browsing. However, applying responsive design to existing web sites often involves major reengineering due to the underlying fluid grid concept. Moreover, applications of responsive design are currently limited to desktop-to-mobile adaptation. This tutorial introduces the main ideas behind responsive design with a focus on the methods and technologies. Based on previous research, we highlight several limitations of the original approach and show how the concepts and methods can be extended to adapt to many different viewing conditions including large-screen settings and touch devices.

Keywords: responsive web design, interface-driven web engineering.

1 Introduction

Application developers in general, and web site providers in particular, currently have to deal with the increased range of new devices and diversity of interface characteristics, not only in terms of screen size and resolution, but also supported input and output modalities. For example, the term "mobile" has traditionally been used to refer to small-form factor, handheld devices such as mobile phones and PDAs with limited screen size and processing power. However, nowadays, this includes a whole new generation of smartphones and tablet computers, such as the iPhone or iPad, that are becoming more and more powerful and commonly provide touch, gesture-based input and other advanced sensing techniques. There are also new kinds of medium-size devices, such as notebooks with support for slate mode, booklets and convertibles, that are often hybrid solutions, but still primarily designed for mobile settings. It is frequently the case that, as well as supporting traditional mouse and keyboard input, they increasingly provide support for an even richer combination of touch, pen and gesture-based input. Looking at the other end of the spectrum, even the term "desktop" may nowadays refer to a wide range of devices with a strong trend towards large, wide-format screens, and there is growing interest in physically much larger, very high-resolution display environments [1]. In addition, research has also suggested extensions of the desktop paradigm towards what has emerged

F. Daniel, P. Dolog, and Q. Li (Eds.): ICWE 2013, LNCS 7977, pp. 510–513, 2013.

as the "tabletop". Many new kinds of large interactive surfaces have been developed and are now becoming commonplace in offices, public spaces and at home. With very small touchscreens [2] and new types of rollable devices [3], recent research has continued to explore different kinds of interaction techniques and is constantly pushing forward both input and output technologies. We can therefore expect an even greater diversification in terms of device characteristics over the coming years.

The rapid evolution and increased diversity of new devices used for web browsing has caused a major rethinking of design strategies. For many years, two strategies, *graceful degradation* [4] and *progressive enhancement* [5], have played a major role. Both aim at a layered approach towards multi-device authoring by adding either more or fewer layers designed for more or less advanced devices in terms of their screen size, input methods and other supported capabilities. Both also follow the well-established separation of concerns in web engineering by distinguishing the different levels of content, navigation and presentation typically using rule-based approaches for selecting appropriate layers. The main difference is that graceful degradation starts from a user interface designed for the "less constrained platform", removing features if the particular device in use does not provide the required support, while progressive enhancement adds layers to the core interface designed for the "lowest common denominator". The two strategies have therefore in common the fact that they try to divide the device landscape into linear partitions, but start at opposite ends of the spectrum. However, this approach has become less feasible nowadays due to the diversification of devices.

A new trend is therefore *responsive web design* [6] which means to build the layout of the web interface on fluid grids that can dynamically adapt to diverse viewing environments. At the technical level, this is achieved by using relative units (percentages or ems) rather than absolute units (pixels or points) for page element sizing as well as CSS3 media queries to apply different CSS rules for the position and floating of elements depending on the size of the browser window. Hence, responsive design promotes a specific way of implementing interfaces that is however difficult to apply to existing web sites without major reengineering [7].

The tutorial is divided into two parts. The first part provides an introduction to responsive web design as a new and significant trend in web development as well as a discussion of current issues. The second part gives an overview of existing, and our own, ongoing research to tackle the different issues in a systematic way. Practitioners not familiar with the concepts and technologies will benefit from the step-by-step introduction. For the ICWE research community, the tutorial provides interesting opportunities for discussing this new web design trend and the implications for web engineering.

2   Tutorial Synopsis

Using various examples, participants will learn about different methods and technologies for achieving responsive design. In particular, the new features of HTML5 and CSS3 will be discussed as well as the problems caused by the fact that these standards themselves are still evolving. While desktop-to-mobile adaptation will be used as the running example in the first part of the tutorial to illustrate the concepts and steps involved in responsive design as a web design method, it also shows the benefits and limitations compared to other context-aware adaptation approaches that have been promoted in research. Specifically, there is an interesting tension and contrast between the interface-driven approach behind responsive web design and model-driven web engineering which has great potential for discussion in the ICWE forum.

The second part of the tutorial addresses some of the issues of responsive design, both from a technological point of view and as a web design method, based on our previous research [8]. First, we present languages, frameworks and tools developed by us and other researchers that tackle the issues of context-aware adaptation at the implementation level. Second, we show how crowdsourcing can be used for the adaptation and evaluation of web sites to make the design and development for the increased proliferation of different forms of devices practical. Finally, we present a set of metrics for measuring the adaptivity of web interfaces and guiding web developers in the adaptation process in order to address contexts of use that are still poorly supported by current design. The methods and tools presented in the second part go beyond the principles of responsive design, not only from a technological and methodological point of view, but also in terms of scenarios and use cases. In particular, we show how the techniques were extended to cater for adaptation to large-screen displays and multi-touch devices as well as distributed interfaces and interaction in multi-device environments.

Therefore, participants will not only receive an overview and introduction to the current trend of responsive web design, but also a sense of the shortcomings of the approach and current issues. For researchers, we highlight interesting opportunities for further research when looking at responsive design in the broader context of web engineering.

Biographical Sketch

Michael Nebeling is a Post-doctoral Researcher and Lecturer at ETH Zurich. His research and teaching interests are at the intersection of Web Engineering and HCI, including context-aware and adaptive systems, multi-device and gesture-based interaction, end-user development and crowdsourcing. His PhD thesis, *Lightweight Informed Adaptation: Methods and Tools for Responsive Design and Development of Very Flexible, Highly Adaptive Web Interfaces* [8], has made several contributions to ICWE and has won best paper awards and nominations at CHI 2011 and EICS 2012.

Moira Norrie has been a Professor at ETH Zurich since 1996 when she established a research group on Global Information Systems. She heads the Institute for Information Systems which is part of the Department of Computer Science. Her main areas of research are information systems engineering, information interaction, web engineering and personal information management.

References

1. Czerwinski, M., Robertson, G., Meyers, B., Smith, G., Robbins, D., Tan, D.: Large display research overview. In: Proc. CHI (2006)
2. Baudisch, P., Chu, G.: Back-of-Device Interaction Allows Creating Very Small Touch Devices. In: Proc. CHI (2009)
3. Steimle, J., Jordt, A., Maes, P.: Flexpad: Highly Flexible Bending Interactions for Projected Handheld Displays. In: Proc. CHI (2013)
4. Florins, M., Vanderdonckt, J.: Graceful Degradation of User Interfaces as a Design Method for Multiplatform Systems. In: Proc. IUI (2004)
5. Desruelle, H., Blomme, D., Gielen, F.: Adaptive Mobile Web Applications: A Quantitative Evaluation Approach. In: Auer, S., Díaz, O., Papadopoulos, G.A. (eds.) ICWE 2011. LNCS, vol. 6757, pp. 375–378. Springer, Heidelberg (2011)
6. Marcotte, E.: Responsive Web Design. A Book Apart (2011)
7. Nebeling, M., Matulic, F., Streit, L., Norrie, M.C.: Adaptive Layout Template for Effective Web Content Presentation in Large-Screen Contexts. In: Proc. DocEng (2011)
8. Nebeling, M.: Lightweight Informed Adaptation: Methods and Tools for Responsive Design and Development of Very Flexible, Highly Adaptive Web Interfaces. PhD thesis, ETH Zurich (2012)

An Introduction to Human Computation and Games with a Purpose

Alessandro Bozzon[1] and Luca Galli[2]

[1] Delft University of Technology, Mekelweg 4, 2628CD, Delft, The Netherlands
a.bozzon@tudelft.nl
[2] Politecnico di Milano, P.zza Leonardo Da Vinci 32, 20133, Milano, Italy
luca.galli@polimi.it

Abstract. Crowdsourcing and human computation are novel disciplines that enable the design of computation processes that include humans as actors for task execution. In such a context, Games With a Purpose are an effective mean to channel, in a constructive manner, the human brainpower required to perform tasks that computers are unable to perform, through computer games. This tutorial introduces the core research questions in human computation, with a specific focus on the techniques required to manage structured and unstructured data. The second half of the tutorial delves into the field of game design for serious task, with an emphasis on games for human computation purposes. Our goal is to provide participants with a wide, yet complete overview of the research landscape; we aim at giving practitioners a solid understanding of the best practices in designing and running human computation tasks, while providing academics with solid references and, possibly, promising ideas for their future research activities.

Keywords: Crowdsourcing, Human Computation, Games With a Purpose.

1 Introduction

The Web has evolved from a publishing platform to a collaborative and social tool, where users spend time online for sharing information and opinions, cooperating in the execution of tasks, playing games, and participating to the collective life of communities. Crowdsourcing [1] and human computation [2] are novel disciplines that exploited such an evolution to enable the design of computation processes that include humans as actors for task execution. In such a context, Games With a Purpose [3] are an effective mean to channel, in a constructive manner, the human brainpower required to perform tasks computers are unable to perform, through computer games. Gamification techniques are applied where the lack of motivation is mining the efficiency of the users. Although these topics are rather new, Human Computation and Games With a Purpose and Gamification rapidly became interesting topics of research, with widespread adoption in industry.

F. Daniel, P. Dolog, and Q. Li (Eds.): ICWE 2013, LNCS 7977, pp. 514–517, 2013.
© Springer-Verlag Berlin Heidelberg 2013

Our tutorial targets academics and practitioners that would like to understand how human computation and game design techniques could be applied to personal and enterprise content management systems. The tutorial is divided into two parts. The first part introduces the core research questions in human computation, with a specific focus on the techniques required to manage structured and unstructured data. The second part delves into the field of game design for serious task, with an emphasis on games for human computation purposes. Our goal is to provide the ICWE research community with a solid understanding of the best practices in designing and running human computation tasks, with references to the most relevant works in the field.

2 Tutorial Synopsis

The tutorial will address several aspects of Human Computation, Games With a Purpose and gamified applications; it will provide an overview of the methods, techniques, and tools that can be used to successfully include crowds in applications and systems.

The intended length of the tutorial is 3 hours over two sessions. The first session will focus on providing a comprehensive background on human computation, introducing the discipline from a historical, industrial, and academic point of view. Attendees will be presented with the best practices in human computation tasks design, with specific insights on performer selection, task allocation, task optimisation, and result aggregation issues. We will then provide an overview on industrial human computation platforms (e.g. Amazon Mechanical Turk[1], Crowdflower[2]) and state-of-the-art systems [4] and frameworks [5]. In addition, we will provide an in-depth analysis for some of these systems, focusing on the ones published in scholarly articles (e.g. CrowdDb [6], CrowdLang [7], Crowdsearcher [8] [9], DeCo [10]); we will discuss the design choices of these systems, analyse their areas of application (e.g. database, information retrieval, multimedia information retrieval), and enumerate desiderata for the next generation of human-enhanced data management systems.

The second session of the tutorial will be centred on describing techniques used to improve the engagement of the performers in a platform. We will introduce two complementary streams of development, respectively represented by *Application Gamification* [11] and *Games with a Purpose* [3], addressing their commonalities and differences. By referring to the best practices used in traditional literature on game design [12] [13] [14], we will analyse the structure of a game, the design of game mechanics, and the development process of a typical digital game. The design process for Gamified Applications and Games with a Purpose will be outlined, with an emphasis on the design of suitable game mechanics for the former and on the design and match of tasks for the latter. During the presentation, the most prominent examples such as ESP Game [15],

---

[1] https://www.mturk.com/mturk/
[2] http://crowdflower.com/

FoldIt [16], Ingress[3], Yahoo! Answers[4] will be showcased. The session will end with a brief introduction to open source or proprietary tools and frameworks for the development of gamified application and digital games for the web, including UserInfuser[5], OpenBadges[6], Badgeville[7], Haxe[8], and Unity[9].

3   Biographical Sketch

Alessandro Bozzon is an Assistant Professor at the Delft University of Technology, with the Web Information Systems group. His research interests are into the fields of data and information management on the Web, with specific focus on Semantic Web technologies, human- and social-computation, and data integration. His current research aims at defining a foundational theory for hybrid human and automatic information management systems, by studying the theoretical models and the technical means to achieve this integration.

Luca Galli is a Phd Student at Politecnico di Milano. His research interests involves Data Mining and Text Mining, Human and Social computation, Game Design and video games development technologies (innovative middleware architectures, game engine architecture, multi platform deployment). His current research aims at integrating traditional game paradigms and gamification techniques in the design and implementation of human enhanced applications.

References

1. Howe, J.: Crowdsourcing: Why the Power of the Crowd Is Driving the Future of Business, 1st edn. Crown Publishing Group, New York (2008)
2. Law, E., von Ahn, L.: Human Computation. Synthesis Lectures on Artificial Intelligence and Machine Learning. Morgan & Claypool Publishers (2011)
3. von Ahn, L.: Games with a purpose. Computer 39(6), 92–94 (2006)
4. Doan, A., Ramakrishnan, R., Halevy, A.Y.: Crowdsourcing systems on the worldwide web. Commun. ACM 54(4), 86–96 (2011)
5. Little, G., Chilton, L.B., Goldman, M., Miller, R.C.: Turkit: tools for iterative tasks on mechanical turk. In: HCOMP 2009, pp. 29–30. ACM (2009)
6. Franklin, M.J., Kossmann, D., Kraska, T., Ramesh, S., Xin, R.: Crowddb: answering queries with crowdsourcing. In: ACM SIGMOD 2011, pp. 61–72. ACM (2011)
7. Minder, P., Bernstein, A.: How to translate a book within an hour: towards general purpose programmable human computers with crowdlang. In: WebScience 2012, Evanston, IL, USA, pp. 209–212. ACM (2012)

---

[3] http://www.ingress.com/
[4] http://answers.yahoo.com/
[5] https://code.google.com/p/userinfuser/
[6] http://openbadges.org/
[7] http://badgeville.com/
[8] http://haxe.org/
[9] http://unity3d.com/

8. Bozzon, A., Brambilla, M., Ceri, S.: Answering search queries with crowdsearcher. In: 21st Int.l Conf. on World Wide Web 2012, WWW 2012, pp. 1009–1018. ACM (2012)
9. Bozzon, A., Brambilla, M., Ceri, S., Mauri, A.: Reactive crowdsourcing. In: 22nd Intl. Conf. on World Wide Web 2013, WWW 2013. ACM (2013)
10. Park, H., Pang, R., Parameswaran, A.G., Garcia-Molina, H., Polyzotis, N., Widom, J.: Deco: A system for declarative crowdsourcing. PVLDB 5(12), 1990–1993 (2012)
11. Deterding, S., Dixon, D., Khaled, R., Nacke, L.: From game design elements to gamefulness: defining "gamification". In: Proceedings of the 15th International Academic MindTrek Conference: Envisioning Future Media Environments, MindTrek 2011, pp. 9–15. ACM, New York (2011)
12. Crawford, C.: The Art of Computer Game Design. Washington State University Vancouver, Vancouver (1982)
13. Fullerton, T., Swain, C., Hoffman, S.: Game Design Workshop: A playcentric approach to creating innovative games. Morgan Kauffmann (2008)
14. Zichermann, G., Cunningham, C.: Gamification by Design: Implementing Game Mechanics in Web and Mobile Apps (2011)
15. von Ahn, L., Dabbish, L.: Labeling images with a computer game. In: Proceedings of the SIGCHI Conference on Human Factors in Computing Systems, CHI 2004, pp. 319–326. ACM, New York (2004)
16. Cooper, S., Treuille, A., Barbero, J., Leaver-Fay, A., Tuite, K., Khatib, F., Snyder, A.C., Beenen, M., Salesin, D., Baker, D., Popović, Z.: The challenge of designing scientific discovery games. In: Proceedings of the Fifth International Conference on the Foundations of Digital Games, FDG 2010, pp. 40–47. ACM, New York (2010)

Current Challenges in Web Crawling

Denis Shestakov

Department of Media Technology, Aalto University
P.O. Box 15500, FI-00076 Aalto, Finland
denis.shestakov@aalto.fi
https://mediatech.aalto.fi/~denis/

Abstract. Web crawling, a process of collecting web pages in an auto-mated manner, is the primary and ubiquitous operation used by a large number of web systems and agents starting from a simple program for website backup to a major web search engine. Due to an astronomical amount of data already published on the Web and ongoing exponential growth of web content, any party that want to take advantage of massive-scale web data faces a high barrier to entry. In this tutorial, we will introduce the audience to five topics: architecture and implementation of high-performance web crawler, collaborative web crawling, crawling the deep Web, crawling multimedia content and future directions in web crawling research.

Keywords: web crawling, web crawler, web spider, web robot, web structure, web growth, web coverage, web graph, collaborative crawling, web ecosystem, web harvesting, crawler architecture, focused crawling, distributed crawling, web mining, web retrieval, deep Web.

1 Introduction

Web crawling [1], a process of collecting web pages in an automated manner, is the primary and ubiquitous operation used by a large number of web systems and agents starting from a simple program for website backup to a major web search engine. For example, search engines such as Google or Microsoft Bing use web crawlers to routinely visit billions of web pages, which are then indexed and made available for answering user search requests. In this way, the characteristics of obtained web crawls such as coverage or freshness directly affect on the quality of web search results served to users. Besides web search, the web crawling tech-nology is central in such applications as web data mining and extraction, social media analysis, digital preservation (i.e., ensuring continued access to informa-tion and all kinds of records, scientific and cultural heritage existing in digital formats), detection of web spam and fraudulent web sites, finding unauthorized use of copyrighted content (music, videos, texts, etc.), identification of illegal and harmful web activities (e.g., terrorist chat rooms), virtual tourism, etc.

Due to an astronomical amount of data already published on the Web and ongoing exponential growth of web content, any party (whether it be an individ-ual, company, government agency, non-profit or educational organization, etc.)

F. Daniel, P. Dolog, and Q. Li (Eds.): ICWE 2013, LNCS 7977, pp. 518–521, 2013.
© Springer-Verlag Berlin Heidelberg 2013

that want to take advantage of massive-scale web data faces a high barrier to entry. Indeed, only network costs associated with the downloading of web-scale size collection by themselves lead to expenses that are not affordable by the majority of potential players.

For those with flexible budgets, there is a next barrier: operating web-scale crawl (at least, hundreds of millions of pages) is a challenging task that requires skills and expertise in distributed data retrieval and processing, not to mention large operational costs. Finally, for the parties who nevertheless manage to overcome the above obstacles but interested in specific subsets of web information, the results of crawl are often wasteful, as majority of retrieved pages do not match their criteria of interest.

As a result, while there are many parties crawling the Web, the large-scale web crawling is done mostly by commercial companies, specifically by web search engines (e.g., Google). Currently, search engines' crawlers are aware of more than one trillion links and probably of more than one hundred billion pages that are re-visited on a regular basis to keep their indexes fresh.[1] Unlike web crawling under the industrial settings, the scale of non-industrial web crawling is modest and does not usually exceed several hundred million pages. Besides the dramatic difference in scale, the crawl datasets collected by commercial web crawlers are not in a public domain, not to mention that their algorithms and techniques are proprietary and kept in secret. As a result, only crawls of small sizes are available to the research community as well as to the general audience. It is clearly unsuitable since such datasets could facilitate research not only in the area of web information retrieval and more generally in computer science but also in other disciplines such as biology, epidemiology, linguistics, sociology, mathematics, etc. [2]. Furthermore, analysis of web datasets (e.g., investigating how web sites are ready to the next 'wave' of users who browse the Web using mobile devices) is of key importance for business and media companies.

In this tutorial, we will address the following topics: architecture and implementation of high-performance web crawler, collaborative web crawling, crawling the deep Web, crawling multimedia content available on the Web, and future directions in web crawling research. We will also provide some background on the structure of the Web and the role of crawling in the Web ecosystem.

2 Tutorial Synopsis

The material will be presented in the following six modules:

- **Web structure&ecosystem.** We start with some necessary background on the structure&ecosystem of the Web [3,4] and provide some useful estimates for the amount of content on the Web [5,6].
- **Architecture and implementation of high-performance web crawler.** Here we present 'traditional' challenges in building an efficient web-scale crawler system and describe state-of-the-art techniques and approaches [7,8].

---

[1] See blog entry at
http://googleblog.blogspot.com/2008/07/we-knew-web-was-big.html

- **Collaborative web crawling.** A collaborative web crawler [9] is a service that crawls the Web on the behalf of its many client applications that define filters to be evaluated against each crawled page.
- **Crawling the deep Web.** We describe the challenges in accessing information available in myriads of online web databases [10] and techniques used in modern web crawlers [11,12]. We also address here complications for web crawlers caused by new web standards, techniques and practices (e.g., rich internet applications) [13].
- **Crawling multimedia content.** We overview this rather unexplored sub-area, which is poorly covered in the literature.
- **Future directions.** Here we discuss some open questions in web crawling research (e.g., crawling utilizing web content structure [14]) and conclude with references to literature, datasets, relevant projects, self-study materials, etc.

3   Biographical Sketch

Denis Shestakov is a postdoctoral researcher at the Department of Media Technology, Aalto University, Finland. He spent one year as a visiting researcher at INRIA Rennes, France. Denis obtained his doctoral degree at University of Turku, Finland in 2008. In his doctoral work [15], Denis addressed the limitations of web crawlers, specifically the poor coverage of information available in online databases (a.k.a. the deep Web). His current research interests lie in the area of distributed algorithms for big data processing, with particular applications in web crawling and large-scale multimedia retrieval. Denis is maintaining an open group on research works in the area of web crawling (see `http://www.mendeley.com/groups/531771/web-crawling/`). Contact him at denis.shestakov@aalto.fi or visit his homepage at `https://mediatech.aalto.fi/~denis/`.

References

1. Olston, C., Najork, M.: Web crawling. Foundations and Trends in Information Retrieval 4(3), 175–246 (2010)
2. Barabasi, A.-L.: Scale-Free networks: A decade and beyond. Science 325(5939), 412–413 (2009)
3. Kleinberg, J.M., Kumar, R., Raghavan, P., Rajagopalan, S., Tomkins, A.S.: The Web as a graph: measurements, models, and methods. In: Asano, T., Imai, H., Lee, D.T., Nakano, S.-I., Tokuyama, T. (eds.) COCOON 1999. LNCS, vol. 1627, pp. 1–17. Springer, Heidelberg (1999)
4. Schonfeld, U., Shivakumar, N.: Sitemaps: Above and beyond the crawl of duty. In: Proc. of WWW 2009, pp. 991–1000 (2009)
5. Bar-Yossef, Z., Gurevich, M.: Random sampling from a search engine's index. JACM 55(5) (2008)
6. Shestakov, D.: Sampling the national deep Web. In: Hameurlain, A., Liddle, S.W., Schewe, K.-D., Zhou, X. (eds.) DEXA 2011, Part I. LNCS, vol. 6860, pp. 331–340. Springer, Heidelberg (2011)

7. Shkapenyuk, V., Suel, T.: Design and implementation of a high-performance distributed web crawler. In: Proc. of ICDE 2002, pp. 357–368 (2002)
8. Lee, H.-T., Leonard, D., Wang, X., Loguinov, D.: IRLbot: Scaling to 6 billion pages and beyond. ACM Transactions on the Web 3(3) (2009)
9. Hsieh, J., Gribble, S., Levy, H.: The architecture and implementation of an extensible web crawler. In: Proc. of NSDI 2010 (2010)
10. Shestakov, D.: Deep Web: databases on the Web. Entry: Handbook of Research on Innovations in Database Technologies and Applications, pp. 581–588 (2009)
11. Madhavan, J., Ko, D., Kot, L., Ganapathy, V., Rasmussen, A., Halevy, A.: Google's deep-Web crawl. In: Proc. of VLDB 2008, pp. 1241–1252 (2008)
12. Shestakov, D.: On building a search interface discovery system. In: Proc. of VLDB Workshops 2009, pp. 81–93 (2009)
13. Duda, C., Frey, G., Kossmann, D., Matter, R., Zhou, C.: AJAX crawl: Making AJAX applications searchable. In: Proc. of ICDE 2009, pp. 78–89 (2009)
14. Lin, S.-H., Ho, J.-M.: Discovering informative content blocks from web documents. In: Proc. of SIGKDD 2002, pp. 588–593 (2002)
15. Shestakov, D.: Search interfaces on the Web: Querying and characterizing. Doctoral thesis, University of Turku (2008)

Enterprise Application Integration - The Cloud Perspective

Jörg Lässig and Markus Ullrich

University of Applied Sciences Zittau/Görlitz
Department of Electronical Engineering and Computer Science
Brückenstr. 1, 02826 Görlitz, Germany
{jlaessig,mullrich}@hszg.de
http://f-ei.hszg.de/ead

Abstract. So far, asynchronous messaging has proven to be the best strategy for enterprise application integration (EAI) success. However, building and deploying messaging solutions causes several problems for developers and new technologies and computing paradigms as cloud computing demand for new solutions. There are more than sixty enterprise integration patterns that are designed to effectively develop messaging solutions for enterprises. The tutorial introduces the visual notation framework to describe large-scale integration solutions across different systems and technologies. This includes examples covering a variety of different integration styles and techniques. In a case study we illustrate the application of the patterns in practice and review existing and emerging standards. Also we try to shed light into the future of EAI. In particular cloud integration is an upcoming trend which is discussed in the tutorial, addressing advantages and limitations of this and other modern EAI strategies and architectures. Looking at open-source solutions for enterprise service buses and messaging systems, we also provide practical advice on designing code that connects an application to a messaging system. This provides information to help the practitioner to design EAI or cloud integration solutions by applying the introduced knowledge.

Keywords: Enterprise application integration, cloud integration, integration styles, enterprise service bus, open-source ESB systems, integration patterns, messaging, business process integration.

1 Introduction

Nowadays requirements for software systems in enterprises are changing frequently due to changes on the business side but also due to emerging new technologies such as significant progress in the cloud computing field. Also, requirements and applied technologies usually differ between enterprises –even in the same industrial sector– significantly. This is due to the availability of various solutions for similar problems, differences in the historic development of an enterprise, different management styles, different business strategies and goals, different levels of process automation and management, etc.

F. Daniel, P. Dolog, and Q. Li (Eds.): ICWE 2013, LNCS 7977, pp. 522–525, 2013.
© Springer-Verlag Berlin Heidelberg 2013

Thus, it is impossible to offer all-in-one software solutions to satisfy all the needs of every enterprise. The obvious practical approach is of course to have different software tools for special purposes and to choose them accordingly from a selection of available systems. In the usual case, the choice is feature-based and hence often systems from different software vendors are applied to different needs within the same enterprise. The need of communication between those systems was/ is often not needed initially but is becoming increasingly important in a globalized environment and in times of the introduction of new paradigms as Industry 4.0 [6] or information partnerships between companies.

1.1 Enterprise Application Integration

According to the above described setting, the selected systems of a company often do not support appropriate interfaces to communicate with each other directly. Also, the coupling of several systems in a pairwise manner is ineffi-cient. This is where enterprise application integration (EAI) comes into play: The need to exchange information between those systems has to be satisfied by a robust and flexible enterprise application integration strategy. According to Gartner there are four major data delivery styles[1]. A frequently used and effec-tive solution for EAI is messaging since it offers the same loose coupling between applications as file transfer and -at the same time- it is almost as consistent and reliable as a shared database but with no obvious performance bottleneck. De-spite those advantageous characteristics, the asynchronous nature of messaging as well as integrating software systems with a variety of different interfaces can be a significant challenge for first time developers of a messaging system.

1.2 Cloud Integration

Currently, the cloud paradigm influences various enterprise IT solutions [7] and the same is true for the development of state of the art EAI solutions [1]. Cloud computing solutions in enterprises also trigger a demand for new integration solutions, e. g., SaaS-to-SaaS (S2S) integration, Cloud-to-Enterprise integration (C2E) or even cloud business process management solutions (Cloud-BPM)[2].

To formalize different approaches, enterprise integration patterns [2] can help to reduce the complexity of integration solutions in a standardized way. Here, basic messaging patterns are considered and the tutorial highlights in which situation which pattern should be applied. This also includes an review of open-source enterprise service bus (ESB) solutions that support messaging, the ap-plication of EAI patterns for common integration scenarios and discussions on how new challenges and technologies can be integrated.

---

[1] E. Thoo, T. Friedman, M. A. Beyer. Critical Capabilities for Data Integration Tools: Common Data Delivery Styles.

[2] G. Johnson. Cloud Integration Defined. Can Cloud BPM Be Far Behind?

2   Tutorial Synopsis

After outlining the need of EAI in modern enterprises to be competitive, we discuss the most frequent challenges when applying EAI strategies in practical settings, such as the integration of critical business functions in the integration scenario or a lack of control concerning participating applications. Typical integration settings range from the integration of a few applications in a single company for special needs up to the integration of various systems and processes in supply chains and enterprise networks or dynamic environments such as virtual enterprises as introduced in [3,4,5].

The attempt to reduce the complexity of integration tasks motivates the development of standards to handle and manage those various flavors of integration scenarios. We feature the common visual notation for integration solutions as introduced by Hohpe and Woolf in [2] so that integration scenarios can be defined and described consistently and high-level.

Next we discuss basic integration styles like file transfer, relational databases and remote procedure calls with a special focus on asynchronous systems and message processing. Here, the topics range from the construction of messages over the characteristics of messaging channels, routing and transformation patterns and also endpoints. Even patterns for managing messaging systems are considered. Additionally, we describe architectural styles and patterns like pipes and filters or message brokers.

Subsequently, we also give an introduction to EAI in the cloud while explaining the different characteristics and levels of cloud integration and the additional challenges of application integration compared to data integration in the cloud. This includes also security considerations in this open and vulnerable environment. Compared to traditional environments new security models across clouds are needed.

On this firm conceptual basis, we review current technologies and standards for EAI solutions and also point out further standardization needs. As one way to implement integration patterns, web services are examined. ESBs are used for the integration of complex and heterogenous EAI scenarios and can be seen as a general approach to implement service-oriented architectures efficiently. There is a high number of different ESB systems available. Focusing further on the implementation side, we showcase some of the most popular open-source ESB solutions for EAI in a live demo and compare them in terms of features, e. g., supported patterns, performance, documentation, usability, maturity or the support of work flows and work flow engines. Typical is, e. g., the support of the WS-Business Processes Execution Language (BPEL) to implement work flows which orchestrate web services.

In a case study we implement an non-trivial exemplary integration scenario and highlight the most important considerations while designing an effective messaging solution, which illustrates certain patterns in a practical setting. The tutorial is concluded with an outlook on emerging trends and future directions of EAI.

3   Bibliographical Sketch

Jörg Lässig is a Full Professor in the field of Enterprise Application Development at the Department of Electrical Engineering and Computer Science at the University of Applied Sciences Zittau/ Görlitz since 2011. He holds degrees in Computer Science and Computational Physics and received a Ph.D. in Computer Science for his research on efficient algorithms and models for the generation and control of cooperation networks at Chemnitz University of Technology, which he finished in 2009. Afterwards he has been participating in various research projects at the International Computer Science Institute at Berkeley, California and at the Universit della Svizzera italiana in Lugano, Switzerland. He is currently focusing on various topics in the context of sustainable information technologies and applications which includes the directions sustainability in enterprise IT, green information systems, logistics and supply and business intelligence.

Markus Ullrich is currently a research associate at the University of Applied Sciences Zittau/Görlitz where he received his M.S. and B.S. in Computer Science in 2010 and 2012, respectively. From 2009 to 2012, he worked as a software developer at the Decision Optimization GmbH where he developed and tested data mining algorithms for predictive maintenance. His current research is focused on cloud computing, cloud integration, distributed systems and privacy preserving data mining.

References

1. Erbes, J., Motahari Nezhad, H.R., Graupner, S.: The future of enterprise it in the cloud. Computer 45(5), 66–72 (2012)
2. Hohpe, G., Woolf, B.: Enterprise integration patterns: Designing, building, and deploying messaging solutions. Addison-Wesley Professional (2004)
3. Lässig, J.: Algorithms and Models for the Generation and Control of Competence Networks. Mensch und Buch Verlag (2009)
4. Lässig, J., Heinrich, S., Dürr, H.: Intelligent support system for enterprise cooperation management. In: Proceedings of the 4th Indian International Conference on Artificial Intelligence, Bangalore, India, pp. 1626–1645 (December 2009)
5. Lässig, J., Trommler, U.: New approaches to enterprise cooperation generation and management. In: Proceedings of the 12th International Conference on Enterprise Information Systems (ICEIS 2010), Funchal, Madeira, Portugal, pp. 350–359 (2010)
6. Meisen, T., Meisen, P., Schilberg, D., Jeschke, S.: Digitale produktion via enterprise application integration. In: Automation, Communication and Cybernetics in Science and Engineering 2009/2010, pp. 609–622. Springer (2011)
7. Ullrich, M., ten Hagen, K., Lässig, J.: Public cloud extension for desktop applications–case study of a data mining solution. In: 2012 Second Symposium on Network Cloud Computing and Applications (NCCA), pp. 53–64. IEEE (2012)

Author Index